6th Edition

Web Development and Design Foundations with HTML5

Terry Ann Felke-Morris, Ed.D.

Professor
Harper College

International Edition contributions by
Piyali Sengupta

PEARSON

Boston   Columbus   Indianapolis   New York   San Francisco   Upper Saddle River
Amsterdam   Cape Town   Dubai   Paris   Montreal   Toronto
Delhi   Mexico City   ngapore   Taipei   Tokyo

Editorial Director, ECS: Marcia Horton
Editor-in-Chief: Michael Hirsch
Acquisitions Editor: Matt Goldstein
Editorial Assistants: Chelsea Kharakozova and
    Emma Snider
Director of Marketing: Patrice Jones
Marketing Manager: Yezan Alayan
Marketing Coordinator: Kathryn Ferranti
Director of Production: Vince O'Brien
Managing Editor: Jeff Holcomb
Publisher, International Edition: Angshuman
    Chakraborty
Acquisitions Editor, International Edition:
    Somnath Basu
Publishing Assistant, International Edition:
    Shokhi Shah
Print and Media Editor, International Edition:
    Ashwitha Jayakumar
Project Editor, International Edition: Jayashree
    Arunachalam

Publishing Administrator, International Edition:
    Hema Mehta
**Senior Manufacturing Controller, Production,
    International Editions:** Trudy Kimber
Cover Designer: Jodi Notowitz
Text Designer: Susan Raymond
Manager, Visual Research: Karen Sanatar
Image Permission Coordinator: Cathy Mazzucca
Manager, Rights and Permissions: Michael Joyce
Permissions Coordinator: Shannon Foreman,
    Electronic Publishing Services, Inc.
Media Editor: Daniel Sandin
Media Project Manager: John Cassar
Full-Service Project Management: Dennis Free,
    Aptara, Inc.
Art: Aptara, Inc.
Cover and Text Printer: Courier/Kendallville

Pearson Education Limited
Edinburgh Gate
Harlow
Essex CM20 2JE
England

and Associated Companies throughout the world

Visit us on the World Wide Web at:
www.pearsoninternationaleditions.com

© Pearson Education Limited 2013

ISBN 10: 0-273-77450-6
ISBN 13: 978-0-273-77450-1

British Library Cataloguing-in-Publication Data
A catalogue record for this book is available from the British Library

10 9 8 7 6 5 4 3 2 1
14 13 12

Typeset in MetaPro-Normal by Aptara, Inc.
Printed and bound by Courier Kendallville in The United States of America

The publisher's policy is to use paper manufactured from sustainable forests.

ISBN 10:   0-273-77450-6
ISBN 13: 978-0-273-77450-1

Preface

Web Development and Design Foundations with HTML5 is intended for use in a beginning web development course. The text covers the basics that web developers need to build a foundation of skills:

- Internet concepts
- Creating web pages with HTML5
- Configuring text, color, and page layout with Cascading Style Sheets (CSS)
- Web design best practices
- Accessibility standards
- The web development process
- Using media and interactivity on web pages
- New CSS3 properties
- Website promotion and search engine optimization
- E-commerce and the Web
- JavaScript

A special feature of this text is the *Web Developer's Handbook*, which is a collection of appendixes that provide resources such as an HTML5 Reference, XHTML Reference, Special Entity Character List, CSS Property Reference, WCAG 2.0 Quick Reference, and FTP Tutorial.

New to This Edition

Building on this textbook's successful fifth edition, the sixth edition features a major update from XHTML to the introduction of HTML5 and CSS3. This textbook continues to integrate HTML and CSS topics such as text configuration, color configuration, and page layout, with an enhanced focus on the topics of design, accessibility, and Web standards. This textbook has a modern approach that prepares students to design web pages that work today, in addition to being ready to take advantage of the new HTML5 coding techniques of the future. XHTML syntax is introduced, but the focus is on HTML5 syntax. New HTML5 elements are presented, with an emphasis on coding web pages that work in both current and future browsers. New features for the sixth edition include the following:

- New sections introducing HTML5 elements and attributes
- New sections introducing CSS3 properties
- Updated code samples, case studies, and web resources
- Updated accessibility coverage for Web Content Accessibility Guidelines (WCAG) 2.0
- Expanded coverage of designing for mobile devices
- Color figures throughout
- Updated reference section for XHTML, HTML5, and CSS
- New FTP Tutorial in the appendix
- New VideoNotes. A series of videos have been developed as a companion for this textbook.

Student files are available for download from the companion website for this textbook at www.pearsoninternationaleditions.com/felke-morris. These files include solutions to the Hands-On Practice exercises, the Website Case Study starter files, and access to the book's companion VideoNotes. See the access card in the front of this textbook for further instructions.

Design for Today and Tomorrow

This textbook has a modern approach that prepares students to design web pages that work today, in addition to being ready to take advantage of the new HTML5 coding techniques of the future. XHTML syntax is introduced, but the focus is on HTML5 syntax. New HTML5 elements are presented, with an emphasis on coding web pages that work in both current and future browsers.

Organization of the Text

This textbook is designed to be used in a flexible manner; it can easily be adapted to suit a variety of course and student needs. Chapter 1 provides introductory material, which may be skipped or covered, depending on the background of the students. Chapters 2 through 4 introduce HTML and CSS coding. Chapter 5 discusses web design best practices and can be covered anytime after Chapter 3 (or even along with Chapter 3). Chapters 6 through 9 continue with HTML and CSS.

Any of the following chapters may be skipped or assigned as independent study, depending on time constraints and student needs: Chapter 7 (More on Links, Layout, and Mobile), Chapter 10 (Web Development), Chapter 11 (Web Multimedia and Interactivity), Chapter 12 (E-Commerce Overview), Chapter 13 (Web Promotion), and Chapter 14 (A Brief Look at JavaScript). A chapter dependency chart is shown in Figure P.1.

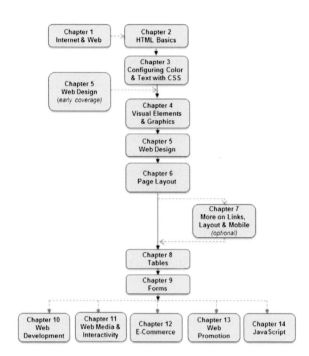

Figure P.1 This textbook is flexible and can be adapted to individual needs

Brief Overview of Each Chapter

Chapter 1: Introduction to the Internet and World Wide Web
This brief introduction covers the terms and concepts related to the Internet and the Web with which Web developers need to be familiar. For many students, some of this will be a review. Chapter 1 provides the base of knowledge on which the rest of the textbook is built.

Chapter 2: HTML Basics
As HTML5 and XHTML are introduced, examples and exercises encourage students to create sample pages and gain useful experience. Solution pages for the Hands-On Practice are available in the student files.

Chapter 3: Configuring Color and Text with CSS
The technique of using Cascading Style Sheets to configure the color and text on web pages is introduced. Students are encouraged to create sample pages as they read through the text. Solutions for the Hands-On Practice are available in the student files.

Chapter 4: Visual Elements and Graphics
This chapter discusses the use of graphics and visual effects on web pages, including image optimization, CSS borders, CSS image backgrounds, new CSS3 visual effects, and new HTML5 elements. Students are encouraged to create web pages as they read through the text. Sample solutions for the Hands-On Practice are available in the student files.

Chapter 5: Web Design
This chapter focuses on recommended web design practices and accessibility. Some of this is reinforcement because tips about recommended website design practices are incorporated into the other chapters.

Chapter 6: Page Layout This chapter continues the study of CSS begun earlier and introduces techniques for positioning and floating web page elements, including a two-column CSS page layout. New HTML5 semantic elements are also introduced. Sample solutions for the Hands-On Practice are available in the student files.

Chapter 7: More on Links, Layout, and Mobile This chapter revisits earlier topics and introduces more advanced techniques related to hyperlinks, using CSS sprites, a three-column page layout, configuring CSS for print, and designing pages for the mobile web. Students are encouraged to create pages as they read through the text. Sample solutions for the Hands-On Practice are available in the student files.

Chapter 8: Tables This chapter focuses on the HTML elements used to create tables. Methods for configuring a table with CSS are introduced. Students are encouraged to create pages as they read through the text. Sample solutions for the Hands-On Practice are available in the student files.

Chapter 9: Forms This chapter focuses on the HTML elements used to create forms. Methods for configuring the form with CSS are introduced. New HTML5 form control elements and attribute values are introduced. Students are encouraged to create sample pages as they read through the text. Sample solutions for the Hands-On Practice are available in the student files.

Chapter 10: Web Development This chapter focuses on the process of website development, including the job roles needed for a large-scale project, the web development process, and web hosting. A web host checklist is included in this chapter.

Chapter 11: Web Multimedia and Interactivity This chapter offers an overview of topics related to adding media and interactivity to web pages. These topics include new HTML5 video and audio, Flash®, Java™ applets, a CSS Image Gallery, new CSS3 transform and transition properties, JavaScript, and AJAX. Students are encouraged to create pages as the topics are discussed. Sample solutions for the Hands-On Practice are available in the student files.

Chapter 12: E-Commerce Overview This chapter introduces e-commerce, security, and order processing on the Web.

Chapter 13: Web Promotion This chapter discusses site promotion from the web developer's point of view and introduces search engine optimization.

Chapter 14: A Brief Look at JavaScript This chapter provides an introduction to client-side scripting using JavaScript. Sample solutions for the Hands-On Practice are available in the student files.

***Web Developer's Handbook* Appendixes:** This handbook contains appendixes that include resources and tutorials that are useful for students, such as an HTML5 Quick Reference, an XHTML Quick Reference, Special Entity Characters, a CSS Property Reference, a WCAG 2.0 Quick Reference, a Web-Safe Color Palette, and an FTP Tutorial.

Features of the Text

Well-Rounded Selection of Topics This text includes both "hard" skills such as HTML5, CSS, and JavaScript (Chapters 2, 3, 4, 6, 7, 8, 9, and 14) and "soft" skills such as web design (Chapter 5), website promotion (Chapter 13), and e-commerce (Chapter 12). This well-rounded foundation will help students as they pursue careers as web professionals. Students and instructors will find classes more interesting because they can discuss, integrate, and apply both hard and soft skills as students create web pages and websites.

Hands-On Practice Web development is a skill and skills are best learned by hands-on practice. This text emphasizes hands-on practice through exercises within the chapters, end-of-chapter exercises, and the development of websites through ongoing real-world case studies. The variety of exercises provides instructors with a choice of assignments for a particular course or semester.

Website Case Studies There are four case studies that continue throughout most of the text (starting with Chapter 2). An additional case study starts in Chapter 5. The case studies serve to reinforce the skills discussed in each chapter. Instructors can cycle assignments from semester to semester or allow students to choose the case study that most interests them. Sample solutions to the case studies are available for download from the Instructor Resource Center at www.pearsoninternationaleditions.com/felke-morris.

Web Research Each chapter offers web research activities that encourage students to further study the topics introduced in the chapter.

Focus on Web Design Most chapters offer additional activities that explore the web design topics related to the chapter. These activities can be used to reinforce, extend, and enhance the course topics.

FAQs In the author's web development courses, she is frequently asked similar questions by students. They are included in this textbook and are marked with the identifying FAQ logo.

Checkpoints Each chapter contains two or three Checkpoints, which are groups of questions to be used by students to self-assess their understanding of the material. A special Checkpoint icon appears with each group of questions.

Focus on Accessibility Developing accessible websites is more important than ever and this textbook is infused with accessibility techniques throughout. The special icon shown here makes accessibility information easy to find.

Focus on
Accessibility

Focus on Ethics Ethics issues related to web development are highlighted throughout the textbook and are marked with the special ethics icon shown here.

Focus on
Ethics

Reference Materials The appendixes in the *Web Developer's Handbook* offer reference materials, including an HTML5 Quick Reference, an XHTML Quick Reference, Special Entity Characters, a CSS Property Reference, a WCAG 2.0 Quick Reference, a Web-Safe Color Palette, and an FTP Tutorial.

VideoNote

VideoNotes VideoNotes are Pearson's new visual tool designed for teaching students key programming concepts and techniques. These short step-by-step videos demonstrate how to solve problems from design through coding. VideoNotes allow for self-placed instruction with easy navigation including the ability to select, play, rewind, fast-forward, and stop within each VideoNote exercise.

Margin icons in your textbook let you know when a VideoNote video is available for a particular concept or homework problem.

Supplemental Materials

Student Resources The student files for the web page exercises, Website Case Study assignments, and access to the book's VideoNotes are available to all readers of this textbook at its companion website www.pearsoninternationaleditions.com/felke-morris. A complimentary access code for the companion website is available with a new copy of this textbook. Subscriptions may also be purchased online.

Instructor Resources The following supplements are available to qualified instructors only. Visit the Pearson Instructor Resource Center (www.pearsoninternationaleditions.com/felke-morris) or for information on how to access them:

- Solutions to the end-of-chapter exercises
- Solutions for the case study assignments
- Test questions
- PowerPoint® presentations
- Sample syllabi

Author's Website In addition to the publisher's companion website for this textbook, the author maintains a website at http://www.webdevfoundations.net. This website contains additional resources, including review activities and a page for each chapter with examples, links, and updates. This website is not supported by the publisher.

Acknowledgments

Very special thanks go to all the folks at Pearson, especially Michael Hirsch, Matt Goldstein, Chelsea Kharakozova, Emma Snider, and Jeff Holcomb.

Thank you to the following people who provided comments and suggestions that were useful for this sixth edition:

James Bell—*Central Virginia Community College*
Carolyn Z. Gillay—*Saddleback College*
Jason Hebert—*Pearl River Community College*
Jean Kent—*Seattle Community College*
Bob McPherson—*Surry Community College*
Teresa Nickerson—*University of Dubuque*
Anita Philipp—*Oklahoma City Community College*

Thank you to those who provided reviews and comments for previous editions:

Carolyn Andres—*Richland College*
James Bell—*Central Virginia Community College*
Ross Beveridge—*Colorado State University*
Karmen Blake—*Spokane Community College*
Jim Buchan—*College of the Ozarks*
Dan Dao—*Richland College*
Joyce M. Dick—*Northeast Iowa Community College*
Elizabeth Drake—*Santa Fe Community College*
Mark DuBois—*Illinois Central College*
Genny Espinoza—*Richland College*
Sharon Gray—*Augustana College*
Lisa Hopkins—*Tulsa Community College*
Barbara James—*Richland Community College*
Nilofar Kadivi—*Richland Community College*
Jean Kent—*Seattle Community College*
Karen Kowal Wiggins—*Wisconsin Indianhead Technical College*
Manasseh Lee—*Richland Community College*
Nancy Lee—*College of Southern Nevada*
Kyle Loewenhagen—*Chippewa Valley Technical College*
Michael J. Losacco—*College of DuPage*
Les Lusk—*Seminole Community College*
Mary A. McKenzie—*Central New Mexico Community College*
Cindy Mortensen—*Truckee Meadows Community College*
John Nadzam—*Community College of Allegheny County*
Brita E. Penttila—*Wake Technical Community College*
Anita Philipp—*Oklahoma City Community College*
Jerry Ross—*Lane Community College*
Noah Singer—*Tulsa Community College*
Alan Strozer—*Canyons College*
Lo-An Tabar-Gaul—*Mesa Community College*
Tebring Wrigley—*Community College of Allegheny County*
Michelle Youngblood-Petty—*Richland College*

A special thank you also goes to Jean Kent, North Seattle Community College, and Teresa Nickerson, University of Dubuque, for taking time to provide additional feedback and sharing student comments about the book.

Thanks are in order to colleagues at William Rainey Harper College for their support and encouragement, especially Ken Perkins, Sarah Stark, Enrique D'Amico, and Dave Braunschweig.

Most of all, I would like to thank my family for their patience and encouragement. My wonderful husband, Greg Morris, has been a constant source of love, understanding, support, and encouragement. Thank you, Greg! A big shout-out to my children, James and Karen, who grew up thinking that everyone's Mom had their own website. Thank you both for your understanding, patience, and timely suggestions!

The publishers would like to thank Soumi Paul of Jadavpur University, Kolkata and Judhajit Sanyal of the Calcutta Institute of Engineering and Management for reviewing the content of the International Edition.

About the Author

Terry Felke-Morris is a Professor of Computer Information Systems at William Rainey Harper College in Palatine, Illinois. She holds a Doctor of Education degree, a Master of Science degree in information systems, and numerous certifications, including Adobe Certified Dreamweaver 8 Developer, WOW Certified Associate Webmaster, Microsoft Certified Professional, Master CIW Designer, and CIW Certified Instructor.

Dr. Felke-Morris has been honored with Harper College's Glenn A. Reich Memorial Award for Instructional Technology in recognition of her work in designing the college's Web Development program and courses. In 2006, she received the Blackboard Greenhouse Exemplary Online Course Award for use of Internet technology in the academic environment. Dr. Felke-Morris received two international awards in 2008: the Instructional Technology Council's Outstanding e-Learning Faculty Award for Excellence and the MERLOT Award for Exemplary Online Learning Resources—MERLOT Business Classics.

With more than 25 years of information technology experience in business and industry, Dr. Felke-Morris published her first website in 1996 and has been working with the Web ever since. A long-time promoter of Web standards, she has been a member of the Web Standards Project Education Task Force. Dr. Felke-Morris is the senior faculty member in the Web Development certificate and degree programs at William Rainey Harper College. For more information about Dr. Felke-Morris, visit http://terrymorris.net.

Contents

CHAPTER 6

Page Layout 241

CHAPTER 7

More on Links, Layout, and Mobile 297

CHAPTER 8

Tables   349

CHAPTER 9

Forms   377

18　　　**Contents**

LOCATION OF VIDEONOTES IN THE TEXT

A series of videos have been developed as a companion for this textbook. VideoNote icons indicate the availability of a video on a specific topic.

Introduction to the Internet and World Wide Web

Chapter Objectives   In this chapter, you will learn how to . . .

- Describe the evolution of the Internet and the Web
- Explain the need for web standards
- Describe universal design
- Identify benefits of accessible web design
- Identify reliable resources of information on the Web
- Identify ethical use of the Web
- Describe the purpose of web browsers and web servers
- Identify networking protocols
- Define URIs and domain names
- Describe HTML, XHTML, and HTML5
- Describe popular trends in the use of the Web

The Internet and the Web are parts of our daily lives.   How did they begin? What networking protocols and programming languages work behind the scenes to display a web page? This chapter provides an introduction to some of these topics and is a foundation for the information that web developers need to know. You'll be introduced to Hypertext Markup Language (HTML), the language used to create web pages; eXtensible Hypertext Markup Language (XHTML), the most recent standardized version of HTML; and HTML5— the newest draft version of HTML.

1.1 The Internet and the Web

The Internet

The **Internet**, the interconnected network of computer networks that spans the globe, seems to be everywhere today. It has become part of our lives. You can't watch television or listen to the radio without being urged to visit a website. Even newspapers and magazines have their place on the Internet.

Birth of the Internet

The Internet began as a network to connect computers at research facilities and universities. Messages in this network would travel to their destination by multiple routes, or paths. This configuration allowed the network to function even if parts of it were broken or destroyed. In such an event, the message would be rerouted through a functioning portion of the network while traveling to its destination. This network was developed by the Advanced Research Projects Agency (ARPA)—and the ARPAnet was born. Four computers (located at UCLA, Stanford Research Institute, University of California Santa Barbara, and the University of Utah) were connected by the end of 1969.

Growth of the Internet

As time went on, other networks, such as the National Science Foundation's NSFnet, were created and connected with the ARPAnet. Use of this interconnected network, or Internet, was originally limited to government, research, and educational purposes. The ban on commercial use of the Internet was lifted in 1991. The growth of the Internet continues: Internet World Stats reported over 2 billion users, about 30% of the world's population, on the Internet in 2011. Figure 1.1 shows the growth of Internet use by geographic area between 2000 and 2011.

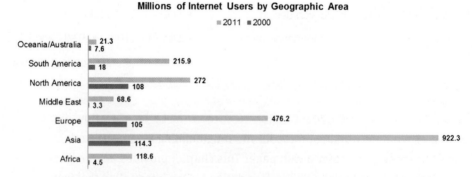

Figure 1.1 Growth of Internet use

The lifting of the restriction on commercial use of the Internet set the stage for future electronic commerce: Businesses were now welcome on the Internet. However, the Internet was still text based and not easy to use. The next set of developments solved this issue.

Birth of the Web

While working at CERN, a research facility in Switzerland, **Tim Berners-Lee** envisioned a means of communication for scientists by which they could easily "hyperlink" to another research paper or article and immediately view it. Berners-Lee created the World Wide Web to fulfill this need. In 1991, Berners-Lee posted the code for the Web in a newsgroup and made it freely available. This version of the World Wide Web used **Hypertext Transfer Protocol (HTTP)** to communicate between the client computer and the web server, used **Hypertext Markup Language (HTML)** to format the documents, and was text based.

VideoNote
Evolution of the Web

The First Graphical Browser

In 1993, Mosaic, the first graphical web browser (shown in Figure 1.2), became available.

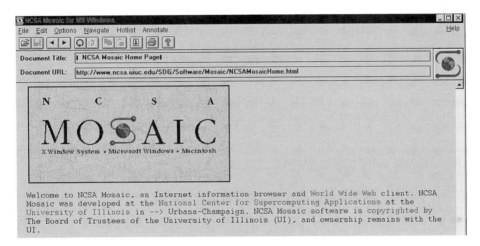

Figure 1.2 Mosaic: The first graphical browser

Marc Andreessen and graduate students working at the National Center for Supercomputing Applications (NCSA) at the University of Illinois Urbana–Champaign developed Mosaic. Some individuals in this group later created another well-known web browser—Netscape Navigator—which is an ancestor of today's Mozilla Firefox browser.

Convergence of Technologies

By the early 1990s, personal computers with easy-to-use graphical operating systems (such as Microsoft's Windows, IBM's OS/2, and Apple's Macintosh OS) were increasingly available and affordable. Online service providers such as CompuServe, AOL, and Prodigy offered low-cost connections to the Internet. The convergence of available computer hardware, easy-to-use operating systems, low-cost Internet connectivity, the HTTP protocol and HTML language, and a graphical browser made information on the Internet much easier to access. The **World Wide Web**—the graphical user interface to information stored on computers running web servers connected to the Internet—had arrived!

Who Runs the Internet?

You may be surprised that there is no single person "in charge" of the global interconnected network of computer networks known as the Internet. Instead, Internet infrastructure standards are overseen by groups such as the **Internet Engineering Task Force (IETF)** and the **Internet Architecture Board (IAB)**. The IETF is the principal body engaged in the development of new Internet protocol standard specifications. It is an open international community of network designers, operators, vendors, and researchers concerned with the evolution of Internet architecture and the smooth operation of the Internet. The actual technical work of the IETF is completed in its working groups. These working groups are organized into areas by topic, such as security and routing.

The IAB is a committee of the IETF and provides guidance and broad direction to the IETF. As a function of this purpose, the IAB is responsible for the publication of the **Request for Comments (RFC)** document series. An RFC is a formal document from the IETF that is drafted by a committee and subsequently reviewed by interested parties. RFCs are available for online review at http://www.ietf.org/rfc.html. Some RFCs are informational in nature, while others are meant to become Internet standards. In the latter case, the final version of the RFC becomes a new standard. Future changes to the standard must be made through subsequent RFCs.

The **Internet Corporation for Assigned Numbers and Names (ICANN)**, http://www.icann.org, was created in 1998 and is a nonprofit organization. Its main function is to coordinate the assignment of Internet domain names, IP address numbers, protocol parameters, and protocol port numbers. Prior to 1998, the **Internet Assigned Numbers Authority (IANA)** coordinated these functions. IANA still performs certain functions under the guidance of ICANN and maintains a website at http://www.iana.org.

Intranets and Extranets

Recall that the Internet is an interconnected network of computer networks that is globally available. When an organization needs the communication capabilities of the Internet, but doesn't want its information to be available to everyone, either an intranet or extranet is appropriate.

An **intranet** is a private network that is contained within an organization or business. Its purpose is to share organizational information and resources among coworkers. When an intranet connects to the outside Internet, usually a gateway or firewall protects the intranet from unauthorized access.

An **extranet** is a private network that securely shares part of an organization's information or operations with external partners such as suppliers, vendors, and customers. Extranets can be used to exchange data, share information exclusively with business partners, and collaborate with other organizations. Privacy and security are important issues in extranet use. Digital certificates, encryption of messages, and virtual private networks (VPNs) are some technologies used to provide privacy and security for an extranet. Digital certificates and encryption used in e-commerce are discussed in Chapter 12.

1.2 Web Standards and Accessibility

Just as with the Internet, no single person or group runs the World Wide Web. However, the **World Wide Web Consortium** (http://www.w3.org), referred to as the W3C, takes a proactive role in developing recommendations and prototype technologies related to the Web. Topics that the W3C addresses include web architecture, standards for web design, and accessibility. In an effort to standardize web technologies, the W3C (logo shown in Figure 1.3) produces specifications called recommendations.

Figure 1.3 The W3C logo

W3C Recommendations

The W3C Recommendations are created in working groups with input from many major corporations involved in building web technologies. These recommendations are not rules; they are guidelines. Major software companies that build web browsers, such as Microsoft, do not always follow the W3C Recommendations. This makes life difficult for web developers because not all browsers will display a web page in exactly the same way. The good news is that there is a convergence toward the W3C Recommendations in new versions of major browsers. There are even organized groups, such as The Web Standards Project, http://webstandards.org, whose mission is to promote W3C Recommendations (often called Web standards) not only to the creators of browsers, but also to web developers and designers. You'll follow W3C Recommendations as you code web pages in this book. Following the W3C Recommendations is the first step toward creating a website that is accessible.

Web Standards and Accessibility

The **Web Accessibility Initiative (WAI)** (http://www.w3.org/WAI), is a major area of work by the W3C. Since the Web has become an integral part of daily life, there is a need for all individuals to be able to access it.

The Web can present barriers to individuals with visual, auditory, physical, and neurological disabilities. An **accessible** website provides accommodations that help individuals overcome these barriers. The WAI has developed recommendations for web content developers, web authoring tool developers, web browser developers, and developers of other user agents to facilitate use of the Web by those with special needs. See the WAI's **Web Content Accessibility Guidelines** (WCAG) at http://www.w3.org/WAI/WCAG20/glance/WCAG2-at-a-Glance.pdf for a quick overview.

Focus on Accessibility

Accessibility and the Law

The **Americans with Disabilities Act** (ADA) of 1990 is a federal civil rights law that prohibits discrimination against people with disabilities. The ADA requires that business, federal, and state services are accessible to individuals with disabilities. A 1996 Department of Justice ruling (http://www.justice.gov/crt/foia/readingroom/frequent_requests/ada_coreletter/cltr204.txt) indicated that ADA accessibility requirements apply to Internet resources.

Focus on Accessibility

Section 508 of the Federal Rehabilitation Act was amended in 1998 to require that U.S. government agencies give individuals with disabilities access to information technology that is comparable to the access available to others. This law requires developers creating information technology (including web pages) for use by the federal government to provide for accessibility. The **Federal IT Accessibility Initiative** (http://www.section508.gov) provides accessibility requirement resources for information technology developers.

In recent years, state governments have also begun to encourage and promote web accessibility. The Illinois Information Technology Accessibility Act (IITAA) guidelines are an example of this trend. (See http://www.dhs.state.il.us/IITAA/IITAAWebImplementationGuidelines.html.)

Universal Design for the Web

The Center for Universal Design defines **universal design** as "the design of products and environments to be usable by all people, to the greatest extent possible, without the need for adaptation or specialized design" (http://www.ncsu.edu/project/design-projects/udi/center-for-universal-design/the-principles-of-universal-design/). Examples of universal design are all around us. The cutouts on curbs that make it possible for people in wheelchairs to access the street also benefit a person pushing a stroller or doing a little rollerblading (Figure 1.4). Doors that open automatically for people with mobility challenges also benefit people carrying packages. A ramp is useful for a person in a wheelchair, a person dragging a rolling backpack or carry-on bag, and so on.

Figure 1.4 Inline skaters benefit from universal design

Awareness of universal design by web developers has been steadily increasing. Forward-thinking web developers design with accessibility in mind because it is the right thing to do. Providing access for visitors with visual, auditory, and other challenges should be an integral part of web design rather than an afterthought.

A person with visual difficulties may not be able to use graphical navigation buttons and may use a screen reader device to provide an audible description of the web page. By making a few simple changes, such as providing text descriptions for the images and perhaps providing a text navigation area at the bottom of the page, web developers can make the page accessible. Often, providing for accessibility increases the usability of the website for all visitors.

Focus on Accessibility

Accessible websites, with alternative text for images, headings used in an organized manner, and captions or transcriptions for multimedia features, are more easily used not only by visitors with disabilities, but also by visitors using a browser on a mobile device such as a phone or tablet. Finally, accessible websites may be more thoroughly indexed by search engines, which can be helpful in bringing new visitors to a site. As this text introduces web development and design techniques, corresponding web accessibility and usability issues are discussed.

1.3 Information on the Web

These days anyone can publish just about anything on the Web. In this section we'll explore how you can tell if the information you've found is reliable and how you can use that information.

Reliability and Information on the Web

There are many websites—but which ones are reliable sources of information? When visiting websites to find information, it is important not to take everything at face value (Figure 1.5).

Questions to ask about web resources are listed as follows;

- **Is the organization credible?**

  Anyone can post anything on the Web! Choose your information sources wisely. First, evaluate the credibility of the website itself. Does it have its own domain name, such as http://mywebsite.com, or is it a free website consisting of just a folder of files hosted on a free web server? The URL of a site hosted on a free web server usually includes part of the free web server's name and might begin with something such as http://mysite.tripod.com or http://www.angelfire.com/foldername/mysite. Information obtained from a website that has its own domain name will usually (but not always) be more reliable than information obtained from a free website.

Figure 1.5 Who really updated that web page you are viewing?

  Evaluate the type of domain name: Is it for a nonprofit organization (.org), a business (.com or .biz), or an educational institution (.edu)? Businesses may provide information in a biased manner, so be careful. Nonprofit organizations and schools will sometimes treat a subject more objectively.

- **How recent is the information?**

  Another item to look at is the date the web page was created or last updated. Although some information is timeless, very often a web page that has not been updated for several years is outdated and may not be the best source of information.

- **Are there links to additional resources?**

  Hyperlinks indicate websites with supporting or additional information that can be helpful to you in your research as you explore a topic. Look for these types of hyperlinks to aid your studies.

- **Is it Wikipedia?**

  Wikipedia is a good place to begin research, but don't accept what you read there for fact, and avoid using Wikipedia as a resource for academic assignments. Why? Well, except for a few protected topics, anyone can update Wikipedia with any-thing! Usually it all gets sorted out eventually—but be aware that the information you read may not be valid.

  Feel free to use Wikipedia to begin exploring a topic, but then scroll down to the bottom of the Wikipedia web page and look for "References"—and then explore those websites and others that you may find. As you gather information on these sites, also consider the other criteria: credibility, domain name, timeliness, and links to additional resources.

Ethical Use of Information on the Web

This wonderful technology called the World Wide Web provides us with information, graphics, and music—all virtually free (after you pay your Internet service provider,

**Focus on
Ethics**

of course). Let's consider the following issues relating to the ethical use of this information:

- Is it acceptable to copy someone's graphic to use on your own website?
- Is it acceptable to copy someone's website design to use on your own site or on a client's site?
- Is it acceptable to copy an essay that appears on a web page and use it, or parts of it, as your own writing?
- Is it acceptable to insult someone on your website or link to that person's site in a derogatory manner?

The answer to all these questions is no. Using someone's graphic without permission is the same as stealing it. In fact, if you link to it, you are actually using up some of the site's bandwidth and may be costing the owner money. Instead, ask the owner of the website for permission to use the graphic. If permission is granted, store the graphic on your own website and be sure to indicate the source of the graphic when you display it on your web page. The key is to request permission before using someone else's resources. Copying the website design of another person or company is also a form of stealing. Any text or graphic on a website is automatically copyrighted in the United States, regardless of whether a copyright symbol appears on the site or not. Insulting a person or company on your website or linking to the person's or company's website in a derogatory manner could be considered a form of defamation.

Issues like these, related to intellectual property, copyright, and freedom of speech, are regularly discussed and decided in courts of law. Good Web etiquette requires that you ask permission before using others' work, give credit for what you use ("fair use" in the U.S. copyright law), and exercise your freedom of speech in a manner that is not harmful to others. The **World Intellectual Property Organization (WIPO)**, http://wipo.int, is dedicated to protecting intellectual property rights internationally.

What if you'd like to retain ownership, but make it easy for others to use or adapt your work? **Creative Commons**, http://creativecommons.org, is a nonprofit organization that provides free services that allow authors and artists to register a type of a copyright license called a Creative Commons license. There are several licenses to choose from, depending on the rights you wish to grant. The Creative Commons license informs others as to exactly what they can and cannot do with your creative work. See http://meyerweb.com/eric/tools/color-blend to view a web page licensed under a Creative Commons Attribution-ShareAlike 1.0 License with "Some Rights Reserved."

 # Checkpoint 1.1

1. Describe the difference between the Internet and the Web.

2. Explain three events that contributed to the commercialization and exponential growth of the Internet.

3. Is the concept of universal design important to web developers? Explain your answer.

1.4 Network Overview

A **network** consists of two or more computers connected for the purpose of communicating and sharing resources. Common components of a network are shown in Figure 1.6 and include the following:

- Server computer(s)
- Client workstation computer(s)
- Shared devices such as printers
- Networking devices (router and switch) and the media that connect them

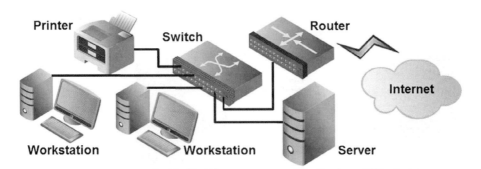

Figure 1.6
Common components of a network

The **clients** are the computer workstations used by individuals, such as a personal computer (PC) on a desk. The **server** receives requests from client computers for resources such as files. Computers used as servers are usually kept in a protected, secure area and are accessed only by network administrators. Networking devices such as hubs and switches provide network connections for computers, and routers direct information from one network to another. The **media** connecting the clients, servers, peripherals, and networking devices may consist of copper cables, fiber optic cables, or wireless technologies.

Networks vary in scale. A **local area network (LAN)** is usually confined to a single building or group of connected buildings. Your school computer lab may use a LAN. If you work in an office, you probably use a computer connected to a LAN. A **wide area network (WAN)** is geographically dispersed and usually uses some form of public or commercial communications network. For example, an organization with offices on both the East and West Coasts of the United States probably uses a WAN to provide a link between the LANs at each of the offices.

A **backbone** is a high-capacity communication link that carries data gathered from smaller links that interconnect with it. On the Internet, a backbone is a set of paths that local or regional networks connect to for long-distance interconnection. The Internet is a group of interconnected networks with very high-speed connectivity provided by the Internet backbones.

1.5 The Client/Server Model

The term **client/server** dates from the last millennium (the 1980s) and refers to personal computers joined by a network. "Client/server" can also describe a relationship between two computer programs—the client and the server. The client requests some type of service (such as a file or database access) from the server. The server fulfills the request and transmits the results to the client over a network. While both the client and the server programs can reside on the same computer, typically they run on different computers (Figure 1.7). It is common for a server to handle requests from multiple clients.

The Internet is a great example of client/server architecture at work. Consider the following scenario: An individual is at a computer using a web browser client to access the Internet. The individual uses the web browser to visit a website, let's say http://www.yahoo.com. The server is the web server program running on the computer with an IP address that corresponds to yahoo.com. It is contacted, locates the web page and related resources that were requested, and responds by sending them to the individual.

Figure 1.7 Web client and web server

Browser
Request

Server
Response

Web Client   Web Server

Here's how to distinguish between web clients and web servers:

Web Client

- Connected to the Internet when needed
- Usually runs web browser (client) software such as Internet Explorer or Firefox
- Uses HTTP
- Requests web pages from a server
- Receives web pages and files from a server

Web Server

- Continually connected to the Internet
- Runs web server software (such as Apache or Internet Information Server)
- Uses HTTP
- Receives a request for the web page
- Responds to the request and transmits the status code, web page, and associated files

When clients and servers exchange files, they often need to indicate the type of file that is being transferred; this is done through the use of a MIME type. **Multipurpose Internet Mail Extensions (MIME)** are rules that allow multimedia documents to be exchanged among many different computer systems. MIME was initially intended to extend the original Internet e-mail protocol, but it is also used by HTTP. MIME provides for the exchange of seven different media types on the Internet: audio, video, image, application, message, multipart, and text. MIME also uses subtypes to further describe the data. The MIME type of a web page is text/html. MIME types of GIF and JPEG images are image/gif and image/jpeg, respectively.

A web server determines the MIME type of a file before the file is transmitted to the web browser. The MIME type is sent along with the document. The web browser uses the MIME type to determine how to display the document.

How does information get transferred from the web server to the web browser? Clients (such as web browsers) and servers (such as a web server) exchange information through the use of communication protocols such as HTTP, TCP, and IP, which are introduced in the next section.

1.6 Internet Protocols

Protocols are rules that describe how clients and servers communicate with each other over a network. There is no single protocol that makes the Internet and Web work; a number of protocols with specific functions are needed.

File Transfer Protocol (FTP)

File Transfer Protocol (FTP) is a set of rules that allow files to be exchanged between computers on the Internet. Unlike HTTP, which is used by web browsers to request web pages and their associated files in order to display a web page, FTP is used simply to move files from one computer to another. Web developers commonly use FTP to transfer web page files from their computers to web servers. FTP is also commonly used to download programs and files from other servers to individual computers.

E-mail Protocols

Most of us take e-mail for granted, but there are two servers involved in its smooth functioning: an incoming mail server and an outgoing mail server. When you send e-mail to others, **Simple Mail Transfer Protocol (SMTP)** is used. When you receive e-mail, **Post Office Protocol** (POP; currently **POP3**) and **Internet Message Access Protocol (IMAP)** can be used.

Hypertext Transfer Protocol (HTTP)

HTTP is a set of rules for exchanging files such as text, images, audio, video, and other multimedia on the Web. Web browsers and web servers usually use this protocol. When the user of a web browser requests a file by typing a website address or clicking on a hyperlink, the browser builds an HTTP request and sends it to the server. The web server in the destination machine receives the request, does any necessary processing, and responds with the requested file and any associated media files.

Transmission Control Protocol/Internet Protocol (TCP/IP)

Transmission Control Protocol/Internet Protocol (TCP/IP) has been adopted as the official communication protocol of the Internet. TCP and IP have different functions that work together to ensure reliable communication over the Internet.

TCP

The purpose of TCP is to ensure the integrity of network communication. TCP starts by breaking files and messages into individual units called **packets**. These packets (see Figure 1.8) contain information such as the destination, source, sequence number, and checksum values used to verify the integrity of the data.

Figure 1.8 TCP packet

TCP is used together with IP to transmit files efficiently over the Internet. IP takes over after TCP creates the packets, using IP addressing to send each packet over the Internet via the best path at the particular time. When the destination address is reached, TCP verifies the integrity of each packet by using the checksum, requests a resend if a packet is damaged, and reassembles the file or message from the multiple packets.

IP

Working in harmony with TCP, IP is a set of rules that controls how data is sent between computers on the Internet. IP routes a packet to the correct destination address. Once sent, the packet gets successively forwarded to the next closest router (a hardware device designed to move network traffic) until it reaches its destination.

Each device connected to the Internet has a unique numeric **IP address**. These addresses consist of a set of four groups of numbers, called octets. The current version of IP, **Internet Protocol Version 4 (IPv4)**, uses 32-bit (binary digit) addressing. This results in a decimal number in the format of xxx.xxx.xxx.xxx, where each xxx is a value from 0 to 255. Theoretically, this system allows for at most 4 billion possible IP addresses (although many potential addresses are reserved for special uses). However, even this many addresses will not be enough to meet the needs of all of the devices expected to be connected to the Internet in upcoming years.

IP Version 6 (IPv6) will be the next standard IP protocol and will provide a huge increase in the number of possible addresses and many technological advances. IPv6 was designed as an evolutionary set of improvements to the current IPv4 and is backwardly compatible with it. Service providers and Internet users can update to IPv6 independently without having to coordinate with each other. IPv6 provides for more Internet addresses because the IP address is lengthened from 32 bits to 128 bits. This means that there are potentially 2^{128} unique IP addresses possible, or 340,282,366,920,938, 463,463,347,607,431,768,211,456 addresses. (Now there will be enough IP addresses for everyone's PC, notebook, cell phone, tablet, toaster, and so on!)

The IP address of a device may correspond to a domain name. The **Domain Name System (DNS)** associates these IP addresses with the text-based URLs and domain names you type into a web browser address box. For example, at the time this book was written, one of Google's IP addresses was 74.125.73.106. You can enter this number in the address text box in a web browser (as shown in Figure 1.9), press Enter, and the Google home page will display. Of course, it's much easier to type "google.com," which is why domain names such as google.com were created in the first place! Since long strings of numbers are difficult for humans to remember, the Domain Name System was introduced as a way to associate text-based names with numeric IP addresses.

Figure 1.9
Entering an IP address in a web browser

1.7 Uniform Resource Identifiers and Domain Names

URIs and URLs

A **Uniform Resource Identifier (URI)** identifies a resource on the Internet. A **Uniform Resource Locator (URL)** is a type of URI which represents the network location of a resource such as a web page, a graphic file, or an MP3 file. The URL consists of the protocol, the domain name, and the hierarchical location of the file on the web server.

The URL http://www.webdevfoundations.net, shown in Figure 1.10, denotes the use of HTTP protocol and the web server named www at the domain name of webdevfoundations.net. In this case, the root file (usually index.html or index.htm) of the chapter1 directory will be displayed.

Figure 1.10 URL
Describing a file within a folder

Domain Names

A **domain name** locates an organization or other entity on the Internet. The purpose of the Domain Name System (DNS) is to divide the Internet into logical groups and understandable names by identifying the exact address and type of the organization. The DNS associates the text-based domain names with the unique numeric IP address assigned to a device.

Let's consider the domain name www.yahoo.com. The ".com" is the top-level domain name. The portion "yahoo.com" is the domain name that is registered to Yahoo! and "yahoo" is considered a second-level domain name. The "www" is the name of the web server (sometimes called **web host server**) at the yahoo.com domain. Taken all together, www.yahoo.com is considered to be a **fully qualified domain name (FQDN)**.

Top-Level Domain Names

A **top-level domain (TLD)** identifies the rightmost part of the domain name, starting with the final period. A TLD is either a generic top-level domain, such as .com for commercial, or a country-code top-level domain, such as .fr for France. ICANN administers the generic top-level domains shown in Table 1.1.

Table 1.1 Top-level domains

Generic TLD	Used By
.aero	Air-transport industry
.asia	Pan-Asia and Asia Pacific community
.biz	Businesses
.cat	Catalan linguistic and cultural community
.com	Commercial entities
.coop	Cooperative
.edu	Restricted to accredited degree-granting institutions of higher education
.gov	Restricted to government use
.info	Unrestricted use
.int	International organization (rarely used)
.jobs	Human resources management community
.mil	Restricted to military use
.mobi	Corresponds to a .com website—the .mobi site is designed for easy access by mobile devices
.museum	Museums
.name	Individuals
.net	Entities associated with network support of the Internet, usually Internet service providers or telecommunication companies
.org	Nonprofit entities
.post	Universal Postal Union, an agency of the United Nations
.pro	Professionals such as accountants, physicians, and lawyers
.tel	Contact information for individuals and businesses
.travel	Travel industry
.xxx	Adult entertainment

The .com, .org, and .net TLD designations are currently used on the honor system, which means that, for example an individual who owns a shoe store (not related to networking) can register shoes.net.

Country-Code Top-Level Domain Names

Two-character country codes have also been assigned as TLD names. These codes were originally intended to be meaningful by designating the geographical location of the individual or organization that registered the name. In practice, however, it is fairly easy to obtain a domain name with a country-code TLD that is not local to the registrant. See http://register.com and many other domain name registration companies for examples. Table 1.2 lists some popular country codes used on the Web.

Table 1.2 Country codes

Country Code TLD	Country
.au	Australia
.de	Germany
.in	India
.jp	Japan
.nl	The Netherlands
.us	United States
.eu	European Union (a group of countries rather than a single country)

The IANA website at http://www.iana.org/cctld/cctld-whois.htm has a complete list of country-code TLDs. Domain names with country codes are often used for municipalities, schools, and community colleges in the United States. For example, the domain name www.harper.cc.il.us denotes, from right to left, the United States, Illinois, community college, Harper, and the web server named "www" as the site for Harper College in Illinois.

The DNS associates domain names with IP addresses. The following happens each time a new URL is typed into a web browser:

1. The DNS is accessed.

2. The corresponding IP address is obtained and returned to the web browser.

3. The web browser sends an HTTP request to the destination computer with the corresponding IP address.

4. The HTTP request is received by the web server.

5. The necessary files are located and sent by HTTP responses to the web browser.

6. The web browser renders and displays the web page and associated files.

The next time you wonder why it is taking so long to display a web page, think about all of the processing that goes on behind the scenes.

FAQ   Will there be any new TLDs soon?

ICANN has approved the expansion of generic TLDs and announced that it will accept applications for new, customized TLDs. Think of the marketing possibilities—your organization's name, product, or service as a TLD! Sound too good to be true? Well, there's a catch. With a $185,000 application fee and an annual $25,000 fee, deep pockets are needed. Visit http://icann.org for more information.

1.8 Markup Languages

Markup languages consist of sets of directions that tell the browser software (and other user agents such as mobile phones) how to display and manage a web document. These directions are usually called tags and perform functions such as displaying graphics, formatting text, and referencing hyperlinks.

Standard Generalized Markup Language (SGML)

SGML is a standard for specifying a markup language or tag set. SGML in itself is not a document language, but a description of how to specify one and create a document type definition (DTD). When Tim Berners-Lee created HTML, he used SGML to create the specification.

Hypertext Markup Language (HTML)

HTML is the set of markup symbols or codes placed in a file intended for display on a web browser. The web browser renders the code in the HTML file and displays the web page document and associated files. The W3C (http://www.w3.org) sets the standards for HTML.

Extensible Markup Language (XML)

XML was developed by the W3C as a flexible method to create common information formats and share the format and the information on the Web. It is a text-based syntax designed to describe, deliver, and exchange structured information. It is not intended to replace HTML, but to extend the power of HTML by separating data from presentation. Using XML, developers can create whatever tags they need to describe their information.

Extensible Hypertext Markup Language (XHTML)

XHTML was developed by the W3C to reformulate HTML 4.01 as an application of XML. It combines the formatting strengths of HTML 4.01 *and* the data structure and extensibility strengths of XML. The primary advantages of XHTML include the ability to extend the language by creating new tags and the promise of increased platform interoperability as mobile devices are used more frequently to access the Web.

HTML5—the Newest Version of HTML

As this was being written, the W3C's HTML Working Group (HTML WG) was busy creating a draft recommendation for **HTML5**, which is intended to be the successor to HTML4 and will replace XHTML. HTML5 incorporates features of both HTML and XHTML, adds new elements, provides new features such as form edits and native video, and is intended to be backward compatible. Although this version still in draft form, much of the proposal is stable and supported by modern browsers. You'll learn to use HTML5 syntax as you work through this textbook.

 ## Checkpoint 1.2

1. Describe the components of the client/server model as applied to the Internet.

2. Identify two protocols used on the Internet to convey information that use the Internet, but do not use the Web.

3. Explain the similarities and differences between a URL and a domain name.

1.9 Popular Uses of the Web

E-Commerce

Continued growth is expected for **e-commerce**, which is the buying and selling of goods and services on the Internet. Forrester Research projects that by 2014, over $248 billion will be spent on online retail sales (http://techcrunch.com/2010/03/08/forrester-forecast-online-retail-sales-will-grow-to-250-billion-by-2014/). With over 2 billion people online worldwide, as reported by Internet World Stats (http://www.internetworldstats.com/emarketing.htm), that's quite a few potential shoppers! As mobile web access becomes more commonplace, e-commerce will be regularly done not only from stationary computers, but also from portable devices—tablets, netbooks, smartphones, and technology we haven't even imagined yet.

Mobile Access

Accessing the Web with devices other than the standard desktop, notebook, and netbook computers is a growing trend. Gartner predicts that by 2013, mobile phones (including smartphones and browser-equipped phones) will "overtake PCs as the most common Web access device worldwide" (http://www.gartner.com/it/page.jsp?id=1278413). SearchBlog reported a Google 2011 projection that "between 15% and 30% of site traffic will come from mobile devices within eighteen months" (http://www.mediapost.com/publications/?fa=Articles.showArticle&art_aid=147794). Bloomberg Businessweek reported that electronics manufacturers expect a huge demand for **tablet** computers (such as the Apple iPad, Motorola Xoom, and Blackberry Playbook) and anticipate $49 billion in sales by 2015 (http://buswk.co/fK2Q9e). Web designers must consider how their pages will display and function not only on personal computers, but also on smartphones, tablets, and other mobile devices.

Blogs

The trend of keeping a web log, or blog, has been driven by individuals as a forum for personal expression. A **blog** is a journal that is available on the Web; it is a frequently updated page with a chronological list of ideas and links. Blog topics range from politics to technical information to personal diaries. Blogs can focus on one subject or range across a diverse group of topics—it's up to the person, called a blogger, who has created and maintains the blog. Bloggers usually update their blogs daily with easy-to-use software designed to allow people with little or no technical background to update and maintain a blog. Many blogs are hosted at blog communities such as http://www.blogger.com, http://www.wordpress.com, and http://www.tumblr.com. Others are hosted at individual websites, such as the blog kept by the web designer Eric Meyer at http://meyerweb.com. Businesses have noted the value of blogs as communication and customer relationship tools. Companies such as Adobe (http://feeds.adobe.com) and IBM (https://www.ibm.com/developerworks/mydeveloperworks/blogs) utilize blogs in this manner.

Wikis

A **wiki** is a website that can be updated immediately at any time by visitors, using a simple form on a web page. Some wikis are intended for a small group of people, such as the members of an organization. The most powerful wiki is Wikipedia (http://wikipedia.org), an online encyclopedia, which can be updated by anyone at any time. Wikis are a form of social software in action—visitors sharing their collective knowledge to create a resource freely used by all. While there have been isolated incidents of practical jokes, and inaccurate information has occasionally been posted at Wikipedia, the given information and linked resources are a good starting point when exploring a topic.

Social Networking

Blogs and wikis provide web visitors with new methods for interacting with websites and other people—a use referred to as **social computing,** or **social networking**. A trendy activity these days is participating in a social networking site such as Facebook (http://www.facebook.com) or LinkedIn (http://www.linkedin.com). Research firm eMarketer predicts that by 2014, close to two-thirds of all Internet users will regularly access social networking sites (http://www.emarketer.com/Report.aspx?code=emarketer_2000644). If it seems to you as if most of your friends are on Facebook, that may be the case: As of 2011, Facebook had over 500 million active users (http://www.digitalbuzzblog.com/facebook-statistics-stats-facts-2011/). While LinkedIn was created with professional and business networking in mind, businesses have also found it useful to create Facebook sites to promote their products and services.

Twitter (http://www.twitter.com) is a social networking site for **microblogging**, or frequently communicating with a brief message (140 characters or less) called a **tweet**. Twitter users (called twitterers) tweet to update a network of friends and followers about their daily activities and observations. Twitter is not limited to personal use. The business world has also discovered the marketing reach that Twitter can provide. Information Week (http://www.informationweek.com/news/hardware/desktop/217801030) reported that Dell attributes $3 million in sales to its use of Twitter.

RSS

Really Simple Syndication, or **Rich Site Summary (RSS)** is used to create newsfeeds from blog postings and other websites. The RSS feeds contain a summary of new items posted to the site. The URL to the RSS feed is usually indicated by the letters XML or RSS in white text within an orange rectangle. A **newsreader** is needed to access the information. Some browsers, such as Firefox, Safari, and Internet Explorer (version 7 or later), can display RSS feeds. Commercial and shareware newsreader applications are also available. The newsreader polls the feed URL at intervals and displays the new headlines when requested. RSS provides web developers with a method to push new content to interested parties and (hopefully) generate return visits to the site.

Podcasts

Podcasts are audio files on the web that take the format of an audio blog, radio show, or interview. Podcasts are typically delivered by an RSS feed, but can also be made available by providing the link to a recorded MP3 file on a web page. These files can be saved to your computer or to an MP3 player (such as an iPod) for later listening.

Web 2.0

Flickr (http://www.flickr.com/) and del.icio.us (http://del.icio.us/) are two social software sites that provide information-sharing opportunities. Flickr, a photo-sharing site, calls itself the "best way to store, search, sort, and share your photos." Once owned by Yahoo!, but sold to AVOS Systems in April 2011, del.icio.us is a collection of users' favorite sites, or bookmarks. Registered users post lists of favorites, share their favorites with others, and discover new sites by looking at others' favorites. Websites such as Wikipedia, Flickr, Twitter, and del.icio.us are examples of what is called **Web 2.0.** While a consensus on the definition of Web 2.0 has yet to be reached, think of it as the next step in the transition of the Web from isolated static websites to a platform that utilizes technology to provide rich interfaces and social networking opportunities. Visit http://www.go2web20.net and use the search engine to find Web 2.0 sites. You may also read Tim O'Reilly's informative Web 2.0 essay at http://oreillynet.com/pub/a/oreilly/tim/news/2005/09/30/what-is-web-20.html for more information on this developing topic.

The single trend that you can expect to remain the same for the foreseeable future is the trend of constant change. Internet and web-related technologies are in a constant state of development and improvement. If constant change and the opportunity to learn something new excite you, web development is a fascinating field. The skills and knowledge you gain in this book should provide a solid foundation for your future learning.

FAQ   **What is the next big thing on the Web?**

The Web is changing by the minute. Check the textbook's companion website at http://www.webdevfoundations.net for a blog that will help you stay current about web trends.

Chapter Summary

This chapter has provided a brief overview of Internet, Web, and introductory networking concepts. Much of this information may already be familiar to you. Visit the textbook's website at http://www.webdevfoundations.net for links to the URLs listed in this chapter and to view updated information.

Key Terms

accessibility
backbone
blog
client/server
clients
domain name
Domain Name System (DNS)
extranet
File Transfer Protocol (FTP)
fully qualified domain name (FQDN)
HTML5
Hypertext Markup Language (HTML)
Hypertext Transfer Protocol (HTTP)
Internet
Internet Architecture Board (IAB)
Internet Assigned Numbers Authority (IANA)
Internet Corporation for Assigned Numbers and Names (ICANN)
Internet Engineering Task Force (IETF)
Internet Message Access Protocol (IMAP)

intranet
IP
IP address
IP Version 4 (IPv4)
IP Version 6 (IPv6)
Local Area Network (LAN)
markup languages
media
microblogging
Multipurpose Internet Mail Extensions (MIME)
network
newsreader
packets
podcasts
Post Office Protocol (POP3)
protocols
Really Simple Syndication or Rich Site Summary (RSS)
Request for Comments (RFC)
server
Simple Mail Transfer Protocol (SMTP)
social computing
social networking

Standard Generalized Markup Language (SGML)
tablet
TCP
top-level domain (TLD)
Transmission Control Protocol/ Internet Protocol (TCP/IP)
tweet
Uniform Resource Indicator (URI)
Uniform Resource Locator (URL)
Web 2.0
Web Accessibility Initiative (WAI)
Web Content Accessibility Guidelines (WCAG)
web host server
Wide Area Network (WAN)
wiki
World Intellectual Property Organization (WIPO)
World Wide Web
World Wide Web Consortium (W3C)
XHTML
XML

Review Questions

Multiple Choice

1. Which of the following is a network that covers a small area, such as a group of buildings or campus?
   a. LAN
   b. WAN
   c. Internet
   d. WWW

2. Which of the following markup languages is intended to extend the power of HTML by separating data from presentation?
   a. XML
   b. XHTML
   c. HTML5
   d. SGML

3. Of the following organizations, which one coordinates applications for new TLDs?
   - a. Internet Assigned Numbers Authority (IANA)
   - b. Internet Engineering Task Force (IETF)
   - c. Internet Corporation for Assigned Numbers and Names (ICANN)
   - d. World Wide Web Consortium (W3C)

4. What is a unique text-based Internet address corresponding to a computer's unique numeric IP address called?
   - a. IP address
   - b. domain name
   - c. URL
   - d. user name

5. Which of the following organizations takes a proactive role in developing recommendations and prototype technologies related to the Web?
   - a. World Wide Web Consortium (W3C)
   - b. Web Professional Standards Organization (WPO)
   - c. Internet Engineering Task Force (IETF)
   - d. Internet Corporation for Assigned Numbers and Names (ICANN)

True or False

6. _____ A URL is one type of URI.

7. _____ Markup languages contain sets of directions that tell the browser software how to display and manage a web document.

8. _____ The World Wide Web was developed to allow companies to conduct e-commerce over the Internet.

9. _____ A domain name that ends in .net indicates that the website is for a networking company.

Fill in the Blank

10. A standard language used for specifying a markup language or tag set is _____.

11. _____ combines the formatting strengths of HTML 4.0 and the data structure and extensibility strengths of XML.

12. _____ is the set of markup symbols or codes placed in a file intended for display on a web browser.

13. The newest version of HTML is called _____.

14. Frequently communicating by posting brief messages at a social networking site is called _____.

15. The purpose of _____ is to ensure the integrity of network communication.

Hands-On Exercise

1. Create a blog to document your learning experiences as you study web development. Visit one of the many sites that offer free blogs, such as http://www.blogger.com, http://www.wordpress.com, or http://www.xanga.com. Follow the site's instructions to establish your own blog. Your blog could be a place to note websites that you find useful or interesting. You might report on sites that contain useful web design resources. You might describe sites that have interesting features, such as compelling graphics or easy-to-use navigation. Write a few sentences about each site that you find intriguing. After you begin to develop your own sites, you could include the URLs and reasons for your design decisions. Share this blog with your fellow students and friends. Display your page in a browser, and print the page. Hand in the printout to your instructor.

Web Research

1. The World Wide Web Consortium creates standards for the Web. Visit its site at http://www.w3c.org and then answer the following questions:

   a. How did the W3C get started?

   b. Who can join the W3C? What does it cost to join?

   c. The W3C home page lists a number of technologies. Choose one that interests you, click on its link, and read the associated pages. List three facts or issues you discover.

2. The Internet Society takes an active leadership role in issues related to the Internet. Visit its site at http://www.isoc.org and then answer the following questions:

   a. Why was the Internet Society created?

   b. Determine which local chapter is closest to you. Visit its website. List the website's URL and an activity or service that the chapter provides.

   c. How can you join the Internet Society? What does it cost to join? Would you recommend that a beginning Web developer join the Internet Society? Why or why not?

3. The World Organization of Webmasters (WOW) is a professional association dedicated to the support of individuals and organizations that create and manage websites. Visit its site at http://www.webprofessionals.org and then answer the following questions:

   a. How can you join WOW? What does it cost to join?

   b. List one of the events in which WOW participates. Would you like to attend this event? Why or why not?

   c. List three ways that WOW can help you in your future career as a web developer.

Focus on Web Design

1. Visit a website that interests you. Print the home page or one other pertinent page from the site. Write a one-page summary of the site that addresses the following topics:

   a. What is the URL of the site?

   b. What is the purpose of the site?

   c. Who is the intended audience?

   d. Do you think that the site reaches its intended audience? Why or why not?

   e. Is the site useful to you? Why or why not?

   f. Does this site appeal to you? Why or why not? Consider the use of color, images, multimedia, organization, and ease of navigation.

   g. Would you encourage others to visit this site? Why or why not?

   h. How could this site be improved?

HTML Basics

Chapter Objectives   In this chapter, you will learn how to . . .

- Describe HTML, XHTML, and HTML5

- Identify the markup language in a web page document

- Use the html, head, body, title, and meta elements to code a template for a web page

- Configure the body of a web page with headings, paragraphs, line breaks, divs, lists, and blockquotes

- Configure text with phrase elements

- Configure special characters

- Use the anchor element to link from page to page

- Create absolute, relative, and e-mail hyperlinks

- Code, save, and display a web page document

- Test a web page document for valid syntax

This chapter gets you started on your very first web page. You'll be introduced to Hypertext Markup Language (HTML), the language used to create web pages; eXtensible Hypertext Markup Language (XHTML), the most recent standardized version of HTML; and HTML5, the newest draft version of HTML. The chapter begins with an introduction to the syntax of XHTML and HTML5; continues with sample web pages; and introduces HTML structural, phrase, and hyperlink elements as more example web pages are created. You will learn more if you work along with the sample pages in the text. Coding HTML is a skill, and every skill improves with practice.

2.1 HTML Overview

Markup languages consist of sets of directions that tell the browser software (and other user agents such as mobile phones) how to display and manage a web document. These directions are usually called tags and perform functions such as displaying graphics, formatting text, and referencing hyperlinks.

The World Wide Web is composed of files containing Hypertext Markup Language (HTML) and other markup languages that describe web pages. Tim Berners-Lee developed HTML using Standard Generalized Markup Language (SGML). SGML prescribes a standard format for embedding descriptive markup within a document and for describing the structure of a document. SGML is not in itself a document language, but rather a description of how to specify one and create a document type definition (DTD). The W3C (http://www.w3c.org) sets the standards for HTML and its related languages. Like the Web itself, HTML is in a constant state of change.

HTML

HTML is the set of markup symbols or codes placed in a file that is intended for display on a web page. These markup symbols and codes identify structural elements such as paragraphs, headings, and lists. HTML can also be used to place media (such as graphics, video, and audio) on a web page and describe fill-in forms. The browser interprets the markup code and renders the page. HTML permits the platform-independent display of information across a network. No matter what type of computer a web page was created on, any browser running on any operating system can display the page.

Each individual markup code is referred to as an **element**, or **tag**. Each tag has a purpose. Tags are enclosed in angle brackets, the < and > symbols. Most tags come in pairs: an opening tag and a closing tag. These tags act as containers and are sometimes referred to as container tags. For example, the text that is between the <title> and </title> tags on a web page would display in the title bar on the browser window. Some tags are used alone and are not part of a pair. For example, a <br> tag that configures a line break on a web page is a stand-alone, or self-contained, tag and does not have a closing tag. Most tags can be modified with **attributes** that further describe their purpose.

XHTML

The most recent standardized version of HTML used today is **eXtensible HyperText Markup Language (XHTML)**. XHTML uses the tags and attributes of HTML4 along with the syntax of XML. HTML was originally developed to provide access to electronic documents via a web browser. Web browsers that evolved along with HTML were written to forgive coding errors, ignore syntax errors, and allow "sloppy" HTML code. Web browsers contain many program instructions that are designed to ignore mistakes such as missing ending tags and to guess how the developer meant the page to display. These extra instructions are not a problem for a personal computer, which has relatively large processing power. However, it could be an issue for electronic devices with fewer resources, such as an Internet tablet or mobile phone.

The purpose of XHTML was to provide a foundation for device-independent web access. XHTML was developed by the W3C to be the reformulation of HTML as an application of XML. XHTML combines the formatting strengths of HTML and the data structure and extensibility strengths of XML. Since XHTML was designed using XML, let's take a quick look at XML.

XML (eXtensible Markup Language) is the W3C standard method for creating new markup languages that will support the display of nontraditional content such as mathematical notation, as well as support a variety of display devices. XML can fulfill these diverse needs because it is an extensible language—that is, it is designed to allow the definition of new tags or markup. The syntax of XML is very exacting so that devices do not have to waste processing power guessing how the document should display, but can instead display information efficiently. An XML document must be well formed. A **well-formed document** is a document that adheres to the syntax rules of the language.

HTML5

As this textbook was being written, the W3C's HTML Working Group (HTML WG) was busy creating a draft recommendation for HTML5, which is intended to be the successor to HTML4 and will replace XHTML. HTML5 incorporates features of both HTML and XHTML, adds new elements of its own, provides new features such as form edits and native video, and is intended to be backward compatible.

It is possible to begin using HTML5 right away! The newest versions of popular browsers, such as Internet Explorer 9, Firefox 4, Safari 5, Google Chrome, and Opera 10, already support some of the new features of HTML5. When new versions of each browser are released, you can expect increased support of HTML5. As you learn to design web pages, you need not only to know what works today in current browsers, but also to get ready to use new HTML5 coding techniques. To meet this challenging goal, this book introduces both XHTML syntax and HTML5 syntax, presents instruction for coding web pages in HTML5 with backward-compatible elements that work in current browsers, and provides practice with the new features of HTML5 that will work only in the latest versions of browsers. Since HTML5 is in draft status and may change after this book is printed, consult http://www.w3.org/TR/html-markup for the most current list of HTML5 elements.

 FAQ What software do I need?

No special software is needed to create a web page document; all you need is a text editor. The Notepad text editor is included with Microsoft Windows. TextEdit is distributed with the Mac OS X operating system. (See http://support.apple.com/kb/TA20406 for configuration information.) An alternative to the operating system's basic text editor is one of the many free or shareware editors that are available, such as Notepad++ for Windows (http://notepad-plus-plus.org/download) and TextWrangler for Macs (http://www.barebones.com/products/textwrangler/download.html). Another commonly used alternative is a commercial web-authoring tool, such as Microsoft Expression Web or Adobe Dreamweaver. Regardless of the software or program you use, having a solid foundation in HTML will be useful.

You will need to test your web pages in the most popular browsers, which are listed as follows, along with the URLs where you can download them for free:

- Internet Explorer (http://microsoft.com/ie9)
- Mozilla Firefox (http://www.mozilla.com/en-US/products/download.html)
- Apple Safari (http://www.apple.com/safari/download/)
- Google Chrome (http://www.google.com/chrome)

You will also find the Web Developer Extension for Firefox (https://addons.mozilla.org/en-us/firefox/addon/web-developer) to be useful.

2.2 Document Type Definition

Because multiple versions and types of HTML and XHTML exist, the W3C recommends identifying the type of markup language used in a web page document with a **Document Type Definition (DTD)**. The DTD identifies the version of HTML contained in your document. Browsers and HTML code validators can use the information in the DTD when processing the web page. The DTD statement, commonly called a **doctype** statement, is placed at the top of a web page document. XHTML is the current standard version of HTML and is supported by popular browsers. HTML5 is the newest version and is currently in draft status. Most of the examples in this book use HTML5 syntax. Except where specifically noted, the HTML5 syntax will display on commonly used browsers.

2.3 Example XHTML Web Page

In this example, we will use the XHTML 1.0 Transitional DTD, which is the least strict version of XHTML 1.0. The DTD for XHTML 1.0 Transitional is as follows:

```
<!DOCTYPE html PUBLIC "-//W3C//DTD XHTML 1.0 Transitional//EN"
"http://www.w3.org/TR/xhtml1/DTD/xhtml1-transitional.dtd">
```

The rest of your web page document will consist of HTML elements and text. After the DTD, each web page begins with an opening `<html>` tag and ends with a closing `</html>` tag. These tags indicate that the text between them is HTML formatted for display in a browser. Every single XHTML web page you create will include the DTD statement, followed by the html, head, title, meta, and body elements. A basic XHTML web page template (found in the student files at chapter2/templatex.html) is as follows:

```
<!DOCTYPE html PUBLIC "-//W3C//DTD XHTML 1.0 Transitional//EN"
"http://www.w3.org/TR/xhtml1/DTD/xhtml1-transitional.dtd">
<html xmlns="http://www.w3.org/1999/xhtml" lang="en" xml:lang="en">
<head>
<title>Page Title Goes Here</title>
<meta http-equiv="Content-Type" content="text/html; charset=utf-8" />
</head>
<body>
... body text and more XHTML tags go here ...
</body>
</html>
```

The XHTML tags are lowercase in the code sample. This format conforms to XML syntax. Notice also that the DTD statement does not follow this syntax. The DTD statement indicates the markup language being used and has mixed-case formatting. With the exception of the specific page title, the first eight lines will usually be the same on every XHTML web page that you create.

When using XHTML, the `<html>` tag also needs to describe the XML namespace (xmlns), which is the location of the documentation for the elements being used. This additional information is added to the `<html>` tag in the form of an **attribute**, which modifies or further describes the function of an element. The xmlns attribute points to the URL of the XHTML namespace used in the document, the standard http://www.w3.org/1999/xhtml. The optional **lang** and **xml:lang** attributes specify the spoken language of the document. For example, `lang="en" xml:lang="en"` indicate the English language. Search engines and screen readers may access these attributes.

Don't worry if the concept of specifying a DTD and the xmlns URL seem a bit overwhelming at first—these lines are reused over and over again in every web page. Once you create your web page template, you'll have these statements ready and waiting for all of your future pages.

2.4 Example HTML5 Web Page

Now that you've seen an example of a web page using XHTML, let's focus on HTML5. The syntax is streamlined and easier to use. We will follow the coding style to use lowercase letters and place quotation marks around attribute values. The HTML5 doctype statement is as follows:

```
<!DOCTYPE html>
```

Just as with XHTML, the doctype statement is the first line in the document. Next, the web page begins with an opening `<html>` tag and ends with a closing `</html>` tag. These tags indicate that the text between them is HTML formatted for display in a browser. Every HTML5 web page contains the doctype statement, followed by the html, head, title, meta, and body elements. A basic HTML5 web page template (found in the student files at chapter2/template.html) is as follows:

```
<!DOCTYPE html>
<html lang="en">
<head>
<title>Page Title Goes Here</title>
<meta charset="utf-8">
</head>
<body>
... body text and more HTML5 tags go here ...
</body>
</html>
```

The next section discusses the purpose of the head, title, meta, and body elements.

2.5 Head, Title, Meta, and Body Elements

There are two sections on a web page: the head and the body. The **head section**, some-times called the header section, contains information that describes the web page document. The **body section** contains the actual tags, text, images, and other objects that are displayed by the browser as a web page.

The Head Section

Elements that are located in the head section include the title of the web page, meta tags that describe the document (such as the character encoding used and information that may be accessed by search engines), and references to scripts and styles. Many of these features do not show directly on the web page. The **head element** contains the head section, which begins with the `<head>` tag and ends with the `</head>` tag. You will always code at least two other elements in the head section: a title element and a meta element.

The first element in the head section, the **title element**, configures the text that will appear in the title bar of the browser window. The text between the `<title>` and `</title>` tags is called the title of the web page and is accessed when web pages are bookmarked and printed. The title should be descriptive. If the web page is for a business or organization, the title should include the name of the organization or business.

The **meta element** describes a characteristic of a web page, such as the character encoding. **Character encoding** is the internal representation of letters, numbers, and symbols in a file such as a web page or other file that is stored on a computer and may be transmitted over the Internet. There are many different character-encoding sets. However, it is common practice to use a character-encoding set that is widely supported, such as utf-8, which is a form of Unicode. The meta tag is not used as a pair of opening and closing tags. It is considered to be a stand-alone, or **self-contained**, tag (referred to as a **void element** in HTML5). The meta tag is coded differently in XHTML and HTML5. The XHTML meta tag has more detailed attributes and is coded with an ending `/>`. The HTML5 meta tag is streamlined and includes only the charset attribute to indicate the character encoding.

XHTML Meta Tag

```
<meta http-equiv="Content-Type" content="text/html; charset=utf-8" />
```

HTML5 Meta Tag

```
<meta charset="utf-8">
```

The Body Section

The body section contains text and elements that display directly on the web page in the browser viewport. The purpose of the body section is to configure the contents of the web page. The **body element** contains the body section, which begins with the `<body>` tag and ends with the `</body>` tag. You will spend most of your time writing code in the body of a web page. If you type text into the body section, it will appear directly on the web page.

2.6 Your First Web Page

 ## Hands-On Practice 2.1

VideoNote
**Your First
Web Page**

Now that you're familiar with basic elements used on every web page, it's your turn to create your first web page.

Create a Folder

You'll find it helpful to create folders to organize your files as you develop the web pages in this book and create your own websites. Use your operating system to create a new folder named mychapter2 on your hard drive or a portable flash drive.

To create a new folder on a Mac:

1. Launch Finder, and select the location where you would like to create the new folder.

2. Choose File > New Folder to create an untitled folder.

3. To rename the folder, select the folder and click on the current name. Type a name for the folder, and press the Return key.

To create a new folder with Windows:

1. Launch Windows Explorer (either press the Windows key or select Start > All Programs > Accessories > Windows Explorer), and navigate to the location where you would like to create the new folder, such as My Documents or your C: drive.

2. Select Organize > New Folder.

3. To rename the New Folder, right-click on it, select Rename from the context-sensitive menu, type in the new name, and press the Enter key.

Your First Web Page

Now you are ready to create your first HTML5 web page. Launch Notepad or another text editor. Type in the following code:

```
<!DOCTYPE html>
<html lang="en">
<head>
<title>My First HTML5 Web Page</title>
<meta charset="utf-8">
</head>
<body>
Hello World
</body>
</html>
```

Notice that the first lines in the file contain the doctype. The HTML code begins with an opening `<html>` tag and ends with a closing `</html>` tag. The purpose of these tags is to indicate that the content between the tags makes up a web page. The head section is delimited by `<head>` and `</head>` tags and contains a pair of title tags with the words "My First HTML5 Web Page" in between, along with a `<meta>` tag to indicate the character encoding. The body section is delimited by `<body>` and `</body>` tags.

The words "Hello World" are typed on a line between the body tags. See Figure 2.1 for a screen-shot of the code as it would appear in Notepad. You have just created the source code for a web page document.

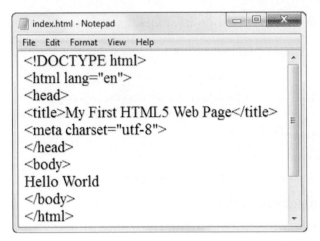

Figure 2.1 Your web page source code displayed in Notepad

 FAQ **Do I have to start each tag on its own line?**

No, you are not required to start each tag on a separate line. A browser can display a page even if all the tags follow each other on one line with no spaces. Humans, however, find it easier to write and read web page code if line breaks and indentation are used.

Save Your File

You will save your file with the name of index.html. A common file name for the home page of a website is index.html or index.htm. Web pages use either a .htm or a .html file extension. The web pages in this book use the .html file extension. Display your file in Notepad or another text editor. Select File from the menu bar, and then select Save As. The Save As dialog box will appear. Navigate to your mychapter2 folder. Using Figure 2.2 as an example, type the file name. Click the Save button after you type the file name. Sample solutions for the exercises are available in the student files. If you like, you can compare your work with the solution in the student files at chapter2/index.html before you test your page.

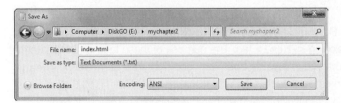

Figure 2.2 The Save As dialog box

FAQ **Why does my file have a .txt file extension?**

In some older versions of Windows, Notepad will automatically append a .txt file extension. If this happens, type the name of the file within quotation marks ("index.html"), and save your file again.

Test Your Page

There are two ways to test your page:

1. Launch Windows Explorer (Windows) or Finder (Mac). Navigate to your index.html file. Double-click index.html. The default browser will launch and will display your index.html page. Your page should look similar to the one shown in Figure 2.3.

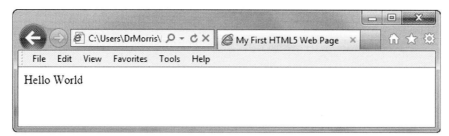

Figure 2.3 Web page displayed by Internet Explorer

2. Launch a browser. (If you are using Internet Explorer 9, right-click in the area at the top of the browser window and select the Menu bar.) Select File > Open > Browse. Navigate to your index.html file. Double-click index.html, and click OK. If you used Internet Explorer, your page should look similar to the one shown in Figure 2.3. A display of the page using Firefox 4 is shown in Figure 2.4.

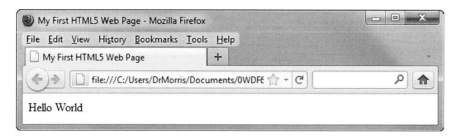

Figure 2.4 Web page displayed by Firefox

Examine your page. Look carefully at the browser window. Notice how the browser title bar or browser tab displays the title text, "My First HTML5 Web Page." Some search engines use the text enclosed within the `<title>` and `</title>` tags to help determine the relevancy of keyword searches, so make certain that your pages contain descriptive titles. The title element is also used when viewers bookmark your page or add it to their Favorites. An engaging and descriptive page title may entice a visitor to revisit your page. If your web page is for a company or an organization, it's a best practice to include the name of the company or organization in the title.

Checkpoint 2.1

1. Describe the origin, purpose, and features of HTML.

2. Describe the software needed to create and test web pages.

3. Which element contains the visible page content of a web page?

2.7 Heading Element

Heading elements are organized into six levels: h1 through h6. The text contained within a heading element is rendered as a "block" of text by the browser (referred to as block display) and displays with empty space (sometimes called "white space") above and below. The size of the text is largest for **<h1>** (called the heading 1 tag) and smallest for **<h6>** (called the heading 6 tag). Depending on the font being used (more on font sizes in Chapter 3), the text contained within **<h4>**, **<h5>**, and **<h6>** tags may be displayed smaller than the default text size. All text contained within heading tags is displayed with bold font weight. Figure 2.5 shows a web page document with six levels of headings.

FAQ   Why doesn't the heading tag go in the head section?

It's common for students to try to code the heading tags in the head section of the document, but someone doing this won't be happy with the way the browser displays the web page. Even though "heading tag" and "head section" sound similar, always code heading tags in the body section of the web page document.

Figure 2.5 Sample headings

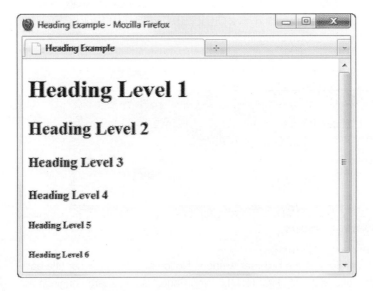

Hands-On Practice 2.2

To create the web page shown in Figure 2.5, launch Notepad or another text editor. Select File > Open to edit the HTML5 template file located at chapter2/template.html in the student files. Modify the title element and add heading tags to the body section as indicated by the following highlighted code:

```
<!DOCTYPE html>
<html lang="en">
<head>
<title>Heading Example</title>
<meta charset="utf-8">
</head>
<body>
<h1>Heading Level 1</h1>
<h2>Heading Level 2</h2>
<h3>Heading Level 3</h3>
<h4>Heading Level 4</h4>
<h5>Heading Level 5</h5>
<h6>Heading Level 6</h6>
</body>
</html>
```

Save the document as heading2.html on your hard drive or flash drive. Launch a browser such as Internet Explorer or Firefox to test your page. It should look similar to the page shown in Figure 2.5. You can compare your work with the HTML5 solution found in the student files (chapter2/heading.html) and the XHTML solution (chapter2/headingxhtml.html). Notice that in this example, the code for both solutions is the same except for the Document Type Declaration, html, and meta tags. This is true for most of the examples in this chapter. The HTML5 solutions for each hands-on practice activity are provided in the student files. The XHTML solution is also provided when deemed useful for comparison.

Accessibility and Headings

Heading tags can help to make your pages more accessible and usable. You create an outline of the page content when you code heading tags numerically as appropriate (h1, h2, h3, and so on) and configure page content in block display elements such as paragraphs and lists. Visually challenged visitors who are using a screen reader can direct the software to display a list of the headings used on a page to focus on the topics that interest them. Your well-organized page will be more usable for every visitor to your site, including those who are visually challenged.

Focus on Accessibility

More Heading Options in HTML5

You may have heard about the new HTML5 header hgroup elements. They offer additional options for configuring headings, but they are supported only in newer browsers. We will introduce these new elements in Chapter 6.

2.8 Paragraph Element

Paragraph elements are used to group sentences and sections of text together. Text that is contained by **<p>** and **</p>** tags display as a "block" (referred to as block display) and will appear with empty space above and below it. Figure 2.6 shows a web page document with a paragraph after the first heading.

Figure 2.6 Web
page using
headings and a
paragraph

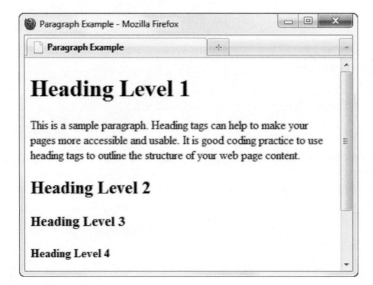

Hands-On Practice 2.3

To create the web page shown in Figure 2.6, launch a text editor. Select File > Open to edit the file
located at chapter2/heading.html in the student files. Modify the page title, and add a paragraph
of text to your page below the line with the `<h1>` tags and above the line with the `<h2>` tags. Use
the following code as an example:

```
<!DOCTYPE html>
<html lang="en">
<head>
<title>Paragraph Example</title>
<meta charset="utf-8">
</head>
<body>
<h1>Heading Level 1</h1>
<p>This is a sample paragraph. Heading tags can help to make your
pages more accessible and usable. It is good coding practice to use
heading tags to outline the structure of your web page content.
</p>
<h2>Heading Level 2</h2>
<h3>Heading Level 3</h3>
<h4>Heading Level 4</h4>
<h5>Heading Level 5</h5>
<h6>Heading Level 6</h6>
</body>
</html>
```

Save the document as paragraph2.html on your hard drive or flash drive. Launch a browser to
test your page. It should look similar to the page shown in Figure 2.6. You can compare your
work with the solution found in the student files (chapter2/paragraph.html). Notice how the text in
the paragraph wraps automatically as you resize your browser window.

Alignment

As you tested your web pages, you may have noticed that the headings and text begin near the left margin. This placement is called **left alignment** and is the default alignment for web pages. There are times, however, when you want a paragraph or heading to be centered or right aligned. The align attribute can be used for this purpose. The purpose of an **attribute** is to modify the properties of an HTML element. In this case, the **align** attribute modifies the element's horizontal alignment (left, center, or right) on a web page. To center an element on a web page, use the attribute `align="center"`. To right-align the text within an element, use the `align="right"` attribute. In XHTML syntax, the align attribute can be used with a number of block display elements, including the paragraph (`<p>`) and heading (`<h1>` through `<h6>`) tags. The align attribute is **obsolete** in HTML5, which means that while it may be used in XHTML, the attribute has been removed from the W3C HTML5 draft specification. In Chapter 6, you will learn how to configure alignment using a more modern approach with Cascading Style Sheets (CSS).

2.9 Line Break Element

The **line break element** causes the browser to advance to the next line before displaying the next element or portion of text on a web page. The line break tag is not coded as a pair of opening and closing tags. It is considered to be a **stand-alone,** or **void**, element. In HTML5 syntax, the line break tag is coded as **
**. In XHTML (which follows XML syntax), the line break tag is coded as <br />. (The ending /> indicates a self-contained tag.) Figure 2.7 shows a web page document with a line break after the first sentence in the paragraph.

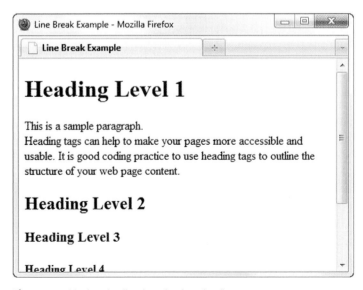

Figure 2.7 Notice the line break after the first sentence

Hands-On Practice 2.4

To create the web page shown in Figure 2.7, launch a text editor. Select File > Open to edit the file located at chapter2/paragraph.html in the student files. Modify the text contained between the title tags to be "Line Break Example". Place your cursor after the first sentence in the paragraph (after "This is a sample paragraph."). Press the Enter key. Save your file. Test your page in a browser, and notice that even though your source code showed the "This is a sample paragraph." sentence on its own line, the browser did not render it that way. A line break tag is needed to configure the browser to display the second sentence on a new line. Edit the file in a text editor, and add a `<br>` tag (the file uses HTML5 syntax) after the first sentence in the paragraph, as shown in the following code snippet:

```
<body>
<h1>Heading Level 1</h1>
<p>This is a sample paragraph. <br> Heading tags can help to make
your pages more accessible and usable. It is good coding practice to
use heading tags to outline the structure of your web page content.
</p>
<h2>Heading Level 2</h2>
<h3>Heading Level 3</h3>
<h4>Heading Level 4</h4>
<h5>Heading Level 5</h5>
<h6>Heading Level 6</h6>
</body>
```

Save your file as linebreak2.html. Launch a browser to test your page. It should look similar to the page shown in Figure 2.7. You can compare your work with the solution found in the student files (chapter2/linebreak.html). An XHTML solution can also be found in the student files (chapter2/linebreakxhtml.html).

FAQ   Why does my web page still look the same?

Often, students make changes to a web page document, but get frustrated because their browser shows an older version of the page. The following troubleshooting tips are helpful when you know you modified your web page, but the changes do not show up in the browser:

1. Make sure you save your page after you make the changes.

2. Verify the location that you are saving your page to—a specific folder on the hard drive or removable storage.

3. Verify the location that your browser is requesting the page from—a specific folder on the hard drive or removable storage.

4. Be sure to click the Refresh or Reload button in your browser.

2.10 Blockquote Element

In addition to organizing text in paragraphs and headings, sometimes you need to add a quotation to a web page. **The blockquote element** is used to display a block of quoted text in a special way—indented from both the left and right margins. A block of indented text begins with a **`<blockquote>`** tag and ends with a **`</blockquote>`** tag. Figure 2.8 shows a web page document with a heading, a paragraph, and a blockquote.

Figure 2.8 The text within the blockquote element is indented

Hands-On Practice 2.5

To create the web page shown in Figure 2.8, launch a text editor. Select File > Open to edit the template file located at chapter2/template.html in the student files. Modify the title element. Add a heading tag, a paragraph tag, and a blockquote tag to the body section as indicated by the following highlighted code:

```
<!DOCTYPE html>
<html lang="en">
<head>
<title>Blockquote Example</title>
<meta charset="utf-8">
</head>
<body>
<h1>The Power of the Web</h1>
<p>According to Tim Berners-Lee, the inventor of the World Wide Web,
at http://www.w3.org/WAI/:</p>
<blockquote>
The power of the Web is in its universality. Access by everyone
regardless of disability is an essential aspect.
</blockquote>
</body>
</html>
```

Save the document as blockquote2.html on your hard drive or flash drive. Launch a browser to test your page. It should look similar to the page shown in Figure 2.8. You can compare your work with the solution found in the student files (chapter2/blockquote.html).

You have probably noticed how convenient the `<blockquote>` tag could be if you need to indent an area of text on a web page. You may have wondered whether it would be OK to use the blockquote element anytime you would like to indent text or whether the blockquote element is reserved only for long quotations. The semantically correct use of the blockquote element is only for displaying large blocks of quoted text within a web page. Why should you be concerned about semantics? Consider the future of the Semantic Web, described in *Scientific American* (http://www.scientificamerican.com/article.cfm?id=the-semantic-web) as "[a] new form of Web content that is meaningful to computers [that] will unleash a revolution of new possibilities." Using HTML in a semantic, structural manner is one step toward the Semantic Web. So, avoid using a blockquote element just to indent text. You will learn modern techniques to configure margins and padding on elements later in this book.

2.11 Phrase Elements

Phrase elements, sometimes referred to as **logical style elements,** indicate the context and meaning of the text between the container tags. It is up to each browser to interpret that style. Phrase elements are displayed right in line with the text (referred to as inline display) and can apply to a section of text or even just a single character of text. For example, the **<strong>** element indicates that the text associated with it has strong importance and should be displayed in a "strong" manner in relation to normal text on the page. Table 2.1 lists common phrase elements and examples of their use. Notice that some tags, such as <cite> and <dfn>, result in the same type of display (italics) as the <em> tag in today's browsers. These tags semantically describe the text as a citation or definition, but the physical display is usually italics in both cases.

Table 2.1 Phrase elements

Element	Example	Usage
<abbr>	WIPO	Identifies text as an abbreviation; configure the title attribute with the full name
<b>	**bold** text	Text that has no extra importance, but is styled in bold font by usage and convention
<cite>	*cite* text	Identifies a citation or reference; usually displayed in italics
<code>	`code` text	Identifies program code samples; usually a fixed-space font
<dfn>	*dfn* text	Identifies a definition of a word or term; usually displayed in italics
<em>	*emphasized* text	Causes text to be emphasized in relation to other text; usually displayed in italics
<i>	*italicized* text	Text that has no extra importance, but is styled in italics by usage and convention
<kbd>	`kbd` text	Identifies user text to be typed; usually a fixed-space font
<mark>	mark text	Text that is highlighted in order to be easily referenced (HTML5 only)
<samp>	`samp` text	Shows program sample output; usually a fixed-space font
<small>	small text	Legal disclaimers and notices ("fine print") displayed in small font size
<strong>	**strong** text	Strong importance; causes text to stand out from surrounding text; usually displayed in bold
<sub>	sub text	Displays a subscript as small text below the baseline
<sup>	sup text	Displays a superscript as small text above the baseline
<var>	*var* text	Identifies and displays a variable or program output; usually displayed in italics

Each phrase element is a container element, so an opening and a closing tag must be used. As shown in Table 2.1, the <strong> element indicates that the text associated with it has "strong" importance. Usually, the browser (or other user agent) will display <strong> text in bold font type. A screen reader, such as JAWS or Window-Eyes, might interpret `<strong>` text to indicate that the text should be more strongly spoken. In the following line, the phone number is displayed with strong importance:

```
Call for a free quote for your web development needs: 888.555.5555
```

The corresponding code is

```
<p>Call for a free quote for your web development needs:
<strong>888.555.5555</strong></p>
```

Notice that the opening `<strong>` and closing `</strong>` tags are contained within the paragraph tags (`<p>` and `</p>`). This code is properly nested and is considered to be **well formed**. When improperly nested, the `<p>` and `<strong>` tag pairs overlap each other instead of being nested within each other. Improperly nested code will not pass validation testing (see Section 2.18, "HTML Validation") and may cause display issues.

Figure 2.9 shows a web page document (also found in the student files at chapter2/em.html) that uses the `<em>` tag to display the emphasized phrase "Access by everyone" in italics.

The code snippet is

```
<blockquote>
The power of the Web is in its universality.
<em>Access by everyone</em>
regardless of disability is an essential aspect.
</blockquote>
```

Figure 2.9 The `<em>` tag in action

2.12 Unordered List

Lists are used on web pages to organize information. When writing for the Web, headings, short paragraphs, and lists make your pages clear and easy to read. HTML can be used to create three types of lists: **description lists**, **ordered lists**, and **unordered lists**. This section focuses on the unordered list, often referred to as a bulleted list when using word processing applications.

An **unordered list** displays a bullet, or list marker, before each entry in the list. This bullet can be one of several types: disc (the default), square, and circle. See Figure 2.10 for a sample unordered list.

Popular Web Servers

- Apache Web Server
- Microsoft IIS
- Oracle iPlanet Web Server

Figure 2.10 Sample unordered list

Unordered lists begin with a **`<ul>`** tag and end with a **`</ul>`** tag. Each list item begins with an **`<li>`** tag and ends with an **`</li>`** tag. The code to configure the heading and unordered list shown in Figure 2.10 is

```
<h1>Popular Web Servers</h1>
<ul>
    <li>Apache Web Server</li>
    <li>Microsoft IIS</li>
    <li>Oracle iPlanet Web Server</li>
</ul>
```

The Type Attribute

The type attribute can be used to change the type of list marker, or bullet. For example, to create an unordered list organized with square list markers, use `<ul type="square">`. Table 2.2 documents the type attribute and its values for unordered lists.

Table 2.2 The type attribute for unordered lists

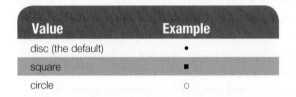

Value	Example
disc (the default)	•
square	■
circle	o

HTML5 and Unordered Lists

The type attribute is widely used in unordered lists and is valid in XHTML. However, be aware that the type attribute on the `<ul>` tag is considered obsolete in HTML5 because it is decorative and does not convey meaning. No worries—you will learn how to configure the list markers in an unordered list with CSS in Chapter 6.

 ## Hands-On Practice 2.6

In this Hands-On Practice, you will use a heading and an unordered list on the same page. To create the web page shown in Figure 2.11, launch a text editor. Select File > Open to edit the template file located at chapter2/template.html in the student files. Modify the title element and add h1, ul, and li tags to the body section as indicated by the following highlighted code:

Figure 2.11 An unordered list

```
<!DOCTYPE html>
<html lang="en">
<head>
<title>Heading and List</title>
<meta charset="utf-8">
</head>
<body>
<h1>Popular Web Servers</h1>
<ul>
    <li>Apache Web Server</li>
    <li>Microsoft IIS</li>
    <li>Oracle iPlanet Web Server</li>
</ul>
</body>
</html>
```

Save your file as ul2.html. Launch a browser and test your page. It should look similar to the page shown in Figure 2.11. You can compare your work with the solution in the student files (chapter2/ul.html). Take a few minutes to experiment with the type attribute. Configure the unordered list to use square bullets. Save your file as ul3.html. Test your page in a browser. You can compare your work with the solution in the student files (chapter2/ulsquare.html).

 FAQ   Can I use images as the "bullets" in unordered lists?

Yes, you can. In Chapter 6, you will learn to use Cascading Style Sheets (CSS) to configure the list markers ("bullets") in an unordered list to display graphic files as list markers.

2.13 Ordered List

An ordered list displays a numbering or lettering system to itemize the information contained in the list. Ordered lists can be organized by the use of numerals (the default), uppercase letters, lowercase letters, uppercase Roman numerals, and lowercase Roman numerals. See Figure 2.12 for a sample ordered list.

Popular Web Servers

1. Apache Web Server
2. Microsoft IIS
3. Oracle iPlanet Web Server

Figure 2.12 Sample ordered list

Ordered lists begin with an **<ol>** tag and end with an **</ol>** tag. Each list item begins with an **<li>** tag and ends with an **</li>** tag. The code to configure the heading and ordered list shown in Figure 2.12 follows:

```
<h1>Popular Web Servers</h1>
<ol>
     <li>Apache Web Server</li>
     <li>Microsoft IIS</li>
     <li>Oracle iPlanet Web Server</li>
</ol>
```

The Type Attribute

The type attribute configures the symbol used for ordering the list. For example, to create an ordered list organized by uppercase letters, use <ol type="A">. Table 2.3 documents the type attribute and its values for ordered lists.

Table 2.3 The type attribute for ordered lists

Value	Symbol
1	Numerals (the default)
A	Uppercase letters
a	Lowercase letters
I	Roman numerals
i	Lowercase Roman numerals

HTML5 and Ordered Lists

Even though unordered lists and ordered lists are similar, HTML5 treats their type attribute differently. In HTML5, the type attribute is obsolete for use with unordered lists. However, the type attribute is valid when used with ordered lists because the sequencing provides information. The **start attribute** is useful when you need a list to begin with an integer value other than 1 (for example, `start="10"`). Use the new HTML5 **reversed attribute** (set `reversed="reversed"`) to configure the list markers to display in descending order.

 ## Hands-On Practice 2.7

In this Hands-On Practice, you will use a heading and an ordered list on the same page. To create the web page shown in Figure 2.13, launch a text editor. Select File > Open to edit the template file located at chapter2/template.html in the student files. Modify the title element and add h1, ol, and li elements to the body section as indicated by the following highlighted code:

```
<!DOCTYPE html>
<html lang="en">
<head>
<title>Heading and List</title>
<meta charset="utf-8">
</head>
<body>
<h1>Popular Web Servers</h1>
<ol>
    <li>Apache Web Server</li>
    <li>Microsoft IIS</li>
    <li>Oracle iPlanet Web Server</li>
</ol>
</body>
</html>
```

Save your file as ol2.html. Launch a browser and test your page. It should look similar to the page shown in Figure 2.13. You can compare your work with the solution in the student files (chapter2/ol.html).

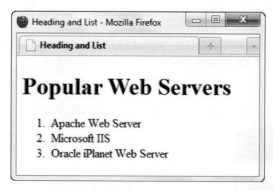

Figure 2.13 An ordered list

Take a few minutes to experiment with the type attribute. Configure the ordered list to use uppercase letters instead of numerals. Save your file as ol3.html. Test your page in a browser. You can compare your work with the solution in the student files (chapter2/ola.html).

2.14 Description List

HTML5 introduces a new element name, **description list**, to replace the definition list element (used in XHTML and earlier versions of HTML). A description list is useful for organizing terms and their descriptions. The terms stand out, and their descriptions can be as long as needed to convey your message. Each term begins on its own line at the margin. Each description begins on its own line and is indented. Description lists are also handy for organizing Frequently Asked Questions (FAQs) and their answers. The questions and answers are offset with indentation. Any type of information that consists of a number of corresponding terms and longer descriptions is well suited to being organized in a description list. See Figure 2.14 for an example of a web page that uses a description list.

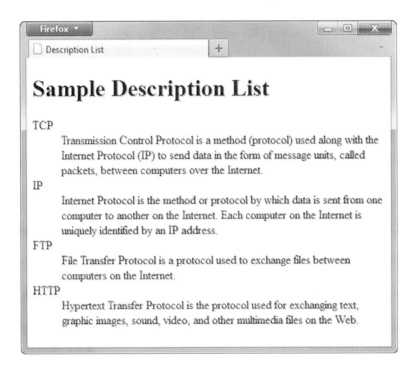

Figure 2.14 A description list

Description lists begin with the **<dl>** tag and end with the **</dl>** tag. Each term or name in the list begins with the **<dt>** tag and ends with the **</dt>** tag. Each description begins with the **<dd>** tag and ends with the **</dd>** tag.

Hands-On Practice 2.8

In this Hands-On Practice, you will use a heading and a description list on the same page. To create the web page shown in Figure 2.14, launch a text editor. Select File > Open to edit the template file located at chapter2/template.html in the student files. Modify the title element and add h1, dl, dd, and dt tags to the body section as indicated by the following highlighted code:

```
<!DOCTYPE html>
<html lang="en">
<head>
<title>Description List</title>
<meta charset="utf-8">
```

```
</head>
<body>
<h1>Sample Description List</h1>
<dl>
    <dt>TCP</dt>
        <dd>Transmission Control Protocol is a method (protocol) used
along with the Internet Protocol (IP) to send data in the form of
message units, called packets, between computers over the Internet.</dd>
    <dt>IP</dt>
        <dd>Internet Protocol is the method or protocol by which data
is sent from one computer to another on the Internet. Each computer
on the Internet is uniquely identified by an IP address.</dd>
    <dt>FTP</dt>
        <dd>File Transfer Protocol is a protocol used to exchange
files between computers on the Internet.</dd>
    <dt>HTTP</dt>
        <dd>Hypertext Transfer Protocol is the protocol used for
exchanging text, graphic images, sound, video, and other multimedia
files on the Web.</dd>
</dl>
</body>
</html>
```

Save your file as description2.html. Launch a browser and test your page. It should look similar to the page shown in Figure 2.14. Don't worry if the word wrap is a little different; the important formatting is that each **<dt>** term should be on its own line and the corresponding **<dd>** description should be indented under it. Try resizing your browser window, and notice how the word wrap on the description text changes. You can compare your work with the solution in the student files (chapter2/description.html).

FAQ   **Why is the HTML code in the Hands-On Practice examples indented?**

Actually, it doesn't matter to the browser if web page code is indented, but humans find it easier to read and maintain code when it is logically indented. Review the description list created in Hands-On Practice 2.7. Notice how the **<dt>** and **<dd>** tags were indented. This makes it easier for you or another web developer to understand the source code in the future. There is no rule as to how many spaces to indent, although your instructor or the organization you work for may have a standard. Consistent indentation helps to create more easily maintainable web pages.

Checkpoint 2.2

1. How do the heading tags help to make a page more accessible to its users?

2. What are the different types of lists that could be created using HTML5?

3. Describe the purpose of the blockquote element.

2.15 Special Characters

In order to use special symbols such as quotation marks, the greater-than sign (>), the less-than sign (<), and the copyright symbol (©) in your web page document, you need to use **special characters**, sometimes called **entity characters**. For example, if you wanted to include a copyright line on your page as follows:

```
© Copyright 2013 My Company. All rights reserved.
```

Use the special character `&copy;` to display the copyright symbol, as shown in the following code:

```
&copy; Copyright 2013 My Company. All rights reserved.
```

Another useful special character is ` `, which stands for nonbreaking space. You may have noticed that web browsers treat multiple spaces as a single space. If you need a small number of spaces in your text, you may use   multiple times to indicate multiple blank spaces. This practice is acceptable if you simply need to tweak the position of an element a little. However, if you find that your web pages contain many   special characters in a row, you should use a different method, such as configuring the padding or margin with Cascading Style Sheets (see Chapters 4 and 6.). Table 2.4 and Appendix C, "Special Entity Characters," provide descriptions of special characters and their corresponding code.

Table 2.4 Common special characters

Character	Entity Name	Code
"	Quotation mark	&quot;
'	Right single quotation mark	&rsquo;
©	Copyright symbol	&copy;
&	Ampersand	&amp;
Empty space	Nonbreaking space	
—	Long dash	&mdash;
		Vertical Bar	|

 ## Hands-On Practice 2.9

Figure 2.15 shows the web page you will create in this Hands-On Practice. Launch a text editor. Select File > Open to edit the template file located at chapter2/template.html in the student files. Modify the title of the web page by changing the text between the `<title>` and `</title>` tags to "Web Design Steps."

The sample page shown in Figure 2.15 contains a heading, an unordered list, and copyright information. Configure the heading "Web Design Steps" as a level 1 heading (`<h1>`) as follows:

```
<h1>Web Design Steps</h1>
```

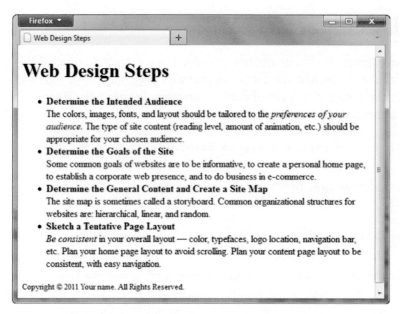

Figure 2.15 The design.html web page

Now create the unordered list. The first line of each bulleted item is the title of the web design step, which should be strong or stand out from the rest of the text. The code for the beginning of the unordered list is as follows:

```
<ul>
  <li><strong>Determine the Intended Audience</strong><br>
The colors, images, fonts, and layout should be tailored to the
<em>preferences of your audience.</em> The type of site content
(reading level, amount of animation, etc.) should be appropriate for
your chosen audience.</li>
```

Now code the entire ordered list in your design.html file. Remember to code the closing `</ul>` tag at the end of the list. Don't worry if your text wraps a little differently; your screen resolution or browser window size may be different from what is displayed in Figure 2.15.

Finally, configure the copyright information with the small element. Use the special character `&copy;` for the copyright symbol. The code for the copyright line is as follows:

```
<p><small>Copyright &copy; 2011 Your name. All Rights Reserved.
</small></p>
```

How did you do? Compare your work to the sample in the student files (chapter2/design.html).

2.16 Div Element

The **div** element configures a structural block area, or "division," on a web page, with empty space above and below. A div element begins with a `<div>` tag and ends with a `</div>` tag. Use a div element when you need to format an area of a web page, such as a logo, navigation, or footer area. The div element is also useful for configuring a section that contains other block display elements, such as `<p>`, `<ul>`, `<blockquote>`, and even other `<div>` elements. You will use Cascading Style Sheets (CSS) later in this book to style and configure the color, text typeface, and layout of div and other structural elements such as headings, paragraphs, and lists. Chapter 6 will introduce new HTML5 structural elements that you can use in modern browsers instead of div elements to configure common page areas, including the header, nav, footer, aside, article, and section elements.

Hands-On Practice 2.10

In this Hands-On Practice, you will practice using the div element as you edit the Trillium Media Design home page, shown in Figure 2.16. Launch a text editor, and open the starter.html file from the chapter2 folder in the student files. Save your page as div2.html.

Figure 2.16 This page uses the div element

The code from the body section is as follows:

```
<body>
<h1>Trillium Media Design</h1>
<p>Home  Services  Contact</p>
<h2>New Media and Web Design</h2>
<p>Trillium Media Design will bring your company&rsquo;s Web presence
to the next level. We offer a comprehensive range of services.</p>
<h2>Meeting Your Business Needs</h2>
<p>Our expert designers are creative and eager to work with you.
Take advantage of the power of Web 2.0!</p>
<p><small>Copyright &copy; 2012 Your Name Here</small></p>
</body>
```

Review the code, and notice that the navigation information and the copyright information are configured in paragraph tags, even though they are not really paragraphs (or even sentences). Both a paragraph element and a div element configure text in a block with empty space above and below. However, when the text is not a true paragraph in meaning, a div element is the better choice. Modify the code to replace the paragraph tags that contain the navigation and copyright information with div tags as follows:

```
<body>
<h1>Trillium Media Design</h1>
<div>Home  Services  Contact</div>
<h2>New Media and Web Design</h2>
<p>Trillium Media Design will bring your company&rsquo;s Web presence
to the next level. We offer a comprehensive range of services.</p>
<h2>Meeting Your Business Needs</h2>
<p>Our expert designers are creative and eager to work with you.
Take advantage of the power of Web 2.0!</p>
<div><small>Copyright &copy; 2012 Your Name Here</small></div>
</body>
```

Save your file and display it in a browser. It should look about the same. However, it is now improved "under the hood"—the div elements are a better semantic choice than paragraph elements to configure content areas that are not actually paragraphs, such as the navigation and copyright areas. The student files contain a sample solution at chapter2/div.html. As you continue to develop web pages, youwill find that div elements are very handy for configuring areas on web pages.

 FAQ   **Are there new structural elements in HTML5 that configure areas on web pages?**

Yes, one of the characteristics of HTML5 is an emphasis on semantics. While the div element is useful, it is also quite generic. HTML5 offers a variety of special-purpose structural elements, including section, article, heading, nav, aside, and footer. You'll explore these elements in Chapter 6.

2.17 Anchor Element

Use the **anchor element** to specify a **hyperlink**, often referred to as a *link*, to another web page or file that you want to display. Each anchor element begins with an **<a>** tag and ends with a **</a>** tag. The opening and closing anchor tags surround the text to click to perform the hyperlink. Use the **href** attribute to configure the hyperlink reference, which identifies the name and location of the file to access. Figure 2.17 shows a web page document with an anchor tag that configures a hyperlink to this book's website, http://webdevfoundations.net.

Figure 2.17
Sample hyperlink

The code for the anchor tag in Figure 2.17 is as follows:

```
<a href="http://webdevfoundations.net">Web Development &amp; Design
Foundations</a>
```

Notice that the href value is the URL for the website. The text that is typed between the two anchor tags displays on the web page as a hyperlink and is underlined by most browsers. When you move the mouse cursor over a hyperlink, the cursor changes to a pointing hand, as shown in Figure 2.17.

Hands-On Practice 2.11

To create the web page shown in Figure 2.17, launch a text editor. Select File > Open to edit the template file located at chapter2/template.html in the student files. Modify the title element and add anchor tags to the body section as indicated by the following highlighted code:

```
<!DOCTYPE html>
<html lang="en">
<head>
<title>Anchor Example</title>
<meta charset="utf-8">
</head>
<body>
<a href="http://webdevfoundations.net">Web Development &amp; Design
Foundations</a>
</body>
</html>
```

Save the document as anchor2.html on your hard drive or flash drive. Launch a browser to test your page. It should look similar to the page shown in Figure 2.17. You can compare your work with the solution found in the student files (chapter2/anchor.html).

FAQ   Can images be hyperlinks?

Yes. Although we'll concentrate on text hyperlinks in this chapter, it's also possible to configure an image as a hyperlink. You'll get practice with image links in Chapter 4.

Absolute Hyperlinks

An **absolute hyperlink** indicates the absolute location of a resource on the Web. Use absolute hyperlinks when you need to link to resources on other websites. The href value for an absolute hyperlink to the home page of a website includes the `http://` protocol and the domain name. The following hyperlink is an absolute hyperlink to the home page of this book's website:

```
<a href="http://webdevfoundations.net">Web Development &amp; Design
Foundations</a>
```

Note that if we want to access a web page other than the home page on the book's website, we could also include a specific folder name and file name. For example, the following anchor tag configures an absolute hyperlink for a file named chapter1.html located in a folder named 6e on this book's website:

```
<a href="http://webdevfoundations.net/6e/chapter1.html">Web Development
&amp; Design Foundations Chapter 1</a>
```

Relative Hyperlinks

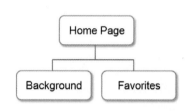

Figure 2.18 Site map

When you need to link to web pages within your site, use a relative hyperlink. The href value for a relative hyperlink does not begin with the http:// and does not include a domain name. For a relative hyperlink, the href value will contain only the file name or file name and folder of the web page you want to display. The hyperlink location is relative to the page currently being displayed. For example, if you were coding a home page (index.html) for the website whose site map is illustrated in Figure 2.18 and wanted to link to a page named contact.html located in the same folder as index.html, you would use the following code sample:

```
<a href="contact.html">Contact Us</a>
```

 Hands-On Practice 2.12

The best way to learn how to code web pages is by actually doing it! Let's practice and create three pages in a sample website.

1. Create a new folder. Name your folder "mypractice". The site we will create here is an example of a personal website. It will contain a home page called index.html and two content pages called background.html and favorites.html. A sample site map (see Figure 2.18) shows

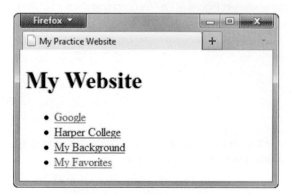

Figure 2.19 Sample index.html displayed in the Firefox browser

the organization of the site: a home page (index.html) with navigation hyperlinks to two other pages (background.html and favorites.html).

2. Now create the home page for your mypractice website, as shown in Figure 2.19. Launch a text editor. Select File > Open to edit the template file located at chapter2/template.html in the student files. Modify the title element and configure the following:

- A "My Website" heading—use `<h1>` tags
- An unordered list with the following:
  - An absolute link to your favorite search engine
  - An absolute link to the website of your school
  - A relative link to background.html
  - A relative link to favorites.html

The body section of your web page will be similar to the following code sample:

```
<body>
<h1>My Website</h1>
<ul>
    <li><a href="http://google.com">Google</a></li>
    <li><a href="http://harpercollege.edu">Harper College</a></li>
    <li><a href="background.html">My Background</a></li>
    <li><a href="favorites.html">My Favorites</a></li>
</ul>
</body>
```

Save your page as index.html in the mypractice folder. Display your page in a browser. It should look similar to the page shown in Figure 2.19. Compare your work to the sample (chapter2/practice/index.html) in the student files. Test your page by clicking each link. When you click the absolute links to your favorite search engine and your school, you should see those pages displayed if you are connected to the Internet. The relative links should not work yet; let's create the background.html page in Step 3.

3. Create the background.html page, as shown in Figure 2.20.

Figure 2.20 Sample background.html page

Let's work efficiently by building on the previous page. Launch a text editor and open the index.html file. Select File > Save As to save the file with the name background.html in the mypractice folder. In order to create a consistent logo for the site, do not change the h1 heading area. Replace the rest of the web page content with the following:

- A subheading of "My Background"—use <h2> tags

- A paragraph that contains one or two sentences about your background

- A navigation bar configured within a div that contains relative hyperlinks to the home page (index.html), the "My Background" page (background.html), and the "My Favorites" page (favorites.html). As shown in Figure 2.20, you will need to add a blank space between each anchor element. The body section of your web page will be similar to the following code sample:

```
<body>
  <h1>My Website</h1>
  <h2>My Background</h2>
     <p>As a college student majoring in Web Design, I'm interested
     in developing my skills in design principles, HTML, and CSS.</p>
  <div><a href="index.html">Home</a>
     <a href="background.html">Background</a>
     <a href="favorites.html">Favorites</a></div>
</body>
```

Save your file. Now test your index.html page again. This time, when you click the "My Background" hyperlink, your browser should display your new page. Click the "Home" hyperlink on your background.html page to redisplay your home page. Don't worry if these hyperlinks do not work perfectly the first time. If you have problems, carefully examine the source code of the pages, and verify the existence and location of the files by using Windows Explorer or the Mac Finder.

4. Using Step 3 as a guide, create the "My Favorites" page (favorites.html), and configure an unordered list of your favorite topics. See an example in the student files (chapter2/practice/favorites.html).

 FAQ **What if my relative hyperlink doesn't work?**

Check the following:

- Did you save files in the specified folder?

- Did you save the files with the names as requested? Use Windows Explorer, My Computer, or Finder (Mac users) to verify the actual names of the files you saved.

- Did you type the file names correctly in the anchor tag's href property? Check for typographical errors.

- When you place your mouse cursor over a link, the file name of a relative link will display in the status bar in the lower edge of the browser window. Verify that the correct file name appears.

On many operating systems, such as UNIX or Linux, the use of uppercase and lowercase in file names matters, so make sure that the file name and the reference to it are in the same case. It's a good practice to use only lowercase letters for file names used on the Web.

E-Mail Hyperlinks

The anchor tag can also be used to create e-mail hyperlinks. An **e-mail link** will automatically launch the default mail program configured for the browser. The href value of an e-mail link begins with "mailto:", followed by a valid e-mail address. For example, to create an e-mail link to the e-mail address help@terrymorris.net, code the following:

```
<a href="mailto:help@terrymorris.net">help@terrymorris.net</a>
```

It's a good practice to configure the e-mail address as the hyperlink text. Not everyone has an e-mail program configured with his or her browser. You increase usability for all your visitors by displaying the e-mail address as text on the web page.

 # Hands-On Practice 2.13

In this Hands-On Practice, you will modify the home page of the website you created in Hands-On Practice 2.12 by adding an e-mail link to the page's footer area. Launch a text editor, and open the index.html file from your mypractice folder. This example uses the index.html file found in the student files in the chapter2/practice folder.

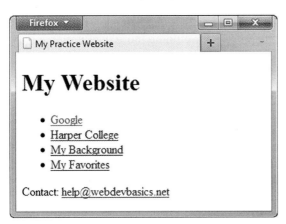

Figure 2.21 E-mail link added to index.html

Configure a div that contains the text "Contact:" and an e-mail hyperlink at the bottom of the page as shown in Figure 2.21. Use your e-mail address as the href value. Save the page, and test it in a browser. The browser display should look similar to the page shown in Figure 2.21. Compare your work with the sample in the student files (chapter2/practice2/index.html). Modify the favorites.html and background.html files in a similar manner. Sample solutions are located in the student files (chapter2/practice2 folder).

 FAQ **Won't displaying my actual e-mail address on a web page increase spam?**

Yes and no. While it's possible that some unethical spammers may harvest web pages for e-mail addresses, chances are that your e-mail application's built-in spam filter will prevent your inbox from being flooded with messages. When you configure an easily readable e-mail hyperlink, you increase the usability of your website for your visitors in the following situations:

- The visitor may be at a public computer with no e-mail application configured. In such a case, clicking the e-mail hyperlink usually causes an error message to display. The visitor will have difficulty contacting you in this manner.

- The visitor may be at a private computer, but prefer not to use the e-mail application (or address) that is configured by default to work with the browser. Perhaps he or she shares the computer with others, or perhaps he or she wishes to preserve the privacy of the default e-mail address.

If you prominently displayed your actual e-mail address, then a visitor in either of these situations can still access your e-mail address and use it to contact you (in either their e-mail application or via a web-based e-mail system such as Google's Gmail). The result is a more usable website for your visitors.

Accessibility and Hyperlinks

Focus on Accessibility

Visually challenged visitors who are using a screen reader can configure the software to display a list of the hyperlinks in the document. However, a list of links is useful only if the text describing each link is actually helpful and descriptive. For example, on your college website, a "Search the course schedule" link would be more useful than a link that simply says, "More information."

Block Anchor

It's typical to use anchor tags to configure phrases, or even just a single word, as a hyperlink. HTML5 provides a new function for the anchor tag: the block anchor. A block anchor can configure one or more elements (even those which display as a block, such as a div, h1, or paragraph) as a hyperlink. See an example in the student files at chapter2/block.html.

 FAQ   What are some tips for using hyperlinks?

- Make your link names descriptive and brief to minimize possible confusion.

- Avoid using the phrase "Click here" in your hyperlinks. In the early days of the Web, this phrase was needed because clicking links was a new experience for web users. Now that the Web is a daily part of our lives, this phrase is slightly redundant, and even archaic.

- Try not to bury hyperlinks within large blocks of text; use lists of hyperlinks instead. Be aware that it is more difficult to read web pages than printed pages.

- Be careful when linking to external websites. The Web is dynamic, and it's possible that the external site may change the name of the page, or even delete the page. If this happens, your link will be broken.

Checkpoint 2.3

1. What is the purpose of a **div** element in HTML?
2. What is the purpose of the **anchor** element in HTML?
3. How would you write an anchor tag for creating an e-mail link?

2.18 HTML Validation

The W3C's free Markup Validation Service, available at http://validator.w3.org, will validate your HTML code and check it for syntax errors. **HTML validation** provides students with quick self-assessment—you can prove that your code uses correct syntax. In the working world, HTML validation serves as a quality assurance tool. Invalid code may cause browsers to render the pages slower than otherwise.

Hands-On Practice 2.14

In this Hands-On Practice, you will use the W3C Markup Validation Service to validate a web page file. This example uses the page completed in Hands-On Practice 2.8 (located in the student files at chapter2/design.html). Open design.html in a text editor. Add an error to the design.html page by deleting the first closing `</strong>` tag. This modification should generate several error messages.

Next, attempt to validate the design.html file. To do so, launch a browser, and visit the W3C Markup Validation Service file upload page at http://validator.w3.org/#validate_by_upload. Click the Browse button, and select the chapter2/design.html file from your computer. Click the Check button to upload the file to the W3C site (Figure 2.22).

An error page will display. Notice the "Errors found while checking this document" message. You can view the errors by scrolling down the page, as shown in Figure 2.23.

VideoNote
HTML Validation

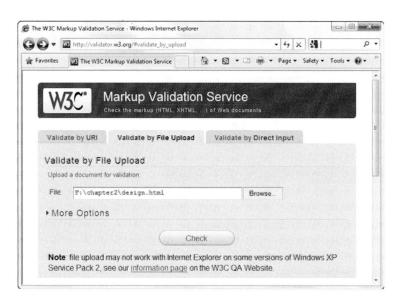

Figure 2.22 Validating a page with the W3C Markup Validation Service

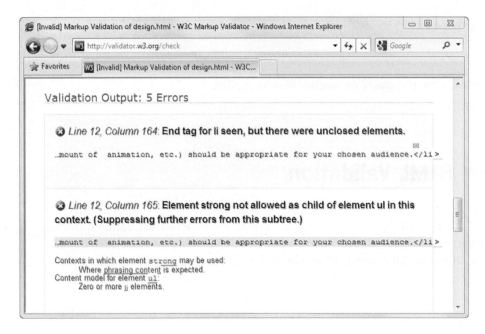

Figure 2.23 The service indicates that the error is on line 12

Notice that the message indicates line 12, which is the first line after the missing closing `</strong>` tag. HTML error messages often point to a line that follows the error. The text of the message, "End tag for li seen, but there were unclosed elements," lets you know that something is wrong. It is up to you to figure out what it is. A good place to start is to check your container tags and make sure they are in pairs. In this case, that is the problem. You can scroll down to view the other errors. However, since multiple error messages are often displayed after a single error occurs, it is a good idea to fix one item at a time and then revalidate.

Edit the design.html file in a text editor, and add the missing `</strong>` tag. Save the file. Launch a browser, and visit http://validator.w3.org/#validate_by_upload. Select your file, select More Options, and verify that the Show Source and Verbose Output check boxes are checked. Click the Revalidate button to begin the validation.

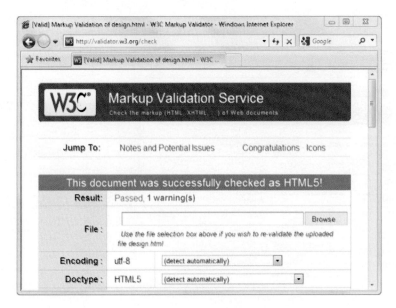

Figure 2.24 The page has passed the validation test

Your display should be similar to that shown in Figure 2.24. Notice the "This document was successfully checked as HTML5!" message. This means that your page passed the validation test. Congratulations, your design.html page is valid! You may also notice a warning message, which you can overlook, indicating that the HTML5 conformance checker is in experimental status.

It is good practice to validate your web pages. However, when validating code, use common sense. Since web browsers still do not completely follow W3C recommendations, there will be situations, such as when adding multimedia to a web page, in which HTML code configured to work reliably across a variety of browsers and platforms will not pass validation.

 FAQ **Are there other ways to validate my HTML?**

In addition to the W3C validation service, there are other tools that you can use to check the syntax of your code. Explore the HTML5 validator at http://html5.validator.nu and the HTML5 "lint" tool at http://lint.brihten.com/html.

Chapter Summary

This chapter has provided an introduction to HTML, XHTML, and HTML5. The basic elements that are part of every web page were demonstrated. Structural HTML elements including div, paragraph, and blockquote were presented. Additional topics included configuring lists and using special characters, phrase elements, and hyperlinks. You have practiced testing your HTML5 code for valid syntax. If you worked along with the samples in the chapter, you should be ready to create some web pages on your own. The Hands-On Exercises and Web Case Studies that follow will provide some additional practice.

Visit this textbook's website at http://www.webdevfoundations.net for links to the URLs listed in this chapter and to view updated information.

Key Terms

&copy;	<meta>	eXtensible HyperText Markup Language (XHTML)
	<ol>	head element
<a>	<p>	head section
<abbr>	<samp>	header
<b>	<small>	heading element
<blockquote>	<strong>	href attribute
<body>	<sub>	HTML5
 	<sup>	hyperlink
<cite>	<title>	Hypertext Markup Language (HTML)
<code>	<ul>	inline display
<dd>	<var>	left alignment
<dfn>	absolute link	obsolete
<div>	anchor element	ordered list
<dl>	attribute	paragraph element
<dt>	block display	phrase element
<em>	body element	relative link
<font>	body section	special character
<h1>	character encoding	tag
<h6>	description list	unordered list
<head>	div element	validation
<html>	DOCTYPE	well-formed document
<i>	document type definition (DTD)	XHTML 1.0 Transitional
<kbd>	element	XML (eXtensible Markup Language)
<li>	e-mail link	XML namespace (xmlns)
<mark>		

Review Questions

Multiple Choice

1. Which of the following is a heading tag?
   a. <head> </head>
   b. <title> </title>
   c. <h3> </h3>
   d. <meta> </meta>

2. Which tag defines a horizontal line?
   a. <hr>
   b.
   c. <dl>
   d. <li>

3. Which tag pair configures a structural area on a web page?

   a. `<area> </area>`

   b. `<div> </div>`

   c. `<cite> </cite>`

   d. `<strong> </strong>`

4. Which of the following is not a legal anchor command?

   a. `<a href="#notes"> See Notes </a>`

   b. `<a href="http://www.w3.org" target="_blank"> Visit W3 Consortium </a>`

   c. `<a href="index.html">Go to Home Page </a>`

   d. `<a href="tom@mysite.com">Send E-mail </a>`

5. Which of the following is not a phrase tag?

   a. `<em>`

   b. `<code>`

   c. `<var>`

   d. `<div>`

6. Which type of list would be the best option for organizing FAQs and their answers?

   a. description list

   b. ordered list

   c. unordered list

   d. none of the above

7. What would you use to make a list beginning with an integer value 5?

   a. start attribute

   b. type attribute

   c. reversed attribute

   d. none of the above

8. When do you need to use a fully qualified URL in a hyperlink?

   a. always

   b. when linking to a web page file on the same site

   c. when linking to a web page file on an external site

   d. never

9. Which tag pair contains the items in an ordered or unordered list?

   a. `<item> </item>`

   b. `<li> </li>`

   c. `<dd> </dd>`

   d. all of the above

10. What does an e-mail link do?

    a. automatically sends you an e-mail message with the visitor's e-mail address as the reply-to field

    b. launches the default e-mail application for the visitor's browser, with your e-mail address as the recipient

    c. displays your e-mail address so that the visitor can send you a message later

    d. links to your mail server

Fill in the Blank

11. The _____ tag provides metadata about the HTML document, which are typically the page description, keywords, author and update information, etc.

12. The _____ tag inserts a single line break.

13. The _____ tag defines a list item in ordered or unordered lists.

14. _____ is the default alignment for web pages.

15. The bullet types available in unordered lists are of three types: _____, _____, and _____, the default being _____.

Short Answer

16. Explain why it is good practice to place the e-mail address on the web page and within the anchor tag when creating an e-mail link.

Apply Your Knowledge

1. **Predict the Result.** Sketch out and briefly describe the web page that will be created with the following HTML code:

```
<!DOCTYPE html>
<html lang="en">
<head>
<title>Predict the Result</title>
<meta charset="utf-8">
</head>
```

```
<body>
<code>
     #include &lt;stdio.h&gt; <br>
     #include &lt;sys/types.h&gt; <br>
     #include &lt;sys/socket.h&gt;<br><br>

     main(int argc, char *argv[])<br>
     {<br>
         char mess[80];<br>
         printf("This is a demo..");<br>
     }<br>
</code><br>
</body>
</html>
```

2. **Fill in the Missing Code.** The web page defined by the given code should display a heading and a description list, but some HTML tags, indicated by <_>, are missing. Fill in the missing code.

```
<!DOCTYPE html>
<html lang="en">
<head>
     <title>Door County Wildflowers</title>
     <meta charset="utf-8">
</head>
<body>
     <_>Door County Wild Flowers<_>
     <dl>
       <dt>Trillium<_>
         <_>This white flower blooms from April through June in
         wooded areas.<_>
       <_>Lady Slipper<_>
         <_>This yellow orchid blooms in June in wooded areas.</dd>
     <_>
</body>
</html>
```

3. **Find the Error.** All the text on the web page defined by the given code displays in large and bold font typeface. Explain why this is happening.

```
<!DOCTYPE html>
<html lang="en">
<head>
<title>Find the Error</title>
<meta charset="utf-8">
</head>
<body>
<h1>Words of Wisdom<h1>
<blockquote>
     <p> The art of being wise is knowing what to overlook.
</p>

          - William Strunk
</blockquote>
</body>
</html>
```

Hands-On Exercises

1. Write the HTML to display the text "HTML is the predominant markup language for web pages". Use the abbr tag for the word 'HTML'.

2. Write the HTML to display the texts "Creating a web page is fun" and "I love HTML5" in two separate lines. Try to use the heart symbol instead of the word 'love' in the second line.

3. Write the HTML to display a hypothetical name and address using the address element.

4. Write the HTML for a nested list that displays your favorite books in three categories: fictions, classics and travel writing. The fiction category should also be divided into three types: adventure, sci-fi, and romance.

5. Write the HTML for an ordered list that uses lowercase Roman numerals to order alcoholic beverages. This ordered list should display the following terms: beer, wine, and whiskey.

6. Write the HTML to display the chemical equation for water:

$$2H_2 + O_2 = 2H_2O$$

7. Modify the following code snippet to indicate that the terms "HTML5" and "Internet" should have strong importance and the group of words "World Wide Web" and "Opera Software" should be hyperlinks to the sites www.w3.org and http://opera.com/, respectively:

```
<p>HTML5 is a language for structuring and presenting content
for the World Wide Web and is a core technology of the Internet
originally proposed by Opera Software.</p>
```

8. Create a web page that uses a description list to display three network protocols (see Chapter 1) and their descriptions. Include a hyperlink to a website that provides information about the protocols. Add an appropriate heading to the page. Save the page as network.html.

9. Create a web page that uses a description list to display various markup languages (i.e., SGML, HTML, XML, XHTML, and HTML5; see Chapter 1) and their descriptions. Include a hyperlink to a website that provides information about the protocols. Add an appropriate heading to the page.

10. Create a web page about your favorite singer. Give an unordered list for albums and a description list for awards won in the year 2011. Include a hyperlink to the singer's personal website.

Web Research

There are many HTML5 tutorials on the Web. Use your favorite search engine to discover them. Choose two that are helpful. For each, print out the home page or other pertinent page and create a web page that contains the answers to the following questions:

a. What is the URL of the website?

b. Is the tutorial geared toward the beginner level, intermediate level, or both levels?

c. Would you recommend this site to others? Why or why not?

d. List one or two concepts that you learned from this tutorial.

Focus on Web Design

You are learning the syntax of HTML5. However, coding alone does not make a web page; design is also very important. Surf the Web and find two web pages, one that is appealing to you and one that is unappealing to you. Print each page. Create a web page that answers the following questions for each of your examples:

a. What is the URL of the website?

b. Is the page appealing or unappealing? List three reasons for your answer.

c. If the page is unappealing, what would you do to improve it?

 # WEBSITE CASE STUDY

Each of the case studies in this section continues throughout most of the text. This chapter introduces each website scenario, presents the site map, and directs you to create two pages for the site.

JavaJam Coffee House

Julio Perez is the owner of the JavaJam Coffee House, a gourmet coffee shop that serves snacks, coffee, tea, and soft drinks. Local folk music performances and poetry readings are held a few nights during the week. The customers of JavaJam are mainly college students and young professionals. Julio would like a web presence for his shop that will display his services and provide a calendar for the performances. He would like a home page, menu page, music performance schedule page, and job opportunities page.

A site map for the JavaJam Coffee House website is shown in Figure 2.25. The site map describes the architecture of the website, which consists of a "Home" page with three main content pages: "Menu," "Music," and "Jobs."

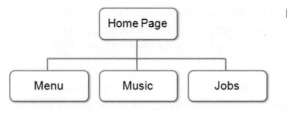

Figure 2.25 JavaJam site map

Figure 2.26 displays a wireframe sketch of the page layout for the website. It contains a site logo, a navigation area, a content area, and a footer area for copyright information.

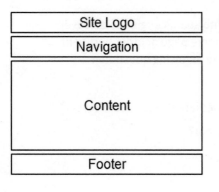

Figure 2.26 JavaJam wireframe

You have three tasks in this case study:

1. Create a folder for the JavaJam website.

2. Create the Home page: index.html.

3. Create the Menu page: menu.html.

Hands-On Practice Case Study

Task 1: Create a folder on your hard drive or portable storage device (thumb drive or SD card) called "javajam" to contain your JavaJam website files.

Task 2: The Home Page. You will use a text editor to create the Home page for the JavaJam Coffee House website. The Home page is shown in Figure 2.27.

Figure 2.27 JavaJam index.html

Launch a text editor, and create a web page with the following specifications:

1. **Web Page Title.** Use a descriptive page title. The company name is a good choice for a business website.

2. **Wireframe Logo.** Use ‹h1› for the JavaJam Coffee House logo.

3. **Wireframe Navigation.** Place the following text within a div element:

   Home Menu Music Jobs

   Code anchor tags so that "Home" links to index.html, "Menu" links to menu.html, "Music" links to music.html, and "Jobs" links to jobs.html. Add extra blank spaces between the hyperlinks with the   special character as needed.

4. **Wireframe Content.**

   a. Configure the following content in an unordered list:

   Specialty Coffee and Tea

   Bagels, Muffins, and Organic Snacks

   Music and Poetry Readings

   Open Mic Night

b. Code the following address and phone number contact information within a div element. Use line break tags to help you configure this area and add extra space between the phone number and the footer area.

12312 Main Street

Mountain Home, CA 93923

1-888-555-5555

5. **Wireframe Footer.** Configure the following copyright and e-mail link information within a div element. Format it with small text size (use the `<small>` tag) and italics font style (use the `<i>` tag).

JavaJam Copyright © 2013 Coffee House

Place your name in an e-mail link on the line under the copyright.

The page in Figure 2.27 may seem a little sparse, but don't worry; as you gain experience and learn to use more advanced techniques, your pages will look more professional. White space (blank space) on the page can be added with `<br>` tags where needed. Your page does not need to look exactly the same as the sample. Your goal at this point should be to practice and get comfortable using HTML.

Save your page in the javajam folder, and name it index.html.

Task 3: The Menu Page. Create the Menu page shown in Figure 2.28. A technique that improves productivity is to create new pages based on existing pages so that you can benefit from your previous work. Your new Menu page will use the index.html page as a starting point.

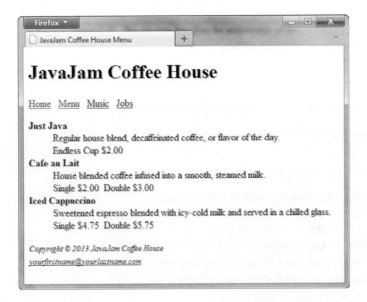

Figure 2.28 JavaJam menu.html

Open the index.html page for the JavaJam website in a text editor. Select File › Save As, and save the file with the new name of menu.html in the javajam folder. Now you are ready to edit the page.

1. **Web Page Title.** Modify the page title. Change the text contained between the `<title>` and `</title>` tags to the following:

JavaJam Coffee House Menu

2. Wireframe Content.

   a. Delete the Home page content unordered list and contact information.

   b. Use a description list to add the menu content to the page. Use the `<dt>` tag to contain each menu item name. Configure the menu item name to have strong importance and display in bold font weight with the `<strong>` tag. Use the `<dd>` tag to contain the menu item description. The menu item names and descriptions are as follows:

Just Java

Regular house blend, decaffeinated coffee, or flavor of the day.

Endless Cup $2.00

Cafe au Lait

House blended coffee infused into a smooth, steamed milk.

Single $2.00 Double $3.00

Iced Cappuccino

Sweetened espresso blended with icy-cold milk and served in a chilled glass.

Single $4.75 Double $5.75

Save your page, and test it in a browser. Test the hyperlink from the menu.html page to index.html. Test the hyperlink from the index.html page to menu.html. If your links do not work, review your work, paying close attention to these details:

- Verify that you have saved the pages with the correct names in the correct folder.
- Verify your spelling of the page names in the anchor tags.

Test again after you make changes.

Fish Creek Animal Hospital

Magda Patel is a veterinarian and owner of the Fish Creek Animal Hospital. Her customers are local pet owners who range from children to senior citizens. Magda would like a website to provide information to her current and potential customers. She has requested a home page, a services page, a page for advice from a veterinarian, and a contact page.

A site map for the Fish Creek Animal Hospital website is shown in Figure 2.29. The site map describes the architecture of the website, which consists of a "Home" page with three main content pages: "Services," "Ask the Vet," and "Contact."

Figure 2.29 Fish Creek site map

Figure 2.30 displays a wireframe sketch of the page layout for the website. It contains a site logo, a navigation area, a content area, and a footer area for copyright information.

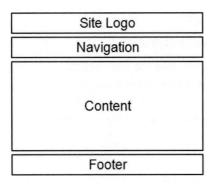

Figure 2.30 Fish Creek wireframe

You have three tasks in this case study:

1. Create a folder for the Fish Creek website.

2. Create the Home page: index.html.

3. Create the Services page: services.html.

Hands-On Practice Case Study

Task 1: Create a folder on your hard drive or portable storage device (thumb drive or SD card) called "fishcreek" to contain your Fish Creek website files.

Task 2: The Home Page. You will use a text editor application to create the Home page for the Fish Creek Animal Hospital website. The Home page is shown in Figure 2.31.

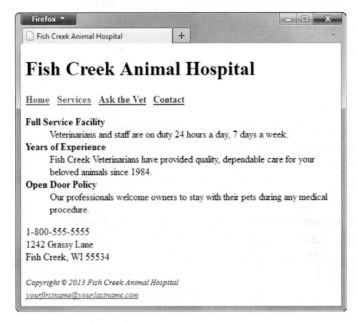

Figure 2.31 Fish Creek index.html

Launch a text editor, and create a web page with the following specifications:

1. **Web Page Title.** Use a descriptive page title. The company name is a good choice for a business website.

2. **Wireframe Logo.** Use ‹h1› for the Fish Creek Animal Hospital logo.

3. **Wireframe Navigation.**   Configure the following text using the <b> phrase element within a div element:

Home Services Ask the Vet Contact

Code anchor tags so that "Home" links to index.html, "Services" links to services.html, "Ask the Vet" links to askvet.html, and "Contact" links to contact. html. Add extra blank spaces between the hyperlinks with the   special character as needed.

4. **Wireframe Content.**

   a. Code the following content in a description list. Configure the text in each dt element to have strong importance and display in bold font weight:

   Full Service Facility

   Veterinarians and staff are on duty 24 hours a day, 7 days a week.

   Years of Experience

   Fish Creek Veterinarians have provided quality, dependable care for your beloved animals since 1984.

   Open Door Policy

   Our professionals welcome owners to stay with their pets during any medical procedure.

   b. Configure the following address and phone number contact information within a div element below the description list. Use line break tags to help you format this area.

   1-800-555-5555

   1242 Grassy Lane

   Fish Creek, WI 55534

5. **Wireframe Footer.** Code the following copyright and e-mail link information within a div element. Format it with small text size (use the `<small>` tag) and italics font style (use the `<i>` tag).

Copyright © 2013 Fish Creek Animal Hospital

Place your name in an e-mail link on the line under the copyright.

The page in Figure 2.31 may seem a little sparse, but don't worry; as you gain experience and learn to use more advanced techniques, your pages will look more professional. White space (blank space) on the page can be added with `<br>` tags where needed. Your page does not need to look exactly the same as the sample. Your goal at this point should be to practice and get comfortable using HTML.

Save your page in the fishcreek folder, and name it index.html.

Task 3: The Services Page. Create the Services page shown in Figure 2.32. A technique that improves productivity is to create new pages based on existing pages so that you can benefit from your previous work. Your new Services page will use the index.html page as a starting point.

Open the index.html page for the Fish Creek website in a text editor. Select File › Save As, and save the file with the new name of services.html in the fishcreek folder. Now you are ready to edit the page.

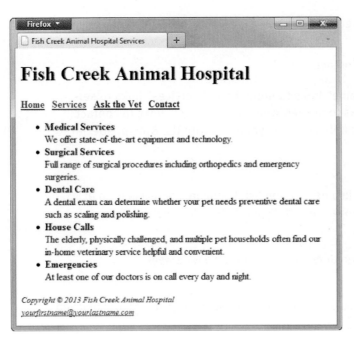

Figure 2.32 Fish Creek services.html

1. **Web Page Title.** Modify the page title. Change the text contained between the `<title>` and `</title>` tags to the following:

   Fish Creek Animal Hospital Services

2. **Wireframe Content.**

   a. Delete the Home page content description list and contact information.

   b. Use an unordered list to add the services content to the page. Configure the name of each services category to use bold font weight and have strong emphasis. (Use the `<strong>` tag.) Use line break tags to help you configure this area. The service categories and descriptions are as follows:

   Medical Services

   We offer state-of-the-art equipment and technology.

   Surgical Services

   Full range of surgical procedures including orthopedics and emergency surgeries.

   Dental Care

   A dental exam can determine whether your pet needs preventive dental care such as scaling and polishing.

   House Calls

   The elderly, physically challenged, and multiple pet households often find our in-home veterinary service helpful and convenient.

   Emergencies

   At least one of our doctors is on call every day and night.

Save your page, and test it in a browser. Test the hyperlink from the services.html page to index.html. Test the hyperlink from the index.html page to services.html. If your links do not work, review your work, paying close attention to these details:

- Verify that you have saved the pages with the correct names in the correct folder.
- Verify your spelling of the page names in the anchor tags.

Test again after you make changes.

Pacific Trails Resort

Melanie Bowie is the owner of Pacific Trails Resort, located on the California North Coast. The resort offers a quiet getaway, with luxury camping in yurts along with an upscale lodge for dining and visiting with fellow guests. The target audience for Pacific Trails Resort is couples who enjoy nature and hiking. Melanie would like a website that emphasizes the uniqueness of the location and accommodations. She would like the website to include a home page, a page about the special yurt accommodations, a reservations page with a contact form, and a page to describe the activities available at the resort.

A site map for the Pacific Trails Resort website is shown in Figure 2.33. The site map describes the architecture of the website, which consists of a "Home" page with three main content pages: "Yurts," "Activities," and "Reservations."

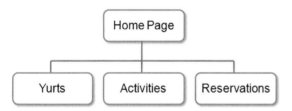

Figure 2.33 Pacific Trails Resort site map

Figure 2.34 displays a wireframe sketch of the page layout for the website. It contains a site logo, a navigation area, a content area, and a footer area for copyright information.

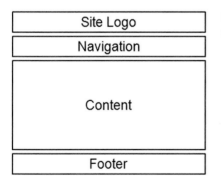

Figure 2.34 Pacific Trails Resort wireframe

You have three tasks in this case study:

1. Create a folder for the Pacific Trails website.
2. Create the Home page: index.html.
3. Create the Yurts page: yurts.html.

Figure 2.35 Pacific Trails Resort index.html

Hands-On Practice Case Study

Task 1: Create a folder on your hard drive or portable storage device (thumb drive or SD card) called "pacific" to contain your Pacific Trails Resort website files.

Task 2: The Home Page. You will use a text editor to create the Home page for the Pacific Trails Resort website. The Home page is shown in Figure 2.35.

Launch a text editor, and create a web page with the following specifications:

1. **Web Page Title.** Use a descriptive page title. The company name is a good choice for a business website.

2. **Wireframe Logo.** Use ‹h1› for the Pacific Trails Resort logo.

3. **Wireframe Navigation.** Configure the following text using the <b> phrase element within a div element:

   Home Yurts Activities Reservations

   Code anchor tags so that "Home" links to index.html, "Yurts" links to yurts.html, "Activities" links to activities.html, and "Reservations" links to reservations.html.

4. **Wireframe Content.**

   a. Code the following text within an h2 element:

      Enjoy Nature in Luxury

   b. Configure the following sentences in a paragraph:

      Pacific Trails Resort offers a special lodging experience on the California North Coast. Relax in serenity with panoramic views of the Pacific Ocean.

   c. Code the following content in an unordered list:

      Private yurts with decks overlooking the ocean

      Activities lodge with fireplace and gift shop

Nightly fine dining at the Overlook Cafe

Heated outdoor pool and whirlpool

Guided hiking tours of the redwoods

d. Configure the following address and phone number contact information within a div element below the unordered list. Use line break tags to help you format this area.

Pacific Trails Resort

12010 Pacific Trails Road

Zephyr, CA 95555

888-555-5555

5. **Wireframe Footer.** Configure the following copyright and e-mail link information within a div element. Format it with small text size (use the `<small>` tag) and italics font style (use the `<i>` tag).

Copyright © 2013 Pacific Trails Resort

Place your name in an e-mail link on the line under the copyright.

The page in Figure 2.35 may seem a little sparse, but don't worry; as you gain experience and learn to use more advanced techniques, your pages will look more professional. White space (blank space) on the page can be added with `<br>` tags where needed. Your page does not need to look exactly the same as the sample. Your goal at this point should be to practice and get comfortable using HTML.

Save your page in the pacific folder, and name it index.html.

Task 3: The Yurts Page. Create the Yurts page shown in Figure 2.36. A technique that improves productivity is to create new pages based on existing pages so that you can benefit from your previous work. Your new Yurts page will use the index.html page as a starting point.

Figure 2.36 Pacific Trails Resort yurts.html

Open the index.html page for the Pacific Trails Resort website in a text editor. Select File ›
Save As, and save the file with the new name of yurts.html in the pacific folder. Now you
are ready to edit the page.

1. **Web Page Title.** Modify the page title. Change the text contained between the
   `<title>` and `</title>` tags to the following:

   Pacific Trails Resort :: Yurts

2. **Wireframe Content.**

   a. Replace the text in the h2 element with the following:

      The Yurts at Pacific Trails Resort

   b. Delete the Home page content paragraph, unordered list, and contact information.

   c. Add the yurts content to the page as a FAQs (frequently asked questions) list by
      using a description list. Configure each question to have strong importance and
      bold font weight (use the `<strong>` phrase element) within a dt element. Config-
      ure each answer within a dd element. The text is shown as follows:

      What is a yurt?

      Our luxury yurts are permanent structures four feet off the ground. Each yurt has
      canvas walls, a wooden floor, and a roof dome that can be opened.

      How are the yurts furnished?

      Each yurt is furnished with a queen-size bed with down quilt and gas-fired stove.
      The luxury camping experience also includes electricity and a sink with hot and
      cold running water. Shower and restroom facilities are located in the lodge.

      What should I bring?

      Bring a sense of adventure and some time to relax! Most guests also pack
      comfortable walking shoes and plan to dress for changing weather with layers
      of clothing.

Save your page, and test it in a browser. Test the hyperlink from the yurts.html page to
index.html. Test the hyperlink from the index.html page to yurts.html. If your links do not
work, review your work, paying close attention to these details:

- Verify that you have saved the pages with the correct names in the correct folder.

- Verify your spelling of the page names in the anchor tags.

Test again after you make the changes.

Prime Properties

Prime Properties is a small real estate company that specializes in residential properties.
The owner, Maria Valdez, would like a website to showcase her listings and provide a
point of contact for her clients, who are mainly middle-class working adults who are
looking for a home in the northwest Chicago suburbs. Maria would like a home page, a
listings page that contains information about her properties, a financing page, and a
contact page.

A site map for the Prime Properties website is shown in Figure 2.37. The site map
describes the architecture of the website, which consists of "Home" page with three
main content pages: "Listings," "Financing," and "Contact."

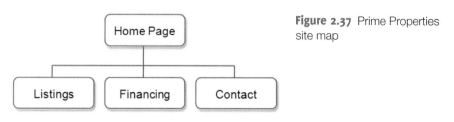

Figure 2.37 Prime Properties site map

Figure 2.38 displays a wireframe sketch of the page layout for the website. It contains a site logo, a navigation area, a content area, and a footer area for copyright information.

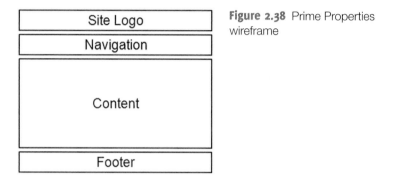

Figure 2.38 Prime Properties wireframe

You have three tasks in this case study:

1. Create a folder for the Prime Properties website.

2. Create the Home page: index.html.

3. Create the Financing page: financing.html.

Hands-On Practice Case Study

Task 1: Create a folder on your hard drive or portable storage device (thumb drive or SD card) called "prime" to contain your Prime Properties web page files.

Task 2: The Home Page. You will use a text editor to create the Home page for the Prime Properties website. The Home page is shown in Figure 2.39.

Figure 2.39 Prime Properties index.html

Launch a text editor, and create a web page with the following specifications:

1. **Web Page Title.** Use a descriptive page title. The company name is a good choice for a business website.

2. **Wireframe Logo.** Use <h1> for the Prime Properties logo.

3. **Wireframe Navigation.** Configure the following text using the <b> phrase element within a div element :

   Home Listings Financing Contact

Code anchor tags so that "Home" links to index.html, "Listings" links to listings.html, "Financing" links to financing.html, and "Contact" links to contact.html.

4. **Wireframe Content.**

   a. Code each line of the following text in its own paragraph:

   Prime Properties is prepared to market and sell your property.

   The philosophy of Prime Properties is to promote our clients, not ourselves.

   We can also help you find the property that meets your needs:

   b. Configure the following content in an unordered list:

   location

   price

   features

   c. Code the following address and phone number contact information within a div element. Use line break tags to help you configure this area and add extra space between the phone number and the footer area.

   Prime Properties

   3055 Bode Road

   Schaumburg, IL 60194

   847-555-5555

5. **Wireframe Footer.** Configure the following copyright and e-mail link information within a div element. Format it with small text size (use the <small> tag) and italics font style (use the <i> tag)

   Copyright © 2013 Prime Properties

   Place your name in an e-mail link on the line under the copyright information.

The page in Figure 2.39 may seem a little sparse, but don't worry; as you gain experience and learn to use more advanced techniques, your pages will look more professional. White space (blank space) on the page can be added with <br> tags where needed. Your page does not need to look exactly the same as the sample. Your goal at this point should be to practice and get comfortable using HTML.

Save your page in the prime folder, and name it index.html.

Task 3: The Financing Page. Create the Financing page shown in Figure 2.40. A technique that improves productivity is to create new pages based on existing pages so that you can benefit from your previous work. Your new Financing page will use the index.html page as a starting point.

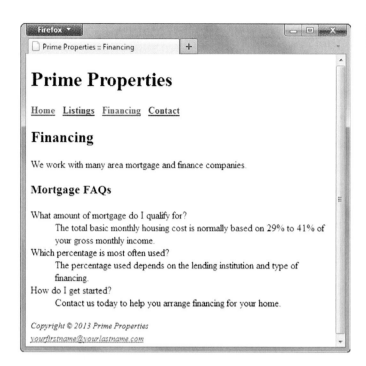

Figure 2.40 Prime Properties
financing.html

Open the index.html page for the Prime Properties website in a text editor. Select File › Save As, and save the file with the new name of financing.html in the prime folder. Now you are ready to edit the page.

1. **Web Page Title.** Modify the page title. Change the text contained between the `<title>` and `</title>` tags to the following:

   Prime Properties :: Financing

2. **Wireframe Content.**

   a. Delete the Home Page content paragraphs, unordered list, and contact information.

   b. Configure the following text in an `<h2>` element:

   Financing

   c. Code the following sentence in a paragraph:

   We work with many area mortgage and finance companies.

   d. Configure the following phrase with an `<h3>` element:

   Mortgage FAQs

   e. Use a description list to configure the FAQs. Configure `<dt>` elements for the questions and `<dd>` elements for the answers. The FAQ questions and answers are as follows:

   What amount of mortgage do I qualify for?

   The total basic monthly housing cost is normally based on 29% to 41% of your gross monthly income.

   Which percentage is most often used?

The percentage used depends on the lending institution and type of financing.

How do I get started?

Contact us today to help you arrange financing for your home.

Save your page, and test it in a browser. Test the hyperlink from the financing.html page to index.html. Test the hyperlink from the index.html page to financing.html. If your links do not work, review your work with close attention to these details:

- Verify that you have saved the pages with the correct names in the correct folder.
- Verify your spelling of the page names in the anchor tags.

Test again after you make the changes.

Configuring Color and Text with CSS

Chapter Objectives   In this chapter, you will learn how to . . .

- Describe the evolution of style sheets from print media to the Web

- List advantages of using Cascading Style Sheets

- Configure background and text color on web pages

- Create style sheets that configure common color and text properties

- Apply inline styles

- Use embedded style sheets

- Use external style sheets

- Configure element, class, id, and contextual selectors

- Utilize the "cascade" in CSS

- Validate CSS

Now that you have been introduced to HTML, let's explore **Cascading Style Sheets (CSS)**. Web designers use CSS to separate the presentation style of a web page from the information on the web page. CSS is used to configure text, color, and page layout. CSS is not new—it was first proposed as a standard by the W3C in 1996. In 1998, additional properties for positioning web page elements were introduced to the language with CSS level 2 (CSS2), which was used for over a decade before reaching official "recommendation" status in 2011. CSS continues to evolve, with proposals for CSS level 3 (CSS3) properties that support features such as embedding fonts, rounded corners, and transparency. This chapter introduces you to the use of CSS on the Web as you explore how to configure color and text.

3.1 Overview of Cascading Style Sheets

Figure 3.1 The CSS Zen Garden home page at http://www.csszengarden.com

For years, style sheets have been used in desktop publishing to apply typographical styles and spacing instructions to printed media. CSS provides this functionality (and much more) for web developers. CSS allows web developers to apply typographic styles (typeface, font size, and so on) and page layout instructions to a web page. The CSS Zen Garden, http://www.csszengarden.com, exemplifies the power and flexibility of CSS (Figure 3.1). Visit this site for an example of CSS in action. Notice how the content looks dramatically different depending on the design (CSS style rules) you select. Although the designs on the CSS Zen Garden are created by CSS masters, at some point these designers were just like you—starting out with CSS basics.

CSS is a flexible, cross-platform, standards-based language developed by the W3C. The W3C's description of CSS can be found at http://www.w3.org/Style. Be aware that even though CSS has been in use for many years, it is still considered an emerging technology, and different browsers do not support it in exactly the same way. We concentrate on aspects of CSS that are well supported by popular browsers.

Advantages of Cascading Style Sheets

There are several advantages to using CSS (see Figure 3.2):

- **Typography and page layout can be better controlled.** These features include font size, line spacing, letter spacing, indents, margins, and element positioning.

- **Style is separate from structure.** The format of the text and colors used on the page can be configured and stored separately from the body section of the web page document.

- **Styles can be stored.** You can store styles in a separate document and associate them with the web page. When the styles are modified, the HTML remains intact. This means, for example, that if your client decides to change the background color of a set of web pages from red to white, you only need to change one file that contains the styles, instead of modifying each web page document.

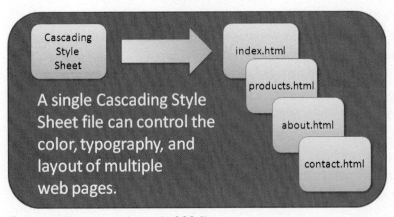

Figure 3.2 The power of a single CSS file

- **Documents are potentially smaller.** The formatting is separate from the document; therefore, the actual documents should be smaller.

- **Site maintenance is easier.** Again, if the styles need to be changed, then it is possible to complete the modifications by changing the style sheet only.

You may be wondering if there are any disadvantages to using CSS. In fact, there is one large disadvantage: CSS technology is not yet uniformly supported by browsers. This disadvantage will be less of an issue in the future as browsers comply with standards. Modern browsers have good support for CSS2 properties. Browser support for new CSS3 features such as rounded corners and color transparency is increasing, although there are differences in syntax, and not all browsers offer the same level of support. See http://caniuse.com/#cats=CSS for a list of CSS3 features supported by various browsers. This book will focus on aspects of CSS that are well supported by modern browsers and note when differences in syntax are needed.

Configuring Cascading Style Sheets

Web developers use four methods to incorporate CSS technology: inline, embedded, external, and imported.

- **Inline styles** are coded in the body of the web page as an attribute of an HTML tag. The style applies only to the specific element that contains it as an attribute.

- **Embedded styles** are defined in the header of a web page. These style instructions apply to the entire web page document.

- **External styles** are coded in a separate text file. This text file is associated with the web page by using a link element in the head section.

- **Imported styles** are similar to external styles in that they can connect styles coded in a separate text file with a web page document. An external style sheet can be imported into embedded styles or into another external style sheet by using the @import directive.

CSS Selectors and Declarations

Style sheets are composed of style rules that describe the styling to be applied. Each **rule** has two parts: a **selector** and a **declaration**:

- **CSS Style Rule Selector** The selector can be an HTML element name, a class name, or an id name. In this section, we will focus on applying styles to element name selectors. We will work with class selectors and id selectors later in this chapter.

- **CSS Style Rule Declaration** The declaration indicates the CSS property you are setting (such as color) and the value you are assigning to the property.

For example, the CSS rule shown in Figure 3.3 would set the color of the text used on a web page to blue. The selector is the body tag, and the declaration sets the color property to the value of blue.

Figure 3.3 Using CSS to set the text color to blue

The `background-color` Property

The CSS **background-color property** configures the background color of an element. The following style rule will configure the background color of a web page to be yellow. Notice how the declaration is enclosed within braces and how the colon symbol (:) separates the declaration property and the declaration value.

```
body { background-color: yellow }
```

The `color` Property

The CSS **color property** configures the text (foreground) color of an element. The following CSS style rule will configure the text color of a web page to be blue:

```
body { color: blue }
```

Configure Background and Text Color

Figure 3.4 displays a web page with a blue text and a yellow background. To configure more than one property for a selector, use a semicolon (;) to separate the declarations as follows:

```
body { color: blue; background-color: yellow; }
```

Figure 3.4 A web page with yellow background color and blue text color

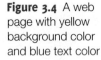
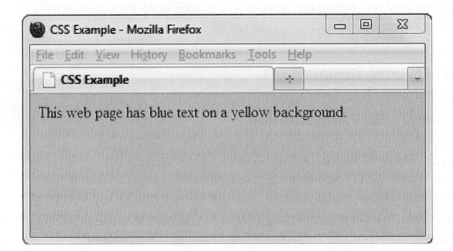

The spaces in these declarations are optional. The ending semicolon (;) is also optional, but useful in case you need to add additional style rules at a later time. The following code samples are also valid:

```
body {color:blue;background-color:yellow}
body { color: blue;
      background-color: yellow; }
body {
    color: blue;
    background-color: yellow;
}
```

You might be asking yourself how you would know what properties and values can be used. See the CSS Property Reference in Appendix D for a detailed list of CSS properties. This chapter introduces you to some of the CSS properties commonly used to configure color and text, shown in Table 3.1. In the next sections, we'll take a look at how color is used on web pages.

Table 3.1 CSS properties used in this chapter

Property	Description	Values
background-color	Background color of an element	Any valid color
color	Foreground (text) color of an element	Any valid color
font-family	Name of a font or font family	Any valid font or a font family such as serif, sans-serif, fantasy, monospace, or cursive
font-size	Size of the font	Varies; a numeric value with pt (standard font point sizes) or px (pixels) units or the unit em (which corresponds to the width of the upper-case M of the current font); a numeric percentage; and the text values xx-small, x-small, small, medium, large, x-large, and xx-large
font-style	Style of the font	normal, italic, or oblique
font-weight	The "boldness" or weight of the font	Varies; the text values normal, bold, bolder, and lighter and the numeric values 100, 200, 300, 400, 500, 600, 700, 800, and 900
line-height	The spacing allowed for the line of text	It is most common to use a percentage for this value; for example, a value of 200% would correspond to double-spacing.
margin	Shorthand notation to configure the margin surrounding an element	A numeric value (px or em); for example, body {margin: 10px} will set the page margins in the document to 10 pixels. When eliminating the margin, do not use the px or em unit—for example, body {margin:0}
margin-left	Configures the space in the left margin of the element	A numeric value (px or em), auto, or 0
margin-right	Configures the space in the right margin of the element	A numeric value (px or em), auto, or 0
text-align	The alignment of text	center, justify, left, or right
text-decoration	Determines whether text is underlined; this style is most often applied to hyperlinks	The value "none" will cause a hyperlink not to be underlined in a browser that normally processes in this manner
width	The width of the content of an element	A numeric value (px or em), numeric percentage, or auto (default)

3.2 Using Color on Web Pages

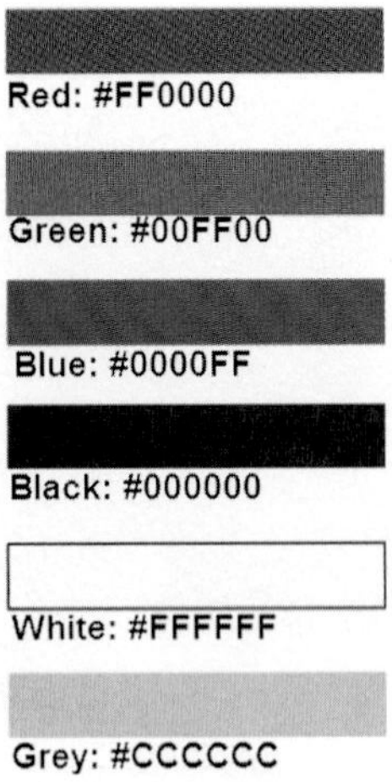

Red: #FF0000

Green: #00FF00

Blue: #0000FF

Black: #000000

White: #FFFFFF

Grey: #CCCCCC

Figure 3.5 Color swatches and hexadecimal color values

Monitors display color as a combination of different intensities of red, green, and blue, a concept known as **RGB color**. RGB intensity values are numerical from 0 to 255. Each RGB color has three values, one each for red, green, and blue. These values are always listed in the same order (red, green, blue) and specify the numerical value of each color used (see the examples in Figure 3.5). You will usually use hexadecimal color values to specify RGB color on web pages.

Hexadecimal Color Values

Hexadecimal is the name for the base-16 numbering system, which uses the characters 0, 1, 2, 3, 4, 5, 6, 7, 8, 9, A, B, C, D, E, and F to specify numeric values. **Hexadecimal color** values specify RGB color with numeric value pairs ranging from 00 to FF (0 to 255 in base 10). Each pair is associated with the amount of red, green, and blue displayed. Using this notation, one would specify the color red as #FF0000 and the color blue as #0000FF. The # symbol signifies that the value is hexadecimal. You can use either uppercase or lowercase letters in hexadecimal color values; #FF0000 and #ff0000 both configure the color red.

Don't worry—you won't need to do calculations to work with web colors. Just become familiar with the numbering scheme. See Figure 3.6 for an excerpt from the color chart at http://webdevfoundations.net/color.

Figure 3.6 Partial color chart

#FFFFFF	#FFFFCC	#FFFF99	#FFFF66	#FFFF33	#FFFF00
#FFCCFF	#FFCCCC	#FFCC99	#FFCC66	#FFCC33	#FFCC00
#FF99FF	#FF99CC	#FF9999	#FF9966	#FF9933	#FF9900
#FF66FF	#FF66CC	#FF6699	#FF6666	#FF6633	#FF6600
#FF33FF	#FF33CC	#FF3399	#FF3366	#FF3333	#FF3300
#FF00FF	#FF00CC	#FF0099	#FF0066	#FF0033	#FF0000

Web-Safe Colors

Back in the day of 8-bit color monitors, web page color could be problematic and it was important to use one of the 216 **web-safe colors**, which display in a similar manner on both the Mac and PC platforms. The hexadecimal color values of web-safe colors use the numerals 00, 33, 66, 99, CC, and FF. The 216 web-safe colors make up the **Web-Safe Color Palette**, shown in Appendix F (also at http://webdevfoundations.net/color). Now that most monitors display millions of colors, using web-safe colors is less important. The Web-Safe Color Palette is rather limited, and it is common for today's web designers to choose colors creatively rather than select them only from the palette.

CSS Color Syntax

CSS syntax allows you to configure colors in a number of ways, including hexadecimal color values, color names, and decimal color values. Table 3.2 shows CSS syntax examples that configure a paragraph with red text.

Table 3.2 CSS color syntax examples

CSS Syntax	Color Type
`p { color: red; }`	Color name
`p { color: #FF0000; }`	Hexadecimal color value
`p { color: #F00; }`	Shorthand hexadecimal (one character for each hexadecimal pair; used only with web-safe colors)
`p { color: rgb(255,0,0); }`	Decimal color value (RGB triplet)

FAQ **Are there other methods to configure color with CSS?**

Yes, the CSS3 Color Module (currently in proposed recommendation status) provides a way for web developers to configure not only color, but also the transparency of the color, with RGBA (Red, Green, Blue, Alpha). You'll explore this technique in Chapter 4.

3.3 Inline CSS with the Style Attribute

Recall that there are four methods for configuring CSS: inline, embedded, external, and imported. In this section, we focus on inline CSS using the style attribute.

The Style Attribute

Inline styles are coded as an attribute on an HTML tag using the **style attribute**. The value of the style attribute is set to the style rule declaration that you need to configure. Recall that a declaration consists of a property and a value. Each property is separated from its value with a colon (:). The following code will use inline styles to set the text color of an `<h1>` tag to a shade of red:

```
<h1 style="color:#cc0000">This is displayed as a red heading</h1>
```

If there is more than one property, they are separated by a semicolon (;). The following code configures the heading with a red text color and a gray background color:

```
<h1 style="color:#cc0000;background-color:#cccccc">
This is displayed as a red heading on a gray background</h1>
```

Hands-On Practice 3.1

In this Hands-On Practice, you will configure a web page with inline styles. The inline styles will specify the following:

- Global body tag styles for an off-white background with teal text. These styles will be inherited by other elements by default. For example:

  ```
  <body style="background-color:#F5F5F5;color:#008080;">
  ```

- Styles for an h1 element with a teal background with off-white text. This style will override the global styles configured on the body element. For example:

  ```
  <h1 style="background-color:#008080;color:#F5F5F5;">
  ```

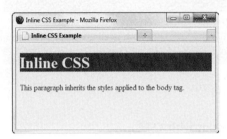

Figure 3.7 Web page using inline styles

A sample is shown in Figure 3.7. Launch a text editor. Select File > Open to edit the template file located at chapter2/template.html in the student files. Modify the title element, and add heading tags, paragraph tags, style attributes, and text to the body section as indicated by the following highlighted code:

```
<!DOCTYPE html>
<html lang="en">
<head>
<title>Inline CSS Example</title>
<meta charset="utf-8">
</head>
<body style="background-color:#F5F5F5;color:#008080;">
<h1 style="background-color:#008080;color:#F5F5F5;">Inline CSS</h1>
<p>This paragraph inherits the styles applied to the body tag.</p>
</body>
</html>
```

Save the document as inline2.html on your hard drive or flash drive. Launch a browser to test your page. It should look similar to the page shown in Figure 3.7. Note that the inline styles applied to the body tag are inherited by other elements on the page (such as the paragraph) unless more-specific styles are specified (such as those coded on the `<h1>` tag). You can compare your work with the solution found in the student files (chapter3/inline.html).

Let's continue and add another paragraph, with the text color configured to be dark gray:

```
<p style="color:#333333">This paragraph overrides the text color
style applied to the body tag.</p>
```

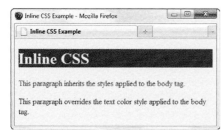

Figure 3.8 The second paragraph's inline styles override the global styles configured on the body tag

Save the document as inline3.html. It should look similar to the page shown in Figure 3.8. You can compare your work with the solution found in the student files (chapter3/inlinep.html). Note that the inline styles applied to the second paragraph override the global styles applied to the body of the web page.

FAQ   **Are inline styles recommended?**

While inline styles can sometimes be useful, you'll find that you won't use this technique much in practice—it's inefficient, adds extra code to the web page document, and is inconvenient to maintain. However, inline styles can be quite handy in some circumstances, such as when you post an article to a content management system or blog and need to tweak the sitewide styles a bit to help get your point across.

3.4 Embedded CSS with the Style Element

In the previous Hands-On Practice, you added inline styles for one of the paragraphs. To do so, you coded a style attribute on the paragraph element. But what if you needed to configure the styles for 10 or 20 paragraphs instead of just one? Using inline styles, you might be doing a lot of repetitive coding! While inline styles apply to one HTML element, embedded styles apply to an entire web page.

Style Element

Embedded styles are placed within a **<style> element** located in the head section of a web page. The opening <style> tag and the closing </style> tag contain the list of embedded-style rules. When using XHTML syntax, the <style> tag requires a **type attribute** with the value of "text/css" to indicate the MIME type. HTML5 syntax does not require the type attribute.

The web page in Figure 3.9 uses embedded styles to set the text color and background color of the web page document with the body element

Figure 3.9 Web page with embedded styles

selector. See the example in the student files at chapter3/embed.html. The code follows:

```
<!DOCTYPE html>
<html lang="en">
<head>
<title>Embedded Styles</title>
<meta charset="utf-8">
<style>
body { background-color: #CCFFFF;
       color: #000033;
}
</style>
</head>
<body>
<h1>Embedded CSS</h1>
<p>This page uses embedded styles.</p>
</body>
</html>
```

Notice the way the style rules were coded, with each rule on its own line. This formatting is not required for the styles to work, but it makes the styles more readable and easier to maintain than one long row of text. The styles are in effect for the entire web page document because they were applied to the <body> tag using the body element selector.

Hands-On Practice 3.2

Launch a text editor, and open the starter.html file from the chapter3 folder in the student files. Save your page as embedded.html, and test it in a browser. Your page should look similar to the one shown in Figure 3.10.

Figure 3.10 The web page without any styles

Open the file in a text editor, and view the source code. Notice that the web page code uses the `<h1>`, `<h2>`, `<div>`, `<p>`, `<ul>`, and `<li>` elements. In this Hands-On Practice, you will code embedded styles to configure selected background and text colors. You will use the body element selector to configure the default background color (`#e6e6fa`) and default text color (`#191970`) for the entire page. You will also use the h1 and h2 element selectors to configure different background and text colors for the heading areas. Edit the embedded.html file in a text editor, and add the following code below the `<title>` element in the head section of the web page:

```
<style>
body { background-color: #e6e6fa; color: #191970; }
h1 { background-color: #191970; color: #e6e6fa; }
h2 { background-color: #aeaed4; color: #191970; }
</style>
```

Save your file, and test it in a browser. Figure 3.11 displays the web page along with corresponding color swatches. A monochromatic color scheme was chosen. Notice how the repetition of a limited number of colors unifies the design of the web page. View the source code for your page, and review the CSS and HTML code. An example of this web page is in the student files at chapter3/embedded.html. Note that all the styles were located in a single place on the web page. Since embedded styles are coded in a specific location, they are easier to maintain over time than inline styles. Also, notice that you coded the styles for the h2 element selector only once (in the head section), and *both* of the `<h2>` elements applied the h2 style. This approach is more efficient than coding the same inline style on each `<h2>` element. However, it is uncommon for a website to have only one page. Repeating the CSS in the head section of each web page file is inefficient and difficult to maintain. In the next section, you'll use a more productive approach—configuring an external style sheet.

Figure 3.11 The web page after embedded styles are configured

FAQ **My CSS doesn't work; what can I do?**

Coding CSS is a detail-oriented process. There are several common errors that can cause the browser not to apply CSS correctly to a web page. With a careful review of your code and the following tips, you should get your CSS working:

- Verify that you are using the colon (:) and semicolon (;) symbols in the right spots—they are easy to confuse. The colon should separate the properties from their values, while the semicolon should be placed between each *property:value* configuration.

- Check that you are not using equal (=) signs instead of colons (:) between each property and its value.

- Verify that curly braces ({ and }) are properly placed around the style rules for each selector.

- Check the syntax of your selectors, the selectors' properties, and the property values for correct usage.

- If part of your CSS works and part doesn't, read through the CSS and determine the first rule that is not applied. Often, the error is in the rule above the rule that is not applied.

- Use a validation application to check your CSS code. The W3C has a free CSS code validator at http://jigsaw.w3.org/css-validator. The W3C's CSS validator can help you find syntax errors. See Section 3.9 for an overview of how to use this tool to validate your CSS.

Checkpoint 3.1

1. List three reasons to use CSS on a web page.

2. When designing a page that uses colors other than the default colors for text and background, explain why it is a good reason to configure both the text color and the background color.

3. Describe one advantage to using embedded styles instead of inline styles.

3.5 Configuring Text with CSS

In Chapter 2, you discovered how to use HTML to configure some characteristics of text on web pages, including phrase elements such as the `<strong>` element. You have also already configured text color using the CSS color property. In this section, you will learn to use CSS to configure font typeface. Using CSS to configure text is more flexible (especially when using an external style sheet, as you will discover later in the chapter) than using HTML elements and is the method preferred by modern web developers.

The `font-family` Property

The **`font-family` property** configures font typeface. A web browser displays text using the fonts that have been installed on the user's computer. When a font is specified that is not installed on your web visitor's computer, the default font is substituted. Times New Roman is the default font displayed by most web browsers. Table 3.3 shows font family categories.

Table 3.3 Common fonts

Font Family Category	Font Family Description	Common Font Typeface Names
serif	Serif fonts have small embellishments ("serifs") on the end of letter strokes; often used for headings	Times New Roman, Georgia, Palatino
sans-serif	Sans-serif fonts do not have serifs; often used for web page text	Arial, Tahoma, Helvetica, Verdana
monospace	Fixed-width font; often used for code samples	Courier New, Lucida Console
cursive	Handwritten style; use with caution— may be difficult to read on a web page	Lucida Handwriting, Brush Script, Comic Sans MS
fantasy	Exaggerated style; use with caution— may be difficult to read on a web page	Jokerman, Impact, Papyrus

Not every computer has the same fonts installed. See http://www.ampsoft.net/webdesign-l/WindowsMacFonts.html for a list of web-safe fonts. Create a built-in backup plan by listing multiple fonts and categories for the value of the font-family property. The browser will attempt to use the fonts in the order listed. The following CSS configures the p element selector to display text in Arial (if installed), Helvetica (if installed), or the default installed sans-serif font:

```
p { font-family: Arial, Helvetica, sans-serif; }
```

FAQ I've heard about "embedding" fonts in order to use special fonts on a web page—what's that all about?

Still in draft form and not yet an official standard, CSS3 introduces @font-face, which can be used to "embed" fonts within web pages, although what actually happens is that you provide the location of the font and the browser downloads it. For example, if you own the rights to freely distribute the font named MyAwesomeFont and it is stored in a file named myawesome-font.otf in the same folder as your web page, the CSS to make it available to your web page visitors is

```
@font-face { font-family: 'MyAwesomeFont';
             src: url('myawesomefont.otf'); }
```

Current browsers support @font-face, but there are file size and copyright issues to consider. You may have purchased a font, but you need to check your license to determine whether you also have the right to freely distribute the font. For more information about @font-face, see http://nimbupani.com/font-in-your-face.html and the textbook's website at http://webdevfoundations.net/6e/chapter3.html. Keep in mind that if you need a nonstandard font just for a logo area or for an image on a web page, there is an easy solution: You are free to use any font that is available to you when you create an image with a graphics application.

More CSS Font Properties

CSS provides you with lots of options for configuring the text on your web pages. In this section, you will explore the font-size, font-weight, font-style, and line-height properties.

The font-size Property

The **font-size property** sets the size of the font. Table 3.4 lists a wide variety of text and numeric values—there are almost too many choices available. See the notes in Table 3.4 for recommended use.

Table 3.4 Configuring font size

Value Category	Values	Notes
Text Value	xx-small, x-small, small, medium (default), large, x-large, xx-large	Scales well when text is resized in browser; limited options for text size
Pixel Unit (px)	Numeric value with unit, such as 10 px	Pixel-perfect display depends on screen resolution; may not scale in every browser when text is resized
Point Unit (pt)	Numeric value with unit, such as 10 pt	Use to configure print version of web page (see Chapter 7); may not scale in every browser when text is resized
Em Unit (em)	Numeric value with unit, such as .75 em	Recommended by W3C; scales well when text is resized in browser; many options for text size
Percentage Value	Numeric value with percentage, such as 75%	Recommended by W3C; scales well when text is resized in browser; many options for text size

The **em unit** is a relative font unit that has its roots in the print industry, dating back to the day when printers set type manually with blocks of characters. An em unit is the width of a square block of type (typically the uppercase M) for a particular font and type size. On web pages, an em unit corresponds to the width of the font and size used in the parent element (typically the body element). So, the size of an em unit is relative to the font typeface and default size. Percentage values work in a similar manner to em units. For example, font-size: 100% and font-size: 1em should render the same in a browser. To compare font sizes on your computer, launch a browser and view chapter3/fonts.html in the student files.

The font-weight Property

The **font-weight property** configures the boldness of the text. Configuring the CSS rule font-weight: bold; has a similar effect as the <strong> or <b> HTML element.

The font-style Property

The **font-style property** typically is used to configure text displayed in italics. Valid values for font-style are normal (the default), italic, and oblique. The CSS font-style: italic; has the same visual effect in the browser as an <i> or <em> HTML element.

The `line-height` Property

The **`line-height` property** modifies the default height of a line of text and is often configured with a percentage value. For example, code `line-height: 200%;` to configure text to appear double spaced.

The `text-align` Property

HTML elements are left-aligned by default; They begin at the left margin. The CSS **`text-align` property** configures the alignment of text and inline elements within block display elements such as headings, paragraphs, and divs. The values for the text-align property are left (default), right, and center. The following CSS code sample configures an h1 element to have centered text:

```
h1 { text-align: center; }
```

While it can be quite effective to center the text displayed in web page headings, be careful about centering text in paragraphs. According to WebAIM (http://www.webaim.org/techniques/textlayout), studies have shown that centered text is more difficult to read than left-aligned text.

The `text-indent` Property

The CSS **`text-indent` property** configures the indentation of the first line of text within an element. The value can be numeric (such as a px, pt, or em unit) or a percentage. The following CSS code sample configures the first line of all paragraphs to be indented:

```
p { text-indent: 5em; }
```

The `text-decoration` Property

The purpose of the CSS **`text-decoration` property** is to modify the display of text. Commonly used values for the text-decoration property include `none`, `underline`, `overline`, and `line-through`. Did you ever wonder why some hyperlinks are not underlined? Although hyperlinks are underlined by default, you can remove the underline with the text-decoration property. The following code sample removes the underline on a hyperlink:

```
a { text-decoration: none; }
```

 # Hands-On Practice 3.3

Now that you've got a collection of new CSS properties for font and text configuration, let's try them out by modifying the embedded.html page. Launch a text editor, and open embedded.html. You will now code additional CSS style rules to configure the text on the page.

Set Default Font Properties for the Page

As you have already seen, CSS rules applied to the body selector apply to the entire page. Modify the CSS for the body selector to display text using a sans-serif font. The new font typeface style rule shown in the following code will apply to the entire web page unless more specific style rules are applied to a selector (such as h1 or p), a class, or an id (more on classes and ids later):

```
body { background-color: #E6E6FA;
       color: #191970;
       font-family: Arial, Verdana, sans-serif; }
```

Save your page as embedded1.html, and test it in a browser. Your page should look similar to the one shown in Figure 3.12. Notice that just a single line of CSS changed the font typeface of all the text on the page!

Figure 3.12 CSS configures the font on the web page

Configure the h1 Selector

Now you will configure the `line-height` and `font-family` CSS properties. Set the `line-height` property to 200%; this will add a bit of empty space above and below the heading text. (In Chapters 4 and 6, you will explore other CSS properties, such as the margin, border, and padding, that are more commonly used to configure space surrounding an element.) Next, modify the h1 selector to use a serif font. When a font name contains spaces, type quotes as indicated in the code that follows. While it is generally recognized that blocks of text using sans-serif fonts are easier to read, it is common to use a serif font to configure page or section headings.

```
h1 { background-color: #191970;
     color: #E6E6FA;
     line-height: 200%;
     font-family: Georgia, "Times New Roman", serif; }
```

Save your page, and test it in a browser. If you notice that the "Trillium Media Design" text seems to crowd the left margin, add a ` ` nonbreaking space special character in the body of the web page after the opening `<h1>` tag.

Configure the h2 Selector

Configure the CSS rule to use the same font typeface as the h1 selector and to display centered text.

```
h2 { background-color: #AEAED4;
     color: #191970;
     font-family: Georgia, "Times New Roman", serif;
     text-align: center; }
```

Configure the Paragraphs

Edit the HTML, and remove the line break tag that is after the first sentence of each paragraph; these line breaks look a bit awkward. Next, configure text in paragraphs to display just slightly smaller than the default text size. Use the `font-size` property set to .90em. Configure the first line of each paragraph to be indented. Use the `text-indent` property to configure a 3em indent.

```
p { font-size: .90em;
    text-indent: 3em; }
```

Configure the Unordered List

Configure the text displayed in the unordered list to be bold.

```
ul { font-weight: bold; }
```

Save your page as embedded2.html, and test it in a browser. Your page should look similar to the one shown in Figure 3.13. The student files contain a sample solution at chapter3/embedded2.html. CSS is quite powerful—just a few lines of code significantly changed the appearance of the web page. You may be wondering if even more customization is possible. For example, what if you did not want all the paragraphs to display in exactly the same way? While you could add inline styles to the web page code, that is usually not the most efficient technique. The next section introduces the CSS class and id selectors, which are widely utilized to configure specific page elements.

Figure 3.13 CSS configures color and text properties on the web page

FAQ   **Is there a quick way to apply the same styles to more than one HTML tag or more than one class?**

Yes, you can apply the same style rules to multiple selectors (such as HTML elements, classes, or ids) by listing the selectors in front of the style rule. Place a comma between each selector. The following code sample shows the `font-size` of 1em being applied to both the paragraph and list-item elements:

```
p, li { font-size: 1em; }
```

3.6 CSS Class, id, and Contextual Selectors

The Class Selector

Use a CSS **class selector** when you need to apply a CSS declaration to certain elements on a web page and not necessarily tie the style to a particular HTML element. See Figure 3.14, and notice that the last two items in the unordered list are displayed in a different color than the others; this is an example of using a class. When setting a style for a class, configure the class name as the selector. Place a dot, or period (.), in front of the class name in the style sheet. The following code configures a class called feature in a style sheet with a foreground (text) color set to red:

```
.feature { color: #FF0000; }
```

The styles set in the new class can be applied to any element you wish. You do this by using the class attribute, such as `class="feature"`. Do not type the dot in front of the class value in the opening tag where the class is being applied. The following code will apply the feature class styles to a `<li>` element:

```
<li class="feature">Usability Studies</li>
```

The id Selector

Use a CSS **id selector** to identify and apply a CSS rule uniquely to a single area on a web page. For example, the copyright information in the page footer in Figure 3.14 displays in small italic text with a gray color (`#333333`). This style could have been configured with a class. However, because the page will have only one footer area, an id is more appropriate. When setting a style for an id, place a hash mark (#) in front of the id name in the style sheet. The following code will configure an id called footer in a style sheet with gray, small, italic text:

```
#footer { color: #333333;
          font-size: .75em;
          font-style: italic; }
```

The styles set in the footer id can be applied to any element you wish by using the id attribute, `id="footer"`. Do not type the # in front of the id value in the opening tag. The following code will apply the footer id styles to a div tag:

```
<div id="footer">This paragraph will be displayed using styles
configured in the footer id.</div>
```

Using CSS with an id selector is similar to using CSS with a class selector. Use an id selector to configure a single element on a web page. Use a class selector to configure one or more elements on a web page.

Figure 3.14 Using classes and ids

Hands-On Practice 3.4

In this Hands-On Practice, you will modify the CSS and the HTML in the Trillium Technologies page to configure the navigation and page footer areas. Launch a text editor, and open embedded2.html.

Configure the Navigation Area

The navigation links would be more prominent if they were displayed in a larger and bolder font. Create a class named nav that sets the font-size and font-weight properties.

```
.nav { font-weight: bold;
       font-size: 1.25em; }
```

Modify the opening div tag of the navigation area. Add a class attribute that associates the div with the nav class as follows:

```
<div class="nav"><a href="index.html">Home</a>
<a href="services.html">Services</a>
<a href="contact.html">Contact</a></div>
```

Configure the Content Area

Trillium Technologies would like to draw attention to its new usability and search optimization services. Create a class named feature that configures the text color to be red (#ff0000).

```
.feature { color: #ff0000; }
```

Modify the last two items in the unordered list. Add a class attribute to each opening li tag that associates the list item with the feature class as follows:

```
<li class="feature">Usability Studies</li>
<li class="feature">Search Engine Optimization</li>
```

Configure the Footer Area

Create an id named footer that sets the text color, font-size, and font-style properties.

```
#footer { color: #333333;
          font-size: .75em;
          font-style: italic; }
```

Modify the opening div tag of the footer area to add an id attribute that associates div with the id class:

```
<div id="footer">Copyright &copy; 2012 Your Name Here</div>
```

Save your file as embedded3.html, and test it in a browser. Your page should look similar to the image shown in Figure 3.14. The student files contain a sample solution at chapter3/embedded3.html. Notice how the class and id styles are applied.

 ## FAQ   **How do you choose class and id names?**

You can choose almost any name you wish for a CSS class or id. However, CSS class names are more flexible and easier to maintain over time if they are descriptive of the structure rather than of specific formatting. For example, a class name of largeBold would no longer be meaningful if the design were changed to display the area differently; however, a structural class name such as nav, header, footer, content, or subheading is meaningful regardless of how the area is configured. Here are more hints for class names:

- Use short, but descriptive, names.
- Both letters and numbers may be used.
- Avoid spaces in class names.
- Class names are not case sensitive, but consistency will make page maintenance easier.

A final tip about CSS classes is to be wary of "classitis"—that is, creating a brand new class each time you need to configure text a bit differently. Decide ahead of time how you will configure page areas, code your classes, and apply them. The result will be a more cohesive and better organized web page.

The Contextual Selector

Use a CSS **contextual selector** when you want to specify an element within the context of its container (parent) element. Contextual selectors are sometimes referred to as descendent selectors. To configure a contextual selector, list the container selector (which can be an element selector, class, or id) followed by the specific selector you are styling. For example, to specify a green text color only for anchor tags located *within* the footer id declared earlier, code the following style rule:

```
#footer a { color: #00ff00; }
```

You will get practice with contextual selectors in Chapters 6 and 7. The next section introduces a new HTML element that is useful when configuring page areas.

3.7 Span Element

Recall from Chapter 2 that the div element configures a section or division on a web page with empty space above and below. The div element is useful when you need to format a section that is physically separated from the rest of the web page, referred to as a block display. In contrast, the **span element** defines a section on a web page that is *not* physically separated from other areas; this formatting is referred to as inline display. Use the `<span>` tag if you need to format an area that is contained within another, such as within a `<p>`, `<blockquote>`, `<li>`, or `<div>` tag.

 ## Hands-On Practice 3.5

You will experiment with the span element in this Hands-On Practice by configuring a new class to format the company name when it is displayed within the text on the page and using the span element to apply this class. Open the embedded3.html file in a text editor. Your web page will look similar to the one shown in Figure 3.15 after the changes are complete.

Figure 3.15 This web page uses the span element

Configure the Company Name

View Figure 3.15, and notice that the company name, Trillium Technologies, is displayed in bold and serif font within the first paragraph. You will code both CSS and HTML to configure this formatting. First, create a new CSS rule that configures a class called companyname in bold, serif font, and 1.25em in size. The code follows:

```
.companyname { font-weight: bold;
               font-family: Georgia, "Times New Roman", serif;
               font-size: 1.25em; }
```

Next, modify the beginning of the first paragraph of HTML to use the span element to apply the class as follows:

```
<p><span class="companyname">Trillium Media Design</span> will bring
```

Save your file, and test it in a browser. Your page should look similar to the one shown in Figure 3.15. The student files contain a sample solution at chapter3/embedded4.html. View the source code for your page, and review the CSS and HTML code. Note that all the styles were located in a single place on the web page. Since embedded styles are coded in a specific location, they are easier to maintain over time than inline styles. Also notice that you needed to code the styles for the h2 element selector only once (in the head section), and *both* of the <h2> elements applied the h2 style. This approach is more efficient than coding the same inline style on each <h2> element. However, it is uncommon for a website to have only one page. Repeating the CSS in the head section of each web page file is inefficient and difficult to maintain. In the next section, you will use a more efficient approach: configuring an external style sheet.

3.8 Using External Style Sheets

VideoNote
External Style Sheets

The flexibility and power of CSS are best utilized when the CSS is external to the web page document. An external style sheet is a text file with a .css file extension that contains CSS style rules. The external style sheet file is associated with a web page by using the link element. This approach provides a way for multiple web pages to be associated with the same external style sheet file. The external style sheet file does not contain any HTML tags; it contains only CSS style rules.

The advantage of external CSS is that styles are configured in a single file. This means that when styles need to be modified, only one file needs to be changed, instead of multiple web pages. On large sites, this approach can save a web developer much time and increase productivity. Let's get some practice with this useful technique.

Link Element

The **link element** associates an external style sheet with a web page. It is placed in the head section of the page and is a stand-alone, void tag. In HTML5 syntax, the link element is coded as <link>. When using XHTML syntax, the link element is coded as <link />. Three attributes are used with the link element: rel, href, and type.

- The value of the **rel** attribute is "stylesheet".
- The value of the **href** attribute is the name of the style sheet file.

- The value of the **type** attribute is `"text/css"`, which is the MIME type for CSS. The type attribute is optional in HTML5 and required in XHTML.

Code the following in the head section of a web page to associate the document with the external style sheet named color.css:

```
<link rel="stylesheet" href="color.css">
```

Hands-On Practice 3.6

Let's practice using external styles. First, you will create an external style sheet. Next, you will configure a web page to be associated with the external style sheet.

Create an External Style Sheet

Launch a text editor, and type in the following style rules to set the background color of a page to blue and the text color to white. Save the file as color.css.

```
body { background-color: #0000FF;
       color: #FFFFFF; }
```

Figure 3.16 shows the external color.css style sheet displayed in Notepad. Notice that there is no HTML in this file. HTML tags are not coded within an external style sheet. Only CSS rules (selectors, properties, and values) are coded in an external style sheet.

Figure 3.16 The external style sheet color.css

Configure the Web Page

To create the web page shown in Figure 3.17, launch a text editor and open the template file located at chapter2/template.html in the student files. Modify the title element, add a link tag to the head section, and add a paragraph to the body section as indicated by the following highlighted code:

```
<!DOCTYPE html>
<html lang="en">
<head>
<title>External Styles</title>
<meta charset="utf-8">
<link rel="stylesheet" href="color.css">
</head>
<body>
<p>This web page uses an external style sheet.</p>
</body>
</html>
```

Save your file as external.html. Launch a browser, and test your page. It should look similar to the page shown in Figure 3.17. You can compare your work with the solution in the student files (chapter3/external.html). The color.css style sheet can be associated with any number of web pages. If you ever need to change the style of formatting, you need to change only a single file (color.css) instead of multiple files (all of the web pages). As mentioned earlier, this technique can boost productivity on a large site.

Figure 3.17 This page is associated with an external style sheet

The advantage of having only a single file to update is significant for both small and large websites. In the next Hands-On Practice, you will modify the Trillium Technologies home page to use an external style sheet.

Hands-On Practice 3.7

In this Hands-On Practice, you will continue to gain experience using external style sheets as you create the external style sheet file named trillium.css, modify the Trillium Technologies home page to use external styles instead of embedded styles, and associate a second web page with the trillium.css style sheet.

A version of the Trillium home page is in the student files. Open the embedded4.html file in a browser. The display should be the same as the web page shown in Figure 3.15 from Hands-On Practice 3.5.

```
trillium.css - Notepad
File  Edit  Format  View  Help
body { background-color: #E6E6FA;
        color: #191970;
        font-family: Arial, Verdana, sans-serif; }
h1 { background-color: #191970;
      color: #E6E6FA;
      line-height: 200%;
      font-family: Georgia, "Times New Roman", serif; }
h2 { background-color: #AEAED4;
      color: #191970;
      font-family: Georgia, "Times New Roman", serif;
      text-align: center;  }
p { font-size: .90em;
     text-indent: 3em;  }
ul { font-weight: bold; }
.nav { font-weight: bold;
        font-size: 1.25em; }
.feature { color: #ff0000;  }
#footer { color: #333333;
           font-size: .75em;
           font-style: italic; }
.companyname { font-weight: bold;
                font-family: Georgia, "Times New Roman", serif;
                font-size: 1.25em; }
```

Figure 3.18 The external style sheet named trillium.css

Now that you've seen what you're working with, let's begin. Launch a text editor, and save the file as index.html in a folder called trillium. You are ready to convert the embedded CSS to external CSS. Select the CSS rules (all the lines of code between, but not including, the opening and closing `<style>` tags). Use Edit > Copy, or press the Ctrl + C keys (Cmd + C keys on a Mac), to copy the CSS code to the clipboard. Now you will place the CSS in a new file. Launch a text editor and create a new file. Use Edit > Paste ,or press the Ctrl + V keys (Cmd + V keys on a Mac), to paste the CSS style rules. Save the file as trillium.css. See Figure 3.18 for a screenshot of the new trillium.css file in Notepad. Notice that there are no HTML elements in trillium.css — not even the `<style>` element. The file contains CSS rules only.

Next, edit the index.html file in a text editor. Delete the CSS code you just copied. Delete the closing `</style>` tag. Replace the opening `<style>` tag with a link element to associate the style sheet named trillium.css. The `<link>` tag code is as follows:

```
<link href="trillium.css" rel="stylesheet">
```

Save the file, and test it in a browser. Your web page should look just like the one shown in Figure 3.15. Although it looks the same, the difference is in the code: The page now uses external, instead of embedded, CSS.

Now, for the fun part — you will associate a second page with the style sheet. The student files contain a services.html page for Trillium at chapter3/services.html. When you display this page in a browser, it should look similar to the one shown in Figure 3.19. Notice that although the structure of the page is similar to the home page, the styling of the text and colors is absent.

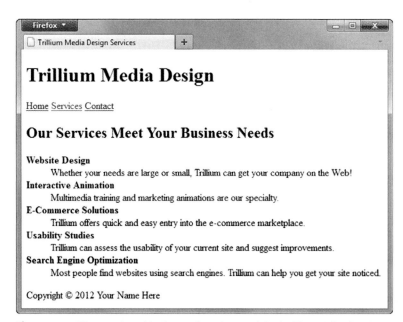

Figure 3.19 The services.html page is not associated with a style sheet

Launch a text editor to edit the services.html file. As you view the HTML code, you will notice that this page is ready for our trillium.css styles — for example, the nav class and footer id have been coded as attributes in the corresponding navigation and page footer areas. All that is left for you to do is to code an HTML `<link>` tag to associate the services.html web page with the trillium.css external style sheet. Place the following code in the header section above the closing `</head>` tag:

```
<link href="trillium.css" rel="stylesheet">
```

Save your file, and test it in a browser. Your page should look similar to Figure 3.20—the CSS rules have been applied!

Figure 3.20
The services.html page has been associated with trillium.css

If you click the Home and Services hyperlinks, you can move back and forth between the index.html and services.html pages in the browser. The student files contain a sample solution in the chapter3/3.7 folder.

Notice that when using an external style sheet, if the use of color or fonts on the page ever needs to be changed, modifications are made only to the external style sheet. Think about how this approach can improve productivity on a site with many pages. Instead of modifying hundreds of pages to make a color or font change, only a single file—the CSS external style sheet—needs to be updated. Becoming comfortable with CSS will be important as you develop your skills and increase your technical expertise.

 # Checkpoint 3.2

1. Describe a reason to use embedded styles. Explain where embedded styles are placed on a web page.

2. Describe a reason to use external styles. Explain where external styles are placed and how web pages indicate that they are using external styles.

3. Write the code to configure a web page to associate with an external style sheet called mystyles.css.

FAQ   **When designing a new web page or website, how do I begin to work with CSS?**

The following guidelines can be helpful when configuring a page using CSS:

- Review the design of the page. Check if common fonts are used. Define global properties (the default for the entire page) for characteristics such as fonts and colors attached to the body element selector.

- Identify typical elements used for organization in the page (such as `<h1>`, `<h2>`, and so on), and declare style rules for these elements if different from the default.

- Identify various page areas such as the logo header, navigation, footer, and so on. List any special configurations needed for these areas. You may decide to configure classes or ids in your CSS to configure these areas.

- Create one prototype page that contains most of the elements you plan to use and test. Revise your CSS as needed.

- Plan and test. These are important activities when designing a website.

3.9 Center HTML Elements with CSS

You learned how to center text on a web page earlier in this chapter—but what about centering the entire web page itself? A popular page layout design that is easy to accomplish with just a few lines of CSS is to center the entire contents of a web page within a browser viewport. The key is to configure a div element that contains, or "wraps," the entire page content. The HTML follows:

```
<body>
<div id="wrapper">
... page content goes here ...
</div>
</body>
```

Next, configure CSS style rules for this container. As will be discussed further in Chapter 6, the **margin** is the empty space surrounding an element. In the case of the body element, the margin is the empty space between the page content and the edges of the browser window. As you might expect, the `margin-left` and `margin-right` properties configure the space in the left and right margins, respectively. The margins can be set to 0, pixel units, em units, percentages, or auto. When margin-left and margin-right are both set to auto, the browser calculates the amount of space available and divides it evenly between the left and right margins. The `width` property configures the width of a block display element. The following CSS code sample sets the width of an id named wrapper to 700 pixels and centers it:

```
#wrapper { width: 700px;
          margin-left: auto;
          margin-right: auto; }
```

You'll practice this technique in the next Hands-On Practice.

Hands-On Practice 3.8

In this Hands-On Practice, you will code CSS properties to configure a centered page layout, using the files from Hands-On Practice 3.7 as a starting point. Create a new folder called trillium2. Locate the chapter3/3.7 folder in the student files. Copy the index.html, services.html, and trillium.css files to your trillium2 folder. Open the trillium.css file in a text editor. Create an id named wrapper. Add the margin-left, margin-right, and width style properties to the style rules as follows:

```
#wrapper { margin-left: auto;
           margin-right: auto;
           width: 80%; }
```

Save the file.

Open the index.html file in a text editor. Add the HTML code to configure a div element assigned to the id wrapper that "wraps," or contains, the code within the body section. Save the file. When you test your index.html file in a browser, it should look similar to the page shown in Figure 3.21. The student files contain a sample solution in the chapter3/3.8 folder.

Figure 3.21 The page content is centered within the browser viewport

FAQ **Is there an easy way to add a comment for documentation purposes in CSS?**

Yes. An easy way to add a comment to CSS is to type "/*" before your comment and "*/" after your comment, as shown in the following example:

```
/* Configure Footer */
#footer { font-size: .80em; font-style: italic; text-align: center; }
```

3.10 The "Cascade"

Figure 3.22 shows the "cascade" (**rules of precedence**) that applies the styles in order from outermost (external styles) to innermost (HTML attributes coded on the page). This set of rules allows the sitewide styles to be configured, but overridden when needed by more granular page-specific styles (such as embedded or inline styles).

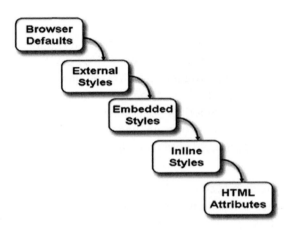

Figure 3.22 The "cascade" of Cascading Style Sheets

External styles can apply to multiple pages. If a web page contains both a link to an external style sheet and embedded styles, the external styles will be applied first, and then the embedded styles will be applied. This approach allows a web developer to override global external styles on selected pages.

If a web page contains both embedded styles and inline styles, the embedded styles are applied first, and then the inline styles are applied. This approach allows a web developer to override pagewide styles for particular HTML tags or classes.

Any XHTML tag or attribute will override styles. For example, a `<strong>` tag will override corresponding font-related styles configured for an element. If no attribute or style is applied to an element, the browser's default is applied. However, the appearance of the browser's default may vary by browser, and you might be disappointed with the result. Use CSS to specify the properties of your text and web page elements. Avoid depending on the browser's default.

In addition to the general cascade of CSS types described previously, the style rules themselves follow rules of precedence. Style rules applied to more local elements (such as a paragraph) take precedence over those applied to more global elements (such as a `<div>` that contains the paragraph).

Let's look at an example of the cascade. Consider the following CSS code:

```
.content { font-family: Arial, sans-serif; }
p { font-family: "Times New Roman", serif; }
```

The CSS has two style rules: a rule creating a class named `content` that configures text using the Arial (or generic sans-serif) font family, and a rule configuring all paragraphs to use the Times New Roman (or generic serif) font family. The HTML on the page contains a `<div>` with multiple elements, such as headings and paragraphs, as shown in the following code:

```
<div class="content">
<h1>Main Heading</h1>
<p>This is a paragraph. Notice how the paragraph is contained in
the div.</p>
</div>
```

Here is how the browser would render the code:

1. The text contained in the heading is displayed with Arial font because it is part of the `<div>` assigned to the `content` class. It inherits the properties from its parent (`<div>`) class. This is an example of **inheritance**, in which certain CSS properties are passed down to elements nested within a container element, such as a `<div>` or `<body>` element. Text-related properties (font-family, color, etc.) are generally inherited, but box-related properties (margin, padding, width, etc.) are not. See http://www.w3.org/TR/CSS21/propidx.html for a detailed list of CSS properties and their inheritance status.

2. The text contained in the paragraph is displayed with Times New Roman font because the browser applies the styles associated with the most local element (the paragraph). Even though the paragraph is contained in (and is considered a child of) the `content` class, the local paragraph style rules takes precedence and are applied by the browser.

Don't worry if CSS and rules of precedence seem a bit overwhelming at this point. CSS definitely becomes easier with practice. You will get a chance to practice with the "cascade" as you complete the next Hands-On Practice.

 Hands-On Practice 3.9

You will experiment with the "cascade" in this Hands-On Practice as you work with a web page that uses external, embedded, and inline styles.

1. Create a new folder named mycascade.

2. Launch a text editor. Open a new file. Save the file as site.css in the mycascade folder. You will create an external style sheet that sets the `background-color` of the web page to a shade of yellow (`#FFFFCC`) and the text color to black (`#000000`). The code follows:

```
body { background-color: #FFFFCC;
       color: #000000; }
```

Save and close the site.css file.

3. Open a new file in the text editor, and save it as mypage1.html in the mycascade folder. The web page will be associated with the external style sheet site.css, use embedded styles to set the global text color to blue, and use inline styles to configure the text color of the

second paragraph. The file mypage1.html will contain two paragraphs of text. The code for mypage1.html follows:

```
<!DOCTYPE html>
<html lang="en">
<head>
<title>The Cascade in Action</title>
<meta charset="utf-8">
<link rel="stylesheet" href="site.css">
<style>
  body { color: #0000FF; }
</style>
</head>
<body>
<p>This paragraph applies the external and embedded styles
&mdash; note how the blue text color that is configured in
the embedded styles takes precedence over the black text color
configured in the external stylesheet.</p>
<p style="color: #FF0000">Inline styles configure this paragraph
to have red text and take precedence over the embedded and
external styles.</p>
</body>
</html>
```

Save mypage1.html, and display it in a browser. Your page should look similar to the sample shown in Figure 3.23. The student files contain a sample solution at chapter3/cascade/mypage1.html.

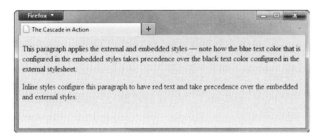

Figure 3.23 Mixing external, embedded, and inline styles

Take a moment to examine the mypage1.html web page and compare it with its source code. The web page picked up the yellow background from the external style sheet. The embedded style configured the text to be the color blue, which overrides the black text color in the external style sheet. The first paragraph in the web page does not contain any inline styles, so it inherits the style rules in the external and embedded style sheets. The second paragraph contains an inline style of red text color; this setting overrides the corresponding external and embedded styles.

3.11 CSS Validation

The W3C has a free Markup Validation Service (http://jigsaw.w3.org/css-validator) that will validate your CSS code and check it for syntax errors. **CSS validation** provides students with quick self-assessment—you can prove that your code uses correct syntax. In the working world, CSS validation serves as a quality assurance tool. Invalid code may cause browsers to render the pages more slowly than otherwise.

VideoNote
CSS Validation

Hands-On Practice 3.10

In this Hands-On Practice, you will use the W3C CSS Validation Service to validate an external CSS style sheet. This example uses the color.css file completed in Hands-On Practice 3.6 (student files chapter3/color.css). Locate color.css, and open it in a text editor. Now add an error to the color.css file By finding the body element selector style rule and deleting the first "r" in the `background-color` property. Add another error by removing the # from the `color` property value. Save the file.

Next, attempt to validate the color.css file. Visit the W3C CSS Validation Service page at http://jigsaw.w3.org/css-validator and select the "by File Upload" tab. Click the Browse button and select the color.css file from your computer. Click the Check button. Your display should be similar to that shown in Figure 3.24. Notice that two errors were found. The selector is listed, followed by the reason an error was noted.

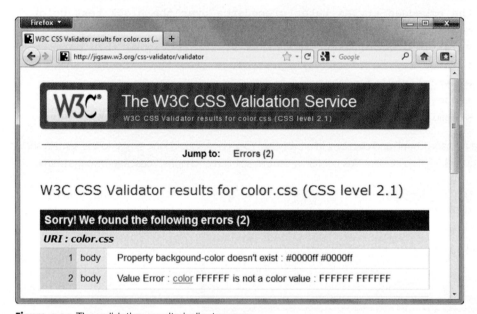

Figure 3.24 The validation results indicate errors

Notice that the first message in Figure 3.24 indicates that the "`backgound-color`" property does not exist. This is a clue to check the syntax of the property name. Edit color.css and correct the first error. Test and revalidate your page. Your browser should now look similar to the one shown in Figure 3.25 and should be reporting only one error.

The error reminds you that `FFFFFF` is not a color value; you are expected to already know that you need to add a "`#`" character to code a valid color value, as in `#FFFFFF`. Notice how any valid CSS rules are displayed below the error messages. Correct the color value, save the file, and test again.

Your results should look similar to those shown in Figure 3.26. There are no errors listed. The Valid CSS Information contains all the CSS style rules in color.css. This means your file passed

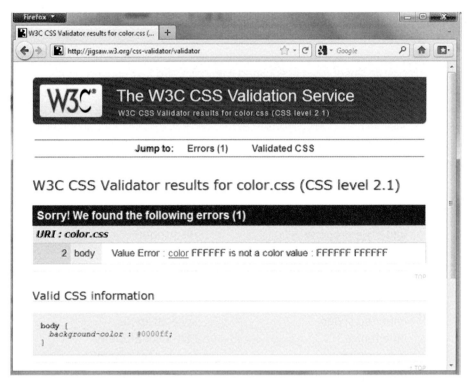

Figure 3.25 The valid CSS code is displayed below the errors (and warnings, if any)

the CSS validation test. Congratulations, your color.css file is valid CSS syntax! It is good practice to validate your CSS style rules. The CSS validator can help you to quickly identify code that needs to be corrected and indicate which style rules a browser is likely to consider valid. Validating CSS code is one of the many productivity techniques that web developers commonly use.

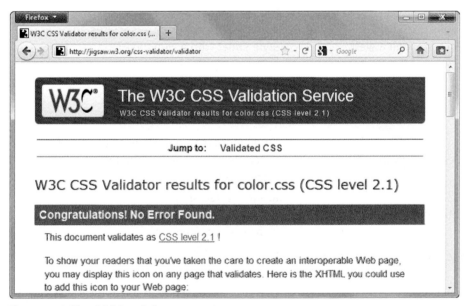

Figure 3.26 The CSS is valid!

Chapter Summary

This chapter has introduced Cascading Style Sheet rules associated with color and text on web pages. There is much more that you can do with CSS, including positioning, hiding and showing page areas, formatting margins, and formatting borders. As you continue your study of web development with this textbook, you will learn about these additional uses. Visit this textbook's website at http://www.webdevfoundations.net for examples, information on the resources described in this chapter, and to view updated information.

Key Terms

`<link>`	font-size property	property
`<span>`	font-style property	rel attribute
`<style>`	font-weight property	RGB color
background-color property	hexadecimal color values	rule
Cascading Style Sheets (CSS)	id attribute	rules of precedence
class attribute	id selector	selector
class selector	imported styles	style attribute
color property	inheritance	text-align property
CSS validation	inline styles	text-indent property
declaration	line-height property	type attribute
em unit	margin-left property	Web-Safe Color Palette
embedded styles	margin-right property	width property
external styles	pixels	
font-family property	point	

Review Questions

Multiple Choice

1. Which of the following is the CSS property used to set the alignment of text on a web page?
   a. text-align
   b. text-alignment
   c. text
   d. align

2. What are embedded styles placed within?
   a. an external CSS file
   b. the `<style>` element
   c. the style attribute in the relevant tag
   d. none of the above

3. How does the background-image property repeat an image by default?
   a. both horizontally and vertically
   b. horizontally only
   c. vertically only
   d. none of the above

4. Which of the following associates an external style sheet with a web page?
   a. the `style` element
   b. the `head` element
   c. the `link` element
   d. the `rel` element

5. When more than one style is specified for an HTML element, which of the following gets the highest priority?
   a. embedded style
   b. external style sheet
   c. browser default
   d. inline styles

6. When more than one style is specified for an HTML element, which of the following gets the lowest priority?
   a. embedded style
   b. external style sheet

c. browser default

d. inline styles

7. Which of the following cannot be a selector?

a. an HTML element name

b. an HTML file name

c. a class name

d. an id name

8. Which of the following values does the font-style property typically have?

a. normal, italic, and oblique

b. serif, sans-serif, and monospace

c. left, right, and center

d. underline, overline, and line-through

9. Which of the following configures a background color of #FFF8DC for a web page using CSS?

a. `body { background-color: #FFF8DC; }`

b. `document { background: #FFF8DC; }`

c. `body { bgcolor: #FFF8DC;}`

d. `document { bgcolor: #FFF8DC; }`

10. Which of the following uses CSS to configure a class called news with red text, large font, and Arial or a sans-serif font?

a.
```
news { color: red;
       font-size: large;
       font-family: Arial,
       sans-serif; }
```

b.
```
.news { color: red;
        font-size: large;
        font-family: Arial,
        sans-serif; }
```

c.
```
.news { text: red;
        font-size: large;
        font-family: Arial,
        sans-serif; }
```

d.
```
#news { text: red;
        font-size: large;
        font-family: Arial,
        sans-serif;}
```

11. Which of the following is true if a web page contains both a link to an external style sheet and embedded styles?

a. Embedded styles will be applied first, and then the external styles will be applied.

b. The inline styles will be used.

c. External styles will be applied first, and then the embedded styles will be applied.

d. The web page will not display.

Fill in the Blank

12. A CSS rule has two main parts: a _____ and one or more _____ .

13. Each declaration consists of a _____ and a _____.

14. You can remove the underline from a hyperlink with the _____ property.

15. The _____ element is useful for block display. In contrast, the _____ element is useful for inline display.

Apply Your Knowledge

1. **Predict the Result.** Draw and write a brief description of the web page that will be created with the following HTML code:

```
<!DOCTYPE html>
<html lang="en">
<head>
<title>Halloween Costumes</title>
<meta charset="utf-8">

<style>
body { background-color: #000000;
       color: #ffffff;
       font-family: Arial,sans-serif; }
```

```
h1 { background-color: #FFFFFF;
     color: #ff0000;
     font-family: cursive;}
.footer { font-size: 80%;
          font-style: italic; }
a { color: #ff0000;}
</style>
</head>
<body>
<h1>Halloween Costumes and other Accessories!!!</h1>
<div>Dresses/Accessories <a href="games.html">Games</a>
<a href="ideas.html">Other Ideas</a>
<a href="contact.html">Contact Us</a>
</div>
<p>Halloween costumes are costumes worn on or around Halloween, a
festival which falls on October 31. <br>
The Halloween costume has a fairly short history. Wearing costumes
has long been associated with other holidays around the time of
Halloween, even Christmas. </p>
<br><br>
<div class="footer">
Copyright &copy; 2012 Fancy Dress Stores
</div>
</body>
</html>
```

2. **Fill in the Missing Code.** Consider the following code, in which some CSS properties and values, indicated by "_", and some HTML tags, indicated by < _ >, are missing:

```
<!DOCTYPE html>
<html lang="en">
<head>
<title>Green Valley Log Cabins</title>
<meta charset="utf-8">
<style>
body { background-color: #FFFFCC;

color: "_"; }

h1{ "_": "_" }
p { "_": "_" }
< _ >
< _ >
<body>
<h1>Find Nature at your Doorstep</h1>
    <p>Come here to discover the natural beauty and quality of
Appalachian Log Cabins and Timber Homes. </p>
<p>Our distinctive log homes feature a variety of styles and great
floor plans. </p>
<p>Each design is energy efficient and speaks of grandeur. </p>
<p>Our Log Homes are the perfect blend of old world charm and
modern conveniences and comfort. </p>
</body>
</html>
```

The web page corresponding to the code should be configured so that the background and text colors have good contrast. The <h1> tag should use Times New Roman, or any sans-serif font in its absence. Other text on the page should be 150% of normal size. Fill in the missing code.

3. **Find the Error.** Why won't the page corresponding to the following code display properly in a browser?

```
<!DOCTYPE html>
<html lang="en">
<head>
<title>Green Valley Log Cabins</title>
<meta charset="utf-8">
<style>
body { background-color: #FFFFCC;
color: #990000 ; }
h1 { color : #336600;
font-family: Times New Roman, sans-serif }
p { font-size: 150%;}
<style>
</head>
<body>
<h1>Find Nature at your Doorstep</h1>
<p>Come here to discover the natural beauty and quality of
Appalachian Log Cabins and Timber Homes. </p>
<p>Our distinctive Log Homes feature a variety of styles
and great floor plans. </p>
<p>Each design is energy efficient and speaks of grandeur.
</p>
<p>Our Log Homes are the perfect blend of old world charm
    and modern conveniences and comfort.
</p>
</body>
</html>
```

Hands-On Exercises

1. Write the HTML for a paragraph that has a text indent of 1em, text color of blue, and text alignment as justify.

2. Write the HTML and CSS code for an embedded style sheet that configures a background color of #doe4fe and a text color of #0000FF. However, the level-1 headings should have the text color as red, and centered text alignment.

3. Write the CSS code for an id selector that specifies that all elements named "center" will have centered text alignment.

4. Write the CSS code for an external style sheet that configures the text to be blue and in Arial, Verdana, or another sans-serif font. The page has a background color of medium-blue, and some sections of text will have a background color of sky-blue. There will be some level-3 headings with a background color of dark-blue and text color of white.

5. Write the HTML and CSS code for an embedded style sheet that configures links without underlines; configures a background color of linen; configures a text color

of lime green; is in Arial, Helvetica, or another sans-serif font; and specifies that all p elements with class="center" will be center-aligned.

6. Write the HTML and CSS code for an embedded style sheet that configures a background color of Aqua; configures a text color of blue; is in Times New Roman, Times, or another serif font; and has a class called notice that should have bold italic and underlined text in red color.

7. **Practice with External Style Sheets.** In this exercise, you will create two external style sheet files and a web page. You will experiment with linking the web page to the external style sheets and note how the display of the page is changed.

   a. Create an external style sheet (call it format1.css) to format as follows: document background color of white, document text color of #000099, and document font family of Arial, Helvetica, or sans-serif. Hyperlinks should have a background color of gray (#CCCCCC). Configure the h1 selector to use the Times New Roman font with red text color.

   b. Create an external style sheet (call it format2.css) to format as follows: document background color of yellow and document text color of green. Hyperlinks should have a background color of white. Configure the h1 selector to use the Times New Roman font with white background color and green text color.

   c. Create a web page about your favorite movie that displays the movie name in an <h1> tag, a description of the movie in a paragraph, and an unordered (bulleted) list of the main actors and actresses in the movie. The page should also have a hyperlink to a website about the movie. Place an e-mail link to yourself on the web page. This page should be associated with the format1.css file. Save the page as moviecss1.html. Be sure to test your page in more than one browser. Modify the moviecss1.html page to link to the format2.css external style sheet instead of the format1.css file. Save the page as moviecss2.html and test it in a browser. Notice how different the page looks!

8. **Practice with the Cascade.** In this exercise, you will create two web pages that link to the same external style sheet. After modifying the configuration in the external style sheet, you will test your pages again and find that they automatically pick up the new style configuration. Finally, you will add an inline style to one of the pages and find that it takes effect and overrides the external style.

   a. Create a web page that includes an unordered list describing at least three advantages of using CSS. The text "CSS Advantages" should be contained within <h1> tags. This page should include a hyperlink to the W3C website. Write the HTML code so that one of the advantages is configured to be a class called news. Place an e-mail link to yourself on the web page. The web page should be associated with the external style sheet called ex8.css. Save the page as advantage.html.

   b. Create an external style sheet (call it ex8.css) to format as follows: document background color of white; document text color of #000099; and document font family of Arial, Helvetica, or sans-serif. Hyperlinks should have a background color of gray (#CCCCCC). <h1> elements should use the Times New Roman font with black text color. The news class should use red italic text.

   c. Launch a browser, and test your work. Display the advantage.html page. It should use the formatting configured in ex8.css. Modify the web page or the CSS file until your page displays as requested.

d. Change the configuration of the external style sheet (ex8.css) to use a document background color of black, document text color of white, and <h1> text color of gray (#CCCCCC). Save the file. Launch a browser, and test the advantage.html page. Notice how it picks up the new styles from the external style sheet.

e. Modify the advantage.html file to use an inline style. The inline style should be applied to the <h1> tag and configure it to have red text. Save the advantage. html page, and test in a browser. Notice how the <h1> text color specified in the style sheet is overridden by the inline style.

9. **Practice Validating CSS.** Choose a CSS external style sheet file to validate; perhaps you have created one for your own website. Otherwise, use an external style sheet file that you worked with in this chapter. Use the W3C CSS validator at http://jigsaw.w3.org/css-validator. If your CSS does not immediately pass the validation test, modify it and test again. Repeat this process until the W3C validates your CSS code. Write a one- or two-paragraph summary about the validation process that answers the following questions: Was the CSS validator easy to use? Did anything surprise you? Did you encounter a number of errors or just a few? How easy was it to determine how to correct the CSS file? Would you recommend the validator to other students? Why or why not?

Web Research

1. This chapter has introduced you to using CSS to configure web pages. Use a search engine to find CSS resources. The following resources can help you get started:

- http://www.w3.org/Style/CSS
- http://positioniseverything.net
- http://www.dezwozhere.com/links.html

Create a web page that provides a list of at least five CSS resources on the Web. For each CSS resource, provide the URL, website name, and a brief description. Configure text and background colors with good contrast. Place your name in the e-mail address at the bottom of the web page.

2. There is still much for you to learn about CSS. A great place to learn about web technology is the Web itself. Use a search engine to search for CSS tutorials. The following resources can help you get started:

- http://www.echoecho.com/css.htm
- http://www.w3schools.com/css
- http://www.davesite.com/webstation/css

Choose a tutorial that is easy to read. Select a section that discusses a CSS technique that was not covered in this chapter. Create a web page that uses this new technique. The web page should provide the URL of your tutorial, the name of the website, and a description of the new technique you discovered. Place your name in the e-mail address at the bottom of the web page.

Focus on Web Design

In this chapter, you have learned how to configure color and text with CSS. In this activity, you will design a color scheme, code an external CSS file for the color scheme, and code an example web page that applies the styles you configured. Use any of the following sites to help you get started with color and web design ideas:

Psychology of Color

- http://www.infoplease.com/spot/colors1.html
- http://www.sensationalcolor.com/meanings.html
- http://designfestival.com/the-psychology-of-color
- http://www.designzzz.com/infographic-psychology-color-web-designers

Color Theory

- http://www.colormatters.com/colortheory.html
- http://colortheory.liquisoft.com/
- http://www.digital-web.com/articles/color_theory_for_the_colorblind

Color Scheme Generators

- http://meyerweb.com/eric/tools/color-blend
- http://colorschemer.com/schemes
- http://www.colr.org
- http://colorsontheweb.com/colorwizard.asp
- http://kuler.adobe.com
- http://colorschemedesigner.com

Complete the following tasks:

a. Design a color scheme. List three hexadecimal color values in addition to neutral colors such as white (#FFFFFF) or black (#000000) in your design.

b. Describe the process you went through as you selected the colors. Describe why you chose these colors. What type of website would they be appropriate for? List the URLs of any resources you used.

c. Create an external CSS file named color1.css that configures font properties, text color, and background color selections for the document, h1 element selector, p element selector, and footer class, using the colors you have chosen.

d. Create a web page named color1.html that shows examples of the CSS style rules.

 WEBSITE CASE STUDY

Implementing CSS

Each of the case studies in this section continues throughout most of the text. This chapter implements CSS in the websites.

JavaJam Coffee House

See Chapter 2 for an introduction to the JavaJam Coffee House Case Study. Figure 2.25 shows a site map for the JavaJam website. The Home page and Menu page were created in Chapter 2. You will develop a new version of the website that uses an external style sheet to configure text and color. Figure 2.26 depicts the wireframe page layout.

You have the following tasks:

1. Create a new folder for this JavaJam case study.

2. Create an external style sheet named javajam.css that configures the color and text for the JavaJam website.

3. Modify the Home page to utilize an external style sheet to configure colors and fonts. The new Home page and color swatches are shown in Figure 3.27.

4. Modify the Menu page to be consistent with the new Home page.

5. Configure centered page layout.

Figure 3.27 New JavaJam index.html

Hands-On Practice Case

Task 1: Create a folder on your hard drive or portable storage device called javajamcss. Copy all the files from your Chapter 2 javajam folder into the javajamcss folder.

Task 2: The External Style Sheet. You will use a text editor to create an external style sheet named javajam.css. Code the CSS to configure the following:

1. Global styles for the document (use the body element selector) with background color #ffffcc; text color #330000; and Verdana, Arial, or any sans-serif font.

2. Styles for the h1 element selector that configure background color #ccaa66, text color #000000, 200% line height, and centered text.

3. Styles for the navigation area (use an id named nav) that configure centered text. *Hint*: Use the CSS text-align property.

4. Styles for the page footer area (use an id named footer) that configure background color #ccaa66, text color #000000, small font size (.60em), italics, and centered text.

Save the file as javajam.css in the javajamcss folder. Check your syntax with the CSS validator (http://jigsaw.w3.org/css-validator). Correct and retest if necessary.

Task 3: The Home Page. Launch a text editor, and open the index.html file. You will modify this file to apply styles from the javajam.css external style sheet as follows:

1. Add a `<link>` element to associate the web page with the javajam.css external style sheet file. Save and test your index.html page in a browser and you'll notice that the styles configured with the body and h1 element selectors are already applied!

2. Configure the navigation area. Assign the div that contains the navigation to the id named nav. *Hint*: `<div id="nav">`.

3. Configure the page footer area. Remove the `<small>` and `<i>` elements, because the `font-size` and `font-style` are configured as part of the footer id. Assign the div that contains the footer information to the id named `footer`.

Save the index.html file, and test it in a browser. Your page should look similar to the one shown in Figure 3.27 except that your page content will be left-aligned instead of centered. Don't worry—you'll center your page layout in Task 5 of this case study.

Task 4: The Menu Page. Launch a text editor, and open the menu.html file. You will modify this file in a similar manner as you modified the home page: Add the `<link>` element, configure the navigation area, and configure the page footer area. Save and test your new menu.html page. It should look similar to the one shown in Figure 3.28, except for the alignment.

Task 5: Center Page Layout with CSS. Modify javajam.css, index.html, and menu.html to configure page content that is centered with 80% width (refer to Hands-On Practice 3.8 if necessary):

1. Launch a text editor, and open the javajam.css file. Add a style rule for an id named wrapper with `width` set to 80%, `margin-right` set to auto, and `margin-left` set to auto.

2. Launch a text editor, and open the index.html file. Add the HTML code to configure a div element assigned to the id `wrapper` that "wraps," or contains, the code within the body section. Save and test your index.html page in a browser and you'll notice that the page content is now centered within the browser viewport as shown in Figure 3.27.

3. Launch a text editor, and open the menu.html file. Add the HTML code to configure a div element assigned to the id `wrapper` that "wraps," or contains, the code within the body section. Save and test your menu.html page in a browser and you'll notice that the page content is now centered within the browser viewport as shown in Figure 3.28.

Experiment with modifying the javajam.css file. Change the page background color, the font family, and so on. Test your pages in a browser. Isn't it amazing how a change in a single file can affect multiple files when external style sheets are used?

Fish Creek Animal Hospital

See Chapter 2 for an introduction to the Fish Creek Animal Hospital Case Study. Figure 2.29 shows a site map for the Fish Creek website. The Home page and Services page were created in Chapter 2. You will develop a new version that uses an external style sheet to configure text and color. Figure 2.30 depicts the wireframe page layout.

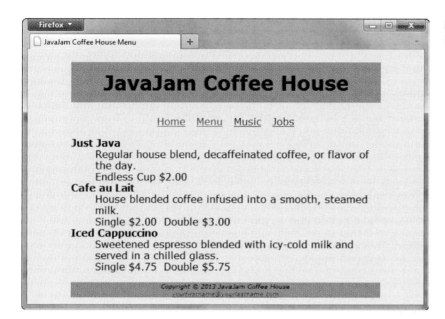

Figure 3.28
New menu.html page

You have the following tasks:

1. Create a new folder for this Fish Creek case study.

2. Create an external style sheet named fishcreek.css that configures the color and text for the Fish Creek website.

3. Modify the Home page to utilize an external style sheet to configure colors and fonts. The new Home page and color swatches are shown in Figure 3.29.

4. Modify the Services page to be consistent with the new Home page.

5. Configure centered page layout.

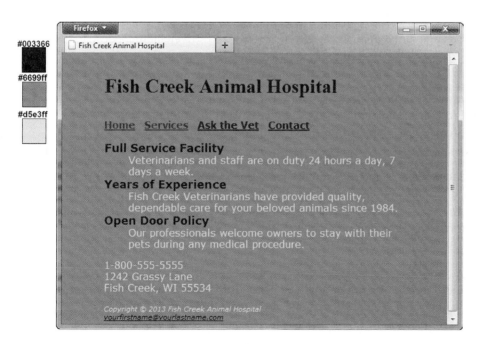

Figure 3.29
New Fish Creek
index.html

Hands-On Practice Case Study

Task 1: Create a folder on your hard drive or portable storage device called fishcreekcss. Copy all the files from your Chapter 2 fishcreek folder into the fishcreekcss folder.

Task 2: The External Style Sheet. You will use a text editor to create an external style sheet named fishcreek.css. Code the CSS to configure the following:

1. Global styles for the document (use the body element selector) with background color #6699ff; text color #d5e3ff; and Verdana, Arial, or any sans-serif font.

2. Styles for the h1 element selector that configure background color #6699ff, text color #003366, serif font, and 200% line height.

3. Styles for a navigation area (use a class named nav) that displays text in bold.

4. Styles for a class named category with bold font, background color #6699ff, text color #003366, and larger font size (1.1em).

5. Styles for the page footer area (use an id named footer) with a small font size (.70em) and italic text.

Save the file as fishcreek.css in the fishcreekcss folder. Check your syntax with the CSS validator (http://jigsaw.w3.org/css-validator). Correct and retest if necessary.

Task 3: The Home Page. Launch a text editor, and open the index.html file. You will modify this file to apply styles from the fishcreek.css external style sheet as follows:

1. Add a <link> element to associate the web page with the fishcreek.css external style sheet file. Save and test your index.html page in a browser and you'll notice that the styles configured with the body and h1 element selectors are already applied!

2. Configure the navigation area. Assign the div that contains the navigation to the class named nav. *Hint*: <div class="nav">. Remove the <b> element from the navigation area, because the CSS will configure the bold font style.

3. Configure each <dt> element to apply the category class. *Hint*: <dt class="category">. Remove the <strong> elements, because the CSS will configure the bold font style.

4. Configure the page footer area. Remove the <small> and <i> elements, because the font-size and font-style are configured as part of the footer id. Assign the div that contains the footer information to the id named footer.

Save the index.html file, and test in a browser. Your page should look similar to the one shown in Figure 3.29 except that your page content will be left-aligned instead of indented from the margins. Don't worry—you'll configure your page layout in Task 5 of this case study.

Task 4: The Services Page. Launch a text editor, and open the services.html file. You will modify this file in a similar manner: Add the <link> element, configure the navigation area, configure the category classes (*Hint*: Use the <span> tag to contain the name of each service offered), and configure the page footer area. Save and test your new services.html page. It should look similar to the one shown in Figure 3.28 except for the alignment.

Task 5: Center Page Layout with CSS. Modify fishcreek.css, index.html, and services. html to configure page content that is centered with 80% width. Refer to Hands-On Practice 3.8 if necessary.

1. Launch a text editor, and open the fishcreek.css file. Add a style rule for an id named wrapper with `width` set to `80%`, `margin-right` set to auto, and `margin-left` set to auto.

2. Launch a text editor, and open the index.html file. Add the HTML code to configure a div element assigned to the id `wrapper` that "wraps," or contains, the code within the body section. Save and test your index.html page in a browser and you'll notice that the page content is now centered within the browser viewport as shown in Figure 3.29.

3. Launch a text editor, and open the services.html file. Add the HTML code to configure a div element assigned to the id `wrapper` that "wraps," or contains, the code within the body section. Save and test your services.html page in a browser and you'll notice that the page content is now centered within the browser viewport as shown in Figure 3.30.

Experiment with modifying the fishcreek.css file. Change the page background color, the font family, and so on. Test your pages in a browser. Isn't it amazing how a change in a single file can affect multiple files when external style sheets are used?

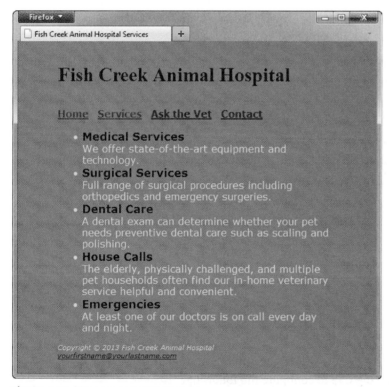

Figure 3.30 New services.html page

Pacific Trails Resort

See Chapter 2 for an introduction to the Pacific Trails Resort Case Study. Figure 2.33 shows a site map for the Pacific Trails Resort website. The Home page and Yurts page were created in Chapter 2. You will develop a new version of this website that uses an external style sheet to configure text and color. Figure 2.34 depicts the wireframe page layout.

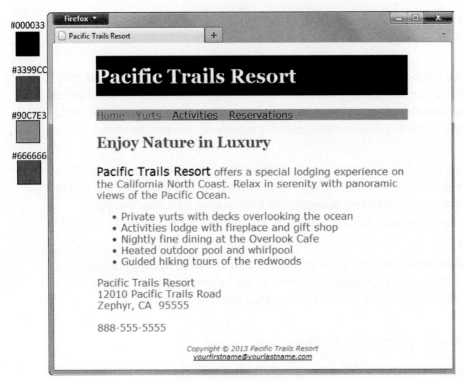

Figure 3.31 New Pacific Trails index.html

You have the following tasks:

1. Create a new folder for this Pacific Trails case study.

2. Create an external style sheet named pacific.css that configures the color and text for the Pacific Trails website.

3. Modify the Home page to utilize an external style sheet to configure colors and fonts. The new Home page and color swatches are shown in Figure 3.31.

4. Modify the Yurts page to be consistent with the new Home page.

5. Configure centered page layout.

Hands-On Practice Case Study

Task 1: Create a folder on your hard drive or portable storage device called pacificcss. Copy all the files from your Chapter 2 pacific folder into the pacificcss folder.

Task 2: The External Style Sheet. You will use a text editor to create an external style sheet named pacific.css. Code the CSS to configure the following:

1. Global styles for the document (use the body element selector) with background color #FFFFFF; text color #666666. and Verdana, Arial, or any sans-serif font.

2. Styles for the h1 element selector that configure background color #000033, text color #FFFFFF, 200% line height, and Georgia or any serif font.

3. Styles for a navigation area (use an id named nav) that displays text in bold and has a sky-blue background color (#90C7E3).

4. Styles for the h2 element selector that configure medium-blue text color (#3399CC) and Georgia or any serif font.

5. Styles for the dt element selector that configure dark-blue text color (#000033).

6. Styles for a class named `resort` that configure dark-blue text color (#000033) and 1.2em font size.

7. Styles for the page footer area (use an id named `footer`) with a small font size (.70em) and italic, centered text.

Save the file as pacific.css in the pacificcss folder. Check your syntax with the CSS validator (http://jigsaw.w3.org/css-validator). Correct and retest if necessary.

Task 3: The Home Page. Launch a text editor, and open the index.html file. You will modify this file to apply styles from the pacific.css external style sheet as follows:

1. Add a `<link>` element to associate the web page with the pacific.css external style sheet file. Save and test your index.html page in a browser and you'll notice that the styles configured with the body, h1, and h2 element selectors are already applied!

2. Configure the navigation area. Assign the div that contains the navigation to the id named nav. *Hint*: `<div id="nav">`. Remove the `<b>` element from the navigation area, because the CSS will configure the bold font weight.

3. Find the company name ("Pacific Trails Resort") in the first paragraph below the h2. Configure a span that contains this text. Assign the span tag to the `resort` class.

4. Configure the page footer area. Remove the `<small>` and `<i>` elements, because the `font-size` and `font-style` are configured as part of the footer id. Assign the div that contains the footer information to the id named `footer`.

Save the index.html file, and test in a browser. Your page should look similar to the one shown in Figure 3.31 except that your page content will be left-aligned instead of indented from the margins. Don't worry—you'll configure your page layout in Task 5 of this case study.

Task 4: The Yurts Page. Launch a text editor, and open the yurts.html file. You will modify this file in a similar manner: Add the `<link>` element, configure the navigation area, and configure the page footer area. Save and test your new yurts.html page. It should look similar to the one shown in Figure 3.32 except for the alignment.

Task 5: Center Page Layout with CSS. Modify pacific.css, index.html, and yurts.html to configure page content that is centered with 80% width. Refer to Hands-On Practice 3.8 if necessary.

1. Launch a text editor, and open the pacific.css file. Add a style rule for an id named wrapper with width set to 80%, margin-right set to auto, and margin-left set to auto.

2. Launch a text editor, and open the index.html file. Add the HTML code to configure a div element assigned to the id wrapper that "wraps," or contains, the code within the body section. Save and test your index.html page in a browser and you'll notice that the page content is now centered within the browser viewport as shown in Figure 3.31.

3. Launch a text editor and open the yurts.html file. Add the HTML code to configure a div element assigned to the id wrapper that "wraps," or contains, the code within the body section. Save and test your yurts.html page in a browser and you'll notice

that the page content is now centered within the browser viewport as shown in Figure 3.32.

Experiment with modifying the pacific.css file. Change the page background color, the font family, and so on. Test your pages in a browser. Isn't it amazing how a change in a single file can affect multiple files when external style sheets are used?

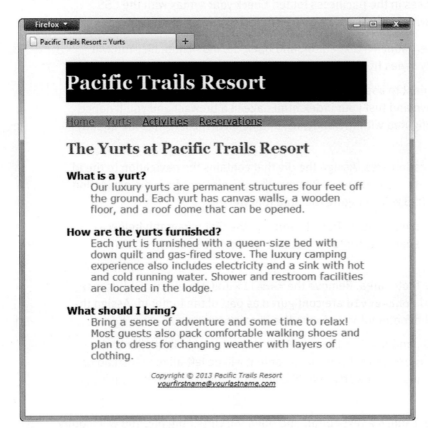

Figure 3.32 New yurts.html page

Prime Properties

See Chapter 2 for an introduction to the Prime Properties Case Study. Figure 2.37 shows a site map for the Prime Properties website. The Home page and Financing page were created in Chapter 2. You will develop a new version of this website that uses an external style sheet to configure text and color. Figure 2.38 depicts the wireframe page layout.

You have the following tasks:

1. Create a new folder for this Prime Properties case study.

2. Create an external style sheet named prime.css that configures the color and text for the Prime Properties website.

3. Modify the Home page to utilize an external style sheet to configure colors and fonts. The new Home page and color swatches are shown in Figure 3.33.

4. Modify the Financing page to be consistent with the new Home page.

5. Configure centered page layout.

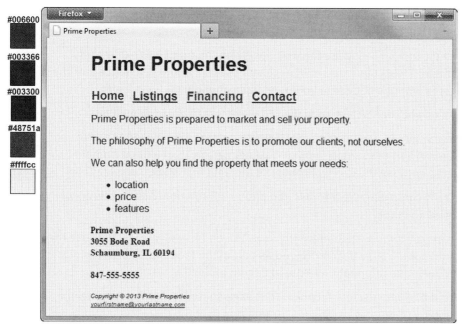

Figure 3.33 New Prime Properties index.html

Hands-On Practice Case Study

Task 1: Create a folder on your hard drive or portable storage device called primecss. Copy all the files from your Chapter 2 prime folder into the primecss folder.

Task 2: The External Style Sheet. You will use a text editor to create an external style sheet named prime.css. Code the CSS to configure the following:

1. Global styles for the document (use the body element selector) with background color #ffffcc; text color #003300; and Arial, Helvetica, or any sans-serif font.

2. Styles for the h2 element selector that configure background color #ffffcc and text color #003366.

3. Styles for the h3 element selector that configure background color #ffffcc and text color #006600.

4. Styles for the dd element selector that configure italics, font size smaller than the default (.90em), and 200% line height.

5. Styles for an id named header that configure background color #ffffcc and text color #48751A.

6. Styles for a navigation area (use a class named nav) that displays text in bold, large (1.2em) font.

7. Styles for a class named contact that configure boldface, font size smaller than the default (.90em), and Times New Roman or any serif font.

8. Styles for the page footer area (use an id named footer) with small font size (.60em) and italic text.

Save the file as prime.css in the primecss folder. Check your syntax with the CSS validator (http://jigsaw.w3.org/css-validator). Correct and retest if necessary.

Task 3: The Home Page. Launch a text editor, and open the index.html file. You will modify this file to apply styles from the prime.css external style sheet.

1. Add a `<link>` element to associate the web page with the prime.css external style sheet file. Save and test your index.html page in a browser and you'll notice that the styles configured with the body selector are already applied!

2. Configure the logo header area. Assign the `<h1>` element to the id named `header`.

3. Configure the navigation area. Assign the div that contains the navigation to the class named `nav`. *Hint*: `<div class="nav">`. Remove the `<b>` element from the navigation area, because the CSS will configure the bold font style.

4. Configure the div containing the address and phone information. Assign this area to the class named `contact`.

5. Configure the page footer area. Remove the `<small>` and `<i>` elements, because the `font-size` and `font-style` are configured as part of the footer id. Assign the div that contains the footer information to the id named footer.

Save the index.html file, and test in a browser. Your page should look similar to the one shown in Figure 3.33.

Task 4: The Financing Page. Launch a text editor, and open the financing.html file. You will modify this file in a similar manner: Add the `<link>` element, configure the logo header area, configure the navigation area, and configure the page footer area. Save and test your new financing.html page. It should look similar to the one shown in Figure 3.34.

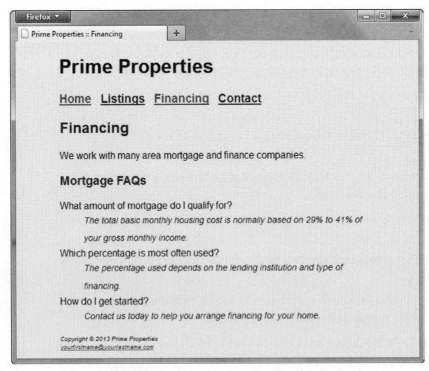

Figure 3.34 New financing.html page

Task 5: Center Page Layout with CSS. Modify prime.css, index.html, and financing.html to configure page content that is centered with 80% width. Refer to Hands-On Practice 3.8 if necessary.

1. Launch a text editor, and open the prime.css file. Add a style rule for an id named `wrapper` with `width` set to `80%`, `margin-right` set to auto, and `margin-left` set to auto.

2. Launch a text editor, and open the index.html file. Add the HTML code to configure a div element assigned to the id `wrapper` that "wraps," or contains, the code within the body section. Save and test your index.html page in a browser and you'll notice that the page content is now centered within the browser viewport as shown in Figure 3.33.

3. Launch a text editor, and open the financing.html file. Add the HTML code to configure a div element assigned to the id `wrapper` that "wraps," or contains, the code within the body section. Save and test your financing.html page in a browser and you'll notice that the page content is now centered within the browser viewport as shown in Figure 3.34.

Experiment with modifying the prime.css file. Change the page background color, the font family, and so on. Test your pages in a browser. Notice how a change in a single file can affect multiple files when external style sheets are used.

Visual Elements and Graphics

Chapter Objectives   In this chapter, you will learn how to . . .

- Create and format lines and borders on web pages

- Decide when to use graphics and what graphics are appropriate

- Apply the image element to add graphics to web pages

- Optimize an image for web page display

- Configure images as backgrounds on web pages

- Configure images as hyperlinks

- Configure rounded corners, box shadow, text shadow, opacity, and gradients with CSS3

- Configure RGBA color with CSS3

- Use HTML5 elements to caption a figure

- Use the HTML5 meter and progress elements

- Find free and fee-based graphics sources

- Follow recommended web design guidelines when using graphics on web pages

A key component of a compelling website   is the use of interesting and appropriate graphics. This chapter introduces you to working with visual elements on web pages.

When you include images on your website, it is important to remember that not all users are able to view them. Some users may have vision problems and need assistive technology such as a screen reader application that reads the web page to them. In addition, search engines send out spiders and robots to walk the web and catalog pages for their indexes and databases; such programs do not access your images. Visitors using a mobile device may have images disabled. As a web developer, strive to create pages that are enhanced by graphical elements, but are usable without them.

4.1 Configuring Lines and Borders

Web designers often use visual elements such as lines and borders to separate or define areas on web pages. In this section, you'll explore two coding techniques to configure a line on a web page: the HTML horizontal rule element and the CSS border and padding properties.

The Horizontal Rule Element

A **horizontal rule element** visually separates areas of a page and configures a horizontal line across a web page. Since the horizontal rule element does not contain any text, it is coded as a void tag and not in a pair of opening and closing tags. XHTML syntax for the horizontal rule is `<hr />`. HTML5 syntax for the horizontal rule is `<hr>`. The horizontal rule element has a new semantic meaning in HTML5, indicating a thematic break. Horizontal rules are centered within their container element by default.

 ## Hands-On Practice 4.1

Open the web page found at chapter4/starter1.html in the student files in a text editor. This file should be familiar to you; it is similar to the web page you worked with in Chapter 3. (See Figure 3.14.) Add an `<hr>` tag above the div element that contains the page footer.

Save your file as hr.html, and test it in a browser. The lower portion of your web page should look similar to the partial screenshot shown in Figure 4.1. Compare your work with the solution in the student files (chapter4/hr.html). While a horizontal rule can be easily created using HTML, a more modern technique for configuring lines on web pages is to use CSS to configure a border.

> ### Meeting Your Business Needs
>
> Our expert designers are creative and eager to work with you. Take advantage of the power of Web 2.0!
>
> Copyright © 2012 Your Name Here

Figure 4.1 The `<hr>` tag configures a horizontal line

The border and padding Properties

As you may have noticed when you configured background colors for heading elements in Chapter 3, block display HTML elements form the shape of a rectangular box on a web page. This is an example of the CSS box model, which you will explore in detail in Chapter 6. For now, let's focus on two CSS properties that can be configured for the "box": the border and padding properties.

The border Property

The **border property** configures the border, or boundary, around an element. By default, the border has a width set to 0 and does not display. You can set the `border-width`, `border-color`, and `border-style` with the border property. And there's more—you can even configure individual settings for the `top`, `right`, `bottom` and `left` borders using the `border-top`, `border-right`, `border-bottom`, and `border-left` properties.

The `border-style` Property

The **border-style** property configures the type of line displayed in the border. The formatting options include `inset`, `outset`, `double`, `groove`, `ridge`, `solid`, `dashed`, and `dotted`. Be aware that these property values are not all uniformly applied by browsers. Figure 4.2 shows how Firefox 4 and Internet Explorer 9 render various border-style values.

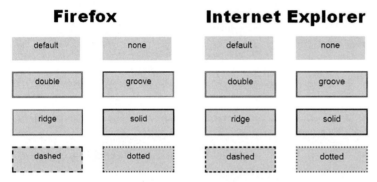

Figure 4.2 Not all `border-style` values are rendered the same way by popular browsers

The CSS to configure the borders shown in Figure 4.2 uses a `border-width` of 3 pixels, the value indicated for the `border-style` property, and a `border-color` of #000000. For example, the style rule to configure the dashed border follows:

```
.dashedborder { border-width: 3px;
                border-style: dashed;
                border-color: #000033; }
```

A shorthand notation allows you to configure all the border properties in one style rule by listing the values of `border-width`, `border-style`, and `border-color`, as in the following example:

```
.dashedborder { border: 3px dashed #000033; }
```

The `padding` Property

The **padding** property configures empty space between the content of the HTML element (usually text) and the border. By default, the padding is set to `0`. If you configure a background color for an element, the color is applied to both the padding and the content areas. You'll apply the padding and border properties in the next Hands-On Practice. You may want to refer to Table 4.1, which presents a description of the CSS properties introduced in Chapter 4, as you work through the Hands-On Practice exercises.

Table 4.1 New CSS properties introduced in this chapter

Property	Description	Values
`background-attachment`	Configures whether the background image scrolls with the page or is fixed in place	`fixed, scroll` (default)
`background-clip`	Configures the background painting area. This CSS3 property is not supported in all browsers.	`padding-box, border-box,` or `content-box`
`background-image`	Background image on an element	To display an image, use `url(imagename.gif)`, `url(imagename.jpg)`, or `url(imagename.png)`. To disable image display, use `none` (default).
`background-origin`	Configures the background positioning area. This CSS3 property is not supported in all browsers.	`padding-box, border-box,` or `content-box`
`background-position`	Position of the background image	Two percentage values or numeric pixel values. The first value configures the horizontal position, and the second configures the vertical position starting from the upper left corner of the container's box. Text values can also be used: `left, top, center, bottom,` and `right`.
`background-repeat`	Controls how the background image will repeat	Text values `repeat` (default), `repeat-y,` (vertical repeat), `repeat-x` (horizontal repeat), and `no-repeat` (no repeat). The new CSS3 values (`space, round`) are not supported in all browsers.
`background-size`	Configures the size of the background image. This CSS3 property is not supported in all browsers.	Two percentages, pixel values, `auto, contain,` or `cover`. The first value indicates width. The second value indicates height. If only one value is provided, the second value defaults to `auto`. The value `contain` causes the background image to be scaled (with aspect ratio intact) to horizontally fill the container. The value `cover` causes the background image to be scaled (with aspect ratio intact) to vertically fill the container.
`border`	Shorthand notation to configure the values for `border-width,` `border-style,` and `border-color` of an element	The values for `border-width, border-style,` and `border-color` separated by spaces—for example, `border: 1px solid #000000;`
`border-bottom`	Shorthand notation to configure the bottom border of an element	The values for `border-width, border-style,` and `border-color` separated by spaces—for example, `border-bottom: 1px solid #000000;`
`border-bottom-left-radius`	Configures rounded corners on the bottom left corner of a border. This CSS3 property is not supported in all browsers.	One numeric value (px or em) or percentage that configures the radius of the corner.
`border-bottom-right-radius`	Configures rounded corners on the bottom right corner of a border. This CSS3 property is not supported in all browsers.	One numeric value (px or em) or percentage that configures the radius of the corner.
`border-color`	The color of the border around an element	Any valid color value
`border-left`	Shorthand notation to configure the left border of an element	The values for `border-width, border-style,` and `border-color` separated by spaces—for example, `border-left: 1px solid #000000;`

Table 4.1 (*Continued*)

Property	Description	Values
`border-radius`	Configures rounded corners on a element. This CSS3 property is not supported in all browsers.	One to four numeric values (px or em) or percentages that configure the radius of the corners. If a single value is provided, it configures all four corners. The corners are configured in order of top left, top right, bottom right, and bottom left.
`border-right`	Shorthand notation to configure the right border of an element	The values for `border-width`, `border-style`, and `border-color` separated by spaces—for example, `border-right: 1px solid #000000;`
`border-style`	The type of border around an element	Text values `double`, `groove`, `inset`, `none` (the default), `outset`, `ridge`, `solid`, `dashed`, `dotted`, and `hidden`
`border-top`	Shorthand notation to configure the top border of an element	The values for `border-width`, `border-style`, and `border-color` separated by spaces—for example, `border-top: 1px solid #000000;`
`border-top-left-radius`	Configures a rounded top left corner. This CSS3 property is not supported in all browsers.	One numeric value (px or em) or percentage that configures the radius of the corner.
`border-top-right-radius`	Configures a rounded top right corner. This CSS3 property is not supported in all browsers.	One numeric value (px or em) or percentage that configures the radius of the corner.
`border-width`	The width of a border around an element	A numeric pixel value (such as 1px) or the text values `thin`, `medium`, and `thick`
`box-shadow`	Configures a drop shadow on an element. This CSS3 property is not supported in all browsers.	Two to four numerical values (px or em) to indicate horizontal offset, vertical offset, blur radius (optional), and spread distance (optional), and a valid color value. Use the `inset` keyword to configure an inner shadow.
`height`	The height of an element	A numeric pixel value or percentage
`linear-gradient`	Configures a linear blending of shades from one color to another. This CSS3 property is not supported in all browsers.	Numerous syntax options for starting points of the gradient and color values. For example, the following configures a two-color linear gradient: `linear-gradient(#FFFFFF, #8FA5CE);`
`min-width`	Configures a minimum width for an element	A numeric pixel value or percentage
`opacity`	Configures the transparency of an element. This CSS3 property is not supported in all browsers.	Numeric values between 1 (fully opaque) and 0 (completely transparent). This property is inherited by all child elements.
`padding`	Shorthand notation to configure the amount of padding—the blank space between the element and its border	1. A single numeric value (px or em) or percentage; configure padding on all sides of the element. 2. Two numeric values (px or em) or percentages; the first value configures the top and bottom padding, and the second value configures the left and right padding—for example, `padding: 20px 10px;` 3. Three numeric values (px or em) or percentages; the first value configures the top padding, the second value configures the left and right padding, the third value configures the bottom padding—for example, `padding: 5px 30px 10px;`

(Continued)

Table 4.1 (*Continued*)

Property	Description	Values
		4. Four numeric values (px or em) or percentages; the values configure the padding in the following order: `padding-top`, `padding-right`, `padding-bottom`, `padding-left`.
`padding-bottom`	Blank space between an element and its bottom border	A numeric value (px or em) or percentage
`padding-left`	Blank space between an element and its left border	A numeric value (px or em) or percentage
`padding-right`	Blank space between an element and its right border	A numeric value (px or em) or percentage
`padding-top`	Blank space between an element and its top border	A numeric value (px or em) or percentage
`radial-gradient`	Configures a radial (circular) blending of shades from one color to another. This CSS3 property is not supported in all browsers.	Numerous syntax options for starting points of the gradient and color values. For example, the following configures a two-color radial gradient: `radial-gradient(#FFFFFF, #8FA5CE);`
`text-shadow`	Configures a drop shadow on the text displayed within an element. This CSS3 property is not supported in all browsers.	Two to four numerical values (px or em) to indicate horizontal offset, vertical offset, blur radius (optional), and spread distance (optional), and a valid color value.

 Hands-On Practice 4.2

In this Hands-On Practice you will work with the border and padding properties. Launch a text editor, and open the web page found at chapter4/starter1.html in the student files. You will modify the CSS style rules for the h1 element selector, h2 element selector, and footer id. When you are finished, your page should look similar to the one shown in Figure 4.3.

Edit the CSS style rules as follows:

1. Modify the style rules for the h1 element selector. Remove the line-height style rule, because you will use padding to configure the empty space. Add a style rule to set the padding to 15 pixels. The code follows:

```
padding: 15px;
```

2. Add a style rule to the h2 element selector to configure a 2-pixel, dashed, bottom border in the color #191970. The code follows:

```
border-bottom: 2px dashed #191970;
```

3. Add a footer id selector to configure a thin, solid, top border in the color #aeaed4 along with 10 pixels of top padding. Also configure the footer to have gray, small, italic text. The code follows:

```
#footer { border-top: thin solid #aeaed4;
          padding-top: 10px;
          color: #333333;
          font-size: .75em;
          font-style: italic; }
```

Edit the HTML, and assign the div that contains the footer information to the id named footer. Save your file as border.html.

Test your page in multiple browsers. Expect your page to look slightly different in various browsers. See Figure 4.3 for a screenshot of the page using Firefox. Figure 4.4 shows the page displayed in Internet Explorer. The student files contain a sample solution (chapter4/border.html).

Figure 4.3 CSS border and padding properties add visual interest to the page

Figure 4.4 Internet Explorer renders the dashed border differently than Firefox

FAQ   **My web page looks different in some browsers. What can I do?**

Do not expect your web pages always to look the same in every browser and every browser version. Web pages that look different in various browsers are a part of life in the world of web developers. The good news is that browser developers are finally beginning to be less inventive and more compliant with the W3C standards. Also, organizations such as The Web Standards Project (http://www.webstandards.org) have lobbied for standards compliance in browsers. Look for improved compliance in the future!

Checkpoint 4.1

1. Is the following code legal? What does it intend to do?

```
h1 { color : #00FF00;
border: #ff0000 solid 5px;
border-bottom-color:#00ff00;
}
```

2. Is the following code legal?

```
h1 { border-style:dotted solid double dashed;}
```

3. True or False: The "border-width" property does not work if it is used alone.

4.2 Types of Graphics

Graphics can make web pages compelling and engaging. This section discusses features of graphic files commonly used on the Web: GIF, JPEG, and PNG. A new web graphic format, WepP, is also introduced.

Graphic Interchange Format (GIF) Images

GIF images are best used for line drawings containing mostly solid tones and simple images such as clip art. The maximum number of colors in a GIF file is 256. GIF images have a .gif file extension. Figure 4.5 shows a logo image created in GIF format.

Figure 4.5 This logo is a GIF

Transparency

The format GIF89A used by GIF images supports image **transparency**. In a graphics application, such as the open-source GIMP, one color (typically the background color) of the image can be set to be transparent. The background color (or background image) of the web page shows through the transparent area in the image. Figure 4.6 displays two GIF images on a blue textured background.

Figure 4.6
Comparison of
transparent and
nontransparent
GIFs

Animation

An **animated GIF** consists of several images or frames, each of which is slightly different. When the frames display on the screen in order, the image appears animated. Animated GIFs can be created in a graphics application such as Adobe Fireworks.

Compression

Lossless compression is used when a GIF is saved. This means that nothing in the original image is lost and that the compressed image, when rendered by a browser, will contain the same pixels as the original.

Optimization

To avoid slow-loading web pages, graphic files should be optimized for the Web. Image **optimization** is the process of creating an image with the lowest file size that still renders a good-quality image—balancing image quality and file size. GIF images are typically optimized by reducing the number of colors in the image by using a graphics application such as Adobe Photoshop, Adobe Fireworks, or GIMP.

Interlacing

Browsers render, or display, web page documents in order, line by line, starting at the top of the document. They display standard images as the files are read in order from top to bottom. The top of a standard image begins to display after 50 percent of the image has been read by a browser. When a GIF graphic file is created, it can be configured as interlaced. An **interlaced** image progressively displays and seems to fade in as it downloads. The image first appears fuzzy but gradually becomes clearer and sharper, which can help to reduce the perceived load time of your web page.

Joint Photographic Experts Group (JPEG) Images

JPEG images are best used for photographs. In contrast to a GIF image, a JPEG image can contain 16.7 million colors. However, JPEG images cannot be made transparent, and they cannot be animated. JPEG images have a .jpg or .jpeg file extension.

Compression

JPEG images are saved using **lossy compression**. This means that some pixels in the original image are lost or removed from the compressed file. When a browser renders the compressed image, the display is similar to, but not exactly the same as, the original image.

Optimization

There are trade-offs between the quality of the image and the amount of compression. An image with less compression will have higher quality and result in a larger file size.

Figure 4.7 A JPEG saved at 80-percent quality (55KB file size) displays well on a web page

Figure 4.8 JPEG saved at 20-percent quality (19KB file size)

Figure 4.9 This small thumbnail image is only 5KB

An image with more compression will have lower quality and result in a smaller file size. Most graphics applications allow you to preview the quality–compression trade-off and choose the image that best suits your needs.

When you take a photo with a digital camera, the file size is too large for optimal display on a web page. Figure 4.7 shows an optimized version of a digital photo with an original file size of 250KB. The image was optimized using a graphics application set to 80-percent quality, is now only 55KB, and displays well on a web page.

Figure 4.8 was saved with 20 percent quality and is only 19KB, but its quality is unacceptable. The quality of the image degrades as the file size decreases. The square blockiness you see in Figure 4.8 is called **pixelation** and should be avoided.

Another technique used with web graphics is to display a small version of the image, called a **thumbnail image**. Often, the thumbnail is configured as an image hyperlink that displays the larger image when clicked. Figure 4.9 shows a thumbnail image.

Progressive JPEG

When a JPEG file is created, it can be configured as progressive. A **progressive JPEG** is similar to an interlaced GIF in that the image progressively displays and seems to fade in as it downloads.

Portable Network Graphic (PNG) Images

PNG images combine the best of GIF and JPEG images and will be a replacement for GIF images in the future. PNG (pronounced "ping") graphics can support millions of colors, support variable transparency levels, and use lossless compression. PNG images also support interlacing.

Table 4.2 Overview of common web graphic file types

Image Type	File Extension	Compression	Transparency	Animation	Colors	Progressive Display
GIF	.gif	Lossless	Yes	Yes	256	Interlacing
JPEG	.jpg or .jpeg	Lossy	No	No	Millions	Progressive
PNG	.png	Lossless	Yes	No	Millions	Interlacing

New WebP Image Format

Google's new **WebP image format** offers improved lossy compression for photographic images, but it's not yet ready for use in commercial websites. WebP (pronounced "weppy") graphics are currently supported only by the Google Chrome browser. Visit http://code.google.com/speed/webp for more information on this new image format.

4.3 Image Element

The **image element** configures graphics on a web page. These graphics can be photographs, banners, company logos, navigation buttons, and so on; you are limited only by your creativity and imagination.

The image element is not coded as a pair of opening and closing tags. It is considered to be a void element. Use `<img  />` for XHTML syntax and `<img>` for HTML5 syntax. The following code example configures an image named logo.gif, which is located in the same folder as the web page:

```
<img src="logo.gif" height="200" width="500" alt="My Company Name">
```

The **src attribute** specifies the file name of the image. The **alt attribute** provides a text replacement, typically a text description, of the image. The browser reserves the correct amount of space for your image if you use the height and width attributes with values either equal to or approximately the size of the image. Table 4.3 lists `<img>` tag attributes and their values. Commonly used attributes are shown in bold.

Table 4.3 Attributes of the <img> tag

Attribute	Value
align	right, left (default), top, middle, bottom; obsolete—use the CSS float or position property instead (see Chapter 6)
alt	Text phrase that describes the image
border	Image border size in pixels; border="0" prevents the border of an image hyperlink from being displayed; obsolete—use the CSS border property instead
height	Height of image in pixels
hspace	Amount of space, in pixels, that is blank to the left and right of the image; obsolete—use the CSS padding property instead
id	Text name—alphanumeric, beginning with a letter, no spaces; the value must be unique and not used for other id values on the same web page document
name	Text name—alphanumeric, beginning with a letter, no spaces; this attribute names the image so that it can be easily accessed by client-side scripting languages such as JavaScript; obsolete—use the id attribute
src	The URL or file name of the image
title	A text phrase containing advisory information about the image; typically more descriptive than the alt text
vspace	Amount of space, in pixels, that is blank above and below the image; obsolete—use the CSS padding property instead
width	Width of image in pixels

Notice that several attributes in Table 4.3 are marked as obsolete. Although obsolete in HTML5, they are still valid in XHTML so you'll see them coded in existing web pages. As you work through this book, you'll use CSS to re-create the functions of these now-obsolete attributes.

FAQ   What if I don't know the height and width of an image?

Most graphics applications can display the height and width of an image. If you have a graphics application such as Adobe Photoshop or Adobe Fireworks handy, launch the application and open the image. These applications include options that will display the properties of the image, such as height and width.

If you don't have a graphics application available, you can determine the dimensions of an image by using a browser. Display the image on a web page. Right-click on the image to display the context-sensitive menu. Select a menu option such as Properties or "View Image Info" to view the dimensions (height and width) of the image. (*Warning*: If the height and width are specified on the web page, those values will be displayed even if the image's actual height and width are different.)

Accessibility and Images

**Focus on
Accessibility**

Use the alt attribute to provide accessibility. Recall from Chapter 1 that Section 508 of the Rehabilitation Act requires the use of accessibility features for new information technology (including websites) associated with the federal government. The alt attribute configures an alternative text description of the image. This alt text is used by the browser in two ways. The browser will show the alt text in the image area before the graphic is downloaded and displayed. Some browsers will also show the alt text as a tool tip whenever a visitor to the web page places the mouse cursor over the image area. Applications such as screen readers will read the text in the alt attribute out loud. A mobile browser may display the alt text instead of the image.

Standard browsers such as Internet Explorer and Safari are not the only type of application or user agent that can access your website. Major search engines run programs called spiders or robots; these programs index and categorize websites. They cannot process text within images, but some process the value of the alt attributes in image tags.

Image Hyperlinks

The code to make an image function as a hyperlink is very easy. To create an **image link,** all you need to do is surround your image element with anchor tags. For example, to place a link around an image called home.gif, use the following HTML code:

```
<a href="index.html"><img src="home.gif" height="19" width="85"
alt="Home"></a>
```

When an image is used as a hyperlink, the default is to show a blue outline (border) around the image. If you would prefer not to display this outline, you could use the `border="0"` attribute in your image tag as follows:

```
<a href="index.html"><img src="home.gif" height="19"
width="85" alt="Home" border="0"></a>
```

A more modern approach is to use CSS to configure the border on the img selector. The next Hands-On Practice will demonstrate this technique as you configure images and add image links to a web page.

Hands-On Practice 4.3

In this Hands-On Practice you will add a graphical logo banner and image navigation buttons to a web page. Then you'll configure the image buttons as image links. Create a new folder called trilliumch4. The graphics used in this Hands-On Practice are located in the student files chapter4/starters folder. Save the trilliumbanner.jpg, home.gif, services.gif, and contact.gif files in your trilliumch4 folder. A starter version of the Trillium Media Design Home page is ready for you in the student files. Save the chapter4/starter2.html file to your trilliumch4 folder. Launch a browser to display the starter2.html web page; notice that a monochromatic green color scheme has been configured with CSS. When you are finished with this Hands-On Practice, your page will look similar to the one shown in Figure 4.10.

Figure 4.10 The new Trillium Home page with a logo banner

Launch a text editor, and open starter2.html in the trilliumch4 folder.

1. Configure the logo banner image:

    ● Replace the text contained between the `<h1>` opening and closing tags. Code an `<img>` element to display trilliumbanner.jpg in this area. Remember to include the `src`, `alt`, `height`, and `width` attributes. Sample code follows:

    ```
    <img src="trilliumbanner.jpg" alt="Trillium Media Design"
    width="700" height="86">
    ```

    ● Edit the embedded CSS to configure the h1 element selector to have the same height as the image. Add the following style rule:

    ```
    height: 86px;
    ```

2. Configure the image links. Notice that the anchor tags are already coded; you'll just need to convert the text links to image links. However, before you start changing the code, let's take a minute to discuss accessibility. Whenever the main navigation consists of media, such as an image, some individuals may not be able to see the images (or may have images turned off in their browser). To provide navigation that is accessible to all, configure a set of plain-text navigation links in the page footer area as follows:

   • Copy the `<div>` element containing the navigation area to the lower portion of the page, and paste it above the page footer.

   • Modify the style rules in the nav class. Change the font size to .75em.

3. Now, focus on the top navigation area. Replace the text contained between each pair of anchor tags with an image element. Use home.gif for the link to index.html, services.gif for the link to services.html, and contact.gif for the link to contact.html. Sample code follows:

   ```
   <a href="index.html"><img src="home.gif" alt="Home" width="120"
   height="40"></a>
   ```

4. Edit the embedded CSS to create a new style rule that configures no border for the img element selector. The code follows:

   ```
   img { border-style: none; }
   ```

Save your page as index.html in the trilliumch4 folder. Launch a browser, and test your page. It should look similar to the one shown in Figure 4.10. *Note*: If an image did not display on your web page, verify that you have saved the trilliumbanner.jpg, home.gif, services.gif, and contact.gif files in the trilliumch4 folder and that you have spelled the file name correctly in the `<img>` element.

As you test your page, resize the browser window, make it smaller, and note how the image links move around. To prevent them from moving, add a new style rule to the body selector that sets a minimum width for the page. This rule will cause the browser to automatically display a horizontal scroll bar if a visitor to the web page resizes the browser window below the size specified. Sample code follows:

```
min-width: 700px;
```

Save and test your page again. The student files contain a sample solution in the chapter4/4.3 folder. Isn't it interesting how just a few images can add visual interest to a web page?

 FAQ **What if my images don't show?**

The following are common reasons for images not displaying on a web page:

   • Are your images really in the website folder? Use Windows Explorer or Mac Finder to double-check.

   • Did you code the HTML and CSS correctly? Check for common mistakes such as typing scr instead of src and missing quotation marks.

   • Do your images have the exact file names that you have used in the background or src attributes in your HTML code? Attention to detail and consistency will be very helpful here.

FAQ How should I name my image files?

Guidelines for naming image files:

- Use all lowercase letters.
- Do not use punctuation symbols and spaces.
- Do not change the file extensions (should be .gif, .jpg, .jpeg, or .png).
- Keep your file names short, but descriptive. Here are some examples:

    i1.gif is probably too short.

    myimagewithmydogonmybirthday.gif is too long.

    dogbday.gif may be just about right.

Optimize an Image for the Web

Photos taken with a digital camera are too large—in both their dimensions and their file size—to display well on a web page. Recall that image optimization requires balancing image quality and file size. It is the process of creating an image with the lowest file size that still renders with good quality. Adobe Photoshop and Adobe Fireworks are often used by web professionals to optimize images for the Web. GIMP (http://gimp.org) is a popular open-source image editor that supports multiple platforms. Pixlr offers a free, easy-to-use, online photo editor at http://pixlr.com/editor.

Hands-On Practice 4.4

In this Hands-On Practice you will configure an image with a caption on a web page. The photo used in this Hands-On Practice is located in the student files chapter4/starters folder. Save the myisland.jpg file in a folder named mycaption.

Step 1: Launch a text editor. Select File > Open to edit the template file located at chapter2/template.html in the student files. Modify the title element. Add an image tag to the body section to display the myisland.jpg image as follows:

```
<img src="myisland.jpg" alt="Tropical Island" height="480" width="640">
```

Save the file as index.html in the mycaption folder. Launch a browser to test your page. It should look similar to the page shown in Figure 4.11.

Figure 4.11 The image is displayed on the web page

Step 2: Configure a figure caption and border for the image. To do so, launch a text editor and open the web page file. Add embedded CSS to the head section that configures an id named figure that is 640 pixels wide, has a border, has padding set to 5px, and has centered text using the Papyrus font typeface (or the default fantasy family font). The code follows:

```
<style>
#figure { width: 640px;
          border: 1px solid #000000;
          padding: 5px;
          text-align: center;
          font-family: Papyrus, fantasy; }
</style>
```

Edit the body section to add a div to contain the image. Add the text "Tropical Island Getaway" below the image but within the div element. Assign the div to the id named figure. Save the file as index.html in the mycaption folder. Launch a browser to test your page. It should look similar to the page shown in Figure 4.12. The student files contains a sample solution in the chapter4/caption folder.

Figure 4.12 CSS configures the placement of the border and figure caption

4.4 HTML5 Visual Elements

In Hands-On Practice 4.4, you configured an image and a caption on a web page. You used a div element to contain the image and text caption. In this section, you'll explore an approach that implements new HTML5 elements and requires a modern browser that supports HTML5 (such as Safari, Firefox, Chrome, Opera, or Internet Explorer 9). You'll use the new HTML5 figure and figcaption elements.

HTML5 Figure Element

The block display `figure` **element** comprises a unit of content that is self-contained, such as an image, along with one optional `figcaption` element.

HTML5 Figcaption Element

The block display `figcaption` **element** provides a caption for a figure.

Hands-On Practice 4.5

In this Hands-On Practice you will configure an area on a web page that contains an image with a caption by using the HTML5 figure and figcaption elements. The graphic used in this Hands-On Practice is located in the student files chapter4/starters folder. Save the myisland.jpg file in a folder named mycaption2.

Step 1: Launch a text editor. Select File > Open to edit the template file located at chapter2/template.html in the student files. Modify the title element. Add an image tag to the body section to display the myisland.jpg image as follows:

```
<img src="myisland.jpg" alt="Tropical Island" height="480"
width="640">
```

Save the file as index.html in the mycaption2 folder. Launch a browser to test your page. It should look similar to the page shown in Figure 4.11.

Step 2: Configure a figure caption and border for the image. Launch a text editor and open the web page file. Add embedded CSS to the head section that configures the figure element selector to be 640 pixels wide, with a border, and with padding set to 5px. Configure the figcaption element selector to have centered text using the Papyrus font typeface (or the default fantasy family font). The code follows:

```
<style>
figure { width: 640px;
         border: 1px solid #000000;
         padding: 5px; }
figcaption { text-align: center;
             font-family: Papyrus, fantasy; }
</style>
```

Edit the body section. Below the image, add a `figcaption` element that contains the following text: "Tropical Island Getaway." Configure a `figure` element that contains both the image and the figcaption. The code follows:

```
<figure>
  <img src="island.jpg" width="640" height="480" alt="Tropical Island">
  <figcaption>
  Tropical Island Getaway
  </figcaption>
</figure>
```

Save the file as index.html in the mycaption2 folder. Launch a browser to test your page. It should look similar to the page shown in Figure 4.13. The student files contains a sample solution in the chapter4/caption2 folder.

Figure 4.13 The HTML5 figure and figcaption elements were used in this web page

You might be wondering why these new HTML5 elements were created when the same design can be configured using a div element as a container. The reason is semantics. The div element is useful but very generic in nature. When the figure and figcaption elements are used, the structure of the content is well defined. However, if you are designing pages for commercial websites, hold off on using the new figure and figcaption elements until browser support of HTML5 is more widespread.

HTML5 Meter Element

The **meter element** displays a visual gauge of a numeric value within a known range, typically as part of a bar chart. At the time this textbook was written, this new HTML5 element was supported only in the Chrome and Opera 11 browsers. The meter element is configured with several attributes, including value (the value displayed), min (the lowest possible value in the range), and max (the highest possible value in the range). The following code snippet (from the student files chapter4/meter.html) configures the display of a monthly browser-usage report that shows total visits and the number of visits by users for each browser:

```
<h1>Monthly Browser Report</h1>
<meter value="14417" min="0" max="14417">14417</meter>14,417 Total
Visits<br>
<meter value="7000" min="0" max="14417">7000</meter> 7,000 Firefox<br>
<meter value="3800" min="0" max="14417">3800</meter> 3,800 Internet
Explorer<br>
<meter value="2062" min="0" max="14417">2062</meter> 2,062 Chrome<br>
<meter value="1043" min="0" max="14417">1043</meter> 1,043 Safari<br>
<meter value="312" min="0" max="14417">312</meter>   
312 Opera<br>
<meter value="200" min="0" max="14417">200</meter>   
200 other<br>
```

Figure 4.14 displays the page in the Opera browser. As time goes on, more browsers will support the new HTML5 meter element. It provides a very handy way to display a bar chart on a web page. Visit http://caniuse.com to get current information on browser support of this element.

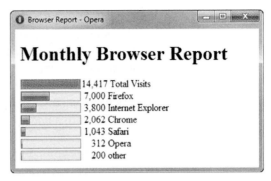

HTML5 Progress Element

The **progress element** displays a bar that depicts a numeric value within a specified range. At the time this textbook was written, this new HTML5 element was supported by the Chrome, Firefox 6, and Opera 11 browsers. The progress element is configured with the `value` (the value displayed) and `max` (highest possible value) attributes. The following code snippet (from the student files chapter4/progress.html) shows 50 percent completion of a task:

Figure 4.14 The `meter` element rendered in the Opera browser

```
<h1>Progress Report</h1>
<progress value="5000" max="10000">5000 </progress>
Progress Toward Our Goal
```

Figure 4.15 displays the page in the Chrome browser. As time goes on, more browsers will support the new HTML5 elements. Visit http://caniuse.com to get current information on browser support of HTML5.

Figure 4.15 The `progress` element rendered in the Chrome browser

4.5 Background Images

Back in Chapter 3, you learned how to configure background color with the CSS `background-color` property. For example, the following CSS code configures the background of a web page to be a soft yellow:

VideoNote
CSS Background Images

```
body { background-color: #ffff99; }
```

The background-image Property

Use the CSS **background-image property** to configure a background image. For example, the following CSS code configures the HTML body selector with a background of the graphic texture1.png located in the same folder as the web page file:

```
body { background-image: url(texture1.png); }
```

Using Both Background Color and a Background Image

You can configure both a background color and a background image. The background color (specified by the `background-color` property) will display first. Next, the image specified as the background will be displayed as it is loaded by the browser.

By coding both a background color and a background image, you provide your visitor with a more pleasing visual experience. If the background image does not load for some reason, the background color will still have the expected contrast with your text color. If the background image is smaller than the web browser window and the web page is configured with CSS not to automatically tile (repeat the image), the background color of the page will display in areas not covered by the background image. The CSS for a page with both a background color and a background image follows:

```
body { background-color: #99cccc;
       background-image: url(background.jpg); }
```

Browser Display of a Background Image

You may think that a graphic created to be the background of a web page would always be about the size of the browser window viewport. However, the dimensions of the background image are often much smaller than the typical viewport. The shape of a background image is often either a thin rectangle or a small rectangular block. Unless otherwise specified in a style rule, browsers repeat, or tile, these images to cover the page's background, as shown in Figures 4.16 and 4.17. The images have small file sizes so that they download as quickly as possible.

Figure 4.16 A long, thin background image tiles down the page

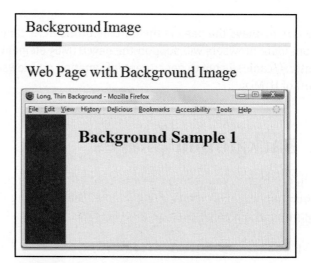

Figure 4.17 A small rectangular background is repeated to fill the web page window

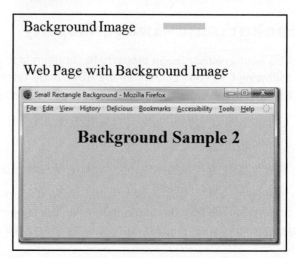

The background-repeat Property

As just discussed, the default behavior of a browser is to repeat, or tile, background images to cover the entire element's background. This behavior also applies to other elements, such as backgrounds for headings, paragraphs, and so on. You can change this tiling behavior with the CSS **background-repeat property**. The values for the background-repeat property include repeat (default), repeat-y (vertical repeat), repeat-x (horizontal repeat), and no-repeat (no repeat). Figure 4.18 provides examples of the actual background image and the result of applying various background-repeat property values.

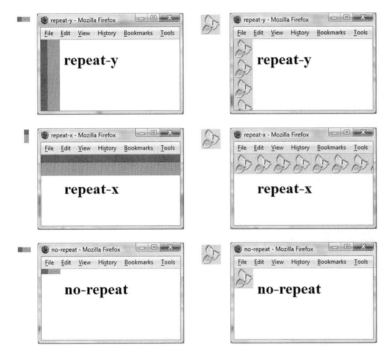

Figure 4.18 Examples of the CSS background-repeat property

CSS3 provides for additional values for the background-repeat property that are not yet well supported by browsers:

- background-repeat: space;

  Repeats the image in the background without clipping (or cutting off) parts of the image by adjusting empty space around the repeated images.

- background-repeat: round;

  Repeats the image in the background and scales (adjusts) the dimensions of the image to avoid clipping.

The background-position Property

You can specify other locations for the background image besides the default top left location by using the **background-position property**. Valid values for the background-position property include percentages; pixel values; or left, top, center, bottom, and

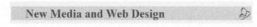
New Media and Web Design

Figure 4.19 The flower background image was configured to display on the right side with CSS

right. The first value indicates horizontal position. The second value indicates vertical position. If only one value is provided, the second value defaults to center. In Figure 4.19, the small flower image has been placed in the background on the right side of the element by using the following style rule:

```
h2 { background-image: url(trilliumbg.gif);
     background-position: right;
     background-repeat: no-repeat; }
```

 Hands-On Practice 4.6

Let's practice using a background image. You will update the index.html file from Hands-On Practice 4.3 (shown in Figure 4.10). In this Hands-On Practice you will configure the h2 element selector with a background image that does not repeat. Obtain the trilliumbullet.gif image from the student files chapter4/starters folder. Save the image in your trilliumch4 folder. When you have completed this exercise, your page should look similar to the one shown in Figure 4.20.

Figure 4.20 The background image in the `<h2>` areas is configured with `background-repeat: no-repeat`

Launch a text editor, and open index.html.

1. Modify the style rule for the h2 element selector to configure the `background-image` and `background-repeat` properties. Set the background image to be trilliumbullet.gif. Set the background not to repeat. The h2 element selector style rules follow:

```
h2 { background-color: #d5edb3;
     color: #5c743d;
     font-family: Georgia, "Times New Roman", serif;
     background-image: url(trilliumbullet.gif);
     background-repeat: no-repeat; }
```

2. Save your page as index.html. Launch a browser, and test your page. You may notice that the text in the h2 element is displayed over the background image. In this case, the page would look more appealing if there were more space, or padding, before the beginning of the text displayed by the h2 elements. Use the CSS `padding-left` property to add empty space within the left side of the element. Add the following declaration to the h2 element selector to add empty space before the text:

```
padding-left: 30px;
```

3. Save and test your page again. It should look similar to the one shown in Figure 4.20. The student files contain a sample solution in the chapter4/4.6 folder.

 FAQ **What if my images are in their own folder?**

It's a good idea to organize your website by placing all your images in a folder. Notice that the CircleSoft website whose file structure is shown in Figure 4.21 contains a folder called images, which contains GIF and JPEG files. To refer to these files in code, you also need to refer to the images folder. The following are some examples:

- The CSS code to configure the background.gif file from the images folder as the page background follows:

```
body { background-image:
       url(images/background.gif); }
```

Figure 4.21 A folder named "images" contains the graphic files

- The HTML to display the logo.jpg file from the images folder follows:

```
<img src="images/logo.jpg"
alt="CircleSoft" width="588" height="120">
```

The background-attachment Property

Use the **background-attachment property** to configure whether the background image remains fixed in place or scrolls along with the page in the browser viewport. Valid values for the background-attachment property include `fixed` and `scroll` (the default).

 ## Checkpoint 4.2

1. What is wrong with this code?

```
<img src="logo.gif" height="200" width="300" text="Company
Name">
```

2. Write a single-line CSS code for a page with background color #FFCC99, background image myfile.gif. The image is positioned at the top right corner.

3. Explain how the browser will render the web page if you use CSS to configure both a background image and a background color.

4.6 More About Images

This section introduces several additional techniques used with images on web pages. Topics discussed include image maps, the favorites icon, image slicing, and CSS Sprites.

Image Maps

An **image map** is an image that can be used as one or more hyperlinks. An image map will typically have multiple clickable or selectable areas that link to another web page or website. The selectable areas are called **hotspots**. You have probably used image maps many times, but never realized it. One common use of image maps is to create interactive maps that website visitors can manipulate to choose a location. Figure 4.22 shows a page in the http://nerrs.noaa.gov website that displays a map of the Ace Islands. When a visitor selects an island, a new web page displays with detailed information about the island.

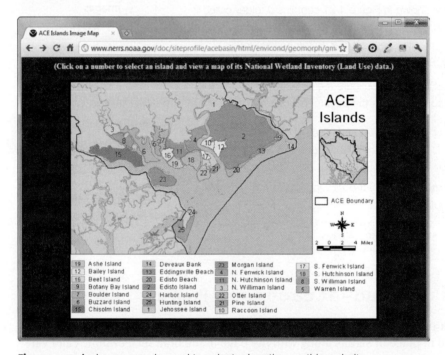

Figure 4.22 An image map is used to select a location on this website

Most web authoring software, such as Adobe Dreamweaver, provides wizards or other tools to help you create image maps quickly and easily. If you don't have access to a web authoring tool to create an image map, the most difficult part is determining the pixel coordinates of the hyperlink area. The coordinates are in pairs of numbers that signify the number of pixels from the top and the number of pixels from the left edge of the image. If you are working with a graphic artist, he or she may be able to supply you with the coordinates. Another option is to open the image in a graphics application such as Adobe Fireworks, Adobe Photoshop, or GIMP to obtain approximate coordinates. You can modify these coordinate values as you work with the HTML on your web page. Image maps can be used to create clickable areas in three shapes: rectangles, circles, and polygons.

An image map uses two new elements: map and area. The **map element** is a container tag and is used to begin and end the image map. The **name attribute** is coded to associate the <map> tag with its corresponding image. Configure the image tag with the **usemap attribute** to indicate which <map> to use. For example, `<img src="fishingboat.jpg" usemap="#boat">` will be associated with the image map described by `<map name="boat" id="boat">`. The id attribute uniquely identifies the map area.

The <area> tag defines the coordinates or edges of the map area and uses shape, coords, alt, and href attributes. XHTML syntax for the horizontal rule is `<area />`. Table 4.4 describes the type of coordinates (coords) needed for each shape value.

Table 4.4 Shape coordinates

Shape	Coordinates	Meaning
rect	"x1,y1, x2,y2"	The coordinates at point (x1,y1) represent the upper-left corner of the rectangle. The coordinates at point (x2,y2) represent the lower-right corner of the rectangle.
circle	"x,y,r"	The coordinates at point (x,y) indicate the center of the circle. The value of r is the radius of the circle, in pixels.
polygon	"x1,y1, x2,y2, x3,y3", etc.	The values of each (x,y) pair represent the coordinates of a corner point of the polygon.

We'll focus on a rectangular image map. For a rectangular image map, the value of the shape attribute is rect, and the coordinates indicate the pixel positions as follows: distance of the upper-left corner from the left side of the image, distance of the upper-left corner from the top of the image, distance of the lower-right corner from the left edge of the image, and distance fo the lower-right corner from the top of the image.

Figure 4.23 shows an image of a fishing boat. The dotted rectangle around the fishing boat indicates the location of the hotspot. The coordinates shown (24, 188) indicate that the top-left corner is 24 pixels from the left edge of the image and 188 pixels from the top of the image. The pair of coordinates in the lower-right corner (339, 283) indicates that this corner is 339 pixels from the left edge of the image and 283 pixels from the top of the image. Visit the textbook's website at http://webdevfoundations.net/6e/chapter4.html to see an image map in action. The HTML code to create this image map follows:

```
<map name="boat" id="boat">
  <area href="http://www.doorcountyvacations.com" shape="rect"
        coords="24, 188, 339, 283" alt="Door County Fishing">
</map>
<img src="fishingboat.jpg" usemap="#boat" alt="Door County" width="416"
height="350">
```

Most web developers do not hand-code image maps. As mentioned previously, the easiest way to create a client-side image map is to use a web authoring tool, such as Adobe Dreamweaver (http://adobe.com/dreamweaver) or Coffee Cup Software's HTML Editor (http://www.coffeecup.com/html-editor).

Figure 4.23 Sample image map

The Favorites Icon

Ever wonder about the small icon you sometimes see in the address bar or tab of a browser? That's a **favorites icon**, usually referred to as a **favicon**, which is a square image (either 16×16 pixels or 32×32 pixels) associated with a web page. The favicon, shown in Figure 4.24, may display in the browser's address bar, tab, or the favorites and bookmarks lists.

Figure 4.24 The favorites icon displays in the browser tab and address bar

You can create a favicon in a graphics application, such as Adobe Fireworks, or at a number of websites including http://www.favicongenerator.com, http://www.favicon.cc, and http://www.freefavicon.com. While some versions of Internet Explorer (version 6 and earlier) expected the file to be named favicon.ico and to reside in the root directory of the web server, a more modern approach is to associate the favicon.ico file with a web page by using the link element. Recall that in Chapter 3, you coded the `<link>` tag in the header section of a web page to associate an external style sheet file with a web page file. You can also use the `<link>` tag to associate a favorites icon with a web page.

Three attributes are used to associate a web page with a favorites icon: `rel`, `href`, and `type`. The value of the `rel` attribute is `icon`. The value of the `href` attribute is the name of the image file. The value of the `type` attribute describes the MIME type of the image—which defaults to `image/x-icon` for .ico files. The HTML code to associate a favorites icon named favicon.ico to a web page follows:

```
<link rel="icon" href="favicon.ico" type="image/x-icon">
```

Note that to be compatible with Internet Explorer and follow Microsoft's proprietary syntax, you'll also need to code a second link tag:

```
<link rel="shortcut icon" href="favicon.ico" type="image/x-icon">
```

Be aware that Internet Explorer's support of the favorites icon is somewhat buggy. You may need to publish your files to the Web (see the FTP tutorial in Appendix G) in order for the favicon to display even in current versions of Internet Explorer. Other browsers, such as Firefox, Safari, Google Chrome, and Opera, display favicons more reliably and also support GIF and PNG image formats.

Hands-On Practice 4.7

Let's practice using a favorites icon. Obtain the favicon.ico file from the student files in the chapter4/starters folder. In this exercise, you will use your files in the trilliumch4 folder from Hands-On Practice 4.6 (also see the student files chapter4/4.6 folder) as a starting point.

1. Launch a text editor, and open index.html. Add the following link tags to the head section of the web page:

   ```
   <link rel="icon" href="favicon.ico" type="image/x-icon">
   <link rel="shortcut icon" href="favicon.ico" type="image/x-icon">
   ```

2. Save your page as index.html. Launch the Firefox browser, and test your page. You should notice the small trillium flower in the Firefox browser tab as shown in Figure 4.25. The student files contain a sample solution in the chapter4/4.7 folder.

Figure 4.25 The favorites icon displays in the Firefox browser tab

Image Slicing

Graphic artists and designers can create complex web page images. Sometimes, parts of these images are better optimized as GIFs than as JPEGs, while other parts of the images may be better optimized as JPEGs than as GIFs. By **image slicing** the single, complex images into multiple, smaller images, you can optimize all portions for the most efficient display. In addition, there may be times when you plan special mouse rollover effects for parts of a large, complex image. In this case, parts of the image need to be individually accessible to scripting languages, and so the image needs to be sliced. When an image is sliced, it is broken into multiple graphic files. Most graphics applications, such as Adobe Fireworks and Adobe Photoshop, have features for image slicing that automatically create the HTML for you. Visit the text-book's website at http://webdevfoundations.net/6e/chapter4.html for more information on image slicing.

CSS Sprites

A modern technique to optimize the use of images on web pages is called CSS Sprites. A **sprite** is an image file that contains multiple small graphics that are configured as background images for various web page elements. The CSS `background-image`, `background-repeat`, and `background-position` properties are used to manipulate the placement of the image. Having just a single image saves download time, because the browser needs to make only one http request for the combined image instead of many requests for the individual smaller images. You'll work with CSS Sprites in Chapter 7.

4.7 Sources and Guidelines for Graphics

Sources of Graphics

There are many ways to obtain graphics: You can create them using a graphics application, download them from a website providing them for free, purchase and download them from a graphics website, purchase a graphics collection on a DVD, take digital photographs, scan photographs, scan drawings, or hire a graphic designer to create graphics for you. Popular graphic applications include Adobe Photoshop and Adobe Fireworks. Popular free graphics applications include GIMP (http://gimp.org), Google's Picasa (http://picasa.google.com), and the Pixlr web application (http://pixlr.com/editor). These applications usually include tutorials and sample images to help you get started. Visit the textbook's website at http://webdevfoundations.net/6e/chapter4.html for tutorials on using Adobe Fireworks and Adobe Photoshop to create a logo banner image.

Focus on Ethics

Sometimes you might be tempted to right-click on an image on a web page and download it for use on your own website. Be aware that materials on a website are copyrighted (even if a copyright symbol or notice does not appear) and are not free to use unless the owner of the site permits it. So, contact the owner of an image and request permission for use rather than just taking it. If you're using Flickr (http://flickr.com) to search for images, select the advanced-search page and check "*Only search within Creative Commons-licensed content.*" Be sure to follow the instructions for attribution when indicated.

There are many web sites that offer free and low-cost graphics. Choose a search engine and search for "free graphics"—you'll get more results than you have time to view. The following are a few sites that you may find helpful when looking for images:

- Microsoft Clip Art: http://office.microsoft.com/clipart/default.aspx
- FamFamFam: http://www.famfamfam.com
- Free Stock Photo Search Engine: http://www.everystockphoto.com
- Free Images: http://www.freeimages.co.uk
- The Stock Solution: http://www.tssphoto.com
- SuperStock: http://www.superstock.com
- iStockphoto: http://www.istockphoto.com

It is also possible to create a banner or button image online. There are a number of sites that offer this feature. Some include advertising with your free image, some offer paid member-ships, and others are simply free. Search for "create free online banner" to find sites offering this service. The following are a few useful sites for creating banners and button images:

- Animation Online: http://www.animationonline.com
- Web 2.0 LogoCreator: http://creatr.cc/creatr
- Cooltext.com: http://www.cooltext.com
- Ad Designer.com: http://www.addesigner.com

Guidelines for Using Images

Images enhance your web page by creating an engaging, interesting user experience. Images can also hurt your web page by slowing down its performance to a crawl and discouraging visitors. This section explores some guidelines for using images on web pages.

Reuse Images

Once an image from your site is requested for a web page, it is stored in the cache on your visitor's hard drive. Subsequent requests for the image will use the file from the hard drive in-stead of another download. This approach results in faster page loads for all pages that use the image. It is recommended that you reuse common graphics such as logos and navigation buttons on multiple pages instead of creating different versions of these common graphics.

Consider the Size vs. Quality Issue

You can choose among varying levels of image quality when using a graphics applica-tion to create or optimize an image. There is a correlation between the quality of the image and the size of the image file: The higher the quality, the larger the file size will be. Choose the smallest file that gives you appropriate quality. You may need to experi-ment until you get the right match.

Consider Image Load Time

Be careful when using images on web pages—it takes time for them to load. Optimize the file size and the dimensions of images for efficient web page display.

Use Appropriate Resolution

Web browsers display images at relatively low **resolution**—72ppi (pixels per inch) or 96ppi. Many digital cameras and scanners can create images with much higher resolution. Of course, higher resolution means larger file size. Even though the browser does not display the depth of resolution, more bandwidth is still used for the large file size. Be careful when taking digital photographs or scanning images. Use a resolution setting appropriate for web pages. A one-inch image saved at 150ppi could appear close to two inches wide on a 72ppi monitor.

Specify Dimensions

Always use accurate height and width attributes on image tags. This will allow the browser to allocate the appropriate space on the web page for the image and load the page faster. Do not try to resize the appearance of an image by modifying the settings of the height and width attributes. While this approach will work, your page will load more slowly, and your image quality may suffer. Instead, use a graphics application to create a smaller or larger version of the graphic when needed.

Be Aware of Brightness and Contrast

Gamma refers to the brightness and contrast of the monitor display. Monitors used with Macintosh and Windows operating systems use a different default gamma setting (Macintosh uses 1.8; Windows uses 2.2). Images that have good contrast on a computer running Windows may look slightly washed out on a Macintosh. Images created on a Macintosh may look darker, with less contrast, when displayed on a computer with a Windows operating system. Be aware that even monitors on the same operating system may have slightly different gamma values than the default for the platform. A web developer cannot control gamma, but should be aware that images will look different on various platforms because of this issue.

Accessibility and Visual Elements

Focus on Accessibility

Even though images help to create a compelling, interesting website, remember that not all your visitors will be able to view your images. The Web Accessibility Initiative's WCAG 2.0 includes a number of guidelines for web developers in the use of color and images:

- Don't rely on color alone. Some visitors may have color perception deficiencies. Use high contrast between background and text color.

- Provide a text equivalent for every nontext element. Use the alt attribute on your image tags.

    - If an image displays text, configure that text as the value of the alt attribute.

    - Use alt="" for an image that is purely decorative.

- If your site navigation uses image hyperlinks, provide simple text links at the bottom of the page.

Vinton Cerf, the co-inventor of TCP/IP and the former chairman of the Internet Society, said, "The Internet is for everyone." Follow web accessibility guidelines to ensure that this is true.

Checkpoint 4.3

1. Search for a site that uses image hyperlinks to provide navigation. List the URL of the page. What colors are used on the image links? If the image links contain text, is there good contrast between the background color and the letters on the image links? Would the page be accessible to a visitor who is sight challenged? How have accessibility issues been addressed? Is the alt attribute used to describe the image link? Is there a row of text links in the footer section of the page? Answer these questions and discuss your findings.

2. When configuring an image map, describe the relationship between the image, map, and area tags.

3. True or False: You should save your images using the smallest file size possible.

4.8 CSS3 Visual Effects

This section introduces new CSS3 properties that provide visual effects on web pages, including background clipping and scaling, multiple background images, rounded corners, box shadows, text shadows, opacity effects, transparent color with RGBA, and gradients.

The CSS3 `background-clip` Property

The new CSS3 **`background-clip` property** confines the display of the background image with the following values:

- `content-box` (clips the display to the area behind the content)

- `padding-box` (clips the display to the area behind the content and padding)

- `border-box` (default; clips the display to the area behind the content, padding, and border; similar to the padding-box property except that the image will display behind a border configured to be transparent)

The background-clip property is supported by modern browsers, although Safari requires the proprietary `-webkit-background-clip` property instead of the W3C draft `background-clip` property. Be aware that when you code the nonstandard property, your CSS will not pass W3C validation. Figure 4.26 shows a background image that is configured to clip to the content box. The sample page is located in the student files (chapter4/clip folder).

The CSS is shown as follows:

Figure 4.26 The CSS3 `background-clip` property

```
.test { background-image: url(myislandback.jpg);
       -webkit-background-clip: content-box;
       background-clip: content-box;
       width: 400px;
       padding: 20px;
       border: 1px solid #000; }
```

The CSS3 background-origin Property

The new CSS3 **background-origin property** positions the background image, using the following values:

- content-box (positions relative to the content area)
- padding-box (default; positions relative to the padding area)
- border-box (positions relative to the border area)

Figure 4.27 The CSS3 background-origin property

Figure 4.27 shows a background image that is configured to display in the lower right corner of the content box. The sample page is located in the student files (chapter4/origin folder).

```
The CSS is shown as follows:
.test { background-image: url(trilliumsolo.jpg);
        background-origin: content-box;
        background-repeat: no-repeat;
        background-position: right bottom;
        width: 400px;
        padding: 20px;
        border: 1px solid #000; }
```

You may have noticed that it's common to use several CSS properties when configuring background images. The properties typically work together. However, be aware that the background-origin property has no effect if the background-attachment property is set to the value "fixed".

The CSS3 background-size Property

The new CSS3 **background-size property** can be used to resize or scale the background image. Valid values for the background-size property can be:

- a pair of percentage values (width, height)
- a pair of pixel values (width, height)
- auto, contain, or cover

If only one numeric or percentage value is provided, the second value defaults to auto. The value contain causes the background image to be scaled (with aspect ratio intact) to vertically fill the container. The value cover causes the background image to be scaled (with aspect ratio intact) to horizontally fill the container. In Figure 4.28 (see the student files chapter4/size folder), the background image has been configured to vertically fill the container using the following style rule:

Figure 4.28 The CSS3 background-size property

```
div { background-image: url(myislandback.jpg);
      background-size: cover;
      background-repeat: no-repeat;
      width: 200px;
      padding: 20px; }
```

When using new CSS3 properties, be mindful that they are supported only in modern browsers. Be sure to test without the CSS3 properties to verify that the pages are still readable and usable. Visit http://www.quirksmode.org/css/contents.html to get current information about browser support of CSS3 properties.

CSS3 Multiple Background Images

Let's explore applying multiple background images to a web page. Although the CSS3 Backgrounds and Borders module is still in working draft status, current versions of most popular web browsers support the use of multiple background images.

Figure 4.29 shows a web page with two background images configured on the body selector: a green gradient image that repeats across the entire browser viewport, and a flower image that displays once in the right footer area. Use the CSS3 `background` property to configure multiple background images. Each image declaration is separated by a comma. You can optionally add property values to indicate the image's position and whether the image repeats. The `background` property uses a shorthand notation: Just list the values that are needed for relevant properties such as `background-position` and `background-repeat`.

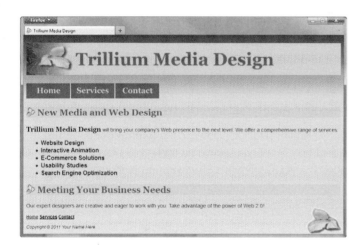

Figure 4.29 The Firefox browser displays multiple background images

Progressive Enhancement

Multiple background images are currently supported by recent versions of Firefox, Chrome, Safari, Opera, and Internet Explorer 9. Be aware that multiple background images are not supported by earlier versions of Internet Explorer. You'll use the technique of **progressive enhancement**, which is defined by web developer and HTML5 evangelist Christian Heilmann as "starting with a baseline of usable functionality, then increasing the richness of the user experience step by step by testing for support for enhancements before applying them." In other words, start with a web page that displays well in most browsers and then add new design techniques, such as multiple background images, in a way that enhances the display for visitors who are using browsers that support the new technique.

To provide for progressive enhancement when using multiple background images, first configure a separate `background-image` property with a single image (rendered by most browsers) before the background property with multiple images (rendered by supporting browsers and ignored by nonsupporting browsers). Figure 4.30 shows the page displayed in Internet Explorer 8, which rendered the standard `background-image` property.

Figure 4.30 Progressive enhancement in action. Although only one background image displays, the web page has a similar display to Figure 4.29

Hands-On Practice 4.8

Let's practice configuring multiple background images. In this Hands-On Practice you will configure the body element selector to display multiple background images on the web page. Obtain the trilliumgradient.png and the trilliumfoot.gif images from the student files chapter4/starters folder. Save the images in your trilliumch4 folder. You'll update the index.html file from the previous Hands-On Practice. Launch a text editor, and open index.html.

1. Modify the style rule for the body element selector. Configure the `background-image` property to display trilliumgradient.png. This style rule will be applied by browsers that do not support multiple background images. Configure a `background` property to display both the trilliumgradient.png image and the trilliumfoot.gif image. The trilliumfoot.gif image should not repeat and should be displayed in the lower right corner. The body selector style rules are as follows:

```
body { background-color: #f4ffe4; color: #333333;
       font-family: Arial; Verdana, sans-serif;
       min-width: 700px;
       background-image: url(trilliumgradient.png);
       background: url(trilliumfoot.gif) no-repeat bottom right,
                  url(trilliumgradient.png); }
```

2. Save your page as index.html. Launch a browser, and test your page. It will look different, depending on which browser you use—similar to either Figure 4.29 (in a browser that supports multiple background images) or Figure 4.30 (in a browser that does not support multiple background images). *Note*: The W3C CSS validator currently defaults to CSS level 2.1, but the `background` property is part of CSS level 3 (CSS3). You need to choose the appropriate CSS level when validating. Visit http://jigsaw.w3.org/css-validator and select "CSS level 3" for the Profile value.

3. There is usually more than one way to design a web page. Let's consider the placement of the flower image in the footer area of the web page. Why not configure the gradient image

as the body element selector background and the flower image as the footer background? This configuration will provide for a similar display on all currently popular browsers. Let's try this out. Edit the index.html file. Remove the background property from the body selector. A code sample is

```
body { background-color: #f4ffe4; color: #333333;
       background-image: url(trilliumgradient.png); }
```

Next, configure the trilliumfoot.gif image as the background for the #footer selector. Configure a height value that will be large enough to display the image. The code is

```
#footer { font-size: .75em; font-style: italic;
          background-image: url(trilliumfoot.gif);
          background-repeat: no-repeat;
          background-position: right;
          height: 90px; }
```

4. Save your page as index2.html. Launch a browser, and test your page. It should look similar to Figure 4.29 on all popular modern browsers. See the chapter4/4.8 folder in the student files for solutions to this Hands-On Practice.

CSS3 Rounded Corners

As you've worked with borders and the box model, you may have begun to notice a lot of rectangles on your web pages! CSS3 introduces the **border-radius property**, which can be used to create rounded corners and soften up those rectangles. Valid values for the border-radius property include one to four numeric values (using pixel or em units) or percentages that configure the radius of the corner. If a single value is provided, it configures all four corners. If four values are provided the corners are configured in order of top left, top right, bottom right, and bottom left. You can configure corners individually with the border-bottom-left-radius, border-bottom-right-radius, border-top-left-radius, and border-top-right-radius properties.

VideoNote
**Rounded Corners
with CSS**

There is a complication when configuring rounded corners, though. Developers of browser-rendering engines, such as **WebKit** (used by Safari and Google Chrome) and **Gecko** (used by Firefox and other Mozilla-based browsers), have created proprietary properties to implement rounded corners. In addition, Internet Explorer 9 is the first version of IE to support the border-radius property. So, you need to code three different style declarations to round those corners:

- -webkit-border-radius (for WebKit browsers)

- -moz-border-radius (for Gecko browsers)

- border-radius (W3C Draft Syntax)

Eventually, all browsers will support CSS3 and the border-radius property, so code this property last in the list. CSS declarations to set a border with rounded corners are shown in the next segment of code. If you would like a visible border to display, configure the border property. Then set the value of the three `border-radius` properties to a value below 20px for best results. For example:

```
border: 3px ridge #330000;
-webkit-border-radius: 15px;
-moz-border-radius: 15px;
border-radius: 15px;
```

See Figure 4.31 (chapter4/box.html in the student files) for an example of this code in action. With progressive enhancement in mind, note that your visitors using older versions of Internet Explorer will see right-angle rather than rounded corners. However, the functionality and usability of the web page will not be affected.

Figure 4.31
Rounded corners
were configured
with CSS

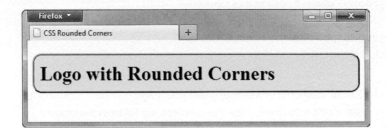

Be aware that when you code the nonstandard properties, your CSS will not pass W3C validation. Also, keep in mind that another approach to getting a rounded look is to create a rounded rectangle background image with a graphics application. However, once CSS3 becomes a well-supported standard, the box model will be easy to "round out" and is a much more efficient way to accomplish rounded corners.

 Hands-On Practice 4.9

You'll configure a logo header area that uses a background image and rounded borders in this Hands-On Practice. When complete, your web page will look similar to the one shown in Figure 4.32.

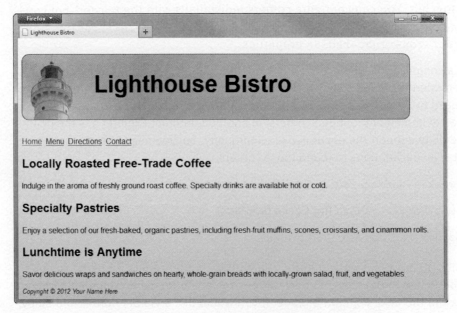

Figure 4.32 The web page with the logo area configured

1. Create a new folder called borderch4. Copy the lighthouselogo.jpg and the background.jpg files in the chapter4/starters folder to your borderch4 folder. A starter file is ready for you in the student files. Save the chapter4/starter3.html file to your borderch4 folder. Launch a browser to display the starter3.html web page shown in Figure 4.33.

Figure 4.33 The starter3.html file

2. Launch a text editor, and open the starter3.html file. Save the file as index.html. Edit the embedded CSS, and add the following style declarations to the h1 selector that will configure the lighthouselogo.jpg image as a background image that does not repeat: height set to 100px, width set to 700px, font size set to 3em, 150px of left padding, 30px of top padding, and a solid dark-blue border (#000033) with a border radius of 15px. The style declarations are as follows:

```
h1 { background-image: url(lighthouselogo.jpg);
     background-repeat: no-repeat;
     height: 100px; width: 700px; font-size: 3em;
     padding-left: 150px; padding-top: 30px;
     border: 1px solid #000033;
     -webkit-border-radius: 15px;
     -moz-border-radius: 15px;
     border-radius: 15px; }
```

3. Save the file. When you test your index.html file in a browser, it should look similar to the one shown in Figure 4.32 if you are using a browser that supports rounded corners. Otherwise the logo will have right-angle corners, but the web page will still be usable. Compare your work with the solution in the student files (chapter4/lighthouse/index.html).

FAQ **After I added the new properties, my CSS no longer passes W3C validation. What should I do?**

Because you are using the browser-proprietary properties `-webkit-border-radius` and `-moz-border-radius` in addition to the CSS3 `border-radius` property, your CSS code will not pass validation, but your pages will display in modern browsers with the visual aesthetic you envisioned. In this case, it's a deliberate decision to choose the visual display over the use of absolutely correct syntax. In time, all browsers will support the border-radius property, you'll be able to remove the proprietary code, and your CSS will pass W3C CSS Level 3 validation testing. In the meantime, if you are intentionally using nonstandard properties to enhance your web pages, don't worry when your CSS validation test generates errors related to those properties.

FAQ   Why do some browsers use proprietary properties?

When adding early support for a CSS effect or proposed property, browser vendors typically use a prefix to identify the property as a browser extension. As time goes by and the W3C specification for the property becomes stable, the browser vendor will eventually support the official property. Since CSS is rendered top down, a standard practice is to code your style rules with the browser-specific properties listed before the W3C standard property.

The CSS3 box-shadow Property

The CSS3 **box-shadow property** can be used to create a shadow effect on block-display elements such as div and paragraph elements. The developers of the WebKit and Gecko browser rendering engines have introduced proprietary properties for the box shadow effect. You'll need to code three style declarations to create a shadow and provide three to five values for each:

- Numeric pixel value for the shadow's horizontal offset:

  Positive value configures a shadow on the right. Negative value configures a shadow on the left.

- Numeric pixel value for the shadow's vertical offset:

  Positive value configures a shadow below. Negative value configures a shadow above.

- Optional: Numeric pixel value for the blur radius:

  Higher values configure more blur for a softer shadow. 0 configures a sharp shadow.

- Optional: Numeric pixel value for the spread distance:

  Positive values cause the shadow to expand. Negative values cause the shadow to contract.

- Valid color value

Here's an example that configures a dark-gray drop shadow with 5px horizontal offset, 5px vertical offset, and a 5px blur radius:

```
-webkit-box-shadow: 5px 5px 5px #828282;
-moz-box-shadow: 5px 5px 5px #828282;
box-shadow: 5px 5px 5px #828282;
```

Eventually, all browsers will support CSS3 and the official box-shadow property, so code this property last in the list. Note that when you include the nonstandard properties, your CSS will not pass W3C validation.

Include the optional inset value to configure an inner shadow. For example:

```
-webkit-box-shadow: inset 5px 5px 5px #828282;
-moz-box-shadow: inset 5px 5px 5px #828282;
box-shadow: inset 5px 5px 5px #828282;
```

The CSS3 `text-shadow` Property

The CSS3 `text-shadow` **property** configures a shadow effect on text and is supported by most recent versions of modern browsers, except for Internet Explorer 9. The property requires four values:

- Numeric pixel value for the shadow's horizontal offset:

  Positive value configures a shadow on the right. Negative value configures a shadow on the left.

- Numeric pixel value for the shadow's vertical offset:

  Positive value configures a shadow below. Negative value configures a shadow below.

- Numerical pixel value for the blur radius:

  Higher values configure more blur. 0 configures a sharp shadow.

- Valid color value

Here's an example:

```
text-shadow: 3px 3px 3px #666;
```

 ## Hands-On Practice 4.10

You'll configure a centered content area and apply the `text-shadow` and `box-shadow` properties in this Hands-On Practice. When complete, your web page will look similar to the one shown in Figure 4.34.

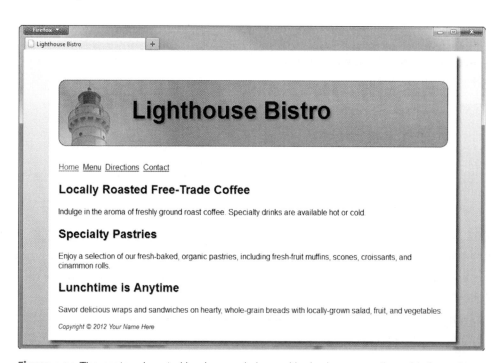

Figure 4.34 The centered neutral background along with shadow properties add dimension

Create a new folder called shadowch4. Copy the lighthouselogo.jpg and the background.jpg files from the chapter4/starters folder to your shadowch4 folder. Launch a text editor, and open the chapter4/lighthouse/index.html file (shown in Figure 4.32). Save the file in your shadowch4 folder.

1. Configure the page content to be centered, with an 800-pixel width, a white background, and some padding.

   a. Edit the HTML. Configure a div element assigned to the id named container that wraps the code within the body section. Code the opening `<div>` tag on a new line after the opening body tag. Code a closing div tag on a new line before the closing body tag.

   b. Edit the embedded CSS to configure a new selector, an id named container. Configure a white background color and 20 pixels of padding. Recall from Chapter 3 the style declarations that will center the page content. Use the `width`, `margin-left`, and `margin-right` properties as follows:

   ```
   #container { background-color: #ffffff;
                padding: 20px;
                width: 800px;
                margin-right: auto;
                margin-left: auto; }
   ```

2. Edit the embedded CSS to add the following style declarations to the #container selector to configure a box shadow:

   ```
   -webkit-box-shadow: 5px 5px 5px #1e1e1e;
   -moz-box-shadow: 5px 5px 5px #1e1e1e;
   box-shadow: 5px 5px 5px #1e1e1e;
   ```

3. Add the following style declaration to the h1 element selector to configure a dark-gray text shadow:

   ```
   text-shadow: 3px 3px 3px #666;
   ```

4. Add the following style declaration to the h2 element selector to configure a light-gray text shadow with no blur:

   ```
   text-shadow: 1px 1px 0 #ccc;
   ```

5. Save the file. When you test your index.html file in a browser, it should look similar to the one shown in Figure 4.34 if you are using a browser that supports the `box-shadow` and `text-shadow` properties. Otherwise the shadows will not display, but the web page will still be usable. See the student files for a solution (chapter4/lighthouse/shadow.html).

Browser support changes with each new browser version. There is no substitute for thoroughly testing your web pages.

However, several resources provide support lists. The following websites provide this information:

- http://westciv.com/wiki/Experimental_CSS_compatibility_table
- http://www.findmebyip.com/litmus
- http://www.quirksmode.org/css/contents.html
- http://www.impressivewebs.com/css3-click-chart

The CSS3 opacity Property

The CSS3 opacity **property** configures the transparency of the background color. Opacity values range from 0 (which is completely transparent) to 1 (which is completely opaque and has no transparency). See Figure 4.35 for an example of using the opacity property to configure a white background that is only 60% opaque.

Figure 4.35 The background of the h1 area is transparent

Hands-On Practice 4.11

In this Hands-On Practice you'll work with the opacity property as you configure the web page shown in Figure 4.35.

1. Create a new folder called opacitych4. Copy fall.jpg file from the chapter4/starters folder to your opacitych4 folder. Launch a text editor and open the chapter2/template.html file. Save it in your opacitych4 folder with the name index.html. Change the page title to "Fall Nature Hikes".

2. Let's create the structure of the web page with a div that contains an h1 element. Add the following code to your web page in the body section:

```
<div id="content">
 <h1>Fall Nature Hikes</h1>
</div>
```

3. Now, add style tags to the head section, and configure the embedded CSS. You'll create an id named content to display the fall.jpg as a background image that does not repeat. The content id also has a width of 640 pixels, a height of 480 pixels, left and right auto margins (which will center the object in the browser viewport), and 20 pixels of top padding. The code is

```
#content { background-image: url(fall.jpg);
           background-repeat: no-repeat;
           margin-left: auto;
           margin-right: auto;
           width: 640px;
           height: 480px;
           padding-top: 20px;}
```

4. Now configure the h1 element selector to have a white background color with opacity set to 0.6, font size set to 4em, and 10 pixels of padding. Sample code is

```
h1 { background-color: #FFFFFF;
     opacity: 0.6;
     font-size: 4em;
     padding: 10px; }
```

5. Save the file. When you test your index.html file in a browser that supports opacity (such as Chrome, Firefox, Safari, or Internet Explorer 9), it should look similar to the page shown in Figure 4.35. See the student files for a solution (chapter4/opacity/index.html). If you look very carefully at the web page, you'll see that the opacity property configured both the background color and the text color of the h1 element to be partially transparent. The opacity property is inherited and would also affect any elements contained within the h1 element. Experiment by changing the opacity property to different values, and observe the results.

Figure 4.36 shows the web page displayed in Internet Explorer 8, which does not support the opacity property. Notice that the visual aesthetic is not exactly the same, but the page is still usable. While Internet Explorer 9 supports opacity, earlier versions support the proprietary `filter` property with an opacity level configured between 1 (transparent) and 100 (opaque). A sample is found in the student files (chapter4/opacity/opacityie.html). The CSS for the filter property is

```
filter: alpha(opacity=60);
```

Figure 4.36 Internet Explorer 8 does not support the opacity property and displays an opaque background color

CSS3 RGBA Color

CSS3 supports new syntax for the color property that configures transparent color, called **RGBA color**. Four values are required: red color, green color, blue color, and alpha (transparency). RGBA color does not use hexadecimal color values. Instead, decimal color values are configured; see the partial color chart in Figure 4.37 and the Web-Safe Color Palette in the Appendix for examples.

#FFFFFF
rgb (255, 255, 255)
	#FFFFCC
	rgb(255, 255, 204)
		#FFFF99
		rgb(255,255,153)
			#FFFF66
			rgb(255,255,102)

#FFFF33
rgb(255,255,51)
	#FFFF00
	rgb(255,255,0)
		#FFCCFF
		rgb(255, 204, 255)
			#FFCCCC
			rgb(255,204,204)

#FFCC99
rgb(255,204,153)
	#FFCC66
	rgb(255,204,102)
		#FFCC33
		rgb(255,204,51)
			#FFCC00
			rgb(255,204,0)

#FF99FF
rgb(255,153,255)
	#FF99CC
	rgb(255,153,204)
		#FF9999
		rgb(255,153,153)
			#FF9966
			rgb(255,153,102)

Figure 4.37 Hexadecimal and RGB decimal color values

The values for red, green, and blue must be decimal values from 0 to 255. The alpha value must be a number between 0 (transparent) and 1 (opaque). Figure 4.38 shows a web page with the text configured to be slightly transparent.

Figure 4.38 CSS3 RGBA color configures the transparent text

Hands-On Practice 4.12

In this Hands-On Practice you'll configure transparent text as you code the web page shown in Figure 4.38.

1. Launch a text editor, and open the file you created in the previous Hands-On Practice (also located in the student files chapter4/opacity/index.html). Save the file with the name rgba.html.

2. Delete the current style declarations for the h1 element selector. You will create new style rules for the h1 selector to configure 10 pixels of right padding and right-aligned sans-serif white text that is 70% opaque, with a font size of 5em. Since not all browsers support RBGA color, you'll configure the color property twice. The first instance will be the standard color value that is supported by all modern browsers; the second instance will configure the RGBA color. Older browsers will not understand the RGBA color and will ignore it. Newer browsers will "see" both of the color style declarations and will apply them in the order they are coded, so the result will be transparent color. The CSS code is

```
h1 { color: #ffffff;
     color: rgba(255, 255, 255, 0.7);
     font-family: Verdana, Helvetica, sans-serif;
     font-size: 5em;
     padding-right: 10px;
     text-align: right; }
```

3. Save the file. When you test your rgba.html file in a browser that supports RGBA color (such as Chrome, Firefox, Safari, or Internet Explorer 9), it should look similar to the page shown in Figure 4.38. See the student files for a solution (chapter4/opacity/rgba.html). If you are using a nonsupporting browser such as Internet Explorer 8 (or earlier), you'll see white text instead of transparent text. While Internet Explorer 9 supports RGBA color, earlier versions support the proprietary filter property; an example is in the student files (chapter4/opacity/rbgaie.html).

FAQ   What's HSLA color all about?

There is another new method to configure color when using CSS3, called HSLA color. The letters in HSLA stand for hue, saturation, lightness, and alpha. It's a different way of thinking about color than the RGB system that web designers typically use. HSLA color is not yet supported on all browsers. Check out the following resources for more information:

- http://www.w3.org/TR/2003/CR-css3-color-20030514/#hsla-color
- http://www.useragentman.com/blog/2010/08/28/coding-colors-easily-using-css3-hsl-notation
- http://css-tricks.com/yay-for-hsla

CSS3 Gradients

CSS3 provides a method to configure color as a **gradient,** which is a smooth blending of shades from one color to another color. A CSS3 gradient background color is defined purely with CSS; no image file is needed! This provides flexibility for web designers, along with a savings in the bandwidth required to serve out gradient background image files.

Sound great? Yes, it does, but there is a catch: The WebKit and Gecko browser rendering engines use a proprietary coding syntax to process CSS gradients. The W3C has added gradient support to the CSS Image Value and Replaced Content Module (in draft status), but at the time this textbook was written, this syntax had not yet been adopted by browsers. This section will provide an example of a CSS3 gradient, along with links to resources for further study.

Figure 4.34 displays a web page with a JPG gradient background image that was configured in a graphics application. The web page shown in Figure 4.39 (available in the student files chapter4/lighthouse/gradient.html) does not use a JPG for the background; CSS3 gradient properties re-created the look of the linear gradient image.

CSS3 Gradients and Progressive Enhancement

It's very important to keep progressive enhancement in mind when using CSS3 gradients. Configure a "fallback" background-color property or background-image property which will be rendered by browsers that do not support CSS3 gradients. In Figure 4.39 the background color was configured to be same value as the ending gradient color.

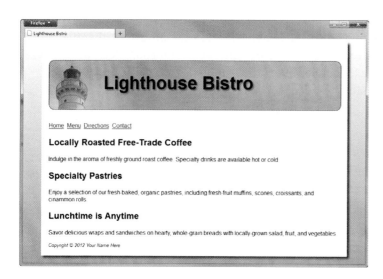

Figure 4.39 The gradient in the background was configured with CSS3 without an image file.

Configuring CSS3 Gradients

Code four style declarations to configure a gradient background:

- `-webkit-gradient` (for Webkit browsers)
- `-moz-linear-gradient` (for Gecko browsers)
- `filter` (for Internet Explorer)
- `linear-gradient` (W3C draft syntax)

Configure the gradient as the value of the background-image property (except for Internet Explorer, which uses its `filter` property). The following CSS code first configures a background color (for nonsupporting browsers) and then configures a linear gradient that blends from white (#FFFFFF) to a medium blue (#8FA5CE):

```
background-color: #8FA5CE;
background-image: -webkit-gradient(linear, left top, left bottom,
                  from(#FFFFFF), to(#8FA5CE));
background-image: -moz-linear-gradient(top, #FFFFFF, #8FA5CE);
filter: progid:DXImageTransform.Microsoft.gradient
        (startColorstr=#FFFFFFFF, endColorstr=#FF8FA5CE);
background-image: linear-gradient(#FFFFFF, #8FA5CE);
```

WebKit Syntax

Examine the WebKit code syntax which is used by the Safari and Google Chrome browsers. In its most basic form, the value of —webkit-gradient lists the type of gradient (linear or radial), starting point, ending point, starting color, and ending color.

Gecko Syntax

Review the Gecko code syntax which is used by browsers such as Firefox and Flock. The value of —moz-linear-gradient lists the starting point and color-stops (in this case there are two colors: #FFFFFF and #8FA5CE).

Internet Explorer Syntax

Internet Explorer version 9 and below implements the filter property rather than the background-image property. The color values are each eight characters long. The first two characters indicate the alpha value (#00 is transparent; #FF is opaque). The next six characters indicate the hexadecimal color value.

W3C Syntax

The W3C syntax uses different functions for linear (linear-gradient) and radial (radial-gradient) gradients. The basic format for a two-color linear gradient lists the value for each color (in this example, #FFFFFF and #8FA5CE).

As shown in the code samples, the syntax for configuring gradients varies by browser engine. It is expected that eventually all browsers will support W3C linear-gradient syntax, so code this declaration last in the list. Recall that the browser-proprietary CSS syntax in this section is nonstandard. Your CSS code will not pass W3C validation when you use these properties.

Experiment with generating CSS3 gradient code at http://www.westciv.com/tools/gradients, http://www.colorzilla.com/gradient-editor, and http://gradients.glrzad.com. For more information about CSS3 gradient syntax, visit the corresponding websites:

- **Webkit**: http://webkit.org/blog/175/introducing-css-gradients

- **Mozilla**: http://developer.mozilla.org/en/CSS/-moz-linear-gradient

- **Internet Explorer:**
  http://msdn.microsoft.com/en-us/library/ms532997(VS.85,loband).aspx

- **W3C:** http://dev.w3.org/csswg/css3-images/#gradients

Chapter Summary

This chapter has introduced the use of visual elements and graphics on web pages. The number-one reason visitors leave web pages is long download times. When using images, be careful to optimize the images for the Web, reducing both the size of the file and the dimensions of the image, in order to minimize download time.

You explored new HTML5 elements and many CSS properties in this chapter. When using the new CSS3 properties and HTML5 elements, be mindful of the concepts of progressive enhancement and accessibility. Verify that the pages display in an acceptable manner even if new techniques are not supported by the browser. Provide text alternatives to images with the alt attribute.

Visit the textbook's website at http://www.webdevfoundations.net for examples, the links listed in this chapter, and updated information.

Key Terms

<area>
<figcaption>
<figure>
<hr>
<img>
<map>
<meter>
<progress>
alt attribute
animated GIFs
background-attachment property
background-clip property
background-image property
background-origin property
background-position property
background-repeat property
background-size property
border property
border-color property
border-radius property

border-style property
border-width property
box-shadow property
favicon
filter property
gamma
Gecko
GIF
gradient
height attribute
hotspots
HSLA color
hspace attribute
image link
image map
image optimization
image slicing
interlaced image
JPEG
longdesc attribute

lossless compression
lossy compression
min-width property
opacity property
padding property
PNG
progressive enhancement
progressive JPEG
RGBA color
resolution
src attribute
text-shadow property
thumbnail image
transparency
usemap attribute
vspace attribute
Webkit
WebP
width attribute

Review Questions

Multiple Choice

1. Which CSS property configures the space between the content and the border area of any HTML element?
   a. border
   b. padding
   c. margin
   d. none of the above

2. Which HTML tag configures a horizontal line on a web page?
   a. <line>
   b.
   c. <hr>
   d. <border>

3. Which of the following creates an image link to the index.html page when the home.gif graphic is clicked?

   a. `<a href="index.html" src="home.gif" alt="Home"></a>`

   b. `<a href="index.html"><img src= "home.gif" alt="Home"></a>`

   c. `<img src="home.gif" href= "index.html" alt="Home">`

   d. `<a href="index.html"><img href= "home.gif" alt="Home"></a>`

4. Why should you include height and width attributes on an `<img>` tag?

   a. They are required attributes and must always be included.

   b. They help the browser render the page faster because it reserves the appropriate space for the image.

   c. They help the browser display the image in its own window.

   d. none of the above

5. Which element provides a handy way to display a bar chart on a web page?

   a. meter

   b. progress

   c. samp

   d. output

6. Which CSS property allows you to configure the background image in such a way that it scrolls along with the page in the browser viewport?

   a. background-image

   b. background-repeat

   c. background-attachment

   d. background-position

7. Which of the following graphic types is best suited to photographs?

   a. GIF

   b. JPG

   c. BMP

   d. PHOTO

8. Which of the following graphic types can be made transparent?

   a. GIF

   b. JPG

   c. BMP

   d. PHOTO

9. Which of the following is the right HTML code to associate a favicon with the icon file favicon.ico with a web page?

   a. `<headrel="icon" href="favicon.ico" type="image/x-icon">`

   b. `<titlerel="icon" href="favicon.ico" type="image/x-icon">`

   c. `<meta rel="icon" href="favicon.ico" type="image/x-icon">`

   d. `<link rel="icon" href="favicon.ico" type="image/x-icon">`

10. Which of the following configures a graphic to repeat vertically down the side of a web page?

    a. `hspace="10"`

    b. `background-repeat:repeat;`

    c. `valign="left"`

    d. `background-repeat: repeat-y;`

Fill in the Blank

11. By default, padding is set to _____.

12. The block display _____ element sets up a caption for a figure.

13. The _____ element displays a bar depicting a numeric value within a specific range, whereas the _____ element displays a bar chart on a web page.

14. An image map is a(n) _____ having multiple _____ areas which are called _____.

15. The CSS3 _____ can be used to resize or scale the background-image.

Apply Your Knowledge

1. **Predict the Result.** Draw and write a brief description of the web page that will be created with the following HTML code:

```
<!DOCTYPE html>
<html lang="en">
<head>
<title>Predict the Result</title>
<meta charset="utf-8">
<style>
figure{ width: 500px;border: 2px solid #0000ff;
padding: 15px; border-radius:25px;
}
figcaption{ text-align:center;font-family:Papyrus,
fantasy;color:blue; }
</style>
</head>
<body>
<p> This page describes Arctic penguins and their habitats.</p>
<figure>
<imgsrc="Penguins.jpg" width="500" height="500" alt="Arctic
Penguins">
<figcaption>
Arctin Penguins and Their Habitats
</figcaption>
</figure>
</body>
</html>
```

2. **Fill in the Missing Code.** This web page contains an image link and should be configured so that the background and text colors have good contrast. The image used on this web page should link to a page called services.html. Some HTML attribute values, indicated by "_", are missing. Some CSS style rules, indicated by "_", are incomplete. The code follows:

```
<!DOCTYPE html>
<html lang="en">
<head>
<title>CircleSoft Design</title>
<meta charset="utf-8">
<style>
body { "_": "_";
       color: "_";
}
</style>
</head>
<body>
  <div>
  <a href="_"><img src="logo.gif" alt="_" height="100"
  width="600">
  <br>Enter CircleSoft Design</a>
</div>
</body>
</html>
```

3. **Find the Error.** This page displays an image called Penguins.jpg. The image is 100 pixels wide by 100 pixels high. When this page is displayed, the image does not

look right. Find the error. Describe the attributes that you would code in the `<img>` tag to provide accessibility. The code follows:

```
<!DOCTYPE html>
<html lang="en">
<head>
<title>Find the Error</title>
<meta charset="utf-8">
</head>
<body>
<p> where is the image?</p>
<img href="Penguins.jpg" height="100" width="100" alt="Arctic
Penguins">
</body>
</html>
```

Hands-On Exercises

1. Write the CSS to configure a graphic named wintermorning.jpg to display once in the background of all `<h1>` elements. Write the HTML code to use this `<h1>` element on your page.

2. Write the HTML to create an image hyperlink. The image is called schaumburgthumb.jpg. It is 100 pixels high by 150 pixels wide. The image should link to a larger image called schaumburg.jpg. There should be no border on the image.

3. You have been asked to survey 100 web developers on the technologies they use on the web. The following table displays the response of these developers, i.e., the number of people who said that they use that particular technology:

Ajax	JackBe	Laszlo	JavaFX	Flex	Silverlight
85	63	72	73	79	68

Write the HTML code to produce a bar chart depicting the survey result on a web page.

4. Experiment with page backgrounds. Locate the erget1.gif file in the student files chapter4/starters folder. Design a web page that uses this file as a background.

5. Experiment with page backgrounds. CSS3 allows you to use several background images for an element. Locate the files erget1.gif and erget2.gif in the student files chapter4/starters folder. Design a web page that uses these files as background images. The first image should be on the top left corner and the second image should be on the bottom right corner of your page.

6. The background-origin property specifies the positioning area of the background images. The background image can be placed within the content-box, padding-box, or border-box area. Write three different classes that will use the image erget1.gif as background image, with three different background origin positions. Observe the effect.

7. Practice with CSS.
   a. Write the CSS for a div element with rounded corners, a light-grey background area, 25 pixels of padding, and solid border in a dark-grey color. Provide enough padding considering the rounded corners.
   b. Write the CSS for a div element with width of 300 pixels and height of 100 pixels, with olive-green background color and a grey box shadow.

   c. Write the CSS for a class named heading with the following characteristics: a light-blue background, dark-blue text color with grey text shading.

   d. Write the CSS for a class named footer with the following characteristics: a solid double grey border top, green text color with .75em text size and italic font style.

   e. Write the CSS for a background with an image named mypic.gif where the background image is stretched to cover the entire content area.

8. You have designed a navigation bar with text hyperlinks and image hyperlinks. You can also build a navigation bar with standard HTML lists. Write the HTML to create a navigation bar using HTML unordered lists. Use the styling list-style-type:none with the ul element and display:inline with the li element. This will be discussed in detail in Chapter 6.

9. Design a web page that provides a list of resources for free clip art and free photographs. The list should contain at least five different websites. Use your favorite graphic sites, the sites suggested in this chapter, or sites you have found on the Web. Save the page as freegraphics.html.

10. Visit the textbook's website at http://webdevfoundations.net/6e/chapter4.html and follow the link to the Adobe Fireworks or Adobe Photoshop tutorial. Follow the instructions to create a logo banner. Hand in the printouts described in the tutorial to your instructor.

Web Research

1. Providing access to the Web for all people is an important issue. Visit the W3C's Web Accessibility Initiative and explore its WCAG 2.0 Quick Reference at http://www.w3.org/WAI/WCAG20/quickref. View additional pages at the W3C's site as necessary. Explore the checkpoints that are related to the use of color and images on web pages. Create a web page that uses color, uses images, and includes the information that you discovered.

2. This chapter has introduced you to several new CSS3 properties. Choose one of them to research further. Create an example web page that demonstrates the use of the property. Use one of the following sites to determine the current browser support of the property, and include a summary of this information (along with the URLs of the resources you used) in your web page:

- http://www.quirksmode.org/css/contents.html
- http://westciv.com/wiki/Experimental_CSS_compatibility_table
- http://www.findmebyip.com/litmus
- http://www.impressivewebs.com/css3-click-chart

Focus on Web Design

Visit a website that interests you. Print the home page or one other pertinent page from the site. Write a one-page summary and reaction to the website you chose to visit. Address the following topics:

   a. What is the purpose of the site?

   b. Who is the intended audience?

    c. Do you believe the site reaches its audience?

    d. Was this site useful to you? Why or why not?

    e. List the colors and/or graphics that are used on the home page of this website: background, backgrounds of page sections, text, logo, navigation buttons, and so on.

    f. How does the use of color and graphics enhance the website?

WEBSITE CASE STUDY
Using Graphics & Visual Elements

Each of the case studies in this section continues throughout most of the text. In this chapter, we add images to the websites, create a new page, and modify existing pages.

JavaJam Coffee House

See Chapter 2 for an introduction to the JavaJam Coffee House Case Study. Figure 2.25 shows a site map for the JavaJam website. The Home page and Menu page were created in earlier chapters. Using the existing website as a starting point, you will modify the design of the pages and create a new page, the Music page. You have five tasks in this case study:

1. Create a new folder for this JavaJam case study, and obtain the starter image files.

2. Modify the Home page to display a logo image, a JPEG image, and a content div as shown in Figure 4.40.

3. Modify the Menu page to be consistent with the Home page.

4. Create a new Music page, as shown in Figure 4.41.

5. Modify the style rules in the javajam.css file as needed.

Figure 4.40 New JavaJam Home page

Hands-On Practice Case

Task 1: Create a folder on your hard drive or portable storage device called javajam4. Copy all the files from your Chapter 3 javajamcss folder into the javajam4 folder. Obtain the images used in this case study from the student files. The images are located in the chapter4/casestudystarters/javajam folder. The images are background.gif, greg.jpg, gregthumb.jpg, javalogo.gif, melanie.jpg, melaniethumb.jpg, and windingroad.jpg. Save them in your javajam4 folder.

Task 2: The Home Page. Launch a text editor, and open the index.html file from your javajam4 folder. Modify the index.html file to look similar to the web page shown in Figure 4.40.

1. Replace the "JavaJam Coffee House" text contained within the h1 element with the javalogo.gif. Be sure to include the alt, height, and width attributes on the `<img>` tag for the graphic.

2. Configure a div element that will contain all the web page content between the navigation area and the footer area.

   - Add a new blank line below the navigation div. Code an opening div tag that is assigned to the id named content.

   - Add a new blank line above the footer div. Code a closing div tag.

3. Add a new blank line below the opening div tag for the content id. Configure the windingroad.jpg image to display. Be sure to include the alt, height, and width attributes. Also configure the image to appear to the right of the unordered list by coding the `align="right"` attribute on the `<img>` tag. *Note*: In Chapter 6 you'll learn to use the CSS float property to configure this type of layout.

Save and test your new index.html page. It will be similar to Figure 4.40, but you'll notice that a few final touches (like the background image) are missing; you'll configure these with CSS in Task 5.

Task 3: The Menu Page. Launch a text editor, and open the menu.html page from your javajam4 folder. Replace the JavaJam Coffee House heading with the javalogo.gif. Configure the content div in the same manner as on the home page. Save and test your new menu.html page.

Task 4: The Music Page. Use the Menu page as the starting point for the Music page. Launch a text editor, and open the menu.html file in the javajam4 folder. Save the file as music.html. Modify the music.html file to look similar to the Music page, as shown in Figure 4.41:

1. Change the page title to an appropriate phrase.

2. Delete the description list from the page.

3. The main content in the page will consist of a paragraph below the navigation and two sections describing music performances.

   - The text of the paragraph follows:

     The first Friday night each month at JavaJam is a special night. Join us from 8pm to 11pm for some music you won't want to miss!

   - *Hint*: Use the special character `&rsquo;` for the apostrophe character.

   - The section describing each music performance consists of an h2 element, a paragraph assigned to the class named details, and an image link.

Figure 4.41 JavaJam music.html

January Music Performance:

- Configure an h2 element with the following text: January

- Code an opening paragraph tag. Assign the paragraph to the class named details.

- Configure the melaniethumb.jpg as an image link to melanie.jpg. Code appropriate attributes on the `<img>` tag.

- Configure the following text within the paragraph after the image:

  Melanie Morris entertains with her melodic folk style. Check out the podcast! CDs are now available.

February Music Performance:

- Configure an h2 element with the following text: February

- Code an opening paragraph tag. Assign the paragraph to the class named details.

- Configure the gregthumb.jpg as an image link to greg.jpg. Code appropriate attributes on the `<img>` tag.

- Configure the following text within the paragraph after the image:
  Tahoe Greg's back from his tour. New songs. New stories. CDs are now available.

- *Hint*: Use the special character `&rsquo;` for the apostrophe character.

Save the music.html file. If you test your page in a browser, you'll notice that it looks different from Figure 4.41—you still need to configure style rules.

Task 5: Configure the CSS. Open javajam.css in a text editor. Edit the style rules as follows:

1. Modify the body element selector style rules. Configure background.gif as the background image.

2. Modify the style rules for the wrapper id. Configure the background color to be #ffffcc. Configure a minimum width of 700px (use `min-width`). Use the `box-shadow` property to configure a drop-shadow effect.

3. Modify the h1 element selector. Remove the line-height style rule.

4. Add a new style rule for the h2 selector that configures a background color (#ccaa66), font size (1.2em), left padding (10px) and bottom padding (5px). The style rules follow:

```
background-color: #ccaa66;
font-size: 1.2em;
padding-left: 10px;
padding-bottom: 5px;
```

5. Modify the footer id. Configure 10 pixels of padding.

6. Add a new style rule for the id named content to configure 25 pixels of padding.

7. Add a new style rule for the class named details to add 20% left and right padding (use `padding-left` and `padding-right`). Notice how this rule adds empty space on either side of the music performance description and image.

8. Add a new style rule for the img element selector not to display a border.

Save the javajam.css file. Test your pages (index.html, menu.html, and music.html) in a browser. If your images do not appear or your image links do not work, examine your work carefully. Use Windows Explorer or Mac Finder to verify that the images are saved in your javajam4 folder. Examine the src attribute on the <img> tags to be sure you spelled the image names correctly. Another useful troubleshooting technique is to validate the HTML and CSS code. See Chapters 2 and 3 for Hands-On Practice exercises that describe how to use these validators.

Fish Creek Animal Hospital

See Chapter 2 for an introduction to the Fish Creek Animal Hospital Case Study. Figure 2.29 shows a site map for Fish Creek. The Home page and Services page were created in earlier chapters. Using the existing website as a starting point, you will modify the design of the pages and create a new page, the Ask the Vet page. You have five tasks in this case study:

1. Create a new folder for this Fish Creek case study, and obtain the starter image files.

2. Modify the Home page to display a logo image and navigation image links as shown in Figure 4.42.

3. Modify the Services page to be consistent with the Home page.

4. Create a new Ask the Vet page, as shown in Figure 4.43.

5. Modify the style rules in the fishcreek.css file as needed.

Figure 4.42 New Fish Creek Home page

Hands-On Practice Case

Task 1: Create a folder on your hard drive or portable storage device called fishcreek4. Copy all the files from your Chapter 3 fishcreekcss folder into the fishcreek4 folder. Obtain the images used in this case study from the student files. The images are located in the chapter4/casestudystarters/fishcreek folder. The images are fishcreeklogo.gif, home.gif, services.gif, askthevet.gif, and contact.gif. Save the files in your fishcreek4 folder.

Task 2: The Home Page. Launch a text editor, and open the index.html file from your fishcreek4 folder. Modify the index.html file to look similar to the web page shown in Figure 4.42.

1. Replace the "Fish Creek Animal Hospital" text contained within the h1 element with the fishcreeklogo.gif. Be sure to include the alt, height, and width attributes on the `<img>` tag for the graphic.

2. Update the navigation area.

   - Since you will be replacing the main navigation with image links, it's a good idea to provide for accessibility by including a set of text navigation links in the footer section of the web page. Copy the nav div, and paste it inside the footer area above the copyright line.

   - Refer to Figure 4.42 , and replace the main navigation text hyperlinks with image links. The home.gif should link to index.html. The services.gif should link to services.html. The askthevet.gif should link to askvet.html. The contact.gif should link to contact.html. Use appropriate attributes on the `<img>` tag: alt, height, and width. Assign the div that contains the main navigation to the id named main. The div tag is coded as follows:

     ```
     <div class="nav" id="main">
     ```

Save and test your new index.html page. It will be similar to Figure 4.42, but you'll notice that a few final touches (like the text shadow on the categories) are missing; you'll configure these with CSS in Task 5.

Task 3: The Services Page. Launch a text editor, and open the services.html page from your fishcreek4 folder. Replace the "Fish Creek Animal Hospital" heading with the fishcreeklogo.gif. Configure the navigation areas in a similar way as the home page. Save and test your new services.html page.

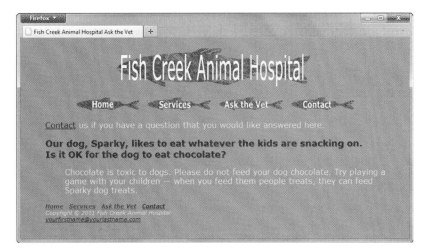

Figure 4.43 Fish Creek askvet.html

Task 4: The Ask the Vet Page. Use the Services page as the starting point for the Ask the Vet page. Launch a text editor, and open the services.html file in the fishcreek4 folder. Save the file as askvet.html. Modify the askvet.html file to look similar to the Ask the Vet page, as shown in Figure 4.43:

1. Change the page title to an appropriate phrase.

2. Delete the unordered list from the page.

3. The page content consists of a paragraph of text followed by a definition list that contains a question and an answer.

   a. Replace the text in the paragraph as follows:

      Contact us if you have a question that you would like answered here.

   b. The word "Contact" should link to the contact.html page.

   c. The description list displays the question and answer. The <dt> element configures the question. Assign the <dt> element to the category class used on the Services page. The <dd> element configures the answer. The content of the description list follows:

      Question: Our dog, Sparky, likes to eat whatever the kids are snacking on. Is it OK for the dog to eat chocolate?"

      Answer: Chocolate is toxic to dogs. Please do not feed your dog chocolate. Try playing a game with your children—when you feed them people treats, they can feed Sparky dog treats.

   d. *Hint*: See Appendix C, "Special Characters," for the character code to display the em dash (—).

Save the askvet.html file. If you test your page in a browser, you'll notice that it looks different from Figure 4.43—you still need to configure style rules.

Task 5: Configure the CSS. Open fishcreek.css in in a text editor. Edit the style rules as follows:

1. The fish navigation image area is quite wide. Modify the style rules to change the width of the page content container id from 80% to 700 pixels.

2. Modify the style rules for the h1 element selector. Delete the existing style rules. Add a new style rule to center the image (use `text-align:center`).

3. Modify the category class to display text with a drop shadow (use `text-shadow: 1px 1px 1px #666`).

4. Add a new style rule for the img element selector to display no border.

5. Add a new style rule for the id named main that configures centered text (use `text-align: center`).

Save the fishcreek.css file. Test your pages (index.html, services.html, and askvet.html) in a browser. If your images do not appear or your image links do not work, examine your work carefully. Use Windows Explorer or Mac Finder to verify that the images are saved in your fishcreek4 folder. Examine the src attribute on the <img> tags to be sure you spelled the image names correctly. Another useful troubleshooting technique is to validate the HTML and CSS code. See Chapters 2 and 3 for Hands-On Practice exercises that describe how to use these validators.

Pacific Trails

See Chapter 2 for an introduction to the Pacific Trails Case Study. Figure 2.33 shows a site map for Pacific Trails. The Home page and Yurts page were created in earlier chapters. Using the existing website as a starting point, you will modify the design of the pages and create a new page, the Activities page. You have five tasks in this case study:

1. Create a new folder for this Pacific Trails case study, and obtain the starter image files.

2. Modify the Home page to display a logo image and scenic photograph as shown in Figure 4.44.

3. Modify the Yurts page to be consistent with the Home page.

4. Create a new Activities page, as shown in Figure 4.45.

5. Modify the style rules in the pacific.css file as needed.

Hands-On Practice Case

Task 1: Create a folder on your hard drive or portable storage device called pacific4. Copy all the files from your Chapter 3 pacificcss folder into the pacific4 folder. Obtain the images used in this case study from the student files. The images are located in the chapter4/casestudystarters/pacific folder. The images are sunset.jpg, coast.jpg, yurt.jpg, trail.jpg, and background.jpg. Save the files in your pacific4 folder.

Task 2: The Home Page. Launch a text editor, and open the index.html file from your pacific4 folder. Modify the index.html file to look similar to the web page shown in Figure 4.44.

1. Configure a div that will contain all the web page content between the navigation area and the footer area.

   • Add a new blank line below the navigation div. Code an opening div tag that is assigned to the id named content.

   • Add a new blank line above the footer div. Code a closing div tag.

2. Add a new blank line below the h2 element. Configure the coast.jpg image to display. Be sure to include the alt, height, and width attributes.

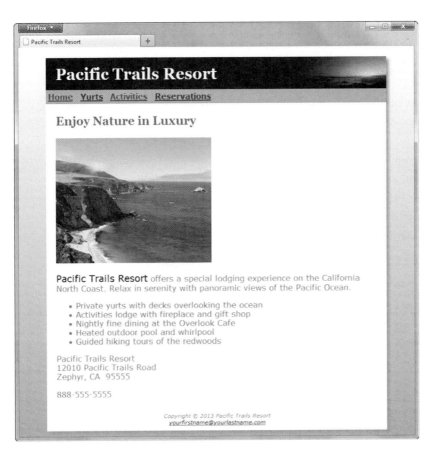

Figure 4.44 New Pacific Trails Resort Home page

Figure 4.45 Pacific Trails activities.html

Save and test your new index.html page. It will be similar to Figure 4.44, but you'll notice that a few final touches (like the sunset image in the logo area) are missing; you'll configure these with CSS in Task 5.

Task 3: The Yurts Page. Launch a text editor, and open the yurts.html page from your pacific4 folder. Add a new blank line below the h2 element. Configure the yurt.jpg image to display. Be sure to include the alt, height, and width attributes. Save and test your new yurts.html page.

Task 4: The Activities Page. Use the Yurts page as the starting point for the Activities page. Launch a text editor, and open the yurts.html file in the pacific4 folder. Save the file as activities.html. Modify the activities.html file to look similar to the Activities page, as shown in Figure 4.45:

1. Change the page title to an appropriate phrase.

2. Change the text in the <h2> to be "Activities at Pacific Trails Resort".

3. Modify the <img> tag to display the trail.jpg image.

4. Delete the description list from the page.

5. Configure the following text, using h3 tags for the headings and paragraph tags for the sentences:

   Hiking

   Pacific Trails Resort has 5 miles of hiking trails and is adjacent to a state park. Go it alone or join one of our guided hikes.

   Kayaking

   Ocean kayaks are available for guest use.

   Bird Watching

   While anytime is a good time for bird watching at Pacific Trails, we offer guided birdwatching trips at sunrise several times a week.

Save the activities.html file. If you test your page in a browser, you'll notice that it looks different from Figure 4.45; you still need to configure style rules.

Task 5: Configure the CSS. Open pacific.css in in a text editor. Edit the style rules as follows:

1. Modify the body element selector style rules. Configure background.jpg as the background image.

2. Modify the style rules for the wrapper id. Configure the background color to be #ffffff. Configure a minimum width of 700px (use min-width). Use the box-shadow property to configure a drop-shadow effect.

3. Modify the style rules for the h1 element selector. Configure the sunset.jpg as a background image that displays on the right and does not repeat. Also configure 20 pixels of left padding. Configure a 72-pixel height (the same height as the background image).

4. Modify the style rules for the nav id. Configure 5 pixels of padding.

5. Modify the style rules for the footer id. Configure 10 pixels of padding.

6. Add a new style rule for the h3 element selector to display #000033 text color.

7. Add a new style rule for an id named content that configures 20 pixels of left and right padding.

8. Have you noticed extra empty space between the logo header area and the navigation? Let's do something about that. We'll need to use the CSS margin property, which you'll explore in depth in Chapter 6. Modify the style rules for the h1 selector to set the bottom margin to 0 with the following code:

```
margin-bottom: 0;
```

Save the pacific.css file. Test your pages (index.html, yurts.html, and activities.html) in a browser. If your images do not appear or your image links do not work, examine your work carefully. Use Windows Explorer or Mac Finder to verify that the images are saved in your pacific4 folder. Examine the src attribute on the `<img>` tags to be sure you spelled the image names correctly. Another useful troubleshooting technique is to validate the HTML and CSS code. See Chapters 2 and 3 for Hands-On Practice exercises that describe how to use these validators.

Prime Properties

See Chapter 2 for an introduction to the Prime Properties Case Study. Figure 2.37 shows a site map for Prime Properties. The Home page and Financing page were created in earlier chapters. Using the existing website as a starting point, you will modify the design of the pages and create a new page, the Listings page. You have five tasks in this case study:

1. Create a new folder for this Prime Properties case study, and obtain the starter image files.

2. Modify the Home page to display a logo image and navigation buttons as shown in Figure 4.46.

3. Modify the Financing page to be consistent with the Home page.

4. Create a new Listings page, as shown in Figure 4.47.

5. Modify the style rules in the prime.css file as needed.

Hands-On Practice Case

Task 1: Create a folder on your hard drive or portable storage device called prime4. Copy all the files from your Chapter 3 primecss folder into the prime4 folder. Obtain the images used in this case study from the student files. The images are located in the chapter4/casestudystarters/prime folder. The images are primelogo.gif, primehomenav.gif, primehomebtn.gif, primelistingsnav.gif, primelistingsbtn.gif, primefinancingnav.gif, primefinancingbtn.gif, primecontactnav.gif, primecontactbtn.gif, schaumburg.jpg, schaumburgthumb.jpg, libertyville.jpg, libertyvillethumb.jpg, primevertical.png, primehorizontal.png, and primediagonal.png. Save the files in your prime4 folder.

Task 2: The Home Page. Launch a text editor, and open the index.html file from your prime4 folder. Modify the index.html file to look similar to the web page shown in Figure 4.46.

1. Replace the "Prime Properties" text contained within the h1 element with the primelogo.gif. Be sure to include the alt, height, and width attributes on the `<img>` tag for the graphic.

2. Update the navigation area.

Figure 4.46 Prime Properties Home page

- Since you will be replacing the main navigation with image links, it's a good idea to provide for accessibility by including a set of text navigation links in the footer section of the web page. Copy the navigation div, and paste it inside the footer area above the copyright line.

- Refer to Figure 4.46, and replace the main navigation text hyperlinks with image links. The navigation buttons use color as a visual cue for visitors. The navigation button for the current page has a blue background. The navigation buttons for other pages have a green background. To configure this area for the Home page, use primehomebtn.gif (link to index.html), primelistingsnav.gif (link to listings.html), primefinancingnav.gif (link to financing.html), and primecontactnav.gif (link to contact.html). Use appropriate attributes on the `<img>` tag: alt, height, and width.

Save and test your new index.html page. It will be similar to Figure 4.46 but you'll notice that a few final touches (like the dark-blue page background) are missing; you'll configure these with CSS in Task 5.

Task 3: The Financing Page. Launch a text editor, and open the financing.html page from your prime4 folder. Replace the "Prime Properties" heading with the primelogo.gif. Configure the navigation areas in a similar way as in the home page. In the top navigation, use primehomenav.gif (link to index.html), primelistingsnav.gif (link to listings.html), primefinancingbtn.gif (link to financing.html), and primecontactnav.gif (link to contact.html). Save and test your new financing.html page.

Task 4: The Listings Page. Use the Financing page as the starting point for the Listings page. Launch a text editor, and open the financing.html file in the prime4 folder. Save the file as listings.html. Modify your file to look similar to the Listings page, as shown in Figure 4.47.

1. Change the title to an appropriate phrase.

2. Configure the top navigation area to display primehomenav.gif (link to index.html), primelistingsbtn.gif (link to listings.html), primefinancingnav.gif (link to financing.html), and primecontactnav.gif (link to contact.html).

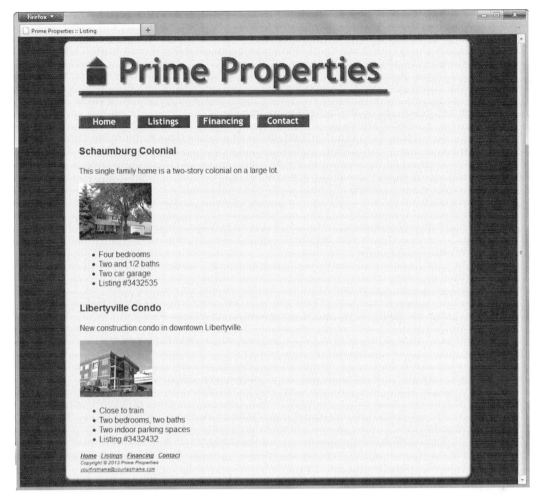

Figure 4.47 Prime Properties listings.html

3. Replace the h2 element text "Financing" with "Listings".

4. Delete the text between the Listings heading and the footer section of the web page.

5. The section describing each listing consists of an h3 element, an image link, a paragraph, and an unordered list.

Schaumburg Colonial Listing

- Configure an h3 element with the following text:

  Schaumburg Colonial

- Configure a paragraph with the following text:

  This single family home is a two-story colonial on a large lot.

- Configure the schaumburgthumb.jpg as an image link to schaumburg.jpg. Code appropriate attributes on the `<img>` tag, including src, alt, height, and width.

- Configure an unordered list with the following text:

  Four bedrooms

  Two and 1/2 baths

  Two car garage

  Listing #3432535

Libertyville Condo Listing

- Configure an h3element with the following text:

    Libertyville Condo

- Configure a paragraph with the following text:

    New construction condo in downtown Libertyville.

- Configure the libertyvillethumb.jpg as an image link to libertyville.jpg. Code appropriate attributes on the `<img>` tag, including src, alt, height, and width.

- Configure an unordered list with the following text:

    Close to train

    Two bedrooms, two baths

    Two indoor parking spaces

    Listing #3432432

Save the listings.html file. If you test your page in a browser, you'll notice that it looks different from Figure 4.47; you still need to configure style rules.

Task 5: Configure the CSS. Open pacific.css in in a text editor. Edit the style rules as follows:

- Modify the style rules for the body element selector to configure a very dark background color (#000033). Choose either primevertical.png, primehorizontal.png or primediagonal.png to use as the background image.

- Modify the style rules for the #wrapper id. Configure #FFFFCC as the background color. Configure a minimum width of 700px (use `min-width`), no top padding, no right padding, 20 pixels of bottom padding, 30 pixels of left padding, and a 1 pixel blue (#00332B) ridge border with rounded corners. Also configure an inset box shadow with the following CSS:

```
-webkit-box-shadow: inset -3px -3px 3px 3px #00332B;
-moz-box-shadow: inset -3px -3px 3px 3px #00332B;
box-shadow: inset -3px -3px 3px 3px #00332B;
```

- Modify the style rules for the h3 element selector to have 10 pixels of top padding.

- The background properties on the header id selector, h2 element selector, and h3 element selector interfere with the inset box shadow in some browsers. Remove the `background-property` style rule from these selectors.

- Configure the img element selector to display no border.

Save the prime.css file. Test your pages (index.html, financing.html, and listing.html) in a browser. If your images do not appear or your image links do not function, examine your work carefully. Use Windows Explorer or Mac Finder to verify that the images are saved in your prime folder. Examine the src attributes on the `<img>` tags to be sure you spelled the image names correctly. Another useful troubleshooting technique is to validate the HTML and CSS code. See Chapters 2 and 3 for Hands-On Practice exercises that describe how to use these validators.

Web Design

Chapter Objectives   In this chapter, you will learn how to . . .

- Describe the most common types of website organization
- Describe the principles of visual design
- Design for your target audience
- Design clear, easy-to-use navigation
- Improve the readability of the text on your web pages
- Use graphics appropriately on web pages
- Apply the concept of universal design to web pages
- Describe web page layout design techniques
- Apply best practices of web design

As a website visitor, you have probably found that certain websites are appealing and easy to use while others seem awkward or just plain annoying. What separates the good from the bad? This chapter discusses recommended web design practices. The topics include site organization, navigation design, page layout design, text design, graphic design, and accessibility considerations.

5.1 Design for Your Target Audience

Whatever your personal preferences, design your website to appeal to your **target audience**—the people who will use your site. Your intended target audience may be specific, such as kids, college students, young couples, or seniors, or you may intend your site to appeal to everyone. The purpose and goals of your visitors will vary—they may be casually seeking information, performing research for school or work, comparison shopping, job hunting, and so on. The design of a website should appeal to and meet the needs of the target audience.

Figure 5.1
The compelling graphic draws you in

For example, NASA's website, http://www.nasa.gov, as shown in Figure 5.1, features compelling graphics and has a different look and feel from the text-based, link-intensive Bureau of Labor Statistics Consumer Price Index web page, http://www.bls.gov/cpi, in Figure 5.2.

Figure 5.2
This text-intensive web page offers numerous choices

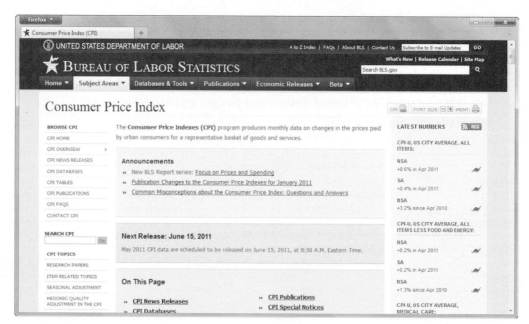

The first site engages you, draws you in, and invites exploration. The second site provides you with a wide range of choices so that you can quickly get down to work. The layout, navigation, and even the use of color and text can work together to appeal to your target audience. Keep your target audience in mind as you explore the web design practices in this chapter.

5.2 Website Organization

How will visitors move around your site? How will they find what they need? This is largely determined by the website's organization or architecture. There are three common types of website organization:

- Hierarchical
- Linear
- Random (sometimes called Web organization)

A diagram of the organization of a website is called a **site map**. Creating the site map is one of the initial steps in developing a website (more on this in Chapter 10).

Hierarchical Organization

Most websites use **hierarchical organization**. A site map for hierarchical organization, such as the one shown in Figure 5.3, is characterized by a clearly defined home page with links to major site sections. Web pages within sections are placed as needed. The home page and the first level of pages in a hierarchical site map typically indicate the hyperlinks on the main navigation bar of each web page.

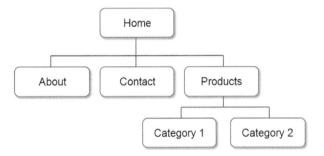

Figure 5.3 Hierarchical site organization

It is important to be aware of the pitfalls of hierarchical organization. Figure 5.4 shows a site design that is too shallow—there are too many major site sections.

This site design needs to be organized into fewer, easily managed topics or units of information, a process called **chunking**. In the case of web page design, each unit

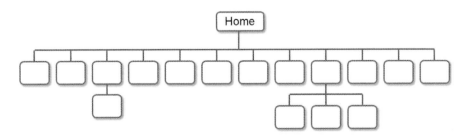

Figure 5.4 This site design uses a shallow hierarchy

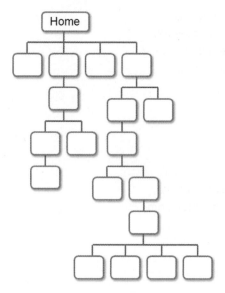

Figure 5.5 This site design uses a deep hierarchy

of information is a page. Nelson Cowan, a research psychologist at the University of Missouri, found that adults typically can keep about four items or chunks of items (such as the three parts of a phone number 888-555-5555) in their short-term memory (http://web.missouri.edu/~cowann/research.html). Following this principle, be aware of the number of major navigation links and try to group them into visually separate sections on the page with each group having no more than about four links.

Another pitfall is designing a site that is too deep. Figure 5.5 shows an example of this. The interface design "three click rule" says that a web page visitor should be able to get from any page on your site to any other page on your site with a maximum of three hyperlinks. In other words, a visitor who cannot get what they want in three mouse clicks will begin to feel frustrated and may leave your site. This rule may be very difficult to satisfy on a large site, but in general, the goal is to organize your site so that your visitors can easily navigate from page to page within the site structure.

Linear Organization

When the purpose of a site or series of pages on a site is to provide a tutorial, tour, or presentation that needs to be viewed sequentially, **linear organization**, as shown in Figure 5.6, is useful.

Figure 5.6 Linear site organization

In linear organization, the pages are viewed one after another. Some websites use hierarchical organization in general, but with linear organization in a few small areas.

Random Organization

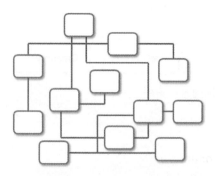

Figure 5.7 Random site organization

Random organization (sometimes called Web organization) offers no clear path through the site, as shown in Figure 5.7. There is often no clear home page and no discernable structure. Random organization is not as common as hierarchical or linear organization and is usually found only on artistic sites or sites that strive to be especially different and original. This type of organization is typically not used for commercial websites.

FAQ **What's a good way to build my site map?**

Sometimes it is difficult to begin creating a site map for a website. Some design teams meet in a room with a blank wall and a package of large Post-it® Notes. They write the titles of topics and subtopics needed in the site on the Post-it® Notes. They arrange the notes on the wall and discuss them until the site structure becomes clear and there is consensus within the group. If you are not working in a group, you can try this on your own and then discuss the organization of the website with a friend or fellow student.

5.3 Principles of Visual Design

There are four visual design principles that you can apply to the design of just about anything: repetition, contrast, proximity, and alignment. Whether you are designing a web page, a button, a logo, a DVD cover, a brochure, or a software interface, the four design principles will help to create the "look," or visual aesthetic, of your project and will determine whether your message is effectively communicated.

VideoNote
Principles of Visual Design

Repetition: Repeat Visual Elements Throughout the Design

When applying the principle of **repetition**, the designer repeats one or more elements throughout the product. The repeating aspect ties the work together. Whether it is color, shape, font, or image, the repetition of elements helps to unify a design.

Contrast: Add Visual Excitement and Draw Attention

To apply the principle of **contrast**, the designer should make the elements very different (add contrast) in order to make the design interesting and to direct attention. When designing web pages, there should be good contrast between the background color and the text.

Proximity: Group Related Items

When designers apply the principle of **proximity**, related items are placed physically close together. Unrelated items should have space separating them. The placing of items close together gives visual clues to the logical organization of the information or functionality.

Alignment: Align Elements to Create Visual Unity

Another principle that helps to create a cohesive web page is **alignment**. When applying this principle, the designer organizes the page so that each element placed has some alignment (vertical or horizontal) with another element on the page.

Repetition, contrast, proximity, and alignment are four principles that can greatly improve your web page designs. If you apply these principles effectively, your web pages will look more professional and you will communicate your message more clearly. Keep these visual design principles in mind as you design and build websites.

5.4 Design to Provide Accessibility

In Chapter 1, you were introduced to the concept of **universal design**. The Center for Universal Design defines universal design as "the design of products and environments to be usable by all people, to the greatest extent possible, without the need for adaptation or specialized design."

Focus on Accessibility

Who Benefits from Universal Design and Increased Accessibility?

Consider the following scenarios:

- Maria, a young woman in her twenties with physical challenges who cannot manipulate a mouse and who uses a keyboard with much effort: Accessible web pages designed to function without a mouse will help Maria to access content.

- Leotis, a college student who is deaf and wants to be a web developer: Captions for audio/video content and transcripts will provide Leotis access to content.

- Jim, a middle-aged man who has a dial-up Internet connection and is using the Web for personal enjoyment: Alternate text for images and transcripts for multimedia will provide Jim improved access to content.

- Nadine, a mature woman with age-related macular degeneration who has difficulty reading small print: Web pages that are designed so that text can be enlarged in the browser will make it easier for Nadine to read.

- Karen, a college student using a smartphone to access the Web: Accessible content organized with headings and lists will make it easier for Karen to surf the Web on a mobile device.

Figure 5.8 Everyone benefits from an accessible web page

- Prakesh, a man in his thirties who is legally blind and needs access to the Web in order to do his job: Web pages that are designed to be accessible (which are organized with headings and lists, display descriptive text for hyperlinks, provide alternate text descriptions for images, and are usable without a mouse) will help Prakesh to access content.

All of these individuals benefit from web pages that are designed with accessibility in mind. A web page that is designed to be accessible is typically more usable for all—even a person who has no physical challenges and is using a broadband connection benefits from the improved presentation and organization of a well-designed web page (Figure 5.8).

Accessible Design Can Benefit Search Engine Listing

Search engine programs (commonly referred to as bots or spiders) walk the Web and follow hyperlinks on websites. An accessible website with descriptive page titles that is well organized with headings, lists, descriptive text for hyperlinks, and alternate text for images is more visible to search engine robots and may result in a better ranking.

Accessibility Is the Right Thing to Do

The Internet and the World Wide Web are such a pervasive part of our culture that accessibility is mandated by law in the United States. Section 508 of the Rehabilitation Act requires electronic and information technology, including web pages, used by federal agencies to be accessible to people with disabilities. At the time this was written, the Section 508 standards were undergoing revision; see http://www.access-board.gov for current information. The accessibility recommendations presented in this text are intended to satisfy the Section 508 standards and the Web Content Accessibility Guidelines 2.0 (WCAG 2.0) recommended by the W3C's Web Accessibility Initiative (WAI). The following four principles are essential to conformance with WCAG 2.0: **P**erceivable, **O**perable, **U**nderstandable, and **R**obust, referred to by the acronym **POUR**.

1. Content must be **Perceivable**. Perceivable content is easy to see or hear. Any graphic or multimedia content should be available in a text format, such as text descriptions for images, closed captions for videos, and transcripts for audio.

2. Interface components in the content must be **Operable**. Operable content has navigation forms, or other interactive features that can be used or operated with either a mouse or a keyboard. Multimedia content should be designed to avoid flashing, which may cause a seizure.

3. Content and controls must be **Understandable**. Understandable content is easy to read, organized in a consistent manner, and provides helpful error messages when appropriate.

4. Content should be **Robust** enough to work with current and future user agents, including assistive technologies. Robust content is written to follow W3C recommendations and should be compatible with multiple operating systems, browsers, and assistive technologies such as screen reader applications.

The WCAG 2.0 Quick Reference in Appendix E contains a brief list of guidelines for designing accessible web pages. See http://www.w3.org/TR/WCAG20/Overview for a detailed description of the WCAG 2.0 guidelines. These guidelines are segmented into three levels of conformance: Level A, Level AA, and Level AAA. In addition to satisfying the Section 508 guidelines, the accessibility recommendations discussed in this textbook are also intended to fully satisfy the WCAG 2.0 Level AA (includes Level A) guidelines and partially satisfy the Level AAA guidelines. Visit http://www.w3.org/WAI/WCAG20/quickref for an interactive checklist of these guidelines. Developing accessible web pages is an important aspect of web design. WebAIM has created a WCAG 2.0 checklist with helpful tips at http://webaim.org/standards/wcag/checklist. The University of Toronto (http://achecker.ca/checker/index.php) provides a free accessibility validation service.

As you work through this book, you'll learn to include accessibility features as you create practice pages. You've already discovered the importance of the title tag, heading tags, descriptive text for hyperlinks, and alternate text for images in Chapters 2, 3, and 4. You're well on your way to creating accessible web pages!

5.5 Writing for the Web

Long-winded sentences and explanations are often found in academic textbooks and romance novels, but they really are not appropriate on a web page. Large blocks of text and long paragraphs are difficult to read on the Web. The following suggestions will help to increase the readability of your web pages.

Organize Your Content

According to web usability expert Jakob Neilsen, people don't really read web pages; they scan them. Organize the text content on your pages to be quickly scanned. Be concise. Use headings, subheadings, brief paragraphs, and unordered lists to organize web page content so that it is easy to read and visitors can quickly find what they need.

Also be aware of line length—use white space and multiple columns if possible. Look ahead to Figure 5.15 for examples of text placement on a web page. While it's fine to center headings and navigation areas, avoid centering all of your text—a paragraph of centered text is more difficult to read than left-aligned text.

Text in Hyperlinks

Hyperlink key words or descriptive phrases; do not hyperlink entire sentences. Avoid use of the words "Click here" in hyperlinks because users know what to do by now. Also, be aware that an increasing number of people are using touch screens so they'll be selecting or tapping rather than clicking.

Reading Level

Match the reading level and style of writing to your target audience. Use vocabulary that they will be comfortable with. Juicy Studio offers a free online readability test at http://juicystudio.com/services/readability.php.

Use Common Fonts

Use common font typefaces such as Arial, Verdana, Georgia, or Times New Roman. Remember that the web page visitor must have the font installed on his or her computer in order for that particular font to appear. Your page may look great with Gill Sans Ultra Bold Condensed, but if your visitor doesn't have the font, the browser's default font will be displayed. Explore the list of "browser safe fonts" at http://www.ampsoft.net/webdesign-l/WindowsMacFonts.html.

Font Size and Weight

Be aware that fonts display smaller on a Mac than on a PC. Even within the PC platform, the default font size displayed by browsers may not be the same. Consider creating prototype pages of your font size settings to test on a variety of browsers and screen resolution settings. **Bold** or *emphasize* important text. However, be careful not to bold everything—that has the same effect as bolding nothing.

Font Color Contrast

Use appropriate color combinations. Newbie web designers sometimes choose color combinations for web pages that they would never dream of using in their wardrobe. An easy way to choose colors that contrast well and look good together is to select colors from an image or logo that you will use for your site.

Spelling and Grammar

Unfortunately, many websites contain misspelled words. Most web authoring tools such as Adobe Dreamweaver have built-in spell checkers; consider using this feature. Finally, be sure that you proofread and test your site thoroughly. It's very helpful if you can find web developer buddies—you check their sites and they check yours. It's always easier to see someone else's mistake than your own.

5.6 Use of Color

Choosing Colors

You may be wondering how to select colors to display on web pages. One easy way to choose colors is to use a monochromatic color scheme—all shades or tints of the same color along with neutrals such as white, black, and/or gray. Try the Color Blender at http://meyerweb.com/eric/tools/color-blend to select colors for a monochromatic color scheme. Another way to create a color scheme is to base it on a photograph or image. If you have a favorite color and would like to create a color scheme around it, visit one of the following sites that suggest color schemes:

- Colors on the Web: http://colorsontheweb.com/colorwizard.asp
- Kuler: http://kuler.adobe.com
- Lee Street Management: http://www.leestreet.com/QuickColor.swf
- Color Scheme Designer: http://colorschemedesigner.com
- ColorJack: http://www.colorjack.com/articles/color_formulas.html

Accessibility and Color

While color can help you create a compelling web page, keep in mind that not all of your visitors will see or be able to distinguish between colors. Some visitors will use a screen reader and will not experience your colors, so your information must be clearly conveyed even if the colors cannot be viewed.

Focus on Accessibility

Your color choices can be crucial. For example, red text on a blue background, as shown in Figure 5.9, is usually difficult for everyone to read. Also avoid using a red and green color scheme or a brown and purple color scheme because individuals with color-deficient vision may have difficulty differentiating the colors. According to Vischeck (http://www.vischeck.com/vischeck), about 1 out of 20 people experience some type of color perception deficiency. Visit http://www.vischeck.com/vischeck/vischeckURL.php to simulate how a person with a color deficiency experiences the colors on a web page. White, black, and shades of blue and yellow are easier for most people to discern.

Can you read this easily?

Figure 5.9
Some color combinations are difficult to read

Choose background and text colors with a high amount of contrast. The WCAG 2.0 guidelines recommend a contrast ratio of 4.5:1 for standard text. If the text has a large font, the contrast ratio can be as low as 3:1. Jonathan Snook's online Colour Contrast Check at http://snook.ca/technical/colour_contrast/colour.html can help you to verify the contrast level of your text and background colors.

See Lighthouse International's website (http://lighthouse.org/accessibility/design/accessible-print-design/effective-color-contrast) for more information on the effective use of color. When choosing color, it's important to consider the preferences of your target audience. The next sections focus on this aspect of web design.

Colors and Your Target Audience

Choose colors that will appeal to your target audience. Younger audiences, such as children and preteens, prefer bright, lively colors along with animation and interactivity. Individuals in their late teens and early twenties generally prefer dark background colors with occasional use of bright contrast, music, and dynamic navigation. For an older target audience, light backgrounds, well-defined images, and large text are appropriate.

If your goal is to appeal to everyone, follow the example of the popular Amazon.com and eBay websites in their use of color. These sites use a neutral white background with splashes of color to add interest and highlight page areas. Use of white as a background color was also reported by Jakob Nielsen and Marie Tahir in *Homepage Usability: 50 Websites Deconstructed*, a book that includes analyses of 50 top websites. According to this study, 84% of the sites used white as the background color and 72% used black as the text color. This maximized the contrast between text and background, providing maximum ease of reading.

You'll also notice that websites targeting "everyone" often include compelling visual graphics while providing the main content on a white background for maximum contrast.

 Checkpoint 5.1

1. List the four basic principles of design. View the home page of your school and describe how each principle is applied.

2. List three best practices used when writing text for the Web. The following text was found on an actual website. The company name and city have been changed. Apply the best practices used when writing for the Web and rewrite the following content:

   Acme, Inc. is a new laboratory instrument repair and service company. Our staff at this time has a combined total of 30 plus years of specimen preparation instrumentation service and repair.

   Our technicians are EPA refrigeration certified. We are fully insured and all of our workers are fully covered by workman's compensation insurance. A proof of insurance certificate can be provided upon request.

   We are located in Chicago, Illinois. Which houses shop repair facilities and offices. Acme, Inc. technicians are factory trained and equipped with the best diagnostic and repair equipment available.

We keep a separate file on every piece of equipment we work on. When a technician is sent on a repair, he has a file which lists the whole repair history on that piece of equipment. These files also help us answer any of your questions about past repairs.

Our rates are $100.00 per hour for Labor and Travel with a 2 hour minimum. $0.40 per mile and all related expenses PARTS are not included.

3. View the following three websites: Walmart (http://www.walmart.com), MuggleNet (http://www.mugglenet.com), and Sesame Street (http://www.sesamestreet.org/muppet). Describe the target audience for each site. How do their designs differ? Do the sites meet the needs of their target audiences?

5.7 Use of Graphics and Multimedia

As shown in Figure 5.1, a compelling graphic can be an engaging element on a web page. However, avoid relying on images to convey meaning. Some individuals may not be able to see your images and multimedia—they may be accessing your site with a mobile device or using an assistive technology such as a screen reader to visit your page. You may need to include text descriptions of important concepts or key points that a graphic image or multimedia file conveys. In this section, you'll explore recommended techniques for the use of graphics and multimedia on web pages.

File Size and Image Dimensions Matter

Keep both the file size and the dimensions of images as small as possible. Try to display only exactly what is needed to get your point across. Use a graphic application to crop an image or create a thumbnail image that links to a larger version of the image.

Antialiased/Aliased Text in Media

Antialiasing introduces intermediate colors to smooth jagged edges in digital images. Graphic applications such as Adobe Photoshop and Adobe Fireworks can be used to create antialiased text images. The graphic shown in Figure 5.10 was created using antialiasing. Figure 5.11 displays an image created without antialiasing; notice the jagged edges.

Antialiased

Figure 5.10 Antialiased text

Use Only Necessary Multimedia

Use animation and multimedia only if it will add value to your site. Don't include an animated GIF or a Flash animation (see Chapter 11) just because you have one. Limit the use of animated items. Only use animation if it makes the page more effective. Consider limiting how long an animation plays.

In general, younger audiences find animation more appealing than older audiences. However, a well-done navigation animation or an animation that describes a product or service could be appealing to almost any target group. Adobe Flash is frequently used on the Web to add visual interest and interactivity to web pages. You'll configure a Flash animation on a web page in Chapter 11.

Figure 5.11 This graphic was not antialiased: The letter "A" has a jagged look

Focus on Accessibility

Provide Alternate Text

As discussed in Chapter 4, each image on your web page should be configured with alternate text. Alternate text may be displayed by mobile devices, displayed briefly when an image is slow to load, and displayed when a browser is configured to not show images. Alternate text is also read aloud when a person with a disability uses a screen reader to access your website. In Figure 5.12, the Firefox Web Developer extension was used to display the alt text for an image on the National Park Service website (http://nps.gov).

To satisfy accessibility requirements, also provide alternate text equivalents for multimedia, such as video and audio. A text transcript of an audio recording can be useful not only to those with hearing challenges, but also to individuals who prefer to read when accessing new information. In addition, the text transcript may be accessed by a search engine and used when your site is categorized and indexed. Captions help to provide accessibility for video files. See Chapter 11 for more on accessibility and multimedia.

Figure 5.12 The alt text is displayed above the image by the Firefox Web Developer extension

5.8 Navigation Design

Ease of Navigation

Sometimes web developers are so close to their sites that they can't see the forest for the trees. A new visitor will wander onto the site and not know what to click or how to find the information he or she seeks. Clearly labeled navigation on each page is helpful. For maximum usability, the navigation should be in the same location on each page.

Navigation Bars

Clear **navigation bars**, either graphic or text based, make it obvious to website users where they are and where they can go next. It's quite common for site-wide navigation to be located either in a horizontal navigation bar placed under the logo or in a vertical navigation bar on the left side of the page. Less common is a vertical navigation bar on the right side of the page because this area can be cut off at lower screen resolutions.

Breadcrumb Navigation

Jakob Nielsen, a well-known usability and web design professional, favors what he calls a breadcrumb trail for larger sites, which indicates the path of web pages a visitor has viewed during the current session. A common design technique is to place the breadcrumb trail navigation at the top of the main content area that indicates the pages the visitor has viewed during a visit.

Using Graphics for Navigation

Focus on Accessibility

Sometimes graphics are used instead of text to provide navigation. When image hyperlinks instead of text hyperlinks provide the main navigation for the site, two techniques provide for accessibility:

- Each image element is configured with an alternate text description (see Chapter 4).
- The page is configured with text hyperlinks in the footer section.

Skip Repetitive Navigation

Focus on Accessibility

Provide a method to skip repetitive navigation links. It is easy for visitors without vision and mobility challenges to scan a web page and quickly focus on the page content. However, long, repetitive navigation bars quickly become tedious to access when utilizing a screen reader or a keyboard to visit a web page. Consider adding a "Skip navigation" or "Skip to content" hyperlink before your main navigation bar that links to a named fragment (see Chapter 7) at the beginning of the content section of your page. Figure 5.13 presents another way to implement the skip navigation feature. Although not immediately visible in the browser, visitors using a screen reader or a keyboard to tab through the page will immediately encounter the "Skip to main content" hyperlink in the upper-left side of the U.S. Department of Transportation web page (http://www.dot.gov).

Figure 5.13 Press the tab key to access the "Skip to content" link on the U.S. Department of Transportation website

Dynamic Navigation

In your experiences visiting websites you've probably encountered navigation menus that display additional options when your mouse cursor moves over an item. This is dynamic navigation, which provides a way to offer many choices to visitors while at the same time avoid overwhelming them. Instead of showing all the navigation links all the time, menu items are dynamically displayed (typically using a combination of HTML and CSS) as appropriate. The additional items are made available when a related top-level menu item has focus or is selected. Visit Dynamic Drive (http://www.dynamicdrive.com/dynamicindex1) for sample code that you can use to create dynamic navigation for your own web pages.

Site Map

Even with clear and consistent navigation, visitors sometimes may lose their way on large websites. A site map provides an outline of the organization of the website with hyperlinks to each major page. This can help visitors find another route to get to the information they seek, as shown in the Ready.gov website in Figure 5.14.

Site Search Feature

Note the search feature in the upper-right corner of the web page in Figure 5.14. This site search feature helps visitors to find information that is not apparent from the navigation or the site map.

Figure 5.14 This large site offers a site search feature and a site map to visitors

5.9 Page Layout Design

Wireframes and Page Layout

A **wireframe** is a sketch or blueprint of a web page that shows the structure (but not the detailed design) of basic page elements such as the logo, navigation, content, and footer. Wireframes are used as part of the design process to experiment with various page layouts, develop the structure and navigation of the site, and provide a basis for communication among project members. Note that the exact content (text, images, logo, and navigation) does not need to be placed in the wireframe diagram. Figure 5.15 depicts a diagram of a web page with a logo, navigation area, content area (with headings, subheadings, images, paragraphs, and unordered lists), and a footer area.

In Chapter 6, you'll learn how to use Cascading Style Sheets (CSS) to configure web pages with multiple columns. Sometimes the page layout for the home page is different from the page layout used for the content pages. Even when this is the case, a consistent logo and color scheme will produce a more cohesive website.

Figure 5.15 This wireframe page layout uses images and columns of various widths

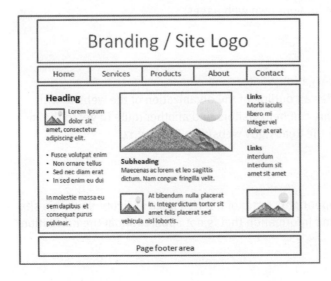

Page Layout Design Techniques

Now that you have been introduced to page layout, it's time to consider three popular techniques for web page layout design: ice, jello, and liquid.

Ice Design

The **ice design** technique is sometimes referred to as a solid or fixed design. The page hugs the left margin and has a fixed width. Websites that use this technique include Federal Student Aid website (http://studentaid.ed.gov) and the League for Innovation in the Community College website (http://www.league.org).

Jello Design

The **jello design** technique configures content that is centered and may be of a fixed width or a percentage width, such as 80%. Regardless of the screen resolution, the content is centered in the page with even margins on both sides. Websites that use this technique include Public Broadcasting Service (http://www.pbs.org), Office Depot (http://www.officedepot.com), and the State of California (http://www.ca.gov).

The **liquid design** technique results in a fluid web page with content that takes up 100% of the browser window regardless of the screen resolution. There is no empty margin on the left or right—the multicolumn content will flow to fill whatever size of window is used to display it. A disadvantage of this page layout is that at high screen resolutions the lines of text may extend quite far across the browser viewport and become more difficult to read. Websites using this technique include Amazon.com (http://www.amazon.com) and Moodle™ (http://moodle.org).

Websites designed using ice, jello, and liquid techniques can be found throughout the Web. Ice designs using a fixed-width layout give the web developer the most control over the page configuration but result in pages with large empty areas when viewed at higher screen resolutions. Liquid designs may become less readable when viewed at high screen resolutions because the page stretches to fill a wider area than originally intended by the developer. Jello designs are often used because the web pages are typically most pleasing to view on a variety of screen resolutions.

Design for the Mobile Web

Access to the Web from cell phones, smartphones, and tablets makes it possible to always be online. The research firm eMarketer (http://emarketer.com) predicts significant growth for mobile access to the Web, with a projected 134.3 million mobile Internet users by 2013. With this growth in mind, it's becoming more important to design web pages that are accessible and usable for your mobile visitors.

There are a few schools of thought on the best way to accomplish this, including developing a new mobile site with a .mobi TLD (see Chapter 1 to review TLDs), creating a separate website hosted within your current domain that is targeted for mobile users, and using CSS to create a style sheet along with new CSS3 media queries to configure your current website for display on mobile devices. You'll practice using these CSS coding techniques in Chapter 7. Whichever method you choose to use, be mindful of the following considerations when designing mobile websites.

Figure 5.16 A text-intensive mobile site features hyperlinks to frequently accessed information

- **Small screen size.** Common mobile phone screen sizes include 320×240, 320×480, 480×800, and 640×960 (Apple iPhone 4). Even on one of the large phones, that's not a lot of pixels to work with!

- **Low bandwidth (slow connection speed).** Although the use of faster 3G and 4G networks is becoming more widespread, many mobile users experience slow connection speeds. Images usually take up quite a bit of bandwidth on a typical website. Depending on the service plan, some mobile web visitors may be paying per kilobyte. Be aware of this and eliminate unnecessary images.

- **Font, color, and media issues.** Mobile devices may have very limited font support. Configure font size using ems or percentages. Include generic font family names in your stylesheet. Mobile devices may have very limited color support. Choose colors carefully to maximize contrast. Many mobile devices do not support Adobe Flash media.

- **Awkward controls; limited processor and memory.** While smartphones with touch controls are becoming more popular, many mobile users will not have access to mouse-like controls. Provide keyboard access to assist these users. Although mobile device processing speed and available memory are improving, they still cannot compare to the resources of a desktop computer. While this won't be an issue for the websites you create for exercises in this textbook, be mindful of this issue in the future as you continue to develop your skills and create web applications.

- **Functionality.** Provide easy access to your website's features with prominent hyperlinks or a prominent search button. The mobile site for the White House (Figure 5.16) is quite text-intensive with links to featured content, a search feature, and a prominent link to the regular (full) website.

5.10 More Design Considerations

Load Time

The last thing you want to happen is for your visitors to leave your page before it has even finished loading! Make sure your pages load as quickly as possible. Web usability expert Jakob Nielsen reports that visitors will often leave a page after waiting more than 10 seconds. It takes just less than 9 seconds at 56Kbps for a browser to display a web page and associated files of 60KB. It's a good practice to try to limit the total file size of a website's home page and all of its associated images and media files to less than 60KB. However, it's common to go over this recommended limit for content pages when you're sure that your visitors will be interested enough to wait to see what your site is presenting.

According to a recent study by the PEW Research Center's Internet and American Life Project, the percentage of U.S. Internet users with a broadband (cable, DSL, and so on) connection at home or at work is rising. Sixty-six percent of adult Americans have access to broadband at home. Even with the trend of increasing bandwidth available to your visitors, keep in mind that 34% of households do not have broadband Internet access. Visit Pew Internet (http://www.pewinternet.org) for the most up-to-date statistics. The chart shown in Figure 5.17 compares file sizes and connection speed download

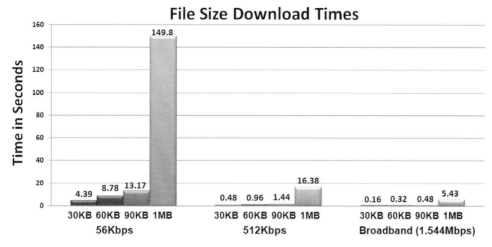

Figure 5.17 File size download times and Internet connection speeds

times, and was created using a File Transfer Time–Data Transfer Speed Calculator (http://www.t1shopper.com/tools/calculate/downloadcalculator.php).

One method to help determine whether the load time of your page is acceptable is to view the size of your website files in Windows Explorer or Mac Finder. Calculate the total file size of your web page plus all of its associated images and media. If the total file size for a single page and its associated files is more than 60KB and it is likely that your target audience may not be using broadband access, take a closer look at your design. Consider whether you really need to use all of the images to convey your message. The **perceived load time** is the amount of time that a web page visitor is aware of waiting while your page is loading. Because visitors often leave a website if a page takes too long to load, it is important to shorten their perception of waiting. A common technique is to shorten the perceived loading time by optimizing images, using CSS Sprites (see Chapter 7), and breaking a long page into multiple smaller pages. Popular web authoring tools such as Microsoft Expression Web and Adobe Dreamweaver will calculate load time at various transmission speeds.

Above the Fold

Placing important information **above the fold** is a technique borrowed from the newspaper industry. When newspapers are placed on counters and in vending machines to be sold, the portion above the fold on the page is viewable. Publishers noticed that more papers were sold when the most important, attention-getting information was placed in this location. You may use this technique to attract visitors to your web pages and to keep them there. At the most popular screen resolution of 1024×768, the amount of screen viewable above the fold (after accounting for browser menus and controls) is about 600 pixels. Avoid placing important information and navigation on the far right side because this area may not be initially displayed by browsers at some screen resolutions.

White Space

This term **white space** is also borrowed from the publishing industry. Placing blank or white space (because paper is usually white) in areas around blocks of text increases the readability of the page. Placing white space around graphics helps them to stand out. Allow for some blank space between blocks of text and images. How much is adequate? It depends—experiment until the page is likely to look appealing to your target audience.

Avoid Horizontal Scrolling

In order to make it easy for visitors to view and use your web pages, avoid creating pages that are too wide to be displayed in the browser window. These pages require the user to scroll horizontally. Currently, the most popular screen resolution is 1024×768. Cameron Moll (http://www.cameronmoll.com/archives/001220.html) suggests that the optimal web page width for display at 1024×768 screen resolution is 960 pixels. Be mindful that not all of your web page visitors will maximize their browser viewport.

Browsers

Unless you are designing for an intranet within an organization, expect your website to be visited using a wide variety of browsers. Just because your web page looks great in your favorite browser doesn't automatically mean that all browsers will render it well. A recent survey by Net Market Share (http://marketshare.hitslink.com/browser-market-share.aspx?qprid=0&qpcustomd=0) indicates that while Microsoft Internet Explorer is still the most popular web browser, the Firefox open-source browser and the Google Chrome browser have been gaining ground. The survey reports that about 54% of website visitors use Internet Explorer (including versions 6 through 9), 22% use Firefox, 13% use Google Chrome, 7% use Safari, 2% use Opera, 1% use the Opera Mini mobile browser, and the remaining 1% use a variety of browsers, including Blackberry, Playstation, and Konqueror.

Apply the principle of **progressive enhancement**. Design the site so that it looks good in browsers commonly used by your target audience and then add enhancements with CSS3 and/or HTML5 for display in modern browsers. Always try to test your pages with the most popular versions of browsers on desktop PC and Mac operating systems. At the time of this writing, these are Internet Explorer 8, Internet Explorer 7, Firefox 4, Google Chrome 11, and Safari. Many web page components, including default text size and default margin size, are different among browsers, browser versions, and operating systems. Also try to test your site on other types of devices such as tablets and smart-phones. Opera offers free simulators for the Opera Mini mobile browser at http://www.opera.com/mobile/demo.

Screen Resolution

Your website visitors will use a variety of screen resolutions. A recent survey by Net Market Share (http://marketshare.hitslink.com/report.aspx?qprid=17) reported the use of more than 90 different screen resolutions, with the top four being 1024×768 (with 19.6%), 1280×800 (15%), 1366×768 (13%), and 1280×1024 (8%). A typical smartphone screen resolution of 320×480 was in use by about 2% of web visitors. Mobile use will vary with the purpose of the website, but it is expected to grow as the use of smart-phones and tablets increases. Be aware that mobile devices have low screen resolution, such as 240×320, 320×480, or 480×800. Popular tablet devices offer a higher screen resolution: Apple iPad (1024×768), Motorola Xoom (1280×800), Samsun Galaxy Tab (1200×800), and Blackberry Playbook (1024×600). In Chapter 7, you'll explore CSS media queries, which is a technique for configuring a web page to display well on various screen resolutions.

5.11 Web Design Best Practices Checklist

Table 5.1 contains a checklist of recommended web design practices. Use this as a guide to help you create easy-to-read, usable, and accessible web pages.

Table 5.1 Web design best practices checklist

Page Layout		
❏	1.	Appealing to target audience
❏	2.	Consistent site header/logo
❏	3.	Consistent navigation area
❏	4.	Informative page title that includes the company/organization/site name
❏	5.	Page footer area—copyright, last update, contact e-mail address
❏	6.	Good use of basic design principles: repetition, contrast, proximity, and alignment
❏	7.	Displays without horizontal scrolling at 1024×768 and higher resolutions
❏	8.	Balance of text/graphics/white space on page
❏	9.	Good contrast between text and background
❏	10.	Repetitive information (header/logo and navigation) takes up no more than one-quarter to one-third of the browser window at 1024×768 resolution
❏	11.	Home page has compelling, interesting information above the fold (before scrolling down) at 1024×768 resolution
❏	12.	Home page downloads within 10 seconds on dial-up connection

Browser Compatibility		
❏	1.	Displays on current versions of Internet Explorer (8+)
❏	2.	Displays on current versions of Firefox (4+)
❏	3.	Displays on current versions of Google Chrome
❏	4.	Displays on current versions of Safari (both Mac and Windows)
❏	5.	Displays on current versions of Opera (10+)
❏	6.	Displays on mobile devices

Navigation		
❏	1.	Main navigation links are clearly and consistently labeled
❏	2.	Navigation is easy to use for target audience
❏	3.	When the main navigation consists of images and/or multimedia, the page footer area contains plain-text hyperlinks (accessibility)
❏	4.	Navigation aids (such as site map, skip to content link, and/or breadcrumbs) are used
❏	5.	All navigation hyperlinks work

(Continued)

Table 5.1 (*Continued*)

Color and Graphics

❏	1.	Use of different colors in page background/text is limited to a maximum of three or four plus neutrals
❏	2.	Color is used consistently
❏	3.	Background and text colors have good contrast
❏	4.	Color is not used alone to convey meaning (accessibility)
❏	5.	Use of color and graphics enhances rather than detracts from the site
❏	6.	Graphics are optimized and do not slow download significantly
❏	7.	Each graphic used serves a clear purpose
❏	8.	Image tags use the alt attribute to configure alternate text replacement (accessibility)
❏	9.	Animated images do not distract from the site and either do not repeat or only repeat a few times

Multimedia (see Chapter 11)

❏	1.	Each audio/video/Flash file used serves a clear purpose
❏	2.	The audio/video/Flash files used enhance rather than distract from the site
❏	3.	Captions or transcripts are provided for each audio or video file used (accessibility)
❏	4.	The file size is indicated for audio or video file downloads
❏	5.	Hyperlinks to downloads for media plug-ins are provided

Content Presentation

❏	1.	Common fonts such as Arial, Verdana, Georgia, or Times New Roman are used
❏	2.	Writing techniques for the Web are used: headings, bullet points, short paragraphs, and so on
❏	3.	Fonts, font sizes, and font colors are consistently used
❏	4.	Content provides meaningful, useful information
❏	5.	Content is organized in a consistent manner
❏	6.	Information is easy to find (minimal clicks)
❏	7.	Timeliness: The date of the last revision and/or copyright date is accurate
❏	8.	Content does not include outdated material
❏	9.	Content is free of typographical and grammatical errors
❏	10.	Avoids the use of "Click here" when writing text for hyperlinks
❏	11.	Hyperlinks use a consistent set of colors to indicate visited/nonvisited status
❏	12.	Alternate text equivalent to content is provided for graphics and media (accessibility)

Functionality

❏	1.	All internal hyperlinks work
❏	2.	All external hyperlinks work
❏	3.	All forms (see Chapter 9) function as expected
❏	4.	No JavaScript (see Chapters 11 and 14) errors are generated by the pages

Table 5.1 (*Continued*)

		Accessibility
❏	1.	When the main navigation consists of images and/or multimedia, the page footer area contains plain-text hyperlinks
❏	2.	Color is not used alone to convey meaning
❏	3.	Image tags use the alt attribute to configure alternate text replacement
❏	4.	Captions or transcripts are provided for each audio or video file used
❏	5.	Attributes designed to improve accessibility, such as alt, title, and summary, are used where appropriate
❏	6.	If the site uses frames, frame titles are configured and meaningful content is placed in the no-frames area
❏	7.	To assist screen readers, the spoken language of the page is indicated with the HTML element's lang attribute

Note: Web Design Best Practices Checklist is copyrighted by Terry Morris (http://terrymorris.net). Used by permission.

 # Checkpoint 5.2

1. View the home page of your school. Use the Web Design Best Practices Checklist (Table 5.1) to evaluate the page. Describe the results.

2. View your favorite website (or a URL provided by your instructor). Maximize and resize the browser window. Decide whether the site uses ice, jello, or liquid design. Adjust the screen resolution on your monitor to a different resolution than you normally use. Does the website look similar or very different? Offer two recommendations for improving the design of the site.

3. List three best practices used when placing graphics on web pages. View the home page of your school. Describe the use of web graphic design best practices on this page.

Chapter Summary

This chapter introduced recommended web design practices. The choices you make in the use of page layout, color, graphics, text, and media depend on your particular target audience. Developing an accessible web site should be the goal of every web developer. Visit the textbook website at http://www.webdevfoundations.net for examples, the links listed in this chapter, and updated information.

Key Terms

above the fold
alignment
antialiased text
breadcrumb trails
chunking
contrast
hierarchical organization
horizontal scrolling
ice design
jello design
linear organization

liquid design
load time
navigation bar
page layout
perceived load time
POUR
progressive enhancement
proximity
random organization
repetition
screen resolution

site map
site search
skip to content
target audience
WAI (Web Accessibility Initiative)
WCAG 2.0 (Web Content
    Accessibility Guidelines 2.0)
white space
wireframe

Review Questions

Multiple Choice

1. Which of the following would a consistent website design *not* have?
   a. a similar navigation area on each content page
   b. the same fonts on each content page
   c. a different background color on each page
   d. the same logo in the same location on each content page

2. Which of the following are the three most common methods for organizing websites?
   a. horizontal, vertical, and diagonal
   b. hierarchical, linear, and random
   c. accessible, readable, and maintainable
   d. none of the above

3. Which of the following is not a web design recommended practice?
   a. Design your site to be easy to navigate.
   b. Colorful pages appeal to everyone.
   c. Design your pages to load quickly.
   d. Limit the use of animated items.

4. Which of the following are the four principles of the Web Content Accessibility Guidelines?
   a. repetition, contrast, proximity, and alignment
   b. perceivable, operable, understandable, and robust
   c. accessible, readable, maintainable, and reliable
   d. hierarchical, linear, random, and sequential

5. Which of the following is a sketch or blueprint of a web page that shows the structure (but not the detailed design) of basic page elements?
   a. drawing
   b. HTML code
   c. site map
   d. wireframe

6. Which of the following are influenced by the intended or target audience of a site?
   a. the amount of color used on the site
   b. the font size and styles used on the site
   c. the overall look and feel of the site
   d. all of the above

7. Which of the following recommended design practices apply to a website that uses images for its main site navigation?
   a. Provide alternative text for the images.
   b. Place text links at the bottom of the page.
   c. Both a and b.
   d. No special considerations are needed.

8. Which of the following is known as white space?
   a. the empty screen area around blocks of text and images
   b. the background color of white used for a page
   c. configuring the color of the text to be white
   d. none of the above

9. Which of the following should you do when creating text hyperlinks?
   a. Create the entire sentence as a hyperlink.
   b. Include the words "Click here" in your text.
   c. Use a key phrase as a hyperlink.
   d. none of the above

10. Which of the following is the design technique used to create pages that stretch to fill the browser window?
   a. ice
   b. liquid
   c. jello
   d. none of the above

Fill in the Blank

11. The most common structure used for commercial websites is _____ organization.

12. All browsers and browser versions _____ display web pages in exactly the same way.

13. The _____ is a group whose mission is to create guidelines and standards for web accessibility.

Short Answer

14. Describe an issue to consider when designing for the mobile Web.

15. Describe one of the four principles of WCAG 2.0.

Hands-On Exercises

1. **Web Design Evaluation.** As you read Chapter 5, you explored web page design, including navigation design techniques and the design principles of repetition, contrast, proximity, and alignment. You'll review and evaluate screenshots of web pages in this hands-on exercise.

   Select a website to review. Provide the following information:
   a. Indicate the type(s) of navigation evident.
   b. Describe how the design principles of repetition, contrast, proximity, and alignment are applied. Be specific.
   c. Complete the Web Design Best Practices Checklist (see Table 5.1).

2. Practice creating site maps for the following situations.

   a. Doug Kowalski is a freelance photographer who specializes in nature photography. He often gets contract work shooting photos for textbooks and journals. Doug would like a website that showcases his talents and provides publishers with an easy way to contact him. He would like a home page, a few pages with samples of his nature photographs, and a contact page. Create a site map based on this scenario.

   b. Mary Ruarez owns a business, named Just Throw Me, which sells handcrafted specialty pillows. She currently sells at craft fairs and local gift shops, but would like to expand her business to the Web. She would like a website with a home page, a page that describes her products, a page for each of her seven pillow styles, and an order page. She has been advised that because she is collecting information from individuals, a page describing her privacy policy would be a good idea. Create a site map based on this scenario.

c. Prakesh Khan owns a dog-grooming business named A Dog's Life. He would like a website that includes a home page, a page about grooming services, a page with a map to his shop, a contact page, and a section that explains how to select a good pet. The content for the part of the website on selecting a pet will be a step-by-step presentation. Create a site map based on this scenario.

3. Practice creating wireframe page layouts for the following situations. Use the style for page layout composition shown in Figure 5.15 where places for logo, navigation, text, and images are indicated. Do not worry about exact wording or exact images.

a. Create sample wireframe page layouts for Doug Kowalski's photography business, described in 2(a). Create a wireframe layout for the home page. Create another wireframe page layout for the content pages.

b. Create sample wireframe page layouts for the Just Throw Me website described in 2(b). Create a wireframe layout for the home page. Create another wireframe page layout for the content pages.

c. Create sample wireframe page layouts for the A Dog's Life website described in 2(c). Create a wireframe layout for the home page and the regular content pages. Create another wireframe page layout for the presentation pages.

4. Choose two sites that are similar in nature or have a similar target audience, such as the following:

- Amazon.com (http://www.amazon.com) and Barnes & Noble (http://www.bn.com)
- Kohl's (http://www.kohls.com) and JCPenney (http://www.jcpenney.com)
- CNN (http://www.cnn.com) and MSNBC (http://www.msnbc.com)

Describe how the two sites you chose to review exhibit the design principles of repetition, contrast, proximity, and alignment.

5. Choose two sites that are similar in nature or have a similar target audience, such as the following:

- Crate & Barrel (http://www.crateandbarrel.com) and Pottery Barn (http://www.potterybarn.com)
- Harper College (http://goforward.harpercollege.edu) and College of Lake County (http://www.clcillinois.edu)
- Chicago Bears (http://www.chicagobears.com) and Green Bay Packers (http://www.packers.com)

Describe how the two sites you chose to review exhibit web design best practices. How would you improve these sites? Recommend three improvements for each site.

6. How would you design a home page for the following businesses using the ice design technique? Create a wireframe page layout for the home page.

a. See 2(a) for the description of Doug Kowalski's photography business.

b. See 2(b) for the description of Just Throw Me.

c. See 2(c) for the description of A Dog's Life.

7. How would you design a home page for the following businesses using the jello design technique? Create a wireframe page layout for the home page.

a. See 2(a) for the description of Doug Kowalski's photography business.

b. See 2(b) for the description of Just Throw Me.

c. See 2(c) for the description of A Dog's Life.

8. How would you design a home page for the following businesses using the liquid design technique? Create a wireframe page layout for the home page.

a. See 2(a) for the description of Doug Kowalski's photography business.

b. See 2(b) for the description of Just Throw Me.

c. See 2(c) for the description of A Dog's Life.

Web Research

This chapter introduced techniques that are useful when writing for the Web. Explore this topic further. Visit the resources listed below to get started.

- Writing for the Web: http://www.useit.com/papers/webwriting
- Writing Well for the Web: http://www.webreference.com/content/writing
- Web Writing that Works!: http://www.webwritingthatworks.com/CGuideJOBAID.htm
- A List Apart: 10 Tips on Writing the Living Web: http://www.alistapart.com/articles/writeliving
- The Yahoo! Style Guide: http://styleguide.yahoo.com/writing

If these resources are no longer available, search the Web for information on "writing for the Web." Read one or more articles. Select five techniques that you would like to share with others. Write a one-page summary of your findings. Include the URLs of your resources.

Focus on Web Design

1. This chapter discusses recommended web design practices. Sometimes it is helpful to learn about good design by examining poor design. Visit Web Pages that Suck (http://www.webpagesthatsuck.com) and read about their examples of poor design. Think about some websites that you have visited. Do any of them have similar qualities? Find two websites that use poor web design practices. Write a one-page report that includes an introduction about the design practices that are not followed at the websites, a link to each site, and a description of how each site has practiced poor website design.

2. Visit any of the websites referenced in this chapter that interest you. Write a one-page summary and reaction to the website you chose to visit. Address the following topics:

- What is the purpose of the site?
- Who is the intended audience?
- Do you think the site reaches the intended audience?
- List three examples of how this website uses recommended web design guidelines.
- How could this site be improved?

WEBSITE CASE STUDY
Web Design Best Practices

Each of the following case studies continues throughout most of this textbook. In this chapter, you are asked to analyze the design of the websites.

JavaJam Coffee House

See Chapter 2 for an introduction to the JavaJam Coffee House case study. Figure 2.25 shows a site map for the JavaJam website. Three pages for this site were created in earlier chapters. In this case study, you will review the site for recommended web design practices.

Hands-On Practice Case

1. Examine the site map in Figure 2.25. What type of site organization is used for the JavaJam website? Is it the most appropriate organization for the site? Why or why not?

2. Review the recommended web design practices from this chapter. Use the Web Design Best Practices Checklist (Table 5.1) to evaluate the JavaJam site that you created in earlier chapters. Cite three design practices that have been well implemented. Cite three design practices that could be implemented in a better way. How else would you improve the website?

Fish Creek Animal Hospital

See Chapter 2 for an introduction to the Fish Creek Animal Hospital case study. Figure 2.29 shows a site map for the Fish Creek website. Three pages for the site were created in earlier chapters. In this case study, you will review the site for recommended web design practices.

Hands-On Practice Case

1. Examine the site map in Figure 2.29. What type of site organization is used for the Fish Creek website? Is it the most appropriate organization for the site? Why or why not?

2. Review the recommended web design practices from this chapter. Use the Web Design Best Practices Checklist (Table 5.1) to evaluate the Fish Creek site that you created in earlier chapters. Cite three design practices that have been well implemented. Cite three design practices that could be implemented in a better way. How else would you improve the website?

Pacific Trails Resort

See Chapter 2 for an introduction to the Pacific Trails Resort case study. Figure 2.33 shows a site map for the Pacific Trails Resort website. Three pages for the site were created in earlier chapters. During this case study, you will review the site for recommended web design practices.

Hands-On Practice Case

1. Examine the site map in Figure 2.33. What type of site organization is used for the Pacific Trails Resort website? Is it the most appropriate organization for the site? Why or why not?

2. Review the recommended web design practices from this chapter. Use the Web Design Best Practices Checklist (Table 5.1) to evaluate the Pacific Trails Resort site that you created in earlier chapters. Cite three design practices that have been well implemented. Cite three design practices that could be implemented in a better way. How else would you improve the website?

Prime Properties

See Chapter 2 for an introduction to the Prime Properties case study. Figure 2.37 shows a site map for the Prime Properties website. Three pages for the site were created in earlier chapters. During this case study, you will review the site for recommended web design practices.

Hands-On Practice Case

1. Examine the site map in Figure 2.37. What type of site organization is used for the Prime Properties website? Is it the most appropriate organization for the site? Why or why not?

2. Review the recommended web design practices from this chapter. Use the Web Design Best Practices Checklist (Table 5.1) to evaluate the Prime Properties site you created in earlier chapters. Cite three design practices that have been well implemented. Cite three design practices that could be implemented in a better way. How else would you improve the website?

Web Project

The purpose of this Web Project case study is to design a website using recommended design practices. Your website might be about a favorite hobby or subject, your family, a church or club you belong to, a company a friend owns, or the company you work for. Your website will contain a home page and at least six (but no more than ten) content pages. Complete the following documents: Topic Approval, Site Map, and Page Layout Design. You will not develop web pages at this point; you will complete that task in later chapters.

Hands-On Practice Case

1. **Web Project Topic Approval.** The topic of your website must be approved by your instructor. Provide the following information:

   - What is the purpose of the website?

     List the reason you are creating the website.

   - What do you want the website to accomplish?

     List the goals you have for the website.

     Describe what needs to happen for you to consider your website a success.

- Who is your target audience?

  Describe your target audience by age, gender, socioeconomic characteristics, and so on.

- What opportunity or issue is your website addressing?

  For example, your website might address the opportunity to provide information about a topic to others or create an initial web presence for a company.

- What type of content might be included in your website?

  Describe the type of text, graphics, and media you will need for the website.

- List the URLs for at least two related or similar websites found on the Web.

2. **Web Project Site Map.** Use the drawing feature of a word processing program, a graphics application, or a paper and pencil to create a site map of your website that shows the hierarchy of pages and relationships between pages.

3. **Web Project Page Layout Design.** Use the drawing feature of a word processing program, a graphics application, or paper and pencil to create wireframe page layouts for the home page and content pages of your site. Unless otherwise directed by your instructor, use the style for page layout composition shown in Figure 5.15. Indicate where the logo, navigation, text, and images will be located. Do not worry about exact wording or exact images.

Page Layout

Chapter Objectives   In this chapter, you will learn how to . . .

- Describe and apply the CSS Box Model

- Configure margins with CSS

- Configure float with CSS

- Configure relative and absolute positioning with CSS

- Create two-column page layouts using CSS

- Configure navigation in unordered lists and style with CSS

- Add interactivity to hyperlinks with CSS pseudo-classes

- Configure web pages with HTML5 structural elements, including section, header, hgroup, nav, aside, and footer

You've already configured the centered page layout with CSS.
We'll add to your toolbox of CSS page layout techniques in this chapter, starting with the box model. You'll explore floating and positioning elements with CSS. You'll be introduced to using CSS to add interactivity to hyperlinks with pseudo-classes and use CSS to style navigation in unordered lists. You will practice coding new HTML5 elements that structure web page content.

6.1 The Box Model

Each element in a document is considered to be a rectangular box. As shown in Figure 6.1, this box consists of a content area surrounded by padding, a border, and margins. This is known as the **box model**.

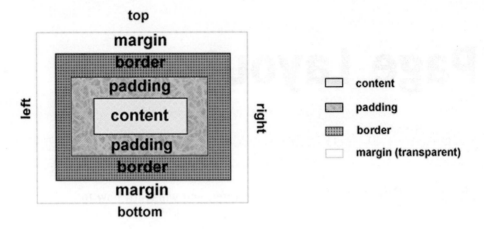

Figure 6.1 The CSS box model

Content

The content area can consist of a combination of text and web page elements such as images, paragraphs, headings, lists, and so on. The visible width of the element on a web page is the total of the content width, the padding width, and the border width. However, the `width` **property** only configures the actual width of the content; it does not include any padding, border, or margin.

Padding

The padding area is between the content and the border. The default padding value is zero. When the background of an element is configured, the background is applied to both the padding and the content areas. Use the `padding` property to configure an element's padding (refer to Chapter 4).

Border

The border area is between the padding and the margin. The default border has a value of 0 and does not display. Use the `border` property to configure an element's border (refer to Chapter 4).

Margin

The margin determines the empty space between the element and any adjacent elements. The solid line in Figure 6.1 that contains the margin area does not display on a web page.

The Margin Property

Use the **margin property** to configure margins on all sides of an element. The margin is always transparent—the background color of the web page or parent element shows in this area. Browsers have default margin values set for the web page document and for certain elements such as paragraphs, headings, forms, and so on. Use the margin property to override the default browser values.

To configure the size of the margin, use a numeric value (px or em). To eliminate the margin, configure it to 0 (with no unit). Use the value `auto` to indicate that the browser should calculate the margin. In Chapters 3 and 4, you used `margin-left: auto;` and `margin-right: auto;` to configure a centered page layout. Table 6.1 shows CSS properties that configure margins.

Table 6.1 Configuring margins with CSS

Property	Description and Common Values
margin	Shorthand notation to configure the margin surrounding an element
	A numeric value (px or em) or percentage; for example, `margin: 10px;`
	The value `auto` causes the browser to automatically calculate the margin for the element
	Two numeric values (px or em) or percentages: The first value configures the top margin and bottom margin, and the second value configures the left margin and right margin; for example, `margin: 20px 10px;`
	Three numeric values (px or em) or percentages: The first value configures the top margin, the second value configures the left margin and right margin, and the third value configures the bottom margin; for example, `margin: 10px 20px 5px;`
	Four numeric values (px or em) or percentages; the values configure the margin in the following order: `margin-top`, `margin-right`, `margin-bottom`, and `margin-left`; for example, `margin: 10px 30px 20px 5px;`
margin-bottom	Bottom margin; a numeric value (px or em), percentage, or `auto`
margin-left	Left margin; a numeric value (px or em), percentage, or `auto`
margin-right	Right margin; a numeric value (px or em), percentage, or `auto`
margin-top	Top margin; a numeric value (px or em), percentage, or `auto`

The Box Model in Action

The web page shown in Figure 6.2 (chapter6/box.html in the student files) depicts the box model in action with an h1 and a div element.

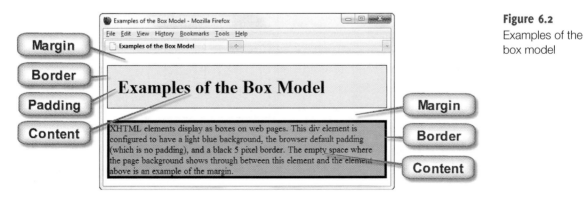

Figure 6.2
Examples of the box model

- The h1 element is configured to have a light-blue background, 20 pixels of padding (the space between the content and the border), and a black, 1 pixel border.

- The empty space where the white web page background shows through is the margin. When two vertical margins meet (such as between the h1 element and the div element), the browser collapses the margin size to be the larger of the two margin values instead of applying both margins.

- The div element has a medium-blue background; the browser default padding (which is no padding); and a black, 5 pixel border.

You will get more practice using the box model in this chapter. Feel free to experiment with the box model and the chapter6/box.html file.

6.2 Normal Flow

Browsers render your web page code line by line in the order it appears in the .html document. This processing is called normal flow. **Normal flow** displays the elements on the page in the order they appear in the web page source code.

Figures 6.3 and 6.4 each display two div elements that contain text content. Let's take a closer look. Figure 6.3 shows a screenshot of two div elements placed one after another on a web page. In Figure 6.4, the boxes are nested inside each other. In both cases, the browser used normal flow (the default) and displayed the elements in the order that they appeared in the source code. As you've worked through the exercises in the previous chapters, you created web pages that the browser has rendered using normal flow.

You'll practice this a bit more in the next Hands-On Practice. Then, later in the chapter, you'll experiment with CSS positioning and float to configure the flow, or placement, of elements on a web page.

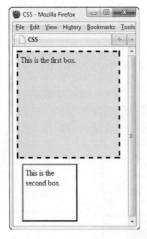

Figure 6.3 Two div elements

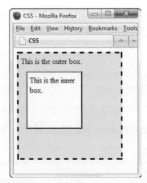

Figure 6.4 Nested div elements

Hands-On Practice 6.1

You will explore the box model and normal flow in this Hands-On Practice as you work with the web pages shown in Figure 6.3 and Figure 6.4.

Practice with Normal Flow

Launch a text editor and open chapter6/starter1.html in the student files. Save the file with the name box1.html. Edit the body of the web page and add the following code to configure two div elements:

```
<div class="div1">
This is the first box.
</div>
<div class="div2">
This is the second box.
</div>
```

Now let's add embedded CSS in the head section to configure the "boxes." Add a new style rule for a class named div1 to configure a light-blue background, dashed border, width of 200 pixels, height of 200 pixels, and 5 pixels of padding. The code is

```
.div1 { width: 200px;
        height: 200px;
        background-color: #D1ECFF;
        border: 3px dashed #000000;
        padding: 5px; }
```

Create a style rule for a class named div2 to configure a width and height of 100 pixels, white background color, ridged border, 10 pixel margin, and 5 pixels of padding. The code is

```
.div2 { width: 100px;
        height: 100px;
        background-color: #ffffff;
        border: 3px ridge #000000;
        margin: 10px
        padding: 5px; }
```

Save the file. Launch a browser and test your page. It should look similar to the one shown in Figure 6.3. The student files contain a sample solution (see chapter6/box1.html).

Practice with Normal Flow and Nested Elements

Launch a text editor and open your box1.html file. Save the file with the name box2.html.

Edit the code. Delete the content from the body section of the web page. Add the following code to configure two div elements—one nested inside the other.

```
<div class="div1">
This is the outer box.
   <div class="div2">
   This is the inner box.
   </div>
</div>
```

Save the file. Launch a browser and test your page. It should look similar to the one shown in Figure 6.4. Notice how the browser renders the nested div elements: The second box is nested inside the first box because it is coded inside the first div element in the web page source code. This is an example of normal flow. The student files contain a sample solution (see chapter6/box2.html).

The examples in this Hands-On Practice happened to use two div elements. However, the box model applies to block display HTML elements in general, not just to div elements. You will get more practice using the box model in this chapter.

A Look Ahead: CSS Layout Properties

You've seen how normal flow causes the browser to render the elements in the order that they appear in the HTML source code. When using CSS for page layout, there are situations in which you will want to specify the location of an element on the page—either the absolute pixel location, the location relative to where the element would normally display, or floating on the page. The CSS properties that configure the placement of elements on a web page are discussed in the following sections.

6.3 CSS Positioning

You've seen how normal flow causes the browser to render the elements in the order that they appear in the HTML source code. When using CSS for page layout, there are situations when you may want more control over the position of an element. This section introduces relative and absolute positioning.

Relative Positioning

Use **relative positioning** to change the location of an element slightly, relative to where it would otherwise appear with normal flow. Configure relative positioning with the `position: relative;` property along with one or more of the following properties: `left`, `right`, `top`, and `bottom`. Table 6.2 lists CSS position and offset properties.

Figure 6.5 shows a web page (see chapter6/relative.html in the student files) that uses relative positioning along with the `left` property to configure the placement of an element in relation to the normal flow. In this case, the container element is the body of the web page.

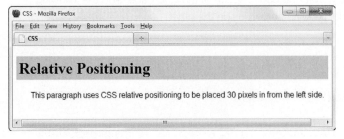

Figure 6.5 The paragraph is configured using relative positioning

Table 6.2 CSS properties for relative and absolute position

Property	Value	Purpose
position	static	Default value; the element is rendered in normal flow
	relative	Configures the location of an element relative to where it would otherwise render in normal flow
	absolute	Configures the location of an element outside of normal flow precisely in its container element
	fixed	Configures the location of an element within the browser viewport; the element does not move when the page is scrolled
left	Numeric value or percentage	The position of the element offset from the left side of the container element
right	Numeric value or percentage	The position of the element offset from the right side of the container element
top	Numeric value or percentage	The position of the element offset from the top of the container element
bottom	Numeric value or percentage	The position of the element offset from the bottom of the container element

The result is that the content of the element is rendered as being offset or shifted 30 pixels from the left, where it would normally be placed at the browser's left margin. Notice also how the padding and background-color properties configure the heading element. The CSS is

```
#myContent { position: relative;
             left: 30px;
             font-family: Arial, sans-serif; }
h1 { background-color: #cccccc;
     padding: 5px;
     color: #000000; }
```

The HTML source code is

```
<h1>Relative Positioning</h1>
<div id="myContent">
<p>This paragraph uses CSS relative positioning to be placed 30 pixels
in from the left side.</p>
</div>
```

Absolute Positioning

Use **absolute positioning** to specify the precise location of an element outside of the normal flow in its container element. Configure absolute positioning with the position: absolute; property along with one or more of the following offset properties: left, right, top, and bottom. See Table 6.2 for a list of CSS position and offset properties.

Figure 6.6 depicts a web page that configures a div element using absolute positioning to display the content 200 pixels in from the left margin and 100 pixels down from the

Figure 6.6 The div element is configured using absolute positioning

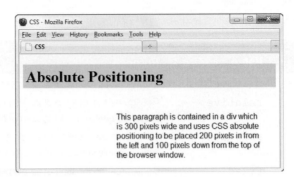

top of its container element, which is the body of the document. The padding and background-color properties configure the heading element. See the student files (chapter8/absolute.html) for an example.

The CSS is

```
#content { position: absolute;
           left: 200px;
           top: 100px;
           font-family: Arial, sans-serif;
           width: 300px; }
h1 { background-color: #cccccc;
     padding: 5px;
     color: #000000; }
```

The HTML source code is

```
<h1>Absolute Positioning</h1>
<div id="content">
<p>This paragraph is contained in a div which is 300 pixels wide and
uses CSS absolute positioning to be placed 200 pixels in from the left
and 100 pixels down from the top of the browser window.</p>
</div>
```

When working with absolute positioning, it is important to be aware that elements not absolutely positioned will be rendered using normal flow by the browser. Elements that are absolutely positioned are rendered outside of normal flow. You'll explore this behavior in the next Hands-On Practice.

 Hands-On Practice 6.2

Figure 6.7 shows screenshots of two web pages with similar HTML content. The web page in the upper screenshot does not have any CSS applied. The web page in the lower screenshot uses CSS to configure text, color, and the absolute position of a paragraph element. Launch a text editor and open chapter6/starter2.html in the student files. When a browser renders the page, it will use normal flow and display the HTML elements in the order in which they are coded: `<h1>`, `<div>`, `<p>`, and `<ul>`. Launch a browser and display the page to verify.

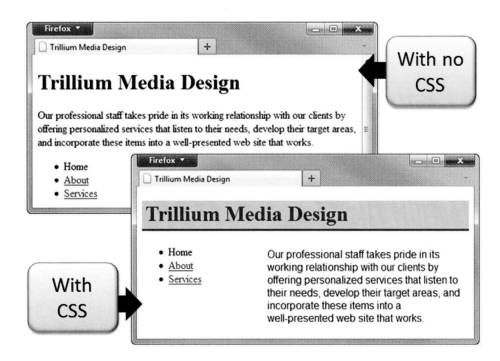

Figure 6.7 The lower web page uses CSS absolute positioning

Let's add the CSS to make this page more engaging, like the lower screenshot in Figure 6.7. Save the file with the name trillium.html. With trillium.html open in a text editor, modify the code as follows:

1. This page uses embedded styles. Code opening and closing `<style>` tags in the head section.

```
<style>
</style>
```

2. Create style rules for the h1 element selector. Configure a background color (#B0C4DE), text color (#000080), a 3 pixel solid bottom border in the color #000080, and 5 pixels of padding on the bottom and left sides.

```
h1 { border-bottom: 3px solid #000080;
     color: #000080;
     background-color: #B0C4DE;
     padding: 0 0 5px 5px; }
```

3. Create style rules for a class named `content`. Configure the position to be absolute, 200 pixels from the left, 75 pixels from the top, a width of 300 pixels, and Arial or sans-serif font typeface.

```
.content { position: absolute;
           left: 200px;
           top: 75px;
           font-family: Arial, sans-serif;
           width: 300px; }
```

4. Assign the paragraph to the `content` class. Add `class="content"` to the opening paragraph tag in the body of the web page.

Save the file. Launch a browser and test your page. It should look similar to the lower web page shown in Figure 6.7. The student files contain a sample solution (see chapter6/trillium.html). Note that even though the unordered list is coded in the page after the paragraph, it's displayed immediately after the heading. This is because the paragraph is absolutely positioned (`position: absolute`). Browsers render absolutely positioned elements outside of normal flow.

Note: This Hands-On Practice used embedded CSS for ease of editing. However, for an actual website with more than one page, the most efficient solution is to use an external CSS file. See Chapter 3 if you'd like to review using external style sheets. You'll use external style sheets later in this chapter.

6.4 CSS Float

Elements that seem to float on the right or left side of either the browser window or another element are often configured using the **float property.** The browser renders these elements using normal flow and then shifts them to either the right or left as far as possible within their container (usually either the browser viewport or a div element).

- Use `float: right;` to float the element on the right side of the container.

- Use `float: left;` to float the element on the left side of the container.

- Specify a width for a floated element unless the element already has an implicit width, such as an img element.

- Other elements and web page content will flow around the floated element.

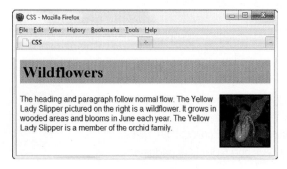

Figure 6.8 The image is configured to float

Figure 6.8 shows a web page with an image configured with `float: right;` to float on the right side of the browser viewport (see chapter6/float.html in the student files). When floating an image, the margin property is useful to configure empty space between the image and text on the page.

View Figure 6.8 and notice how the image stays on the right side of the browser viewport. An id called `yls` was created that applies the `float`, `margin`, and `border` properties. The attribute `id="yls"` was placed on the image tag. The CSS is

```
h1 { background-color: #A8C682;
     padding: 5px;
     color: #000000; }
p { font-family: Arial, sans-serif; }
#yls { float: right;
       margin: 0 0 5px 5px;
       border: 1px solid #000000; }
```

The HTML source code is

```
<h1>Wildflowers</h1>
<img id="yls" src="yls.jpg" alt="Yellow Lady Slipper" height="100"
width="100">
```

```
<p>The heading and paragraph follow normal flow. The Yellow Lady
Slipper pictured on the right is a wildflower. It grows in wooded
areas and blooms in June each year. The Yellow Lady Slipper is a
member of the orchid family.</p>
```

Hands-On Practice 6.3

In this Hands-On Practice, you'll use the CSS float property as you configure the web page shown in Figure 6.9.

Figure 6.9 The CSS float property left-aligns the image

Create a folder named ch6float. Copy the starter3.html and yls.jpg files from the chapter6 folder in the student files into your ch6float folder. Launch a text editor and open starter3.html. Notice the order of the images and paragraphs. Note that there is no CSS configuration for floating the images. Display starter3.html in a browser. The browser renders the page using normal flow and displays the HTML elements in the order they are coded.

Let's add CSS to float the image. Save the file as floatyls.html in your ch6float folder. With floatyls.html open in a text editor, modify the code as follows:

1. Add a style rule for a class name **float** that configures float, margin, and border properties.

```
.float { float: left;
        margin-right: 10px;
        border: 3px ridge #000000; }
```

2. Assign the image element to the class named float (use `class="float"`).

Save the file as index.html. Launch a browser and test your page. It should look similar to the web page shown in Figure 6.9. The student files contain a sample solution (seechapter6/floatyls.html).

The Floated Element and Normal Flow

Take a moment to examine your file in a browser (see Figure 6.9) and consider how the browser rendered the page. The div element is configured with a light background color to demonstrate how floated elements are rendered outside of normal flow. Observe that the image and the first paragraph are contained within the div element. The h2 element follows the div. If all the elements were rendered using normal flow, the area with the light background color would contain both child elements of the div: the image and the first paragraph. In addition, the h2 element would be placed on its own line under the div element.

However, once the image is placed vertically on the page, it is floated outside of normal flow—that's why the light background color only appears behind the first paragraph and why the h2 element's text begins immediately after the first paragraph and appears next to the floated image. In the following sections, you'll explore properties that can "clear" this float and improve the display.

6.5 CSS: Clearing a Float

The `clear` Property

The **clear property** is often used to terminate, or clear, a float. You can set the value of the clear property to `left`, `right`, or `both`, depending on the type of float you need to clear.

Review Figure 6.9 and the code sample (see chapter6/floatyls.html in the student files). Notice that although the div element contains both an image and the first paragraph, the light background color of the div only displays behind the screen area occupied by the first paragraph—it stops a bit earlier than expected. Clearing the float will help take care of this display issue.

Clear a Float with a Line Break

A common technique to clear a float within a container element is to add a line break element configured with the `clear` property. See chapter6/floatylsclear1.html in the student files for an example. Observe that a CSS class is configured to clear the left float:

```
.clearleft { clear: left; }
```

Also, a line break tag assigned to the `clearleft` class is coded before the closing `div` tag. The code for the div element is

```
<div>
<img class="float" src="yls.jpg" alt="Yellow Lady Slipper"
height="100" width="100">
<p>The Yellow Lady Slipper grows in wooded areas and blooms in June
each year. The flower is a member of the orchid family.</p>
<br class="clearleft">
</div>
```

Figure 6.10 displays a screen shot of this page. Review Figure 6.9 and note two changes: the light background color of the div element extends farther down the page and the h2 element's text begins on its own line under the image.

Another Technique to Clear a Float

If you are not concerned about the light background color display, another option is to omit the line break tag and, instead, apply the `clearleft` class to the h2 element, which is the first block display element after the div. This does not change the display of the light background color, but it does force the h2 element's text to begin on its own line, as shown in Figure 6.11 (see chapter6/floatylsclear2.html in the student files).

Figure 6.10 The clear property is applied to a line break tag

Figure 6.11 The clear property is applied to the h2 element

The `overflow` Property

The **`overflow` property** is often used to clear a float, although its intended purpose is to configure how content should display if it is too large for the area allocated. See Table 6.3 for a list of commonly used values for the overflow property.

Table 6.3 The `overflow` property

Value	Purpose
`visible`	Default value; the content is displayed, and if it's too large, the content will overflow and extend outside the area allocated to it
`hidden`	The content is clipped to fit the area allocated to the element in the browser viewport
`auto`	The content fills the area allocated to it and, if needed, scrollbars are displayed to allow access to the remaining content
`scroll`	The content is rendered in the area allocated to it and scrollbars are displayed

Clear a Float

Review Figure 6.9 and the code sample (chapter6/floatyls.html in the student files). Observe the div element, which contains the floated image and first paragraph on the page. Notice that although the div element contains both an image and the first paragraph, the light background color of the div element does not extend as far as expected; it is only visible in the area occupied by the first paragraph. You can use the `overflow` property assigned to the container element to resolve this display issue and clear the float. In this case, we'll apply the `overflow` and `width` properties to the div selector. The CSS to configure the div in this manner is

```
div { background-color: #F3F1BF;
      overflow: auto;
      width: 100%; }
```

This will clear the float. The web page will display as shown in Figure 6.12 (see chapter6/floatylsoverflow.html in the student files).

Figure 6.12 The overflow property is applied to the div selector

Figure 6.13 The browser displays scrollbars

Notice that using the `overflow` property (see Figure 6.12) and applying the `clear` property to a line break tag (see Figure 6.10) result in a similar web page display. You may be wondering about which CSS property (`clear` or `overflow`) is the best one to use when you need to clear a float.

Although the `clear` property is widely used, in this example, it is more efficient to apply the `overflow` property to the container element (for example, a div element). This will clear the float, avoid adding an extra line break tag, and ensure that the container element expands to enclose the entire floated element. You'll get more practice with the `float`, `clear`, and `overflow` properties as you continue working through this textbook. Floating elements is a key technique for designing multicolumn page layouts with CSS.

Configure Scrollbars

The web page in Figure 6.13 demonstrates the use of `overflow: auto;` to automatically display scrollbars if the content exceeds the space allocated to it. In this case, the div that contains the paragraph and the floated image was configured with a width of 300px and a height of 100px.

See the example web page (chapter6/floatylsscroll.html in the student files). The CSS for the div is shown below:

```
div { background-color: #F3F1BF;
      overflow: scroll;
      width: 300px;
      height: 100px; }
```

 Checkpoint 6.1

1. List the components of the box model from innermost to outermost.

2. What are the four values of the position property?

3. Describe the purpose of the CSS float property.

6.6 CSS Two-Column Page Layout

A common design for a web page is a two-column layout. This can be accomplished with CSS by configuring one of the columns to float on the web page. This section introduces you to two formats for the two-column page layout.

Two Columns with Left Navigation

See Figure 6.14 for a wireframe for a two-column web page. The left column will contain navigation.

The HTML template for the page layout is

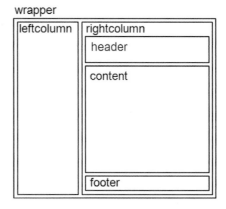

Figure 6.14
Wireframe for a
two-column layout
with left navigation

```
<div id="wrapper">
    <div id="leftcolumn">
    </div>
    <div id="rightcolumn">
        <div id="header">
        </div>
        <div id="content">
        </div>
        <div id="footer">
        </div>
    </div>
</div>
```

The web page in Figure 6.15 implements a two-column layout with the navigation on the left (see chapter6/twocolumn1.html in the student files). The key to this layout is that the left column is coded to float to the left with the float property. The browser renders the other content on the page using normal flow.

- The wrapper is centered and takes up 80% of the web page width. This area is assigned a medium-blue background color that will display behind the left column:

  ```
  #wrapper { width: 80%;
            margin-left: auto;
            margin-right: auto;
            background-color: #b3c7e6; }
  ```

Figure 6.15
A two-column
page layout with
left navigation

- The left column is assigned a fixed width and configured to float to the left. Because no background color is configured, the background color of the container element (the wrapper div) displays:

```
#leftcolumn { float: left;
              width: 150px; }
```

- The right column is assigned a margin on the left that is equal to or greater than the width of the left column. This margin creates the look of two columns (often called faux columns). A white background color is assigned to the right column, which overrides the background color configured in the wrapper:

```
#rightcolumn { margin-left: 155px;
               background-color: #ffffff; }
```

Two Columns with Top Header and Left Navigation

See Figure 6.16 for a wireframe for a web page with that has a top logo header spanning two columns with a navigation area in the left column.

The HTML template for the page layout is

```
<div id="wrapper">
   <div id="header">
   </div>
   <div id="leftcolumn">
   </div>
   <div id="rightcolumn">
      <div id="content">
      </div>
      <div id="footer">
      </div>
   </div>
</div>
```

The web page shown in Figure 6.17 implements a two-column layout with a top header (see chapter6/twocolumn2.html in the student files). The CSS that configures the

Figure 6.16 Wireframe for a two-column layout with a top logo area

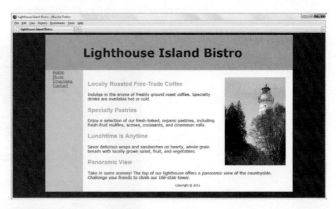

Figure 6.17 A two-column page layout with a top logo and left navigation

`wrapper`, `leftcolumn`, and `rightcolumn` areas is the same as for the web page shown in Figure 6.15. However, notice that the location of the div assigned to the `header` id is different. It is now coded as the first div element within the wrapper and displays before the left and right columns.

FAQ   **Do I have to use a wrapper?**

No, you are not required to use a wrapper or container for a web page layout. However, it does make it easier to get the two-column look because the background color of the wrapper div will display behind any of its child elements that do not have their own background color configured. This technique also provides you with the option of configuring a different background color or background image for the page (as shown in Figure 6.17) using the body element selector.

Not Yet Ready for Prime Time

There is one more aspect of the two-column layout web page design to consider before it is ready for "prime time." The navigation area is a list of hyperlinks. In order to more closely semantically describe the navigation area, the hyperlinks should be configured in an unordered list. In the next section, you'll learn techniques to configure horizontal and vertical navigation hyperlinks in unordered lists.

6.7 Hyperlinks in an Unordered List

One of the advantages of using CSS for page layout involves the use of semantically correct code. Writing semantically correct code means choosing the markup tag that most accurately reflects the purpose of the content. Using the various levels of heading tags for content headings and subheadings or placing paragraphs of text within paragraph tags (rather than using line breaks) are examples of writing semantically correct code. This type of coding is a step in the direction of supporting the Semantic Web. Leading Web developers such as Eric Meyer, Mark Newhouse, Jeffrey Zeldman, and others have promoted the idea of using unordered lists to configure navigation menus. After all, a navigation menu is a list of hyperlinks.

Configuring navigation with a list also helps to provide accessibility. Screen reader applications offer easy keyboard access and verbal cues for information organized in lists, such as the number of items in the list.

Focus on Accessibility

Configure List Markers with CSS

Recall that the default display for an unordered list is to show a disc marker (often referred to as a bullet) in front of each list item. The default display for an ordered list is to show a decimal number in front of each list item. When you configure navigation hyperlinks in an unordered list, you may not always want to see those list markers. It's easy to configure them with CSS. Use the `list-style-type` property to configure the marker for an unordered or ordered list. See Table 6.4 for common property values.

Table 6.4 CSS properties for ordered and unordered list markers

Property	Description	Value	List Marker Display
`list-style-type`	Configures the style of the list marker	`none`	No list markers display
		`disc`	Circle
		`circle`	Open circle
		`square`	Square
		`decimal`	Decimal numbers
		`upper-alpha`	Uppercase letters
		`lower-alpha`	Lowercase letters
		`lower-roman`	Lowercase Roman numerals
`list-style-image`	Image replacement for the list marker	The `url` keyword with parentheses surrounding the file name or path for the image	Image displays in front of each list item
`list-style-position`	Configures placement of the list marker	`inside`	Markers are indented; text wraps under the markers
		`outside` (default)	Markers have default placement

Figure 6.18 shows an unordered list configured with square markers using the following CSS:

```
ul { list-style-type: square; }
```

Figure 6.19 shows an ordered list configured with uppercase letter markers using the following CSS:

```
ol { list-style-type: upper-alpha; }
```

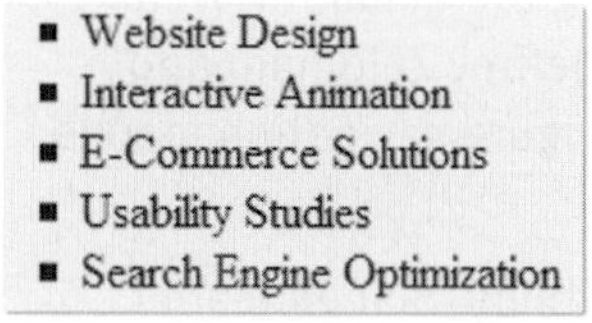
Website Design
Interactive Animation
E-Commerce Solutions
Usability Studies
Search Engine Optimization

Figure 6.18 The unordered list markers are square

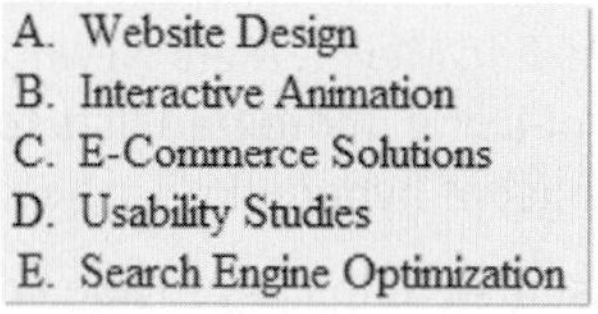
A. Website Design
B. Interactive Animation
C. E-Commerce Solutions
D. Usability Studies
E. Search Engine Optimization

Figure 6.19 The ordered list markers use uppercase letters

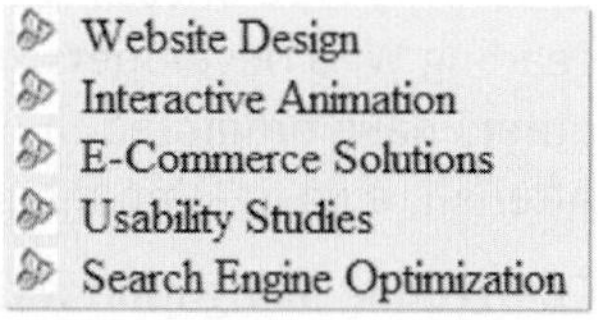
Website Design
Interactive Animation
E-Commerce Solutions
Usability Studies
Search Engine Optimization

Figure 6.20 The list markers are replaced with an image

Configure an Image as a List Marker

Use the `list-style-image` property to configure an image as the marker in an unordered or ordered list. In Figure 6.20, an image named trillium.gif was configured to replace the list markers using the following CSS:

```
ul {list-style-image: url(trillium.gif); }
```

Vertical Navigation with an Unordered List

Figure 6.21 shows the navigation area of a web page (see chapter6/twocolumn3.html in the student files) that uses an unordered list to organize the navigation links. The HTML is

Figure 6.21
Navigation in an
unordered list

```
<ul>
<li><a href="index.html">Home</a></li>
<li><a href="menu.html">Menu</a></li>
<li><a href="directions.html">Directions</a></li>
<li><a href="contact.html">Contact</a></li>
</ul>
```

Configure with CSS

OK, so now that we're semantically correct, how about improving the visual aesthetic? Let's use CSS to eliminate the list marker. We also need to make sure that our special styles only apply to the unordered list in the navigation area (within the leftcolumn id), so we'll use a contextual selector. The CSS to configure the list in Figure 6.22 is

```
#leftcolumn ul { list-style-type: none; }
```

Figure 6.22 The list
markers have been
eliminated with CSS

Remove the Underline with CSS

The **text-decoration property** modifies the display of text in the browser. This property is most often used to eliminate the underline from the navigation hyperlinks with text-decoration: none;.

The CSS to configure the list in Figure 6.23 (see chapter6/twocolumn4.html in the student files) that eliminates the underline on the hyperlinks in the navigation area (within the leftcolumn id) is

```
#leftcolumn a { text-decoration: none; }
```

Figure 6.23 The
CSS text-decoration
property has been
applied

Horizontal Navigation with an Unordered List

You may be wondering how to use an unordered list for a horizontal navigation menu. The answer is CSS! List items are block display elements. They need to be configured as inline display elements to display in a single line. The CSS display **property** configures how the browser renders, or displays, an element on a web page. See Table 6.5 for a list of commonly used values.

Table 6.5 The display property

Value	Purpose
none	The element will not display
inline	The element will display as an inline element in the same line as the surrounding text and/or elements
block	The element will display as a block element with a margin above and below

Home Menu Directions Contact

Figure 6.24
Navigation in an
unordered list

Figure 6.24 shows the navigation area of a web page (see chapter6/navigation.html in the student files) with a horizontal navigation area organized in an unordered list. The HTML is

```
<div id="nav">
<ul>
   <li><a href="index.html">Home</a></li>
   <li><a href="menu.html">Menu</a></li>
   <li><a href="directions.html">Directions</a></li>
   <li><a href="contact.html">Contact</a></li>
</ul>
</div>
```

Configure with CSS

The following CSS was applied in this example:

- To eliminate the list marker, apply `list-style-type: none;` to the ul element selector:

  `#nav ul { list-style-type: none; }`

- To render the list items horizontally instead of vertically, apply `display: inline;` to the li element selector:

  `#nav li { display: inline; }`

- To eliminate the underline from the hyperlinks, apply `text-decoration: none;` to the a element selector. Also, to add some space between the hyperlinks, apply `padding-right: 10px;` to the a element selector:

  `#nav a { text-decoration: none; padding-right: 10px; }`

6.8 CSS Interactivity with Pseudo-Classes

VideoNote
Interactivity with
CSS pseudo-classes

Have you ever visited a website and found that the text hyperlinks changed color when you moved the mouse pointer over them? Often, this is accomplished using a CSS **pseudo-class**, which can be used to apply a special effect to a selector. The five pseudo-classes that can be applied to the anchor element are shown in Table 6.6.

Table 6.6 Commonly used CSS pseudo-classes

Pseudo-Class	When Applied
`:link`	Default state for a hyperlink that has not been clicked (visited)
`:visited`	Default state for a visited hyperlink
`:focus`	Triggered when the hyperlink has keyboard focus
`:hover`	Triggered when the mouse pointer moves over the hyperlink
`:active`	Triggered when the hyperlink is actually clicked

Notice the order in which the pseudo-classes are listed in Table 6.6. Anchor element pseudo-classes *must be coded in this order* (although it's OK to omit one or more of those listed). If you code the pseudo-classes in a different order, the styles will not be reliably applied. It's common practice to configure the :hover, :focus, and :active pseudo-classes with the same styles.

To apply a pseudo-class, write it after the selector. The following code sample will configure text hyperlinks to be red initially. The sample also uses the :hover pseudo-class to configure the hyperlinks to change their appearance when the visitor places the mouse pointer over them so that the underline disappears and the color changes.

```
a:link { color: #ff0000; }
a:hover { text-decoration: none;
          color: #000066; }
```

Figure 6.25 shows part of a web page that uses a similar technique. Note the position of the mouse pointer over the Print This Page hyperlink. The text color has changed and has no underline. Most modern browsers support CSS pseudo-classes.

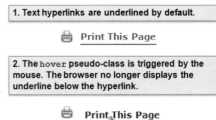

Figure 6.25 Using the hover pseudo-class

Hands-On Practice 6.4

You will use pseudo-classes to create interactive hyperlinks in this Hands-On Practice. Create a folder named ch6hover. Copy the lighthouseisland.jpg, lighthouselogo.jpg, and starter3.html files from the chapter6 folder in the student files into your ch6hover folder. Display the web page in a browser. It should look similar to Figure 6.26. Notice that the navigation area needs to be configured.

Launch a text editor and open starter3.html. Save the file as index.html in your ch6hover folder.

Figure 6.26 The navigation area needs to be styled in this two-column page layout

1. Review the code for this page, which uses a two-column layout. Examine the `leftcolumn` id and modify the code to configure the navigation in an unordered list.

```
<ul>
    <li><a href="index.html">Home</a></li>
    <li><a href="menu.html">Menu</a></li>
    <li><a href="directions.html">Directions</a></li>
    <li><a href="contact.html">Contact</a></li>
</ul>
```

   Let's add CSS to the embedded styles to configure the unordered list elements in the `leftcolumn` id. Eliminate the list marker and set the padding to 10 pixels.

```
#leftcolumn ul { list-style-type: none;
                 padding: 10px; }
```

2. Next, configure basic interactivity with pseudo-classes.

   - Configure the anchor tags in the `leftcolumn` id to have 10 pixels of padding, use bold font, and display no underline.

```
#leftcolumn a { text-decoration: none;
                padding: 10px;
                font-weight: bold; }
```

   - Use pseudo-classes to configure anchor tags in the `leftcolumn` id to display white (#ffffff) text for unvisited hyperlinks, light-gray (#eaeaea) text for visited hyperlinks, and dark-blue (#000066) text when the mouse pointer hovers over hyperlinks:

```
#leftcolumn a:link { color: #ffffff; }
#leftcolumn a:visited { color: #eaeaea; }
#leftcolumn a:hover { color: #000066; }
```

Save your page and test in a browser. Move your mouse pointer over the navigation area and notice the change in the text color. Your page should look similar to Figure 6.27 (see chapter6/hover/index.html in the student files).

Figure 6.27 CSS pseudo-classes add interactivity to the navigation

6.9 Practice with CSS Two-Column Layout

You've had some experience with a two-column layout, organizing navigation links in an unordered list, and configuring CSS pseudo-classes. Let's reinforce these skills with a Hands-On Practice.

Hands-On Practice 6.5

In this Hands-On Practice, you'll create a new version of the Lighthouse Island Bistro home page with a top header section spanning two columns, content in the left column, navigation in the right column, and a footer section below the two columns. See Figure 6.28 for a wireframe. You will configure the CSS in an external style sheet. Create a new folder named ch6practice. Copy the starter4.html, lighthouseisland.jpg, and lighthouselogo.jpg files from the chapter6 folder in the student files into your ch6practice folder.

Figure 6.28 Wireframe for a two-column layout with a top header area

1. Launch a text editor and open starter4.html. Save the file as index.html. Add a link element to the head section of the web page that associates this file with an external style sheet named lighthouse.css. A code sample follows.

   ```
   <link href="lighthouse.css" rel="stylesheet">
   ```

2. Save the index.html file. Launch a text editor and create a new file named lighthouse.css in your ch6practice folder. Configure the CSS for the wireframe sections as follows:

   • The body element selector: very-dark-blue background (#00005D) and Verdana, Arial, or the default sans-serif font typeface

   ```
   body { background-color: #00005D;
          font-family: Verdana, Arial, sans-serif; }
   ```

   • The wrapper id: centered, width set to 80% of the browser viewport, minimum width of 960px, display text in a dark-blue color (#000066), and display a medium-blue (#B3C7E6) background color (*this color will display behind the nav section*)

   ```
   #wrapper { margin: 0 auto;
           width: 80%;
           min-width: 960px;
           background-color: #B3C7E6;
           color: #000066; }
   ```

- The `header` id: slate-blue (#869DC7) background color; very-dark-blue (#00005D) text color; 150% font size; top, right, and bottom padding of 10px; 155 pixels of left padding; and the lighthouselogo.jpg background image

```
#header { background-color: #869DC7;
        color: #00005D;
        font-size: 150%;
        padding: 10px 10px 10px 155px;
        background-repeat: no-repeat;
        background-image: url(lighthouselogo.jpg); }
```

- The h1 element selector: Configure 20 pixels of bottom margin to prevent an Internet Explorer display issue.

```
h1 { margin-bottom: 20px; }
```

- The `nav` id: float on the right, width set to 150px, display bold text, letter spacing of 0.1 em

```
#nav { float: right;
      width: 150px;
      font-weight: bold;
      letter-spacing: 0.1em; }
```

- The `content` id: white background color (#FFFFFF), black text color (#000000), 10 pixels of padding on the top and bottom, 20 pixels of padding on the left and right, and overflow set to auto

```
#content { background-color: #ffffff;
          color: #000000;
          padding: 10px 20px;
          overflow: auto; }
```

- The `footer` id: 70% font size, centered text, 10 pixels of padding, slate-blue background color (#869DC7), and clear set to both

```
#footer { font-size: 70%;
         text-align: center;
         padding: 10px;
         background-color: #869DC7;
         clear: both;}
```

Save the file and display it in a browser. Your display should be similar to Figure 6.29.

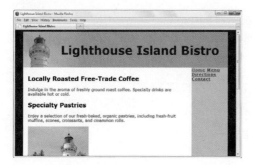

Figure 6.29 Home page with major sections configured using CSS

3. Continue editing the lighthouse.css file to style the h2 element selector and floating image. Configure the h2 element selector with slate-blue text color (#869DC7) and Arial or sans-serif font typeface. Configure the `floatright` id to float on the right side with 10 pixels of margin.

```
h2 { color: #869DC7;
     font-family: Arial, sans-serif; }
#floatright { float: right;
              margin: 10px; }
```

4. Continue editing the lighthouse.css file and configure the navigation bar.

- The ul element selector: Eliminate the list markers. Set a zero margin and zero padding.

```
#nav ul { list-style-type: none; margin: 0; padding: 0; }
```

- The a element selector: no underline, 20 pixels of padding, medium-blue background color (#B3C7E6), and 1 pixel solid white bottom border

  Use `display: block;` to allow the web page visitor to click anywhere on the anchor "button" to activate the hyperlink.

```
#nav a { text-decoration: none;
         padding: 20px;
         display: block;
         background-color: #B3C7E6;
         border-bottom: 1px solid #FFFFFF; }
```

Configure the `:link`, `:visited`, and `:hover` pseudo-classes as follows:

```
#nav a:link { color: #FFFFFF; }
#nav a:visited { color: #EAEAEA; }
#nav a:hover { color: #869DC7;
               background-color: #EAEAEA; }
```

Save your files. Open your index.html file in a browser. Move your mouse pointer over the navigation area and notice the interactivity, as shown in Figure 6.30 (see chapter6/practice/index.html in the student files).

Figure 6.30 CSS pseudo-classes add interactivity to the page

6.10 CSS Resources

CSS Debugging Techniques

Using CSS for page layout requires some patience. It takes a while to get used to it. Fixing problems in code is called **debugging**. This term dates back to the early days of programming when an insect (a bug) lodged inside the computer and caused a malfunction. Debugging CSS can be frustrating and requires patience. One of the biggest issues is that even modern browsers implement CSS in slightly different ways. Browser support changes with each new browser version. Testing is crucial. Expect your pages to look slightly different in various browsers. Although Internet Explorer's support of the CSS standard is improving, there still are differences in compliance. The following are helpful techniques to use when your CSS isn't behaving properly:

Verify Correct HTML Syntax

Invalid HTML code can cause issues with CSS. Use the W3C Markup Validation Service at http://validator.w3.org to verify the correct HTML syntax.

Verify Correct CSS Syntax

Sometimes a CSS style does not apply because of a syntax error. Use the W3C CSS Validation Service at http://jigsaw.w3.org/css-validator to verify your CSS syntax. Carefully check your code. Many times, the error is in the line *above* the style that is not correctly applied.

Configure Temporary Background Colors

Sometimes your code is valid but the page is not rendered in the way that you would expect. If you temporarily assign distinctive background colors such as red or yellow and test again, it should be easier to see where the boxes are ending up.

Configure Temporary Borders

Similar to the temporary background colors, you could temporarily configure an element with a 3 pixel red solid border. This will really jump out at you and help you recognize the issue quickly.

Use Comments to Find the Unexpected Cascade

Style rules and HTML attributes configured farther down the page can override earlier style rules. If your styles are misbehaving, try "commenting out" (see below) some styles and test with a smaller group of statements. Then add the styles back in one by one to see where or when the breakdown occurs. Work patiently and test the entire style sheet in this manner.

Browsers ignore code and text that is contained between comment markers. A CSS comment begins with /* and ends with */. The comment below is an example of documentation that explains the purpose of a style rule.

```
/* Set Page Margins to Zero */
body { margin: 0; }
```

Comments can span multiple lines. The comment on next page begins on the line above the nav class and ends on the line below the nav class. This causes the browser to skip the nav class when applying the style sheet. This technique can be useful for testing when you are experimenting with a number of properties and may need to temporarily disable a style rule.

```
/* temporarily commented out during testing
.nav { text-decoration: none; }
*/
```

A common mistake when using comments is to type the beginning /* without subsequently typing */ to end the comment. As a result, *everything* after the /* is treated as a comment by the browser.

CSS Web Resources

This chapter introduces you to CSS for page layout configuration and should get you started in your exploration of this technology. It may help you to know that you are not alone in your quest to learn CSS. There are many resources with documentation, tutorials, and support for this technology. The page layout techniques discussed in this textbook are just an introduction to using this technology. There are many websites that offer additional insight and techniques for configuring page layout with CSS. The following are a few that you may find useful:

- CSS Layout Techniques: For Fun and Profit: Large collection of CSS page layouts and links to tutorials http://glish.com/css

- The Layout Reservoir: A collection of CSS page layouts http://www.bluerobot.com/web/layouts

- Listamatic: Vertical and horizontal lists with CSS http://css.maxdesign.com.au/listamatic

- W3C Cascading Style Sheets http://www.w3.org/Style/CSS

- Experimental CSS Compatibility Table http://westciv.com/wiki/Experimental_CSS_compatibility_table

- HTML5 and CSS3 Browser Support Chart http://www.findmebyip.com/litmus

- CSS Contents and Browser Compatibility: Peter-Paul Koch's site is dedicated to studying and defeating browser incompatibility related to CSS and JavaScript. http://www.quirksmode.org/css/contents.html

- Position Is Everything: John and Holly Bergevin's site focuses on CSS bugs in modern browsers. It contains some great sample CSS page layouts. http://www.positioniseverything.net

- CSS3 Click Chart http://www.impressivewebs.com/css3-click-chart

- SitePoint CSS Reference http://reference.sitepoint.com/css

 # Checkpoint 6.2

1. Open chapter6/practice/index.html from Hands-On Practice 6.5 in a browser. Resize the browser window. Describe what happens. What type of page design layout (ice, jello, or liquid) is being used?

2. What do you understand by contextual selectors?

3. Describe how to choose whether to configure an HTML element selector, create a class, or create an id when working with CSS.

6.11 HTML5 Structural Elements

HTML5 introduces a number of semantic structural elements that you can use to configure areas on a web page. These new block display elements are not intended to completely replace the div element, but are intended to be used along with div and other elements to structure web page documents in a more meaningful manner that indicates the purpose of the structural areas.

Standard HTML4 and XHTML coding practice is to use only one h1 element on a web page and configure the heading-level elements in outline format. Outlining is different in HTML5. Instead of a heading-level outline, the outline is also configured by sectioning elements (such as section, article, nav, and aside) with heading levels within each section. Try out an HTML5 outliner at http://gsnedders.html5.org/outliner. We'll explore the HTML5 header, hgroup, nav, footer, section, article, aside, and time elements in this section. Let's first take a closer look at the header, hgroup, nav, and footer elements.

Header Element

The **header element** contains the headings of either a web page document or an area in the document such as a section or article. The header element begins with the `<header>` tag and ends with the `</header>` tag. The header element is block display and will typically contain one or more heading-level elements (h1 through h6) and, optionally, the hgroup element.

Hgroup Element

The **hgroup element** groups heading-level tags and is useful if the logo header area of a web page contains both the website name and a **tagline** (a phrase that identifies and captures the essence of a business, e.g., the tagline of L. L. Bean [http://www.llbean.com] is "GUARANTEED TO LAST"). The hgroup element is block display and begins with the `<hgroup>` tag and ends with the `</hgroup>` tag. When there is more than one heading-level element in an hgroup, only the first heading element is placed in the page outline.

Nav Element

The **nav element** contains a section of navigation hyperlinks. The block display nav element begins with the `<nav>` tag and ends with the `</nav>` tag.

Footer Element

The **footer element** contains the footer content of a web page, section, article, paragraph, or even the blockquote element. The block display footer element begins with the `<footer>` tag and ends with the `</footer>` tag.

Remember that these new HTML5 elements are not supported by all browsers. However, you can begin to practice with them today.

Hands-On Practice 6.6

In this Hands-On Practice, you'll start with the two-column Lighthouse Island Bistro home page from Hands-On Practice 6.5 (shown in Figure 6.30) and modify it to use HTML5 structural elements. You'll also add a tagline to the header area. Create a new folder named ch6structure. Copy the index.html, lighthouse.css, lighthouseisland.jpg, and lighthouselogo.jpg files from the chapter6/practice folder in the student files and save them in your ch6structure folder.

1. Launch a text editor and open index.html. Replace the div assigned to the `header` id with an HTML5 header element that contains an hgroup. Also add the tagline "the best coffee on the coast" with an h2 element. The new code is

```
<header>
  <hgroup>
    <h1>Lighthouse Island Bistro</h1>
    <h2>the best coffee on the coast</h2>
  </hgroup>
</header>
```

2. Replace the opening and closing tags for the div assigned to the `nav` id with the HTML5 nav element.

3. Replace the opening and closing tags for the div assigned to the `footer` id with the HTML5 footer element.

4. Recall that the HTML5 figure and figcaption elements were introduced in Chapter 4. Code a figure element that contains the image. Code a figcaption element that displays the text "Island Lighthouse, Built in 1870" within the figure container below the image. Remove `id="floatright"` from the image element. You'll configure the entire figure element to float in step 9. The code is shown below:

```
<figure>
    <img src="lighthouseisland.jpg" width="250" height="355"
alt="Lighthouse Island">
    <figcaption>Island Lighthouse, Built in 1870</figcaption>
</figure>
```

5. Save the index.html file.

6. Open lighthouse.css in a text editor. Edit the CSS to use HTML element selectors for the header, nav, and footer elements. Replace the `#header` selector with the HTML header element selector. Replace all instances of the `#nav` selector with the HTML nav element selector. Replace the `#footer` selector with the HTML footer element selector.

7. Configure CSS for the h1 and h2 elements in the header. Use contextual HTML selectors. Set the h1 bottom margin to 0. Set the h2 with 20 pixels of right padding; no margins; and .80em italic, right-aligned, #00005D color text. The CSS is

```
header h1 { margin-bottom: 0; }
header h2 { margin: 0;
            padding-right: 20px;
            font-size: .80em;
            font-style: italic;
            text-align: right;
            color: #00005D; }
```

8. Clean up some leftover CSS. Remove the `#floatright` style rule and the h1 element style rule from the CSS.

9. Configure the style rules for the figure and figcaption element selectors. The figure element selector is set as follows: float to the right, 260 pixels in width, and 10 pixel margin. The figcaption element selector is set to render small, italic, centered text. The CSS is

```
figure { float: right;
         width: 260px;
         margin: 10px; }
figcaption { text-align: center;
             font-size: .80em;
             font-style: italic; }
```

10. The most recent versions of Internet Explorer, Firefox, Safari, Chrome, and Opera support the HTML5 elements that you have coded. But how can you help older browsers understand the HTML5 code? One technique is to use CSS to configure the HTML5 element selectors as block display elements. At the time that this was written, popular browsers (except Internet Explorer 8 and earlier versions) correctly applied this style declaration. Add the following CSS:

```
header, nav, footer, figure, figcaption { display: block; }
```

11. Save your lighthouse.css file.

12. Display your index.html page in a modern browser. It should look similar to the page shown in Figure 6.31 (see chapter6/structure/index.html in the student files).

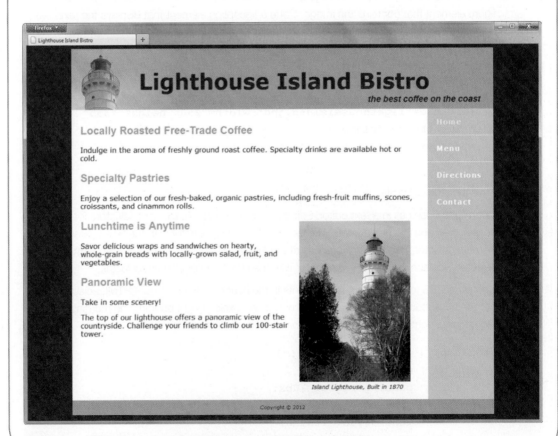

Figure 6.31 HTML5 structural elements were used on this web page

As you completed the Hands-On Practice, you might have noticed that some of the id names used for standard page areas, such as `header`, `nav`, and `footer`, were also the names of new HTML5 structural elements. This is a great way to prepare for HTML5, even if you are still coding XHTML! Become accustomed to the new HTML5 element names by configuring divs with these names as id or class values. Then, later, when it's time to always code in HTML5 syntax, you've got a head start! The HTML5 Gallery at http://html5gallery.com contains many examples of how HTML5 is being used on the Web today. Next, we'll explore the HTML5 section, article, aside, and time elements.

Section Element

The section element contains a "section" of a document, such as a chapter or topic. The block display section element begins with the `<section>` tag and ends with the `</section>` tag. A section element might contain header, footer, article, aside, div, and other elements needed to display the content. Section elements can contain other section elements.

Article Element

The article element contains an independent entry, such as a blog posting, comment, or e-zine article that could stand on its own. The block display article element begins with the `<article>` tag and ends with the `</article>` tag. An article element is block display and might contain header, footer, section, aside, div, and other elements needed to display the content.

Aside Element

The aside element is block display and contains a sidebar, a note, or other tangential content. The aside element begins with the `<aside>` tag and ends with the `</aside>` tag.

Time Element

The time element represents a date or a time and could be useful to date articles or blog postings. The inline display time element begins with the `<time>` tag and ends with the `</time>` tag. An optional `datetime` attribute can be used to specify a calendar date and/or time in machine-readable format. Use YYYY-MM-DD for a date. Use a 24-hour clock and HH:MM for time. See HTML: The Markup Language at http://www.w3.org/TR/html-markup/time.html for additional `datetime` syntax options.

Hands-On Practice 6.7

In this Hands-On Practice, you'll begin with the HTML5 Lighthouse Island Bistro home page (shown in Figure 6.31) and modify the content to use a blog format that is structured with the new HTML5 elements article, header, aside, and time. Create a new folder named ch6blog. Copy the index.html, lighthouseisland.jpg, and lighthouselogo.jpg files from the chapter6/structure folder in the student files into your ch6blog folder.

1. Launch a text editor and open index.html. Delete the text and elements contained within the div assigned to the **content** id. Replace them with an HTML5 section element (assigned to the content id) that contains an h1 element with "Bistro Blog" and two blog articles. Use the section, article, header, aside, and time elements to create two blog postings for the home page. Configure the new section as follows and save the file.

```
<section id="content">
  <h1>Bistro Blog</h1>
  <article>
      <header><h1>Valentine Wrap</h1></header>
      <time datetime="2011-02-02">February 2, 2011</time>
      <aside>Watch for the March Madness Wrap next month!</aside>
      <p>The February special sandwich is the Valentine Wrap &mdash;
      heart-healthy organic chicken with roasted red peppers on a
      whole wheat wrap.</p>
  </article>
  <article>
      <header><h1>New Coffee of the Day Promotion</h1></header>
      <time datetime="2011-01-11">January 11, 2011</time>
      <p>Enjoy the best coffee on the coast in the comfort of your
      home. We will feature a different flavor of our gourmet,
      locally roasted coffee each day with free bistro tastings
      and a discount on one-pound bags.</p>
  </article>
</section>
```

2. Open lighthouse.css in a text editor. Recall that the aside element contains content that is tangential to the main content. Configure CSS to display the aside element on the right (use float) in a light-gray rectangle about 120 pixels wide, a 10 pixel left margin, 5 pixels of padding, 80% font size, and a drop-shadow effect.

```
aside { float: right;
        background-color: #eaeaea;
        width: 120px;
        padding: 5px;
        margin-left: 10px;
        font-size: 80%;
        -webkit-box-shadow: 5px 5px 5px #828282;
        -moz-box-shadow: 5px 5px 5px #828282;
        box-shadow: 5px 5px 5px #828282; }
```

Save the lighthouse.css file. Launch a modern browser and test your index.html page. You might be surprised by the way that the section and article headings display. We'll need to code CSS declarations specifically for the article header and for the h1 in the content id. Use contextual selectors. Launch a text editor and open lighthouse.css again. Add the following new CSS code:

```
article header { background-color: #FFFFFF;
                 background-image: none;
                 padding: 0;
                 font-size: 80%;}
```

```
#content h1 { color: #869dc7;
               font-family: Arial, sans-serif;
               font-size: 1.5em;}
```

3. Recall from Hands-On Practice 6.6 the CSS technique that helps older browsers to render HTML5 elements as expected. Add the section, article, and aside HTML element selectors to the CSS. The new style rule is

```
header, nav, footer, figure, figcaption, section, article, aside
{ display: block; }
```

4. Save the lighthouse.css file. Display your index.html page in a modern browser. It should look similar to the page shown in Figure 6.32 (see chapter6/blog/index.html in the student files).

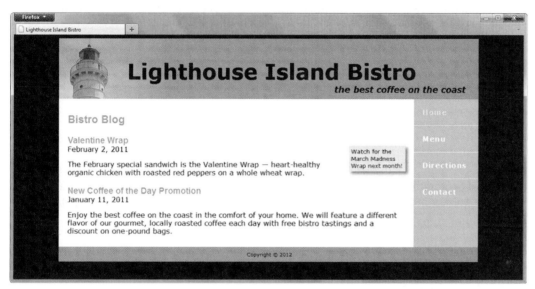

Figure 6.32 The HTML5 section, article, and aside elements were used on this page

HTML5 and Today's Browsers

Internet Explorer 9 and current versions of Safari, Chrome, Firefox, and Opera offer good support of HTML5 structural elements. The issue is that many people still use earlier versions of browsers. There are two different approaches that you can follow if you'd like to begin using HTML5 today: a conservative, straightforward approach and a progressive, enthusiastic approach that is more involved and requires JavaScript (see Chapter 11).

Conservative Approach to Using HTML5 Today

For the best chance at compatibility, code using either HTML5 or XHTML syntax and avoid using the new HTML5 elements. Instead, use the new element names as class names or id names. In this way, you'll become acquainted with the new element names and it will be easier to update the pages to all HTML5 later on. See chapter6/blog/all.html for an example of this technique. As time goes by and older browsers are used less and less, you'll be all set!

Progressive Approach to Using HTML5 Today

For starters, use Hands-On Practice 6.6 and 6.7 as an example: Code using the new HTML5 elements and include CSS that configures older non-supporting browsers to render the HTML5 header, figure, figcaption, footer, nav, section, article, and aside elements as block display (use `display: block;`). This will work well in all browsers except for Internet Explorer 8 and earlier versions.

So, what to do about Internet Explorer 8 and earlier versions? Remy Sharp offers a solution to enhance the support of Internet Explorer 8 and earlier versions (see http://remysharp.com/2009/01/07/html5-enabling-script). The technique uses conditional comments that are only supported by Internet Explorer and are ignored by other browsers. The conditional comments cause Internet Explorer to interpret JavaScript statements that configure it to recognize and process CSS for the new HTML5 element selectors. Sharp has uploaded the script to Google's code project and has made it available for anyone to use. Add the following code to the head section of a web page after CSS to cause Internet Explorer 8 and earlier versions to correctly render your HTML5 code:

```
<!--[if lt IE 9]>
<script src="http://html5shim.googlecode.com/svn/trunk/html5.js">
</script>
<![endif]-->
```

What's the drawback to this approach? Be aware that your web page visitors using Internet Explorer 8 and earlier versions may see a warning message and must have JavaScript enabled for this method to work. Try out an example (see chapter6/blog/today.html in the student files).

 Checkpoint 6.3

1. Why should you use HTML5 structural elements instead of div elements for some page areas?

2. What is the purpose of the article element?

3. What is the purpose of the hgroup element?

Chapter Summary

This chapter introduced CSS page layout techniques and HTML5 structural elements. Techniques for positioning and floating elements and configuring two-column page layouts were demonstrated. This topic is very deep and you have much to explore. Visit the resources cited in the chapter to continue learning about this technology.

Visit the textbook website at http://www.webdevfoundations.net for examples, the links listed in this chapter, and updated information.

Key Terms

:active	`<time>`	margin
:focus	absolute positioning	margin property
:hover	border	normal flow
:link	box model	`overflow` property
:visited	clear property	padding
`<article>`	content	position property
`<aside>`	display property	pseudo-class
`<footer>`	float property	relative positioning
`<header>`	left property	right property
`<hgroup>`	list marker	top property
`<nav>`	list-style-image property	visible width
`<section>`	list-style-type property	width property

Review Questions

Multiple Choice

1. If four numeric values are given for the margin of an element, what would be their right order?

   a. top, right, bottom, left

   b. top, left, bottom, right

   c. top, bottom, right, left

   d. none of the above

2. Which of the following, from outermost to innermost, are components of the box model?

   a. margin, border, padding, content

   b. content, padding, border, margin

   c. content, margin, padding, border

   d. margin, padding, border, content

3. With respect to what does fixed positioning configure the location of an element?

   a. its position in the normal flow

   b. browser viewport

   c. container element

   d. none of the above

4. With respect to what does absolute positioning configure the location of an element?

   a. its position in the normal flow

   b. browser viewport

   c. container element

   d. none of the above

5. Which of the following configures a class called gallery to float to the left?

   a. .gallery { left: float; }

   b. .gallery { float: left; }

   c. .gallery {position: left;}

   d. .gallery {position: float;}

6. Which of the following is an example of using a contextual selector to configure the anchor tags within the .nav class?

   a. nav. a

   b. a nav.

   c. .nav a

   d. a#nav

7. Which of the following sets of positioning properties removes an element from its normal flow?
   a. relative and absolute
   b. relative and static
   c. absolute and fixed
   d. static and fixed

8. How is the overflow property used?
   a. to specify what happens if content overflows an element's box
   b. to clear a float
   c. to provide scroll bars to the content
   d. all of the above

9. Which of the following pseudo-classes is used to modify the display of a hyperlink when a mouse pointer passes over it?
   a. :hover
   b. :link
   c. :onclick
   d. :visited

10. Which of the following properties can be used to clear a float?
    a. float or clear
    b. clear or overflow
    c. position or clear
    d. overflow or float

Fill in the Blank

11. The default CSS positioning value of an element is _____.

12. If an element is configured with float: right;, the other content on the page will appear to its _____.

13. The HTML5 element _____ provides tangential content.

14. The _____ property allows images and any other elements to align on the left or right margin, and the content wraps around it.

15. The _____ determines the empty space between the element and any adjacent elements.

Apply Your Knowledge

1. **Predict the Result.** Draw and write a brief description of the web page that will be created with the following HTML code:

```
<!DOCTYPE html>
<html lang="en">
<head>
<title>CircleSoft Web Design</title>
<meta charset="utf-8">
<style>
  h1 { border-bottom: 1px groove #333333;
       color: #006600;
       background-color: #cccccc }
  #content { position: absolute;
             left: 200px;
             top: 75px;
             font-family: Arial, sans-serif;
             width: 300px; }
  .nav a { font-weight: bold; }
</style>
</head>
<body>
<h1>CircleSoft Web Design</h1>
<div id="content">
```

```
<p>Our professional staff takes pride in its working relationship
with our clients by offering personalized services that listen to
their needs, develop their target areas, and incorporate these
items into a website that works.</p>
</div>
<ul class="nav">
  <li>Home</li>
  <li><a href="about.html">About</a></li>
  <li><a href="services.html">Services</a></li>
</ul>
</body>
</html>
```

2. **Fill in the Missing Code.** This web page should be configured as a two-column
   page layout with a right column that is 150 pixels wide. The right column should
   have a 1 pixel border. The margin in the left-column content area needs to allow for
   space that will be used by the right column. Some CSS selectors, properties, and
   values, indicated by "_", are missing. Fill in the missing code.

```
<!DOCTYPE html>
<html lang="en">
<head>
<title>Trillium Media Design</title>
<meta charset="utf-8">
<style>
#rightcolumn { "_": "_";
               width: "_";
               background-color: #cccccc;
               border: "_"; }
#logo { background-color: #cccccc;
        color: #663333;
        font-size: x-large;
        border-bottom: 1px solid #333333; }
.content { margin-right: "_"; }
.footer { font-size: x-small;
          text-align: center;
          clear: "_"; }
#"_" a { color: #000066;
         text-decoration: none; }
ul {list-style-type: "_"; }
</style>
</head>
<body>
<div id="rightcolumn">
<ul>
  <li><a href="index.html">Home</a></li>
  <li><a href="products.html">Products</a></li>
  <li><a href="services.html">Services</a></li>
  <li><a href="about.html">About</a></li>
</ul>
</div>
```

```
<div class="content">
<div id="logo">
<h1>Trillium Media Design</h1>
</div>
<p>Our professional staff takes pride in its working relationship
with our clients by offering personalized services that listen to
their needs, develop their target areas, and incorporate these
items into a website that works.</p>
</div>
<div class="footer">
Copyright &copy; 2012 Trillium Media Design<br>
Last Updated on 06/08/12
</div>
</body>
</html>
```

3. **Find the Error.** When this page is displayed in a browser, the heading information obscures the floating image and paragraph text. Correct the errors and describe the process that you followed.

```
<!DOCTYPE html>
<html lang="en">
<head>
<title>CSS Float</title>
<meta charset="utf-8">
<style>
body { width: 500px; }
h1 { background-color: #eeeeee;
     padding: 5px;
     color: #666633;
     position: absolute;
     left: 200px;
     top: 20px; }
p { font-family: Arial, sans-serif;
    position; absolute;
    left: 100px;
    top: 100px; }
#yls { float: right;
       margin: 0 0 5px 5px;
       border: solid; }
</style>
</head>
<body>
<h1>Floating an Image</h1>
<img id="yls" src="yls.jpg" alt="Yellow Lady Slipper" height="100"
width="100">
<p>The Yellow Lady Slipper pictured on the right is a wildflower.
It grows in wooded areas and blooms in June each year. The Yellow
Lady Slipper is a member of the orchid family.</p>
</body>
</html>
```

Hands-On Exercises

1. Write the CSS for a div element class named page which will be used for centering a page. Assume the page width to be 800 pixels.

2. Write the CSS for a web page which will be centered on the browser viewport and will have an image floating on the right side of the page. Provide colors of your own choice that will give proper contrast.

3. Write the CSS for an id named note with the following attributes: absolutely positioned on a page 80 pixels from the left and 200 pixels from the top with an olive background.

4. Write the CSS for a class of paragraphs named important with the following attributes: relatively positioned, background color grey, text color white, 20 pixels from the left, and 10 pixels from the top.

5. Write the CSS to configure a class named gallery which will be used to create an image gallery. The width and height of each image in the gallery will be 150 pixels and 120 pixels, respectively. Keep a margin of 5 pixels.

6. Write the HTML code to configure an image gallery utilizing the gallery class created in Exercise 5. Also use the wrapper class from Exercise 2 to center the page.

7. Write the HTML to configure a header element that contains an hgroup element with an h1 element, h2 element, and h3 element. Configure your school name as the h1 element. Configure your major as the h2 element. Configure the name of your current web development course as the h3 element.

8. Write the HTML to configure a section element that contains an h1 element, an h2 element, and an article element. Choose a topic of your choice. Configure the name of the topic as the h1 element. Configure a sub-heading as the h2 element. Configure a brief description of the topic within the article element.

9. Use the mylinks.html file you created in 8 as a starting point. Modify the web page to use external rather than embedded CSS. Save the CSS file as links.css.

10. Create an HTML5 web page about one of your favorite hobbies. Choose a hobby and either take a relevant photo or select a relevant royalty-free photo from the Web (refer to Chapter 4). Decide on a heading for your page. Write one or two brief paragraphs about the hobby. The page must use valid HTML5 syntax and include the following HTML5 elements: header, article, and footer. Include a hyperlink to a website that is relevant to the hobby. Include your name in an e-mail address in the page footer area. Configure the text, color, and layout with embedded CSS. Refer to the section "HTML5 and Today's Browser" and review the techniques for configuring HTML5 pages to display in both modern and older versions of browsers. Modify the CSS and HTML of your page for cross-browser display. Save the file as myhobby.html.

11. Use the myhobby.html file you created in 10 as a starting point. Modify the web page to use external rather than embedded CSS. Save the file as hobby.css.

Web Research

This chapter introduced using CSS to configure web page layout. Use the resources listed in the textbook as a starting point. You can also use a search engine to search for CSS resources. Create a web page that provides a list of at least five CSS resources on the Web. For each CSS resource, provide the URL (configured as a hyperlink), the name of the website, a brief description, and a rating that indicates how helpful it is to beginning web developers.

Focus on Web Design

There is still much for you to learn about CSS. A great place to learn about web technology is on the Web itself. Use a search engine to search for CSS page layout tutorials. Choose a tutorial that is easy to read. Select a section that discusses a CSS technique that was not covered in this chapter. Create a web page that uses this new technique. Consider how the suggested page layout follows (or does not follow) principles of design such as contrast, repetition, alignment, and proximity (see Chapter 5). The web page should provide the URL of your tutorial (configured as a hyperlink), the name of the website, a description of the new technique you discovered, and a discussion of how the technique follows (or does not follow) principles of design.

WEBSITE CASE STUDY

Implementing a CSS Two-Column Page Layout

Each of the following case studies continues throughout most of the textbook. This chapter implements a CSS two-column page layout in the websites.

JavaJam Coffee House

See Chapter 2 for an introduction to the JavaJam Coffee House case study. Figure 2.25 shows a site map for the JavaJam. In this case study, you will implement a new two-column CSS page layout for JavaJam. Figure 6.33 shows a wireframe for a two-column page layout with wrapper, header, left column, right column, floating, and footer areas.

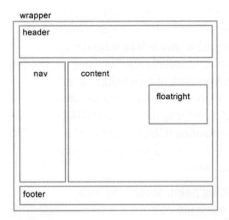

Figure 6.33 Wireframe for a two-column page layout for the JavaJam website

You will modify the external style sheet and the Home, Menu, and Music pages. Use the Chapter 4 JavaJam website as a starting point for this case study. You have five tasks in this case study:

1. Create a new folder for this JavaJam case study.

2. Modify the style rules in the javajam.css file to configure a two-column page layout, as shown in Figure 6.33.

Figure 6.34 The new JavaJam two-column layout (index.html)

3. Modify the Home page to implement the two-column page layout, as shown in Figure 6.34.

4. Modify the Menu page to be consistent with the Home page.

5. Modify the Music page (Figure 6.35) to be consistent with the Home page.

Hands-On Practice Case

Task 1: Create a Folder. Create a folder called javajam6. Copy all of the files from your Chapter 4 javajam4 folder into the javajam6 folder. You will modify the javajam.css file and each web page file (index.html, menu.html, and music.html) to implement the two-column page layout shown in Figure 6.33. See the new JavaJam Home page, as shown in Figure 6.34.

Task 2: Configure the CSS. Open javajam.css in a text editor. Edit the style rules as follows:

1. Configure the header area. Create a new id named `header` with a background (#ccaa66) and text (#000000) color, center alignment (`text-align: center;`), and no margin (`margin: 0;`). Remove the h1 element selector and style rules.

2. Configure the left-column navigation area. Add style rules to the `nav` id to configure an area that floats to the left, is 100 pixels wide, displays centered text, and has 10 pixels of padding on the top.

3. Configure the navigation hyperlinks. Use a contextual selector to add a new style rule for the anchor tags within the `nav` id. Configure this selector with 15 pixels of bottom padding and no underline on hyperlinks.

```
#nav a { text-decoration: none;
         padding-bottom: 15px; }
```

4. Configure the `:link`, `:visted`, and `:hover` pseudo-classes for the navigation hyperlinks. Use the following text colors: #996633 (unvisited hyperlinks), #ccaa66 (visited hyperlinks), and #330000 (hyperlinks with `:hover`). For example,

```
#nav a:link { color: #996633; }
```

5. You will organize the navigation hyperlinks within an unordered list in later tasks. The navigation area in Figure 6.33 does not show list markers. Use a contextual selector to configure unordered lists in the navigation area to display without list markers.

```
#nav ul { list-style-type: none; }
```

6. Modify the content id style rules for the right column. Change the padding to 10 pixels top, 30 pixels bottom, 20 pixels left, and 20 pixels right. Configure a 150 pixel left margin, background (#f2eab7) color, and text (#000000) color.

7. Configure an area that floats to the right. Notice how the winding road graphic shown in Figure 6.33 floats on the right side—this is configured with the floatright class. Images are more compelling when they are separated from other elements (such as text) by empty space. Add 20 pixels of padding to the left side of this area.

8. Modify the footer id style rules. Change the padding to 20 pixels top and bottom. Configure the footer to clear all floats.

9. Configure the :link, :visited, and :hover pseudo-classes for the footer hyperlink. Use the following text colors: #ffffcc (unvisited hyperlink), #f2eab7 (visited hyperlink), and #330000 (hyperlink with :hover).

10. Modify the h2 element selector style rules. View the Music page shown in Figure 6.35 and notice that the <h2> tags are styled differently, with all uppercase text (using a new property, text-transform) and different background and text colors, font size, bottom border, padding, and margin. Also configure styles to clear floats on the left. Replace the h2 element selector style rules with the following:

```
h2 { text-transform: uppercase;
     background-color: #ffffcc;
     color: #663300;
     font-size: 1.2em;
     border-bottom: 1px solid #000000;
     padding: 5px 0 0 5px;
     margin-right: 20px;
     clear: left; }
```

11. Refer to the Music page shown in Figure 6.35 and notice how the images float on the left side of the paragraph description. Configure a new class named floatleft that floats to the left with 20 pixels of right and bottom padding.

12. Configure a new class named clear that clears the left float.

Save the javajam.css file.

Task 3: The Home Page. Open index.html in a text editor. Edit the code as follows:

1. Configure the header area. Assign the <h1> element to the header id.

2. Configure the left-column navigation area, which is the div assigned to the nav id. Remove any   characters that may be present. Code an unordered

list to organize the navigation hyperlinks. Each hyperlink should be contained within `<li>` tags.

3. Configure the image that floats to the right. Modify the winding road image element. Remove the `align="right"` attribute and add `class="floatright"` to the winding road image element.

Save the index.html file. It should look similar to the web page shown in Figure 6.34. Remember that validating your HTML and CSS can help you find syntax errors. Test and correct this page before you continue.

Task 4: The Menu Page. Open menu.html in a text editor. Configure the header area, left-column navigation area, and navigation hyperlinks in the same manner as the home page. Save your new menu.html page and test it in a browser. Use the CSS and HTML validators to help you find syntax errors.

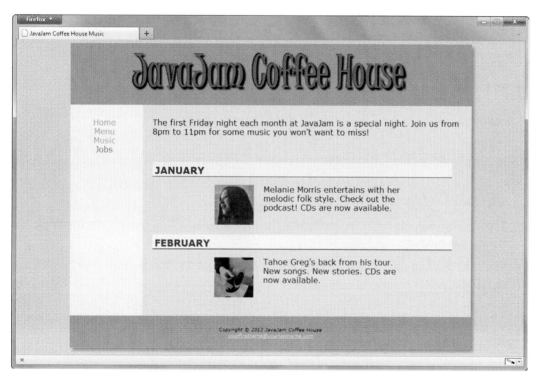

Figure 6.35 The new JavaJam Music page

Task 5: The Music Page. Open music.html in a text editor. Configure the header area, left-column navigation area, and navigation hyperlinks in the same manner as the home page.

1. Configure the thumbnail images to float to the left. Add `class="floatleft"` to the image tag for each thumbnail image.

2. Add a blank line above the closing div tag for the `content` id. Clear the last floated thumbnail image by coding a line break tag that is assigned to the `clearleft` class.

Save your new menu.html page and test it in a browser. Use the CSS and XHTML validators to help you find syntax errors.

In this case study, you changed the page layout of the JavaJam website. Notice that with just a few changes in the CSS and HTML code, you configured a two-column page layout.

OPTIONAL: JavaJam Case Study: HTML5 Extension

Get more practice with the new HTML5 structural elements by creating a new version of the JavaJam website. Create a folder called javajam6HTML5 to contain your JavaJam website files. Copy the files from the javajam6 folder.

1. Modify the javajam.css file in a text editor. Configure new styles and use HTML element selectors for the header, nav, and footer elements.

   - All style declarations previously associated with the `header` id will apply to the header element selector. Replace the `header` id with the header element selector.

   - Configure an h1 element selector with a zero margin.

   - Replace all instances of the `#nav` selector with the nav element selector.

   - Replace all instances of the `#footer` selector with the footer element selector.

   - Modify the `details` class. Configure 35 pixels of bottom padding.

   - Add the following CSS to be compatible with most older browsers:

     ```
     header, nav, figure, footer { display: block; }
     ```

2. Modify each web page in a text editor. Configure HTML5 elements.

   - Configure an HTML5 header element to contain the h1 element. Remove `id="header"` from the h1 tag.

   - Replace the opening and closing tags for the div assigned to the `nav` id with the HTML5 nav element.

   - Replace the opening and closing tags for the div assigned to the `footer` id with the HTML5 footer element.

   - Note the image on the home page. Use the HTML5 figure element to contain the image element. Configure the figure element to use the `floatright` class. Remove the `floatright` class from the image tag.

   - Note the image links on the Music page. Use the HTML5 figure element to contain each image link. Configure the figure element to use the `floatleft` class. Remove the `floatleft` class from the image tags. Also replace the paragraph tags assigned to the `details` class with div tags assigned to the `details` class.

   - Add the following code in the head section of the web page after the link element to assist Internet Explorer 8 and earlier versions):

     ```
     <!--[if lt IE 9]>
     <script src="http://html5shim.googlecode.com/svn/trunk/html5.js">
     </script>
     <![endif]-->
     ```

Save your files. Display your pages in a modern browser. Your new case study web pages should look similar to the previous version. This optional exercise provided you with additional practice using new HTML5 elements.

Fish Creek Animal Hospital

See Chapter 2 for an introduction to the Fish Creek Animal Hospital case study. Figure 2.29 shows a site map for Fish Creek. In this case study, you will implement a redesign with a new two-column CSS page layout. Figure 6.36 displays a wireframe for a two-column page layout with wrapper, logo header, left column, right column, and footer areas.

Figure 6.36 Wireframe for a two-column page layout for the Fish Creek website

You will modify the external style sheet and the Home, Services, and Ask the Vet pages. Use the Chapter 4 Fish Creek website as a starting point for this case study. You have five tasks in this case study:

1. Create a new folder for this Fish Creek case study.

2. Modify the style rules in the fishcreek.css file to configure a two-column page layout, as shown in Figure 6.36.

3. Modify the Home page to implement the two-column page layout, as shown in Figure 6.37.

4. Modify the Services page to be consistent with the Home page.

5. Modify the Ask the Vet page to be consistent with the Home page.

Hands-On Practice Case

Task 1: Create a Folder. Create a folder called fishcreek6. Copy all of the files from your Chapter 4 fishcreek4 folder (except the fish navigation images home.gif, services.gif, askvet.gif, and contact.gif) into the fishcreek6 folder. You will modify the fishcreek.css file and each web page file (index.html, services.html, and askvet.html) to implement the two-column page layout, as shown in Figure 6.36. See the new Fish Creek home page, as shown in Figure 6.37.

Task 2: Configure the CSS. Open fishcreek.css in a text editor. Edit the style rules as follows:

1. Configure a background image for the body element selector. Use the chapter6/gradientblue.jpg file found in the student files.

2. Modify the wrapper id. Configure a white background color (#FFFFFF) and dark-blue text color (#000066) for this area. Change the width to 80%. Set the minimum width to 700 pixels.

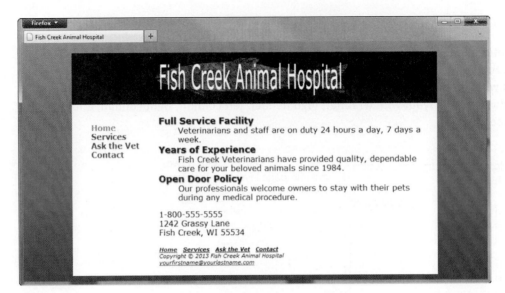

Figure 6.37 The new Fish Creek two-column home page (index.html)

3. Configure the header area. Remove the h1 element selector and style rules. Create a new id named `header` with centered text, a dark-blue background color (#000066), and 10 pixels of padding.

4. Configure the left column area. Add a new style rule for the `leftcolumn` id to configure an area that floats to the left and is 150 pixels wide.

5. You will organize the navigation hyperlinks within an unordered list in later tasks. The navigation area in Figure 6.37 does not show list markers. Use a contextual selector to configure unordered lists in the left column area to display without list markers and no padding.

```
#leftcolumn ul { list-style-type: none;
                 padding-left: 0;}
```

6. Configure the anchor tags in the `leftcolumn` id to display no underline.

```
#leftcolumn a { text-decoration: none; }
```

7. Configure the `:link`, `:visited`, and `:hover` pseudo-classes for the `leftcolumn` hyperlinks. Use the following text colors: #3262A3 (unvisited hyperlinks), #6699FF (visited hyperlinks), and #CCCCCC (hyperlinks with `:hover`). For example,

```
#leftcolumn a:link { color: #3262A3; }
```

8. Configure the right column area. Add a new style rule for the `rightcolumn` id to configure an area with a 180 pixel left margin, 10 pixels of right padding, and 20 pixels of bottom padding.

9. Remove the `main` id. It is no longer used.

10. Modify the `category` class. Remove the background color style rule.

Save the fishcreek.css file.

Task 3: Modify the Home Page. Open index.html in a text editor and modify the code as follows:

1. Configure the header area. Assign the <h1> to the id header.

2. Configure the left column. Modify the div tag that contains this area. Change id="main" to id="leftcolumn".

3. Rework the navigation area. Remove any   characters that may be present. Replace the fish image links with text image links. Then, code an unordered list to organize the navigation hyperlinks. Each hyperlink should be contained within <li> tags.

4. Configure the right column. This area contains the description list, the div with the contact information, and the footer div. Code a div element to contain this area. Assign the div to the id rightcolumn.

Save the index.html file. It should look similar to the web page shown in Figure 6.37. Remember that validating your HTML and CSS can help you find syntax errors. Test and correct this page before you continue.

Task 4: Modify the Services Page. Open services.html in a text editor. Configure the header area, left-column navigation area, navigation hyperlinks, and right-column content area in the same manner as the home page. Save your new services.html page and test it in a browser. Use the CSS and HTML validators to help you find syntax errors.

Task 5: Modify the Ask the Vet Page. Open askvet.html in a text editor. Configure the header area, left-column navigation area, and navigation hyperlinks in the same manner as the home page. Save your new askvet.html page and test it in a browser. Use the CSS and HTML validators to help you find syntax errors.

In this case study, you changed the page layout of the Fish Creek website. Notice that with just a few changes in the CSS and HTML code, you configured a two-column page layout with a completely new visual aesthetic.

OPTIONAL: Fish Creek Case Study: HTML5 Extension

Get more practice with the new HTML5 structural elements by creating a new version of the Fish Creek website. Create a folder called fishcreek6HTML5 to contain your Fish Creek website files. Copy the files from the fishcreek6 folder.

1. Modify the fishcreek.css file in a text editor. Configure new styles and use HTML element selectors for the header, nav, and footer elements.

   - All style declarations previously associated with the header id will apply to the header element selector. Replace the header id with the header element selector.

   - Replace all instances of the #leftcolumn selector with the nav element selector.

   - Replace all instances of the #footer selector with the footer element selector.

   - Add the following CSS to be compatible with most older browsers:

```
header, nav, footer { display: block; }
```

2. Modify each web page in a text editor. Configure HTML5 elements.

- Configure an HTML5 header element to contain the h1 element. Remove `id="header"` from the h1 tag.

- Replace the opening and closing tags for the first div assigned to the `nav` class with the HTML5 nav element.

- Replace the opening and closing tags for the div assigned to the `footer` id with the HTML5 footer element.

- Add the following code in the head section of the web page after the link element to assist Internet Explorer 8 and earlier versions:

```
<!--[if lt IE 9]>
<script src="http://html5shim.googlecode.com/svn/trunk/html5.js">
</script>
<![endif]-->
```

Save your files. Display your pages in a modern browser. Your new case study web pages should look similar to the previous version. This optional exercise provided you with additional practice using new HTML5 elements.

Pacific Trails Resort

See Chapter 2 for an introduction to the Pacific Trails Resort case study. Figure 2.33 shows a site map for Pacific Trails. The pages were created in earlier chapters. In this case study, you will implement a new two-column CSS page layout. Figure 6.38 displays a wireframe for a two-column page layout with wrapper, header, nav, content, and footer areas.

Figure 6.38 Wireframe for a two-column page layout for the Pacific Trails website

You will modify the external style sheet and the Home, Yurts, and Activities pages. Use the Chapter 4 Pacific Trails website as a starting point for this case study. You have five tasks in this case study:

1. Create a new folder for the Pacific Trails case study.

2. Modify the style rules in the pacific.css file to configure a two-column page layout, as shown in Figure 6.38.

3. Modify the Home page to implement the two-column page layout, as shown in Figure 6.39.

4. Modify the Yurts page to be consistent with the Home page.

5. Modify the Activities page to be consistent with the Home page.

Hands-On Practice Case

Task 1: Create a Folder. Create a folder called pacific6. Copy all of the files from your Chapter 4 pacific4 folder (except the navigation button images) into the pacific6 folder. You will modify the pacific.css file and each web page file (index.html, yurts.html, and activities.html) to implement the two-column page layout, as shown in Figure 6.38. See the new Pacific Trails home page, as shown in Figure 6.39.

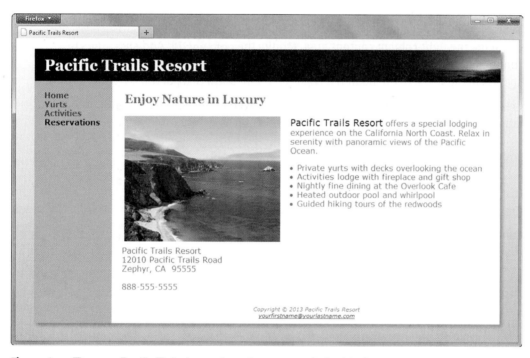

Figure 6.39 The new Pacific Trails two-column home page (index.html)

Task 2: Configure the CSS. Open pacific.css in a text editor. Edit the style rules as follows:

1. Modify the `wrapper` id. Change the background color to blue (#90C7E3), which will be the background behind the navigation area. Configure a minimum width of 960 pixels.

2. Configure the left-column navigation area. Modify the `nav` id. Keep the style rule that configures bold text. Remove the background color property. The nav area will inherit the background color of the `wrapper` id. Add style rules to configure this area to float to the left with a width of 160 pixels. Also configure 20 pixels top padding, 5 pixels right padding, 5 pixels bottom padding, and 20 pixels left padding.

3. Configure the navigation hyperlinks. Use a contextual selector to add a new style rule for the anchor tags within the `nav` id that removes the underline from hyperlinks.

```
#nav a { text-decoration: none; }
```

4. Configure the :link, :visited, and :hover pseudo-classes for the navigation hyperlinks. Use the following text colors: #000033 (unvisited hyperlinks), #344873 (visited hyperlinks), and #FFFFFF (hyperlinks with :hover). For example,

```
#nav a:link { color: #000033; }
```

5. You will organize the navigation hyperlinks within an unordered list in later tasks. The navigation area in Figure 6.39 does not show list markers. Use a contextual selector to configure unordered lists in the navigation area to display without list markers. Also configure the unordered list to have no margin and no left padding.

```
#nav ul { list-style-type: none;
          margin: 0;
          padding-left: 0; }
```

6. Configure the right-column content area. Modify the content id. Add style rules to configure a white (#FFFFFF) background, 160 pixels of left margin (this value corresponds to the width of the floated navigation area), and 1 pixel of top padding.

7. Create a new style rule to configure images displayed in the content id to float to the left with 20 pixels of right padding. Use a contextual selector.

```
#content img { float: left;
               padding-right: 20px }
```

8. Create a new class named clear that clears a float.

9. Configure the unordered lists in the content id to display list markers inside rather than outside of the list.

```
#content ul {list-style-position: inside; }
```

Save the pacific.css file.

Task 3: Modify the Home Page. Open index.html in a text editor and modify the code as follows:

1. Configure the left-column navigation area, which is the div assigned to the nav id. Remove any   characters that may be present. Code an unordered list to organize the navigation hyperlinks. Each hyperlink should be contained within <li> tags.

2. Locate the div that contains the address information. Assign this div to the class named clear.

3. The page layout in Figure 6.38 shows the footer id contained within the content id. Move the closing div tag for the content id and place it on a new line after the closing div tag for the footer id.

Save the index.html file. It should look similar to the web page shown in Figure 6.39. Remember that validating your HTML and CSS can help you find syntax errors. Test and correct this page before you continue.

Task 4: Modify the Yurts Page. Open yurts.html in a text editor. Configure the left-column navigation area, navigation hyperlinks, and footer location in the same manner as the home page. Save your new yurts.html page and test it in a browser. Use the CSS and HTML validators to help you find syntax errors.

Task 5: Modify the Activities Page. Open yurts.html in a text editor. Configure the left-column navigation area, navigation hyperlinks, and footer location in the same manner as the home page. Save your new activities.html page and test it in a browser. Use the CSS and HTML validators to help you find syntax errors.

In this case study, you changed the page layout of the Pacific Trails Resort website. Notice that with just a few changes in the CSS and HTML code, you configured a two-column page layout.

OPTIONAL: Pacific Trails Case Study: HTML5 Extension

Get more practice with the new HTML5 structural elements by creating a new version of the Pacific Trails website. Create a folder called pacific6HTML5 to contain your Pacific Trails website files. Copy the files from the pacific6 folder.

1. Modify the pacific.css file in a text editor. Configure new styles and use HTML element selectors for the header, nav, and footer elements.

   - Replace all instances of the #nav selector with the nav element selector.

   - Replace all instances of the #footer selector with the footer element selector.

   - Replace the #content img selector with a #content figure selector. Add a style rule to configure a zero margin.

   - Add the following CSS to be compatible with most older browsers:

     ```
     header, nav, figure, footer { display: block; }
     ```

2. Modify each web page in a text editor. Configure HTML5 elements.

   - Configure an HTML5 header element to contain the h1 element.

   - Replace the opening and closing tags for the div assigned to the nav id with the HTML5 nav element.

   - Replace the opening and closing tags for the div assigned to the footer id with the HTML5 footer element.

   - Note the image on each page in the content area. Use the HTML5 figure element to contain the image element. Configure the figure element to use the floatleft class. Remove the floatleft class from the image tag.

   - Add the following code in the head section of the web page after the link element to assist Internet Explorer 8 and earlier versions):

     ```
     <!--[if lt IE 9]>
     <script src="http://html5shim.googlecode.com/svn/trunk/html5.js">
     </script>
     <![endif]-->
     ```

Save your files. Display your pages in a modern browser. Your new case study web pages should look similar to the previous version. This optional exercise provided you with additional practice using new HTML5 elements.

Prime Properties

See Chapter 2 for an introduction to the Prime Properties case study. Figure 2.37 shows a site map for Prime Properties. In this case study, you will implement a new two-column CSS page layout for Prime Properties. Figure 6.40 displays a wireframe for a two-column page layout with a wrapper, header, left column, right column, and footer area.

Figure 6.40 Wireframe for a two-column page layout for the Prime Properties website

You will modify the external style sheet and the Home, Listings, and Financing pages. Use the Chapter 4 Prime Properties website as a starting point for this case study. You have five tasks in this case study:

1. Create a new folder for the Prime Properties case study.

2. Modify the style rules in the prime.css file to configure a two-column page layout, as shown in Figure 6.40.

3. Modify the Home page to implement the two-column page layout, as shown in Figure 6.41.

4. Modify the Listings page to be consistent with the Home page.

5. Modify the Financing page to be consistent with the Home page.

Hands-On Practice Case

Task 1: Create a Folder. Create a folder called prime6. Copy all of the files from your Chapter 4 prime4 folder into the prime6 folder. You will modify the prime.css file and each web page file (index.html, listings.html, and financing.html) to implement the two-column page layout shown in Figure 6.40. See the new Prime Properties home page in Figure 6.41.

Task 2: Configure the CSS. Open prime.css in a text editor. Edit the style rules as follows:

1. Configure the left column area. Add a new style rule for the `left` id to configure an area that floats to the left and is 150 pixels wide.

2. Configure the navigation hyperlinks to use CSS for the background color and border instead of using image links. We'll set up the CSS in this step.

   a. Use a contextual selector to add a new style rule for the anchor tags within the `nav` id that removes the underline from hyperlinks. Also configure the anchor tags to

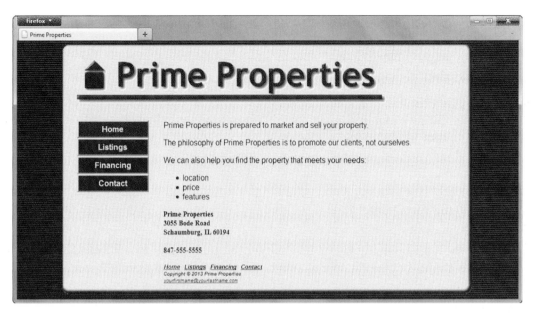

Figure 6.41 The new Prime Properties two-column home page (index.html)

use block display, centered text, bold font, text color #FFFFCC, a 3 pixel gray (#CCCCCC) outset border, and 5 pixels of padding.

```
#left a { text-decoration: none;
        display: block:
        text-align: center;
        color: #FFFFCC;
        font-weight: bold;
        border: 3px outset #CCCCCC;
        padding: 5px;}
```

b. Configure the :link, :visited, and :hover pseudo-classes for the navigation hyperlinks. Use the following background colors: #003366 (unvisited hyperlinks) and #48751A (visited hyperlinks). Configure a 3 pixel inset #333333 border for hyperlinks in the hover state.

```
#left a:link { background-color: #003366; }
#left a:visited { background-color: #48751A; }
#left a:hover { border: 3px inset #333333; }
```

3. You will organize the navigation hyperlinks within an unordered list in later tasks. The navigation area in Figure 6.41 does not show list markers. Use a contextual selector to configure unordered lists in the navigation area to display without list markers. Also configure the unordered list to have no margin and no left padding.

```
#left ul { list-style-type: none;
        margin: 0;
        padding-left: 0; }
```

4. Configure the right column area. Add a new style rule for the `right` id to configure an area with a 180 pixel left margin and 20 pixels of right and bottom padding (`padding: 0 20px 20px 0;`).

5. Modify the `footer` id. Configure a style rule to clear floats.

6. Refer to the Listings page in Figure 6.42 and notice how the images float on the left side of the description. Configure a new class named `floatleft` that floats to the left with 20 pixels of right and bottom padding.

7. Configure a new class named `clear` that clears the left float.

Save the prime.css file.

Task 3: Modify the Home Page. Open index.html in a text editor and modify the code as follows:

1. Configure the left column. Locate the div assigned to `class="nav"` that is immediately below the h1 element. Remove `class="nav"` and assign this div to `id="left"`.

2. The navigation image links are the only content in the left column. Remove other code, including any ` ` characters that may be present. Replace the image links with text image links. Then, code an unordered list to organize the navigation hyperlinks. Each hyperlink should be contained within `<li>` tags.

3. Configure the right column. This area contains the content (paragraphs, unordered list, and contact information) and the footer section. Code a `<div>` that surrounds this area. Assign the `<div>` to `id="right"`.

Save the index.html file. It should look similar to the web page shown in Figure 6.41. Remember that validating your HTML and CSS can help you find syntax errors. Test and correct this page before you continue.

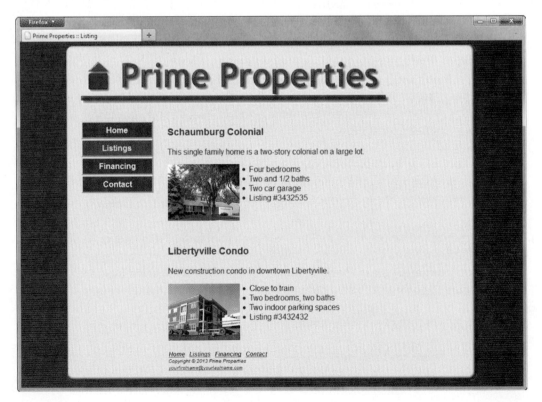

Figure 6.42 The new Prime Properties two-column Listings page

Task 4: Modify the Listings Page. Open listings.html in a text editor.

1. Configure the left-column navigation area, navigation hyperlinks, and right column in the same manner as the home page.

2. Configure the house and condo images to float to the left. Add `class="floatleft"` to these image elements.

3. Add a blank line above the second h3 element on the page. Clear the first floated thumbnail image by coding a line break tag that is assigned to the `clear` class.

Save your new listings.html page and test it in a browser. Use the CSS and HTML validators to help you find syntax errors.

Task 5: Modify the Financing Page. Open financing.html in a text editor. Configure the left-column navigation area, navigation hyperlinks, and right column in the same manner as the home page. Save your new financing.html page and test it in a browser. Use the CSS and HTML validators to help you find syntax errors.

In this case study, you changed the page layout of the Prime Properties website. Notice that with just a few changes in the CSS and HTML code, you configured a two-column page layout.

OPTIONAL: Prime Properties Case Study: HTML5 Extension

Get more practice with the new HTML5 structural elements by creating a new version of the Prime Properties website. Create a folder called prime6HTML5 to contain your Prime Properties website files. Copy the files from the prime6 folder.

1. Modify the prime.css file in a text editor. Configure new styles and use HTML element selectors for the header, nav, and footer elements.

   - All style declarations previously associated with the `header` id will apply to the header element selector. Replace the `header` id with the header element selector.

   - Replace all instances of the `#left` selector with the nav element selector.

   - Replace all instances of the `#footer` selector with the footer element selector.

   - Add the following CSS to be compatible with most older browsers:

     ```
     header, nav, figure, footer { display: block; }
     ```

2. Modify each web page in a text editor. Configure the HTML5 elements.

   - Configure an HTML5 header element to contain the h1 element. Remove `id="header"` from the h1 tag.

   - Replace the opening and closing tags for the div assigned to the `left` id with the HTML5 nav element.

   - Replace the opening and closing tags for the div assigned to the `footer` id with the HTML5 footer element.

   - Note the image links on the Listings page. Use the HTML5 figure element to contain each image link. Configure the figure element to use the `floatleft` class. Remove the `floatleft` class from the image tags. Code a line break above the footer element that is assigned to the `clear` class.

- Add the following code in the head section of the web page after the link element to assist Internet Explorer 8 and earlier versions:

```
<!--[if lt IE 9]>
<script src="http://html5shim.googlecode.com/svn/trunk/html5.js">
</script>
<![endif]-->
```

Save your files. Display your pages in a modern browser. Your new case study web pages should look similar to the previous version. This optional exercise provided you with additional practice using the new HTML5 elements.

Web Project

See Chapter 5 for an introduction to the Web Project case study. As you completed the Chapter 5 Web Project case study activities, you completed a Web Project Topic Approval, Web Project Site Map, and Web Project Page Layout Design. In this case study, you will use your design documents as a guide as you develop the pages for your Web Project using CSS in an external style sheet for both formatting and page layout.

Hands-On Practice Case

1. Create a folder called project. All of your project files and graphics will be organized in this folder and in subfolders as needed.

2. Refer to your Site Map to view the pages that you need to create. Jot down a list of the file names. Add these to the Site Map.

3. Refer to the Page Layout Design. Make a list of the common fonts and colors used on the pages. These may become the CSS you configure for the body element. Note where typical elements used for organization (such as headings, lists, paragraphs, and so on) may be used. You may want to configure CSS for these elements. Identify various page areas such as header, navigation, footer, and so on, and list any special configurations needed for these areas. These will be configured as classes in your CSS. Create an external style sheet, called project.css, which contains these configurations.

4. Using your design documents as a guide, code a representative page for your site. Use CSS to format text, color, and layout. Apply classes and ids where appropriate. Associate the web page to the external style sheet.

   Save and test the page. Modify both the web page and the project.css file as needed. Test and modify them until you have achieved the look you want.

5. Using the completed page as a template wherever possible, code the rest of the pages on your site. Test and modify them as needed.

6. Experiment with modifying the project.css file. Change the page background color, the font family, and so on. Test your pages in a browser. Notice how a change in a single file can affect multiple files when external style sheets are used.

More on Links, Layout, and Mobile

Chapter Objectives   In this chapter, you will learn how to . . .

- Code relative hyperlinks to web pages in folders within a website
- Configure a hyperlink to a named fragment internal to a web page
- Configure images with CSS sprites
- Configure a three-column page layout using CSS
- Configure CSS for printing
- Configure CSS for mobile display
- Utilize CSS3 media queries to target mobile devices

Now that you've had some experience coding HTML and CSS,
you're ready to explore a variety of techniques in this chapter, including relative hyperlinks and named fragment hyperlinks, CSS sprites, three-column page layout, styling for print, styling for mobile browsers, and configuring CSS3 media queries to target mobile devices.

7.1 Another Look at Hyperlinks

Hyperlinks make the Web a "web" of interconnected information. In this section, you'll revisit the topic of hyperlinks and explore coding relative links using the target attribute to open web pages in a new browser window, as well as coding hyperlinks that are internal to a web page.

More on Relative Linking

As indicated earlier in Chapter 2, a relative hyperlink is used to link to web pages within your site. You've been coding relative links to display web pages within the same folder. There are times when you need to link to files in other folders on your website. Let's consider the example of a website for a dog groomer that highlights services and products. The web developer for this site created separate folders called services and products in order to organize the site. See the folder and file listing shown in Figure 7.1.

Figure 7.1 The dog groomer site contains the images, products, and services folders

Relative Link Examples

To review, when linking to a file in the same folder or directory, the value of the href is the name of the file. For example, to link to the contact.html page from the home page (index.html), code the anchor element as follows:

```
<a href="contact.html">Contact</a>
```

When linking to a folder located within the current directory, use both the folder name and the file name in the relative link. For example, to link to the collars.html page in the products folder from the home page (index.html), code the anchor element as follows:

```
<a href="products/collars.html">Collars</a>
```

In Figure 7.1, the collars.html page is located in a subfolder of the groomer folder. The home page for the site (index.html) is located in the groomer folder. When linking to a file that is up one directory level from the current page, use the "../" notation. To link to the home page for the site from the collars.html page, code the anchor element as follows:

```
<a href="../index.html">Home</a>
```

When linking to a file that is in a folder on the same level as the current folder, the href value will use the "../" notation to indicate moving up one level and then down to the chosen folder. For example, to link to the bathing.html page in the services folder from the collars.html page in the products folder, code the anchor element as follows:

```
<a href="../services/bathing.html">Dog Bathing</a>
```

Don't worry if the use of "../" notation and linking to files in different folders seems new and different. In most of the exercises in this book, you will code either absolute links to other websites or relative links to files in the same folder.

Fragment Identifiers

VideoNote
Linking to a Named Fragment

Browsers begin the display of a web page at the top of the document. However, there are times when you need to provide the capability to link to a specific portion of a web page instead of the top. You can accomplish this by coding a hyperlink to a **fragment identifier** (sometimes called a named fragment or fragment id), which is simply an HTML element assigned to an id. Lists of frequently asked questions (FAQs) often use this technique.

There are two components to your coding when using fragment identifiers:

1. The tag that identifies the **named fragment** of a web page: The tag must be assigned to an id. For example, `<div id="content">`

2. The anchor tag that links to the named fragment on a web page.

Linking to a named fragment is often seen on long web pages. You might see a "Back to top" hyperlink that a visitor could select to cause the browser to quickly scroll the page back to the top of the page for easy site navigation.

Another use of fragment identifiers helps to provide for accessibility. Web pages may have a fragment identifier to indicate the beginning of the actual page content. When the visitor clicks on the "Skip to content" hyperlink, the browser links to the fragment identifier and shifts focus to the content area of the page. This "Skip to content" or "Skip navigation" link provides a way for screen reader users to skip repetitive navigation links (see Figure 7.2). This is accomplished in two steps as follows:

Focus on Accessibility

1. **Establish the Target.** Create the "Skip to content" fragment identifier by configuring a div that contains the page content with an id. For example,

   ```
   <div id="content">
   ```

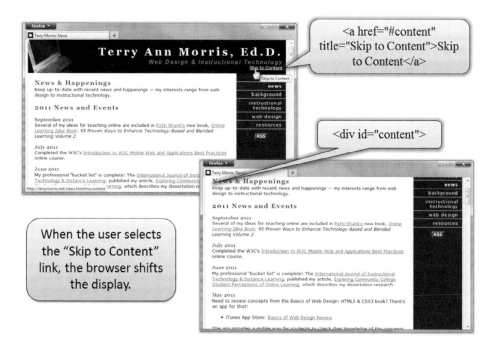

Figure 7.2 The "Skip to Content" link in action

2. **Reference the Target.** At the point of the page where you want to place a hyper-link to the content, type an anchor element. Use the href attribute and place a # (called a **hash mark**) before the name of the fragment identifier. The HTML for a hyperlink to the named fragment "content" is

```
<a href="#content">Skip to Content></a>
```

The hash mark indicates that the browser should search for an id on the same page. If you forget to type the hash mark, the browser will not look on the same web page; it will look for an external file.

Hands-On Practice 7.1

You will work with fragment identifiers in this Hands-On Practice. Locate chapter7/starter1.html in the student files. Figure 7.3 shows a screenshot of this web page.

Launch a text editor and open starter1.html. Save the file as favorites.html. Examine the source code and notice that the top portion of the page contains an unordered list with categories of in-terest (such as Hobbies, HTML, Mobile Web Display, and Professional Organizations) that corre-spond to the text displayed in the h2 elements below. Each h2 element is followed by a definition list of topics and URLs related to that category. It might be helpful to web page visitors if they can click a category item and immediately jump to the page area that has information related to that item. This could be a useful application of linking to fragment identifiers!

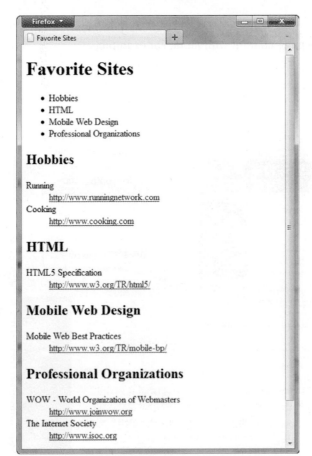

Figure 7.3 You will add hyperlinks to fragment identifiers

Modify the page as follows:

1. Code a named fragment for each h2 element in the definition list. For example,

```
<h2 id="hobbies">Hobbies</h2>
```

2. Add hyperlinks to the items in the unordered list so that each entry will link to its corresponding heading.

3. Add a named fragment near the top of the page.

4. Near the bottom of the favorites.html page, add a hyperlink to return to the top of the page.

Save the file and test it in a browser. Compare your work with the sample found in the student files (chapter7/favorites.html).

There may be times when you need to link to a named fragment on another web page. To accomplish this, place a "#" followed by the fragment identifier id value after the file name in the anchor tag. So, to link to the "Professional Organizations" (given that it is a named fragment called "prof") from any other page on the same website, you could use the following HTML:

```
<a href="favorites.html#prof">Professional Organizations</a>
```

FAQ   Why don't some of my hyperlinks to fragment identifiers work?

The web browser fills the browser window (viewport) with the web page and will scroll to display the named fragment at the top of the viewport. However, if there is not enough "page" left below the named fragment, the content where the named fragment is located will not be displayed at the top of the browser viewport. The browser tries to do the best it can while still filling the viewport with the web page content. Try adding some blank lines (use the `<br>` tag) or padding to the lower portion of the web page. Save your work and test your hyperlinks again.

The Target Attribute

You may have noticed in Hands-On Practice 7.1 that when a visitor clicks on a hyperlink, the new web page will automatically open in the same browser window. You can configure the **target attribute** on an anchor tag with `target="_blank"` to open a hyperlink in a new browser window or browser tab. For example,

`<a href="http://yahoo.com" target="_blank">Yahoo!</a>` will open Yahoo! home page in a new browser window or tab.

Note that you cannot control whether the web page opens in a new window or opens in a new tab; this is dependent upon your visitor's browser configuration. Why not create a test page and try it? The target attribute with the value "_blank" configures the web page to open in a new browser window or tab.

Hands-On Practice 7.2

You will work with the target attribute in this Hands-On Practice. Locate chapter7/favorites.html in the student files. Launch a text editor and open favorites.html. Save the file as target.html. Let's practice using the target attribute. Choose one of the external hyperlinks to modify. And add `target="_blank"` so that the hyperlink opens in a new browser window or tab. The code is shown below:

```
<a href="http://www.isoc.org"
target="_blank">http://www.isoc.org</a>
```

Save the file. Launch a browser and test the file. When you click on the hyperlink that you modified, the new page will display in a new browser window or tab. You can compare your work to the solution in the student files (chapter7/target.html).

Block Anchor

It's typical to use anchor tags to configure phrases or even just a single word as a hyperlink. HTML5 provides a new function for the anchor tag—the block anchor. A block anchor can configure one or more elements (even those that display as a block, such as a div, h1, or paragraph) as a hyperlink. See an example in the student files (chapter7/block.html).

Telephone and Text Message Hyperlinks

If a web page displays a phone number, wouldn't it be handy for a person using a smartphone to be able to tap on the phone number and place a call or send an SMS (Short Message Service) text message? It's very easy to configure a telephone hyperlink or SMS hyperlink for use by smartphones.

According to RFC 3966, you can configure a telephone hyperlink by using a telephone scheme: Begin the href value with `tel:` followed by the phone number. For example, to configure a telephone hyperlink on a web page for use by mobile browsers, code as follows: `<a href="tel:888-555-5555">Call 888-555-5555</a>`.

RFC 5724 indicates that an SMS scheme hyperlink intended to send a text message can be configured by beginning the href value with `sms:` followed by the phone number, as shown in the following code:

```
<a href="sms:888-555-5555">Text 888-555-5555</a>.
```

Not all mobile browsers and devices support telephone and text hyperlinks, but expect increased use of this technology in the future. You'll get a chance to practice using the `tel:` scheme in the Chapter 7 case study.

7.2 CSS Sprites

When browsers display web pages, they must make a separate http request for every file used by the page, including .css files and image files such as .gif, .jpg, and .png files. Each http request takes time and resources. As mentioned in Chapter 4, a **sprite** is an image file that contains multiple small graphics. Using CSS to configure the small graphics combined in the sprite as background images for various web page elements is called **CSS sprites**, a technique made popular by David Shea (http://www.alistapart.com/articles/sprites).

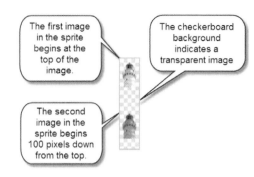

Figure 7.4 The sprite consists of two images in a single graphics file

The CSS sprites technique uses the CSS `background-image`, `background-repeat`, and `background-position` properties to manipulate the placement of the background image. The single graphics file saves download time because the browser only needs to make one http request for the combined image instead of many requests for the individual smaller images. Figure 7.4 shows a sprite with two lighthouse images on a transparent background. These images are configured as background images for the navigation hyperlinks with CSS as shown in Figure 7.5. You'll see this in action as you complete the next Hands-On Practice.

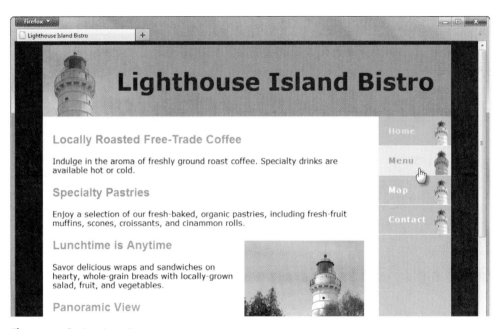

Figure 7.5 Sprites in action

Hands-On Practice 7.3

You will work with CSS sprites in this Hands-On Practice as you create the web page shown in Figure 7.5. Create a new folder named sprites. Locate chapter7/starter2.html in the student files. Copy starter2.html into your sprites folder. Copy the following files from chapter7/starters into your sprites folder: lighthouseisland.jpg, lighthouselogo.jpg, and sprites.gif. The sprites.gif, shown in Figure 7.4, contains two lighthouse images. The first lighthouse image starts at the top of the graphics file. The second lighthouse image begins 100 pixels down from the top of the graphics file. We'll use the value 100 when we configure the display of the second image.

Launch a text editor and open starter2.html. Save the file as index.html. You will edit the embedded styles to configure background images for the navigation hyperlinks.

1. Configure the background image for navigation hyperlinks. Add the following styles to the `#nav a` selector to set the background image to the sprites.gif with no repeat. The value `right` in the `background-position` property configures the lighthouse image to display at the right of the navigation element. The value `0` in the `background-position` property configures the display at offset 0 from the top (at the very top) so the first lighthouse image displays.

```
#nav a {  text-decoration: none;
          display: block;
          padding: 20px;
          background-color: #b3c7e6;
          border-bottom: 1px solid #ffffff;
          background-image: url(sprites.gif);
          background-repeat: no-repeat;
          background-position: right 0;  }
```

2. Configure the second lighthouse image to display when the mouse pointer passes over the hyperlink. Add the following styles to the `#nav a:hover` selector to display the second lighthouse image. The value `right` in the `background-position` property configures the lighthouse image to display at the right of the navigation element. The value `-100px` in the `background-position` property configures the display at an offset of 100 pixels down from the top so the second lighthouse image appears.

```
#nav a:hover {  background-color: #eaeaea;
                color: #869dc7;
                background-position: right -100px;  }
```

Save the file and test it in a browser. Your page should look similar to Figure 7.5. Move your mouse pointer over the navigation hyperlinks to see the background images change. Compare your work with the sample found in the student files (chapter7/sprites/index.html).

FAQ How can I create my own sprite graphics file?

Most web developers use a graphics application such as Adobe Photoshop, Adobe Fireworks, or GIMP to edit images and save them in a single graphics file for use as a sprite. Or, you could use a web-based sprite generator such as the ones listed below:

- CSS Sprites Generator: http://csssprites.com
- CSS Sprite Generator: http://spritegen.website-performance.org
- SpriteMe: http://spriteme.org

If you already have a sprite graphic, check out the online tool at Sprite Cow (http://www.spritecow.com) that can generate pixel-perfect `background-position` property values for a sprite.

Checkpoint 7.1

1. Why should you organize the files in a website using folders and subfolders?

2. Which attribute configures a hyperlink to open the file in a new browser window or tab?

3. State an advantage of using CSS sprites in a website.

7.3 Three-Column CSS Page Layout

Often a web page layout will consist of a header across the top of the page with three columns below: navigation, content, and sidebar. If you are thinking about this layout as a series of boxes—you're thinking correctly for configuring pages using CSS! Figure 7.6 shows a wireframe of this page layout design. Figure 7.7 shows a web page configured using this design. You will create this page in the next Hands-On Practice.

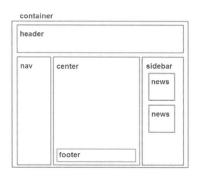

Figure 7.6 Wireframe for a three-column page layout

Figure 7.7 This three-column page layout is designed using CSS

Hands-On Practice 7.4

In this Hands-On Practice, you will develop your first three-column web page using CSS. The same techniques that you used to configure the two-column page will apply here. Think of the page as a series of elements or boxes. Using a wireframe as a guide, configure the basic page structure with HTML. Then code CSS to configure page areas; use ids or classes when appropriate. Recall that a key technique for creating a two-column web page with left-column navigation was to design the left column to float to the left. A key technique for our three-column page is to code the left column with `float:left` and the right column with `float:right`. The center column occupies the middle of the browser window. Refer to Figures 7.6 and 7.7 as you complete this Hands-On Practice.

Getting Started

Locate the showybg.jpg, plsthumb.jpg, and trillium.jpg files in the chapter7/starters folder in the student files. Create a new folder called wildflowers3. Copy the files to the folder.

Part 1: Code the HTML

Review Figures 7.6 and 7.7. Notice the page elements: a header area with a background image; a left column with a navigation area and an image; a center column with paragraphs of text, headings, and an image that floats to the right; a right column with two news items; and a footer. These will all be coded to use ids and classes that correspond to CSS, which configures a number of properties, including the float, margin, border, font-family, and so on. The navigation menu hyperlinks will be configured using an unordered list. As you code the HTML document, you will place the elements on the page and assign id and class values that correspond to the wireframe areas in Figure 7.6. Launch a text editor and type in the following HTML:

```
<!DOCTYPE html>
<html lang="en">
<head>
<title>Door County Wildflowers</title>
<meta charset="utf-8">
</head>
<body>
<div id="container">
  <div id="header">
     <span><a href="#center">Skip to Content</a></span>
     <h1>Door County Wildflowers</h1>
  </div>
  <div id="nav">
    <ul>
      <li><a href="index.html">Home</a></li>
      <li><a href="spring.html">Spring</a></li>
      <li><a href="summer.html">Summer</a></li>
      <li><a href="fall.html">Fall</a></li>
      <li><a href="winter.html">Winter</a></li>
    </ul>
    <img src="plsthumb.jpg" width="100" height="100" alt="Showy Lady
    Slipper">
</div>
<div id="sidebar">
    <h3>The Ridges</h3>
    <p class="news">The Ridges Nature Sanctuary offers wild orchid
hikes during the summer months. For more info, visit <a href=
"http://www.ridgesanctuary.org">The Ridges</a>.</p>
```

```
    <h3>Newport State Park</h3>
    <p class="news">The <a href="http://www.newportwildernesssociety.org">
Newport Wilderness Society</a> sponsors free meadow hikes at 9am
every Saturday. Stop by the park office to register.</p>
</div>
<div id="center">
    <h2>Door County</h2>
    <p>Wisconsin&rsquo;s Door County Peninsula is a unique,
ecologically diverse place with upland and boreal forest, bogs,
swamps, sand and rock beaches, limestone escarpments, and
farmlands.</p>
    <p>A wide array of wildflowers grow in the county because of this
variety of ecosystems.</p>
    <img src="trillium.jpg" width="200" height="150" alt="Trillium"
    id="floatright">
    <h3>Explore the beauty <br>of Door County Wildflowers. . . .</h3>
    <p>With five state parks, tons of county parks, and private nature
sanctuaries, Door County is teeming with natural areas for you to
stalk your favorite wildflowers.</p>
    <div id="footer"> Copyright &copy; 2012 Door County Wild Flowers<br>
    </div>
    </div>
</div>
</body>
</html>
```

Save your page as index.html in your wildflowers3 folder. Test the page in a browser. Your display will not look like Figure 7.7 because you have not yet configured the CSS. The top of your page should look similar to the page shown in Figure 7.8.

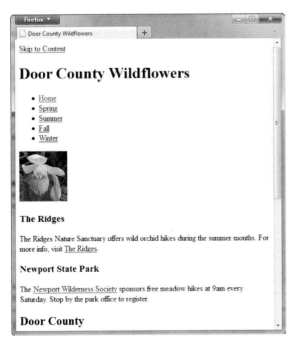

Figure 7.8 The three-column page before CSS is applied

Part 2: Code the Basic CSS

For ease of editing, in this Hands-On Practice, you will code the CSS as embedded styles in the header section of the web page. However, if you were creating an entire website, you would most likely use an external style sheet. Launch a text editor and open index.html. Let's take a moment to consider the main elements used on the page shown in Figure 7.6: header, left-column navigation area, right-column sidebar area, center column, and footer. The left column will contain a navigation area and a small image. The center column will contain paragraphs, a heading, and a right-floating image. The right column will contain a series of headings and news items. Locate these areas on the sketch in Figure 7.6. Notice also that the same font is used throughout the page and the page begins immediately at the browser margin.

With your file open in a text editor, modify the head section of your document and code a `<style>` tag. Now let's consider the CSS configuration. Type the CSS in your document as indicated below:

1. **Body Element Selector.** Set the margin to 0. Configure the background color to #ffffff.

```
body { margin:0;
       background-color: #ffffff; }
```

2. **Container.** Configure this area with background (#eeeeee) and text (#006600) colors, a minimum width of 960 pixels, and a font family of Verdana, Arial, or sans-serif.

```
#container { background-color: #eeeeee;
             color: #006600;
             min-width: 960px;
             font-family: Verdana, Arial, sans-serif; }
```

3. **Header.** Configure a background color (#636631) and a background image (position showybg.jpg at the bottom of the element to repeat horizontally). Set the height to 120 pixels, text color to #cc66cc, text alignment to right, no top padding, no bottom padding, 20 pixels left padding, and 20 pixels right padding. Configure a 2 pixel solid black border across the bottom of this area.

```
#header { background-color: #636631;
          background-image: url(showybg.jpg);
          background-position: bottom;
          background-repeat: repeat-x;
          height: 120px;
          color: #cc66cc;
          text-align: right;
          padding: 0 20px;
          border-bottom: 2px solid #000000; }
```

4. **Left Column.** One of the keys to this three-column page layout is that the left navigation column is designed to float to the left of the browser window. Configure a width of 150 pixels.

```
#nav { float: left;
width: 150px; }
```

5. **Right Column.** One of the keys to this three-column page layout is that the right sidebar column is designed to float to the right of the browser window. Configure a width of 200 pixels.

```
#sidebar { float: right;
           width: 200px; }
```

6. **Center.** The center column will take up all of the room that is available after the left and right columns float. The content area has a special need for margins because the left and right columns are floating on either side. Set the left margin to 160 pixels, the right margin to 210 pixels, and the remaining margins to 0. Also configure the padding for this area. Set the background (#ffffff) and text (#006600) colors.

```
#center { margin: 0 210px 0 160px;
          padding: 1px 10px 20px 10px;
          background-color: #ffffff;
          color: #006600; }
```

7. **Footer.** Configure the page footer with very small text that is centered. Configure the background (#ffffff) and text (#006600) colors for this area. Set the top padding to 10 pixels. Clear the floated image in the center content area.

```
#footer { font-size: .70em;
          text-align: center;
          color: #006600;
          background-color: #ffffff;
          padding-top: 10px;
          clear: both; }
```

At this point, you have configured the main elements of the three-column page layout. Code the closing HTML style tag with `</style>`. Save index.html in the wildflowers3 folder. It's a good idea to open your page in a browser to make sure you are on the right track. It should look similar to the one shown in Figure 7.9. Note that there is still some detail work to do, but you are well on your way!

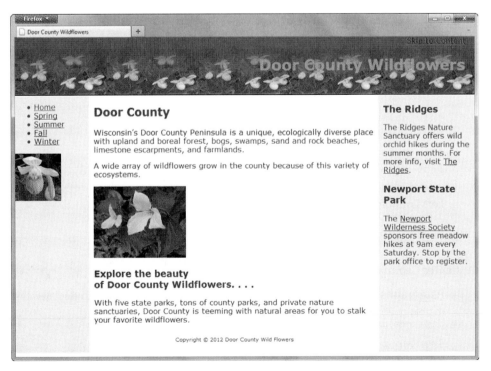

Figure 7.9 The CSS for the basic elements of the three-column layout has been completed

Part 3: Continue Coding CSS

Now you are ready to continue with your styles. Open index.html in a text editor and position your cursor on a blank line above the closing style tag.

1. **Header Area.**

   a. **The h1 Element Selector.** Notice the extra space above the "Door County Wildflowers" text, which is contained within the `<h1>` element in the header area. You can reduce this extra space by setting a 0 top margin for the h1 element selector. Also configure left alignment, text shadow, and a font size of 3em for the h1 selector.

   ```
   h1 { margin-top: 0;
        font-size: 3em;
        text-align: left;
        text-shadow: 2px 2px 2px #000000; }
   ```

   b. **Skip to Content.** Configure the "Skip to Content" hyperlink in the header area with a 0.80em font size. Also configure pseudo-classes for `:link`, `:visited`, `:hover`, `:active`, and `:focus` with text color as shown below.

   ```
   #header a {font-size: 0.80em; }
   #header a:link, #header a:visited { color: #ffffff; }
   #header a:focus, #header a:hover { color: #eeeeee; }
   ```

2. **Left Navigation Column.**

   a. **Navigation Menu.** Configure the unordered list in the `nav` id to provide for a 20 pixel top margin and not to display any list markers.

   ```
   #nav ul { margin-top: 20px;
             list-style-type: none; }
   ```

   The navigation links should have no underline (`text-decoration: none`) and a 1.2em font size. Configure pseudo-classes for `:link`, `:visited`, `:hover`, `:active`, and `:focus` with text color as shown below.

   ```
   #nav a { text-decoration: none;
            font-size: 1.2em; }
   #nav a:link { color:#006600;}
   #nav a:visited { color: #003300; }
   #nav a:focus, #nav a:hover { color: #cc66cc; }
   #nav a:active { color: #000000;}
   ```

   b. **Left Column Image.** Configure images in the `nav` id with a margin of 30 pixels.

   ```
   #nav img { margin: 30px;}
   ```

3. **Center Column.**

   a. **Paragraphs.** Configure the center area's paragraph element selector to display with a margin of 20 pixels.

   ```
   #center p { margin: 20px; }
   ```

b. **Headings.** Configure the h2 and h3 element selectors in the center area with the same text color as the logo header text and the same background color as the main body of the page.

```
#center h2, #center h3 { color: #cc66cc;
                         background-color: #ffffff; }
```

c. **Image Floating at the Right.** Create a `floatright` id to use a 10 pixel margin and float to the right.

```
#floatright { margin: 10px;
              float: right; }
```

4. **Right Sidebar Column.**

a. **Headings.** Configure the h2 element selector in this area with a 1 pixel black solid bottom border, 2 pixels of padding at the bottom, a 10 pixel margin, 0.90em font size, and the same text color as the logo header text.

```
#sidebar h3 { padding-bottom: 2px;
              border-bottom: 1px solid #000000;
              margin: 10px;
              font-size: 0.90em;
              color: #cc66cc;}
```

b. **News Items.** Configure a class called `news` that uses a small font and has a 10 pixel margin.

```
.news { font-size: 0.80em;
        margin: 10px; }
```

Save index.html in the wildflowers3 folder.

Part 4: Test the Page

Now that your styles are coded, test the index.html page again. Your page should look similar to the screenshot shown in Figure 7.7. Recall that Internet Explorer does not support the `text-shadow` property. If there are other differences, verify the id and class values in your HTML. Also check the syntax of your CSS. You may find the W3C CSS Validation Service at http://jigsaw.w3.org/css-validator to be helpful when verifying CSS syntax. The student files contain a copy of this page in the chapter7/wildflowers folder.

7.4 CSS Styling for Print

Even though the "paperless society" has been talked about for decades, the fact is that many people still love paper and you can expect your web pages to be printed. CSS offers you some control over what gets printed and how the printouts are configured. This is easy to do using external style sheets. Create one external style sheet with the configurations for browser display and a second external style sheet with the special printing configurations. Associate both of the external style sheets to the web page using two link elements. The link elements will utilize the **media attribute**, which indicates the media type for which the styles are intended, such as screen display or print display. See a list of media attribute values in Table 7.1.

Table 7.1 The media attribute

Value	Purpose
screen	Default value; Indicates the style sheet that configures the typical browser viewport display on a color computer screen
print	Indicates the style sheet that configures the printed formatting
handheld	Although this value is intended by the W3C to indicate the style sheet that configures display on handheld mobile devices, in practice, the attribute value is not reliably applied (see Return of the Mobile Stylesheet at http://www.alistapart.com/articles/return-of-the-mobile-stylesheet for more information). The next section will describe other methods for configuring the design of mobile web pages.

Modern browsers will use the correct screen or print style sheet, depending on whether they are rendering a screen display or preparing to print a document. Configure the link element for your browser display with media="screen". Configure the link element for your printout with media="print". An example of the HTML follows:

```
<link rel="stylesheet" href="wildflower.css" media="screen">
<link rel="stylesheet" href="wildflowerprint.css" media="print">
```

Print Styling Best Practices

You might be wondering how a print style sheet should differ from the CSS used to display the web page in a browser. Commonly used techniques for styling print are listed below.

Hide Non-Essential Content

It's common practice to prevent banner ads, navigation, or other extraneous areas from appearing on the printout. Use the display: none; style declaration to hide content that is not needed on a printout of the web page.

Configure Font Size and Color for Printing

Another common practice is to configure the font sizes on the print style sheet to use pt units. This will better control the text on the printout. You might also consider configuring the text color to black (#000000) if you envision the need for visitors to print your pages often. The default setting on most browsers prevent background colors and background images from printing, but you can also prevent background image display in your print style sheet.

Control Page Breaks

Use the CSS **page-break-before** or **page-break-after** properties to control page breaks when printing the web page. Well-supported values for these properties are always (the page break will always occur as designated), avoid (if possible, the page break will occur before or after, as designated), and auto (default). For example, to configure a page break at a specific point in the document (in this case, right before an element assigned to the class named `newpage`), configure the CSS as shown below:

```
.newpage { page-break-before: always; }
```

Print URLs for Hyperlinks

Consider whether a person would find it useful to see the actual URL for a resource when reading the printout of your web page. You can use CSS to display the value of the href attribute right on the page using two CSS coding techniques: a CSS pseudo-element and the CSS `content` property. The purpose of a CSS **pseudo-element** is to apply some type of effect to its selector. Table 7.2 lists pseudo-elements and their purpose.

Table 7.2 CSS 2.1 pseudo-elements

Pseudo-element	Purpose
`:after`	Inserts generated content after the selector: Configure the generated content with the content property
`:before`	Inserts generated content before the selector: Configure the generated content with the content property
`:first-letter`	Applies styles to the first letter of text
`:first-line`	Applies styles to the first line of text

Use the CSS `content` **property** along with the `:after` and `:before` pseudo-elements to generate content. A useful feature of the content property is the `attr(X)` function, which returns the value of the HTML attribute provided. You can use this to print the URL of a hyperlink (the value of the `href` attribute). Use quotation marks to contain additional text or characters, such as parentheses. The CSS below will display the URL for each hyperlink in the sidebar area within parentheses after the text hyperlink.

```
#sidebar a:after { content: " (" attr(href) ") "; }
```

Figure 7.10 shows the print preview of the content page you created in Hands-On Practice 7.4 (see Figure 7.7). Notice that the print preview includes the navigation area.

Figure 7.10 Print preview of the page displayed in Figure 7.7

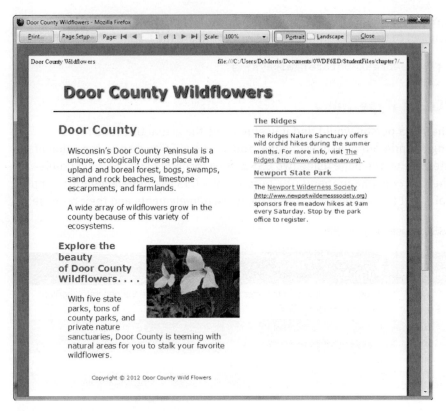

Figure 7.11 Print preview using CSS to configure for printing

Figure 7.11 displays an alternate version of the page that uses CSS to prevent the display of the navigation area, configures pt units for font sizes, and prints the URL for the hyperlinks in the sidebar area. You will explore these techniques in the next Hands-On Practice.

Hands-On Practice 7.5

In this Hands-On Practice, you will code special styles for use when printing a web page. We will use the Door County Wildflowers index.html page from Hands-On Practice 7.4 as a starting point. Figure 7.7 shows a browser display of the index.html page. You will create a new version of index.html that is associated with two external style sheets: one for the screen display and the other for printing. When you are finished, your printed page should resemble Figure 7.11.

Getting Started

Create a new folder named wildflowersPrint. Copy into your new folder index.html, plsthumb.jpg, showybg.jpg, and trillium.jpg from the chapter7/wildflowers folder in the student files.

Part 1: Create a Style Sheet for Screen Display

Launch a text editor and open index.html. Copy all of the style rules between the opening and closing style tags. Use your text editor to create a new file and save it as wildflower.css in your wildflowersPrint folder. Paste the style rules into wildflower.css and save the file.

Part 2: Edit the HTML

Edit index.html and remove the style tags. Code a link element to associate the web page with the external style sheet that you just created (wildflower.css). Add the `media` attribute with the value of `"screen"` to the link element for wildflower.css. Code a second link element to invoke an external style sheet called wildflowerprint.css for printing (`media="print"`). The HTML is as follows:

```
<link rel="stylesheet" href="wildflower.css" media="screen">
<link rel="stylesheet" href="wildflowerprint.css" media="print">
```

Save index.html in the wildflowersPrint folder.

Part 3: Code the New Style Sheet for Print Display

Launch a text editor and open wildflower.css. Because you want to keep most of the styles for printing, you will modify a copy of the screen display external style sheet. Save wildflower.css as wildflowerprint.css in the wildflowersPrint folder. You will modify several areas on this style sheet, including the `container` id, h1 element selector, `header` id, `nav` id, `center` id, and the hyperlinks located in the `header` and `sidebar` ids.

Remove the style declaration for minimum width (`min-width`) from the `container` id.

1. Modify the h1 element selector so that the printer will use 24 point font size. Remove the `text-align` property.

   ```
   h1 { margin-top: 0;
        font-size: 24pt;
        text-shadow: 2px 2px 2px #000000; }
   ```

2. Modify the `header` id style rules. Configure a white background color (#ffffff). Remove the background image declaration. The height property is also not needed because there is no longer a background image. Also remove the text alignment and padding properties.

   ```
   #header { color: #cc66cc;
             background-color: #ffffff;
             border-bottom: 2px solid #000000;
             padding: 0 20px; }
   ```

3. Configure the "Skip to Content" hyperlink in the `header` id to not display. Replace all style rules associated with `#header a` with the following:

   ```
   #header a { display: none; }
   ```

4. Configure the navigation area to not display. Remove all style rules associated with `#nav` and add the following:

   ```
   #nav { display: none; }
   ```

5. Configure the center area. Modify the style rule for `#center`. Set the left margin to 0, the right margin to 40%, and the font size to 12pt.

```
#center { margin: 0 40% 0 0;
          padding: 1px 10px 20px 10px;
          font-size: 12pt;
          background-color: #ffffff;
          color: #006600; }
```

6. Configure the width of the sidebar to 40%.

```
#sidebar { float: right;
           width: 40%; }
```

7. Configure the **news** class. Modify the style rule to configure the font size to 10pt.

```
.news { font-size: 10pt;
        margin: 10px; }
```

8. Configure the hyperlinks in the sidebar area so that the URLs are printed in 8pt black font. Add the following CSS:

```
#sidebar a:after { content " (" attr(href) ") ";
                   font-size: 8pt;
                   color: #000000; }
```

9. Look through the style rules and configure the `background-color` for each h2 and h3 element selector to be white (#ffffff).

Save your file in the wildflowersPrint folder.

Part 4: Test Your Work

Test index.html in a browser. Select File > Print > Preview. Your display should look similar to the page shown in Figure 7.11. The font sizes have been configured and the navigation does not display. The URLs appear after the hyperlink text in the sidebar area. The student files contain a solution in the chapter7/print folder.

Note that there is a change in CSS3 syntax, which requires two colons in front of each pseudo-element (for example, CSS3 uses `::after` instead of `:after`). However, we'll stick with the CSS2 pseudo-elements and syntax for now because there is broader browser support.

7.5 CSS Styling for the Mobile Web

Chapter 5 introduced you to three methods that can be used to provide access for website visitors who use mobile devices. One option is to design and publish a second website with a .mobi TLD. Visit JCPenney at http://jcp.com and http://jcp.mobi to see this in practice. Another option is to design and publish a separate website within your own domain that is optimized for mobile use. This technique is utilized by the White House at http://www.whitehouse.gov (Figure 7.12). The mobile version of the White House website can be viewed at http://m.whitehouse.gov (Figure 7.13). The third option is to configure one

Figure 7.12 The regular White House website (http://www.whitehouse.gov) viewed in a browser

website with separate styles for mobile and desktop browser display. Before we focus on coding, let's consider design techniques for the mobile web.

Mobile Web Design Best Practices

Mobile web users are typically on-the-go, need information quickly, and may be easily distracted. A web page that is optimized for mobile access should try to serve these needs. Take a moment to review Figures 7.12 and 7.13 and observe how the design of the mobile website addresses the design considerations discussed in Chapter 5:

- **Small screen size.** The size of the header area is reduced to accommodate a small screen display.

- **Low bandwidth (slow connection speed).** Note that the large images visible in Figure 7.12 are not displayed on the mobile version of the web page.

- **Font, color, and media issues.** Common font typefaces are utilized. There is also good contrast between text and background color.

- **Awkward controls, and limited processor and memory.** The mobile website uses a single-column page layout that facilitates keyboard tabbing and will be easy to control by touch. The page is mostly text, which will be quickly rendered by a mobile browser.

- **Functionality.** Hyperlinks to popular site features display directly under the header. A search feature is also provided.

Figure 7.13 The mobile version of the White House website (http://m.whitehouse.gov)

Let's build on this base of design considerations and expand them.

Optimize Layout for Mobile Use

Figure 7.14
Wireframe for a typical single-column mobile page layout

A single-column page layout (Figure 7.14) with a small header, key navigation links, content, and page footer works well for a mobile device display. Mobile screen resolutions vary greatly (for example, 320×240 [BlackBerry Pearl], 320×480 [Apple iPhone3, Android HTC Dream], 360×640 [Nokia], 480×800 [Android HTC Desire, Windows HTC Pro], and 640×690 [Apple iPhone4, but with a higher pixel density than iPhone3]). W3C recommendations include the following:

- Limit scrolling to one direction.
- Use heading elements.
- Use lists to organize information (such as unordered lists, ordered lists, and definition lists).
- Avoid using tables (see Chapter 8) because they typically force both horizontal and vertical scrolling on mobile devices.
- Provide labels for form controls (see Chapter 9).
- Avoid using pixel units in style sheets.
- Avoid absolute positioning in style sheets.
- Hide content that is not essential for mobile use.

Optimize Navigation for Mobile Use

Easy-to-use navigation is crucial on a mobile device. The W3C recommends the following:

- Provide minimal navigation near the top of the page.
- Provide consistent navigation.
- Avoid hyperlinks that open files in new windows or pop-up windows.
- Try to balance both the number of hyperlinks on a page and the number of levels of links needed to access information.

Optimize Graphics for Mobile Use

Graphics can help to engage visitors, but be aware of the following W3C recommendations for mobile use:

- Avoid displaying images that are wider than the screen width (assume a 320 pixel screen width on a smartphone display).
- Configure alternate small, optimized background images.
- Some mobile browsers will downsize all images, so images with text may become difficult to read.
- Avoid the use of large graphic images.
- Specify the size of images.
- Provide alternate text for graphics and other non-text elements.

Optimize Text for Mobile Use

It can be difficult to read text on a small mobile device. The following W3C recommendations will aid your mobile visitors.

- Configure good contrast between text and background colors.
- Use common font typefaces.
- Configure font size with em units or percentages.
- Use a short, descriptive page title.

The W3C has published Mobile Web Best Practices 1.0, a list of 60 mobile web design best practices, at http://www.w3.org/TR/mobile-bp. Visit http://www.w3.org/2007/02/mwbp_flip_cards.html for flipcards that summarize the Mobile Web Best Practices 1.0 document.

Design for One Web

The W3C mission of building **"One Web"** refers to the concept of providing a single resource that is configured for optimal display on multiple types of devices. This is more efficient than creating multiple versions of a web document. With the "One Web" in mind, we'll next explore using the viewport meta tag and CSS media queries to target and deliver style sheets that are optimized for mobile display to mobile devices.

Viewport Meta Tag

There are multiple uses for meta tags. You've used the meta tag since Chapter 2 to configure the character encoding on a web page. Now, we'll explore the new **viewport meta tag,** which was created as an Apple extension that helps with displays on mobile devices such as iPhones and Android smartphones by setting the width and scale of the viewport. Figure 7.15 displays a screen shot of a web page displayed on an Android smartphone without the viewport meta tag. Examine Figure 7.15 and notice that the mobile device zoomed out to display the entire web page on the tiny screen. The text on the web page is difficult to read.

Figure 7.16 shows the same web page after the viewport meta tag was added to the head section of the document. The code is shown below:

```
<meta name="viewport"
content="width=device-width, initial-scale=1.0">
```

Code the viewport meta tag with the HTML `name="viewport"` and `content` attributes. The value of the HTML `content` attribute can be one or more **directives** (also referred to as properties by Apple), such as the `device-width` directive and directives that control zooming and scale. Table 7.3 lists viewport meta tag directives and their values.

Figure 7.15 Mobile display of a web page

Figure 7.16 The viewport meta tag helps with mobile displays

Table 7.3 Viewport meta tag directives

Directive	Values	Purpose
`width`	Numeric value or `device-width` which indicates actual width of the device screen	The width of the viewport in pixels
`height`	Numeric value or `device-height` which indicates actual height of the device screen	The height of the viewport in pixels
`initial-scale`	Numeric multiplier; Set to 1 for 100% initial scale	Initial scale of the viewport
`minimum-scale`	Numeric multiplier; Mobile Safari default is 0.25	Minimum scale of the viewport
`maximum-scale`	Numeric multiplier; Mobile Safari default is 1.6	Maximum scale of the viewport
`user-scalable`	`yes` allows scaling, `no` disables scaling	Determines whether a user can zoom in or out

Now that you've scaled the page to be readable, what about styling it for optimal mobile use? That's where CSS comes into play.

CSS Media Queries

Earlier in the chapter, you used the link element along with `media="print"` to configure styles for printing web pages. The attribute value `media="handheld"` was originally intended to serve the same purpose, but it has not been well supported. So, with `media="handheld"` not working, what can you do? Use a **media query** (see

Figure 7.17 CSS media queries help to configure the page for mobile display

http://www.w3.org/TR/css3-mediaqueries) to determine the capability of the mobile device, such as screen resolution and orientation (portrait or landscape), and direct browsers to styles configured specifically for those capabilities. Figure 7.17 shows the same web page as Figures 7.15 and 7.16 , but it looks quite different because of a link element that includes media queries and is associated with a style sheet configured for optimal mobile display. The HTML is shown below:

```
<link href="lighthousemobile.css" rel="stylesheet"
media="only screen and (max-device-width: 480px)">
```

The code sample above will configure an optimal display for the most popular smartphones. The value `only` is a keyword that will hide the media query from outdated browsers. The value `screen` targets devices with screens. The `max-device-width` **media feature** (see Table 7.4) is set to `480px`, which will target the most popular smartphone viewport dimensions. Commonly used **media types** and keywords include the following:

- `all` targets all devices
- `screen` targets screens
- `only` causes older nonsupporting browsers to ignore the media query
- `print` targets printout

Table 7.4 Commonly used media query features

Features	Values	Criteria
max-device-height	Numeric value	The height of the screen size of the output device in pixels is smaller than or equal to the value
max-device-width	Numeric value	The width of the screen size of the output device in pixels is smaller than or equal to the value
min-device-height	Numeric value	The height of the screen size of the output device in pixels is greater than or equal to the value
min-device-width	Numeric value	The width of the screen size of the output device in pixels is greater than or equal to the value
max-height	Numeric value	The height of the viewport in pixels is smaller than or equal to the value; (reevaluated when screen is resized)
min-height	Numeric value	The height of the viewport in pixels is greater than or equal to the value; (reevaluated when screen is resized)
max-width	Numeric value	The width of the viewport in pixels is smaller than or equal to the value; (reevaluated when screen is resized)
min-width	Numeric value	The width of the viewport in pixels is greater than or equal to the value; (reevaluated when screen is resized)
orientation	Portrait or landscape	The orientation of the device

Testing Mobile Display

The best way to test the mobile display of a web page is to publish it to the Web and access it from a mobile device. (See Appendix G for an introduction to publishing a website with FTP.) However, not everyone has access to a smartphone. Several options for emulating a mobile display are listed below:

- **Opera Mobile Emulator** (Windows Only download and install)
  http://www.opera.com/developer/tools/mobile
  Supports media queries.

- **Mobilizer** (Windows and Mac download and install)
  http://www.springbox.com/mobilizer
  Supports media queries.

- **Web-Based Opera Mini 4.2 Simulator** (Runs in a browser window)
  http://www.opera.com/mobile/demo/?ver=4
  Disables background images; supports media queries.

- **Web-Based Opera Mini 6 Simulator** (Runs in a browser window)
  http://www.opera.com/mobile/demo
  Disables background images; supports media queries.

- **iPhone Emulator** (Runs in a browser window)
  http://www.testiphone.com
  Does not support media queries.

- **iPhoney** (Mac only download and install)
  http://www.marketcircle.com/iphoney
  Does not support media queries.

Figure 7.18 A desktop browser was used to approximate the mobile display

Testing with a Desktop Browser

What if you don't have a smartphone and are unable to publish your files to the Web? You can *approximate* the mobile display of your site using a desktop browser by using the following technique:

1. Modify the link element to point to your mobile CSS style sheet.

2. Display your page in a desktop browser and then reduce the width and height of the viewport until it approximates a mobile screen size (such as 320×480).

Figure 7.18 demonstrates this technique. The Firefox browser was used to display the same website using the mobile style sheet (see Figure 7.17).

For Serious Developers Only

If you are a software developer or information systems major, you may want to explore the SDKs (Software Developer Kits) for the iOS and Android platforms. Each SDK includes a mobile device emulator.

- **iOS SDK** (Mac only)   http://developer.apple.com/programs/ios/develop.html

- **Android SDK**   http://developer.android.com/sdk/index.html

Now that you're aware of some mobile design considerations, how to target a mobile device, and options for mobile testing and emulation, let's apply your new knowledge by configuring the web page shown in Figure 7.17.

Hands-On Practice 7.6

Create a new folder named mobile. Locate chapter7/starter2.html in the student files. Copy starter2.html into your mobile folder. Rename the starter2.html file as index.html. Copy the following files from chapter7/starters into your mobile folder: lighthouseisland.jpg, lighthouselogo.jpg, and mobilelogo.jpg. Launch a browser and view starter2.html as shown in Figure 7.19. You will configure the web page to use the viewport meta tag and media queries to target mobile devices. You'll configure CSS for both desktop and mobile display.

Part 1: Create a New Style Sheet

Launch a text editor and open index.html. Copy all the style rules between the opening and closing style tags. Use your text editor to create a new file and save it as lighthouse.css in your mobile folder. Paste the style rules into lighthouse.css and save the file.

Part 2: Edit the HTML

1. Edit index.html and remove the style tags. Code a link element to associate the web page with the external style sheet that you just created (lighthouse.css). Add the **media** attribute with the value of **screen** to the link element for lighthouse.css. Code a second link element to invoke an external style sheet called lighthousemobile.css for mobile display. The HTML code follows:

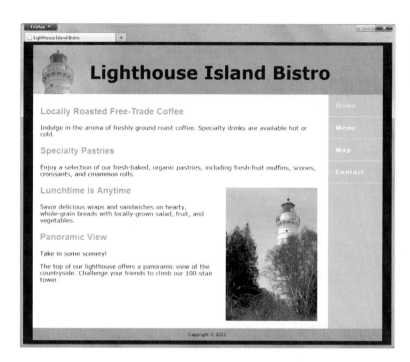

Figure 7.19 Web page displayed in a desktop browser

```
<link href="lighthouse.css" rel="stylesheet" media="screen">
<link href="lighthousemobile.css" rel="stylesheet"
      media="only screen and (max-device-width: 480px)">
```

2. Configure a viewport meta tag below the link elements. The HTML code follows:

```
<meta name="viewport"
content="width=device-width, initial-scale=1.0">
```

3. The mobile display will benefit from a "Back to Top" link at the bottom of the page. Add a div assigned to an id named **backtotop** at the bottom of the content area that contains a hyperlink to the **#header** id. The HTML code follows:

```
<div id="backtotop"><a href="#header">Back to Top</a></div>
```

Save the index.html file in the mobile folder.

Part 3: Code the New CSS

Launch a text editor and open lighthouse.css. Because you will want to keep most of the styles for mobile display, you will start by creating a new version of the external style sheet. Save the lighthouse.css file as lighhousemobile.css in the mobile folder. You will modify several areas on this style sheet, including the body element selector, **wrapper** id, h1 element selector, **header** id, **nav** id, **content** id, **footer** id, and the navigation hyperlinks.

1. Modify the body element selector. Add a style rule to configure no margins.

```
body { font-family: Verdana, Arial, sans-serif;
       background-color: #00005D;
       margin: 0; }
```

2. Modify the `wrapper` id style rules to also configure 100% width, no margin, no padding, and no minimum width.

```
#wrapper { background-color: #b3c7e6;
           color: #000066;
           width: 100%;
           margin: 0;
           padding: 0;
           min-width: 0; }
```

3. Modify the `header` id style rules. Change the padding as indicated below. Change the font size to 100%. Configure the mobilelogo.jpg as a background image that does not repeat. Set the position of the background image to display at the top on the right side.

```
#header { background-color: #869dc7;
          color: #00005D;
          font-size: 100%;
          padding: 0.5em 0 0 0.5em;
          background-image: url(mobilelogo.jpg);
          background-repeat: no-repeat;
          background-position: right top; }
```

4. Eliminate the margin configured for the h1 element selector.

```
h1 { margin: 0; }
```

5. Modify the `nav` id style rules. Remove the float. Set the width to 100% and the font size to 120%.

```
#nav { float: none;
       width: 100%;
       font-size: 120%;
       letter-spacing: 0.1em;
       font-weight: bold; }
```

6. Modify the `content` id style rules. Change the padding to 0.5em.

```
#content { background-color: #ffffff;
           color: #000000;
           padding: 0.5em;
           overflow: auto; }
```

7. Modify the `footer` id style rules. Set the padding to 0.

```
#footer { font-size: 70%;
          text-align: center;
          padding: 0;
          background-color: #869dc7;
          clear: both; }
```

8. Eliminate the margin for the h2 element selector.

```
h2 { color: #869dc7;
     font-family: Arial, sans-serif;
     margin: 0; }
```

9. Configure the paragraph element selector to have a 0.05em margin.

```
p {margin: 0.05em; }
```

10. Configure the `floatright` class to not float and to have no margin.

```
#floatright { margin: 0;
              float: none; }
```

11. Configure a new style rule for li elements in the `nav` id. Set the padding to 0.

```
#nav li { padding: 0; }
```

12. Modify the styles for hyperlinks in the `nav` id. Set the padding as shown below:

```
#nav a { text-decoration: none;
         display: block;
         padding: 0.5em;
         background-color: #b3c7e6;
         border-bottom: 1px solid #ffffff; }
```

13. Configure a new style rule for the `backtotop` id. Set the display to block.

```
#backtotop {display: block; }
```

Save your file in the mobile folder.

Part 4: Update the Desktop CSS

Open lighthouse.css in a text editor. Add CSS to configure the id named `backtotop` to not display.

```
#backtotop { display: none; }
```

Save the file.

Part 5: Test Your Work

Test your index.html file in a desktop browser. It should look similar to Figure 7.19. Then, test your index.html file in a mobile emulator. It should look similar to Figure 7.17 (Android smartphone) or Figure 7.18 (desktop browser approximation). The student files contain a suggested solution in the chapter7/mobile folder.

More on Media Queries

Modern web developers are using media queries to target not only smartphones but also to optimize display for other devices, including tablets and netbooks. The Media Queries website at http://mediaqueri.es displays a gallery of sites that demonstrate **responsive web design**, which Ethan Marcotte (http://www.alistapart.com/articles/responsive-web-design) describes as progressively enhancing a web page for different viewing contexts (such as smartphones and tablets) through the use of techniques, including media queries. The screen captures in the gallery at http://mediaqueri.es show web pages at the following screen widths: 320px (smartphone display), 768px (tablet display), 1024px (netbook display), and 1600px (desktop display). Visit Hardboiled CSS3 Media Queries at http://www.stuffandnonsense.co.uk/blog/about/hardboiled_css3_media_queries to explore sample media query code that targets a variety of device types and displays.

Although the examples in this book use separate style sheets for desktop and mobile display, you could include all of the styles in a single style sheet and write media queries directly in the CSS using the `@media` **rule**. The sample code below displays a different background image specifically for smartphone display.

```
@media only screen and (max-device-width: 480px) {
#header { background-image: url(mobile.gif); }
```

FAQ   **Does using media queries save on bandwidth?**

While using media queries to target mobile devices creates a useful and functional web page for your mobile web visitors, the technique does not save bandwidth. While media queries should cause browsers to apply only specific styles, current browsers still download all of the style sheets and resources (such as background images) associated with your web page just in case they are needed. So, it's still a good idea to optimize all of your images to reduce the amount of bandwidth required by mobile devices. Hopefully, future versions of browsers will only download the resources that are initially needed when a page displays.

This section provided an introduction to mobile web design. You created a style sheet that configured a single-column mobile page layout for an existing website. If you are designing a new website, an alternate approach is to design the mobile style sheet first and then develop alternate style sheets for tablet and/or desktop browsers that progressively enhance the design with multiple columns and larger images. You can find out more about this "Mobile First" approach at http://www.lukew.com/ff/entry.asp?933. As mobile devices evolve and usage increases, there are sure to be new developments in this area of web design. If you are interested in exploring this topic further, you'll find the following resources to be helpful:

- Opera Mini: Web Content Authoring Guidelines: http://dev.opera.com/articles/view/opera-mini-web-content-authoring-guidelines

- W3C Mobile Web Best Practices 1.0: http://www.w3.org/TR/mobile-bp

- W3C Mobile Web Initiative: http://www.w3.org/Mobile

- Mobile Web Development:
  http://www.slideshare.net/estellevw/web-development-for-mobile

- Mobile First Helps with Big Issues: http://www.lukew.com/ff/entry.asp?1117

 Checkpoint 7.2

1. State an advantage of using CSS to style for print.

2. Describe a design consideration when configuring a web page for mobile display.

3. True or False? The `media="handheld"` attribute reliably targets mobile devices.

Chapter Summary

This chapter explored a variety of web development topics, including relative hyperlinks and linking to fragment identifiers, CSS sprites, three-column page layout, styling for print, and styling for mobile devices. Visit the textbook website at http://www.webdevfoundations.net for examples, the links listed in this chapter, and updated information.

Key Terms

:after
:before
:first-letter
:first-line
content property
CSS sprite
directive

fragment identifier
media attribute
media feature
media query
media type
named fragment
One Web

`page-break-after` property
`page-break-before` property
pseudo-element
responsive web design
sprite
target attribute
viewport meta tag

Review Questions

Multiple Choice

1. Which of the following attributes define a fragment identifier on a page?
   a. id
   b. href
   c. fragment
   d. bookmark

2. How would you link to the named fragment `#jobs` on the page employ.html from the home page of the site?
   a. `<a href="employ.html#jobs">Jobs</a>`
   b. `<a name="employ.html#jobs">Jobs</a>`
   c. `<a link="employ.html#jobs">Jobs</a>`
   d. `<a href="#jobs">Jobs</a>`

3. Which of the following causes an element not to display?
   a. `display: block;`
   b. `display: 0px;`
   c. `display: none;`
   d. `display: 0;`

4. Which attribute below can be applied to an anchor tag to open a link in a new browser window?
   a. window
   b. target
   c. rel
   d. media

5. Which of the following is the attribute used to indicate whether the style sheet is for printing or screen display?
   a. rel
   b. type
   c. media
   d. content

6. Which meta tag is used to configure display for mobile devices?
   a. viewport
   b. handheld
   c. mobile
   d. screen

7. Which pseudo-element can be used to generate content that precedes an element?
   a. `:after`
   b. `:before`
   c. `:content`
   d. `:first-line`

8. Which of the following is a mobile web design best practice?
   a. Configure a multiple-column page layout.
   b. Avoid using lists to organize information.
   c. Configure a single-column page layout.
   d. Embed text in images wherever possible.

9. Which of the following font units is recommended for mobile display?

    a. pt unit

    b. px unit

    c. em unit

    d. cm unit

10. Which of the following is an image file that contains multiple small graphics?

    a. viewport

    b. sprite

    c. background-image

    d. media

Fill in the Blank

11. To indicate that an external style sheet is used to configure printing, code _____ on the link element.

12. _____ determine the capability of the mobile device, such as browser viewport dimensions and resolution.

13. The concept of _____ relates to providing a single resource that is configured for optimal display on multiple types of devices.

14. Provide _____ navigation near the top of the page when optimizing for mobile display.

15. When using CSS media queries, code the _____ keyword to hide the query from older nonsupporting browsers.

Apply Your Knowledge

1. **Predict the Result.** Draw and write a brief description of the web page that will be created with the following HTML code:

```
<!DOCTYPE html>
<html lang="en">
<head>
<title>Predict the result</title>
<style type="text/css">
body {background-color: blue;}
#container { position: relative; border: solid: 1px;
margin: auto; width: 80%; background-color:white;}
#masthead { height: 70px; background: #ccc;
text-align: center; }
#main { margin: 0 210px 0 160px; }
#navigation { float:left; top: 70px; left: 0px;
width: 150px; background: #eee;}
#news { float:right; top: 70px; right: 0px;
width: 150px; background: #eee;}
#footer{ margin: 0 160px; padding: 15px;
</style>
</head>
<body>
<div id="container">

<div id="masthead">
<h1> CSS Floating </h1>
</div>
```

```
<div id="navigation">
<ul>
<li><a href="#default">Home</a></li>
<li><a href="#news">News</a></li>
<li><a href="#contact">Contact</a></li>
<li><a href="#about">About</a></li>
</ul>
</div>
<div id="news">
<h3>Announcements</h3>
Watch out for interesting announcements.
</div>
<div id="main" >
<h1>CSS tips</h1>
<p>Elements could be floated only horizontally, i.e., an element can
only be floated left or right, not up or down. A floated element will
move as far to the left or the right as it can. Usually this means all
the way to the left or the right of the containing element. The
elements after the floating element will flow around it. The elements
before the floating element are not affected by it. If an image is
floated to the right, a following text flows around it to the left. </p>
</div>
<div id="footer">
<p>copyright information</p>
</div></div>
</body>
</html>
```

2. **Fill in the Missing Code.** This web page should be configured so that the main content stays on the left side of the browser window and the navigation column remains on the right side. Instead, the navigation column is going below the content. CSS properties and values, indicated by "_" (underscore), are missing. Fill in the missing code to correct the error.

```
<!DOCTYPE html>
<html lang="en">
<head>
<title>Fill in the Missing Code</title>
<meta charset="utf-8">
<style>
.masthead { background: #ccc; padding: 15px;}
.main { "__": "__"; width: 70%; margin-right: 3%; margin-left: 3%}
.footer { clear: left; padding: 15px; background: #666; }
img {float:left;}
</style>
</head>
<body>
<div class="masthead">
<h1> CSS Float </h1>
</div>
<div class="main" >
```

```
<p>The float property allows images and any other element to align
to the left or right margin and the content to wrap around it. </p>
<imgsrc="css.jpg" />
</div>
<div>
<ul>
<li><a href="#default">Home</a></li>
<li><a href="#news">News</a></li>
<li><a href="#contact">Contact</a></li>
<li><a href="#about">About</a></li>
</ul>
</div>
<div class="footer">
<p> copyright information <p>
</div>
</body>
</html>
```

3. **Find the Error.** The page below is intended for the image to display on the left side of the browser window and the content to wrap around the image. What needs to be changed to make this happen?

```
<!DOCTYPE html>
<html lang="en">
<head>
<title>Fill in the Missing Code</title>
<meta charset="utf-8">

<style>
.masthead { background: #ccc; padding: 15px;}
.main { float: left; width: 70%; margin-right: 3%; margin-left: 3%}
.footer { clear: left; padding: 15px; background: #666; }
</style>
</head>
<body>
<div class="masthead">
<h1> CSS Float </h1>
</div>
<div class="main" >
<p>The float property allows images and any other element to align to
the left or the right margin and the content to wrap around it. </p>
<imgsrc="css.jpg" />
<p>Elements that seem to float on the right or left side of either
the browser window or another element are often configured using the
float property. </p>
</div>
<div>
<ul>
<li><a href="#default">Home</a></li>
<li><a href="#news">News</a></li>
<li><a href="#contact">Contact</a></li>
```

```
<li><a href="#about">About</a></li>
</ul>
</div>
<div class="footer">
<p> copyright information <p>
</div>
</body>
</html>
```

Hands-On Exercises

1. Write the HTML to create a fragment identifier at the beginning of a web page designated by "top".

2. Write the HTML to create a hyperlink to the named fragment designated by "top".

3. Write the HTML to associate a web page with an external style sheet named myprint. css to configure a printout.

4. Write the HTML to associate a web page with an external style sheet named mobile. css to configure display for mobile devices.

5. Write the CSS to configure a graphic named mysprite.gif to display as a background image on the left side of a hyperlink. Note that mysprite.gif contains two different images. Configure the image that is located 72 pixels from the top of the sprites.gif graphic to display.

6. Configure Printing for Hands-On Practice 7.3. Configure special printing for the Lighthouse Island Bistro index.html file created in Hands-On Practice 7.3. This file is in the chapter7/sprites folder in the student files. Modify the web page so that it is associated with an external style sheet called lighthouse.css instead of using embedded styles. Save and test your page. Create a new style sheet called myprint. css, which will prevent the navigation from displaying when the page is printed. Modify the index.html page to be associated with this file. Review the use of the media attribute on the link element. Save all files and test your page. Select File › Print › Preview to test the print styles.

7. Extending Hands-On Practice 7.4. In Hands-On Practice 7.4, you created the home page for the Door County Wildflowers website. This file is also available in the chapter7/wildflowers folder in the student files. In this exercise, you will create two additional content pages for the Door County Wildflowers site (spring.html and summer.html). Make sure that all CSS is placed in an external style sheet (mywildflower.css). Modify index.html to use this style sheet. The following is some content to include on the new pages:

Spring Page (spring.html):

- Use the trillium.jpg image (see the chapter7/starters folder in the student files).
- Trillium facts: 8–18 inches tall; perennial; native plant; grows in rich, moist deciduous woodlands; white flowers turn pink with age; fruit is a single red berry; protected flower species

Summer Page (summer.html):

- Use the yls.jpg image (see the chapter7/starters folder in the student files).
- Yellow Lady's Slipper facts: 4–24 inches tall; perennial; native plant; grows in wet, shaded deciduous woods, swamps, and bogs; an orchid; official flower of Door County

8. **Modify the Design of Hands-On Practice 7.4.** Locate the index.html page you created in Hands-On Practice 7.4. This file is in the chapter7/wildflowers folder in the student files. Recall from Chapter 5 that a web page using jello design has content in the center of the web page with blank margins on either side. Configure the style rules for index.html to display the page in this manner.

9. **Create a Mobile Design for Hands-On Practice 7.4.** Locate the index.html page you created in Hands-On Practice 7.4. This file is in the chapter7/wildflowers folder in the student files. Modify the web page so that it links to an external style sheet (flowers.css) instead of using embedded styles. Save and test your page. Create a new style sheet (mymobile.css), which will configure the page for mobile display with a single-column layout (see Figure 7.14). Modify the index.html page to be associated with this file. Configure the viewport meta tag and CSS media queries for smartphone mobile display. Save all files and test your page with both a desktop browser and a mobile device or emulator.

10. **Practice Validating CSS.** Choose a CSS external style sheet file to validate (perhaps you have created one for your own website). Otherwise, use an external style sheet file that you worked on in this chapter. Use the free W3C CSS Validation Service (http://jigsaw.w3.org/css-validator). If your CSS does not immediately pass the validation test, modify it and test again. Repeat this process until W3C validates your CSS code. Write a one- or two-paragraph summary about the validation process. Answer the following questions: Was it easy to use? Did anything surprise you? Did you encounter a number of errors or just a few? How easy was it to determine how to correct the CSS file? Would you recommend this to other students? Why or why not?

Web Research

As you read about mobile web design best practices in this chapter, you may have noticed some overlap with techniques that provide for accessibility, such as alternate text and use of headings. Explore the Web Content Accessibility and Mobile Web document at http://www.w3.org/WAI/mobile. Explore related links that interest you. Write a one-page, double-spaced summary that describes areas of overlap and how web developers can support both accessibility and mobile devices.

Focus on Web Design

Take a few moments and visit the CSS Zen Garden at http://www.csszengarden.com. Explore the site and note the widely different designs. What thought processes and decisions are needed as a person creates a new design for this site? Visit Sheriar Designs (http://manisheriar.com/blog/anatomy-of-a-design-process) or Behind the Scenes of Garden Party (http://www.bobbyvandersluis.com/articles/gardenparty.php) for a behind-the-scenes look at how web developers have approached this task. Reflect on their stories and suggestions. Write a one-page, double-spaced essay that describes ideas about the design process that you'll be able to use as you begin to design websites for personal or professional use. Be sure to include the URL of the resources that you used.

WEBSITE CASE STUDY

Styling for the Mobile Web

Each of the following case studies continues throughout most of the text. This chapter configures the website for display on mobile devices.

JavaJam Coffee House

See Chapter 2 for an introduction to the JavaJam Coffee House case study. Figure 2.25 shows a site map for the JavaJam website. In this case study, you will configure the website to display in mobile devices using the single-column layout shown in Figure 7.14. You will create a new mobile style sheet; modify the current styles; and update the Home, Menu, and Music pages. Use the Chapter 6 JavaJam website as a starting point for this case study. When you are finished, the website will look the same in desktop browsers (see Figure 6.34). The mobile display should be similar to Figure 7.20 or 7.21. You have six tasks in this case study:

1. Create a new folder for this JavaJam case study.

2. Modify the Home page to target mobile devices and deliver a mobile style sheet.

3. Modify the Menu page to be consistent with the Home page.

4. Modify the Music page to be consistent with the Home page.

5. Create a new style sheet (javajammobile.css) that configures a single-column page layout.

6. Modify the desktop style sheet (javajam.css).

Figure 7.20 The new mobile home page displayed on smartphone

Figure 7.21 It's possible to approximate the mobile display of a web page using a desktop browser

Hands-On Practice Case Study

Task 1: Create a Folder. Create a folder called javajam7. Copy all the files from your Chapter 6 javajam6 folder into the javajam7 folder. Copy the javalogomobile.gif file from the chapter7/starters folder in the student files.

Task 2: Modify the Home Page. Open index.html in a text editor. Edit the code as follows:

1. Configure a new link element in the head section that associates the web page with javajammobile.css. Use CSS media queries to target smartphone mobile devices.

2. Configure a viewport meta tag that configures the width to the device-width and sets the initial-scale to 1.0.

3. The JavaJam logo image is too wide for display on a mobile device. If a mobile browser scales down the image, the text may be difficult to read. Your design strategy will be to remove the img tag from the web page and configure "JavaJam Coffee House" within the h1 element. You'll configure this area with CSS in Tasks 5 and 6. The HTML code is

   ```
   <h1 id="header">JavaJam Coffee House</h1>
   ```

4. The home page displays a phone number in the contact information area. Wouldn't it be handy if a person using a smartphone could click on the phone number to call the coffee house? You can make that happen by using tel: in a hyperlink. Configure a hyperlink assigned to an id named mobile that contains the phone number as shown below:

   ```
   <a id="mobile" href="tel:888-555-5555">1-888-555-5555</a>
   ```

   But wait a minute, a telephone link could confuse those visiting the site with adesktop browser. Code another phone number directly after the hyperlink. Code a span element assigned to an id named desktop around the phone number as shown below:

   ```
   <span id="desktop">1-888-555-5555</span>
   ```

   Don't worry about the two phone numbers that are now on the page. You'll configure CSS in Tasks 5 and 6 to show the appropriate phone number (with or without the telephone link) to your website visitors.

Save the index.html file. It should look similar to the web page shown in Figure 7.22 when displayed in a desktop browser. Remember that validating your HTML can help you find syntax errors. Test and correct this page before you continue.

Task 3: Modify the Menu Page. Open menu.html in a text editor. Add the link element and viewport meta tag in a manner consistent with the home page. Reconfigure the header area and logo image in the same manner as the home page. Save and test your new menu.html page in a browser. Use the HTML validator to help you find syntax errors.

Task 4: Modify the Music Page. Open music.html in a text editor. Add the link element and viewport meta tag in a manner consistent with the home page. Reconfigure the header area and logo image in the same manner as the home page. Save and test your new music.html page in a browser. Use the HTML validator to help you find syntax errors.

Figure 7.22 Temporary desktop browser display before new styles are configured

Task 5: Configure the Mobile CSS. Create the mobile style sheet based on the desktop style sheet. Open javajam.css in a text editor. Save the file as javajammobile.css. Edit the style rules as follows:

1. Modify the body element selector. Set the margin and padding to 0. There's no need to display the background image. Set the `background-image` property to the value `none`.

2. Modify the `wrapper` id selector. Set left margin to 0, right margin to 0, width to `100%`, and minimum width to 0.

3. Modify the `header` id selector. Set the text alignment to left. Recall that in Tasks 2, 3, and 4 you removed the logo image element from the web page background. Configure the small logo (javalogomobile.gif) as a background image with center `background-position` and no repeats, and height to 80px, which corresponds to the new background image height.

4. Configure an h1 element selector. Set the margin to 0. Recall that the h1 element contains the text "JavaJam Coffee House". Use the `text-indent` property (refer to Chapter 3) to make this text available to screen readers but not display directly on the web page. The new style rule is

   ```
   h1 { text-indent: -99999px;
        margin: 0; }
   ```

5. Configure the `nav` id selector. The mobile layout uses a single column. Set the float to none, 100% width, 0 top padding, and 0 top margin.

6. Configure the anchor tags in the `nav` id. Modify the style declaration for the `#nav a` selector. Set the display to `block`, padding to 0.2em, font size to 1.3em, font weight to bold. Also configure a 1 pixel bottom border (use #330000 for the border color).

7. Modify the `#nav ul` selector. Set padding and margin to 0.

8. Modify the `content` id selector. Set padding to 0.5em. Set margin to 0.

9. Modify the h2 element selector. Set 0.5em top padding, 0 right padding, 0 bottom padding, and 0.5em left padding. Set the right margin to 0.5em.

10. Modify the `details` class selector. Set left and right padding to 0.

11. Modify the `floatright` class selector. This selector is used by the winding road image on the home page, which will take up too much screen area on mobile devices. Add a new style rule to set display to `none`.

12. Modify the `floatleft` class selector. Set left and right padding to 0.5em.

13. Modify the `footer` id selector. Set top and bottom padding to zero.

14. Remember the telephone number hyperlink you created in Task 2? Configure the CSS for the phone number display as shown below:

```
#mobile { display: inline; }
#desktop { display: none; }
```

Save the javajammobile.css file. Use the CSS validator to help you find syntax errors.

Task 6: Modify the Desktop CSS. Open javajam.css in a text editor. Edit the style rules as follows:

1. Modify the `header` id selector. Set the text alignment to left. Recall that in Tasks 2, 3, and 4 you removed the logo image element from the web page background. Configure the desktop logo (javalogo.gif) as a background image with center `background-position` and no repeats, and height to 100px, which corresponds to the background image height.

2. Configure an h1 element selector. Use the `text-indent` property (refer to Chapter 3) to make this text available to screen readers but not display directly on the web page. The new style rule is

```
h1 {text-indent: -99999px; }
```

3. Remember the telephone number hyperlink you created in Task 2? Configure the CSS for the phone number display as shown below:

```
#mobile { display: none; }
#desktop { display: inline; }
```

Save the javajam.css file. Use the CSS validator to help you find syntax errors.

Display your pages in a desktop browser. The pages should look the same as they did before you started this case study (see Figure 6.34). Next, test the mobile display. Either publish your pages to the Web and display with a mobile device/emulator OR temporarily modify the href value (change javajam.css to javajammobile.css) on the first link element. Display your page and reduce the width of the browser. Your mobile display should be similar to Figure 7.20 or 7.21. Select the hyperlinks to view the Menu and Music pages. They should be similar to the home page. JavaJam is mobile!

Fish Creek Animal Hospital

See Chapter 2 for an introduction to the Fish Creek Animal Hospital case study. Figure 2.29 shows a site map for the Fish Creek website. In this case study, you configure the website to display in mobile devices using the single-column layout shown in Figure 7.14. You will create a new mobile style sheet; modify the current styles; and update the Home,

Services, and Ask the Vet pages. Use the Chapter 6 Fish Creek website as a starting point for this case study. When you are finished, the website will look like Figure 7.26 in desktop browsers. The mobile display should be similar to Figure 7.23 or 7.24. You have six tasks in this case study:

1. Create a new folder for this Fish Creek case study.

2. Modify the Home page to target mobile devices and deliver a mobile style sheet.

3. Modify the Services page to be consistent with the Home page.

4. Modify the Ask the Vet page to be consistent with the Home page.

5. Create a new style sheet (fishcreekmobile.css), which configures a single-column page layout.

6. Modify the desktop style sheet (fishcreek.css).

Figure 7.23 The new mobile home page displayed on smartphone

Figure 7.24 It's possible to approximate the mobile display of a web page using a desktop browser

Hands-On Practice Case Study

Task 1: Create a Folder. Create a folder called fishcreek7. Copy all of the files from your Chapter 6 fishcreek6 folder into the fishcreek7 folder. Copy the bigfish.gif and lilfish.gif files from the chapter7/starters folder in the student files.

Task 2: Modify the Home Page. Open index.html in a text editor. Edit the code as follows:

1. Configure a new link element in the head section that associates the web page with fishcreekmobile.css. Use CSS media queries to target smartphone mobile devices.

2. Configure a viewport meta tag that configures the width to the `device-width` and sets the `initial-scale` to 1.0.

3. The Fish Creek logo image is too wide for display on a mobile device. If a mobile browser scales down the image, the text may be difficult to read. Your design strategy will be to remove the img tag from the web page and configure "Fish Creek Animal

Hospital" text within the h1 element. You'll configure this area with CSS in Tasks 5 and 6. The HTML code is

```
<h1 id="header">Fish Creek Animal Hospital</h1>
```

4. The home page displays a phone number in the contact information area. Wouldn't it be handy if a person using a smartphone could click on the phone number to call the animal hospital? You can make that happen by using `tel:` in a hyperlink. Configure a hyperlink assigned to an id named `mobile` that contains the phone number as shown below:

```
<a id="mobile" href="tel:888-555-5555">1-888-555-5555</a>
```

But wait a minute, a telephone link could confuse those visiting the site with a desktop browser. Code another phone number directly after the hyperlink. Code a span element assigned to an id named `desktop` around the phone number as shown below:

```
<span id="desktop">1-888-555-5555</span>
```

Don't worry about the two phone numbers that are now on the page. You'll configure CSS in Tasks 5 and 6 to show the appropriate phone number (with or without the telephone link) to your website visitors.

Save the index.html file. It should look similar to the web page shown in Figure 7.25 when displayed in a desktop browser. Remember that validating your HTML can help you find syntax errors. Test and correct this page before you continue.

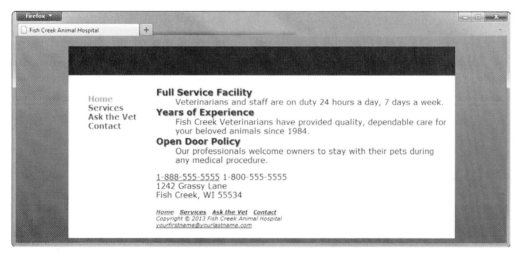

Figure 7.25 Temporary desktop browser display before new styles are configured

Task 3: Modify the Services Page. Open services.html in a text editor. Add the link element and viewport meta tag in a manner consistent with the home page. Reconfigure the header area and logo image in the same manner as the home page. Save and test your new services.html page in a browser. Use the HTML validator to help you find syntax errors.

Task 4: Modify the Ask the Vet Page. Open askvet.html in a text editor. Add the link element and viewport meta tag in a manner consistent with the home page. Reconfigure the header area and logo image in the same manner as the home page. Save and test your new askvet.html page in a browser. Use the HTML validator to help you find syntax errors.

Task 5: Configure the Mobile CSS. Create the mobile style sheet based on the desktop style sheet. Open fishcreek.css in a text editor. Save the file as fishcreekmobile.css. Edit the style rules as follows:

1. Modify the body element selector. Set margin and padding to 0. Set background color to white (#ffffff). There's no need to display the background image. Set the background-image property to the value none.

2. Modify the wrapper id selector. Set left margin to 0, right margin to 0, width to 100%, and minimum width to 0.

3. Modify the header id selector. Recall that in Tasks 2, 3, and 4 you removed the logo image element from the web page background. Configure the small fish logo (lilfish.gif) as a background image with center background-position and no repeats, and height to 40px, which corresponds to the new background image height. Configure white text color, 2em font size, 120% line height, and a gray (#CCCCCC) text-shadow. Set the padding to 0.2em.

4. Configure the leftcolumn id selector. The mobile layout uses a single column. Set the float to none, 100% width, 0 top padding, and 0 top margin.

5. Configure the anchor tags in the leftcolumn id. Modify the style declaration for the #leftcolumn a selector. Set display to block, padding to 0.2em, and font size to 1.3em. Also configure a 1 pixel bottom border (use #330000 for the border color).

6. Modify the #leftcolumn ul selector. Set padding and margin to 0.

7. Modify the rightcolumn id selector. Set 0 top padding, 0 right padding, 0 bottom padding, and 0.4em left padding. Set margin to 0 and font size to 90%.

8. Modify the category class selector. While the text-shadow property can work well in the logo header area, it can make content text difficult to read on a mobile device. Set text-shadow to none.

9. Modify the footer id selector. Set padding and margin to 0.

10. Configure the navigation links in the footer section to not display. The code is shown below:

```
#footer .nav { display: none; }
```

11. Remember the telephone number hyperlink you created in Task 2? Configure the CSS for the phone number display as shown below:

```
#mobile { display: inline; }
#desktop { display: none; }
```

Save the fishcreekmobile.css file. Use the CSS validator to help you find syntax errors.

Task 6: Modify the Desktop CSS. Open fishcreek.css in a text editor. Edit the style rules as follows:

1. Modify the `header` id selector. Set the text alignment to left. Recall that in Tasks 2, 3, and 4 you removed the logo image element from the web page background. Configure the big fish logo (bigfish.gif) as a background image with center `background-position` and no repeats, and height to 80px, which corresponds to the background image height. Configure white text color, 3em font size, 150% line height, and a gray (#CCCCCC) `text-shadow`.

2. Modify the `wrapper` id selector. Change the minimum width to 960px.

3. Remember the telephone number hyperlink you created in Task 2? Configure the CSS for the phone number display as shown below:

```
#mobile { display: none; }
#desktop { display: inline; }
```

Save the fishcreek.css file. Use the CSS validator to help you find syntax errors.

Display your pages in a desktop browser. The home page should look similar to Figure 7.26. Next, test the mobile display. Either publish your pages to the Web and display with a mobile device/emulator OR temporarily modify the href value (change fishcreek.css to fishcreekmobile.css) on the first link element. Display your page and reduce the width of the browser. Your mobile display should be similar to Figure 7.23 or 7.24. Select the hyperlinks to view the Services and Ask the Vet pages. They should be similar to the home page. Fish Creek is mobile!

Figure 7.26 The new header area displayed on a desktop browser

Pacific Trails Resort

See Chapter 2 for an introduction to the Pacific Trails Resort case study. Figure 2.33 shows a site map for the Pacific Trails website. In this case study, you will configure the website to display on mobile devices using the single-column layout shown in Figure 7.14. You will create a new mobile style sheet; modify the current styles; and update the Home, Yurts, and Activities pages. Use the Chapter 6 Pacific Trails website as a starting point for this case study. When you have finished, the website will look the same in desktop browsers (see Figure 6.39). The mobile display should be similar to Figure 7.27 or 7.28. You have six tasks in this case study:

1. Create a new folder for this Pacific Trails case study.

2. Modify the Home page to target mobile devices and deliver a mobile style sheet.

3. Modify the Yurts page to be consistent with the Home page.

4. Modify the Activities page to be consistent with the Home page.

5. Create a new style sheet (pacificmobile.css), which will configure a single-column page layout.

6. Modify the desktop style sheet (pacific.css).

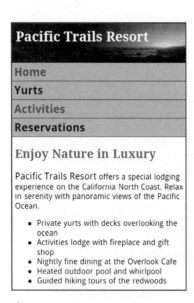

Figure 7.27 The new mobile home page displayed on smartphone

Figure 7.28 It's possible to approximate the mobile display of a web page using a desktop browser

Hands-On Practice Case Study

Task 1: Create a Folder. Create a folder called pacific7. Copy all of the files from your Chapter 6 pacific6 folder into the pacific7 folder.

Task 2: Modify the Home Page. Open index.html in a text editor. Edit the code as follows:

1. Configure a new link element in the head section that associates the web page with pacificmobile.css. Use CSS media queries to target smartphone mobile devices. Refer to Section 7.5.

2. Configure a viewport meta tag that configures the width to the `device-width` and sets the `initial-scale` to 1.0. Refer to Section 7.5.

3. The home page displays a phone number in the contact information area. Wouldn't it be handy if a person using a smartphone could click on the phone number to call the

resort? You can make that happen by using `tel:` in a hyperlink. Configure a hyperlink assigned to an id named `mobile` that contains the phone number as shown below:

```
<a id="mobile" href="tel:888-555-5555">888-555-5555</a>
```

But wait a minute, a telephone link could confuse those visiting the site with a desktop browser. Code another phone number directly after the hyperlink. Code a span element assigned to an id named `desktop` around the phone number as shown here:

```
<span id="desktop">888-555-5555</span>
```

Don't worry about the two phone numbers that are now on the page. You'll configure CSS in Tasks 5 and 6 to show the appropriate phone number (with or without the telephone link) to your website visitors.

Save the index.html file. It should look similar to the web page shown in Figure 6.39 (except for temporarily displaying two phone numbers) when displayed in a desktop browser. Remember that validating your HTML can help you find syntax errors. Test and correct this page before you continue.

Task 3: Modify the Yurts Page. Open yurts.html in a text editor. Add the link element and viewport meta tag in a manner consistent with the home page. Save and test your new yurts.html page in a browser. Use the HTML validator to help you find syntax errors.

Task 4: Modify the Activities Page. Open activities.html in a text editor. Add the link element and viewport meta tag in a manner consistent with the home page. Save and test your new activities.html page in a browser. Use the HTML validator to help you find syntax errors.

Task 5: Configure the Mobile CSS. Create the mobile style sheet based on the desktop style sheet. Open pacific.css in a text editor. Save the file as pacificmobile.css. Edit the style rules as follows:

1. Modify the body element selector. Set the margin and padding to 0. Set text color to black (#000000). There's no need to display the background image. Set the `background-image` property to the value `none`.

2. Modify the `wrapper` id selector. Set left margin to 0, right margin to 0, width to 100%, and minimum width to 0.

3. Configure the h1 element selector. Set margin to 0, font size to 1.5em, and left padding to 0.3em.

4. Configure the `nav` id selector. The mobile layout uses a single column. Set float to none, 100% width, 0 padding, and 0 margin.

5. Configure the anchor tags in the `nav` id. Modify the style declaration for the `#nav a` selector. Set display to `block`, padding to 0.2em, and font size to 1.3em. Also configure a 1 pixel bottom border (use #330000 for the border color).

6. Modify the `#nav ul` selector. Set padding to 0.

7. Modify the `content` id selector. Set 0.1em top padding, 0 right padding, 0 bottom padding, and 0.4em left padding. Set margin to 0 and font size to 90%.

8. Modify the `#content img` selector to not display. Add a new style rule to set display to `none`. Set float to `none`. Set `padding-right` to 0.

9. Modify the `#content ul` selector to use `list-style-position: outside;`.

10. Modify the h1 element selector. Set left padding to 0.3em, height to 20 pixels, and line height to 120%.

11. Modify the `footer` id selector. Set padding and margin to 0.

12. Modify the `clear` class. Set top padding to 0.

13. Remember the telephone number hyperlink you created in Task 2? Configure the CSS for the phone number display as shown below:

```
#mobile { display: inline; }
#desktop { display: none; }
```

Save the pacificmobile.css file.

Task 6: Modify the Desktop CSS. Open pacific.css in a text editor. Edit the style rules. Remember the telephone number hyperlink you created in Task 2? Configure the CSS for the phone number display as shown below:

```
#mobile { display: none; }
#desktop { display: inline; }
```

Display your pages in a desktop browser. The pages should look the same as they did before you started this case study (see Figure 6.39). Next, test the mobile display. Either publish your pages to the Web and display with a mobile device/emulator OR temporarily modify the href value (change pacific.css to pacificmobile.css) on the first link element. Display your page and reduce the width of the browser. Your mobile display should be similar to Figure 7.27 or 7.28. Select the hyperlinks to view the Yurts and Activities pages. They should be similar to the home page. Pacific Trails is mobile!

Prime Properties

See Chapter 2 for an introduction to the Prime Properties case study. Figure 2.37 shows a site map for the Prime Properties website. In this case study, you will configure the website to display on mobile devices using the single-column layout shown in Figure 7.14. You will create a new mobile style sheet, modify the current styles, and update the Home, Financing, and Listings pages. Use the Chapter 6 Prime Properties website as a starting point for this case study. When you are finished, the website will look the same (see Figure 6.41) in desktop browsers. The mobile display should be similar to Figure 7.29 or 7.30. You have six tasks in this case study:

1. Create a new folder for this Prime Properties case study.

2. Modify the Home page to target mobile devices and deliver a mobile style sheet.

3. Modify the Financing page to be consistent with the Home page.

4. Modify the Listings page to be consistent with the Home page.

5. Create a new style sheet (primemobile.css), which will configure a single-column page layout.

6. Modify the desktop style sheet (prime.css).

Figure 7.29 The new mobile home page displayed on smartphone

Figure 7.30 It's possible to approximate the mobile display of a web page using a desktop browser

Hands-On Practice Case Study

Task 1: Create a Folder. Create a folder called prime7. Copy all of the files from your Chapter 6 prime6 folder into the prime7 folder. Copy the primemobile.gif file from the chapter7/starters folder in the student files.

Task 2: Modify the Home Page. Open index.html in a text editor. Edit the code as follows:

1. Configure a new link element in the head section that associates the web page with primemobile.css. Use CSS media queries to target smartphone mobile devices. Refer to Section 7.5.

2. Configure a viewport meta tag that configures the width to the `device-width` and sets the `initial-scale` to 1.0. Refer to Section 7.5.

3. The Prime Properties logo image is too wide for display on a mobile device. If a mobile browser scales down the image, the text may be difficult to read. Your design strategy will be to remove the img tag from the web page and configure "Prime Properties" text within the h1 element. You'll configure this area with CSS in Tasks 5 and 6. The HTML code is

```
<h1 id="header">Prime Properties</h1>
```

4. The home page displays a phone number in the contact information area. Wouldn't it be handy if a person using a smartphone could click on the phone number to call the company? You can make that happen by using `tel:` in a hyperlink. Configure a hyperlink assigned to an id named `mobile` that contains the phone number as shown below:

```
<a id="mobile" href="tel:847-555-5555">847-555-5555</a>
```

But wait a minute, a telephone link could confuse those visiting the site with a desktop browser. Code another phone number directly after the hyperlink. Code a span element assigned to an id named `desktop` around the phone number as shown below:

```
<span id="desktop">847-555-5555</span>
```

Don't worry about the two phone numbers that are now on the page. You'll configure CSS in Tasks 5 and 6 to show the appropriate phone number (with or without the telephone link) to your website visitors.

Save the index.html file. It should look similar to the web page shown in Figure 7.31 when displayed in a desktop browser. Remember that validating your HTML can help you find syntax errors. Test and correct this page before you continue.

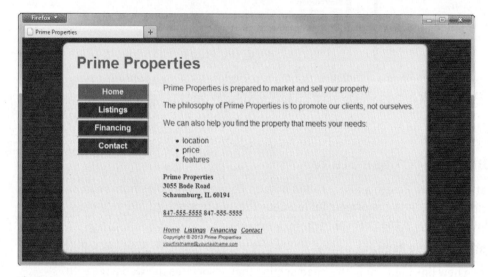

Figure 7.31 Temporary desktop browser display before new styles are configured

Task 3: Modify the Financing Page. Open financing.html in a text editor. Add the link element and viewport meta tag in a manner consistent with the home page. Reconfigure the header area and logo image in the same manner as the home page. Save and test your new financing.html page in a browser. Use the HTML validator to help you find syntax errors.

Task 4: Modify the Listings Page. Open listings.html in a text editor. Add the link element and viewport meta tag in a manner consistent with the home page. Reconfigure the header area and logo image in the same manner as the home page. Save and test your new listings.html page in a browser. Use the HTML validator to help you find syntax errors.

Task 5: Configure the Mobile CSS. Create the mobile style sheet based on the desktop style sheet. Open prime.css in a text editor. Save the file as primemobile.css. Edit the style rules as follows:

1. Modify the body element selector. Set margin and padding to 0. There's no need to display the background image. Set the `background-image` property to the value none.

2. Modify the `wrapper` id selector. Set left margin to 0, right margin to 0, padding to 0, width to 100%, and minimum width to 0.

3. Modify the `header` id selector. Recall that in Tasks 2, 3, and 4 you removed the logo image element from the web page background. Configure the small logo (primemobile.gif) as a background image with no repeats. Set the height to 70 pixels to correspond to the background image. Configure 0.4em bottom padding, no margin, and a 1 pixel `text-shadow` (use #000033 shadow color).

4. Configure an h1 element selector. Set left padding to 2em. The text "Prime Properties" will display in the header area on mobile devices. Set the `text-indent` property to 0.

5. Configure the `left` id selector. The mobile layout uses a single column. Set float to none, 100% width, 0 padding, and 0 margin.

6. Configure the anchor tags in the `left` id. Modify the style declaration for the `#left a` selector. Set padding to 0.3em. Set width to 92%.

7. Modify the `#left ul` selector. Set padding and margin to 0.

8. Modify the `right` id selector. Set padding to 0.5em, margin to 0, and font size to 90%.

9. Modify the `floatleft` class selector. Set the float property to `none`. Set right and bottom padding to 0.

10. Modify the h3 element selector. Set top padding to 0. Set margin to 0.

11. Modify the h2 element selector. Set margin to 0.

12. Modify the dd element selector. Set the `line-height` property to 100%.

13. Modify the `footer` id selector. Set top and bottom padding to 0.

14. Configure a new style rule to set a 0.3em margin for p, dt, dd, and ul elements in the content area (`right` id).

    ```
    #right p, #right ul, #right dd, #right dt { margin: 0.3em; }
    ```

15. Modify the `nav` class (the repeated navigation in the footer section of the page). Use `display: none;` to prevent it from displaying.

16. Remember the telephone number hyperlink you created in Task 2? Configure the CSS for the phone number display as shown below:

    ```
    #mobile { display: inline; }
    #desktop { display: none; }
    ```

Save the primemobile.css file. Use the CSS validator to help you find syntax errors.

Task 6: Modify the Desktop CSS. Open prime.css in a text editor. Edit the style rules as follows:

1. Modify the `header` id selector. Set the text alignment to left. Recall that in Tasks 2, 3, and 4 you removed the logo image element from the web page background. Configure the desktop logo (primelogo.gif) as a background image that does not repeat. Set the height to 100 pixels, which corresponds to the height of the background image.

2. Configure an h1 element selector. Use the `text-indent` property (refer to Chapter 3) to make this text available to screen readers but not display directly on the web page. The new style rule is

    ```
    h1 { text-indent: -99999px; }
    ```

3. Remember the telephone number hyperlink you created in Task 2? Configure the CSS for the phone number display as shown below:

```
#mobile { display: none; }
#desktop { display: inline; }
```

Save the prime.css file. Use the CSS validator to help you find syntax errors.

Display your pages in a desktop browser. The pages should look the same as they did before you started this case study (see Figure 6.41). Next, test the mobile display. Either publish your pages to the Web and display with a mobile device/emulator OR temporarily modify the href value (change prime.css to primemobile.css) on the first link element. Display your page and reduce the width of the browser. Your mobile display should be similar to Figure 7.29 or 7.30. Select the hyperlinks to view the Listings and Financing pages. They should be similar to the home page. Prime Properties is mobile!

Web Project

See Chapters 5 and 6 for an introduction to the Web Project case study. In this case study, you configure the website to display in mobile devices using the single-column layout shown in Figure 7.14. You will create a new mobile style sheet and modify the web pages as indicated in Section 7.5.

Hands-On Practice Case Study

1. Create a new style sheet for mobile display.

2. Modify each web page to associate with the new style sheet for mobile display.

3. Display your pages in a desktop browser. The pages should look the same as they did before you started this case study. Next, display your pages in a mobile device or emulator. Your pages should be optimized for mobile display.

Tables

Chapter Objectives   In this chapter, you will learn how to . . .

- Create a table on a web page

- Apply attributes to format tables, table rows, and table cells

- Increase the accessibility of a table

- Style an HTML table with CSS

While back in the day   tables were often used to format the layout of a web page, CSS is the page layout tool of choice for modern web developers. In this chapter, you'll become familiar with coding HTML tables to organize information on a web page.

8.1 Table Overview

VideoNote
Configure a Table

The purpose of a table is to organize information. In the past, before CSS was well supported by browsers, tables were also used to format web page layouts. An HTML table is composed of rows and columns, like a spreadsheet. Each individual table cell is at the intersection of a specific row and column.

Name	Birthday	Phone
Jack	5/13	857-555-5555
Sparky	11/28	303-555-5555

Figure 8.1 Table with three rows, three columns, and a border

- Each table begins with a `<table>` tag and ends with a `</table>` tag.

- Each table row begins with a `<tr>` tag and ends with a `</tr>` tag.

- Each cell (table data) begins with a `<td>` tag and ends with a `</td>` tag.

- Table cells can contain text, graphics, and other HTML elements.

Figure 8.1 shows a sample table with three rows, three columns, and a border. The sample HTML for this table is

```
<table border="1">
  <tr>
    <td>Name</td>
    <td>Birthday</td>
    <td>Phone</td>
  </tr>
  <tr>
    <td>Jack</td>
    <td>5/13</td>
    <td>857-555-5555</td>
  </tr>
  <tr>
    <td>Sparky</td>
    <td>11/28</td>
    <td>303-555-5555</td>
  </tr>
</table>
```

Notice how the table is coded row by row. Also, each row is coded cell by cell. This attention to detail is crucial for the successful use of tables. An example can be found in the student files (chapter8/table1.html).

Table Element

Table elements are block display elements that contain tabular information. The table begins with a **`<table>`** tag and ends with a **`</table>`** tag. See Table 8.1 for the common attributes of the table element.

Table 8.1 Commonly used attributes of the table element

Attribute	Value	Purpose
align	left (default), right, center	Horizontal alignment of the table (obsolete in HTML5)
bgcolor	Valid color value	Background color of the table (obsolete in HTML5)
border	0	Default; there is no visible border (obsolete in HTML5)
	1–100	Visible border with pixel width specified
cellpadding	Numeric value	Specifies the number of pixels of padding between the content of a table cell and its border (obsolete in HTML5)
cellspacing	Numeric value	Specifies the number of pixels of space between the borders of each cell in a table (obsolete in HTML5)
summary	Text description	Provides accessibility with a text description that gives an overview of and the context for the information in the table (at the time this was written, the summary attribute was obsolete in HTML5, but efforts were underway for reinstatement; check the textbook website for further information)
title	Text description	A brief text description that provides an overview of the table; may be displayed by some browsers as a tooltip
width	Numeric value or percentage	Specifies the width of the table (obsolete in HTML5)

Table Captions

The **caption element** is often used with a data table to describe its contents. The caption begins with a **<caption>** tag and ends with a </caption> tag. The text contained within the caption element displays on the web page above the table, although you'll see later in the chapter that you can configure the placement with CSS. The table shown in Figure 8.2 uses the caption element to set the table caption to "Bird Sightings". Notice that the caption element is coded on the line immediately after the opening <table> tag. An example can be found in the student files (chapter8/table2.html). The HTML for the table is

Figure 8.2 The caption for this table is "Bird Sightings"

```
<table border="1">
<caption>Bird Sightings</caption>
  <tr>
    <td>Name</td>
    <td>Date</td>
  </tr>
  <tr>
    <td>Bobolink</td>
    <td>5/25/10</td>
  </tr>
  <tr>
    <td>Upland Sandpiper</td>
    <td>6/03/10</td>
  </tr>
</table>
```

8.2 Table Rows, Cells, and Headers

Table Row Element

The **table row element** configures a row within a table on a web page. The table row begins with a `<tr>` tag and ends with a `</tr>` tag. See Table 8.2 for common attributes of the table row element.

Table 8.2 Commonly used attributes of the table row element

Attribute	Value	Purpose
`align`	`left` (default), `right`, `center`	Horizontal alignment of the table (obsolete in HTML5)
`bgcolor`	Valid color value	Background color of the table (obsolete in HTML5)

Table Data Element

The **table data element** configures a cell within a row in a table on a web page. The table cell begins with a `<td>` tag and ends with a `</td>` tag. See Table 8.3 for common attributes of the table data cell element.

Table 8.3 Commonly used attributes of the table data and table header cell elements

Attribute	Value	Purpose
`align`	`left` (default), `right`, `center`	Horizontal alignment of the table (obsolete in HTML5)
`bgcolor`	Valid color value	Background color of the table (obsolete in HTML5)
`colspan`	Numeric value	The number of columns spanned by a cell
`headers`	The id value(s) of a column or row header cell	Associates the table data cells with table header cells; may be accessed by screen readers
`height`	Numeric value or percentage	Height of the cell (obsolete in HTML5)
`rowspan`	Numeric value	The number of rows spanned by a cell
`scope`	`row`, `col`	The scope of the table header cell contents (row or column); may be accessed by screen readers
`valign`	`top`, `middle` (default), `bottom`	The vertical alignment of the contents of the cell (obsolete in HTML5)
`width`	Numeric value or percentage	Width of the cell (obsolete in HTML5)

Name	Birthday	Phone
Jack	5/13	857-555-5555
Sparky	11/28	303-555-5555

Figure 8.3 Using `<th>` tags to indicate column headings

Table Header Element

The **table header element** is similar to a table data element and configures a cell within a row in a table on a web page. Its purpose is to configure column and row headings. Text displayed within a table header element is centered and bold. The table header element begins with a **`<th>`** tag and ends with a **`</th>`** tag. See Table 8.3 for common attributes of the table data cell element. Figure 8.3 shows a table with column headings configured by `<th>` tags. The HTML for the table shown in Figure 8.3 is as follows (also see chapter8/table3.html in the student files). Notice that the first row uses `<th>` instead of `<td>` tags.

```
<table border="1">
  <tr>
    <th>Name</th>
    <th>Birthday</th>
    <th>Phone</th>
  </tr>
  <tr>
    <td>Jack</td>
    <td>5/13</td>
    <td>857-555-5555</td>
  </tr>
  <tr>
    <td>Sparky</td>
    <td>11/28</td>
    <td>303-555-5555</td>
  </tr>
</table>
```

Hands-On Practice 8.1

In this Hands-On Practice, you will create a web page similar to Figure 8.4 that describes two schools you have attended. Use the caption "School History Table." The table has three rows and three columns. The first row will have table header elements with the headings School Attended, Years, and Degree Awarded. You will complete the second and third rows with your own information within table data elements.

To get started, launch a text editor and open chapter2/template.html in the student files. Save the file as mytable.html. Modify the title element. Use table, table row, table header, table data, and caption elements to configure a table similar to Figure 8.4.

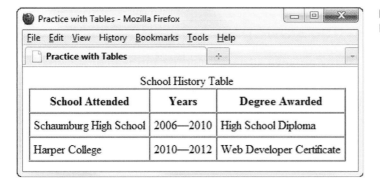

Figure 8.4 School History Table

Hints:

- The table has three rows and three columns.

- To configure a border, use `border="1"` on the `<table>` tag.

- To eliminate space between the cell borders, use `cellspacing="0"` on the `<table>` tag.

- To configure padding within each cell, use `cellpadding="5"` on the `<table>` tag.

- Use the table header element for the cells in the first row.

A sample solution is found in the student files (chapter8/table4.html). Your HTML5 code will not pass W3C validation testing when using obsolete attributes such as `border`, `cellspacing`, and `cellpadding`. This chapter introduces these obsolete attributes because they are still valid in XHTML and are still used often on the Web. Don't worry, you'll get practice configuring a table with CSS properties later in the chapter.

8.3 Span Rows and Columns

You can alter the gridlike look of a table by applying the `colspan` and `rowspan` attributes to table data or table header elements. As you get into more complex table configurations like these, be sure to sketch the table on paper before you start typing the HTML.

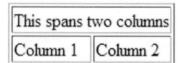

Figure 8.5 Table with a row that spans two columns

The `colspan` Attribute

The `colspan` **attribute** specifies the number of columns that a cell will occupy. Figure 8.5 shows a table cell that spans two columns.

The HTML for the table is

```
<table border="1">
  <tr>
    <td colspan="2">This spans two columns</td>
  </tr>
  <tr>
    <td>Column 1</td>
    <td>Column 2</td>
  </tr>
</table>
```

Figure 8.6 Table with a column that spans two rows

The `rowspan` Attribute

The `rowspan` **attribute** specifies the number of rows that a cell will occupy. An example of a table cell that spans two rows is shown in Figure 8.6.

The HTML for the table is

```
<table border="1">
  <tr>
    <td rowspan="2">This spans two rows</td>
    <td>Row 1 Column 2</td>
  </tr>
  <tr>
    <td>Row 2 Column 2</td>
  </tr>
</table>
```

An example of the tables in Figures 8.5 and 8.6 can be found in the student files (chapter8/table5.html).

Hands-On Practice 8.2

You will practice with the `rowspan` attribute in this Hands-On Practice. To create the web page shown in Figure 8.7, launch a text editor and open chapter2/template.html in the student files. Save the file as myrowspan.html. Modify the title element. Use table, table row, table head, and table data elements to configure the table.

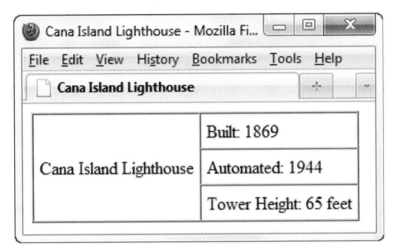

Figure 8.7
Practice with the
`rowspan` attribute

1. Code the opening `<table>` tag. Configure a border with `border="1"`, eliminate space between the cell borders with `cellspacing="0"`, and configure padding within each cell with `cellpadding="5"`.

2. Begin the first row with a `<tr>` tag.

3. The table data cell with "Cana Island Lighthouse" spans three rows. Code a table data element. Use the `rowspan="3"` attribute.

4. Code a table data element that contains the text "Built: 1869".

5. End the first row with a `</tr>` tag.

6. Begin the second row with a `<tr>` tag. This row will only have one table data element because the cell in the first column is already reserved for "Cana Island Lighthouse".

7. Code a table data element that contains the text "Automated: 1944".

8. End the second row with a `</tr>` tag.

9. Begin the third row with a `<tr>` tag. This row will only have one table data element because the cell in the first column is already reserved for "Cana Island Lighthouse".

10. Code a table data element that contains the text "Tower Height: 65 feet".

11. End the third row with a `</tr>` tag.

12. Code the closing `</table>` tag.

Save the file and view it in a browser. A sample solution is found in the student files (chapter8/table6.html). The use of the `border`, `cellpadding`, and `cellspacing` attributes will cause your web page to fail HTML5 validation. However, these attributes are still valid in XHTML syntax. Notice how the "Cana Island Lighthouse" text is vertically aligned in the middle of the cell, which is the default vertical alignment. You can modify the vertical alignment using the `valign` attribute on the td element. While this example uses HTML attributes, the modern approach is to configure tables using CSS, which you'll explore later in this chapter.

8.4 Configure an Accessible Table

Focus on Accessibility

Tables can be useful to organize information on a web page, but what if you couldn't see the table and were relying on assistive technology like a screen reader to read the table to you? You'd hear the contents of the table just the way it is coded—row by row, cell by cell. This might be difficult to understand. This section discusses coding techniques to improve the accessibility of tables.

Bird Sightings

Name	Date
Bobolink	5/25/10
Upland Sandpiper	6/03/10

Figure 8.8 This simple data table uses <th> tags and the caption element to provide accessibility

For a simple informational data table like the one shown in Figure 8.8, the W3C Web Accessibility Initiative (WAI) Web Content Accessibility Guidelines 2.0 (WCAG 2.0) recommend the following:

- Use table header elements (<th> tags) to indicate column or row headings.
- Use the caption element to provide a text title or caption for the table.

An example web page is in the student files (chapter8/table7.html). The HTML is

```
<table border="1">
<caption>Bird Sightings</caption>
  <tr>
    <th>Name</th>
    <th>Date</th>
  </tr>
  <tr>
    <td>Bobolink</td>
    <td>5/25/10</td>
  </tr>
  <tr>
    <td>Upland Sandpiper</td>
    <td>6/03/10</td>
  </tr>
</table>
```

However, for more complex tables, the W3C recommends specifically associating the table data cell values with their corresponding headers. The technique that is recommended uses the id attribute (usually in a <th> tag) to identify a specific header cell and the **headers attribute** in a <td> tag. The code to configure the table in Figure 8.8 using headers and ids is as follows (also see chapter8/table8.html in the student files):

```
<table border="1">
<caption>Bird Sightings</caption>
  <tr>
    <th id="name">Name</th>
    <th id="date">Date</th>
  </tr>
  <tr>
    <td headers="name">Bobolink</td>
    <td headers="date">5/25/10</td>
  </tr>
```

```
<tr>
  <td headers="name">Upland Sandpiper</td>
  <td headers="date">6/03/10</td>
</tr>
</table>
```

FAQ   What about the `summary` attribute?

At the time this was written, the `summary` attribute was deemed obsolete in HTML5, but efforts were underway for reinstatement. Check the textbook website for further information. The `summary` attribute was used for many years and is still valid in XHTML. The purpose of coding a `summary` attribute on a table element is to provide an overview of the purpose and organization of the table, setting the context for the information in the table. The information in the `summary` attribute is available to screen readers but does not display in the browser viewport. An example of using the `summary` attribute for the table shown in Figure 8.8 follows:

```
<table border="1" summary="A list of bird sightings with one bird
listed in each row. The first column contains the name of the bird.
The second column contains the date the bird was identified.">
```

New for the HTML5 specification, W3C suggests the following techniques to provide context for the information in a table: Configure descriptive text in the caption element, provide an explanatory paragraph directly on the web page, or simplify the table.

FAQ   What about the `scope` attribute?

The `scope` attribute specifies the association of table cells and table row or column headers. It is used to indicate whether a table cell is a header for a column (`scope="col"`) or row (`scope="row"`). An example of the code for the table in Figure 8.8 that uses this attribute is as follows (also see chapter8/table9.html in the student files):

```
<table border="1">
<caption>Bird Sightings</caption>
  <tr>
    <th scope="col">Name</th>
    <th scope="col">Date</th>
  </tr>
  <tr>
    <td>Bobolink</td>
    <td>5/25/10</td>
  </tr>
  <tr>
    <td>Upland Sandpiper</td>
    <td>6/03/10</td>
  </tr>
</table>
```

As you reviewed the code sample in the previous page, you may have noticed that using the `scope` attribute to provide accessibility requires less coding than implementing the `headers` and `id` attributes. However, because of inconsistent screen reader support of the `scope` attribute, the WCAG 2.0 recommendations for coding techniques encourage the use of `headers` and `id` attributes rather than the `scope` attribute.

 Checkpoint 8.1

1. What is the purpose of using a table on a web page?

2. To which elements are the `colspan` and `rowspan` attributes applied? What are their respective purposes?

3. What is the purpose of the `headers` attribute in a `<td>` tag?

8.5 Style a Table with CSS

Back in the day, it was common practice to configure the visual aesthetic of a table with HTML attributes. A more modern approach is to use CSS to style a table. In this section, you'll explore using CSS to style the border, padding, alignment, width, height, vertical alignment, and background of table elements. Table 8.4 lists corresponding CSS properties with the HTML attributes used to style tables.

Table 8.4 CSS properties used to style tables

HTML Attribute	CSS Property

align	To align a table, configure the `width` and `margin` properties for the table selector. For example, to center a table, use
	
	`table { width: 75%;`
	`         margin: auto; }`
	
	To align items within table cells, use `text-align`

width	width
height	height
cellpadding	padding
cellspacing	`border-spacing`; a numeric value (px or em) or percentage. If you set a value to 0, omit the unit. One numeric value with unit (px or em) configures both horizontal and vertical spacing. Two numeric values with unit (px or em): The first value configures the horizontal spacing and the second value configures the vertical spacing. `border-collapse` configures the border area. The values are `separate` (default) and `collapse`. Use `border-collapse: collapse;` to remove extra space between table and table cell borders.
bgcolor	background-color
valign	`vertical-align` specifies the vertical placement of content. The values are numeric pixel or percentage, `baseline` (default), `sub` (subscript), `super` (superscript), `top`, `text-top`, `middle`, `bottom`, and `text-bottom`
border	border, border-style, border-spacing
none	background-image
none	`caption-side` specifies the placement of the caption. Values are `top` (default) and `bottom`

Hands-On Practice 8.3

In this Hands-On Practice, you will code CSS style rules to configure an informational table on a web page. Create a folder named ch8table. Copy the starter.html file from the chapter8 folder to your ch8table folder. We'll use embedded styles for ease of editing and testing your page. Open the starter.html file in a browser. The display should look similar to the one shown in Figure 8.9.

Specialty Coffee	Description	Price
Lite Latte	Indulge in a shot of organic, locally roasted espresso with steamed, skim milk.	$3.50
Mocha Latte	Chocolate lovers will enjoy a shot of organic, locally roasted espresso, steamed milk, and your choice of melted dark, milk, or white chocolate.	$4.00
Turtle Treasure	A lucious mocha latte with caramel and pecan syrup — a candy bar in a cup.	$4.50

Lighthouse Island Bistro Specialty Coffee Menu

Figure 8.9 This table is configured with HTML

Launch a text editor and open starter.html from your ch8table folder.

1. Review the web page code and notice the attributes on the `<table>` tag that configure the border, width, alignment, cell padding, and cell spacing of the table. Delete these attributes from the `<table>` tag. You will code embedded CSS style rules to replace their functions.

2. Configure the table element selector. Locate the embedded styles in the head section of the web page. Add a style rule for the table element selector in this area that configures the table to be centered, have a border, and have a width of 600px.

```
table { margin: auto;
        border: 1px solid #5c743d;
        width: 600px; }
```

Save the file as menu.html. Open your page in a browser. Notice that there is a border surrounding the entire table but not surrounding each table cell.

3. Configure the td and th element selectors. Add a style rule that configures a border and padding. Configure these selectors to use Arial or the default sans-serif font typeface.

```
td, th { border: 1px solid #5c743d;
         padding: 5px;
         font-family: Arial, sans-serif; }
```

Save the file and open your page in a browser. Each table cell should now be outlined with a border and should display text in a sans-serif font.

4. Notice the empty space between the borders of the table cells. The `border-spacing` **property** can be used to eliminate this space. Add a `border-spacing: 0;` declaration to the table element selector. Save the file and open your page in a browser.

5. Configure the caption to be displayed with Verdana or the default sans-serif font typeface, bold font weight, 1.2em font size, and 5 pixels of bottom padding. Configure a style rule as follows:

```
caption { font-family: Verdana, sans-serif;
          font-weight: bold;
          font-size: 1.2em;
          padding-bottom: 5px; }
```

6. Let's experiment and configure background colors for the rows instead of cell borders. Modify the style rule for the td and th element selectors and remove the border declaration. The new style rule for the cells is

```
td, th { padding: 5px;
         font-family: Arial, sans-serif; }
```

7. Create a new class called `altrow` that sets a background color.

```
.altrow { background-color: #eaeaea; }
```

8. Modify the `<tr>` tags in the HTML. Assign the second and fourth `<tr>` tags to the `altrow` class. Save the file and open your page in a browser. The table area should look similar to the one shown in Figure 8.10.

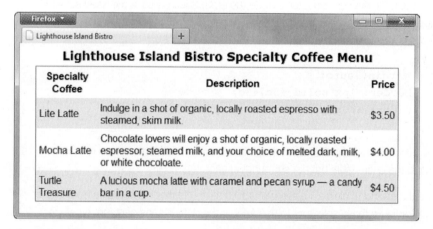

Figure 8.10 Rows are configured with alternating background colors

Notice how the background color of the alternate rows adds subtle interest to the web page. Compare your work with the sample in the student files (chapter8/menu.html). In this Hands-On Practice, you configured the display of an HTML table using CSS. You'll see this coding technique used increasingly in the future.

FAQ   Is there a way to create a table-like page layout with CSS?

Yes, if you'd like to explore using CSS to style table-like layouts on web pages, check out the CSS `display` property. As you may recall from previous chapters, the CSS `display` property configures whether and how an element is displayed. You've already worked with `display: none`, `display: block`, and `display: inline`. Internet Explorer 8 was the last major browser to add support for the `display: table` property values. Rachel Andrew's article, "Everything You Know About CSS Is Wrong" (http://www.digital-web.com/articles/everything_you_know_about_CSS_Is_wrong), encourages developers to embrace the `display: table` coding methods. Be aware that this technique is still quite limited. For example, there is no built-in mechanism to emulate the `rowspan` or `colspan` attribute in HTML tables. However, this is in the works with the CSS3 draft recommendation at http://www.w3.org/Style/CSS/current-work, which includes new CSS specifications for working with multicolumn layouts and grid positioning.

8.6 CSS3 Structural Pseudo-Classes

In the previous section, you configured CSS and applied a class to every other table row to configure alternating background colors, often referred to as "zebra striping." You may have found this to be a bit inconvenient and wondered if there was a more efficient method. Well, there is! CSS3 **structural pseudo-class selectors** allow you to select and apply classes to elements based on their position in the structure of the document, such as every other row. CSS3 pseudo-classes are supported by current versions of Firefox, Opera, Chrome, Safari, and Internet Explorer 9. Earlier versions of Internet Explorer do not support CSS3 pseudo-classes, so consider using this coding technique only for enhancements to a web page. Table 8.5 lists common CSS3 structural pseudo-class selectors and their purpose.

Table 8.5 Common CSS3 structural pseudo-classes

Pseudo-Class	Purpose
`:first-of-type`	Applies to the first element of the specified type
`:first-child`	Applies to the first child of an element (CSS2 selector)
`:last-of-type`	Applies to the last element of the specified type
`:last-child`	Applies to the last child of an element
`:nth-of-type(n)`	Applies to the "nth" element of the specified type Values: a number, `odd`, or `even`

To apply a pseudo-class, write it after the selector. The following code sample will configure the first item in an unordered list to display with red text.

```
li:first-of-type { color: #FF0000; }
```

Hands-On Practice 8.4

In this Hands-On Practice, you will rework the table you configured in Hands-On Practice 8.3 to use CSS3 structural pseudo-class selectors to configure color.

1. Launch a text editor and open menu.html in your ch8table folder (it can also be found as chapter8/menu.html in the student files). Save the file as menu2.html.

2. View the source code and notice that the second and fourth tr elements are assigned to the `altrow` class. You won't need this class assignment when using CSS3 structural pseudo-class selectors. Delete `class="altrow"` from the tr elements.

3. Examine the embedded CSS and locate the `altrow` class. Change the selector to use a structural pseudo-class that will apply the style to the even-numbered table rows. Replace `.altrow` with `tr:nth-of-type (even)` as shown in the following CSS declaration:

```
tr:nth-of-type(even) { background-color: #eaeaea; }
```

4. Save the file and open your page in a browser. The table area should look similar to the one shown in Figure 8.10 if you are using a modern browser that supports CSS3 structural pseudo-classes.

5. Let's configure the first row to have a dark-gray background (#666) and light-gray text (#eaeaea) with the `:first-of-type` structural pseudo-class. Add the following to the embedded CSS:

```
tr:first-of-type { background-color: #666;
                   color: #eaeaea; }
```

6. Save the file and open your page in a browser. The table area should look similar to the one shown in Figure 8.11 if you are using a modern browser that supports CSS3 structural pseudo-classes. A sample solution is available in the student files (chapter8/menucss.html).

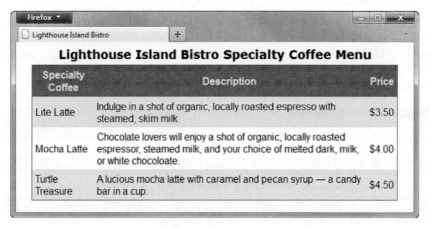

Figure 8.11 CSS3 pseudo-class selectors style the table rows

CSS structural pseudo-classes are convenient to use, but be aware that Internet Explorer 8 and earlier versions do not support this technology. Although browser support will increase in the future, today it's best to apply these pseudo-classes with progressive enhancement in mind.

8.7 Configure Table Sections

There are a lot of configuration options for coding tables. Table rows can be put together into three types of groups: table head with `<thead>`, table body with `<tbody>`, and table footer with `<tfoot>`.

These groups can be useful when you need to configure the areas in the table in different ways, using either attributes or CSS. The `<tbody>` tag is required if you configure a `<thead>` or `<tfoot>` area, although you can omit either the table head or table footer if you like. When you use table row groups, the `<thead>` and `<tfoot>` sections must be coded *before* the `<tbody>` section to pass W3C XHTML validation. The code sample in this section uses HTML5 syntax with the `<tfoot>` coded after the `<tbody>`, which is more intuitive.

The following code sample (see chapter8/tfoot.html in the student files) configures the table shown in Figure 8.12 and demonstrates the use of CSS to configure a table head, table body, and table footer with different styles.

The CSS styles a centered 200-pixel-wide table with a caption that is rendered in large, bold font; a table head section with a light-gray (#eaeaea) background color; a table body section styled with slightly smaller text (.90em) using Arial or sans-serif font; table body td element selectors set to display with some left padding and a dashed bottom border; and a table footer section that has centered, bold text and a light-gray background color (#eaeaea). The CSS code is

Figure 8.12 CSS configures the thead, tbody, and tfoot element selectors

```
table { width: 200px;
        margin: auto; }
caption { font-size: 2em;
          font-weight: bold; }
thead { background-color: #eaeaea; }
tbody { font-family: Arial, sans-serif;
        font-size: .90em; }
tbody td { border-bottom: 1px #000033 dashed;
           padding-left: 25px; }
tfoot { background-color: #eaeaea;
        font-weight: bold;
        text-align: center; }
```

The HTML for the table is

```
<table>
<caption>Time Sheet</caption>
    <thead>
       <tr>
          <th id="day">Day</th>
          <th id="hours">Hours</th>
       </tr>
    </thead>
    <tbody>
       <tr>
          <td headers="day">Monday</td>
          <td headers="hours">4</td>
       </tr>
       <tr>
          <td headers="day">Tuesday</td>
          <td headers="hours">3</td>
       </tr>
```

```
        <tr>
            <td headers="day">Wednesday</td>
            <td headers="hours">5</td>
        </tr>
        <tr>
            <td headers="day">Thursday</td>
            <td headers="hours">3</td>
        </tr>
        <tr>
            <td headers="day">Friday</td>
            <td headers="hours">3</td>
        </tr>
    </tbody>
    <tfoot>
        <tr>
            <td headers="day">Total</td>
            <td headers="hours">18</td>
        </tr>
    </tfoot>
</table>
```

This example demonstrates the power of CSS in styling documents. The `<td>` tags within each table row group element selector (thead, tbody, and tfoot) inherited the font styles configured for their parent group element selector. Notice how a contextual selector configures the padding and border only for `<td>` tags that are contained within (actually, "children of") the `<tbody>` element. Sample code is located in the student files (chapter8/tfoot.html). Take a few moments to explore the web page code and open the page in a browser.

 Checkpoint 8.2

1. What are the equivalent CSS properties for HTML table attributes `cellpadding` and `cellspacing`?

2. What is the purpose of the `border-collapse` property?

Chapter Summary

This chapter introduces both the HTML techniques used to code tables to organize information and the CSS properties that configure the display of tables on web pages. Visit the textbook website at http://www.webdevfoundations.net for examples, the links listed in this chapter, and updated information.

Key Terms

`<caption>`	`:last-child`	cellspacing attribute
`<table>`	`:last-of-type`	colspan attribute
`<tbody>`	`:nth of type`	headers attribute
`<td>`	align attribute	rowspan attribute
`<tfoot>`	border attribute	scope attribute
`<th>`	border-collapse property	summary attribute
`<thead>`	border-spacing property	title attribute
`<tr>`	caption-side property	vertical-align property
`:first-child`	cell	valign attribute
`:first-of-type`	cellpadding attribute	

Review Questions

Multiple Choice

1. Which of the following HTML codes specifies a table caption?

   a. `<caption>Monthly Rainfall </caption>`

   b. `<table>Monthly Rainfall</table>`

   c. `<td><caption>Monthly Rainfall </caption></td>`

   d. `<th><caption>Monthly Rainfall </caption></th>`

2. Which of the following HTML codes specifies a table summary?

   a. `<summary>my table summary </summary>`

   b. `<tfoot>my table summary</tfoot>`

   c. `<table summary= "my table summary"> ... </table>`

   d. `<td summary = "my table summary"> ... </td>`

3. Which of the following HTML codes specifies a distance of 10 pixels between the edges of each cell?

   a. `<table cellborder="10">`

   b. `<table cellpadding="10">`

   c. `<table border="10" >`

   d. `<table cellspacing="10">`

4. Which of the following HTML codes specifies a distance of 10 pixels between the cell content and the cell border?

   a. `<table cellborder="10">`

   b. `<table cellpadding="10">`

   c. `<table border="10" >`

   d. `<table cellspacing="10">`

5. Which of the following HTML codes specifies a header cell that spans two columns?

   a. `<tdcolspan="2">Telephone:</td>`

   b. `<thcolspan="2">Telephone:</th>`

   c. `<throwspan="2">Telephone:</th>`

   d. `<trrowspan="2">Telephone:</tr>`

6. Which of the following HTML codes specifies a header cell that spans two rows?

   a. `<tdcolspan="2">Telephone:</td>`

   b. `<thcolspan="2">Telephone:</th>`

   c. `<throwspan="2">Telephone:</th>`

   d. `<trrowspan="2">Telephone:</tr>`

7. Which of the following HTML code snippets specifies a table border of 2 pixels?

   a. `<table border="2">...</table>`

   b. `<table cellspacing="2">`

   c. `<td border="2">...</td>`

   d. `<tr border="2">...</tr>`

8. Which of the following CSS codes will specify the background color of the odd-numbered table columns to be olive?

   a. `td:nth-of-type(even) { background-color: olive; }`

   b. `td:nth-of-type(odd) { background-color: olive; }`

   c. `tr:nth-of-type(even) { background-color: olive; }`

   d. `tr:nth-of-type(odd) { background-color: olive; }`

9. Which CSS property specifies the vertical placement of the content of a table?

   a. `valign`

   b. `height`

   c. `vertical-align`

   d. `margin`

10. Which CSS property allows the removal of extra space between the table and the table cell borders?

   a. `border`

   b. `padding`

   c. `cellspacing`

   d. `border-collapse`

Fill in the Blank

11. The CSS _____ property is used to configure the background color of a table.

12. The CSS pseudo-class _____ applies to the first element of a specified type.

13. The CSS pseudo-class _____ applies to the last element of a specified type.

14. The HTML _____ attribute specifies the horizontal alignment of the table.

15. The _____ attribute specifies the association of table cells and table row or column headers.

Apply Your Knowledge

1. **Predict the Result.** Draw and write a brief description of the web page that will be created with the following HTML code:

```
<!DOCTYPE html>
<html lang="en">
<head>
<title>Predict the Result</title>
<meta charset="utf-8">
</head>
<body>
<table border="1" cellpadding = "5" cellspacing = "5">
<caption><strong>Exam Schedule:</strong></caption>
<tr>
<td> </td>
<th>9 A.M.</th>
<th>12 P.M.</th>
</tr>
<tr>
<th>Monday: 2nd Jan, 2012</th>
<td>Math</td>
<td>Computer Science</td>
</tr>
<tr>
<th>Tuesday: 3rd Jan, 2012</th>
<td>Physics</td>
<td>Chemistry</td>
</tr>
</table>
</body>
</html>
```

2. **Fill in the Missing Code.** This web page should have a table with a background color of #cccccc and a border. Some CSS properties and values, indicated by "_", are missing. Fill in the missing code.

```
<!DOCTYPE html>
<html lang="en">
<head>
<title>CircleSoft Web Design</title>
<meta charset="utf-8">
<style>
table { "_":"_";
        "_":"_"; }
</style>
</head>
<body>
<h1>CircleSoft Web Design</h1>
<table>
<caption>Contact Information</caption>
    <tr>
        <th>Name</th>
        <th>Phone</th>
    </tr>
    <tr>
        <td>Mike Circle</td>
        <td>920-555-5555</td>
    </tr>
</table>
</body>
</html>
```

3. **Find the Error.** Why doesn't the table information display in the order it was coded?

```
<!DOCTYPE html>
<html lang="en">
<head>
<title>CircleSoft Web Design</title>
<meta charset="utf-8">
</head>
<body>
<h1>CircleSoft Web Design</h1>
<table>
<caption>Contact Information</caption>
<tr>
    <th>Name</th>
    <th>Phone</th>
</tr>
<tr>
    <tr>Mike Circle</td>
    <td>920-555-5555</td>
</tr>
</table>
</body>
</html>
```

Hands-On Exercises

1. Write the HTML for a two-column table that contains your monthly savings. The first row of the table should span two columns and contain the following heading: Monthly Savings. The first column of the table should have the names of months and the content should be right aligned, while the second column should hold the savings and be left aligned. Include at least five months' data in your table.

2. Write the HTML for a three-column table to describe a list of hotels in your state. The columns should contain the name of the hotel, facilities provided, and the contact number. The first row of the table should use th tags and contain descriptive headings for the columns. Use the table row grouping tags <thead> and <tbody> in your table. The text in the table should be center aligned.

3. Modify the table you created in Hands-On Exercise 8.2 to be centered on the page with a width of 800 pixels. Use a background color of #CCCC99, and display text in Arial, Helvetica, or the browser default sans-serif font. Configure this table using CSS instead of obsolete HTML attributes. Add a <tfoot> row grouping that will contain your contact address and e-mail.

4. Write a three-column table to describe the commonly used attributes of the table element. The columns should contain the following headings: attribute, value, and purpose. Use Table 8.1 (page 351) for data and header cells. Configure alternating rows to use the background color #CCCCCC.

5. Use CSS to configure the table created in the previous exercise in such a way that it should be centered on the page and have 80% of the page width. The first row should have a background color #0000cc and text color white. Alternating even rows should have a background color of #99ccff. The text in the header row should be horizontally and vertically centered. The top row of the table should have rounded corners with radius 25 pixels.

6. Create a web page about your favorite recipe with a three-column table that lists the ingredients and the directions for the preparation, and shows a photograph. The ingredients should be provided in an unordered list, and the directions should be provided in an ordered list. Use embedded CSS to style the table border and background color, and center the table on the web page. Place an e-mail link to yourself on the web page.

7. Create a web page about your favorite movie that uses a three-column table containing details about the movie. Use CSS to style the table border and background color. Include the following in the table:

   - Title of the movie
   - Director or producer
   - Leading actor
   - Leading actress
   - A brief description of the movie

   The third column will span all the rows except the header row and should have a still photo from the movie.

8. Create a web page about your favorite music CD that uses a four-column table. The column headings should be as follows:

   - **Group:** Place the name of the group and the names of its principal members in this column.
   - **Tracks:** List the title of each music track or song.

- **Year:** List the year the CD was recorded.
- **Links:** Place at least two absolute links to sites about the group in this column.

  Include an e-mail link to yourself on the web page. Save the page as band8.html.

9. Create a web page about your favorite authors and their best works. The information should be catalogued in three columns: the name and a brief introduction to the author, his or her best works, and a link to his or her personal web page, or to the Wikipedia page in the absence of a personal web page.

Web Research

Search the Web and find a web page configured with one or more HTML tables. Print the browser view of the page. Print out the source code of the web page. On the printout, highlight or circle the tags related to tables. On a separate sheet of paper, create some HTML notes by listing the tags and attributes related to tables found on your sample page, along with a brief description of their purpose. Hand in the browser view of the page, source code printout, and your HTML notes page to your instructor.

Focus on Web Design

Good artists view and analyze many paintings. Good writers read and evaluate many books. Similarly, good web designers view and scrutinize many web pages. Surf the Web and find two web pages, one that is appealing to you and one that is unappealing to you. Print out each page. Create a web page that answers the following questions for each of your examples:

a. What is the URL of the website?

b. Does this page use tables? If so, for what purpose (page layout, organization of information, or another reason)?

c. Does this page use CSS? If so, for what purpose (page layout, text and color configuration, or another reason)?

d. Is this page appealing or unappealing? List three reasons for your answer.

e. If this page is unappealing, what would you do to improve it?

 # WEB SITE CASE STUDY
Using Tables

Each of the following case studies continues throughout most of the textbook. This chapter incorporates an HTML table in the case study websites.

JavaJam Coffee House

See Chapter 2 for an introduction to the JavaJam Coffee House case study. Figure 2.25 shows a site map for JavaJam. Use the Chapter 6 JavaJam website as a starting point for this case study. You will modify the Menu page (menu.html) to display information in an HTML table. You will use CSS to style the table. You have three tasks in this case study:

1. Create a new folder for this JavaJam case study.
2. Modify the style sheet (javajam.css) to configure style rules for the new table.
3. Modify the Menu page to use a table to display information as shown in Figure 8.13.

Figure 8.13 Menu page with a table

Hands-On Practice Case Study

Task 1: Create a Folder. Create a folder called javajam8. Copy all the files from your Chapter 6 javajam6 folder into the javajam8 folder.

Task 2: Configure the CSS. Modify the external style sheet (javajam.css). Open javajam.css in a text editor. Review Figure 8.13 and note the menu descriptions, which are coded in an HTML table. Add style rules to the javajam.css external style sheet to configure a table that is centered, has td and th selectors with 10 pixels of padding, and displays a background color of #ccaa66 in alternate rows (use a class or the :nth-of-type pseudo-class to configure odd table rows). Save the javajam.css file.

Task 3: Modify the Menu Page. Open menu.html in a text editor. The menu descriptions are configured with a description list. Replace the description list with a table that has three rows and two columns. Use th and td elements where appropriate. Save your page and test it in a browser. If the page does not display as you intended, review your work, validate the CSS, validate the HTML, modify as needed, and test again.

Fish Creek Animal Hospital

See Chapter 2 for an introduction to the Fish Creek Animal Hospital case study. Figure 2.29 shows a site map for Fish Creek. Use the Chapter 6 Fish Creek website as a starting point for this case study. You will modify the Services page (services.html) to display information in an HTML table. You will use CSS to style the table. You have three tasks in this case study:

1. Create a new folder for this Fish Creek case study.

2. Modify the style sheet (fishcreek.css) to configure style rules for the new table.

3. Modify the Services page to use a table to display information as shown in Figure 8.14.

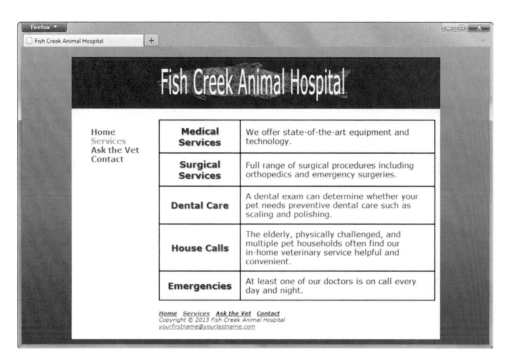

Figure 8.14 Services page with a table

Hands-On Practice Case Study

Task 1: Create a Folder. Create a folder called fishcreek8. Copy all of the files from your Chapter 6 fishcreek6 folder into the fishcreek8 folder.

Task 2: Configure the CSS. Modify the external style sheet (fishcreek.css). Open fishcreek.css in a text editor. Review Figure 8.14 and note the services descriptions, which are coded in an HTML table. Add style rules to the fishcreek.css external style sheet as indicated:

1. Configure a table that has a solid, dark-blue, 2 pixel border.

2. Configure the borders in the table to collapse.

3. Configure td and th element selectors with 10 pixels of padding and a solid, dark-blue, 1 pixel border.

Save the fishcreek.css file.

Task 3: Modify the Services Page. Open services.html in a text editor. The services descriptions are configured with an unordered list. Replace the unordered list with a table that has five rows and two columns. Use th and td elements where appropriate. *Hint*: Assign the th element to the category class. Save your page and test it in a browser. If the page does not display as you intended, review your work, validate the CSS, validate the HTML, modify as needed, and test again.

Pacific Trails Resort

See Chapter 2 for an introduction to the Pacific Trails Resort case study. Figure 2.33 shows a site map for Pacific Trails. Use the Chapter 6 Pacific Trails website as a starting point for this case study. You will modify the Yurts page (yurts.html) to display additional information in an HTML table. You will use CSS to style the table. You have three tasks in this case study:

1. Create a new folder for this Pacific Trails case study.

2. Modify the style sheet (pacific.css) to configure style rules for the new table.

3. Modify the Yurts page to use a table to display information as shown in Figure 8.15.

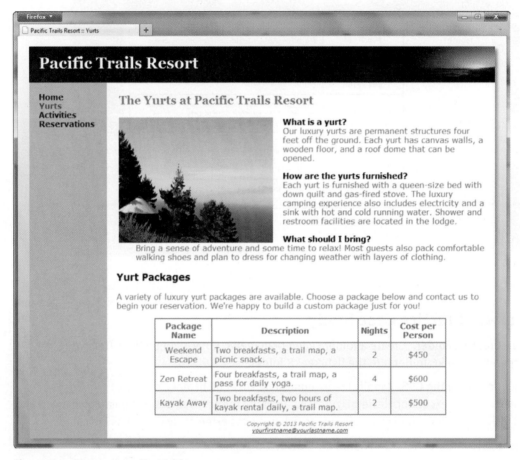

Figure 8.15 Yurts page with a table

Hands-On Practice Case Study

Task 1: Create a Folder. Create a folder called pacific8. Copy all the files from your Chapter 6 pacific6 folder into the pacific8 folder.

Task 2: Configure the CSS. Modify the external style sheet (pacific.css). Open pacific.css in a text editor. Add styles to configure the table on the Yurts page as shown in Figure 8.15.

1. Configure the table. Code a new style rule for the table element selector that configures a centered table with a 1 pixel solid-blue border (#3399cc), 600 pixel width, and no cell spacing (use `border-spacing: 0;`).

2. Configure the table cells. Code a new style rule for the td and th element selectors that configure 5 pixels of padding and a 1 pixel solid-blue border (#3399cc).

3. Center the td content. Code a new style rule for the td element selector that centers text (use `text-align: center;`).

4. Configure the `.text` class. Notice that the content in the table data cells that contain the text description is not centered. Code a new style rule for a class named `text` that will override the td style rule and left-align the text (use `text-align: left;`).

5. Configure alternate-row background color. The table looks more appealing if the rows have alternate background colors, but it is still readable without them. Apply the `:nth-of-type` CSS3 pseudo-class to configure the odd table rows with a light-blue background color (#F5FAFC).

6. Save the pacific.css file.

Task 3: Modify the Yurts Page. Open yurts.html in a text editor.

1. Add a blank line above the footer div. Configure an h3 element with the following text: "Yurt Packages".

2. Below the new h3 element, configure a paragraph with the following text:

   A variety of luxury yurt packages are available. Choose a package below and contact us to begin your reservation. We're happy to build a custom package just for you!

3. You are ready to configure the table. Position your cursor on a blank line under the paragraph and code a table with four rows and four columns. Use the table, th, and td elements. Use the summary attribute on the table element. Assign the td elements that contain the detailed descriptions to the class named `text`. The content for the table is as follows.

Package Name	Description	Nights	Cost per Person
Weekend Escape	Two breakfasts, a trail map, a picnic snack	2	$450
Zen Retreat	Four breakfasts, a trail map, a pass for daily yoga	4	$600
Kayak Away	Two breakfasts, two hours of kayak rental daily, a trail map	2	$500

Save your page and test it in a browser. If the page does not display as you intended, review your work, validate the CSS, validate the HTML, modify as needed, and test again.

Prime Properties

See Chapter 2 for an introduction to the Prime Properties case study. Figure 2.37 shows a site map for Prime Properties. Use the Chapter 6 Prime Properties website as a starting point for this case study. You will modify the Listings page (listings.html) to display the information in an HTML table. You will use CSS to style the table. You have three tasks in this case study:

1. Create a new folder for this Prime Properties case study.

2. Modify the style sheet (prime.css) to configure style rules for the new table.

3. Modify the Listings page to use a table to display information as shown in Figure 8.16.

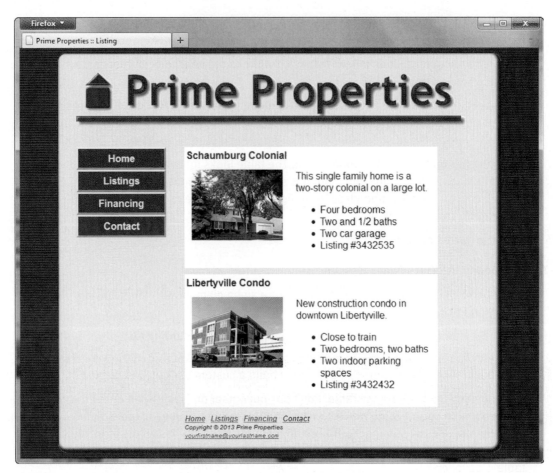

Figure 8.16 Listings page with tables

Hands-On Practice Case Study

Task 1: Create a Folder. Create a folder called prime8. Copy all the files from your Chapter 6 prime6 folder into the prime8 folder.

Task 2: Configure the CSS. Modify the external style sheet (prime.css). Open prime.css in a text editor. Review Figure 8.16 and note the property listing information, which is coded in two HTML tables. Add style rules to the prime.css external style sheet to configure the following:

1. A table with a background color (#ffffff), 80% width, no border, and a 10 pixel bottom margin

2. A th element selector with left-aligned text in a green color (#006600)

3. A td element selector that is aligned vertically to the top and has 10 pixels of padding

4. No top margin for the paragraphs and h3 elements in the table

Save the prime.css file.

Task 3: Modify the Listings Page. Open listings.html in a text editor. The listings information currently uses the <h3>, image, paragraph, and unordered lists elements. You will reconfigure this area with two tables—one for each real estate listing. Each table will have two rows. Refer to Figure 8.16. The first row in each table consists of one table cell which spans two columns that contain the real estate listing name. The second row in each table consists of two table cells. The first table cell in this row contains the image (remove the `floatleft` class from the image element). The second table cell contains the paragraph and unordered list.

Save your page and test it in a browser. If the page does not display as you intended, review your work, validate the CSS, validate the HTML, modify as needed, and test again.

Web Project

See Chapters 5 and 6 for an introduction to the Web Project case study. You will modify the design of one of the pages to display information in an HTML table. Use CSS to style the table.

Hands-On Practice Case Study

1. Choose one of your project web pages to modify. Sketch a design of the table you plan to create. Decide on borders, background color, padding, alignment, and so on.

2. Modify your project's external CSS file (project.css) to configure the table (and table cells) as needed.

3. Update your chosen web page and add the HTML code for a table.

Save and test the page. Modify both the web page and the project.css file as needed. Test and modify until you have achieved the look you want.

Forms

Forms are used for many purposes all over the Web. They are used by search engines to accept keywords and by online stores to process e-commerce shopping carts. Websites use forms to help with a variety of functions, including accepting visitor feedback, encouraging visitors to send a news story to a friend or colleague, collecting e-mail addresses for a newsletter, and accepting order information. This chapter introduces a very powerful tool for web developers—forms that accept information from web page visitors.

9.1 Overview of Forms

Every time you use a search engine, place an order, or join an online mailing list, you use a **form**. A form is an HTML element that contains and organizes objects called **form controls**, including text boxes, check boxes, and buttons, that can accept information from website visitors.

For example, look at Google's search form shown in Figure 9.1. You may have used this many times but never thought about how it works. The form is quite simple; it contains just two form controls: the text box that accepts the keywords used in the search and the search button that submits the form and gets the search started.

Figure 9.1 The search form on Google's home page

Figure 9.2 shows a more detailed form that is used to enter shipping information at the IRS website (http://www.irs.gov). This form contains text boxes to accept information such as name and address. Select lists (sometimes called drop-down boxes) are used to capture information with a limited number of correct values, such as state and country information. When a visitor clicks the continue button, the form information is submitted and the ordering process continues. Whether a form is used to search for web pages or to order a publication, the form alone cannot do all of the processing. The form needs to invoke a program or script on the web server in order to search a database or record an order. There are usually two components of a form:

1. The HTML form itself, which is the web page user interface

2. The server-side processing, which works with the form data and sends e-mail, writes to a text file, updates a database, or performs some other type of processing on the server

Figure 9.2 This form accepts order information

Form Element

Now that you have a basic understanding of what forms do, let's focus on the HTML code to create a form. The **form element** contains a form on a web page. The

`<form>` tag specifies the beginning of a form area. The closing `</form>` tag specifies the end of a form area. There can be multiple forms on a web page, but they cannot be nested inside one another. The form element can be configured with attributes that specify which server-side program or file will process the form, how the form information will be sent to the server, and the name of the form. These attributes are listed in Table 9.1.

Table 9.1 Attributes of the form element

Attribute	Value	Purpose
action	URL or file name/path of server-side processing script	Required; indicates where to send the form information when the form is submitted; mailto:e-mailaddress will launch the visitor's default e-mail application to send the form information
autocomplete	on	HTML5 attribute; default value; browser will use autocomplete to fill form fields
	off	HTML5 attribute; browser will not use autocomplete to fill form fields
id	Alphanumeric, no spaces; the value must be unique and not used for other id values on the same web page document	Optional; provides a unique identifier for the form
method	get	Default value; the value of get causes the form data to be appended to the URL and sent to the web server
	post	The post method is more private and transmits the form data in the body of the HTTP response; this method is preferred by the W3C
name	Alphanumeric, no spaces, begins with a letter; choose a form name value that is descriptive but short (for example, OrderForm is better than Form1 or WidgetsRUsOrderForm)	Optional; names the form so that it can be easily accessed by client-side scripting languages, such as JavaScript, to edit and verify the form information before the server-side processing is invoked

For example, to configure a form with the name attribute set to the value "order", using the post method and invoking a script called demo.php on your web server, the code is

```
<form name="order" method="post" id="order" action="demo.php">
```

. . . form controls go here . . .

```
</form>
```

Form Controls

The purpose of a form is to gather information from a web page visitor. Form controls are the objects that accept the information. Types of form controls include text boxes, scrolling text boxes, select lists, radio buttons, check boxes, and buttons. HTML5 offers new form controls, including those that are customized for e-mail addresses, URLs, dates, times, numbers, and even date selection. HTML elements that configure form controls will be introduced in the following sections.

9.2 Input Element Form Controls

The **input element** is a stand-alone tag that is used to configure several different types of form controls. The input element is coded as `<input>` when using HTML5 syntax and as `<input />` when using XHTML syntax. Use the `type` attribute to specify the type of form control that the browser should display.

Sample Text Box

E-mail:

Figure 9.3 The `<input>` tag with `type="text"` configures this form element

Text Box

The `<input>` tag with `type="text"` configures a text box. The text box form control accepts text or numeric information such as names, e-mail addresses, phone numbers, and other text. Common input element attributes for text boxes are listed in Table 9.2. A sample text box is shown in Figure 9.3.

The code for the text box is shown below:

```
E-mail: <input type="text" name="email" id="email">
```

Table 9.2 Common text box attributes

Attribute	Value	Purpose
type	text	Configures a text box
name	Alphanumeric, no spaces, begins with a letter	Names the form element so that it can be easily accessed by client-side scripting languages (such as JavaScript) or by server-side processing; the name should be unique
id	Alphanumeric, no spaces, begins with a letter	Provides a unique identifier for the form element
size	Numeric value	Configures the width of the text box as displayed by the browser; if size is omitted, the browser displays the text box with its own default size
maxlength	Numeric value	Configures the maximum length of data accepted by the text box
value	Text or numeric characters	Assigns an initial value to the text box that is displayed by the browser; accepts information typed in the text box; this value can be accessed by client-side scripting languages and by server-side processing
disabled	disabled	Form control is disabled
readonly	readonly	Form control is for display; cannot be edited
autocomplete	on	HTML5 attribute; default; browser will use autocomplete to fill the form control
	off	HTML5 attribute; browser will not use autocomplete to fill the form control
autofocus	autofocus	HTML5 attribute; browser places cursor in the form control and sets the focus
list	Datalist element id value	HTML5 attribute; associates the form control with a datalist element
placeholder	Text or numeric characters	HTML5 attribute; brief information intended to assist the user
required	required	HTML5 attribute; browser verifies entry of information before submitting the form
accesskey	Keyboard character	Configures a hot key for the form control
tabindex	Numeric value	Configures the tab order of the form control

Several attributes are new in HTML5. The new **required attribute** is exciting because it will cause supporting browsers to perform form validation. Browsers that support the HTML5 required attribute will automatically verify that information has been entered in the text box and display an error message when the condition is not met. A code sample is

```
E-mail: <input type="text" name="email" id="email"
required="required">
```

Figure 9.4 shows an error message automatically generated by Firefox 4 that is displayed after the user clicked the form's submit button without entering information in the required text box. Browsers that do not support HTML5 or the required attribute will ignore the attribute.

Although web designers are enthusiastic about the required attribute and other new form-processing functions offered by HTML5, it will be some time before all browsers support these new features. In the meantime, be aware that verification and validation of form information also must be done the old-fashioned way—with client-side or server-side scripting.

Figure 9.4 The Firefox 4 browser displayed an error message

 FAQ **Why use both the name and id attributes on form controls?**

The name attribute names the form element so that it can be easily accessed by client-side scripting languages such as JavaScript or by server-side processing languages such as PHP. The value given to a name attribute for a form element should be unique for that form. The id attribute is included for use with CSS and scripting. The value of the id attribute should be unique to the entire web page document that contains the form. Typically, the values assigned to the name and id attributes on a particular form element are the same.

Submit Button

The **submit button** form control is used to submit the form. When clicked, it triggers the action method on the form element and causes the browser to send the form data (the name and value pairs for each form control) to the web server. The web server will invoke the server-side processing program or script listed on the form's action property.

The input element with type="submit" configures a submit button. For example,

```
<input type="submit">
```

Reset Button

The **reset button** form control is used to reset the form fields to their initial values. A reset button does not submit the form.

The input element with type="reset" configures a reset button. For example,

```
<input type="reset">
```

A form with a text box, a submit button, and a reset button is shown in Figure 9.5.

Common attributes for submit buttons and reset buttons are listed in Table 9.3.

Figure 9.5 This form contains a text box, a submit button, and a reset button

Table 9.3 Common attributes for submit and reset buttons

Attribute	Value	Purpose
type	submit	Configures a submit button
	reset	Configures a reset button
name	Alphanumeric, no spaces, begins with a letter	Names the form element so that it can be easily accessed by client-side scripting languages (such as JavaScript) or by server-side processing; the name should be unique
id	Alphanumeric, no spaces, begins with a letter	Provides a unique identifier for the form element
value	Text or numeric characters	Configures the text displayed on the button; a submit button displays the text "Submit Query" by default; a reset button displays "Reset" by default
accesskey	Keyboard character	Configures a hot key for the form control
tabindex	Numeric value	Configures the tab order of the form control

Hands-On Practice 9.1

You will code a form in this Hands-On Practice. To get started, launch a text editor and open chapter2/template.html in the student files. Save the file as form1.html. You will create a web page with a form similar to the example in Figure 9.6.

Figure 9.6 The text on the submit button says "Sign Me Up!"

1. Modify the title element to display the text "Form Example".

2. Configure an h1 element with the text "Join Our Newsletter".

    You are ready to configure the form area. A form begins with the form element. Insert a blank line under the heading you just added and type in a `<form>` tag as follows:

    ```
    <form method="get">
    ```

    In your first form, we are using the minimal HTML needed to create the form; we'll begin working with the **action** attribute later in the chapter.

3. To create the form control for the visitor's e-mail address to be entered, type the following code on a blank line below the form element:

    ```
    E-mail: <input type="text" name="email" id="email"><br><br>
    ```

This places the text "E-mail:" in front of the text box used to enter the visitor's e-mail address. The input element has a `type` attribute with the value of `text` that causes the browser to display a text box. The `name` attribute assigns the name `e-mail` to the information entered into the text box (the `value`) and could be used by server-side processing. The `id` attribute uniquely identifies the element on the page. The `<br>` elements configure line breaks.

4. Now you are ready to add the submit button to the form on the next line. Add a value attribute set to "Sign Me Up!":

```
<input type="submit" value="Sign Me Up!">
```

This causes the browser to display a button with "Sign Me Up!" instead of the default value of "Submit Query".

5. Add a blank space after the submit button and code a reset button:

```
<input type="reset">
```

6. Next, code the closing form tag:

```
</form>
```

Save form1.html and test your web page in a browser. It should look similar to the page shown in Figure 9.6.

You can compare your work with the solution found in the student files (chapter9/form1.html). Try entering some information into your form. Try clicking the submit button. Don't worry if the form redisplays but nothing seems to happen when you click the button—you haven't configured this form to work with any server-side processing. Connecting forms to server-side processing is demonstrated later in this chapter. The next sections will introduce you to more form controls.

Check Box

The check box form control allows the user to select one or more of a group of predetermined items. The input element with `type="checkbox"` configures a check box. Common check box attributes are listed in Table 9.4.

Figure 9.7 shows an example with several check boxes. Note that more than one check box can be selected by the user. The HTML is

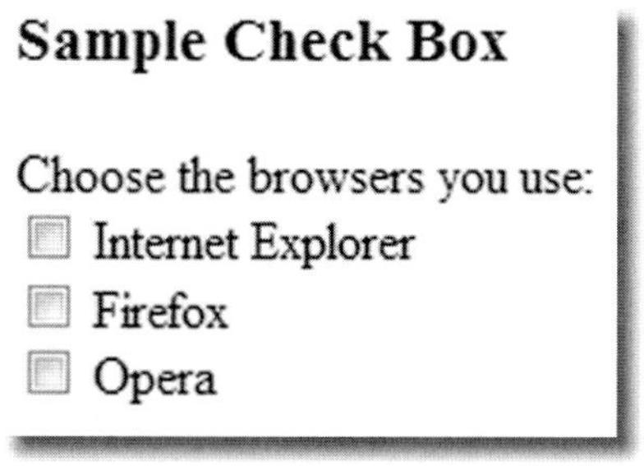

Sample Check Box

Choose the browsers you use:
☐ Internet Explorer
☐ Firefox
☐ Opera

Figure 9.7 Sample check box

```
Choose the browsers you use: <br>
<input type="checkbox" name="IE" id="IE" value="yes">
Internet Explorer<br>
<input type="checkbox" name="Firefox" id="Firefox" value="yes">
Firefox<br>
<input type="checkbox" name="Opera" id="Opera" value="yes">
Opera<br>
```

Table 9.4 Common check box attributes

Attribute	Value	Purpose
type	checkbox	Configures a check box
name	Alphanumeric, no spaces, begins with a letter	Names the form element so that it can be easily accessed by client-side scripting languages (such as JavaScript) or by server-side processing; the name should be unique
id	Alphanumeric, no spaces, begins with a letter	Provides a unique identifier for the form element
checked	checked	Configures the check box to be checked by default when displayed by the browser
value	Text or numeric characters	Assigns a value to the check box that is triggered when the check box is checked; this value can be accessed by client-side and server-side processing
disabled	disabled	Form control is disabled
readonly	readonly	Form control is for display; cannot be edited
autofocus	autofocus	HTML5 attribute; browser places cursor in the form control and sets the focus
required	required	HTML5 attribute; browser verifies entry of information before submitting the form
accesskey	Keyboard character	Configures a hot key for the form control
tabindex	Numeric value	Configures the tab order of the form control

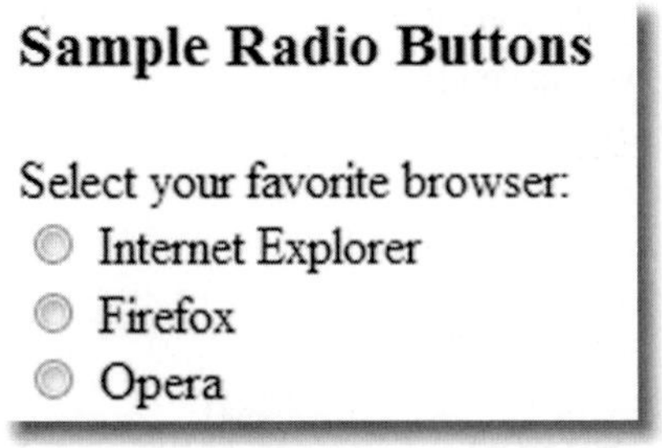

Sample Radio Buttons

Select your favorite browser:
- Internet Explorer
- Firefox
- Opera

Figure 9.8 Use radio buttons when only one choice is an appropriate response

Radio Button

The **radio button** form control allows the user to select exactly one (and only one) choice from a group of predetermined items. Each radio button in a group is given the same name attribute and a unique value attribute. Because the name attribute is the same, the elements are identified as part of a group by the browsers and only one may be selected.

The input element with type="radio" configures a radio button. Figure 9.8 shows an example with a radio button group. Note that only one radio button can be selected at a time by the user. Common radio button attributes are listed in Table 9.5. The HTML is

```
Select your favorite browser:<br>
<input type="radio" name="favbrowser" id="favIE" value="IE"> Internet
Explorer<br>
<input type="radio" name="favbrowser" id="favFirefox" value="Firefox">
Firefox<br>
<input type="radio" name="favbrowser" id="favOpera" value="Opera">
Opera<br>
```

Notice that all the name attributes have the same value: favbrowser. Radio buttons with the same name attribute are treated as a group by the browser. Each radio button in the same group can be uniquely identified by its value attribute.

Table 9.5 Common radio button attributes

Attribute	Value	Purpose
type	radio	Configures a radio button
name	Alphanumeric, no spaces, begins with a letter	Names the form element so that it can be easily accessed by client-side scripting languages (such as JavaScript) or by server-side processing; the name should be unique
id	Alphanumeric, no spaces, begins with a letter	Provides a unique identifier for the form element
checked	checked	Configures the radio button to be selected by default when displayed by the browser
value	Text or numeric characters	Assigns a value to the radio button that is triggered when the radio button is selected; this should be a unique value for each radio button in a group; this value can be accessed by client-side and server-side processing
disabled	disabled	Form control is disabled
readonly	readonly	Form control is for display; cannot be edited
autofocus	autofocus	HTML5 attribute; browser places cursor in the form control and sets the focus
required	required	HTML5 attribute; browser verifies entry of information before submitting the form
accesskey	Keyboard character	Configures a hot key for the form control
tabindex	Numeric value	Configures the tab order of the form control

Hidden Input Control

The **hidden input control** stores text or numeric information, but it is not visible in the browser viewport. Hidden controls can be accessed by both client-side scripting and server-side processing.

The input element with `type="hidden"` configures a hidden input control. Common attributes for hidden input controls are listed in Table 9.6. The HTML to create a hidden input control with the `name` attribute set to "sendto" and the `value` attribute set to an e-mail address is

```
<input type="hidden" name="sendto" id="sendto" value="order@site.com">
```

Table 9.6 Common hidden input control attributes

Attribute	Value	Purpose
type	hidden	Configures a hidden element
name	Alphanumeric, no spaces, begins with a letter	Names the form element so that it can be easily accessed by client-side scripting languages (such as JavaScript) or by server-side processing; the name should be unique
id	Alphanumeric, no spaces, begins with a letter	Provides a unique identifier for the form element
value	Text or numeric characters	Assigns a value to the hidden control; this value can be accessed by client-side scripting languages and server-side processing
disabled	disabled	Form control is disabled

Password Box

The **password box** form control is similar to the text box, but it is used to accept information that must be hidden as it is entered, such as a password.

Sample Password Box

Password: *******

Figure 9.9 The characters secret9 were typed, but the browser displays ******* (Note: Your browser may use a different symbol, such as a stylized circle, to hide the characters)

The input element with `type="password"` configures a password box. When the user types information in a password box, asterisks (or another symbol, depending on the browser) are displayed instead of the characters that have been typed, as shown in Figure 9.9. This hides the information from someone looking over the shoulder of the person typing. The actual characters typed are sent to the server and the information is not really secret or hidden. See Chapter 12 for a discussion of encryption and security.

A password box is a specialized text box. See Table 9.2 for a list of text box attributes.

The HTML is

```
Password: <input type="password" name="pword" id="pword">
```

9.3 Scrolling Text Box

Textarea Element

The **scrolling text box** form control accepts free-form comments, questions, or descriptions. The **textarea element** configures a scrolling text box. The `<textarea>` tag denotes the beginning of the scrolling text box. The closing `</textarea>` tag denotes the end of the scrolling text box. Text contained between the tags will display in the scrolling text box area. A sample scrolling text box is shown in Figure 9.10.

Sample Scrolling Text Box

Comments:

Enter your comments here

Figure 9.10
Scrolling text box

Common attributes for scrolling text boxes are listed in Table 9.7. The HTML is

```
Comments:<br>
<textarea name="comments" id="comments" cols="40" rows="2"> Enter your
comments here</textarea>
```

Table 9.7 Common scrolling text box attributes

Attribute	Value	Purpose
name	Alphanumeric, no spaces, begins with a letter	Names the form element so that it can be easily accessed by client-side scripting languages (such as JavaScript) or by server-side processing; the name should be unique
id	Alphanumeric, no spaces, begins with a letter	Provides a unique identifier for the form element
cols	Numeric value	Required; configures the width in character columns of the scrolling text box; if cols is omitted, the browser displays the scrolling text box with its own default width
rows	Numeric value	Required; configures the height in rows of the scrolling text box; if rows is omitted, the browser displays the scrolling text box with its own default height
maxlength	Numeric value	Configures the maximum length of data accepted by the text box
disabled	disabled	Form control is disabled
readonly	readonly	Form control is for display; cannot be edited
autofocus	autofocus	HTML5 attribute; browser places cursor in the form control and sets the focus
placeholder	Text or numeric characters	HTML5 attribute; brief information intended to assist the user
required	required	HTML5 attribute; browser verifies entry of information before submitting the form
wrap	hard or soft	HTML5 attribute; configures line breaks within the information entered
accesskey	Keyboard character	Configures a hot key for the form control
tabindex	Numeric value	Configures the tab order of the form control

Hands-On Practice 9.2

In this Hands-On Practice, you will create a contact form (see Figure 9.11) with the following form controls: a First Name text box, a Last Name text box, an E-mail text box, and a Comments scrolling text box. You'll use the form you created in Hands-On Practice 9.1 (see Figure 9.6) as a starting point. Launch a text editor and open chapter9/form1.html in the student files. Save the file as form2.html.

Figure 9.11 A typical contact form

1. Modify the title element to display the text "Contact Form".

2. Configure the h1 element with the text "Contact Us".

3. A form control for the e-mail address is already coded. Refer to Figure 9.11 and note that you'll need to add text box form controls for the first name and last name above the e-mail form control. Add the following code on new lines below the opening form tag to accept the name of your web page visitor:

```
First Name: <input type="text" name="fname" id="fname"><br><br>
Last Name: <input type="text" name="lname" id="lname"><br><br>
```

4. Now you are ready to add the scrolling text box form control to the form using a `<textarea>` tag on a new line below the e-mail form control. The code is

```
Comments:<br>
<textarea name="comments" id="comments"></textarea><br><br>
```

Save your file and display your web page in a browser to view the default display of a scrolling text box. Note that this default display will differ by browser. At the time this was written, Internet Explorer always rendered a vertical scroll bar, but the Firefox browser only rendered scroll bars once enough text was entered to require them. The writers of browser rendering engines keep the lives of web designers interesting!

5. Let's configure the `rows` and `cols` attributes for the scrolling text box form control. Modify the `<textarea>` tag and set `rows="4"` and `cols="40"` as follows:

```
Comments:<br>
<textarea name="comments" id="comments" rows="4"
cols="40"></textarea><br><br>
```

6. Next, modify the text displayed on the submit button. Set the value attribute to "Contact". Save form2.html and test your web page in a browser. It should look similar to the page shown in Figure 9.11.

You can compare your work with the solution found in the student files (chapter9/form2.html). Try entering some information into your form. Try clicking the submit button. Don't worry if the form redisplays but nothing seems to happen when you click the button—you haven't configured this form to work with any server-side processing. Connecting forms to server-side processing is demonstrated later in this chapter.

FAQ How can I send form information in an e-mail?

Forms usually need to invoke some type of server-side processing to perform functions such as sending e-mail, writing to text files, updating databases, and so on. Another option is to set up a form to send information using the e-mail program configured to work with the web page visitor's browser. In what is sometimes called using a mailto: URL, the `<form>` tag is coded to use your e-mail address in the action attribute:

```
<form method="post" action="mailto:lsnblf@yahoo.com">
```

When a form is used in this manner, the web visitor will see a warning message. The warning message presents a nonprofessional image and is not the best way to inspire trust and confidence in your website or business.

Be aware that information sent in e-mail messages is not secure. Sensitive information, such as credit card numbers, should not be transmitted using e-mail. See Chapter 12 for information about using encryption to transmit data securely.

There are other reasons not to use mailto: URL. For example, when people share a computer, they may not be using the default e-mail application. In this case, filling out the form is a waste of time. Even if the person using the computer also uses the default e-mail application, perhaps he or she may not want to divulge this particular e-mail address. Perhaps they have another e-mail address that is used for forms and newsletters, and do not want to waste time filling out your form. In either case, the result is an unhappy website visitor. So, while using mailto: URL is easy, it does not always create the most usable web form for your visitors. What's a web developer to do? Use server-side processing (see Hands-On Practice 9.5) to handle form data instead of mailto: URL.

9.4 Select List

The **select list** form control shown in Figures 9.12 and 9.13 is also known by several other names, including select box, drop-down list, drop-down box, and option box. A select list is configured with one select element and multiple option elements.

Select Element

The **select element** contains and configures the select list form control. The `<select>` tag denotes the beginning of the select list. The closing `</select>` tag denotes the end of the select list. Attributes configure the number of options to display and whether more than one option item may be selected. Common attributes for select elements are listed in Table 9.8.

Table 9.8 Common select element attributes

Attribute	Value	Purpose
name	Alphanumeric, no spaces, begins with a letter	Names the form element so that it can be easily accessed by client-side scripting languages (such as JavaScript) or by server-side processing; the name should be unique
id	Alphanumeric, no spaces, begins with a letter	Provides a unique identifier for the form element
size	Numeric value	Configures the number of choices the browser will display; if set to 1, the element functions as a drop-down list (see Figure 9.12); scroll bars are automatically added by the browser if the number of options exceeds the space allowed
multiple	multiple	Configures a select list to accept more than one choice; by default, only one choice can be made from a select list
disabled	disabled	Form control is disabled
tabindex	Numeric value	Configures the tab order of the form control

Option Element

The **option element** contains and configures an option item displayed in the select list form control. The `<option>` tag denotes the beginning of the option item. The closing `</option>` tag denotes the end of the option item. Attributes configure the value of the option and whether they are preselected. Common attributes for option elements are listed in Table 9.9.

Table 9.9 Common option element attributes

Attribute	Value	Purpose
value	Text or numeric characters	Assigns a value to the option; this value can be accessed by client-side and server-side processing
selected	selected	Configures an option to be initially selected when displayed by a browser
disabled	disabled	Form control is disabled

The HTML for the select list in Figure 9.12 is

```
<select size="1" name="favbrowser" id="favbrowser">
  <option>Select your favorite browser</option>
  <option value="Internet Explorer">Internet Explorer</option>
  <option value="Firefox">Firefox</option>
  <option value="Opera">Opera</option>
</select>
```

The HTML for the select list in Figure 9.13 is

```
<select size="4" name="jumpmenu" id="jumpmenu">
    <option value="index.html">Home</option>
    <option value="products.html">Products</option>
    <option value="services.html">Services</option>
    <option value="about.html">About</option>
    <option value="contact.html">Contact</option>
</select>
```

Select List: One Initial Visible Item

Figure 9.12 A select list with size set to 1 functions as a drop-down box when the arrow is clicked

Select List: Four Items Visible

Figure 9.13 Because there are more than four choices, the browser displays a scroll bar

 FAQ   **How does the menu in Figure 9.13 display the selected page?**

Well, it doesn't work, yet. It needs JavaScript (see Chapter 14) to check for the selected item and direct the browser to display the new document. Because it requires JavaScript to work, this type of menu would not be a good choice for your main navigation, but it might be useful for a secondary navigation area.

Checkpoint 9.1

1. You are designing a website for a client who sells items in a retail store. They want to create a customer list for e-mail marketing purposes. Your client sells to consumers and needs a form that accepts a customer's name and e-mail address. Would you recommend using two input boxes (one for the name and one for the e-mail) or three input boxes (one each for the first name, last name, and e-mail address)? Explain your answer.

2. A question on a survey asks participants to indicate their favorite browsers. Most people will select more than one response. What type of form control would you use to configure this question on the web page? Explain your answer.

3. True or False? In a radio button group, the `value` attribute is used by the browser to process the separate radio buttons as a group.

9.5 Image Buttons and the Button Element

As you have worked with forms in this chapter, you may have noticed that the standard submit button (see Figure 9.11) is a little plain. You can make the form control that visitors select to submit the form a bit more compelling and visually interesting in two ways:

1. Configure an image with the input element.

2. Create a custom image that is configured with the button element.

Image Button

Figure 9.14 shows an image used in place of the standard submit button. This is called an **image button**. When an image button is clicked or tapped, the form is submitted. The image button is coded using the `<input>` tag along with `type="image"` and a `src` attribute with the value of the name of the image file. For example, to use the image called login.gif as an image button, the HTML code is

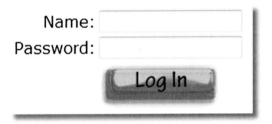

Figure 9.14 The web page visitor will select the image button to submit the form

```
<input type="image" src="login.gif" alt="Login Button">
```

Button Element

Another way to add more interest to a form is to use the **button element**, which can be used to configure not only images but also blocks of text as the selectable area that can submit or reset a form. Any web page content that is between the `<button>` and `</button>` tags is configured to be part of the button. Common attributes for button elements are listed in Table 9.10.

Figure 9.15 shows a form that has an image (signup.gif) configured as a submit button using the button element.

Figure 9.15 The button element configured as a submit button

Table 9.10 Common button element attributes

Common Attributes	Values	Purpose
type	submit	Functions as a submit button
	reset	Functions as a reset button
	button	Functions as a button
name	Alphanumeric, no spaces, begins with a letter	Names the form element so that it can be easily accessed by client-side scripting languages (such as JavaScript) or by server-side processing; the name should be unique
id	Alphanumeric, no spaces, begins with a letter	Provides a unique identifier for the form element
alt	Brief text description of the image	Provides accessibility to visitors who are unable to view the image
value	Text or numeric characters	A value given to a form element that is passed to the form handler

The following HTML code creates the button shown in Figure 9.15:

```
<button type="submit">
<img src="signup.gif" width="80" height="28" alt="Sign up for free
newsletter">
</button>
```

As you visit web pages and view their source code, you will find that the button element is not used as often as the standard submit button or the image button.

9.6 Accessibility and Forms

Focus on Accessibility

In this section, you'll explore techniques to increase the accessibility of form controls, including the label element, fieldset element, legend element, tabindex attribute, and accesskey attribute, which make it easier for individuals with vision and mobility challenges to use your form pages. The use of label, fieldset, and legend elements may increase the readability and usability of the web form for all visitors.

Label Element

Focus on Accessibility

The **label element** is a container tag that associates a text description with a form control. This is helpful to visually challenged individuals who are using assistive technology such as a screen reader to match up the text descriptions on forms with their corresponding form controls. The label element also benefits individuals who have difficulty with fine motor control. Clicking anywhere on either a form control or its associated text label will set the cursor focus to the form control.

There are two different methods to associate a label with a form control.

1. The first method places the label element as a container around both the text description and the HTML form element. Notice that both the text label and the form control must be adjacent elements. The code is

```
<label>E-mail: <input type="text" name="email" id="email"></label>
```

2. The second method uses the `for` attribute to associate the label with a particular HTML form element. This is more flexible and is does not require the text label and the form control to be adjacent. The code is

```
<label for="email">E-mail: </label>
<input type="text" name="email" id="email">
```

Notice that the value of the **for attribute** on the label element is the same as the value of the `id` attribute on the input element. This creates the association between the text label and the form control. The input element uses both the `name` and `id` attributes for different purposes. The `name` attribute can be used by client-side scripting and server-side processing. The `id` attribute creates an identifier that can be used by the label element, anchor element, and CSS selectors. The label element does not display on the web page—it works behind the scenes to provide for accessibility.

Hands-On Practice 9.3

In this Hands-On Practice, you will add the label element to the text box and scrolling text area form controls on the form you created in Hands-On Practice 9.2 (see Figure 9.11) as a starting point. Launch a text editor and open chapter9/form2.html in the student files. Save the file as form3.html.

1. Locate the text box for the first name. Add a label element to wrap around the input tag as follows:

```
<label>First Name: <input type="text" name="fname"
id="fname"></label>
```

2. Using the method shown previously, add a label element for the last name and e-mail form controls.

3. Configure a label element to contain the text "Comments". Associate the label with the scrolling text box form control. The sample code is

```
<label for="comments">Comments:</label><br>
<textarea name="comments" id="comments" rows="4"
cols="40"></textarea>
```

Save form3.html and test your web page in a browser. It should look similar to the page shown in Figure 9.11—the label elements do not change the way that the page displays, but a web visitor with physical challenges should find the form easier to use.

You can compare your work with the solution found in the student files (chapter9/form3.html). Try entering some information into your form. Try clicking the submit button. Don't worry if the form redisplays but nothing seems to happen when you click the button—you haven't configured this form to work with any server-side processing. Connecting forms to server-side processing is demonstrated later in this chapter.

Fieldset and Legend Elements

A technique that can be used to create a more visually pleasing form is to group elements of a similar purpose together using the **fieldset element,** which will cause the browser to render a visual cue, such as an outline or a border, around form elements grouped together within the fieldset. The <fieldset> tag denotes the beginning of the grouping. The closing </fieldset> tag denotes the end of the grouping.

The **legend element** provides a text description for the fieldset grouping. The <legend> tag denotes the beginning of the text description. The closing </legend> tag denotes the end of the text description. The HTML to create the grouping shown in Figure 9.16 is

```
<fieldset>
<legend>Billing Address</legend>
<label>Street: <input type="text" name="street" id="street"
        size="54"></label><br><br>
<label>City: <input type="text" name="city" id="city"></label>
<label>State: <input type="text" name="state" id="state" maxlength="2"
        size="5"></label>
<label>Zip: <input type="text" name="zip" id="zip" maxlength="5"
        size="5"></label>
</fieldset>
```

Fieldset and Legend

Billing Address
Street: _____
City: _____ State: ____ Zip: ____

Figure 9.16 Form controls that are all related to a mailing address

Focus on Accessibility

The grouping and visual effect of the fieldset element creates an organized and appealing web page containing a form. Using the fieldset and legend elements to group form controls enhances accessibility by organizing the controls both visually and semantically. The fieldset and legend elements can be accessed by screen readers and are useful tools for configuring groups of radio buttons and check boxes on web pages.

Hands-On Practice 9.4

In this Hands-On Practice, you will modify the contact form (form3.html) you worked with in Hands-On Practice 9.3 to use the fieldset and legend elements (see Figure 9.17).

Launch a text editor and open the form3.html file that you created in Hands-On Practice 9.3. Perform the following edits:

1. Add an opening <fieldset> tag after the opening <form> tag.

2. Immediately after the opening <fieldset> tag, code a legend element that contains the following text: "Customer Information".

3. Code the closing `</fieldset>` tag before the label element for the Comments scrolling text box.

4. Save your file as form4.html and test your web page in a browser. It should look similar to the one shown in Figure 9.17. You can compare your work with the solution found in the student files (chapter9/form4.html). You may notice that when you activate the submit button, the form redisplays. This is because there is no action property in the form element. You'll work with setting the action property in Section 9.8.

5. How about a quick preview of styling a form with CSS? Figures 9.17 and 9.18 show the same form elements, but the form in Figure 9.18 is styled with CSS, which gives it the same functionality with increased visual appeal.

Figure 9.18 The fieldset, legend, and label elements are configured with CSS

Open form4.html in a text editor and add embedded styles to the head section as indicated below:

```
fieldset { width: 320px;
    border: 2px ridge #ff0000;
    padding: 10px;
    margin-bottom: 10px; }
legend { font-family: Georgia, "Times New Roman", serif;
        font-weight: bold; }
label { font-family: Arial, sans-serif; }
```

Save your file as form5.html and test your web page in a browser. It should look similar to the one shown in Figure 9.18. You can compare your work with the solution found in the student files (chapter9/form5.html).

Focus on Accessibility

The `tabindex` Attribute

Some of your website visitors may have difficulty using a mouse and will access your form with a keyboard. The Tab key can be used to move from one form control to another. The default action for the Tab key within a form is to move to the next form control in the order in which the form controls are coded in the web page document. This is usually appropriate. However, if the tab order needs to be changed for a form, use the **tabindex attribute** on each form control.

For each form tag (`<input>`, `<select>`, and `<textarea>`), code a `tabindex` attribute with a numeric value, beginning with 1, 2, 3, and so on in numerical order. The HTML code to configure the customer e-mail text box as the initial position of the cursor is

```
<input type="text" name="Email" id="Email" tabindex="1">
```

If you configure a form control with `tabindex="0"`, it will be visited after all of the other form controls that are assigned a `tabindex` attribute. If you happen to assign two form controls the same tabindex value, the one that is coded first in the HTML will be visited first.

You can configure the `tabindex` attribute for anchor tags in a similar manner. The default action for the Tab key and anchor tags is to move from hyperlink to hyperlink in the order they are coded on the page. Use the `tabindex` attribute if you need to modify this behavior.

Focus on Accessibility

The `accesskey` Attribute

Another technique that can make your form keyboard-friendly is the use of the **accesskey attribute** on form controls. You can also configure the `accesskey` attribute on an anchor tag. Assigning the `accesskey` attribute a value of one of the characters (a letter or number) on the keyboard will create a hot key that your website visitor can press to move the cursor immediately to a form control or hyperlink.

The method used to access this hot key varies depending on the operating system. Windows users will press the Alt key and the character key. Mac users will press the Ctrl key and the character key. For example, if the form shown in Figure 9.11 had the customer e-mail text coded with `accesskey="E"`, the web page visitor using Windows could press the Alt and E keys to move the cursor immediately to the e-mail text box. The HTML code for this is

```
<input type="text" name="email" id="email" accesskey="E">
```

Note that you cannot rely on the browser to indicate that a character is an access key, also called a hot key. You will have to manually code information about the hot key. A visual cue may be helpful, such as displaying the hot key in bold or by placing a message such as (Alt+E) after a form control or hyperlink that uses a hot key. When choosing accesskey values, avoid combinations that are already used by the operating system (such as Alt+F to display the File menu). Testing hot keys is crucial.

Checkpoint 9.2

1. Describe the purpose of the fieldset and legend elements.

2. Describe the purpose of the `accesskey` attribute and how it supports accessibility.

3. When designing a form, should you use the standard submit button, an image button, or a button tag? Are these different in the way in which they provide for accessibility? Explain your answer.

9.7 Styling a Form

This section introduces three methods to style and configure the display of a form—from the old-fashioned (using an HTML table), transitional (using an HTML table and CSS), to the modern (using CSS).

Table Structure

The form in Figure 9.11 (from Hands-On Practice 9.2) looks a little "messy" and you might be wondering how that can be improved. A while back, web designers always used a table to configure the design of form elements, typically placing the text labels and form field elements in separate table data cells. An example of this technique is shown in Figure 9.19 and is found in chapter9/formtable.html in the student files.

Figure 9.19 The form controls are well aligned

The HTML is

```
<form method="get">
<table border="0">
  <tr>
    <td align="right">First Name:</td>
    <td><input type="text" name="fmail" id="fmail"></td>
  </tr>
```

```
<tr>
  <td align="right">Last Name:</td>
  <td><input type="text" name="lmail" id="lmail"></td>
</tr>
<tr>
  <td align="right">E-mail:</td>
  <td><input type="text" name="email" id="email"></td>
</tr>
<tr>
  <td align="right" valign="top">Comments:</td>
  <td><textarea name="comments" id="comments" rows="4" cols="40">
  </textarea></td>
</tr>
<tr>
  <td> </td>
  <td><input type="submit" value="Contact">  
  <input type="reset"></td>
</tr>
</table>
</form>
```

Another approach is to organize a form with an HTML table but configure it with CSS rather than with HTML attributes. While this is not a completely table-less design, using a table to configure a small portion of a page that otherwise uses CSS is a method to be considered. It would be best to reserve the use of a table for pure tabular data, such as price lists and budgets. However, the purpose of this example is to show how CSS can be used to streamline even the HTML needed by a table. Later in the chapter, you'll explore how to configure the layout and styling of a form with only CSS—without using an HTML table.

Figure 9.20 This page uses a table styled with CSS

Transitional Approach

Figure 9.20 shows a web page (see chapter9/formtable2.html in the student files) with the form area coded with a table but styled with CSS. The CSS to style the table configures table, th, and td element selectors with properties that would otherwise be defined with HTML attributes. The table element selector is configured with a light-gray background color, no border, 20em width, and Arial or sans-serif font. Recall that th elements display text as bold and centered by default. The th element selector configures normal-weight font, right-aligned text, and top vertical alignment. Finally, the td and th elements are configured with 5 pixels of padding. The CSS is

```
table { background-color: #eaeaea;
        border-style: none;
        width: 20em;
        font-family: Arial, sans-serif; }
th { font-weight: normal;
     text-align: right;
     vertical-align: top; }
td, th { padding: 5px; }
```

Because we are styling the table with CSS, the HTML border and align attributes are no longer needed. Another HTML change is that the text label for each form control is now contained in a th element instead of in a td element.

```
<form method="post">
<table>
  <tr>
    <th>Name:</th>
    <td><input type="text" name="Name" id="Name"></td>
  </tr>
  <tr>
    <th>E-mail:</th>
    <td><input type="text" name="myEmail" id="myEmail"></td>
  </tr>
  <tr>
    <th>Comments:</th>
    <td><textarea name="myComments" id="myComments" rows="2"
        cols="20"></textarea></td>
  </tr>
  <tr>
    <td> </td>
    <td><input type="submit" value="Submit"></td>
  </tr>
</table>
</form>
```

The result is more streamlined, flexible code. Further style changes can be easily made in CSS, leaving the structure of the form's table intact. But the most flexible option of all is not using a table and relying on CSS to configure the entire form. You'll explore this technique next.

Style a Form with CSS

Many web developers cruise along using CSS for page layout until they need to code a form. As discussed in a previous section, tables have long been used to configure forms. This section will demonstrate a more modern approach, using CSS to style a form layout without using an HTML table.

With this method, the CSS box model is used to create a series of boxes, as shown in Figure 9.21. The outermost box defines the form area. Other boxes indicate label elements and form controls. CSS is used to configure these components.

Figure 9.22 displays a web page with a form configured in this manner (see chapter9/formcss.html in the student files). As you view the following CSS and HTML, note that the label element selector is configured with block display, a 100 pixel width, and floats to the left side of the form, and clears any previous left floats. The input and textarea elements have a top margin and are also configured with block display. The submit button is assigned to an id with a left margin. The styles result in a well-aligned form.

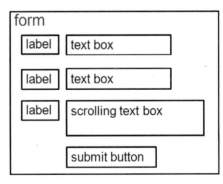

Figure 9.21 Wireframe for a form

Figure 9.22 This form is configured with CSS

The CSS is

```
form { background-color:#eaeaea;
       font-family: Arial, sans-serif;
       width: 350px;
       padding: 10px; }
label { float: left;
        width: 100px;
        display: block;
        clear: left;
        text-align: right;
        padding-right: 10px;
        margin-top: 10px; }
input, textarea { margin-top: 10px;
                  display: block; }
#mySubmit { margin-left: 110px; }
```

The HTML code is

```
<form>
    <label for="myName">Name:</label>
    <input type="text" name="myName" id="myName">
    <label for="myEmail">E-mail:</label>
    <input type="text" name="myEmail" id="myEmail">
    <label for="myComments">Comments:</label>
    <textarea name="myComments" id="myComments" rows="2"
    cols="20"></textarea>
    <input id="mySubmit" type="submit" value="Submit">
</form>
```

This section provided you with a method to style a form with CSS. Testing the way that different browsers render the form is crucial.

As you've coded and displayed the forms in this chapter, you may have noticed that when you click the submit button, the form just redisplays—the form doesn't do anything. This is because there is no action attribute in the <form> tag. The next section focuses on the second component of using forms on web pages—server-side processing.

9.8 Server-Side Processing

Your web browser requests web pages and their related files from a web server. The web server locates the files and sends them to your web browser. Then the web browser renders the returned files and displays the requested web pages. Figure 9.23 illustrates the communication between the web browser and the web server.

Sometimes a website needs more functionality than static web pages, possibly a site search, order form, e-mail list, database display, or other type of interactive, dynamic processing. This is when server-side processing is needed. Early web servers used a protocol called **Common Gateway Interface** (CGI) to provide this functionality. CGI is a protocol, or standard method, for a web server to pass a web page user's request (which

Browser Request

Server Response

Web Client

Web Server

Figure 9.23 The web browser (client) communicates with the web server

is typically initiated through the use of a form) to an application program and to accept information to send to the user. The web server typically passes the form information to a small application program that is run by the operating system and that processes the data, usually sending back a confirmation web page or message. Perl and C are popular programming languages for CGI applications.

Server-side scripting is a technology by which a server-side script is run on a web server to dynamically generate web pages. Examples of server-side scripting technologies include PHP, Ruby on Rails, Microsoft Active Server Pages, Adobe ColdFusion, Sun JavaServer Pages, and Microsoft .NET. Server-side scripting differs from CGI in that it uses **direct execution**: The script is run either by the web server itself or by an extension module to the web server.

A web page invokes server-side processing by either an attribute on a form or by a hyperlink (the URL of the script is used). Any form data that exists is passed to the script. The script completes its processing and may generate a confirmation or response web page with the requested information. When invoking a server-side script, the web developer and the server-side programmer must communicate about the form `method` **attribute** (`get` or `post`), form `action` **attribute** (the URL of the server-side script), and any special form element control(s) expected by the server-side script.

The `method` attribute is used on the form tag to indicate the way in which the name and value pairs should be passed to the server. The method attribute value of `get` causes the form data to be appended to the URL, which is easily visible and not secure. The method attribute value of `post` does not pass the form information in the URL; it passes it in the entity body of the HTTP request, which makes it more private. The W3C recommends the `method="post"` method.

The `action` attribute is used on the `<form>` tag to invoke a server-side script. The `name` attribute and the `value` attribute associated with each form control are passed to the server-side script. The `name` attribute may be used as a variable name in the server-side processing. In the next Hands-On Practice, you will invoke a server-side script from a form.

VideoNote
Connect a Form to Server-Side Processing

Hands-On Practice 9.5

In this Hands-On Practice, you will configure a form to invoke a server-side script. Please note that your computer must be connected to the Internet when you test your work. When using a server-side script, you will need to obtain some information, or documentation, from the person or organization providing the script. You will need to know the location of the script, whether it requires any specific names for the form controls, and whether it requires any hidden form elements.

A server-side script has been created at the author's website
(http://webdevbasics.net/scripts/demo.php) for students to use for this exercise. The documentation for the server-side script is listed below:

- Script URL: http://webdevbasics.net/scripts/demo.php

- Form method: `post`

- Script purpose: This script will accept form input and display the form control
  names and values in a web page. This is a sample script for student assignments. It
  demonstrates that server-side processing has been invoked. A script used by an
  actual website would perform a function such as sending an e-mail message or
  updating a database.

Now you will add the configuration required to use the demo.php server-side processing with a
form. Launch a text editor and open formcss.html (see chapter9/formcss.html in the student files).
Modify the `<form>` tag by adding a `method` attribute with a value of "`post`" and an `action`
attribute with a value of "`http://webdevbasics.net/scripts/demo.php`". The HTML
code for the revised `<form>` tag is

```
<form method="post" action="http://webdevbasics.net/scripts/demo.php">
```

Save your file as contact.html and test your web page in a browser. Your screen should look
similar to the one shown in Figure 9.22. Now you are ready to test your form. You must be
connected to the Internet to test your form successfully. Enter information in the form controls
and click the submit button. You should see a confirmation page similar to the one shown in
Figure 9.24.

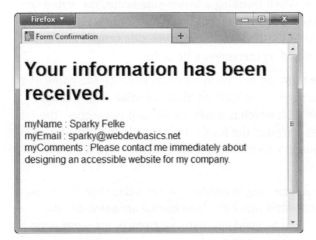

Figure 9.24 The server-side script has created this web
page in response to the form

The demo.php script creates a web page that displays a message and the form information
that you entered. Where did this confirmation page originate? This confirmation page was
created by the server-side script on the `action` attribute in the form element. Sometimes
students wonder what code is used in the demo.php file. Writing scripts for server-side
processing is beyond the scope of this textbook. However, if you are curious, visit
http://webdevfoundations.net/6e/chapter9.html to see the source code for this script.

FAQ **What do I do if nothing happened when I tested my form?**

Try these troubleshooting hints:

- Verify that your computer is connected to the Internet.
- Verify the spelling of the script location in the `action` attribute.
- Attention to detail is crucial!

Privacy and Forms

You've just learned how to collect information from your website visitors. Do you think that your visitors may want to know how you plan to use the information that you collect? The guidelines that you develop to protect the privacy of your visitors' information is called a **privacy policy**. Websites either indicate this policy on the form page itself or create a separate page that describes the privacy policy (and other company policies). For example, the order form page at MyMoney.gov (http://www.mymoney.gov/privacy.html) indicates the following:

> "We do not give, sell or transfer personal information to third parties unless required by law, such as the Freedom of Information Act."

If you browse popular sites such as Amazon.com or eBay.com, you'll find links to their privacy policies (sometimes called a privacy notice) in the page footer area. The privacy policy of the Better Business Bureau can be found at http://www.bbb.org/us/privacy-policy. Include a privacy notice on your site to inform your visitors how you plan to use the information that they share with you.

Server-Side Processing Resources

Sources of Free Remote-Hosted Form Processing

If your web host provider does not support server-side processing, free remotely hosted scripts may be an option. The script is not hosted on your server so you don't need to worry about installing it or whether your web host provider will support it. The disadvantage is that there usually is some advertising displayed. The following are a few sites that offer this service:

- FormBuddy.com: http://formbuddy.com
- ExpressDB: http://www.expressdb.com
- FormMail: http://www.formmail.com
- Master.com: http://www.master.com

Sources of Free Server-Side Scripts

To use free scripts, you need to have access to a web server that supports the language used by the script. Contact your web host provider to determine what is supported. Be aware that many free web host providers do not support server-side processing (you get what you pay for!). The following are a few sites that offer free scripts and other resources:

- The PHP Resource Index: http://php.resourceindex.com
- ASP101: http://www.asp101.com

- HotScripts: http://www.hotscripts.com
- Matt's Script Archive: http://www.scriptarchive.com
- ScriptSearch.com: http://www.scriptsearch.com

Exploring Server-Side Processing Technologies

Many types of technologies can be used for server-side scripting, form processing, and information sharing:

- PHP: http://www.php.net
- Sun JavaServer Pages Technology: http://www.oracle.com/technetwork/java/javaee/jsp
- Active Server Pages: http://msdn.microsoft.com/en-us/library/ms972337.aspx
- Adobe ColdFusion and Web Applications: http://www.adobe.com/products/coldfusion
- Ruby on Rails: http://www.rubyonrails.org
- Microsoft .NET: http://www.microsoft.com/net

Any of these technologies would be a good choice for future study. Web developers often learn the client side first (HTML, CSS, and JavaScript) and then progress to learning a server-side scripting or programming language.

 Checkpoint 9.3

1. Describe server-side processing.

2. Why is communication needed between the developer of a server-side script and the web page designer?

9.9 HTML5 Form Controls

HTML5 offers a variety of new form controls for web developers that provide increased usability for web page visitors who are using modern browsers. For example, some new form controls offer built-in browser edits and validation. Future web designers will probably take these features for granted someday, but you are right in the middle of this huge advance in web page coding, so now is a great time to become familiar with these new elements. The display and support of the new HTML5 form controls will vary by browser, but you can use them right now! Browsers that do not support the new input types will display them as text boxes and ignore unsupported attributes or elements. In this section, you'll explore the new HTML5 e-mail address, URL, telephone number, search field, datalist, slider, spinner, calendar, and color form controls.

E-mail Address Input

The **e-mail address input** form control is similar to the text box. Its purpose is to accept information that must be in e-mail format, such as "DrMorris2010@gmail.com". The input element with `type="email"` configures an e-mail address input form control. Only browsers that support the HTML5 `email` attribute value will verify the format of the information. Other browsers will treat this form control as a text box. Attributes supported by the e-mail address input form control are listed in Table 9.2.

Figure 9.25 (see chapter9/email.html in the student files) shows an error message displayed by the Opera 11 browser when text other than an e-mail address is entered. Note that the browser does not verify that the e-mail address actually exists, just that the text entered is in the correct format. The HTML is

```
<label for="email">E-mail:</label>
<input type="email" name="myEmail" id="myEmail">
```

URL Input

The **URL input** form control is similar to the text box. It is intended to accept any valid type of URL or URI, such as "http://webdevfoundations.net". The input element with `type="url"` configures a URL input form control. Only browsers that support the HTML5 `url` attribute value will verify the format of the information. Other browsers render this form control as a text box. Attributes supported by the URL input form control are listed in Table 9.2.

Figure 9.26 (see chapter9/url.html in the student files) shows an error message displayed by Firefox 4 when text other than a URL is entered. Note that the browser does not verify that the URL actually exists, just that the text entered is in the correct format. The HTML is

```
<label for="myWebsite">Suggest a Website:</label>
<input type="url" name="myWebsite" id="myWebsite">
```

Figure 9.25 The Opera 11 browser displays an error message

Figure 9.26 The Firefox 4 browser displays an error message

Telephone Number Input

The **telephone number** input form control is similar to the text box. Its purpose is to accept a telephone number. The input element with `type="tel"` configures a telephone number input form control. An example is in the student files (chapter9/tel.html). Attributes supported by the telephone number input form control are listed in Table 9.2. Browsers that do not support `type="tel"` will render this form control as a text box. The HTML is

```
<label for="mobile">Mobile Number:</label>
<input type="tel" name="mobile" id="mobile">
```

Search Field Input

The **search field** is similar to the text box and is used to accept a search term. The input element with `type="search"` configures a search field input form control. An example is in the student files (chapter9/search.html). Attributes supported by the search field control are listed in Table 9.2. Browsers that do not support `type="search"` will render this form control as a text box. The HTML is

```
<label for="keyword">Search:</label>
<input type="search" name="keyword" id="keyword">
```

FAQ   How can I tell which browsers support the new HTML5 form elements?

There's no substitute for testing. With that in mind, several resources are listed below that provide information about browser support for new HTML5 elements:

- When can I use …: http://caniuse.com
- HTML5 and CSS3 Support: http://findmebyip.com/litmus
- HTML5 and CSS3 Readiness: http://html5readiness.com
- The HTML5 Test: http://html5test.com
- HTML5 Web Forms and Browser Support: http://www.standardista.com/html5

Datalist Form Control

Figure 9.27 shows the **datalist** form control in action. Notice how a selection of choices is offered to the user along with a text box for entry. The datalist is configured using three elements: an input element, the datalist element, and one or more option elements. Only browsers that support the HTML5 datalist element will display and process the datalist items. Other browsers ignore the datalist element and render the form control as a text box.

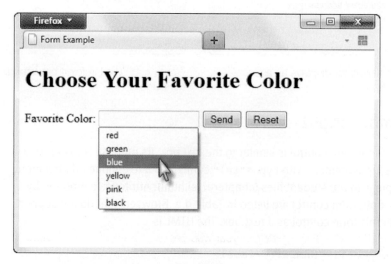

Figure 9.27 Firefox 4 displays the datalist form control

The source code for the datalist is available in the student files (chapter9/list.html). The HTML is

```
<label for="color">Favorite Color:</label>
<input type="text" name="color" id="color" list="colors">
  <datalist id="colors">
    <option value="red">
    <option value="green">
    <option value="blue">
    <option value="yellow">
    <option value="pink">
    <option value="black">
</datalist>
```

Notice that the value of the **list attribute** on the input element is the same as the value of the id attribute on the datalist element. This creates the association between the text box and the datalist form control. One or more option elements can be used to offer predefined choices to your web page visitor. The option element's value attribute configures the text displayed in each list entry. The web page visitor can choose an option from the list (see Figure 9.27) or type directly in the text box, as shown in Figure 9.28.

Figure 9.28 The list disappeared when the user began typing in the text box

The datalist form control offers a convenient way to offer choices yet provide for flexibility on a form. At the time this was written, only the Firefox 4 browser supported this new HTML5 element. See http://webdevfoundations.net/6e/chapter9.html for new developments on this intriguing form control.

FAQ Why should I learn about the new HTML5 form controls if they are not yet supported by all browsers?

The new form controls offer increased usability for your web page visitors who have modern browsers. And, they are backward compatible with older browsers, too. Browsers that do not support the new input types will display them as text boxes and ignore unsupported attributes or elements. Figure 9.29 depicts the display of a datalist in the Google Chrome browser. Notice that, unlike Firefox 4, this version of the Chrome browser does not render the list—it only renders a text box.

Figure 9.29 Browsers that do not support the datalist form control display a text box

Slider Form Control

The **slider** form control provides a visual, interactive user interface that accepts numerical information. The input element with `type="range"` configures a slider control in which a number within a specified range is chosen. The default range is from 1 to 100. Only browsers that support the HTML5 `range` attribute value will display the interactive slider control, shown in Figure 9.30 (see chapter9/range.html in the student files). Note the position of the slider in Figure 9.30; this resulted in the value 80 being chosen. The nondisplay of the value to the user may be a disadvantage of the slider control. Nonsupporting browsers render this form control as a text box, as shown in Figure 9.31.

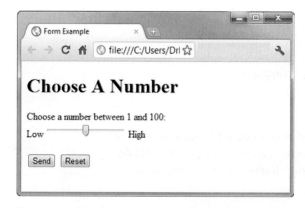

Figure 9.30 The Chrome browser displays the range form control

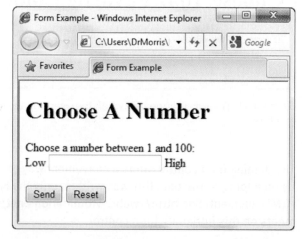

Figure 9.31 Internet Explorer 8 renders the range form control as a text box

The slider control accepts attributes listed in Tables 9.2 and 9.11. The `min`, `max`, and `step` attributes are new. Use the **`min` attribute** to configure the minimum range value. Use the **`max` attribute** to configure the maximum range value. The slider controls sets numeric values in increments, or steps, of 1. Use the **`step` attribute** to configure a value for the incremental steps between values to be other than 1.

The HTML for the slider control rendered in Figures 9.30 and 9.31 is

```
<label for="myChoice">Choose a number between 1 and 100:</label><br>
Low <input type="range" name="myChoice" id="myChoice"> High
```

Table 9.11 Additional attributes for slider, spinner, and date/time form controls

Attribute	Value	Purpose
max	Maximum numeric value	HTML5 attribute for range, number, and date/time input controls; specifies a maximum value
min	Minimum numeric value	HTML5 attribute for range, number, and date/time input controls; specifies a minimum value
step	Incremental numeric step value	HTML5 attribute for range, number, and date/time input controls; specifies a value for incremental steps

Spinner Form Control

The **spinner** form control displays an interface that accepts numerical information and provides feedback to the user. The input element with `type="number"` configures a spinner control in which the user can either type a number into the text box or select a number from a specified range. Only browsers that support the HTML5 `number` attribute value will display the interactive spinner control, shown in Figure 9.32 (see chapter9/spinner.html in the student files). Other browsers render this form control as a text box. You should expect increased support in the future.

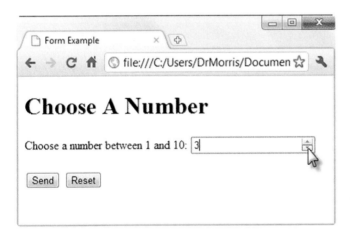

Figure 9.32 A spinner control displayed in the Google Chrome browser

The spinner control accepts attributes listed in Tables 9.2 and 9.11. Use the `min` attribute to configure the minimum value. Use the `max` attribute to configure the maximum value. The spinner control sets numeric values in increments, or steps, of 1. Use the `step` attribute to configure a value for the incremental step between values to be other than 1. The HTML for the spinner control displayed in Figure 9.32 is

```
<label for="myChoice">Choose a number between 1 and 10:</label>
<input type="number" name="myChoice" id="myChoice" min="1" max="10">
```

Calendar Form Control

HTML5 provides a variety of **calendar form controls** to accept date- and time-related information. Use the input element and configure the type attribute to specify a date or time control. Table 9.12 lists the HTML5 calendar date and time controls.

Table 9.12 Date and time controls

Type Attribute Value	Purpose	Format
date	A date	YYYY-MM-DD Example: January 2, 2014 is represented by "2014-01-02"
datetime	A date and time with time zone information; note that the time zone is indicated by the offset from UTC time	YYYY-MM-DDTHH:MM:SS-##:##Z Example: January 2, 2014, at exactly 9:58 a.m. Chicago time (CST) is represented by "2014-01-02T09:58:00-06:00Z"
datetime-local	A date and time without time zone information	YYYY-MM-DDTHH:MM:SS Example: January 2, 2014, at exactly 9:58 a.m. is represented by "2014-01-02T09:58:00"
time	A time without time zone information	HH:MM:SS Example: 1:34 p.m. is represented by "13:34:00"
month	A year and month	YYYY-MM Example: January 2014 is represented by "2014-01"
week	A year and week	YYYY-W##, where ## represents the week in the year Example: The third week in 2014 is represented by "2014-W03"

The form in Figure 9.33 (see chapter9/date.html in the student files) uses the input element with type="date" to configure a calendar control with which the user can select a date. The HTML is

```
<label for="myDate">Choose a Date</label>
<input type="date" name="myDate" id="myDate">
```

Figure 9.33 A date form control displayed in the Opera browser

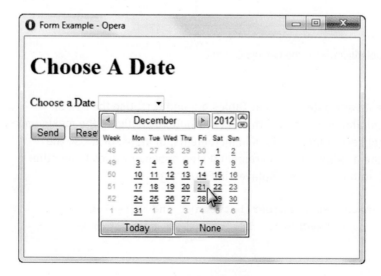

The date and time controls accept attributes listed in Tables 9.2 and 9.11. At the time this was written, only the Opera browser displayed a calendar interface for date and time controls. Other browsers currently render the date and time form controls as a text box, but you should expect increased support in the future.

Color-well Form Control

The **color-well** form control displays an interface that offers a color-picker interface to the user. The input element with `type="color"` configures a control with which the user can choose a color. Only browsers that support the HTML5 color attribute value will display a color-picker interface, shown in Figure 9.34 (see chapter9/color.html in the student files). Other browsers render this form control as a text box.

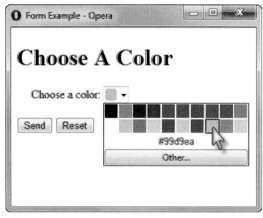

Figure 9.34 The Opera browser supports the color-well form control

The HTML for the color-well form control rendered in Figure 9.34 is

```
<label for="myColor">Choose a color:</label>
<input type="color" name="myColor" id="myColor">
```

In the next Hands-On Practice, you'll get some experience with the new HTML5 form controls.

Hands-On Practice 9.6

In this Hands-On Practice, you will code HTML5 form controls as you configure a form that accepts a name, e-mail address, rating value, and comments from a website visitor. Figure 9.35 displays the form in the Opera 11 browser, which supports the HTML5 features used in the Hands-On Practice. Figure 9.36 displays the form in Internet Explorer 9, which does not support the HTML5 features. Notice that the form is enhanced in Opera 11, but is still usable in both browsers, demonstrating the concept of progressive enhancement.

Figure 9.35 The form displayed in the Opera 11 browser

Figure 9.36 The form displayed in the Internet Explorer 9 browser

To get started, launch a text editor and open chapter9/formcss.html in the student files, shown in Figure 9.22. Save the file as form5.html. You will modify the file to create a web page similar to the examples in Figures 9.35 and 9.36.

1. Modify the title element to display the text "Comment Form". Configure the text contained within the h1 element to be "Send Us Your Comments". Add a paragraph to indicate "Required fields are marked with an asterisk *."

2. Modify the embedded styles:

   a. Change the width of the label element selector to 150 pixels.

   b. Change the left margin of `#mySubmit` to 160 pixels.

3. Modify the form element to submit the form information, using the `post` method, to the form processor at http://webdevbasics.net/scripts/demo.php:

   ```
   <form method="post" action="http://webdevbasics.net/scripts/demo.php">
   ```

4. Modify the form controls.

   a. Configure the name, e-mail, and comment information to be required. Use an asterisk to inform your web page visitor about the required fields.

   b. Code `type="email"` instead of `type="input"` for the e-mail address.

   c. Use the `placeholder` attribute (refer to Table 9.2) to provide hints to the user in the name and e-mail form controls.

5. Add a slider control (use `type="range"`) to generate a value from 1 to 10 for the rating.

   Modify the HTML as follows:

   ```
   <form method="post"
   action="http://webdevbasics.net/scripts/demo.php">
     <label for="myName">*Name:</label>
     <input type="text" name="myName" id="myName"
            required="required" placeholder="your first and last name">
     <label for="myEmail">*E-mail:</label>
   ```

```
      <input type="text" name="myEmail" id="myEmail"
            required="required" placeholder="you@yourdomain.com">
      <label for="myRating">Rating (1 - 10):</label>
      <input type="range" name="myRating" id="myRating" min="1" max="10">
      <label for="myComments">*Comments:</label>
      <textarea name="myComments" id="myComments" rows="2" cols="20"
            required="required"></textarea>
      <input id="mySubmit" type="submit" value="Submit">
   </form>
```

6. Save form5.html and test your web page in a browser. If you use a browser that supports the HTML5 features used in the form (such as Opera 11), your page should look similar to Figure 9.35. If you use a browser that does not support the form's HTML5 attributes (such as Internet Explorer 8), your form should look similar to Figure 9.36. The display in other browsers will depend on the level of HTML5 support. See HTML5 Web Forms and Browser Support (http://www.standardista.com/html5/html5-web-forms) for an HTML5 browser support list.

7. Try submitting the form without entering any information. Figure 9.37 shows the result when using Opera 11. Note the error message which indicates that the name field is required. Compare your work with the solution in the student files (chapter9/form5.html).

Figure 9.37 The Opera 11 browser displays an error message

As this Hands-On Practice demonstrated, support of the new HTML5 form control attributes and values is not uniform. It will be some time before all browsers support these new features. Design forms with progressive enhancement in mind and be aware of both the benefits and the limitations of using the new HTML5 features.

HTML5 and Progressive Enhancement

Use HTML5 form elements with the concept of progressive enhancement in mind. Nonsupporting browsers will display text boxes in place of form elements that are not recognized. Supporting browsers will display and process the new form controls. This is progressive enhancement in action: Everyone sees a usable form and visitors who are using modern browsers benefit from the enhanced features.

Chapter Summary

This chapter introduced the use of forms on web pages. You learned how to configure form controls, provide for accessibility, and configure a form to access server-side processing. You also explored new HTML5 form elements. Visit the textbook website at http://www.webdevfoundations.net for examples, the links listed in this chapter, and updated information.

Key Terms

`<button>`	Common Gateway Interface (CGI)	reset button
`<fieldset>`	datalist form control	scrolling text box
`<form>`	date and time form control	search field input
`<input>`	e-mail input	select list
`<label>`	for attribute	server-side scripting
`<legend>`	form	slider form control
`<option>`	form control	spinner form control
`<select>`	hidden input control	submit button
`<textarea>`	list attribute	tabindex attribute
accesskey attribute	method attribute	telephone number input
action attribute	name attribute	text box
button	password box	URL input
check box	privacy policy	value attribute
color-well form control	radio button	

Review Questions

Multiple Choice

1. Which of the following HTML5 text box attributes enforces browser validation?
   a. required
   b. autocomplete
   c. autofocus
   d. form

2. What are the two possible values the method attribute in the `<form>` tag can have?
   a. name and action
   b. get and action
   c. post and action
   d. get and post

3. What does the action attribute in the form tag do?
   a. indicates where to send the form information when the form is submitted
   b. causes the form data to be appended to the URL and sent to the web server
   c. transmits the form data in the body of the HTTP response
   d. none of the above

4. You need a form input as a `<name, value>` pair that would be returned to you but would not show up anywhere on the web page when displayed in the browser. Which of the following form controls will you use?
   a. text box controls
   b. hidden control
   c. e-mail control
   d. labels

5. Which of the following code snippets will configure a button with the text "Submit" on it?
   a. `<button type = "submit">`
   b. `<input type = "submit">`
   c. both of the above
   d. none of the above

6. Which of the following controls allows the user to select only one choice from a group of items?

a. check box
b. select list
c. radio button
d. button

7. What will happen if you configure a form control with `tabindex = "0"`?

a. It will not be visited by the tab key.
b. It will be visited after all the form controls assigned a tab index.
c. It will be visited before all the form controls assigned a tab index.
d. It will be visited by the tab key randomly.

8. Which of the following is a valid HTML code for configuring a password control?

a. `<input type = "password" name = "password" >`
b. `<input type = "text" name = "password">`
c. `<input type = "text" value = "password">`
d. `<input type = "text" value = "*">`

9. Which of the following is not an HTML5 input type?

a. email
b. url
c. range
d. datalist

10. Choose the HTML that would associate a label displaying the text "E-mail:" with the e-mail text box.

a. `E-mail <input type="textbox" name="email" id="email">`
b. `<label>E-mail: </label><input type="text" name="email" id="email">`

c. `<label for="email">E-mail: </label> <input type="text" name="email" id="emailaddress">`
d. `<label for="email">E-mail: </label> <input type="text" name="email" id="email">`

11. What will happen when a browser encounters a new HTML5 form control that it does not support?

a. The computer will shut down.
b. The browser will crash.
c. The browser will display an error message.
d. The browser will display an input text box.

Fill in the Blank

12. The _____ element provides a text description for the fieldset grouping.

13. The _____ attribute(s) create(s) a hotkey for a form control.

14. The datalist is configured using three elements: a(n) _____ element, the _____ element, and one or more _____ elements.

Short Answer

15. Describe at least three form controls that could be used to allow a visitor to your web page to select a color.

Apply Your Knowledge

1. Predict the Result. Draw and write a brief description of the web page that will be created with the following HTML code:

```
<!DOCTYPE html>
<html lang="en">
<head>
<title>Predict the Result</title>
<meta charset="utf-8">
</head>
```

```
<body>
<h1>Contact Us</h1>
<form action="myscript.php">
<fieldset><legend>Complete the form and a consultant will contact
you.</legend>
E-mail: <input type="text" name="email" id="email" size="40">
<br>Please indicate which services you are interested in:<br>
<select name="inquiry" id="inquiry" size="1">
    <option value="development">Web Development</option>
    <option value="redesign">Web Redesign</option>
    <option value="maintain">Web Maintenance</option>
    <option value="info">General Information</option>
</select>
<br>
<input type="submit">
</fieldset>
</form>
<div><a href="index.html">Home</a> <a href="services.html">
Services</a> Contact</div>
</body>
</html>
```

2. **Fill in the Missing Code.** This web page configures a survey form to collect information on the favorite search engine used by web page visitors. The form action should submit the form to the server-side script, called survey.php. Some HTML tags and their attributes, indicated by < _>, are missing. Some HTML attribute values, indicated by "_", are missing.

```
<!DOCTYPE html>
<html lang="en">
<head>
<title>Fill in the Missing Code</title>
<meta charset="utf-8">
</head>
<body>
<h1>Vote for your favorite Search Engine</h1>
<form method="_" action="_">
  <input type="radio" name="_" id="Ysurvey" value="Yahoo"> Yahoo!<br>
  <input type="radio" name="survey" id="Gsurvey" value="Google">
  Google<br>
  <input type="radio" name="_" id="Bsurvey" value="Bing"> Bing<br>
  <_>
</form>
</body>
</html>
```

3. **Find the Error.** Find the coding errors in the following subscription form:

```
<!DOCTYPE html>
<html lang="en">
<head>
<title>Find the error:</title>
<meta charset="utf-8">
</head>
```

```
<body>
<form method="" action="">
Select your favorite site:
<select name="search_engine">
<option value="google">Google</option>
<option value="msn">MSN</option>
<option value="yahoo">Yahoo</option>
<option value="bing">Bing</option>
</select>
First name: <input type="text" name="firstname" ><br>
Last name: <input type="text" name="lastname" ><br>
<button type="submit">
</form>
</body>
</html>
```

Hands-On Exercises

1. Write the HTML code to create the following:
   a. Two text boxes named name and addr to accept the name and the address of a user. Ensure that the user can type up to 30 characters in both the boxes.
   b. A multi-line text input control that would accept 10 lines of text with each line having maximum 50 characters
   c. A radio button list of two options: male and female
   d. A check box list of the options: student, professional, entrepreneur, and others
   e. A button of width 30 pixels and height 10 pixels, with the text 'Cancel' on it
   f. A spinner control that allows the user to enter numbers from 1 to 10
   g. A color picker for the user
   h. A calendar control for the user

2. Write the HTML to create a form that asks for user information for registering users to your site. The form should have the following fields: username, email, and comments. It should also have a check box confirming whether the user wants to subscribe to your site's mailing list, a submit button, and a reset button.

3. Write the HTML to add a fieldset and legend with the text "Contact us" around the form created in the previous exercise. Change the form height to 300 pixels and width to 500 pixels.

4. Create a web page with a form that accepts user information for a shipping company. The form should have a fieldset and legend with the text "Shipping Address" around the following form controls: AddressLine1, AddressLine2, City, State, ZIP.

   You have learned styling a form using either table structure or CSS. However, a similar effect could be created using HTML lists, where each list item may contain a label and the related input. Try to use this methodology in your form design.

5. Write the HTML to create a form that accepts requests for user registration for a site. The form should allow the users to enter two sets of information: personal information like date of birth, sex, mobile number, etc., and site registration information like username and password. Apply appropriate CSS styles to your form.

6. Write a web page that contains a music survey form similar to the example shown in Figure 9.38.

Figure 9.38
Sample music
survey form

Include the following form controls:

- Text box for name

- E-mail address input form control for the e-mail address

- A scrolling text box that is 60 characters wide and 3 rows high

- A radio button group with at least three choices

- A check box group with at least three choices

- A select box that initially shows three items but contains at least four items

- A submit button

- A reset button

- Use the fieldset and legend elements as shown in Figure 9.38 to configure the display of form areas with radio buttons and check boxes.

Use a CSS to configure the display of your form. Place your name and e-mail address at the bottom of the page. *Hint:* Draw a sketch of your form and the table before you begin coding the HTML and CSS.

Web Research

1. This chapter mentioned a number of sources of free remotely hosted scripts, including FormBuddy.com (http://formbuddy.com), FormMail (http://www.formmail.com), Response-o-Matic (http://response-o-matic.com), and Master.com (http://master.com). Visit two of these sites or use a search engine to find other resources for free remotely hosted scripts. Register (if necessary) and examine the website to see

exactly what is offered. Most sites that provide remotely hosted scripts have a demo you can view or try. If you have time (or your instructor asks you to), follow the directions and access a remotely hosted script from one of your web pages. Now that you've at least been through a demo of the product or tried it yourself (even better!), it's time to write your review.

Create a web page that lists the two resource sites you chose and provides a comparison of what they offer. List the following for each website:

- Ease of registration
- Number of scripts or services offered
- Types of scripts or services offered
- Site banner or advertisement
- Ease of use
- Your recommendation

Provide links to the resource sites you reviewed and place your name and e-mail address at the bottom of the page.

2. Search the Web for a web page that uses an HTML form. Print the browser view of the page. Print out the source code of the web page. Using the printout, highlight or circle the tags related to forms. On a separate sheet of paper, create some HTML notes by listing the tags and attributes related to the forms found on your sample page along with a brief description of their purpose.

3. Choose one server-side technology mentioned in this chapter: PHP, ASP, JSP, Ruby on Rails, or ASP.NET. Use the resources listed in the chapter as a starting point, but also search the Web for additional resources on the server-side technology you have chosen. Create a web page that lists at least five useful resources along with information about each that provides the name of the site, the URL, a brief description of what is offered, and a recommended page (such as a tutorial, free script, and so on). Place your name in an e-mail link on the web page.

Focus on Web Design

The design of a form, such as the justification of the labels, the use of background colors, and even the order of the form elements can either increase or decrease the usability of a form. Visit some of the following resources to explore form design:

- Web Application Form Design: http://www.uie.com/articles/web_forms
- 10 Tips to a Better Form:
  http://particletree.com/features/10-tips-to-a-better-form
- Sensible Forms: http://www.alistapart.com/articles/sensibleforms
- Best Practices for Form Design:
  http://www.lukew.com/resources/articles/WebForms_LukeW.pdf

Create a web page that lists the URLs of at least two useful resources along with a brief description of the information you found most interesting or valuable. Design a form on the web page that applies what you've just learned in your exploration of form design. Place your name in an e-mail link on the web page.

WEBSITE CASE STUDY
Adding a Form

Each of the following case studies continues throughout most of the textbook. This chapter adds a page containing a form that invokes server-side processing to the websites.

JavaJam Coffee House

See Chapter 2 for an introduction to the JavaJam Coffee House case study. Figure 2.25 shows a site map for the JavaJam site. Use the Chapter 8 JavaJam website as a starting point for this case study. You will create the new Jobs page that contains a form. You have three tasks in this case study:

1. Create a new folder for this JavaJam case study.

2. Modify the style sheet (javajam.css) to configure style rules for the new form.

3. Create the new Jobs page shown in Figure 9.39.

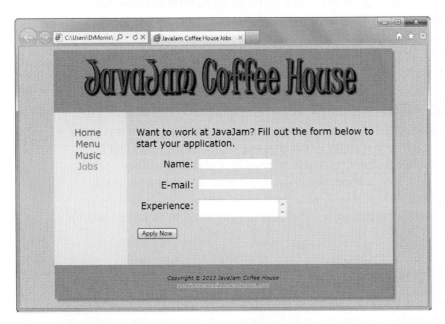

Figure 9.39
JavaJam Jobs page

Hands-On Practice Case Study

Task 1: Create a Folder. Create a folder called javajam9. Copy all of the files from your Chapter 8 javajam8 folder into the javajam9 folder.

Task 2: Configure the CSS. Modify the external style sheet (javajam.css). Open javajam.css in a text editor. Review Figure 9.39 and the wireframe in Figure 9.40. Notice how the text labels for the form controls are on the left side of the content area but contain right-aligned text. Notice the empty vertical space between each form control. Configure CSS as indicated below:

1. Create a label element selector to float to the left with block display. Set the text alignment to right, assign a width of 120 pixels, and set an appropriate amount of right padding.

2. Configure the input element and textarea element selectors with block display and 20 pixels of bottom margin.

Save the javajam.css file.

Task 3: Create the Jobs Page. Use the Menu page as the starting point for the Jobs page. Launch a text editor and open menu.html. Save the file as jobs.html. Modify your jobs.html file to look similar to the Jobs page (shown in Figure 9.39) as follows:

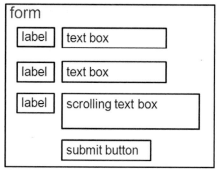

Figure 9.40 Wireframe for the form

1. Change the page title to an appropriate phrase.

2. The Jobs page will contain a paragraph and a form in the content div. Delete the table in the content div.

3. Add a paragraph that contains the following text: "Want to work at JavaJam? Fill out the form below to start your application."

4. Prepare to code the HTML for the form area. Begin with a form element that uses the post method and the action attribute to invoke server-side processing. Unless directed otherwise by your instructor, configure the action attribute to send the form data to http://webdevbasics.net/scripts/javajam.php.

5. Configure the form control for the Name information. Create a label element that contains the text "Name:". Create a text box named myName. Use the for attribute to associate the label element with the form control.

6. Configure the form control for the E-mail information. Create a label element that contains the text "E-mail:". Create a text box named myEmail. Use the for attribute to associate the label element with the form control.

7. Configure the Experience area on the form. Create a label element that contains the text "Experience:". Create a textarea element named myExperience with rows set to 2 and cols set to 20. Use the for attribute to associate the label element with the form control.

8. Configure the submit button. Code an input element with type="submit" and value="Apply Now".

9. Code an ending </form> tag on a blank line after the submit button.

Save your file and test your web page in a browser. It should look similar to the page shown in Figure 9.39. If you are connected to the Internet, submit the form. This will send your form information to the server-side script configured in the form tag. A confirmation page that lists the form information and their corresponding names will be displayed.

OPTIONAL ACTIVITY: Configure the form with HTML5 attributes and values. Get more practice with the new HTML5 elements by modifying the form on the Jobs page to use HTML5 attributes and values. Modify the jobs.html file in a text editor.

1. Add the following sentence to the paragraph above the form: "Required fields are marked with an asterisk (*)."

2. Use the required attribute to require the name, e-mail, and experience form controls to be entered. Add an asterisk at the beginning of each label text.

3. Configure the input element for the e-mail address with type="email".

Save your file and display your web page in a browser. Submit the form with missing information or only a partial e-mail address. Depending on the browser's level of HTML5 support, the browser may perform form validation and display an error message. Figure 9.41 shows the Jobs page rendered in the Firefox 5 browser with an incorrectly formatted e-mail address.

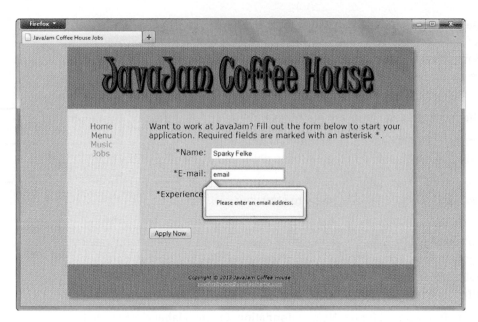

Figure 9.41 The Jobs page with HTML5 form controls

The optional activity in this case study provided you with additional practice using the new HTML5 attributes and values. The display and functioning of browsers will depend on the level of HTML5 support. See HTML5 Web Forms and Browser Support (http://www.standardista.com/html5/html5-web-forms) for an HTML5 browser support list.

Fish Creek Animal Hospital

See Chapter 2 for an introduction to the Fish Creek Animal Hospital case study. Figure 2.29 shows a site map for Fish Creek. Use the Chapter 8 Fish Creek website as a starting point for this case study. You will create the new Contact page that contains a form. You have three tasks in this case study:

1. Create a new folder for this Fish Creek case study.

2. Modify the style sheet (fishcreek.css) to configure style rules for the new form.

3. Create the new Contact page shown in Figure 9.42.

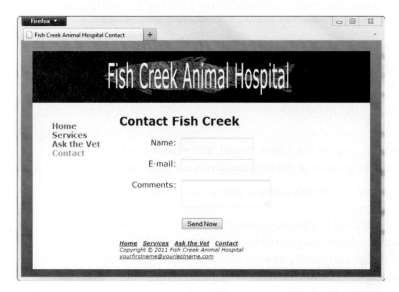

Figure 9.42 Fish Creek Contact page

Hands-On Practice Case Study

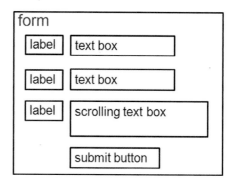

Figure 9.43 Wireframe for the form

Task 1: Create a Folder. Create a folder called fishcreek9. Copy all of the files from your Chapter 8 fishcreek8 folder into the fishcreek9 folder.

Task 2: Configure the CSS. Modify the external style sheet (fischcreek.css). Open fishcreek.css in a text editor. Review Figure 9.42 and the wireframe in Figure 9.43. Notice how the text labels for the form controls are on the left side of the content area but contain right-aligned text. Notice the empty vertical space between each form control. Configure CSS as indicated below:

1. Create a label element selector to float to the left with block display. Set the text alignment to right, assign a width of 120 pixels, and set an appropriate amount of right padding.

2. Configure the input element and textarea element selectors with block display and 20 pixels of bottom margin.

3. Configure an id named `mySubmit` with a 130 pixel left margin.

Save the fishcreek.css file.

Task 3: Create the Contact Page. Use the Ask the Vet page as the starting point for the Contact page. Launch a text editor and open askvet.html. Save the file as contact.html. Modify your contact.html file to look similar to the Contact page (shown in Figure 9.42) as follows:

1. Change the page title to an appropriate phrase.

2. The Contact page will display a form in the `#rightcolumn` div. Delete the paragraph and description list in the `#rightcolumn` div.

3. Add an h2 element that contains the following text: "Contact Fish Creek".

4. Prepare to code the HTML for the form area. Begin with a form element that uses the post method and the action attribute to invoke server-side processing. Unless directed otherwise by your instructor, configure the action attribute to send the form data to http://webdevbasics.net/scripts/fishcreek.php.

5. Configure the form control for the Name information. Create a label element that contains the text "Name:". Create a text box named myName. Use the `for` attribute to associate the label element with the form control.

6. Configure the form control for the E-mail information. Create a label element that contains the text "E-mail:". Create a text box named myEmail. Use the `for` attribute to associate the label element with the form control.

7. Configure the Comments area on the form. Create a label element that contains the text "Comments:". Create a textarea element named myComments with `rows` set to 2 and `cols` set to 20. Use the `for` attribute to associate the label element with the form control.

8. Configure the submit button on the form. Configure "Send Now" to display on the button. Assign the input element to the id named `mySubmit`.

9. Code an ending `</form>` tag on a blank line after the submit button.

Save your file and test your web page in a browser. It should look similar to the page shown in Figure 9.42. If you are connected to the Internet, submit the form. This will send your form information to the server-side script configured in the form tag. A confirmation page that lists the form information and their corresponding names will be displayed.

OPTIONAL ACTIVITY: Configure the form with HTML5 attributes and values. Get more practice with the new HTML5 elements by modifying the form on the Contact page to use HTML5 attributes and values Modify the contact.html file in a text editor.

1. Add a paragraph above the form with the following sentence: "Required fields are marked with an asterisk (*)."

2. Use the `required` attribute to require the name, e-mail, and comments form controls to be entered.

3. Configure the input element for the e-mail address with `type="email"`.

Save your file and display your web page in a browser. Submit the form with missing information or only a partial e-mail address. Depending on the browser's level of HTML5 support, the browser may perform form validation and display an error message. Figure 9.44 shows the Contact page rendered in the Opera 11 browser with missing required information.

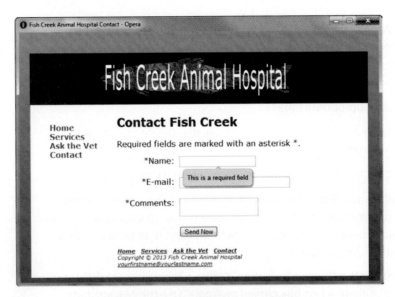

Figure 9.44 The Contact page with HTML5 form controls

The optional activity in this case study provided you with additional practice using the new HTML5 attributes and values. The display and functioning of browsers will depend on the level of HTML5 support. See HTML5 Web Forms and Browser Support (http://www.standardista.com/html5/html5-web-forms) for an HTML5 browser support list.

Pacific Trails Resort

See Chapter 2 for an introduction to the Pacific Trails Resort case study. Figure 2.33 shows a site map for Pacific Trails. Use the Chapter 8 Pacific Trails website as a starting point for this case study. You will create the new Contact page that contains a form. You have three tasks in this case study:

1. Create a new folder for this Pacific Trails case study.

2. Modify the style sheet (pacific.css) to configure style rules for the new form.

3. Create the new Reservations page shown in Figure 9.45.

Figure 9.45 Pacific Trails Reservations page

Hands-On Practice Case Study

Task 1: Create a Folder. Create a folder called pacific9. Copy all of the files from your Chapter 8 pacific8 folder into the pacific9 folder.

Task 2: Configure the CSS. Modify the external style sheet (pacific.css). Open pacific. css in a text editor. Review Figure 9.45 and the wireframe in Figure 9.46. Notice how the text labels for the form controls are on the left side of the content area but contain right-aligned text. Notice the empty vertical space between each form control. Configure CSS as indicated below:

1. Create a label element selector to float to the left with block display. Set the text alignment to right, assign a width of 120 pixels, and set an appropriate amount of right padding.

2. Configure the input element and textarea element selectors with block display and 20 pixels of bottom margin.

3. Configure an id named `mySubmit` with a 130 pixel left margin.

Save the pacific.css file.

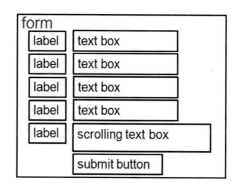

Figure 9.46 Wireframe for the form

Task 3: Create the Reservations Page. Use the Home page as the starting point for the Reservations page. Launch a text editor and open index.html. Save the file as reservations.html. Modify your reservations.html file to look similar to the Reservations page (shown in Figure 9.45) as follows:

1. Change the page title to an appropriate phrase.

2. Delete the image, paragraph, and unordered list in the content area. Do not delete the logo header, navigation, address, or page footer areas of the page.

3. Replace the text contained within the `<h2>` tags with: "Reservations at Pacific Trails".

4. Configure an h3 element on a new line with the following text: "Contact Us".

5. Prepare to code the HTML for the form area. Begin with a form element that uses the post method and the action attribute to invoke server-side processing. Unless directed otherwise by your instructor, configure the action attribute to send the form data to http://webdevbasics.net/scripts/pacific.php.

6. Configure the form control for the First Name information. Create a label element that contains the text "First Name:". Create a text box named myFName. Use the `for` attribute to associate the label element with the form control.

7. Configure the form control for the Last Name information. Create a label element that contains the text "Last Name:". Create a text box named myLName. Use the `for` attribute to associate the label element with the form control.

8. Configure the form control for the E-mail information. Create a label element that contains the text "E-mail:". Create a text box named myEmail. Use the `for` attribute to associate the label element with the form control.

9. Configure the form control for the Phone information. Create a label element that contains the text "Phone:". Create a text box named myPhone. Use the `for` attribute to associate the label element with the form control.

10. Configure the Comments area on the form. Create a label element that contains the text "Comments:". Create a textarea element named myComments with `rows` set to 2 and `cols` set to 20. Use the `for` attribute to associate the label element with the form control.

11. Configure the submit button on the form. Configure "Submit" to display on the button. Assign the input element to the id named `mySubmit`.

12. Code an ending `</form>` tag on a blank line after the submit button.

Save your file and test your web page in a browser. It should look similar to the page shown in Figure 9.45. If you are connected to the Internet, submit the form. This will send your form information to the server-side script configured in the form tag. A confirmation page that lists the form information and their corresponding names will be displayed.

OPTIONAL ACTIVITY: Configure the form with HTML5 attributes and values. Get more practice with the new HTML5 elements by modifying the form on the Reservations page to use HTML5 attributes and values Modify the reservations.html file in a text editor.

1. Use the `required` attribute to require the first name, last name, e-mail, and comments form controls to be entered.

2. Configure the input element for the e-mail address with `type="email"`.

3. Configure the input element for the phone number with `type="tel"`.

4. Add a calendar form control to process a reservation request date (use `type="date"`).

5. Add a spinner form control to process a value between 1 and 14 to indicate the number of nights for the length of stay (use `type="number"`). Use the `min` and `max` attributes to configure the range of values.

Save your file and display your web page in a browser. Submit the form with missing information or only a partial e-mail address. Depending on the browser's level of HTML5 support, the browser may perform form validation and display an error message. Figure 9.47 shows the Reservations page rendered in the Opera 11 browser with an incorrectly formatted e-mail address.

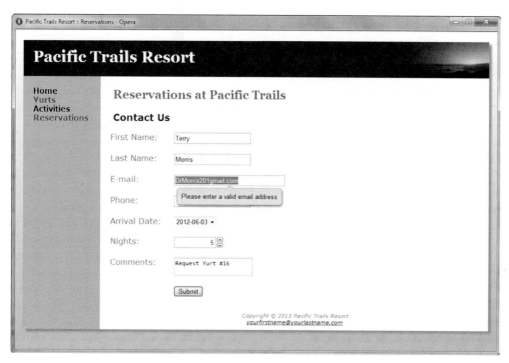

Figure 9.47 The Reservations page with HTML5 form controls

The optional activity in this case study provided you with additional practice using the new HTML5 attributes and values. The display and functioning of browsers will depend on the level of HTML5 support. See HTML5 Web Forms and Browser Support (http://www.standardista.com/html5/html5-web-forms) for an HTML5 browser support list.

Prime Properties

See Chapter 2 for an introduction to the Prime Properties case study. Figure 2.37 shows a site map for Prime Properties. Use the Chapter 8 Prime Properties website as a starting point for this case study. You will create the new Contact page that uses a form. You have three tasks in this case study:

1. Create a new folder for this Prime Properties case study.

2. Modify the style sheet (prime.css) to configure style rules for the new table.

3. Create the Contact page shown in Figure 9.48.

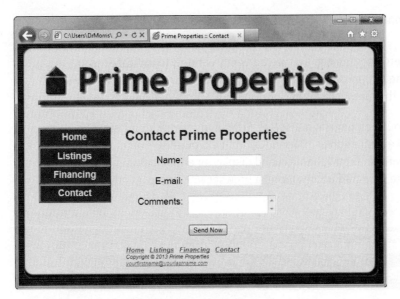

Figure 9.48 Prime Properties Contact page

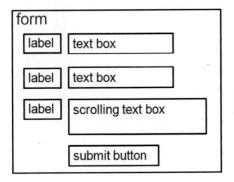

Figure 9.49 Wireframe for the form

Hands-On Practice Case Study

Task 1: **Create a Folder.** Create a folder called prime9. Copy all of the files from your Chapter 8 prime8 folder into the prime9 folder.

Task 2: **Configure the CSS.** Modify the external style sheet (prime.css). Open prime.css in a text editor. Review Figure 9.48 and the wireframe in Figure 9.49. Notice how the text labels for the form controls are on the left side of the content area but contain right-aligned text. Notice the empty vertical space between each form control. Configure CSS as indicated below:

1. Create a label element selector to float to the left with block display. Set the text alignment to right, assign a width of 120 pixels, and set an appropriate amount of right padding.

2. Configure the input element and textarea element selectors with block display and 20 pixels of bottom margin.

3. Configure an id named mySubmit with a 130 pixel left margin.

Save the prime.css file.

Task 3: Create the Contact Page. Use the Financing page as the starting point for the Contact page. Launch a text editor and open financing.html. Save the file as contact.html. Modify your contact.html file to look similar to the Contact page (shown in Figure 9.48) as follows:

1. Change the page title to an appropriate phrase.

2. The Contact page will display a form in the #right div. Delete the paragraph, h3, and description list in the #right div.

3. Change the text in the h2 element to "Contact Prime Properties".

4. Prepare to code the HTML for the form area. Begin with a form element that uses the post method and the action attribute to invoke server-side processing. Unless

directed otherwise by your instructor, configure the action attribute to send the form data to http://webdevbasics.net/scripts/prime.php.

5. Configure the form control for the Name information. Create a label element that contains the text "Name:". Create a text box named myName. Use the `for` attribute to associate the label element with the form control.

6. Configure the form control for the E-mail information. Create a label element that contains the text "E-mail:". Create a text box named myEmail. Use the `for` attribute to associate the label element with the form control.

7. Configure the Comments area on the form. Create a label element that contains the text "Comments:". Create a textarea element named myComments with `rows` set to 2 and `cols` set to 20. Use the `for` attribute to associate the label element with the form control.

8. Configure the submit button on the form. Configure "Send Now" to display on the button. Assign the input element to the id named `mySubmit`.

9. Code an ending `</form>` tag on a blank line after the submit button.

Save your file and test your web page in a browser. It should look similar to the page shown in Figure 9.48. If you are connected to the Internet, submit the form. This will send your form information to the server-side script configured in the form tag. A confirmation page that lists the form information and their corresponding names will be displayed.

OPTIONAL ACTIVITY: Configure the form with HTML5 attributes and values. Get more practice with the new HTML5 elements by modifying the form on the Contact page to use HTML5 attributes and values Modify the contact.html file in a text editor.

1. Use the `required` attribute to require the name, e-mail, and comments form controls to be entered.

2. Configure the input element for the e-mail address with `type="email"`.

Save your file and display your web page in a browser. Submit the form with missing information or only a partial e-mail address. Depending on the browser's level of HTML5 support, the browser may perform form validation and display an error message. Figure 9.50 shows the Contact page rendered in the Firefox 5 browser with missing required information.

Figure 9.50 The Contact page with HTML5 form controls

The optional activity in this case study provided you with additional practice using new HTML5 attributes and values. The display and functioning of browsers will depend on the level of HTML5 support. See HTML5 Web Forms and Browser Support (http://www.standardista.com/html5/html5-web-forms) for an HTML5 browser support list.

Web Project

See Chapters 5 and 6 for an introduction to the Web Project case study. You will either add a form to an existing page in your website or create a new page that contains a form. Use CSS to style the form.

Hands-On Practice Case Study

1. Choose one of your project web pages to contain the form. Sketch a design of the form you plan to create.

2. Modify your project's external CSS file (project.css) to configure the form areas as needed.

3. Update your chosen web page and add the HTML code for the form.

4. The form element should use the post method and action attributes to invoke server-side processing. Unless directed otherwise by your instructor, configure the action attribute to send the form data to http://webdevbasics.net/scripts/demo.php.

Save and test the page. If you are connected to the Internet, submit the form. This will send your form information to the server-side script configured in the form element. A confirmation page that lists the form information and their corresponding names will be displayed.

Web Development

Chapter Objectives   In this chapter, you will learn how to . . .

- Describe the skills, functions, and job roles needed to develop a successful web project

- Utilize the stages in the standard System Development Life Cycle

- Identify other common system development methodologies

- Apply the System Development Life Cycle to the development of web projects

- Identify opportunities and determine goals during the Conceptualization phase

- Determine information topics and site requirements during the Analysis phase

- Create the site map, page layout, prototype, and documentation as part of the Design phase

- Complete the web pages and associated files during the Production phase

- Verify the functionality of the website and use a test plan during the Testing phase

- Obtain client approval and launch a website

- Modify and enhance the website during the Maintenance phase

- Compare the goals of the website to the results as part of the Evaluation phase

- Find the right web hosting provider for your website

- Choose a domain name for your website

This chapter discusses the skills needed for successful large-scale project development and introduces you to common web development methods, choosing a domain name, and options for hosting a website.

10.1 Successful Large-Scale Project Development

Large-scale projects are not completed by only one or two individuals. They are created by a group of people working together as a team. The job roles of project manager, information architect, marketing representative, copywriter, editor, graphic designer, database administrator, network administrator, and web developer/designer are usually needed for large projects. In smaller companies or organizations, each person can wear many hats and juggle his or her job roles. For a smaller-scale project, one of the web developers may double as the project manager, web designer, graphic designer, database administrator, and/or information architect. It is important to realize that each project is unique; each has its own needs and requirements. Choosing the right people to work on a web project team can make it or break it.

Project Job Roles

Project Manager

The **project manager** oversees the website development process and coordinates team activities. The project manager creates the project plan and schedule. This individual is accountable for reaching project milestones and producing results. Excellent organizational, managerial, and communication skills are required.

Information Architect

The **information architect** clarifies the mission and goals of the site; assists in determining the functionality of the site; and is instrumental in defining the site organization, navigation, and labeling. Web developers and/or the project manager sometimes take on this role.

Marketing Representative

The **marketing representative** handles the organization's marketing plan and goals. He or she works with the web designers to create a **web presence**, or a look and feel, that aligns with the marketing goals of the organization. The marketing representative also helps to coordinate the website with other media used for marketing, such as print, radio, and television marketing.

Copywriter and Editor

The **copywriter** prepares and evaluates copy. When material from existing brochures, newsletters, and white papers will be used on the website, it must be repurposed or reworked for the web media. The content manager or **editor** may work with the copywriter to check the text for correct grammar and consistency.

Content Manager

The **content manager** participates in the strategic and creative development and enhancement of the website. He or she oversees changes in content. The skill set of a successful content manager includes editing, copywriting, marketing, technology, and communications. The person in this dynamic job role must be able to facilitate change.

Graphic Designer

The **graphic designer** determines the appropriate use of color and graphics on the site, designs wireframes and page layouts, creates logos and graphic images, and optimizes images for display on the Web.

Database Administrator

A **database administrator** is needed if the site accesses information stored in databases. Database administrators create databases, create procedures to maintain databases (including backup and recovery), and control access to databases.

Network Administrator

The **network administrator** configures and maintains the **web server**, installs and maintains system hardware and software, and controls access security.

Web Developer/Web Designer

The job titles of web developer and web designer are often used interchangeably, but typically a web developer has more of a coding and scripting focus and a web designer has more of a design and graphics focus. The **web designer** writes HTML and CSS code and may fulfill some graphic designer job duties, such as determining the appropriate use of color, designing wireframes and page layouts, creating logos and graphics, and optimizing images for display on the Web. The **web developer**, sometimes referred to as a **front-end web developer**, writes HTML, CSS, and client-side scripting such as JavaScript. Some web developers may specialize in writing server-side scripting with database access. Typically, there are multiple web designers and web developers assigned to a large project, each with his or her area of expertise.

Project Staffing Criteria

Whether the project is large or small, finding the right people to work on it is crucial. When selecting staff for a project, consider each individual's work experience, portfolio, formal education, and industry certifications.

Another option for staffing a web project (or developing an entire website) is to outsource the project—that is, hire another company to do the work for you. Sometimes portions of a project are outsourced, such as graphics creation, multimedia animation, or server-side scripting. When this option is chosen, communication between the project manager and the external organization is crucial. The outsourcing team needs to be aware of the project goals and deadlines.

Large or small, developed in-house or outsourced, the success of a website project depends on planning and communication. Formal project development methodology is used to coordinate and facilitate the planning and communication needed for a successful web project.

10.2 The Development Process

Large corporate and commercial websites don't just happen. They are carefully built, usually by following a project development methodology. A methodology is a step-by-step plan that encompasses the life cycle of a project from start to finish. It comprises a

Figure 10.1 The System Development Life Cycle (SDLC)

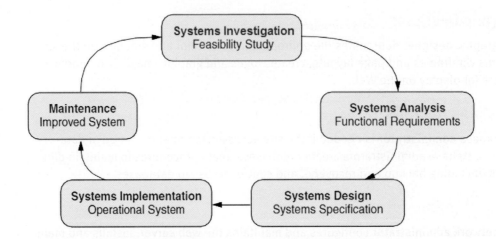

series of **phases**, each having specific activities and deliverables. Most modern methodologies have their roots in the **System Development Life Cycle (SDLC)**, a process that has been used for several decades to build large-scale information systems. The SDLC comprises a set of phases, sometimes called steps or stages. Each phase is usually completed before beginning the activities in the next phase. The basic phases of the standard SDLC (see Figure 10.1) are systems investigation, systems analysis, systems design, systems implementation, and maintenance.

Websites are often developed using a variation of the SDLC that is modified to apply to web projects. Large companies and web design firms usually create their own special methodology for use on projects. The Website Development Cycle is a guide to successful web project management. Depending on the scope and complexity of a particular project, some steps can be completed in a single meeting; other steps can take weeks or months.

The Website Development Cycle, shown in Figure 10.2, usually consists of the following steps: Conceptualization, Analysis, Design, Production, Testing, Launch, Maintenance, and Evaluation.

Figure 10.2 The Website Development Cycle

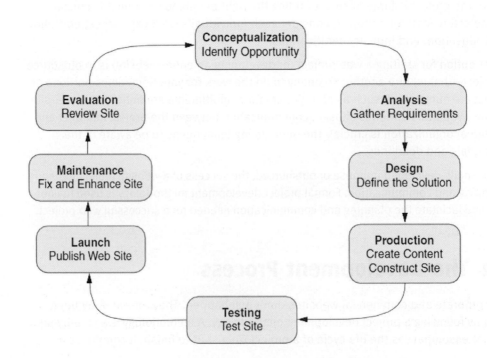

FAQ **What about other development methodologies?**

The development methodology presented in this chapter is a version of the traditional SDLC modified for website development. Other development methods include the following:

- **Prototyping.** A small working model is created and shown to the client. It is continually revised by the developer until it is usable for the intended purpose. This method can easily be included in the Website Development Cycle during the Design phase.

- **Spiral System Development.** This is excellent for very-large-scale or phased projects where it is important to reduce risk. Small portions of the project are completed one after another in a spiral system of development.

- **Joint Application Development (JAD).** This type of development focuses on group meetings and collaboration between the users and developers of a website or system. It is generally used only with in-house development.

- **Agile Software Development.** This development methodology is viewed as innovative in that it stresses responsiveness based on generating and sharing knowledge within a development team and with the client. The philosophy emphasizes code over documentation and results in the project being developed in many small, iterative steps.

- **Organization-Specific Development Methodologies.** Large companies and web development firms often create their own version or interpretation of a site development methodology to be used for projects.

An important aspect of website development is that you are never finished—your site needs to be kept fresh and up-to-date, there will be errors or omissions that need to be corrected, and new components and pages will be needed. The first step is to decide why the website is needed in the first place.

Conceptualization

What opportunity or issue is the site addressing? What is the motivation for the site? Perhaps your client owns a retail store and wishes to sell products over the Internet. Perhaps your client's competitor just launched a website and your client needs to create one just to keep up. Perhaps you have a great idea that will be the next eBay!

Because the focus of your work is to make the site usable and appealing to your target audience, you must determine the site's intended audience. It is crucial to be aware of who your audience is and what their preferences are.

Another task during **conceptualization** is to determine the site's long-term and short-term goals or mission. Perhaps a short-term goal is simply to publish a home page. Perhaps a long-term goal is for 20% of a company's product sales to be made on the website or you may simply want a certain number of website visitors each month. Whatever they are, it is better if the objectives are measurable. Decide how you will measure the success (or failure) of your website.

Determining the purpose and goals of a site is usually done with the cooperation of the client, project manager, and information architect. In a formal project environment, a document that details the results of this step is created and then approved by the client before development can proceed.

Analysis

The Analysis phase involves meetings and interviews with key client personnel. **Analysis** is usually completed by the project manager, information architect or other analyst, and the client's marketing representative and related personnel. The network administrator and database administrator may be interviewed depending on the scope of the project. Common tasks completed during the Analysis phase are as follows:

- **Determine Information Topics.** Organize the information to be presented on the site into categories and create a hierarchy. These **information topics** will be used later as a starting point for developing the site navigation.

- **Determine Functionality Requirements.** State what the site will do, not how it will do it. For example, state that "the site will accept credit card orders from customers," not "the site will perform order processing using PHP to look up each price and sales tax information in MySQL databases and use real-time credit card verification supplied by somewebsite.com." Note the difference in the level of detail in these **functionality requirements**.

- **Determine Environmental Requirements.** What **environmental requirements**, such as hardware, operating system, memory capacity, screen resolution, and bandwidth, will your site visitors use? What type of hardware and software requirements will the web server need?

- **Determine Content Requirements.** Does content already exist in another format (for example, brochures, catalogs, white papers)? Determine who is responsible for creating and repurposing the content for the site. Does the client company or marketing department have any **content requirements** that must be met? For example, is there a specific visual aesthetic or corporate branding component that must be present on the site?

- **Compare the Old Approach to the New Approach.** Perhaps you are not creating a new website, but modifying an existing one. What benefits or added value will the new version provide?

- **Review Your Competitors' Sites.** A careful review of your competitors' web presence will help you design a site that will stand out from the crowd and be more appealing to your shared customer base. Note the good and bad components of these sites.

- **Estimate Costs.** Create an estimate of the costs and time involved to create the site. A formal project plan is often created or modified at this point. Often, an application such as Microsoft Project is used to estimate costs and plan project schedules.

- **Do a Cost/Benefit Analysis.** Create a document that compares the costs and benefits of the site. Measurable benefits are the most useful and most appealing to clients. In a formal project environment, a document that details the results of this **cost/benefit analysis** must be approved by the client before the team can proceed.

Design

Once everyone knows what is needed, it is time to determine how it can be accomplished. The Design phase involves meetings and interviews with key client personnel. **Design** tasks are usually completed by the project manager, information architect or other analyst, graphic designer(s), senior web developer(s), and the client's marketing representative and related personnel. Common tasks during the Design phase include the following:

- **Choose a Site Organization.** As discussed in Chapter 5, common website organizational forms are hierarchical, linear, and random. Determine which is best for the project site and create a site map.

- **Design the Prototype.** As a starting point, sketch out the design on paper. Sometimes it's useful to sketch within an empty browser frame (see chapter10/sketch.doc in the student files). Often, a graphics application is used to create sample web page mock-ups, or wireframes. These can be shown to clients as a prototype, or working model, of the system for approval. They can also be shown to focus groups for **usability testing**.

- **Design a Page Layout.** Determine the visual aesthetic and layout with wireframes and sample page mock-ups. Items such as the site color scheme, the size of logo graphics, button graphics, and text should be determined. Using the page layout design and site map, create sample layouts for the home page and content pages. Use a graphic application to create mock-ups of these pages to get a good idea of how the site will function. If you use a web authoring tool at this early stage, you run the risk of your manager or client thinking that you already have the site half done and insisting on early delivery.

- **Document Each Page.** While this may seem unnecessary, lack of content is a frequent cause of website project delays. Prepare a content sheet for each page, such as the one shown in Figure 10.3 (see chapter10/contentsheet.doc in the student files), which describes the functionality of the document, text and graphic content requirements, source of content, and approver of content.

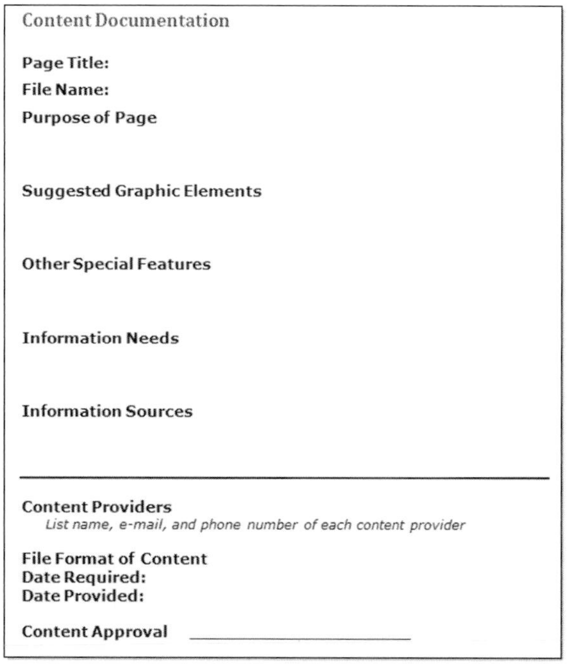

Content Documentation

Page Title:
File Name:
Purpose of Page

Suggested Graphic Elements

Other Special Features

Information Needs

Information Sources

Content Providers
List name, e-mail, and phone number of each content provider

File Format of Content
Date Required:
Date Provided:

Content Approval _____

Figure 10.3
Sample content sheet

The site map and page design prototypes are usually approved by the client before the team can progress to the Production phase.

Production

During **production**, all the previous work comes together (hopefully) in a usable and effective website. During the Production phase, the web designers and web developers are on the critical path—their work must be completed as scheduled or the project will be late. The other project members are consulted, as needed, for clarification and approval. Common tasks of the Production phase include the following:

- **Choose a Web Authoring Tool.** The use of a web authoring tool, such as Adobe Dreamweaver or Microsoft Expression Web, can greatly increase productivity. Specific productivity aids include designer notes, page templates, task management, and web page check-in and check-out to avoid overlapping page updates. The use of an authoring tool will serve to standardize the HTML used in the project pages. Any standards related to indentation, comments, and so on should be determined at this time.

- **Organize Your Site Files.** Consider placing images and media in their own folder. Also, place server-side scripts in a separate folder. Determine naming conventions for web pages, images, and media.

- **Develop and Individually Test Components.** During this task, the graphic designers and web developers create and individually test their contributions to the site. As the images, web pages, and server-side scripting are developed, they are individually tested. This is called **unit testing**. On some projects, a senior web developer or the project manager will review the components for quality and standards compliance.

Once all components have been created and unit tested, it's time to put them together and begin the Testing phase.

Testing

The components should be published to a test web server. This test web server should have the same operating system and web server software that the production (actual) web server will be using. Some common site **testing** considerations follow:

- **Test on Different Browsers and Browser Versions.** It is very important to test your pages on commonly used browsers and versions of those browsers.

- **Test with Different Screen Resolutions.** Although, as a web developer, you may use a very high screen resolution, not everyone uses 1920×1200 screen resolution. The most commonly used screen resolutions at the time of this writing are 1024×768, 1280×800, and 1366×768. Be sure to test your web pages on various resolutions—you might be surprised at the results.

- **Test Using Different Bandwidths.** If you live and work in a metropolitan area, everyone you know may have broadband access to the Internet. However, many people still use dial-up connections to access the Web. It is important to test your site on both slow and fast connections. Images that look great over your school's T3 line may load very slowly over a 56K modem.

- **Test from Another Location.** Be sure to test your website using a computer other than the one the website was developed on, in order to simulate the web page visitor's experience more closely.

- **Test Using Mobile Devices.** Mobile use of the Web is increasing all the time—test your site on one or more of the currently popular smartphones. See Chapter 7 for mobile web testing tools.

- **Test, Test, Test.** There is no such thing as too much testing. Humans make mistakes. It is much better for you and your team to find the errors than for your client to point them out to you when they review the website.

Does this sound like a lot to keep track of? It is. That's why it's a good idea to create a **test plan**, which is a document that describes what will be tested on each page of a website. A sample test plan for a web page, shown in Figure 10.4 (see chapter10/testplan.pdf in the student files), can help you organize your testing as you check your document in different browsers and screen resolutions. The document validation section covers content, links, and any forms or scripting that are required for the page. Search engine optimization meta tags are discussed in Chapter 13. However, at this point, you should be able to verify that the page title is descriptive and includes the company or organization's name. Testing your page using different bandwidths is important because web pages that take too long to download are often abandoned.

Figure 10.4
Sample test plan

Web Page Document Test Plan

| File Name: | | | | | | | | | | Date: | |
| Page Title: | | | | | | | | | | Tester: | |

Browser Compatibility

	1024x768	1280x800	800x600	Other	PC	Mac	Linux	Images Disabled	CSS Disabled	Other	Notes
Internet Explorer (Version #)											
Internet Explorer (Version #)											
Firefox (Version #)											
Safari (Version #)											
Opera (Version #)											
Chrome (Version #)											
JAWS Screen Reader											
Mobile (Device Name)											
Other											

Document Validation

	Pass	Fail	Notes
XHTML Validation			
CSS Validation			
Check Spelling			
Check for Required Content			
Check for Required Graphics			
Check Alt Attributes			
Test Hyperlinks			
Accessibility Testing			
Form Processing			
Scripting/Dynamic Effects			
Usability Testing			
Other			

Search Engine Optimization

	Notes
Meta tag (description)	
Keywords in page title	
Keywords in headings	
Keywords in content	
Other	

Download Time Check

	Time	Notes
56 6Kbps		
128Kbps		
512Kbps		
T1/DS1		
Other		

Notes

Automated Testing Tools and Validators

The web authoring tool you use for your project will provide some built-in site reporting and testing features. Web authoring applications such as Adobe Dreamweaver and Microsoft Expression Web provide functions such as spell-check, link checks, and load time calculations. Each application has unique features. Dreamweaver's reporting includes link checking, accessibility, and code validation. There are other **automated testing** tools and **validators** available. The W3C Markup Validation Service (http://validator.w3.org) can be used to validate both HTML and XHTML. Test CSS for proper syntax using the W3C CSS Validation Service (http://jigsaw.w3.org/css-validator). Analyze the download speed of your page using the Web Page Analyzer (http://www.websiteoptimization.com/services/analyze).

Adobe also offers cross-browser testing at BrowserLab (http://browserlab.adobe.com). Testing tools that offer additional features such as spell-check, browser compatibility, page load time, and broken link checking are available from NetMechanic (http://www.netmechanic.com) and others.

Accessibility Testing

Focus on Accessibility

Accessible web pages can be used by all individuals, including those with visual, hearing, mobility, and cognitive challenges. As you've worked through this book, accessibility has been an integral part of your web page design and coding rather than an afterthought. You've configured headings and subheadings, navigation within unordered lists, images with alternate text, and associations between text and form controls. These techniques all increase the accessibility of a web page.

Web Accessibility Standards

Section 508 of the Rehabilitation Act.   Section 508 (http://www.access-board.gov/sec508/guide/1194.22.htm) requires electronic and information technology, including web pages, that are used by U.S. federal agencies to be accessible to people with disabilities. At the time this was written, the Section 508 standards were undergoing revision.

Web Content Accessibility Guidelines (WCAG 2.0).   WCAG 2.0 (http://www.w3.org/TR/WCAG20) considers an accessible web page to be perceivable, operable, and understandable for people with a wide range of abilities. The page should be robust enough to work with a variety of browsers and other user agents, such as assistive technologies (for example, screen readers) and mobile devices. The guiding principles of WCAG 2.0 are known as POUR:

1. Content must be **P**erceivable.

2. Interface components in the content must be **O**perable.

3. Content and controls must be **U**nderstandable.

4. Content should be **R**obust enough to work with current and future user agents, including assistive technologies.

Prove your compliance with accessibility standards by performing **accessibility testing** on your site. There are a variety of accessibility checkers available. Adobe Dreamweaver includes a built-in accessibility checker. WebAIM Wave (http://wave.webaim.org) and ATRC AChecker (http://www.achecker.ca/checker) are two popular free online accessibility evaluation tools. Several browser toolbars are available that can be used to assess accessibility, including the Web Developer Extension (http://chrispederick.com/work/web-developer), WAT-C Web Accessibility Toolbar (http://www.wat-c.org/tools), and the AIS Web Accessibility Toolbar (http://www.visionaustralia.org.au/ais/toolbar).

It's important not to rely completely on automated tests—you'll want to review the pages yourself. For example, while an automated test can check for the presence of an alt attribute, it takes a human to critically think and decide whether the text of the alt attribute is an appropriate description for a person who cannot view the image. WebAIM provides a detailed checklist (http://www.webaim.org/standards/wcag/checklist) that prompts you with items to review in order to verify compliance with WCAG 2.0 requirements.

Usability Testing

Usability is the measure of the quality of a user's experience when interacting with a website. It's about making a website that is easy, efficient, and pleasant for your visitors. Usability.gov (http://usability.gov) describes five factors that affect the user's experience:

- **Ease of Learning.** How easy is it to learn to use the website? Is the navigation intuitive? Does a new visitor consider it easy to learn to perform basic tasks on the website or is he or she frustrated?

- **Efficiency of Use.** How do experienced users perceive the website? Once they are comfortable, are they able to complete tasks efficiently and quickly or are they frustrated?

- **Memorability.** When a visitor returns to a website, does he or she remember enough to use it productively or is the visitor back at the beginning of the learning curve (and frustrated)?

- **Error Frequency and Severity.** Do website visitors make errors when navigating or filling in forms on the website? Are they serious errors? Is it easy to recover from errors or are visitors frustrated?

- **Subjective Satisfaction.** Do users like using the website? Are they satisfied? Why or why not?

Testing how actual web page visitors use a website is called **usability testing**. It can be conducted at any phase of a website's development and is often performed more than once. A usability test is conducted by asking users to complete tasks on a website, such as placing an order, looking up the phone number of a company, or finding a product. The exact tasks will vary depending on the website being tested. The users are monitored while they try to perform these tasks. They are asked to think out loud about their doubts and hesitations. The results are recorded (often on video tape) and discussed with the web design team. Often, changes are made to the navigation and page layouts based on these tests. Perform the small-scale usability test in Hands-On Exercise 5 at the end of this chapter to become more familiar with this technique.

If usability testing is done early in the development phase of a website, it may use the paper page layouts and site map. If the development team is struggling with a design issue, sometimes a usability test can help to determine which design idea is the better choice. When usability is done during a later phase, such as the Testing phase, the actual website is tested. This can lead to confirmation that the site is easy to use and well designed, to last minute changes in the website, or to a plan for website enhancements in the near future.

Launch

Your client—whether another company or another department in your organization—needs to review and approve the test website before the files are published to the live site. Sometimes this approval takes place at a face-to-face meeting. Other times, the test URL is given to the client and the client e-mails approval or requested changes.

Once the test website has been approved, it is published to your live production website (this is called a **launch**). If you think you are finished, think again! It is crucial to test all site components after publishing to make sure the site functions properly in its new environment. Marketing and promotional activities for the website (see Chapter 13) usually take place at this time.

Maintenance

A website is never finished. There are always errors or omissions that were overlooked during the development process. Clients usually find many new uses for a website once they have one and request modifications, additions, and new sections (this is called site **maintenance**). At this point, the project team identifies the new opportunity or enhancement and begins another loop through the development process.

Other types of updates needed may be relatively small—perhaps a link is broken, a word is misspelled, or a graphic needs to be changed. These small changes are usually made as soon as they are noticed. The question of who makes the changes and who approves them is often a matter of company policy. If you are a freelance web developer, the situation is more straightforward—you will make the changes and your client will approve them.

Evaluation

Remember the goals set for the website in the Conceptualization phase? During the **evaluation** phase, it's time to review them and determine whether your website meets them. If not, consider how you can enhance the site and begin another loop through the development process.

Checkpoint 10.1

1. Describe the role of the project manager.

2. Explain why many different roles are needed on a large-scale web project.

3. List three different techniques used to test a website. Describe each technique in one or two sentences.

VideoNote
**Choosing a
Domain Name**

10.3 Domain Name Overview

A crucial part of establishing an effective web presence is choosing a **domain name**; it serves to locate your website on the Internet. If your business or organization is new, then it's often convenient to select a domain name while you are deciding on a company name. If your organization is well established, choose a domain name that relates to your existing business presence. Although many domain names have already been purchased, there are still a lot of available options.

Choosing a Domain Name

- **Describe Your Business.** Although there is a long-standing trend to use "fun" words as domain names (for example, yahoo.com, google.com, bing.com, woofoo.com, and so on), think carefully before doing so. Domain names for traditional businesses and organizations are the foundation of the organization's web presence and should include the business name or purpose.

- **Be Brief, If Possible.** While most people find new websites with search engines, some of your website visitors will type your domain name in a browser. A shorter domain name is preferable to a longer one—it's easier for your visitors to remember.

- **Avoid Hyphens (-).** Using the hyphen character (commonly called a dash) in a domain name makes it difficult to pronounce the name. Also, someone typing your domain name may forget the dash and end up at a competitor's site! If you can, avoid the use of dashes in a domain name.

- **There's More Than .com.** While the .com top-level domain name (TLD) is still the most popular for commercial and personal websites, consider also registering your domain name with other TLDs, such as .biz, .net, .us, .mobi, and so on. Commercial businesses should avoid the .org TLD, which is the first choice for nonprofit organizations. You don't have to create a website for each domain name that you register. You can arrange with your domain name registrar (for example, Register.com [http://www.register.com]) for the extra domain names to point visitors to the domain name where your website is located. This is called **domain name redirection**.

- **Brainstorm Potential Keywords.** Think about words that a potential visitor might type into a search engine when looking for your type of business or organization. This is the starting point for your list of **keywords**. If possible, work one or more keywords into your domain name (but still keep it as short as possible).

- **Avoid Trademarked Words or Phrases.** The U.S. Patent and Trademark Office (USPTO) defines a **trademark** as a word, phrase, symbol, or design, or a combination of words, phrases, symbols, or designs, that identifies and distinguishes the source of the goods of one party from those of others. A starting point in researching trademarks is the USPTO Trademark Electronic Search System (TESS); visit http://tess2.uspto.gov. See http://www.uspto.gov for more information about trademarks.

- **Know the Territory.** Explore the way your potential domain name and keywords are already used on the Web. It's a good idea to type your potential domain names (and related words) into a search engine to see what may already exist.

- **Verify Availability.** Check with one of the many **domain name registrars** to determine whether your domain name choices are available. A few of the many sites that offer domain name registration services are listed below:

  - Register.com: http://www.register.com

  - Network Solutions: http://www.networksolutions.com

  - GoDaddy.com: http://www.godaddy.com

  Each of these sites offers a search feature that provides you with a way to determine whether a potential domain name is available, and if it is owned, who owns it. Often the domain name is already taken. If that's the case, the sites listed previously will provide you with alternate suggestions that may be appropriate. Don't give up; a domain name is out there waiting for your business.

Registering a Domain Name

Once you've found your perfect domain name, don't waste any time in registering it. The cost to register a domain name varies, but it is quite reasonable. The top rate for a .com 1-year registration is currently $35 (and there are numerous opportunities for discounts with multiyear packages or bundled web hosting services). It's perfectly okay to register a domain name even if you are not ready to publish your website immediately. There are many companies that provide domain name registration services, as listed previously. When you register a domain name, your contact information (your name, phone number, mailing address, and e-mail address) will be entered into the WHOIS database and is available to anyone unless you choose the option for private registration. While there is usually a small annual fee for **private registration**, it shields your personal information from unwanted spam and curiosity seekers.

Obtaining a domain name is just one part of establishing a web presence. You also need to host your website somewhere. The next section introduces you to the factors involved in choosing a web host.

10.4 Web Hosting

Where is the appropriate place for your web project to "live"? Choosing the most appropriate web hosting provider for your business or client could be one of the most important decisions you make. A good web hosting service will provide a robust, reliable home for your website. A poor web hosting service will be a source of problems and complaints. Which would you prefer?

Web Hosting Providers

A **web hosting provider** is an organization that offers storage for your website files along with the service of making them available on the Internet. Your domain name, such as webdevfoundations.net, is associated with an IP address that points to your website on the web server at the web hosting provider. It is common for web hosting providers to charge a setup fee in addition to the monthly hosting fee.

Hosting fees vary widely. The cheapest hosting company is not necessarily the one to use. Never consider using a free web hosting provider for a business website. These free sites are great for kids, college students, and hobbyists, but they are unprofessional. The last thing you or your client wants is to be perceived as unprofessional or not serious about the business at hand. As you consider different web hosting providers, try contacting their support phone numbers and e-mail addresses to determine just how responsive they really are. Word of mouth, web searches, and online directories such as Hosting Review (http://www.hosting-review.com) are all resources in your quest for the perfect web hosting provider.

Types of Web Hosting

- **Virtual Hosting**, or shared hosting, is a popular choice for small websites (Figure 10.5). The web hosting provider's physical web server is divided into a number of virtual domains and multiple websites are set up on the same computer. You have the authority to update files in your own website space, while the web hosting provider maintains the web server computer and Internet connectivity.

- **Dedicated Hosting** is the rental and exclusive use of a computer and connection to the Internet that is housed on the web hosting company's premises. A dedicated server is usually needed for a website that could have a considerable amount of traffic, such as tens of millions of hits a day. The server can usually be configured and operated remotely from the client's company, or you can pay the web hosting provider to administer it for you.

Figure 10.5 Virtual web hosting

- **Co-Located Hosting** uses a computer that your organization has purchased and configured. Your web server is housed and connected to the Internet at the web host's physical location, but your organization typically administers this computer.

10.5 Choosing a Virtual Host

A number of factors to consider when choosing a web host have been discussed, including bandwidth, disk storage space, technical support, and the availability of e-commerce packages. For a handy list of these factors and others to consider in your quest for a virtual web host, review the web host checklist shown in Table 10.1.

FAQ **Why do I care about knowing which operating system my web hosting provider uses?**

Knowing the operating system used by your web hosting provider is important because it can help you with troubleshooting your website. Often, students' websites work great on their own PC (usually with a Windows-based operating system) but fall apart (with broken links and images that do not load) after being published on a free web server that uses a different operating system.

Some operating systems, such as Windows, treat uppercase and lowercase letters in exactly the same way. Other operating systems, such as UNIX and Linux, consider uppercase and lowercase letters to be different. This is called being **case-sensitive**. For example, when a web server running on a Windows operating system receives a request generated by an anchor tag coded as `<a href="MyPage.html">My Page</a>`, it will return a file named with any combination of uppercase or lowercase letters. The values MyPage.html, mypage.html, and myPage.html can all be used. However, when the request generated by the same anchor tag is received by a web server running on a UNIX system (which is case-sensitive), the file would only be found if it were really saved as MyPage.html. If the file were named mypage.html, a 404 Not Found error would result. This is a good reason to be consistent when naming files; consider always using lowercase letters for file names.

Table 10.1 Web host checklist

Operating System	❏ UNIX ❏ Linux ❏ Windows	Some web hosts offer a choice of these platforms. If you need to integrate your website with your business systems, choose the same operating system for both.
Web Server	❏ Apache ❏ IIS	These two web server applications are the most popular. Apache usually runs on a UNIX or Linux operating system. Internet Information Services (IIS) is bundled with selected versions of Microsoft Windows.
Bandwidth	❏ _____ GB per month ❏ _____ Charge for overage	Some web hosts carefully monitor your data transfer bandwidth and charge you for overages. While unlimited bandwidth is great, it is not always available. A typical low-traffic website may transfer between 100 and 500MB per month. A medium-traffic site should be okay with about 20GB of data transfer bandwidth per month.
Technical Support	❏ E-mail ❏ Chat ❏ Forum ❏ Phone	Review the description of technical support on the web host's site. Is it available 24 hours a day, 7 days a week? E-mail or phone a question to test it. If the organization is not responsive to you as a prospective customer, be leery about the availability of its technical support later.
Service Agreement	❏ Uptime guarantee ❏ Automatic monitoring	A web host that offers a Service Level Agreement (SLA) with an uptime guarantee shows that they value service and reliability. The use of automatic monitoring will inform the web host technical support staff when a server is not functioning.
Disk Space	❏ _____ GB	Many virtual hosts routinely offer several gigabytes of disk storage space. If you have a small site that is not graphics-intensive, you may never even use 100MB of disk storage space.
E-mail	❏ _____ Mailboxes	Most virtual hosts offer multiple e-mail boxes per site. These can be used to filter messages (customer service, technical support, general inquiries, and so on).
Uploading Files	❏ FTP Access ❏ Web-based File Manager	A web host that offers FTP access will allow you the most flexibility. Others only allow updates through a web-based file manager application. Some web hosts offer both options.
Canned Scripts	❏ Form processing	Many web hosts supply canned, pre-written scripts to process form information.
Scripting Support	❏ PHP ❏ .NET ❏ _____ Other	If you plan to use server-side scripting on your site, determine which, if any, scripting is supported by your web host.
Database Support	❏ MySQL ❏ MS Access ❏ MS SQL	If you plan to access a database with your scripting, determine which, if any, database is supported by your web host.
E-Commerce Packages	❏ _____	If you plan to enter into e-commerce (see Chapter 12), it may be easier if your web host offers a shopping cart package. Check to see if one is available.
Scalability	❏ Scripting ❏ Database ❏ E-commerce	You probably will choose a basic (low-end) plan for your first website. Note the scalability of your web host: Are there other available plans with scripting, database, e-commerce packages, and additional bandwidth or disk space as your site grows?
Backups	❏ Daily ❏ Periodic ❏ No backups	Most web hosts will back up your files regularly. Check to see how often the backups are made and if they are accessible to you. Be sure to make your own site backups as well.
Site Statistics	❏ Raw log file ❏ Log reports ❏ No log access	The web server log contains useful information about your visitors, how they find your site, and what pages they visit. Check to see if the log is available to you. Some web hosts provide reports about the log. See Chapter 13 for more information on web server logs.
Domain Name	❏ Required to register with host ❏ OK to register on your own	Some web hosts offer a package that includes registering your domain name. However, you will retain control of your domain name account if you register it yourself.
Price	❏ $_____ setup fee ❏ $_____ per month	Price is last in this list for a reason. Do not choose a web host based on price alone—the old adage "you get what you pay for" is definitely true here. It is not unusual to pay a one-time setup fee and then a periodic fee—monthly, quarterly, or annually.

Checkpoint 10.2

1. Describe the type of web host that would meet the needs of a small company for its initial web presence.

2. What is the difference between a dedicated web server and a co-located web server?

3. Explain why price is not the most important consideration when choosing a web host.

Chapter Summary

This chapter introduced the System Development Life Cycle and its application to web development projects. The job roles related to website development were discussed. The chapter also included an introduction to choosing a domain name and a website host provider. Visit the textbook website at http://www.webdevfoundations.net for examples, the links listed in this chapter, and updated information.

Key Terms

accessibility testing	editor	Service Level Agreement (SLA)
analysis	environmental requirements	System Development Life
automated testing	evaluation	Cycle (SDLC)
co-located web server	functionality requirements	test plan
conceptualization	graphic designer	testing
content manager	information architect	trademark
content requirements	information topics	unit testing
copywriter	keywords	usability testing
cost-benefit analysis	launch	validators
database administrator	maintenance	virtual hosting
dedicated web server	marketing representative	web developer
design	network administrator	web hosting provider
domain name	phases	web presence
domain name redirection	production	web server
domain name registrars	project manager	

Review Questions

Multiple Choice

1. Which of the following should be included when testing a website?
   a. checking all of the hyperlinks within the site
   b. viewing the site in a variety of web browsers
   c. viewing the site in a variety of screen resolutions
   d. all of the above

2. Which of the following are included in the role of an information architect?
   a. being instrumental in defining the site organization, navigation, and labeling
   b. attending all meetings and collecting all information
   c. managing the project
   d. none of the above

3. What is the purpose of private registration for a domain name?
   a. It protects the privacy of your website.
   b. It is the cheapest form of domain name registration.

   c. It protects the privacy of your contact information.
   d. none of the above

4. Which methodology is often used by web project teams?
   a. the SDLC
   b. a derivative of the SDLC that is similar to the one discussed in this chapter
   c. a methodology that is decided as the project is built
   d. no development methodology is necessary

5. What do team members do during the Analysis phase of a website project?
   a. determine what the site will do—not how it will be done
   b. determine the information topics of the site
   c. determine the content requirements of the site
   d. all of the above

6. In which phase is a prototype of the website often created?

   a. the Design phase
   b. the Conceptualization phase
   c. the Production phase
   d. the Analysis phase

7. Which of the following occurs during the Production phase?

   a. A web authoring tool is often used.
   b. The graphics, web pages, and other components are created.
   c. The web pages are individually tested.
   d. all of the above

8. Which of the following occurs during the Evaluation phase?

   a. The goals for the site are reviewed.
   b. The web designers are evaluated.
   c. The competition is evaluated.
   d. none of the above

9. Which of the following is true about domain names?

   a. It is recommended to register multiple domain names that are redirected to your website.
   b. It is recommended to use long, descriptive domain names.

   c. It is recommended to use hyphens in domain names.
   d. There is no reason to check for trademarks when you are choosing a domain name.

10. Which web hosting option is appropriate for the initial web presence of an organization?

    a. dedicated hosting
    b. free web hosting
    c. virtual hosting
    d. co-located hosting

Fill in the Blank

11. _____ can be described as testing how actual web page visitors use a website.

12. The _____ determines the appropriate use of graphics on the site and creates and edits graphics.

13. The _____ operating system(s) treat uppercase and lowercase letters differently.

Short Answer

14. Why should the websites of competitors be reviewed when designing a website?

15. Why should you try to contact the technical support staff of a web hosting provider before you become one of its customers?

Hands-On Exercises

1. Skip this exercise if you have completed Hands-On Practice 2.14 in Chapter 2. In this exercise, you will validate a web page. Choose one of the web pages that you have created. Launch a browser and visit the W3C Markup Validation Service (http://validator.w3.org). Click on the Validate by File Upload tab. Click the Browse button, select a file from your computer, and click the Check button to upload the file to the W3C site. Your page will be analyzed and a Results page will be generated that shows a report of violations of the doctype that is used by your web page. The error messages display the offending code along with the line number, column number, and a description of the error. Don't worry if your web page does not pass the validation the first time. Many well-known websites have pages that do not validate—even Yahoo! (http://www.yahoo.com) had validation errors at the time this was written. Modify your web page document and revalidate it until you see a message that states "This document was successfully checked as HTML5!" (see Figure 10.6).

   You can also validate pages directly from the Web. Try validating the W3C's home page (http://www.w3.org), Yahoo! (http://www.yahoo.com), and your school's home page. Visit the W3C Markup Validation Service (http://validator.w3.org) and notice the Validate by URI area. Enter the URL of the web page you would like to validate in the Address text box. Click the Check button and view the results. Experiment with the character encoding and doctype options. The W3C's page

Figure 10.6
Message indicating that the web page has passed the validation

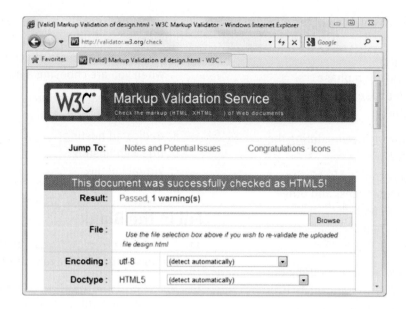

should pass the validation. Don't worry if the other pages do not validate. Validation is not required for web pages. However, web pages that pass the validation should display well in most browsers. (*Note:* If you have published pages to the web, try validating one of them instead of your school's home page.)

2. Run an automated accessibility test on the home page of your school's website. Use both the WebAIM Wave (http://wave.webaim.org) and ATRC AChecker (http://www.achecker.ca/checker) automated tests. Describe the differences in the way these tools report the results of the test. Did both tests find similar errors? Write a one-page report that describes the results of the tests. Include your recommendations for improving the website.

3. The Web Page Analyzer (http://www.websiteoptimization.com/services/analyze) calculates download times for a web page and associated assets, along with providing suggestions for improvement. Visit this site and test your school's home page (or a page assigned by your instructor). After the test is run, a web page speed report will display file sizes and include suggestions for improvement. Print out the browser view of this results page and write a one-page report that describes the results of the test and your own recommendations for improvement.

4. The Dr. Watson site (http://watson.addy.com) offers free web page validation. Visit this site and test your school's home page (or a page assigned by your instructor). After the test is run, a report is displayed with categories such as server response, estimated download speed, syntax and style analysis, spell-check, link verification, images, search engine compatibility (see Chapter 13), site link popularity (see Chapter 13), and source code. Print out the browser view of this results page and write a one-page report that describes the results of the test and your own recommendations for improvement.

5. Perform a small-scale usability test with a group of other students. Decide who will be the typical users, the tester, and the observer. You will perform a usability test on your school's website.

- The typical users are the test subjects.

- The tester oversees the usability test and emphasizes that the users are not being tested; the website is being tested.

- The observer takes notes on the user's reactions and comments.

Step 1 The tester welcomes the users and introduces them to the website that they will be testing.

Step 2 For each of the following scenarios, the tester introduces the scenario and questions the users as they work through the task. The tester should ask the users to indicate when they are in doubt, confused, or frustrated. The observer takes notes.

- Scenario 1: Find the phone number of the contact person for the web development program at your school.

- Scenario 2: Determine when to register for the next semester.

- Scenario 3: Find the requirements for earning a degree or certificate in web development or a related area.

Step 3 The tester and the observer organize the results and write a brief report. If this were a usability test for a website that you were developing, the development team would meet to review the results and discuss the necessary improvements to the site.

Step 4 Hand in a report with your group's usability test results. Complete the report using a word processor. Write no more than one page about each scenario. Write one page of recommendations for improving your school's website.

Note: For more information on usability testing, see Keith Instone's classic presentation at http://instone.org/files/KEI-Howtotest-19990721.pdf. Another good resource is Steven Krug's book, *Don't Make Me Think*.

6. See the description of usability testing in Hands-On Exercise 5. In a small group, perform usability tests on two similar websites, such as the following:

- Barnes and Noble (http://www.bn.com) and Powell's Books (http://powells.com)

- AccuWeather.com (http://accuweather.com) and Weather Underground (http://www.wunderground.com)

- Running.com (http://running.com) and Cool Running (http://www.coolrunning.com)

Select and list three scenarios to test. Decide who will be the users, the tester, and the observer. Follow the steps listed in Hands-On Exercise 5.

7. Pretend that you are on a job interview. Choose a role on a web project team that interests you. In three or four sentences, describe why you would be an excellent addition to a web development team in that role.

Web Research

1. This chapter discussed options for hosting websites. In this research exercise, you will search for web hosting providers and report on three that meet the following criteria:

- Support PHP and MySQL.

- Offer e-commerce capabilities.

- Provide at least 100MB disk space.

Use your favorite search engine to find web hosting providers or visit web host directories such as Hosting Review (http://www.hosting-review.com) and HostIndex.com (http://www.hostindex.com). The web server survey results provided by

Netcraft (http://uptime.netcraft.com/perf/reports/Hosters) may also be useful. Create a web page that presents your findings. Include links to your three web hosting providers. Your web page should include a table of information such as the setup fees, monthly fees, domain name registration costs, amount of disk space, type of e-commerce package, and cost of e-commerce package. Use color and graphics appropriately on your web page. Place your name and e-mail address at the bottom of your web page.

2. This chapter discussed the different job functions that are needed to develop large websites. Choose a job role that interests you. Search for information about available jobs in your geographical area. Search for technology jobs with your favorite search engine or visit a job site such as Monster.com (http://www.monster.com), Dice (http://www.dice.com), Indeed (http://www.indeed.com), or CareerBuilder. com (http://www.careerbuilder.com) and search for your desired location and job type. Find three possible job positions that interest you and report on them. Create a web page that includes a brief description of the job role you have chosen, a description of the three available positions, a description of the types of experience and/or educational background required for the positions, and the salary range (if available). Use color and graphics appropriately on your web page. Place your name and e-mail address at the bottom of your web page.

Focus on Web Design

The U.S. Department of Health and Human Services offers a free online PDF book, *Research-Based Web Design & Usability Guidelines* (http://www.usability.gov/guidelines/guidelines_book.pdf). The book suggests guidelines for a variety of topics, including navigation, text appearance, scrolling and paging, writing content, usability testing, and accessibility. Choose one chapter topic that interests you. Read the chapter. Note four guidelines that you find intriguing or useful. In a one-page report, describe why you chose the chapter topic and the four guidelines you noted.

 # WEBSITE CASE STUDY
Testing Phase

This case study continues throughout the rest of the text. In this chapter, you will test the Web Project case study.

Web Project

See Chapter 5 for an introduction to the Web Project. In this chapter, you will develop a test plan for the project. You will review the documents created in the previous chapters' Web Project and create a test plan.

Hands-On Practice Case Study

Part 1: Review the Design Documents and Completed Web Pages. Review the Topic Approval, Site Map, and Page Layout Design documents that you created in the Chapter 5 Web Project. Review the web pages that you have created and/or modified in the Chapter 6 through Chapter 9 Web Project activities.

Part 2: Prepare a Test Plan. See Figure 10.4 for a sample test plan document (Chapter10/testplan.pdf in the student files). Create a test plan document for your website, including CSS validation, HTML validation, and accessibility testing.

Part 3: Test Your Website. Implement your test plan and test each page that you have developed for your Web Project. Record the results. Create a list of suggested improvements.

Part 4: Perform Usability Testing. Describe three scenarios that typical visitors to your site may encounter. Using Hands-On Exercise 5 as a guide, conduct a usability test for these scenarios. Write a one-page report about your findings. What improvements would you suggest for the website?

Web Multimedia and Interactivity

Chapter Objectives   In this chapter, you will learn how to . . .

- Describe the purpose of plug-ins, helper applications, media containers, and codecs

- Describe the types of multimedia files used on the Web

- Configure hyperlinks to multimedia files

- Apply the object element to display audio and video files

- Apply the object element to display Adobe Flash multimedia on a web page

- Configure audio and video on a web page with HTML5 elements

- Describe features and common uses of Flash

- Configure a Flash animation on a web page

- Describe features and common uses of Java applets

- Configure a Java applet on a web page

- Create an interactive image gallery with CSS

- Configure the CSS3 transform and transition properties

- Describe features and common uses of JavaScript

- Describe the purpose of the HTML5 canvas element

- Describe features and common uses of Ajax

- Locate Flash, Java applets, JavaScript, and Ajax resources on the Web

As the saying goes, "A picture is worth a thousand words."   You already are aware that graphics help to make web pages compelling. Other types of media, such as audio and video, are introduced in this chapter. Appropriate movies and sounds on your web pages can make them more interesting and informative. Sources of these media types, the HTML code needed to place media on a web page, and suggested uses of media are introduced.

You began to work with interactivity in Chapter 6 when you used CSS pseudo-classes to respond to mouse movements over hyperlinks. You'll expand your CSS skill set as you configure an interactive image gallery and explore CSS3 transition and transform properties. Adding the right touch of interactivity to a web page can make it engaging and compelling for your visitors.

Technologies commonly used to add interactivity to web pages include Flash, Java applets, JavaScript, and Ajax. This chapter introduces you to these techniques. Each of these topics is explored more fully in other books; each technology could be the sole subject of an entire book or college course. As you read this chapter and try the examples, concentrate on learning the features and capabilities of each technology, rather than trying to master the details.

11.1 Plug-Ins, Containers, and Codecs

Web browsers are designed to display web pages and GIF, JPG, and PNG images, among others. When the media is not one of these types, the browser searches for a **plug-in** or **helper application** that is configured to display the file type. If it cannot find a plug-in or helper application (which runs in a separate window from the browser) on the visitor's computer, the web browser offers the visitor the option of saving the file to their computer. Several commonly used plug-ins are listed as follows:

- **Adobe Flash Player (http://www.adobe.com/products/flashplayer).** The Flash Player displays SWF files. These can contain audio, video, and animation, along with interactivity.

- **Adobe Shockwave Player (http://www.adobe.com/products/shockwaveplayer).** The Shockwave Player displays high-performance multimedia created using the Adobe Director application.

- **Adobe Reader (http://www.adobe.com/products/acrobat/readstep2.html).** Adobe Reader is commonly used to display information stored in PDF format, such as printable brochures, documents, and white papers.

- **Java Runtime Environment (http://www.java.com/en/download/manual.jsp).** The Java Runtime Environment (JRE) is used to run applications and applets utilizing Java technology.

- **RealPlayer (http://www.real.com).** The RealPlayer plug-in plays streaming audio, video, animation, and multimedia presentations on the Web.

- **Windows Media Player (http://www.microsoft.com/windows/windowsmedia/ download).** The Windows Media Player plug-in plays streaming audio, video, animation, and multimedia presentations on the Web.

- **Apple QuickTime (http://www.apple.com/quicktime/download).** The Apple QuickTime plug-in displays QuickTime animation, music, audio, and video directly within the web page.

The plug-ins and helper applications listed previously have been used on the Web for many years. What is new about HTML5 audio and video is that it is native to the browser; no plug-ins are needed. When working with native HTML5 audio and video, you need to be aware of the **container** (which is designated by the file extension) and the **codec** (which is the algorithm used to compress the media).

Explore Table 11.1 and Table 11.2, which list common media file extensions, the container file type, and a description with codec information (if applicable for HTML5).

Table 11.1 Common audio file types

Extension	Container	Description
.wav	Wave	Created by Microsoft; standard on the PC platform; also supported on the Mac platform.
.aiff and .aif	Audio Interchange	Popular audio file format on the Mac platform; also supported on the PC platform.
.mid	Musical Instrument Digital Interface (MIDI)	Contains instructions to recreate a musical sound rather than a digital recording of the sound itself; a limited number of types of sounds can be reproduced.
.au	Sun UNIX Sound File	Older type of sound file that generally has poorer sound quality than the newer audio file formats.
.mp3	MPEG-1 Audio Layer-3	Popular for music files because of the MP3 codec, which supports two channels and advanced compression.
.ogg	OGG	Open-source audio file format (see http://www.vorbis.com) that uses the Vorbis codec.
.m4a	MPEG-4 Audio	Audio-only MPEG-4 format that uses the Advanced Audio Coding (AAC) codec; supported by QuickTime, iTunes, and mobile devices such as the iPod and iPad.

Table 11.2 Common video file types

Extension	Container	Description
.mov	QuickTime	Created by Apple and initially used on the Mac platform, it is also supported by Windows.
.avi	Audio Video Interleaved	Microsoft's original standard video format for the PC platform.
.flv	Flash Video	Flash-compatible video file container; supports the H.264 codec.
.wmv	Windows Media Video	Streaming video technology developed by Microsoft; the Windows Media Player supports this file format.
.mpg	MPEG	Developed under the sponsorship of the Moving Picture Experts Group (MPEG) (http://www.chiariglione.org/mpeg); supported on both Windows and Mac platforms.
.m4v and .mp4	MPEG-4	MPEG-4 (MP4) codec and H.264 codec; played by QuickTime, iTunes, and mobile devices such as the iPod and iPad.
.3gp	3GPP Multimedia	H.264 codec; a standard for delivery of multimedia over third-generation, high-speed wireless networks.
.ogv or .ogg	OGG	Open-source video file format (see http://www.theora.org) that uses the Theora codec.
.webm	WebM	Open media file format (see http://www.webmproject.org) sponsored by Google; uses the VP8 video codec and Vorbis audio codec.

11.2 Getting Started with Audio and Video

As you read this chapter, you'll explore different ways to provide audio and video for your website visitors, including providing a hyperlink, XHTML solutions with the object and param elements, and the new HTML5 audio and video elements. We'll get started with the easiest method, which is coding a hyperlink.

Provide a Hyperlink

The easiest way to give your website visitors access to an audio or a video file is to create a simple hyperlink to the file. For example, the code to hyperlink to a sound file named WDFpodcast.mp3 is

```
<a href="WDFpodcast.mp3">Podcast Episode 1</a> (MP3)
```

When your website visitor clicks on the hyperlink, the plug-in for MP3 files that is installed on the computer (such as QuickTime) typically will display embedded in a new browser window or tab. Your web page visitor can then use the plug-in to play the sound. If your website visitor right-clicks on the hyperlink, the media file can be downloaded and saved.

 Hands-On Practice 11.1

In this Hands-On Practice, you will create a web page similar to Figure 11.1 that contains an h1 tag and a hyperlink to an MP3 file. The web page will also provide a hyperlink to a text transcript of that file to provide for accessibility. It's useful to your web page visitors to also indicate the type of file (such as an MP3) and, optionally, the size of the file to be accessed.

Figure 11.1 The default MP3 player will launch in the browser when the visitor clicks on Podcast Episode 1

Copy the podcast.mp3 and podcast.txt files from the chapter11/starters folder in the student files and save them to a folder named podcast. Use the chapter2/template.html file as a starting point and create a web page with the heading "Web Design Podcast", a hyperlink to the MP3 file, and a hyperlink to the text transcript. Save your web page as podcast2.html and display it in a browser. Test your web page in different browsers, using different versions. When you click on the MP3 hyperlink, an audio player (whichever player or plug-in is configured for the browser) will launch to play the file. When you click on the hyperlink for the text transcript, the text will display in the browser. Compare your work to chapter11/podcast/podcast.html in the student files.

11.3 XHTML Object and Param Elements

Object Element

Another way to include multimedia on your web page is to embed the audio or video file in the page and optionally display a control panel or player for the multimedia. When coding in XHTML syntax (refer to Chapter 2), the object element is used for this purpose. The code in this section uses XHTML syntax, but the object and param elements may also be used in HTML5. The **object element** is a multipurpose container tag for adding various types of objects to a web page. The object element begins with the `<object>` tag and ends with the `</object>` tag. Additional configuration values, called parameters, will usually need to be coded using the param element. Table 11.3 lists the common attributes of the object element.

Table 11.3 Common attributes of media object elements

Attribute	Value	Usage
data	File name	Required; provides the media's file name
classid	Uniquely identifies the player software	Optional; used with Windows; the `classid` identifies an ActiveX control that must be installed on the visitor's PC
	QuickTime: `classid="clsid:02BF25D5-8C17-4B23-BC80-D3488ABDDC6B"`	
	Windows Player: `classid="6BF52A52-394A-11d3-B153-00C04F79FAA6"`	
	Flash Shockwave Player: `classid="clsid:D27CDB6E-AE6D-11cf-96B8-444553540000"`	
codebase	Specifies a relative path for the location of the plug-in	Optional; facilitates the location and download of the plug-in if needed; not used with Windows Media Player 7
	QuickTime: `codebase="http://www.apple.com/qtactivex/qtplugin.cab"`	
	Flash Shockwave Player: `codebase="http://download.macromedia.com/pub/shockwave/cabs/flash/swflash.cab#Version=8,0,22,0"`	
height	Numeric, number of pixels	Optional; configures the height of the media control console
title	Brief text description	Optional; may be displayed by browsers or assistive technologies
type	Valid MIME type	Optional; specifies the MIME type of the media file, such as `audio/mpeg` or `video/quicktime`
width	Numeric, number of pixels	Optional; configures the width of the media control console

Param Element

The **param element** is a self-contained tag with two attributes: name and value. Use `<param />` for XHTML syntax and `<param>` for HTML5 syntax. All the `<param />` tags for the object appear before the ending `</object>` tag. The player's documentation will indicate whether parameters are needed and the format you should use. Table 11.4 lists common param element attribute values.

Table 11.4 Common param element media attribute values

Attribute	Value	Usage
src	Valid file name, name of media file	Required; provides the name of the file to be played
autoplay	true or false	Optional; determines whether the media will play automatically when the page is loaded (if omitted, the media may not automatically play)
controller	true or false (not uniformly supported)	Optional; indicates whether the media console will display
hidden	true (not uniformly supported)	Optional; hides the default media console
loop	Numeric value or true for continuous play (not uniformly supported)	Optional; determines how many times the media file will repeat

Audio on a Web Page

The basic XHTML code to use the <object> tag to embed a sound loop within a player on a web page is

```
<object data="soundloop.mp3" height="50" width="100"
  type="audio/mpeg" title="Music Sound Loop">
  <param name="src" value="soundloop.mp3" />
  <param name="controller" value="true" />
  <param name="autoplay" value="false" />
</object>
```

A sample page using this <object> tag can be found in the student files (chapter11/musicbase.html). See Figure 11.2 for a screenshot of this page displayed in the Chrome (left screenshot) and Internet Explorer (right screenshot) browsers. If you see warning messages when the object element is used to play media, click through the warning message and consider consulting your network administrator or lab support staff for recommended security settings and/or plug-in installation.

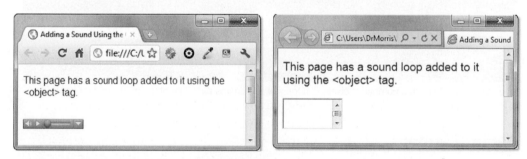

Figure 11.2 The Google Chrome browser (left screenshot) correctly renders the multimedia object; the Internet Explorer browser (right screenshot) does not properly configure the object

Review Figure 11.2. Notice that the Chrome browser (left screenshot) correctly renders the object element and displays a media player for the MP3. However, even though the

XHTML is valid and satisfies W3C recommendations, Internet Explorer (right screenshot) does not properly configure the object. Don't worry, there is a solution for this issue: Configure another object element that only Internet Explorer will process. This technique is described by Elizabeth Castro in "Bye Bye Embed" (http://www.alistapart.com/articles/byebyeembed).

Internet Explorer requires the `classid` attribute (to indicate the player's ActiveX control) and its associated `codebase` attribute in order to properly render an object element configured for audio or video files. The code to play an audio file with QuickTime within Internet Explorer is

```
<object data="soundloop.mp3" height="50" width="100"
    type="audio/mpeg"
    classid="clsid:02BF25D5-8C17-4B23-BC80-D3488ABDDC6B"
    codebase="http://www.apple.com/qtactivex/qtplugin.cab">
  <param name="src" value="soundloop.mp3" />
  <param name="controller" value="true" />
  <param name="autoplay" value="false" />
</object>
```

Castro describes a technique in her article that uses *both* `<object>` tags, along with conditional comments (which only Internet Explorer follows), to direct non-Internet Explorer browsers to the standard code. The solution (see chapter11/music.html in the student files) is

```
<object data="soundloop.mp3" height="50" width="100"
type="audio/mpeg"
    classid="clsid:02BF25D5-8C17-4B23-BC80-D3488ABDDC6B"
    codebase="http://www.apple.com/qtactivex/qtplugin.cab">
  <param name="src" value="soundloop.mp3" />
  <param name="controller" value="true" />
  <param name="autoplay" value="false" />
  <!--[if !IE]>-->
    <object data="soundloop.mp3" height="50" width="100"
    type="audio/mpeg">
      <param name="src" value="soundloop.mp3" />
      <param name="controller" value="true" />
      <param name="autoplay" value="false" />
    </object>
  <!--<![endif]-->
</object>
```

Browsers render in a top-down, line-by-line manner. Only Internet Explorer understands the conditional comments. In this case, the conditional comment indicates that Internet Explorer should ignore the code within the comments. The conditional comment begins with `<!--[if !IE]>-->` and ends with `<!--<![endif]-->`. So, Internet Explorer will render the first `<object>` tag and skip the second, while other browsers will process one after another (within the same area in the browser viewport) and render using the code from the second `<object>` tag. If this sounds complicated, it is! Life would be so much less complex if browsers behaved in a more similar manner. You'll get some experience with the object element in the next Hands-On Practice.

Hands-On Practice 11.2

In this Hands-On Practice, you will create a web page that displays a controller to play a sound (see Figure 11.3). Copy the music1.mp3 audio file from the student files (chapter11/music1.mp3) and save the file in a folder named music. Launch a text editor and open the XHTML web page template found in the student files (chapter2/templatex.html).

1. Configure a relevant page title.

2. Code an h1 element with the text "Playing Sounds with the Object Tag".

3. Use the `<object>` tag and `<param />` tag to configure a console that lets the web page visitor control the audio file. Use the previous code and the list of attributes and values in Table 11.3 and Table 11.4 as a guide. Save your web page as objectaudio.html in the music folder and test it in a browser.

4. Experiment with the object element's width attribute: Try the values 25, 50, 100, and 110, and notice how the display of the controller changes. Explore the param element's `autoplay` value to configure the sound to automatically play when the page loads. Use the param element's `loop` value to cause the sound to loop continuously. Test your web page in different browsers, using different versions. Compare your work to chapter11/object.html in the student files.

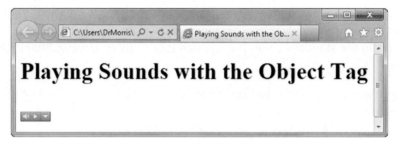

Figure 11.3 This page uses the object element with width="50"

FAQ   How can I make a podcast?

Podcasts are audio files on the web that may take the format of an audio blog, radio show, or interview. There are three steps in publishing a podcast:

1. **Record the podcast.** The Windows and Mac operating systems contain audio recording utilities. Apple's Quicktime Pro (available at http://apple.com/quicktime/pro for both Windows and Mac) is a low-cost application that can be used to record audio. If you are using a Mac, another option is Apple's GarageBand, which is a pre-installed music application that offers a range of options for recording and editing audio. Audacity is a free cross-platform digital audio editor (available at http://audacity.sourceforge.net for both Windows and Mac). You can use Audacity to record your voice for a podcast and mix in music loops to add interest. Once the WAV file is created, the LAME encoder (http://lame.sourceforge.net) or a similar application can be used to convert to an MP3 format.

2. **Upload the podcast.** Upload the MP3 to your website. If your web host does not permit MP3 files, an alternative is to upload to a site that accepts audio files at no cost such as Internet Archive (http://www.archive.org) or OurMedia (http://ourmedia.org).

3. **Make the podcast available.** The most straightforward method is to code a hyperlink to the audio file. The hyperlink allows website visitors to access the podcast MP3 file, but does

not make the podcast available for subscription. An RSS feed must be created in order for your visitors to subscribe to your current and future podcasts. An RSS feed for a podcast is an XML file that lists information about your podcast. With a bit of patience, you can code your own RSS feed using a text editor (see Stephen Downes's website at http://www.downes.ca/cgi-bin/page.cgi?post=56 or Robin Good's website at http://www.masternewmedia.org/news/2006/03/09/how_to_create_a_rss.htm). However, a number of websites, such as FeedBurner (http://feedburner.google.com), and IceRocket (http://rss.icerocket.com), provide a service that generates and hosts the RSS feed for you. After the RSS feed is uploaded to the Web (either your own or the RSS feed generator's site), you can code a link to the RSS file. Apple provides instructions for submitting your podcast to iTunes at http://apple.com/itunes/whatson/podcasts/specs.html. Web visitors using software such as Apple's iTunes or a free RSS feed reader website such as FeedReader3 (http://feedreader.com) can locate and automatically download your podcast.

Video on a Web Page

Embedding video using an object element and param element is similar to embedding audio in a web page. Refer to the previous section for an overview of these elements. The code in this section uses XHTML syntax. Keep in mind that the object and param elements may also be used in HTML5, although HTML5 introduces new audio and video elements that you'll explore in the next section. A sample page using the object element to display a video can be found in the student files (chapter11/video.html) and is shown in Figure 11.4.

The page was created using Castro's technique (http://www.alistapart.com/articles/byebyeembed) of coding two <object> tags and using Internet Explorer conditional comments. The code to play the sparky.mov video with QuickTime is

Figure 11.4 Playing a video file

```
<object data="sparky.mov" height="150" width="160"
    type="video/quicktime"
    classid="clsid:02BF25D5—8C17—4B23-BC80-D3488ABDDC6B"
    codebase="http://www.apple.com/qtactivex/qtplugin.cab"
    title="Video of a cute Pekingese dog barking">
  <param name="src" value="sparky.mov" />
  <param name="controller" value="true" />
  <param name="autoplay" value="false" />
<!--[if !IE]>-->
  <object data="sparky.mov" height="150" width="160"
    type="video/quicktime"
        title="Video of a cute Pekingese dog barking">
    <param name="src" value="sparky.mov" />
    <param name="controller" value="true" />
    <param name="autoplay" value="false" />
    <p>A video of a cute Pekingese dog barking.</p>
  </object>
<!--<![endif]-->
</object>
```

Depending on your browser plug-ins, the video may not display on this page using the `<object>` tag. The sample pages were tested using the QuickTime plug-in for MOV files. This plug-in issue can be a problem for video components. Testing with your target audience in mind, as well as giving your visitors hints on the most appropriate plug-ins, will help.

What happens if a browser or other user agent cannot display the video? Carefully review the code and notice that there is a descriptive phrase coded before each closing `</object>` tag. This phrase will display on the web page if the object (in this case, the video player) cannot be rendered. Also, to help provide accessibility, the title attribute has been configured with a brief text description of the video. This area will be read by some assistive technologies such as screen readers.

 Hands-On Practice 11.3

In this Hands-On Practice, you will create the web page shown in Figure 11.5, which uses the object and param elements to play a video clip for a web page visitor. Copy the lighthouse.mov file from the chapter11 folder in the student files and save the file in a folder named movie. Launch a text editor and open the XHTML web page template found in the student files (chatper2/templatex.html).

1. Configure a relevant page title.

2. Code an h1 element with the text "Door County Lighthouse Tours".

3. Use the `<object>` tag and `<param />` tag to configure a console that lets the web page visitor control the audio file. Use the previous code and the list of attributes and values in Table 11.3 and Table 11.4 as a guide. Save your web page as objectvideo.html in the movie folder and test it in a browser.

4. Experiment with the object element's height and width attributes. Explore the param element's `autoplay` and `loop` attributes. Test your web page in different browsers, using different versions. Compare your work to the student files (chapter11/lighthouse.html).

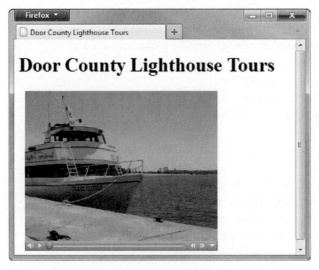

Figure 11.5 Using the `<object>` tag to embed video

Working with Multimedia on the Web

More About Audio Files

There are a number of ways that you can obtain audio files. You can record your own sounds, download sounds or music from a free site, record music from a CD, or purchase a DVD of sounds. There are some ethical issues related to using sounds and music created by others. You may only publish sounds or music that you have created yourself or for which you have obtained the rights (sometimes called a license) to publish. When you purchase a CD or DVD, you have not purchased the rights for publishing to the Web. Contact the owner of the copyright to request permission to use the music.

Focus on Ethics

There are many sources of audio files on the Web. Some offer free files, such as Microsoft's Clip Art and Media (http://office.microsoft.com/clipart), Loopasonic (http://www.loopasonic.com), and FreeAudioClips.com (http://www.freeaudioclips.com). Others, like SoundRangers (http://www.soundrangers.com), may offer one or two free sounds, but ultimately they are in the business of selling soundtracks and CDs. An interesting resource for free sound is the Flash Kit site (http://www.flashkit.com); click on the Sound Loops link. While this site is intended for Adobe Flash developers, the sound files can be used without Flash.

Audio files can be quite large and it is important to be aware of the amount of time required to download them for play. If you decide to use an audio file on a web page, make it as brief as possible. If you are recording your own audio files, be aware that the sampling rate and bit depth will affect the file size. A **sampling rate** is a value related to the number of digital sound samples taken per second when the sound is recorded. It is measured in kilohertz (kHz). Common sampling rates vary from 8 kHz (AM radio quality sound or sound effects) to 44.1 kHz (music CD quality sound). As you would expect, a sound recorded at 44.1 kHz has a much larger file size than a sound recorded at 8 kHz. Bit depth or resolution is another factor in audio file size. A sound recorded with 8-bit resolution (useful for a voice or other simple sounds) will have a smaller file size than a sound recorded using 16-bit resolution (music CD quality).

The Windows and Mac operating systems contain audio recording utilities. Audacity is a free cross-platform digital audio editor (available at http://audacity.sourceforge.net for both Windows and Mac). Apple's Quicktime Pro (available at http://apple.com/quicktime/pro for both Windows and Mac) is a low-cost application that can be used to record audio. If you are using a Mac, another option is Apple's GarageBand, which is a low-cost music application that offers a range of options for recording and editing audio. Apple provides tutorials and documentation for GarageBand (see http://www.apple.com/support/garageband/podcasts/recording for a tutorial about podcasting with GarageBand).

More About Video Files

Just as with audio files, there are a number of ways that you can obtain video files, including recording your own, downloading videos, purchasing a DVD that contains videos, or searching for video files on the Web. Be aware that there are ethical issues related to using videos that you did not create yourself. You must obtain the rights or license to publish videos created by other individuals before publishing them on your website.

Focus on Ethics

Many digital cameras have the capability to take still photographs as well as short MP4 movies. This can be an easy way to create short video clips. Digital video cameras and webcams record digital videos. Once you have created your video, software such as Adobe Premiere (http://www.adobe.com/products/premiere), Apple QuickTime Pro (http://www.apple.com/quicktime/pro), Apple iMovie (http://www.apple.com/ilife/imovie), or Microsoft Movie Maker (http://windows.microsoft.com/en-US/windows7/products/features/movie-maker/) can be used to edit and configure your video masterpiece. Many digital cameras and smartphones provide the ability record to videos and immediately upload them to YouTube to share with the world. You'll work with a YouTube video in Chapter 13.

Multimedia and Accessibility Issues

Focus on Accessibility

Provide alternate content for the media files you use on your website in transcript, caption, or printable PDF format. Provide a text transcript for audio files such as podcasts. Often, you can use the podcast script as the basis of the text transcript file that you create as a PDF and upload to your website. Provide captions for video files. Applications such as Media Access Generator (MAGpie) can add captioning to videos. See the National Center for Accessible Media's website (http://ncam.wgbh.org/webaccess/magpie) for the most up-to-date information on the application. Apple QuickTime Pro includes a captioning function. View an example of a captioned video in the student files (chapter11/starters/sparkycaptioned.mov). When you upload a video to YouTube (http://www.youtube.com), captions are automatically generated (although you'll probably want to make some corrections). You can also create a transcript or text captions for an existing YouTube video (see http://www.google.com/support/youtube/bin/answer.py?answer=100077). Visit WebAIM (http://webaim.org/techniques/captions) for more information about video captioning.

Browser Compatibility Issues

As you completed the Hands-On Practice, you may have encountered playback issues in various browsers. Playing audio and video files on the Web depends on the plug-ins installed in your visitor's web browsers. A page that works perfectly on your home computer may not work for all visitors; it depends on the configuration of the computer. Some visitors will not have the plug-ins properly installed. Some visitors may have file types associated with incorrect plug-ins or incorrectly installed plug-ins. Some visitors may be using low bandwidth and have to wait an overly long time for your media file to download. Are you detecting a pattern here? Sometimes media on the Web can be problematic.

In a response to these browser plug-in compatibility issues and in an effort to reduce reliance on a proprietary technology like Adobe Flash, HTML5 introduces new audio and video elements that are native to the browser. However, because HTML5 is not yet supported by commonly used browsers (such as older versions of Internet Explorer), web designers still need to provide a fallback option, such as providing a hyperlink to the media file or displaying a Flash version of the multimedia. You'll work with HTML5 audio and video later in this chapter, but first, let's explore Adobe Flash.

11.4 Adobe Flash

Adobe Flash is a popular application used to create multimedia that adds visual interest and interactivity to web pages with slide shows, animation, and multimedia effects.

Flash animation is stored in a file with a **.swf** file extension. Unlike other media, SWF files play as they download and give the perception of speedy display of complex graphic animation. The animation can be as simple as the Flash effect shown in Figure 11.6 (see chapter11/flash1.html in the student files). Flash can also be used to play audio and video files, and to create many more complex effects, including full-screen animation, banner ads, and interactive site navigation using integrated audio clips. Flash animation can be interactive; it can be scripted, with a language called ActionScript, to respond to mouse clicks, accept information in text boxes, and invoke server-side scripting.

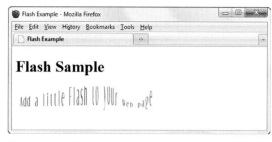

Figure 11.6 This web page displays a Flash SWF file

Flash requires a browser plug-in, which is free and readily available for download from Adobe. According to Adobe, 99% of Internet-enabled desktops have a Flash plug-in installed (http://adobe.com/products/player_census/flashplayer). Recall that playing standard format audio and video files on web pages is extremely dependent on the browser plug-ins that visitors have installed. There was increased use of Adobe Flash technology to play audio and video files on web pages until the Apple iPhone and iPad were released without Flash support. However, Flash is supported by other mobile devices such as Android tablets, Android smartphones, and RIM's Blackberry Playbook.

Flash can be used to create interactive ads on web pages that respond to a visitor's mouse movements with sound and animation. The results of a study by DoubleClick (http://static.googleusercontent.com/external_content/untrusted_dlcp/ www.google.com/en/us/doubleclick/pdfs/DoubleClick-06-2009-The-Brand-Value-of-Rich-Media-and-Video-Ads.pdf) about the value of rich media ads indicated that rich media (such as Flash with video) increases brand awareness, brand favorability, and purchase intent significantly more than other types of ads such as plain image ads or simple Flash banners. Flash can also be used to create entire websites, including navigation, content, and forms. A compelling example is 2Advanced Studios (http://2advanced.com). All the interactivity—navigation, animation, and content—is coded in the Flash SWF file.

Adobe licenses the Adobe Flash file format to third-party developers. This means that you can use applications other than Adobe Flash to create a Flash (SWF file) effect. TechSmith's Camtasia (http://www.techsmith.com) and SWiSH (http://www.swishzone.com) are just two of the third-party tools that can be used to create media in the SWF format.

Today's web developer needs to know how to add a Flash SWF file to a web page. If you are working on a large project, a graphic designer may create the effect and pass it to you for placement on a page. If you are working on a small project, you may be expected to create Flash SWF files yourself. Adobe offers a free trial download of the Flash application, including a few tutorials and lessons on using Flash.

Flash Animation on a Web Page

Modern desktop browsers support the display of Flash media with the object and param elements. As previously discussed, the object element is a multipurpose tag for adding various types of objects to a web page. The object element's attributes vary, depending on the type of object being referenced. The minimum attributes required when working with Flash media are described in Table 11.5.

Table 11.5 Minimal Flash media attributes

Attribute	Description and Value
accesskey	Optional; specifies a hotkey for keyboard access: Windows users press the hotkey and the Ctrl key at the same time
type	The MIME type of the object; use `type="application/x-shockwave-flash"`
data	File name of the Flash media (SWF file)
height	Specifies the height of the object area in pixels
tabindex	Optional; a numeric value that specifies the tabbing order of the Flash media
title	Optional; specifies a brief text description that may be displayed by browsers or assistive technologies
width	Specifies the width of the object area in pixels

The Flash object uses special values, called parameters, to configure the name of the SWF file, the quality of the media, and the background color of the page areas. These are configured with `<param>` tags. The parameters used with Flash media are shown in Table 11.6.

Table 11.6 Flash media parameters

Parameter	Description and Value
movie	File name of the Flash media (SWF file)
quality	Optional; describes the quality of the media; usually the value "high" is used
bgcolor	Optional; background color of the Flash media area; uses a hexadecimal color value
loop	Optional; indicates whether the SWF loops; values are "true" and "false"
wmode	Optional; configures the transparent background of the Flash media area in browsers that support this feature; the value is "transparent"

The following code configures the Flash SWF file shown in Figure 11.6:

```
<object type="application/x-shockwave-flash" data="flashlogo.swf"
    width="300" height="70">
    <param name="movie" value="flashlogo.swf">
    <param name="bgcolor" value="#ffffff">
    <param name="quality" value="high">
    <p>Add a little Flash to your web page.</p>
</object>
```

Notice the code placed before the closing `</object>` tag in the previous example. It is displayed if the browser does not support the multimedia object. Include a link to a web page that contains alternate text content if needed. While the developers of assistive technologies such as screen readers are working toward the support of Flash media, it is not yet universal.

Hands-On Practice 11.4

In this Hands-On Practice, you will create a web page that displays a Flash slide show of photographs. Your web page will look like the one shown in Figure 11.7.

Figure 11.7 Flash slide show of images

Let's get started. Create a folder called lighthouse. Copy the lighthouse.swf file from the student files (chapter11/starters folder) and save it in your lighthouse folder. Use the chapter2/template.html file as a starting point and create a web page with the heading "Door County Lighthouse Cruise" and the appropriate object and param elements to display a Flash file named lighthouse.swf, which is 320 pixels wide and 240 pixels high.

The code is

```
<object type="application/x-shockwave-flash" data="lighthouse.swf"
    width="320" height="240" title="Door County Lighthouse Cruise">
    <param name="movie" value="lighthouse.swf">
    <param name="bgcolor" value="#ffffff">
    <param name="quality" value="high">
    <p>Door County Lighthouse Cruise</p>
</object>
```

Save your web page as lighthouse2.html and test it in a browser. Compare your work to the student files(chapter11/lighthouse/lighthouse.html).

HTML5 Embed Element

Although used for many years to configure media and Flash on web pages, the embed element was never an official W3C element until HTML5. One of the design principles of HTML5 is to "pave the cowpaths," meaning to smooth the way for the valid use of techniques that, although supported by browsers, were not part of the official W3C standard. Figure 11.8 (see chapter11/flashembed.html in the student files) shows a web page using an embed element to display a Flash SWF file.

Figure 11.8 The embed element was used to configure the Flash media

The **embed element** is a self-contained, or void, element that provides a way to add content that requires a plug-in or player to a web page. The embed element can be used to display a Flash SWF file on a web page. The attributes of the embed element commonly used with Flash media are listed in Table 11.7.

Table 11.7 Embed element attributes

Attribute	Description and Value
`src`	File name of the Flash media (SWF file)
`height`	Specifies the height of the object area in pixels
`type`	The MIME type of the object; use `type="application/x-shockwave-flash"`
`width`	Specifies the width of the object area in pixels
`bgcolor`	Optional; hexadecimal value for the background color of the Flash
`quality`	Optional; describes the quality of the media, usually set to "high"
`title`	Optional; specifies a brief text description that may be displayed by browsers or assistive technologies
`wmode`	Optional; set to "transparent" to configure a transparent background in supporting browsers

The following code configures the Flash SWF file shown in Figure 11.7:

```
<embed type="application/x-shockwave-flash"
       src="fall5.swf"
       width="640"
       height="100"
       quality="high"
       title="Fall Nature Hikes">
```

Focus on Accessibility

Notice the value of the title attribute in the previous code. The descriptive text could be accessed by assistive technologies such as a screen reader.

Hands-On Practice 11.5

In this Hands-On Practice, you will launch a text editor and create a web page that displays a Flash slide show of photographs. Your web page will look like the one shown in Figure 11.9.

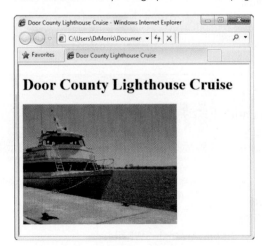

Figure 11.9 Flash slide show of images configured with the embed element

Create a folder called embed. Copy the lighthouse.swf file from the student files (chapter11/starters folder) and save it in your embed folder. Use the chapter2/template.html file as a starting point and create a web page with the heading "Door County Lighthouse Cruise" and an embed element to display a Flash file named lighthouse.swf that is 320 pixels wide and 240 pixels high. The code is

```
<embed type="application/x-shockwave-flash"
       src="lighthouse.swf" quality="high"
       width="320" height="240"
       title="Door County Lighthouse Cruise">
```

Save your web page as index.html in the embed folder and test it in a browser. Compare your work to chapter11/lighthouse/embed.html in the student files.

Flash Resources

There are many sources of free Flash animation and Flash tutorials on the Web. In addition to resources at the Adobe site (http://adobe.com), the following websites contain tutorials and news about Flash:

- Flash Kit: http://flashkit.com

- ActionScript: http://www.actionscript.org

- ScriptOcean: http://www.scriptocean.com/flashn.html

- Kirupa: http://www.kirupa.com/developer/flash/index.htm

As you visit these and other Flash resource sites, keep in mind that some Flash media is copyrighted. Obtain permission from the creator of the media before using it on your site and follow any instructions for giving credit to the source. Some sites allow personal use of their Flash media for free, but require licenses for commercial use.

Focus on Ethics

Adobe has been working toward increasing the accessibility of Flash objects. Recent versions of Flash are accessible to assistive technologies, such as the Window-Eyes screen reader, enabling rich content for a wider audience of web page visitors. Flash supports Microsoft Active Accessibility (MSAA), which provides both a standard method for client technology to communicate with assistive technologies and a technique for developers to use to ensure that the client software that they create in compliance with this standard can include Adobe Flash support. Visit Adobe's website (http://www.adobe.com/accessibility/products/flash) for the most up-to-date information on the issue of Flash accessibility.

Focus on Accessibility

 FAQ   **What's Microsoft Silverlight?**

Silverlight (http://www.silverlight.net) is a plug-in for delivering media experiences and rich interactive applications for the Web. Microsoft Expression Blend is an application that creates interactive media for display by the Silverlight plug-in.

FAQ **What will happen if the browser my web page visitor uses does not support Flash?**

If you used the code in this section to display Flash media on a web page and your visitor's browser does not support Flash, the browser typically will display a message about the need for a missing plug-in. The code in this section passes W3C validation and is the minimum code needed to display Flash media on a web page. If you'd like more features, such as being able to offer an express installation of the latest Flash player to your visitors, explore SWFObject (http://code.google.com/p/swfobject/wiki/documentation), which uses JavaScript to embed Flash content and is W3C standards compliant.

At the time this was written, there was no Flash support for the iPhone, iTouch, or iPad; however, these devices have been configured to support the new HTML5 audio and video elements that are introduced in the next section.

Checkpoint 11.1

1. List three common web browser plug-ins and describe their use.

2. Describe the issues involved with adding media such as audio or video to a web page.

3. Describe a disadvantage of using Flash on a web page.

11.5 HTML5 Audio and Video Elements

The new HTML5 audio and video elements enable browsers to natively play media files without the need for browser plug-ins. When working with native HTML5 audio and video, you need to be aware of the **container** (which is designated by the file extension) and the **codec** (which is the algorithm used to compress the media). Refer to Table 11.1 and Table 11.2, which list common media file extensions, the container file type, and a description with codec information (if applicable for HTML5). If this were a perfect world, all browsers would support all media codecs. Well, it's not perfect and there is no single codec that is supported by all popular browsers. For example, the H.264 codec requires licensing fees and is not supported by the Firefox and Opera web browsers, which support OGG and WebM. Internet Explorer and Safari support the H.264 video, but do not support OGG or WebM. At the time this was written, the Google Chrome browser supported H.264, OGG, and WebM, but planned to drop support of H.264 in the future. See http://www.ibm.com/developerworks/web/library/wa-html5video/index.html?ca= drs-#table2 for an up-to-date browser compatibility chart. When you work with HTML5 audio and video, you'll need to offer multiple versions of the media file in various containers/codecs. Let's get started using the HTML5 audio element.

Audio Element

The new HTML5 **audio element** supports native play of audio files in the browser without the need for plug-ins or players. The audio element begins with the `<audio>` tag and ends with the `</audio>` tag. Table 11.8 lists the attributes of the audio element.

Table 11.8 Audio element attributes

Attribute	Value	Usage
src	File name	Optional; audio file name
type	MIME type	Optional; the MIME type of the audio file, such as audio/mpeg or audio/ogg
autoplay	autoplay	Optional; indicates whether audio should start playing automatically; use with caution
controls	controls	Optional; indicates whether controls should be displayed; recommended
loop	loop	Optional; indicates whether audio should be played over and over
preload	none, metadata, auto	Optional; values: none (no preload), metadata (only download media file metadata), and auto (download the media file)
title	Text description	Optional; specifies a brief text description that may be displayed by browsers or assistive technologies

You'll need to supply multiple versions of the audio file because of the browser support of different codecs. Plan to supply audio files in at least two different containers, including OGG and MP3. It is typical to omit the src and type attributes from the audio tag and, instead, configure multiple versions of the audio file with the source element.

Source Element

The **source element** is a self-contained, or void, tag that specifies a media file and a MIME type. The src attribute identifies the file name of the media file. The type attribute indicates the MIME type of the file. Code type="audio/mpeg" for an MP3 file. Code type="audio/ogg" for audio files using the Vorbis codec. Configure a source element for each version of the audio file. Place the source element before the closing audio tag.

HTML5 Audio on a Web Page

The following code configures the web page shown in Figure 11.10 (see chapter11/audio. html in the student files) to display a controller for an audio file:

```
<audio controls="controls">
   <source src="soundloop.mp3" type="audio/mpeg">
   <source src="soundloop.ogg" type="audio/ogg">
   <a href="soundloop.mp3">Download the Audio File</a> (MP3)
</audio>
```

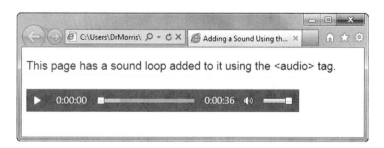

Figure 11.10
Internet Explorer 9 supports the HTML5 audio element

Current versions of Safari, Chrome, Firefox, and Opera also support the HTML5 audio element. While Internet Explorer 9 supports the audio element, earlier versions of Internet Explorer offer no support. The controls displayed by each browser are different.

Review the previous code and note the hyperlink placed between the second source element and the closing audio tag. Any HTML elements or text placed in this area is rendered by browsers that do not support the HTML5 audio element. This is referred to as fallback content; if the audio element is not supported, the MP3 version of the file is made available for download. Figure 11.11 shows a screen shot of Internet Explorer 8 displaying the web page.

Figure 11.11 Internet Explorer 8 does not recognize the audio element

 ## Hands-On Practice 11.6

In this Hands-On Practice, you will launch a text editor and create a web page (see Figure 11.12) that displays an audio control to play a podcast.

Figure 11.12 Using the audio element to provide access to a podcast

Copy the podcast.mp3, podcast.ogg, and podcast.txt files from the chapter11/starters folder in the student files and save them to a folder named audio5. Use the chapter2/template.html file as a starting point and create a web page with the heading "Web Design Podcast", an audio control (use the audio element and two source elements), and a hyperlink to the text transcript. Configure a hyperlink to the MP3 file as the fallback content. The code for the audio element is

```
<audio controls="controls">
  <source src="podcast.mp3" type="audio/mpeg">
  <source src="podcast.ogg" type="audio/ogg">
  <a href="podcast.mp3">Download the Podcast</a> (MP3)
</audio>
```

Save your web page as index.html in the audio5 folder and display it in a browser. Test your web page in different browsers, using different versions. Recall that Internet Explorer versions prior to Version 9 do not support the audio element, but they will display the fallback content. When you click on the hyperlink for the text transcript, the text will display in the browser. Compare your work to chapter11/podcast/podcast5.html in the student files.

FAQ   **How can I convert an audio file to the Ogg Vorbis codec?**

The open-source Audacity application supports Ogg Vorbis. See http://audacity.sourceforge.net for download information. If you're looking for a free Web-based converter, you can upload and share an audio file at the Internet Archive (http://www.archive.org) and an OGG format file will automatically be generated.

Video Element

The new HTML5 **video element** supports native play of video files in the browser without the need for plug-ins or players. The video element begins with the `<video>` tag and ends with the `</video>` tag. Table 11.9 lists the attributes of the video element.

Table 11.9 Video element attributes

Attribute	Value	Usage
src	File name	Optional; video file name
type	MIME type	Optional; the MIME type of the video file, such as video/mp4 or video/ogg
autoplay	autoplay	Optional; indicates whether video should start playing automatically; use with caution
controls	controls	Optional; indicates whether controls should be displayed; recommended
height	number	Optional; video height in pixels
loop	loop	Optional; indicates whether video should be played over and over
poster	File name	Optional; specifies an image to display if the browser cannot play the video
preload	none, metadata, auto	Optional; values: none (no preload), metadata (only download media file metadata), and auto (download the media file)
title	Text description	Optional; specifies a brief text description that may be displayed by browsers or assistive technologies
width	Number	Optional; video width in pixels

You'll need to supply multiple versions of the video file because of the browser support of different codecs. Plan to supply video files in at least two different containers, including MP4 and OGG (or OGV). It is typical to omit the `src` and `type` attributes from the video tag and, instead, configure multiple versions of the audio file with the source element.

Source Element

Recall from the previous section that the **source element** is a self-contained, or void, tag that specifies a media file and a MIME type. The `src` attribute identifies the file name of the media file. The `type` attribute indicates the MIME type of the file. Code `type="video/mp4"` for video files using the MP4 codec. Code `type="video/ogg"` for video files using the Theora codec. Configure a source element for each version of the video file. Place the source elements before the closing video tag.

Figure 11.13 The Opera browser

HTML5 Video on a Web Page

The following code configures the web page shown in Figure 11.13 (chapter11/sparky2.html in the student files) with the native HTML5 browser controls to display and play a video:

```
<video controls="controls" poster="sparky.jpg"
width="160" height="150">
   <source src="sparky.m4v" type="video/mp4">
   <source src="sparky.ogv" type="video/ogg">
   <a href="sparky.mov">Sparky the Dog</a> (.mov)
</video>
```

Figure 11.14 Internet Explorer 8 displays the fallback option

Current versions of Safari, Chrome, Firefox, and Opera support the HTML5 video element. Internet Explorer 9 supports the video element, but earlier versions do not. The controls displayed by each browser are different. Review the code just given and note the anchor element placed between the second source element and the closing video tag. Any HTML elements or text placed in this area is rendered by browsers that do not support the HTML5 video element. This is referred to as fallback content. In this case, a hyperlink to a QuickTime (.mov) version of the file is supplied for the user to download. Another fallback option is to configure an embed element to play a Flash SWF version of the video. Figure 11.14 shows Internet Explorer 8 displaying the web page.

VideoNote
HTML5 Video

Hands-On Practice 11.7

In this Hands-On Practice, you will launch a text editor and create the web page in Figure 11.15, which displays a video control to play a movie.

Figure 11.15 HTML5 video element

Copy the lighthouse.m4v, lighthouse.ogv, lighthouse.swf, and lighthouse.jpg files from the chapter11/starters folder in the student files and save them to a folder named video. Open chapter2/template.html in a text editor and configure a web page with the heading "Lighthouse Cruise" and a video control (use the video element and two source elements). While we could configure a hyperlink to a video file as fallback content, in this example, we'll configure an embed element to display the Flash media file (lighthouse.swf) as fallback content. Configure the lighthouse.jpg file as a poster image, which will display if the browser supports the video element, but it cannot play any of the video files. The code for the video element is

```
<video controls="controls" poster="lighthouse.jpg" width="320"
height="240">
  <source src="lighthouse.m4v" type="video/mp4">
  <source src="lighthouse.ogv" type="video/ogg">
  <embed type="application/x-shockwave-flash"
    src="lighthouse.swf" quality="high" width="320" height="240"
    title="Door County Lighthouse Cruise">
</video>
```

Save your web page as index.html in the video folder and display it in a browser. Test your web page in different browsers. Compare your work to Figure 11.15 and chapter11/video/video.html in the student files.

FAQ **How can I convert a video file to the new codecs?**

You can use Firefogg (http://firefogg.org) to convert your video file to the Ogg Theora codec. Online-Convert offers free conversion to WebM (http://video.online-convert.com/convert-to-webm). The free, open-source MiroVideoConverter (http://www.mirovideoconverter.com) can convert most video files to MP4, WebM, or OGG formats.

11.6 Multimedia Files and Copyright Law

Focus on Ethics

It is very easy to copy and download an image, audio, or video file from a website. It may be very tempting to place someone else's file in one of your own projects, but that may not be ethical or lawful. Only publish web pages, images, and other media that you have personally created or have obtained the rights or license to use. If another individual has created an image, sound, video, or document that you think would be useful on your own website, ask permission to use the material instead of simply taking it. All work (web pages, images, sounds, videos, and so on) is copyrighted, even if there is no copyright symbol and date on the material.

Be aware that there are times when students and educators can use portions of another's work and not be in violation of copyright law. This is called **fair use**. Fair use is the use of a copyrighted work for purposes such as criticism, reporting, teaching, scholarship, or research. The criteria used to determine fair use are as follows:

- The use must be educational rather than commercial.
- The nature of the work copied should be factual rather than creative.
- The amount copied must be as small a portion of the work as possible.
- The copy does not impede the marketability of the original work.

Visit the U.S. Copright Office (http://copyright.gov) and Copyright Website (http://www.copyrightwebsite.com) for some additional information about copyright issues.

Some individuals may want to retain ownership of their work, but make it easy for others to use or adapt it. Creative Commons (http://creativecommons.org) provides a free service that allows authors and artists to register a type of copyright license called a **Creative Commons license**. There are several licenses to choose from, depending on the rights you wish to grant as the author. The Creative Commons license informs others exactly what they can and cannot do with the creative work.

11.7 CSS3 and Interactivity

CSS Image Gallery

Recall from Chapter 6 that the CSS `:hover` pseudo-class provides a way to configure styles to display when the web page visitor moves the mouse over an element. You'll use this basic interactivity, along with CSS positioning and display properties, to configure an interactive image gallery with CSS and HTML. Figure 11.16 shows the gallery in action (see chapter11/gallery/gallery.html in the student files). When you place the mouse over a thumbnail image, the larger version of the image is displayed, along with a caption. If you click on the thumbnail, the image displays in its own browser window.

Figure 11.16 An interactive image gallery with CSS

Waves Crashing in on the Coast

Hands-On Practice 11.8

In this Hands-On Practice, you will create the image gallery web page in Figure 11.16. Copy the following images from the chapter11/starters folder in the student files: photo1.jpg, photo2.jpg, photo3.jpg, photo4.jpg, photo5.jpg, photo6.jpg, photo1thumb.jpg, photo2thumb.jpg, photo3thumb.jpg, photo4thumb.jpg, photo5thumb.jpg, and photo6thumb.jpg. Save them to a folder named gallery.

Launch a text editor and modify chapter2/template.html to configure a web page as indicated:

1. Configure the text "Image Gallery" within an h1 element.

2. Code a div assigned to the id named gallery. This div will contain the thumbnail images.

3. Configure an unordered list within the div. Code six li elements, one for each thumbnail image. The thumbnail images will function as image links with a `:hover` pseudo-class that

causes the larger image to display on the page. We'll make this all happen by configuring a hyperlink element that contains both the thumbnail image and a span element that comprises the larger image, along with descriptive text. An example of the first li element is

```
<li><a href="photo1.jpg"><img src="photo1thumb.jpg"
width="100" height="75" alt="Golden Gate Bridge">
  <span><img src="photo1.jpg" width="400" height="300"
  alt="Golden Gate Bridge"><br>Golden Gate Bridge</span></a>
</li>
```

4. Configure all six li elements in a similar manner. Substitute the actual name of each image file for the href and src values in the code. Write your own descriptive text for each image. Use photo2.jpg and photo2thumb.jpg in the second li element. Use photo3.jpg and photo3thumb.jpg in the third li element, and so on. Save the file as index.html in the gallery folder. Display your web page in a browser. You'll see an unordered list with the thumbnail images, the larger images, and the descriptive text. Figure 11.17 shows a partial screen capture.

Figure 11.17 The web page display before CSS

5. Now, let's add embedded CSS. Open your file in a text editor and code a style element in the head section. The gallery id will use relative positioning. This does not change the location of the gallery, but instead sets the stage to use absolute positioning on the span element in relation to its container (#gallery) instead of in relation to the entire web page document. This won't matter too much for our very basic example, but it would be very helpful if the gallery was part of a more complex web page. Code embedded CSS to configure the gallery with relative positioning; the unordered list with a width of 300 pixels and no list marker; the list items with inline display, left float, and 10 pixels of padding; the images with no border;

the anchor tags with no underline, dark gray color (#333), and italic font; and the span to not display by default. The CSS is

```
#gallery { position: relative; }
#gallery ul { width: 300px;
              list-style-type: none; }
#gallery li { display: inline;
              float: left;
              padding: 10px; }
#gallery img { border-style: none; }
#gallery a { text-decoration: none;
             color: #333;
             font-style: italic; }
#gallery span {display: none; }
```

Next, configure the span to display *only* when the web visitor hovers the mouse over the thumbnail image link. Set the location of the span to use absolute positioning. Locate the span 10 pixels down from the top and 300 pixels in from the left. Center the text within the span:

```
#gallery a:hover span { display: block;
                        position: absolute;
                        top: 10px;
                        left: 300px;
                        text-align: center; }
```

Save your web page and display it in a browser. Your gallery should work well in modern browsers. Note that the outdated Internet Explorer 6 does not support the dynamic display of the larger image, but instead displays the unordered list and processes the thumbnail image links. Compare your work to Figure 11.16 and chapter11/gallery/gallery.html in the student files.

CSS3 Transform Property

CSS3 provides a method to change or transform the display of an element. The **transform** property allows you to rotate, scale, skew, or move an element. Both two-dimensional (2D) and three-dimensional (3D) transforms are possible. Transforms are often used in conjunction with the CSS3 transition property (introduced in the next section).

Developers of browser-rendering engines, such as WebKit (used by Safari and Google Chrome) and Gecko (used by Firefox and other Mozilla-based browsers), have created their own proprietary properties to implement the transform property. So, you need to code multiple style declarations to configure a transform:

- `-webkit-transform` (for Webkit browsers)
- `-moz-transform` (for Gecko browsers)
- `-o-transform` (for the Opera browser)
- `-ms-transform` (for Internet Explorer 9)
- `transform` (W3C draft syntax)

Eventually, all browsers will support CSS3 and the `transform` property, so code this property last in the list. The web page in Figure 11.18 (see chapter11/transform/transform.html in the student files) demonstrates the use of the CSS3 transform property to slightly rotate the figure. CSS is also used to configure a border, text caption, and box shadow for the div that contains the image.

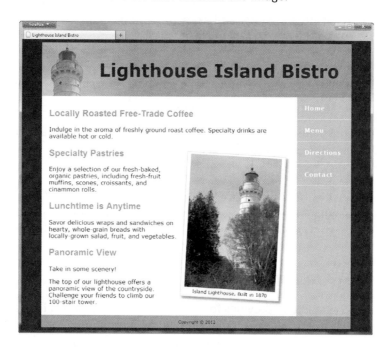

Figure 11.18 The transform property in action

Configuring a CSS3 Rotation Transform

The `rotate()` transform type takes a value in degrees (like an angle in geometry). Rotate to the right with a positive value. Rotate to the left with a negative value. The rotation is around the origin, which, by default, is the middle of the element. The following CSS code first configures a class named figure to float to the right, with a 260 pixel width; 20 pixel margin; 5 pixels of padding; a white background; a gray, solid 1 pixel border; and centered text 0.80em in size. CSS3 is configured next to rotate 3 degrees and apply a box shadow. The code is

```
.figure { float: right;
        width: 260px;
        margin: 20px;
        padding: 5px;
        background-color: #FFF;
        border: 1px solid #CCC;
        text-align: center;
        font-size: 0.80em;
        -webkit-transform: rotate(3deg);
        -moz-transform: rotate(3deg);
        -o-transform: rotate(3deg);
        -ms-transform: rotate(3deg);
        transform: rotate(3deg);
        -webkit-box-shadow: 5px 5px 5px #828282;
        -moz-box-shadow: 5px 5px 5px #828282;
        box-shadow: 5px 5px 5px #828282; }
```

Recall that the browser proprietary CSS syntax in this section is nonstandard. Your CSS code will not pass W3C validation when you use these properties.

This section provided an overview of one type of transform: the rotation of an element. Visit Westciv–Tools & Resources for Web Professionals http://www.westciv.com/tools/transforms/index.html to generate the CSS for rotate, scale, translate, and skew transforms.

For more information about the syntax used in transforms, visit the corresponding websites:

- **Webkit:** http://www.webkit.org/blog/130/css-transforms

- **Mozilla:** https://developer.mozilla.org/en/CSS/-moz-transform

- **Opera:** http://dev.opera.com/articles/view/css3-transitions-and-2d-transforms/#transforms

- **Internet Explorer:** http://msdn.microsoft.com/en-us/ie/ff468705.aspx#_CSS3_2D_Transforms

- **W3C:** http://www.w3.org/TR/css3-2d-transforms and http://www.w3.org/TR/css3-3d-transforms

CSS3 Transition Property

A CSS3 **transition** provides for changes in property values to display in a smoother manner over a specified time. Four different properties can be used with transitions: `transition-property`, `transition-duration`, `transition-timing-function`, and `transition-delay`. The properties can be combined in a single shorthand **transition property**. Table 11.10 lists the transition properties and their purpose.

Table 11.10 CSS transition properties

Property	Description
`transition-property`	Indicates the CSS property to which the transition applies; a list of applicable properties is available at http://www.w3.org/TR/css3-transitions
`transition-duration`	Indicates the length of time to apply the transition; a default value of 0 configures an immediate transition; otherwise, use a numeric value to specify time (usually in seconds)
`transition-timing-function`	Configures changes in the speed of the transition by describing how intermediate property values are calculated; common values include `ease` (default), `linear`, `ease-in`, `ease-out`, `ease-in-out`
`transition-delay`	Indicates the beginning of the transition; a default value of 0 configures no delay; otherwise, use a numeric value to specify time (usually in seconds)
`transition`	Shorthand property; list the value for `transition-property`, `transition-duration`, `transition-timing-function`, and `transition-delay` separated by spaces; default values can be omitted, but the first unit of time applies to `transition-duration`

Browser vendor prefixes are needed to configure transitions. Transitions are supported by current versions of most modern browsers. However, transitions are not currently supported by Internet Explorer. Code four style declarations to configure a transition:

- `-webkit-transition` (for Webkit browsers)
- `-moz-transition` (for Gecko browsers)
- `-o-transition` (for the Opera browser)
- `transition` (W3C draft syntax)

The web page in Figure 11.19 (see chapter11/gallery/transition.html in the student files) demonstrates the use of the CSS3 transition property to straighten the lighthouse photo when the web page visitor hovers over it with the mouse. Compare the position of the lighthouse photo in Figures 11.18 and 11.19 to see the result of the transition.

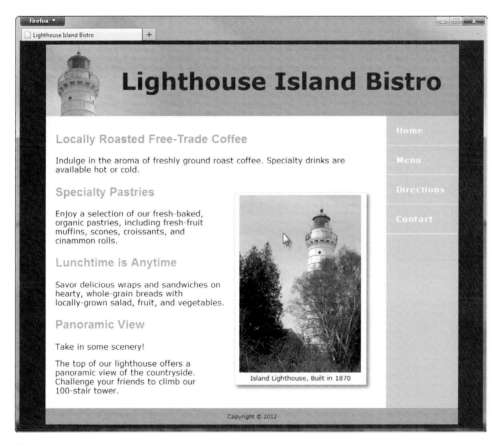

Figure 11.19 The interactive CSS3 transition effect

Configuring a CSS3 Transition

The transition was applied to the `transform` property and uses the shorthand `transition` property to configure a rotation back to 0 degrees in 1/2 second with smooth, linear timing. The key is to configure a style rule for the `.figure:hover` pseudo-class with a style declaration with the ending value of the `transform` property in addition to style declarations for the `transition` property. The new CSS code has a lot of repetition because of the browser vendor prefixes on the CSS3 properties:

```
.figure:hover { -webkit-transform: rotate(0deg);
               -moz-transform: rotate(0deg);
               -o-transform: rotate(0deg);
               transform: rotate(0deg);
               -webkit-transition: -webkit-transform .5s linear;
               -moz-transition: -moz-transform .5s linear;
               -o-transition: -o-transform .5s linear;
               transition: transform .5s linear; }
```

As shown in the previous code, the syntax for configuring transforms varies by browser engine. It is expected that eventually all browsers will support W3C `transition` syntax, so code this declaration last in the list. Recall that the browser proprietary CSS syntax in this section is nonstandard. Your CSS code will not pass W3C validation when you use these properties.

Hands-On Practice 11.9

In this Hands-On Practice, you will modify the web page shown in Figure 11.19 to also change the background color of the .figure class from white to light gray when a web page visitor hovers the mouse over the lighthouse photo. Create a folder named transition and copy the lighthouseisland.jpg and lighthouselogo.jpg files from the chapter11/starters folder in the student files. Launch a text editor and open transition.html, which is located in the chapter11/transform folder in the student files. Display the page in a browser and mouse over the lighthouseisland.jpg image. If your browser supports transitions, your display should be similar to Figure 11.19.

Edit the embedded CSS in the file and modify the `.figure:hover` selector to change the background color to #cccccc over a period of 1 second with ease-in timing. Notice how you can configure transitions for more than one property by separating them with a comma.

```
.figure:hover { background-color: #cccccc;
               -webkit-transform: rotate(0deg);
               -moz-transform: rotate(0deg);
               -o-transform: rotate(0deg);
               transform: rotate(0deg);
               -webkit-transition: -webkit-transform .5s linear,
                                   background-color 1s ease-in;
               -moz-transition: -moz-transform .5s linear,
                                background-color 1s ease-in;
               -o-transition: -o-transform .5s linear,
                              background-color 1s ease-in;
               transition: transform .5s linear,
                           background-color 1s ease-in; }
```

Save your file as index.html in your transition folder and test it in a browser that supports transitions. When you hover over the lighthouse photo, you still should see it rotate and you also should see the background color of the photo area change. A solution is available in the student files (chapter11/transform/transition2.html).

See the following resources for more examples of CSS transforms and transitions:

- CSS Transitions 101:
  http://www.webdesignerdepot.com/2010/01/css-transitions-101

- Using CSS Transforms and Transitions:
  http://return-true.com/2010/06/using-css-transforms-and-transitions

- CSS Fundamentals: CSS3 Transitions: http://net.tutsplus.com/tutorials/
  html-css-techniques/css-fundametals-css-3-transitions

11.8 Java

Java is an object-oriented programming (OOP) language developed by Sun Microsystems, which was later acquired by Oracle. An object-oriented program consists of a group of cooperating objects that exchange messages for the purpose of achieving a common objective. Java is not the same language as JavaScript. It is more powerful and much more flexible than JavaScript. Java can be used to develop both stand-alone executable applications and applets that are invoked by web pages.

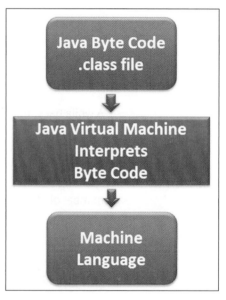

Java applets are platform independent, which means that they can be written and run on any platform: Mac, UNIX, Linux, and Windows. Java applets are compiled (translated from the English-like Java statements to an encoded form) and saved as **.class** files, which contain byte code. The byte code is interpreted by the **Java Virtual Machine (JVM)** in the web browser. The JVM interprets the byte code into the proper machine language for the operating system. The applet is then executed and appears on the web page. See Figure 11.20 for a diagram that shows this process. When a Java applet loads, the area reserved for it on the web page displays an empty rectangular area until the applet begins to execute.

Figure 11.20 The Java Virtual Machine interprets the byte code into machine language

Java applets can process interactive navigation bars on web pages. Visit Java Boutique (http://javaboutique.internet.com/navigation/menu.html) and Apycom (http://apycom.com) for a variety of navigation and menu Java applets. Online games are a popular use of Java applets; try some classic Java applet games at Java on the Brain (http://www.javaonthebrain.com/brain.html). Java applets can also be used to create image and text effects, such as the sample applet shown in Figure 11.21 (see chapter11/java1.html in the student files). While text effects and games are fun, the use of Java applets in business applications has been increasing for functions such as financial calculations and visualization. JARS (http://www.jars.com) provides a Java applet review service and describes applets that are useful in a business environment, such as NetCharts from Visual Mining (http://www.visualmining.com). This type of applet often connects to databases on a web server and can be a very powerful tool if you need to display live data visually. Java applets can perform a variety of functions on web pages. As a web developer, your usual role will not be that of a Java software developer—that is, you should not be expected to write Java applets. However, you could be asked to work with a Java developer to place his or her applet on your website. Whether you obtain an applet from a coworker or find one on a free site, you need to code HTML to display the applet.

Figure 11.21 A Java applet that provides changing text

Adding a Java Applet to a Web Page

A while back, the now-obsolete **applet** element was typically used along with the param element to configure a Java applet on a web page. The W3C recommends using the multipurpose object element to configure a Java applet on a web page. The `<object>` tag specifies the beginning of an applet area in the body of a web page. Its closing tag, `</object>`, specifies the ending of an applet area in the body of a web page. The object element has a number of attributes that are used with Java applets, as described in Table 11.11.

Table 11.11 Object element attributes used with Java applets

Attribute	Value
type	Specifies the MIME type of the Java applet: `application/x-java-applet`
height	Specifies the height of the applet area in pixels
width	Specifies the width of the applet area in pixels
title	Optional; brief text description that may be displayed by browsers or assistive technologies

The software developer who creates an applet determines the parameter values and names required by a specific Java applet. Therefore, expect each applet to require different parameters. Other parameter names and expected values will be provided in the applet documentation. The parameters will be different, depending on the function of the applet. One parameter might be used to set a background color; another parameter could be used to contain a person's name. Parameters are configured with the param element. The code parameter indicates the name of the Java applet.

Hands-On Practice 11.10

In this Hands-On Practice, you will launch a text editor and create a web page that contains a Java applet. This example will use the fader26 applet (provided by Johannes Schellen). This applet displays text messages one at a time. The list of text messages is obtained from a text file (.txt file extension) that you will create. An example of this applet at work can be found in the student files (chapter11/java1.html).

Let's get started. Create a folder called testapplet. Copy the applet file (fader26.class) from the chapter11 folder in the student files and save it in the testapplet folder. Do not change the name of the applet.

Whether you obtain an applet from a free website or from a coworker, each applet should have some accompanying documentation that indicates what parameter it expects. Documentation for the fader26 applet appears in Table 11.12.

Table 11.12 Documentation for fader26 applet

Parameter Name	Parameter Value
code	fader26.class
AppletHome	http://www.crosswinds.net/~fader
Data	The name of the text file that contains the message to be displayed; each line in the text file should begin with text=
bgColor	This is the background color of the Java applet area; uses a hexadecimal color value

Use the chapter2/template.html file as a starting point. Configure a web page with the heading "Java Applet" and the appropriate object and param elements to display a Java applet named fader26.class that is 610 pixels wide and 30 pixels high, has a white background (bgColor parameter), and accesses a text file named message.txt (Data parameter). Also provide a descriptive title and configure http://www.crosswinds.net/~fader as the value of the AppletHome parameter. The code is

```
<object type="application/x-java-applet" width="610" height="30"
title="This Java Applet displays a message that describes what Java
Applets can be used for.">
  <param name="code" value="fader26.class">
  <param name="AppletHome" value="http://www.crosswinds.net/~fader/">
  <param name="Data" value="message.txt">
  <param name="bgColor" value="#FFFFFF">
  Java Applets can be used to display text, manipulate graphics, play
games, and more.
  Visit <a href="http://download.oracle.com/javase/tutorial/">Oracle</a>
for more information.
</object>
```

Save the file in the testapplet folder with the file name java.html. You are not yet ready to test the page because you need to create and format the text file that the applet expects. This applet expects each line of text to begin with **text=**. Figure 11.22 shows a sample text file created using Notepad.

Use this as a guide to create your text file. Save your text file as message.txt in the testapplet folder. The name of the text file must match the value of the Data parameter in the HTML code.

Now launch your web page in a browser. The applet should display your text one line at a time (your browser may display a warning message about the fader26.class applet being created using an earlier version of Java—just click OK or Continue). Be aware that the disadvantage of using Java applets is the lag between the time that the web page is initially loaded and the time that the applet actually begins to execute. Your web page visitor will see a box in the area reserved for the applet until it begins executing.

Figure 11.22 This is the text file needed by the fader26 Java applet

FAQ   Why doesn't my Java applet work?

If your applet does not function as expected, verify the following:

- Are Java applets enabled in your browser?
- Is the applet saved in the testapplet folder?
- Is the applet saved with the name fader26.class (all letters must be lowercase)?
- Are the java.html and message.txt files saved in the testapplet folder?

Java Applet Resources

There are many resources for free and commercial Java applets on the Web. Here are a few helpful sites:

- Java on the Brain: http://www.javaonthebrain.com
- Java Applet Archive: http://www.echoecho.com/freeapplets.htm

Focus on Ethics

As you visit these and other Java resource sites, keep in mind that some Java applets are copyrighted. Be sure to obtain permission from the creator of the applet before using it on your site. There may be some requirements for giving credit to the creator either by name or by linking to their website. Follow the instructions provided with the applet. Some applets are free for use on personal websites, but require licenses for commercial use.

FAQ   Can you share an example of using the obsolete applet element?

Sure! Although the applet element is obsolete, you'll probably run across web pages that still use it. An example of using the applet element to display a Java applet is

```
<applet code="fader26.class" width="610" height="30"
  alt="Displays a message that describes uses of Java applets.">
  <param name="AppletHome" value="http://www.crosswinds.net/~fader/" />
  <param name="Data" value="message.txt" />
  <param name="bgColor" value="#FFFFFF" />
  Java Applets can be used to display text, manipulate graphics,
play games, and more.
  <a href="http://download.oracle.com/javase/tutorial/">Oracle</a>
</applet>
```

Checkpoint 11.2

1. Describe a benefit of using the new HTML5 audio and video elements.
2. What is the purpose of the transform property?
3. Describe a disadvantage of using Java applets on web pages.

11.9 JavaScript

JavaScript is an object-based scripting language. In JavaScript, you work with the objects associated with a web page document: the window, the document, and elements such as forms, images, and links. JavaScript, developed by Netscape, was originally called LiveScript. When Netscape collaborated with Sun Microsystems on modifications to the language, it was renamed JavaScript. JavaScript is not the same as the Java programming language. Unlike Java, JavaScript cannot be used to write stand-alone programs that can run outside of a web browser. JavaScript statements can be placed in a separate file (with a .js extension) that is accessed by a web browser; however, JavaScript statements are often embedded directly on the web page along with the HTML. In either case, the web browser interprets the JavaScript statements. JavaScript is considered to be a client-side scripting language because it runs on the client side (the browser), not the web server. Note that although some web servers (such as the Sun Java System Web Server) can process server-side JavaScript, the language is most commonly used for client-side scripting.

FAQ **Don't all browsers support JavaScript?**

Most modern browsers support JavaScript. However, they also offer the option to disable JavaScript. Some assistive technologies, such as screen readers, may not support JavaScript. You can't assume that every person who visits your website allows JavaScript. It's a good idea to offer your web page visitors an alternative (plain-text links, a phone number to call, and so on) if the features on your website are dependent upon JavaScript.

JavaScript is often used to respond to events such as moving the mouse, clicking a button, and loading a web page. This technology is also often used to edit and verify information on HTML form controls such as text boxes, check boxes, and radio buttons. JavaScript can be used to create pop-up windows, display the current date, perform calculations, and so on. Figure 11.23 shows a website that uses JavaScript to determine and display the current date.

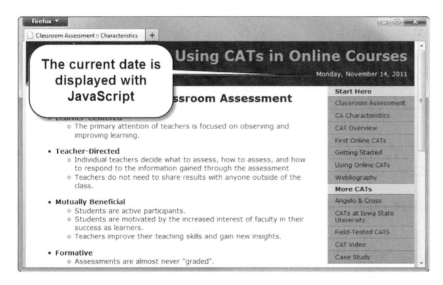

Figure 11.23 This web page displays the current date with JavaScript

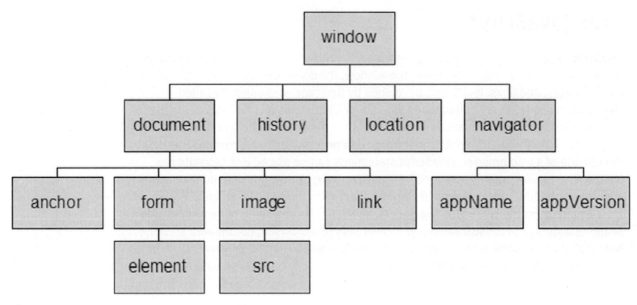

Figure 11.24 The Document Object Model (DOM)

There is an introduction to coding JavaScript in Chapter 14. An important part of working with JavaScript is manipulating the **Document Object Model (DOM).** The DOM defines every object and element on a web page. Its hierarchical structure can be used to access page elements and apply styles to page elements. A portion of a basic DOM that is common to most browsers is shown in Figure 11.24.

JavaScript Resources

There is a lot to learn about JavaScript, but there are many free resources for JavaScript code and JavaScript tutorials on the Web. Here are a few sites that offer free tutorials or free scripts:

- JavaScript Tutorial: http://echoecho.com/javascript.htm
- JavaScript for the Total Non-Programmer: http://www.webteacher.com/javascript
- JavaScript Tutorial: http://www.w3schools.com/JS

Once you are comfortable with HTML and CSS, the JavaScript language is a good technology to learn as you continue your studies. Try some of the resources listed and get your feet wet. See Chapter 14 for a more detailed introduction to JavaScript. The next section introduces Ajax, a technology that uses JavaScript.

11.10 Ajax

Ajax is not a single technology, but a combination of different technologies. Ajax stands for Asynchronous JavaScript and XML. These technologies are not new, but recently have been used together to provide a better experience for web visitors and create interactive web applications. Jesse James Garrett of Adaptive Path (http://adaptivepath.com/ideas/ajax-new-approach-web-applications) is credited with coining the term "Ajax". The technologies utilized in Ajax are as follows:

- Standards-based HTML and CSS

- The Document Object Model

- XML (and the related XSLT technology)

- Asynchronous data retrieval using XMLHttpRequest

- JavaScript

Some of these technologies may be unfamiliar to you. That's okay at this point in your web development career. You're currently creating a strong foundation in HTML and CSS and may decide to continue your studies in the future and learn additional web technologies. Right now, it's enough to know that these technologies exist and what they can be used for.

Ajax is part of the **Web 2.0** movement—the transition of the Web from isolated static websites to a platform that uses technology to provide rich interfaces and social networking opportunities for people. See "What Is Web 2.0?" (http://www.oreillynet.com/pub/a/oreilly/tim/news/2005/09/30/what-is-Web-20.html) by Tim O'Reilly, who was instrumental in the creation of the term "Web 2.0".

Ajax is a web development technique for creating interactive web applications. Recall the client/server model discussed in Chapters 1 and 9. The browser makes a request to the server (often triggered by clicking a link or a submit button), and the server returns an entire new web page for the browser to display. Ajax pushes more of the processing on the client (browser) using JavaScript and XML and often uses behind-the-scenes asynchronous requests to the server to refresh a portion of the browser display instead of the entire web page. The key is that when using Ajax technology, JavaScript code (which runs on the client computer within the confines of the browser) can communicate directly with the server, exchanging data and modifying parts of the web page display without reloading the entire web page. For example, as soon as a website visitor types a zip code into a form, the value could be looked up in a zip code database and the city/state automatically populated using Ajax—and all of this takes place while the visitor is entering the form information before they click the submit button. The result is that the visitor perceives the web page as being more responsive and has a more interactive experience. See CSS Property Review (http://webdevfoundations.net/css) for an example of Ajax in action. As shown in Figure 11.19, hints are provided as you type the name of a CSS property without refreshing the page.

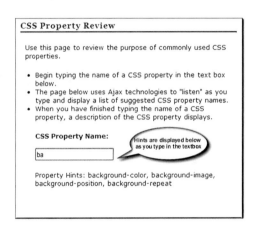

Figure 11.25 Ajax technologies are used to update the page as the visitor types

Developers are using Ajax to support the web applications that are part of Web 2.0: Flickr photo sharing (http://www.flickr.com), the Delicious shared collection of favorite sites (http://www.delicious.com), Google e-mail (http://gmail.google.com), the Amazon A9 search engine (http://www.a9.com), and Microsoft Live (http://www.live.com).

Ajax Resources

Ajax is a very hot topic on the Web right now and there are many resources and articles available. Some helpful sites are listed here:

- Getting Started with Ajax: http://www.alistapart.com/articles/gettingstartedwithajax

- Ajax Tutorial: http://www.tizag.com/ajaxTutorial

11.11 HTML5 Canvas Element

The HTML5 **canvas element** configures dynamic graphics. It provides a way to dynamically draw and transform lines, shapes, images, and text on web pages. If that wasn't enough, the canvas element also provides methods to interact with actions taken by the user, like moving the mouse.

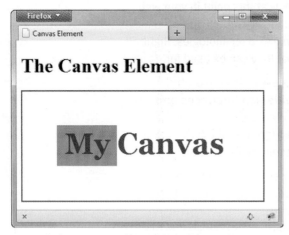

Figure 11.26 The canvas element

The canvas element begins with the `<canvas>` tag and ends with the `</canvas>` tag. However, the canvas element is configured through an **application programming interface** (API), which means that a programming or scripting language, such as JavaScript, is needed to implement it. The canvas API provides methods for two-dimensional (2D) bitmap drawing, including lines, strokes, arcs, fills, gradients, images, and text. However, instead of drawing visually using a graphics application, you draw programmatically by writing JavaScript statements. A very basic example of using JavaScript to draw within the canvas element is shown in Figure 11.26 (see chapter11/canvas.html in the student files). The code is

```
<!DOCTYPE html>
<html lang="en">
<head>
<title>Canvas Element</title>
<meta charset="utf-8">
<style>
canvas { border: 2px solid red; }
</style>
<script type="text/javascript">
function drawMe() {
  var canvas = document.getElementById("myCanvas");
  if (canvas.getContext) {
    var ctx = canvas.getContext("2d");
    ctx.fillStyle = "rgb(255, 0, 0)";
    ctx.font = "bold 3em Georgia";
    ctx.fillText("My Canvas", 70, 100);
    ctx.fillStyle = "rgba(0, 0, 200, 0.50)";
    ctx.fillRect(57, 54, 100, 65);
  }
}
</script>
</head>
<body onload="drawMe()">
<h1>The Canvas Element</h1>
<canvas id="myCanvas" width="400" height="175"></canvas>
</body>
</html>
```

If some of the code looks like a foreign language to you, don't worry: JavaScript IS a different language than CSS and HTML; it has its own syntax and rules. Here's a quick overview of the code:

- The red outline was created by applying CSS to the canvas selector.

- The JavaScript function drawMe() is invoked when the browser loads the page. JavaScript looks for a canvas element assigned to the "myCanvas" id. JavaScript tests for browser support of canvas and, if true, performs the following actions:

  - Sets the canvas context to 2D.

  - Draws the "My Canvas" text.

  - Uses the fillStyle attribute to set the drawing color to red.

  - Uses the font attribute to configure font weight, font size, and font family.

  - Uses the fillText method to specify the text to display, followed by the x-value (pixels in from the left) and y-value (pixels down from the top).

  - Draws the rectangle.

  - Uses the fillStyle attribute to set the drawing color to blue with 50% opacity.

  - Uses the fillRect method to set the x-value (pixels in from the left), y-value (pixels down from the top), width, and height of the rectangle.

The promise of the canvas element is that it can be used to provide interactions as sophisticated as those developed with Adobe Flash. At the time this was written, all modern browsers (with the exception of Internet Explorer) support the canvas element. Use a browser other than Internet Explorer to see virtuoso examples of the canvas element in action at the following websites:

- Implementing a HTML5 Canvas-based, Tilt Sensing Snow Globe: http://blog.webreakstuff.com/2010/11/building-a-canvas-snowglobe

- Canvas Demos: Applications, games, tools, and tutorials for the HTML5 canvas element: http://www.canvasdemos.com

This section provided a very quick overview of the canvas element. If you'd like additional examples and practice with this intriguing new element, visit the following resources:

- HTML5 Canvas Expand Image on Hover: http://www.html5canvastutorials.com

- HTML5 Canvas Cheat Sheet: http://blog.nihilogic.dk/2009/02/html5-canvas-cheat-sheet.html

 Checkpoint 11.3

1. What are two uses of JavaScript?

2. Describe two technologies used in Ajax.

3. What is the purpose of the HTML5 canvas element?

11.12 Accessibility and Multimedia/Interactivity

Focus on Accessibility

Multimedia and interactivity can help to create a compelling, engaging experience for your website visitors. Please keep in mind that not every web visitor will be able to experience these features, so incorporate the following into your website:

- Provide links to free downloads for the plug-ins used by your multimedia.

- Text descriptions and equivalent content (such as captions) of audio and video will provide access for those with hearing challenges and will also assist visitors using mobile devices or slow Internet connections.

- When you work with multimedia developers and programmers to create Flash animation or Java applets for your site, request features that provide accessibility, such as keyboard access, text descriptions, and so on. If you use Flash or a Java applet for site navigation, be sure that it can be accessed with a keyboard and/or provide plain-text navigation links in the footer section of the pages. Adobe provides good resources for web developers on their Accessibility web page (http://www.adobe.com/resources/accessibility).

- WCAG 2.0 Guideline 2.3.1 recommends that a web page not contain any item that flashes more than three times per second. This is to prevent optically induced seizures. You may need to work with your multimedia developer to ensure that dynamic effects perform within a safe range.

- If you use JavaScript, be aware that some visitors may have JavaScript disabled or are unable to manipulate the mouse. In order to be in compliance with Section 508 of the Rehabilitation Act, your site must be functional at a basic level, even if your visitor's browser does not support JavaScript. A site using Ajax to redisplay a portion of the browser window may have issues when accessed using an assistive technology or text browser. The importance of testing cannot be overemphasized. W3C has developed ARIA (Accessible Rich Internet Applications), which is a protocol that supports accessibility for scripted and dynamic content, such as the web applications created using Ajax. At the time this was written, ARIA was not uniformly supported by all commonly used browsers. See WAI-ARIA Overview (http://www.w3.org/WAI/intro/aria.php) for more information about ARIA.

When you design with multimedia/interactivity accessibility in mind, you help those visitors who have physical challenges, as well as those who are using low bandwidth or who may be missing plug-ins on their browser. As a last resort, consider creating a separate text-only version of the page if the multimedia and/or interactivity used on a page cannot comply with accessibility guidelines.

Chapter Summary

This chapter introduced technologies to add media and interactivity to web pages. HTML techniques used to configure sound and video were discussed. Adobe Flash, Java applets, JavaScript, Ajax, and the HTML5 canvas element were introduced. You configured an interactive CSS image gallery and explored the new CSS3 transition and transform properties. Accessibility and copyright issues related to these technologies were addressed. Visit the textbook website at http://www.webdevfoundations.net for examples, the links listed in this chapter, and updated information.

Key Terms

.aiff	`<applet>`	helper application
.au	`<audio>`	interactivity
.avi	`<canvas>`	Java
.class	`<embed>`	Java applet
.flv	`<object>`	Java Virtual Machine (JVM)
.m4a	`<param>`	JavaScript
.m4v	`<script>`	media
.mid	`<source>`	playback
.mov	`<video>`	plug-in
.mp3	Ajax	podcasting
.mp4	codec	RSS feed
.mpg	container	sampling rate
.ogg	copyright	transform property
.ogv	Creative Commons license	transition property
.swf	Document Object Model (DOM)	transitions
.wav	fair use	Web 2.0
.wmv	Flash	

Review Questions

Multiple Choice

1. What should you be aware of while working with HTML5 audio and video elements?

   a. plug-ins

   b. container and codec

   c. both of the above

   d. none of the above

2. Which of the following is invalid?

   a. `<a href="mymusic.mp3"> Play the Music</a>`

   b. `<embed height="50px" width="100px" src="mymusic.mp3" />`

   c. `<object height="50px" width="100px" data="mymusic.mp3"></object>`

   d. none of the above

3. What is the purpose of the XHTML `<object>` element?

   a. to embed the audio or video file in the page

   b. to support HTML plug-ins

   c. to display a control panel or player for the multimedia

   d. all of the above

4. Which of the following is not true about the HTML5 audio element?

   a. It supports native play of audio files in the browser.

   b. It begins with the `<audio>` tag and ends with the `</audio>` tag.

   c. It needs plug-ins or players for the respective media.

   d. You may omit the `src` and the `type` attributes while using this element.

5. The _____ element is a self-contained tag that specifies multiple media resources for media elements.
   a. source
   b. param
   c. embed
   d. audio

6. To specify that the video should start over again every time it is completed, you should use the _____ attribute of the `<video>` element.
   a. `loop`
   b. `autoplay`
   c. `preload`
   d. none of the above

7. Which of the following elements can be used with the HTML5 video element to provide fallback content?
   a. anchor element
   b. embed element
   c. object element
   d. all of the above

8. Which of the following is not true about JavaScript?
   a. It adds interactivity to HTML pages.
   b. You can't use JavaScript without a license.
   c. It is a scripting language.
   d. It is an interpreted language, i.e., the script is executed without preliminary compilation.

9. Which of the following can be described as the purpose of JavaScript?
   a. reacting to events
   b. validating form data
   c. detecting a visitor's browser and creating cookies
   d. all of the above

10. Which of the following technologies presents an HTML document as a tree structure?
    a. JavaScript
    b. HTML DOM
    c. Ajax
    d. Java applets

Fill in the Blank

11. The CSS3 _____ property allows move, scale, turn, spin, or stretch elements.

12. The CSS3 _____ property allows adding an effect when changing from one style to another.

13. The HTML5 _____ element is used to draw graphics on a web page.

14. When displaying a Java applet, the browser invokes the _____ to interpret the bytecode into the appropriate machine language.

15. Ajax stands for _____ JavaScript and XML.

Short Answer

16. List at least two reasons not to use audio or video on a web page.

17. Describe a type of copyright license that empowers the author/artist to grant some, but not all, rights for using his or her work.

Apply Your Knowledge

1. **Predict the Result.** Draw and write a brief description of the web page that will be created with the following HTML code:

```
<!DOCTYPE html>
<html lang="en">
<head><title>CircleSoft Designs</title>
<meta charset="utf-8">
<style>
body { background-color: #FFFFCC;
color: #330000;
font-family: Arial,Helvetica,sans-serif; }
.content { width: 750px; }
</style>
</head>
```

```
<body>
<div class="content">
<h1>Musical Instrument Digital Interface (MIDI)</h1>
<div><strong>Tips: Do not put inline sound on your page, as most
people find it annoying. </strong>
<p> MIDI files contain instructions to recreate a musical sound
rather than
a digital recording of the sound itself; a limited number of
types of sounds can be reproduced. </p>
<p><a href="song1.mid" title="Musical Bonanza">Play the sample
music</a>
</p>
</div>
</div>
</body>
</html>
```

2. **Fill in the Missing Code.** This web page should display a Flash media file named slideshow.swf that is 200 pixels wide and 175 pixels high. Some HTML attributes, indicated by "_", are missing. Fill in the missing code.

```
<!DOCTYPE html>
<html lang="en">
<head>
<title>Fill in the Missing Code</title>
<meta charset="utf-8">
</head>
<body>
<h1>Trillium Media Design</h1>
<p>Visual Tour of Our Services</p><br>
<embed type="application/x-shockwave-flash"
       "_"="slideshow.swf" quality="high"
       "_"="200" "_"="175"
       title="slideshow">
</body>
</html>
```

3. **Find the Error.** The purpose of the following web page is to play an audio file. However, the rendered page is not showing the player and asking for a plug-in instead. Correct the code to make it work.

```
<!DOCTYPE html>
<html lang="en">
<head>
<title>HTML media</title>
<meta charset="utf-8">
</head>
<body>
    <embed height="50px" width="100px" src="song1.mid" />
    <object height="50px" width="100px"
data="song1.mid"></object>
  </body>
  </html>
```

Hands-On Exercises

1. You have created multiple versions of a video file named video1.mp4. You have the versions video1.swf, video1.ogg, and video1.webm. Write the best HTML code to display the video in all possible browsers. The video is 420 pixels high and 340 pixels wide.

2. Write the HTML to embed an audio file called lesson1.wav on a web page that can be controlled by the visitor.

3. Write the HTML to add a Flash file called birdy.swf to your web page. The effect needs an area that is 300 pixels wide and 70 pixels high.

4. You have created multiple versions of an audio file named song1.mp3. You also have the version song1.ogg of the same music. Write the best HTML code to play the audio in all possible browsers.

5. Write the CSS3 code to create a div element 100 pixels wide and 100 pixels high, with the background color gray. When a user hovers over this element, its dimensions change to 200 pixels, the background color changes to blue, and the text color change to white. Write a simple HTML to use this element.

6. Write the CSS3 code to create an image element 420 pixels high and 340 pixels wide and rotated at an angle of 30 degrees. Write the HTML code to use this style to render an image named panorama.jpg on your web page.

7. Create a web page about your favorite music group that uses either the Java applet described in Hands-On Practice 11.9 or a Java applet of your choice. The applet should display the names of songs performed by the group. Place an e-mail link to yourself on the web page. Save the page as java11.html.

8. Visit the textbook website at http://webdevfoundations.net/flashcs5 and follow the instructions to create a Flash logo banner. Configure a web page to display the logo banner. Place an e-mail link to yourself on the web page. Save the page as flash11.html.

Web Research

1. This chapter mentioned some software applications that can be used to create and edit media files. With those as a starting point, search for more applications on the Web. Create a web page that lists at least five media authoring applications. Organize your web page with a list that provides the name of the software application, the URL, a brief description, and the price. Place your name in an e-mail link on the web page. Your web page should include a hyperlink to a music audio file. Include an audio file (soundloop.mp3) from this chapter, record your own, or find an appropriate sound file on the Web. Place your name in an e-mail link on the web page.

2. Issues related to copyright law were discussed in this chapter. With the resources provided as a starting point, search for additional information related to copyright

law and the Web. Create a web page that provides five helpful facts about copyright law and the Web. Provide the URLs of the websites you used as resources. Place a media console on the page to allow visitors to play an audio file while they read your web page. Include an audio file (soundloop.mp3) from this chapter, record your own, or find an appropriate sound file on the Web. Place your name in an e-mail link on the web page.

3. Choose one method of web interactivity discussed in this chapter: JavaScript, Java applets, Flash, or Ajax. Use the resources listed in the chapter as a starting point, but also search the Web for additional resources on the interactivity method you have chosen. Create a web page that lists at least five useful resources along with a brief description of each. Organize your web page with a list that provides the name of the site, the URL, a brief description of what is offered, and a recommended page (such as a tutorial or free script) for each resource. Place your name in an e-mail link on the web page.

4. Choose one method of web interactivity discussed in this chapter: JavaScript, Java applets, or Flash. Use the resources listed in the chapter as a starting point, but also search the Web for additional resources on the interactivity method you have chosen. Find either a tutorial or a free download that uses the method of web interactivity you are researching. Create a web page that uses the code or download that you found. Describe the effect and list the URL of the resource on the web page. Place your name in an e-mail link on the web page.

Focus on Web Design

1. Ajax is a relatively new technology and there are web design usability and accessibility issues associated with it. Visit the following sites to become aware of these issues:

   - Ajax Usability Mistakes: http://ajaxian.com/archives/ajax-usability-mistakes
   - Usability and Accesibility with Ajax:
     http://www.sitepoint.com/blogs/2005/03/10/usability-and-accessibility-with-ajax
   - Ajax and Accessibility:
     http://www.standards-schmandards.com/2005/ajax-and-accessibility
   - Flash, Ajax, Usability, and SEO:
     http://www.clickz.com/clickz/column/1702189/flash-ajax-usability-seo

   Write a one-page report that describes Ajax usability issues that web designers should be aware of. Cite the URLs of the resources you used.

2. In a 2007 interview
   (http://www.guardian.co.uk/technology/2007/apr/05/adobe.newmedia), Mark Anders, the senior principal scientist at Adobe, recommended Flash as "a great platform for building the next generation of rich Internet applications." Although Flash is well-supported in standard desktop browsers, many mobile devices do not support Flash. In 2011 Adobe dropped development of the Flash player for mobile browsers (http://blogs.adobe.com/conversations/2011/11/flash-focus.html). After you review the sources listed, decide on your own opinion of Flash and when, as a designer, you would recommend its use. Write a one-page paper that persuasively presents your opinion. Cite the URLs of your resources.

WEBSITE CASE STUDY
Adding Multimedia

Each of the following case studies continues throughout most of the text. This chapter adds media and interactivity to the websites.

JavaJam Coffee House

See Chapter 2 for an introduction to the JavaJam Coffee House case study. Figure 2.25 shows a site map for the JavaJam website. Use the Chapter 9 JavaJam website as a starting point for this case study. You have three tasks in this case study:

1. Create a new folder for this JavaJam case study.

2. Configure a hyperlink to an audio file on the Music page (music.html).

3. Replace javalogo.gif with a Flash animated banner called javalogo.swf on each page. Figure 11.27 shows the home page with the new Flash banner.

Figure 11.27 The new Flash banner on the home page

Hands-On Practice Case Study

Task 1: Create a Folder. Create a folder called javajam11. Copy all the files from your Chapter 9 javajam9 folder into the javajam11 folder. Copy greg.mp3 and javalogo.swf from the chapter11/casestudystarters folder in the student files and save them to your javajam11 folder.

Task 2: Update the Music Page. Open music.html in a text editor. Modify music.html so that the text "New songs" links to greg.mp3. See Hands-On Practice 11.1 as a guide. Save your web page and test it using several browsers. You should hear the sound when you click on the hyperlink.

Task 3: Update the Logo Header Area on Each Page. Launch a text editor and edit the home page (index.html). Replace the logo header image with the Flash javalogo.swf file.

The Flash media is 620 pixels in width and 117 pixels in height. See Hands-On Practice 11.5 for help. Save your web page and test it using several browsers. You should see the logo animate. Next, update the other pages (menu.html, music.html, and jobs.html) in the same way so that your website has a consistent design. Save your web pages and test them in a browser.

Fish Creek Animal Hospital

See Chapter 2 for an introduction to the Fish Creek Animal Hospital case study. Figure 2.29 shows a site map for the Fish Creek website. Use the Chapter 9 Fish Creek website as a starting point for this case study. You have four tasks in this case study:

1. Create a new folder for this Fish Creek case study.

2. Modify fishcreek.css to configure the placement of the Flash logo and video.

3. Replace fishcreeklogo.gif with a Flash animated banner called fishcreeklogo.swf on each page.

4. Add a video to the Ask the Vet page (askvet.html). See Figure 11.28 for a sample screenshot.

Figure 11.28 Fish Creek Ask the Vet page with HTML5 video element

Hands-On Practice Case Study

Task 1: Create a Folder. Create a folder called fishcreek11. Copy all the files from your Chapter 9 fishcreek9 folder into the fishcreek11 folder. Copy fishcreeklogo.swf and sparky.webm from the chapter11/casestudystarters folder in the student files and save them to your fishcreek11 folder. Copy sparky.mov, sparky.m4v, sparky.ogv, and sparky.jpg from the chapter11 folder in the student files and save them to your fishcreek11 folder.

Task 2: Configure the CSS. Modify the external style sheet (fishcreek.css). Open fishcreek.css in a text editor. Edit the CSS and code a new video html selector that floats to the right and has 20 pixel left and right margins. Save the fishcreek.css file.

Task 3: Update the Logo Header Area on Each Page. Launch a text editor and edit the home page (index.html). Replace the logo header image with the Flash fishcreeklogo.swf file. The Flash media is 600 pixels in width and 100 pixels in height. See Hands-On Practice 11.5 for help. Save your web page and test it using several browsers. You should see the logo animate. Next, update the other pages (services.html, askvet.html, and contact.html) in the same way so that your website has a consistent design. Save and test your web pages in a browser.

Task 4: Configure a Video on the Ask the Vet Page. Launch a text editor and edit the Ask the Vet page (askvet.html). Configure the Sparky video (sparky.mov, sparky.m4v, sparky.ogv, and sparky.jpg files) to display to the left of the paragraph and description list. Use the HTML5 video and source elements. Configure a 200 pixel height, 2200 pixel width, and a hyperlink to the sparky.mov file as fallback content in browsers that do not support the video element. See Section 11.5 as a guide. Save your web page and test it using several browsers.

Pacific Trails Resort

See Chapter 2 for an introduction to the Pacific Trails Resort case study. Figure 2.33 shows a site map for the Pacific Trails website. Use the Chapter 9 Pacific Trails website as a starting point for this case study. You have three tasks in this case study:

1. Create a new folder for this Pacific Trails case study.

2. Add a video to the home page (index.html) and update the external CSS file. See Figure 11.29 for a sample screenshot.

3. Configure an image gallery on the Activities page (activities.html) and update the external CSS file. See the example web page in Figure 11.30.

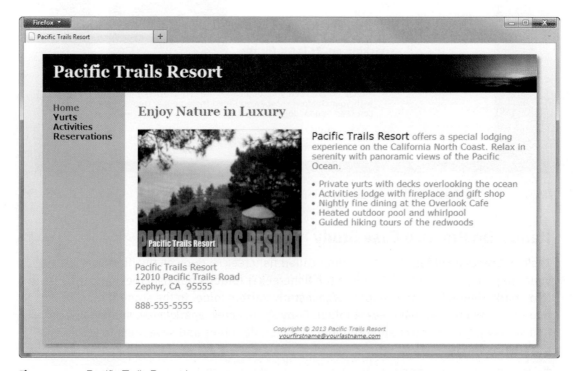

Figure 11.29 Pacific Trails Resort home page

Hands-On Practice Case Study

Task 1: Create a Folder. Create a folder called pacific11. Copy all of the files from your Chapter 9 pacific9 folder into the pacific11 folder. Copy the following files from the chapter11/casestudystarters folder in the student files and save them in your pacific11 folder: pacifictrailsresort.mp4, pacifictrailsresort.ogv, pacifictrailsresort.jpg, and pacifictrailsresort.swf. Copy the following files from the chapter11/starters folder in the student files and save them in your pacific11 folder: photo2.jpg, photo3.jpg, photo4.jpg, photo6.jpg, photo2thumb.jpg, photo3thumb.jpg, photo4thumb.jpg, and photo6thumb.jpg.

Task 2: Configure the Video. Launch a text editor and open the home page (index.html). Replace the image with an HTML5 video control. Configure the video, source, and embed elements to work with the following files: pacifictrailsresort.mp4, pacifictrailsresort.ogv, pacifictrailsresort.swf, and pacifictrailsresort.jpg. The dimensions of the video are 320 pixels wide by 240 pixels high. Save the file. Check your HTML syntax using the W3C validator (http://validator.w3.org). Correct and retest if necessary.

Next, configure the CSS. Launch a text editor and open pacific.css. Locate the `#content img` selector which is configured with style rules to float to the left and have padding on the right. Add the `#content video` and `#content embed` selectors to the style rule as follows:

```
#content img, #content video, #content embed { float: left;
                                               padding-right: 20px; }
```

Save the pacific.css file. Launch a browser and test your new index.html page. It should look similar to Figure 11.29.

Task 3: Configure the Image Gallery. Launch a text editor and open activities.html. Modify the page by adding an image gallery above the footer area. You'll need to modify both the activities.html file and the pacific.css file. Use Hands-On Practice 11.8 as a guide and configure a div assigned to the gallery id. This gallery will display four thumbnail images. Code an unordered list within the gallery div that has four li elements, one for each thumbnail image. The thumbnail images will function as image links with a `:hover` pseudo-class that causes the larger image to display on the page. Within each li element, configure an anchor element to contain both the thumbnail image and a span element that contains the larger image along with descriptive text. Configure the dimensions of the larger images to be 200 pixels wide by 150 pixels high. Save the activities.html file.

Open pacific.css in a text editor. Code the CSS for the gallery as shown in Hands-On Practice 11.8, but configure the position of the span to be located farther in from the left (use `left: 340px;`). By default, the images in the gallery inherit the left float configured for the `#content img` selector. To remove this inheritance, code a `float: none;` style rule on the `#gallery img` selector. Also add a style declaration to the `#footer` selector to clear all floats. Save the pacific.css file.

Launch a browser and test your new Activities page (activities.html). It should look similar to Figure 11.30.

Figure 11.30 New Pacific Trails Activities page

Prime Properties

See Chapter 2 for an introduction to the Prime Properties case study. Figure 2.37 shows a site map for the Prime Properties website. Use the Chapter 9 Prime Properties website as a starting point for this case study. You have four tasks:

1. Create a new folder for this Prime Properties case study.

2. Configure the home page to display an audio control for a podcast.

3. Modify prime.css to configure the placement of a Flash slide show.

4. Modify the home page to display a Flash slide show.

Hands-On Practice Case Study

Task 1: Create a Folder. Create a folder called prime11. Copy all of the files from your Chapter 9 prime9 folder into the prime11 folder. Copy the following files from the chapter11/casestudystarters folder in the student files and save them in your prime11 folder: prime.swf, primepodcast.mp3, primepodcast.ogg, and primepodcast.txt.

Task 2: Configure the Audio. Launch a text editor and open the home page (index.html). Modify index.html so that a heading and an HTML5 audio control displays above the name and address area on the page (see Figure 11.31). Use an h3 element to display the text "Podcast Episode #1,247". Refer to Hands-On Practice 11.6 when you create the audio control. Configure the audio and source elements to work with the following files:

primepodcast.mp3 and primepodcast.ogg. Configure a hyperlink to the podcast transcript (primepodcast.txt) as a fallback if the audio element is not supported. Save the file. Check your HTML syntax using the W3C validator (http://validator.w3.org). Correct and retest if necessary.

Figure 11.31 The Prime Properties home page displays an HTML5 audio control and a Flash slide show

Task 3: Configure the CSS. Modify the external style sheet (prime.css). Open prime.css in a text editor and edit the CSS to configure a new class called `floatright`. Configure the `floatright` class to float to the right, and have a 20 pixel left margin and a 60 pixel right margin. Save the prime.css file.

Task 4: Configure the Flash Slide Show. Launch a text editor and open the home page (index.html). Write the HTML needed to display the Flash slide show prime.swf file (using an embed element configured with a 213 pixel width and 163 pixel height) in the right column above the first paragraph. Refer to Hands-On Practice 11.5. Assign the embed element to the `floatright` class. Save your web page and test it in a browser.

Web Project

See Chapter 5 for an introduction to the Web Project case study. Review the goals of your website and determine whether the use of media or interactivity would add value to your site. If so, you will add either media and/or interactivity to your project site. Check with your instructor regarding the required use of any specific media or technology that supports interactivity in your web project.

Select one or more from the following:

1. Media: Choose one of the examples from the chapter, record your own audio or media file, or search the Web for royalty-free media.

2. Flash: Choose one of the examples from the chapter, create your own SWF file, or search the Web for additional SWF files.

3. Java applet: Choose one of the examples from the chapter, write your own if you have programming skills, or search the Web for free Java applets.

4. CSS image gallery: Create or locate images that relate to your web project. Using Hands-On Practice 11.8 as an example, configure a CSS image gallery.

5. Decide where to apply the media and/or interactive technology to your site. Modify, save the page(s), and test in various browsers.

E-Commerce Overview

E-commerce is the buying and selling of goods and services on the Internet. Whether business-to-business, business-to-consumer, or consumer-to-consumer, websites that support e-commerce are everywhere. This chapter provides an overview of this topic.

12.1 What Is E-Commerce?

A formal definition of **e-commerce** is the integration of communications, data management, and security technologies, which allows individuals and organizations to exchange information related to the sale of goods and services. The major functions of e-commerce include the buying of goods, the selling of goods, and the performance of financial transactions on the Internet.

Advantages of E-Commerce

There are a number of advantages for both businesses and consumers when engaging in e-commerce. For businesses, the many advantages include the following:

- **Reduced Costs.** Online businesses can stay open 24 hours a day without the overhead of a brick-and-mortar facility. Many businesses establish a website before attempting e-commerce. When they add e-commerce functions to their website, the site becomes a source of revenue and, in many cases, pays for itself in short order.

- **Increased Customer Satisfaction.** Businesses can use their websites to improve communication with customers and increase customer satisfaction. E-commerce sites often contain a page for frequently asked questions (FAQs). The availability of customer service representatives by e-mail, discussion forums, or even online chats (see LivePerson at http://www.liveperson.com) can improve customer relations.

- **More Effective Data Management.** Depending on the level of automation, e-commerce sites can perform credit card verification and authorization, update inventory levels, and interface with order fulfillment systems, thereby managing the organization's data more efficiently.

- **Potentially Higher Sales.** An e-commerce store that is open 24 hours a day, 7 days a week and is available to everyone on the planet has the potential for higher sales than a traditional brick-and-mortar storefront.

Businesses aren't the only beneficiaries of e-commerce; consumers see some advantages as well, including the following:

- **Convenience.** Consumers can shop at any time of the day. There is no travel time to get to the store. Some consumers prefer website shopping over traditional catalog shopping because they can view additional images and join discussion forums about the products.

- **Easier Comparison Shopping.** There is no driving from store to store to check the price of an item. Customers can easily surf the Web to compare prices and value.

- **Wider Selection of Goods.** Because it is convenient to shop and compare, consumers have a wider selection of goods available for purchase.

As you can see, e-commerce provides a number of advantages for both businesses and consumers.

Risks of E-Commerce

There are risks involved in any business transaction and e-commerce is no exception. The possible risks for businesses include the following:

- **Loss of Sales if Technology Fails.** If your website isn't available or your e-commerce form processing doesn't work, customers may not return to your site. It is always important to have a user-friendly, reliable website, but when you engage in e-commerce, reliability and ease of use are critical factors in the success of your business.

- **Fraudulent Transactions.** Fraudulent credit card purchases or crank orders placed by vandals (or 13-year-olds with time on their hands) are risks that businesses need to deal with.

- **Customer Reluctance.** Although more and more consumers are willing to purchase on the Web, the target market of your business may not be. However, by offering incentives such as free shipping or a "no questions asked" returns policy, your business may be able to attract these consumers.

- **Increased Competition.** Because the overhead for an e-commerce site can be much lower than that of a traditional brick-and-mortar store, a company operating out of a basement can be just as impressive as a long-standing business if its website looks professional. Because it is much easier to enter the marketplace with an e-commerce store, your business will have increased competition.

Businesses are not alone in needing to deal with the risks associated with e-commerce. Consumers may perceive the following risks:

- **Security Issues.** Later in this chapter, you will learn how to determine whether a website uses a Secure Sockets Layer (SSL) protocol for the encryption and security of information. The general public may not know how to determine whether a website is using this encryption method and be wary of placing a credit card order. Another, possibly more important, issue is what the site does with information after it is transmitted over the Internet. Is the database secure? Are the database backups secure? These questions are difficult to answer. It's a good idea to purchase only from sites that you consider to be reputable.

- **Privacy Issues.** Many sites post privacy policy statements. These describe what the site will do (or will not do) with the information they receive. Some sites use the data for internal marketing purposes only. Other sites sell the data to outside companies. Websites can and do change their privacy policies over time. Consumers may be leery of purchasing online because of the potential lack of privacy.

- **Purchasing Based on Photos and Descriptions.** There is nothing like holding and touching an item before you purchase it. Consumers run the risk of purchasing a product that they will not be happy with because they are making purchasing decisions based on photographs and written descriptions. If an e-commerce site has a generous returns policy, consumers will feel more confident about making a purchase.

- **Returns.** It is often more difficult to return an item to an e-commerce store than to a brick-and-mortar store. Consumers may not want to risk this inconvenience.

12.2 E-Commerce Business Models

Both businesses and consumers are riding the e-commerce wave. There are four common e-commerce business models: business-to-consumer, business-to-business, consumer-to-consumer, and business-to-government.

- **Business-to-Consumer (B2C).** Most of the business-to-consumer selling takes place at online stores. Some, like Amazon.com (http://www.amazon.com), are online only. Others are click-and-mortar—electronic storefronts for well-known brick-and-mortar stores such as Sears (http://www.sears.com).

- **Business-to-Business (B2B).** E-commerce between two businesses often takes the form of exchanging business supply chain information among vendors, partners, and business customers. Electronic Data Interchange (EDI) is also included in this category.

- **Consumer-to-Consumer (C2C).** Individuals are selling to each other on the Internet. The most common format is that of the auction. The most well-known auction site is eBay (http://www.ebay.com), which was founded in 1995.

- **Business-to-Government (B2G).** Businesses are selling to the government on the Internet. There are very strict usability standards for businesses that target governmental agencies. Section 508 of the Rehabilitation Act requires that electronic and information technology (including web pages) used by federal agencies is accessible to people with disabilities. See http://www.section508.gov for more information.

Businesses began exchanging information electronically using EDI many years before the Web came into existence.

12.3 Electronic Data Interchange (EDI)

Electronic Data Interchange is the transfer of structured data between companies over a network. This facilitates the exchange of standard business documents, including purchase orders and invoices. EDI is not new; it has been in existence since the 1960s. Organizations that exchange EDI transmissions are called trading partners.

The Accredited Standards Committee X12 (ASC X12) is chartered by the American National Standards Institute (ANSI) to develop and maintain EDI standards. These standards include transaction sets for common business forms, such as requisitions and invoices. This allows businesses to reduce paperwork and communicate electronically.

EDI messages are placed in transaction sets, which consist of a header; one or more data segments, which are strings of data elements separated by delimiters; and a trailer. Newer technologies such as XML and web services are allowing trading partners virtually unlimited opportunities to customize their information exchange over the Internet.

Now that you are aware of the possibilities of e-commerce and the types of business models, you may be wondering where the most money is being made. The next section discusses some statistics related to e-commerce.

12.4 E-Commerce Statistics

You may be surprised to discover that the most money is being made in B2B e-commerce—businesses selling to other businesses. According to the U.S. Census Bureau, in 2009, B2B transactions accounted for 91% of e-commerce in the United States. The U.S. Census Bureau reported that online retail sales increased from $34 billion in 2002 to $165 billion in 2010.

Although e-commerce growth stalled during the recent economic downturn, it is again demonstrating growth. eMarketer (http://www.emarketer.com/Report.aspx?code=emarketer_2000770) reported that while e-commerce only grew 1.6% in 2009, more than 14% growth was demonstrated in 2010. The research firm forecasts more than 13% growth in e-commerce in 2011 and cites mobile commerce, social commerce, and daily deal sites such as Groupon (http://www.groupon.com) as contributing to growth. According to a TechCrunch report (http://tinyurl.com/3m7vwku), Forrester Research predicts online retail sales growth at a 10% compound annual rate, reaching more than $248 billion by 2014.

You may be wondering what people are buying online. A report compiled by the U.S. Census Bureau (http://www.census.gov/compendia/statab/2011/tables/11s1055.xls) indicated that the top 10 categories for online retail sales in 2008 (the most recent year with actual sales figures) were the following:

1. Clothing, accessories, and footwear ($17 billion)
2. Computer hardware and software ($14.3 billion)
3. Electronics and appliances ($13 billion)
4. Furniture and home furnishings ($9.8 billion)
5. Books, music, and videos ($9 billion)
6. Office equipment and supplies ($5.8 billion)
7. Drugs, health aids, and beauty aids ($5.5 billion)
8. Sporting goods ($3.9 billion)
9. Toys, hobby goods, and games ($3.3 billion)
10. Food, beer, and wine ($2.3 billion)

Now that you know what is selling the best online, who are your potential online consumers? eMarketer forecasts that in 2011, close to 179 million Americans ages 14 and older will shop online. A survey by the PEW Internet and American Life Project (http://www.pewinternet.org/Static-Pages/Trend-Data/Whos-Online.aspx) indicated that while about the same percentage of men and women are online, Internet usage varies by age, income, and education. Table 12.1 shows an excerpt from this research.

Table 12.1 Online population

Category	Percentage Who Use the Internet
Men	78%
Women	76%
Age: 18–29	90%
Age: 30–49	84%
Age: 50–64	76%
Age: 65 and older	46%
Household Income: Less than $30,000	63%
Household Income: $30,000 to $49,999	79%
Household Income: $50,000 to $74,999	92%
Household Income: $75,000 or higher	96%
Education: Did not graduate high school	40%
Education: High school graduate	69%
Education: Some college	89%
Education: College graduate	93%

12.5 E-Commerce Issues

Doing business on the Internet is not without its problems. The following are some common issues:

- **Intellectual Property.** There has been some recent controversy regarding intellectual property rights and domain names. **Cybersquatting** is the practice of registering a domain name that is a trademark of another entity in the hopes of profiting by selling the domain name to the entity. The Internet Corporation for Assigned Names and Numbers (ICANN) sponsors the Uniform Domain Name Dispute Policy at http://www.icann.org/udrp/udrp.htm, which can be used to combat cybersquatters.

- **Security.** Security is a constant issue on the Internet. Distributed denial of service (DDoS) attacks have shut down popular e-commerce sites. Some of these attacks are carried out by script kiddies (teenagers with technical knowledge and sometimes malicious intent), who literally have nothing better to do than cause havoc on the Web.

- **Fraud.** Fraudulent websites that ask for credit card numbers without any intent of delivering products or with fraudulent intent are an understandable source of concern for consumers.

- **Taxation.** State governments and local municipalities need sales tax to fund education, public safety, health, and many other essential services. When an item is purchased at a retail store, the sales tax is collected from the purchaser by the seller at the time of the sale and periodically remitted by the seller to the state in which the sale occurred.

  When an item is purchased on the Internet, the seller usually does not collect and remit the sales tax. In this situation, many states require that consumers file a use tax and pay the amount that would have been collected. In reality, few consumers do this and few states attempt to enforce it. Our local governments are losing revenue for funding worthwhile programs.

There have been some movements to require that sales tax is collected on all Internet purchases. At the time this was written, the moratorium on Internet sales tax was still in effect. However, state and local governments are losing sources of revenue as more consumers turn to online shopping. Look for the topic of Internet sales tax to continue to be controversial.

- **International Commerce.** Websites that target a global audience have additional concerns. If a site will be offered in multiple languages, there are options of automatic translation programs such as SYSTRANLinks (http://www.systranlinks.com) and companies that provide customized website translation services such as WorldLingo (http://www.worldlingo.com). Be aware that the graphical user interface (GUI) that works with English may not work with other languages. For example, comparable words and phrases often take quite a few more letters in German than in English. If your GUI has minimal white space in the English version of the site, how will it look in the German version?

  How will your international customers pay you? If you accept credit cards, the credit card company will perform the currency conversion. What about the culture of your target international audience? Have you studied the target countries and made certain that your site is appealing and not offensive? Another issue related to international commerce is the cost of shipping and the availability of delivery to remote destinations.

Now that you are familiar with the concept of e-commerce, let's take a closer look at encryption methods and security. The next section introduces encryption methods, SSL, and digital certificates.

12.6 E-Commerce Security

Encryption

Encryption is used to ensure privacy within an organization and on the Internet. **Encryption** is the conversion of data into an unreadable form, called a **ciphertext**. Ciphertext cannot be easily understood by unauthorized individuals. **Decryption** is the process of converting the ciphertext into its original form, called plain text or **clear text**, so that it can be understood. The process of encryption and decryption requires an algorithm and a key. An **algorithm** involves a mathematical calculation. A **key** is a numeric code that should be long enough so that its value cannot easily be guessed.

Encryption is important on the Internet because information in a packet can be intercepted as it travels the communications media. If a hacker or business competitor intercepts an encrypted packet, he or she will not be able to use the information (such as a credit card number or business strategy) because it cannot be read.

A number of types of encryption are commonly used on the Internet, including **symmetric-key encryption** and **asymmetric-key encryption**.

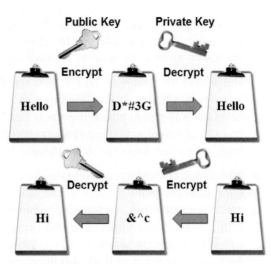

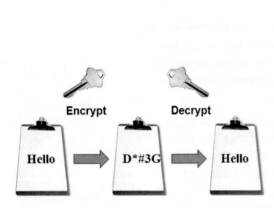

Figure 12.1 Symmetric-key encryption uses a single key

Figure 12.2 Asymmetric-key encryption uses a key pair

Symmetric-Key Encryption

Symmetric-key encryption, shown in Figure 12.1, is also called single-key encryption because both the encryption and decryption use the same key. Because the key must be kept secret from others, both the sender and the receiver must know the key before communicating using encryption. An advantage of symmetric-key encryption is speed.

Asymmetric-Key Encryption

Asymmetric-key encryption is also called public-key encryption because there is no shared secret. Instead, two keys are created at the same time. This key pair contains a public key and a private key. The public key and the private key are mathematically related in such a way that it is unlikely that anyone would guess one of the pair even with knowledge of the other. Only the public key can decrypt a message encrypted with the private key and only the private key can decrypt a message encrypted with the public key (see Figure 12.2). The public key is available via a digital certificate (more on that later). The private key should be kept secure and secret. It is stored on the web server (or other computer) of the key owner. Asymmetric-key encryption is much slower than symmetric-key encryption.

Integrity

The encryption methods described above help to keep the contents of a message secret. However, e-commerce security is also concerned with making sure that messages have not been altered or damaged during transmission. A message is said to have **integrity** if it can be proven that is has not been altered. **Hash functions** provide a way to ensure the integrity of messages. A hash function, or hash algorithm, transforms a string of characters into a usually shorter, fixed-length value or key, called a **digest**, which represents the original string.

These security methods—especially the techniques of symmetric-key and asymmetric-key encryption—are used as part of SSL, the technology that helps to make commerce on the Internet secure. The next section introduces this technology.

Secure Sockets Layer (SSL)

Secure Sockets Layer is a protocol that allows data to be privately exchanged over public networks. It was developed by Netscape and is used to encrypt data sent between a client (usually a web browser) and a web server. SSL utilizes both symmetric and asymmetric keys.

SSL provides secure communication between a client and a server by using the following:

- Server and (optionally) client digital certificates for authentication
- Symmetric-key cryptography with a "session key" for bulk encryption
- Public-key cryptography for transfer of the session key
- Message digests (hash functions) to verify the integrity of the transmission

You can tell that a website is using SSL by the protocol in the web browser address text box—it shows https instead of http. Also, browsers typically display a lock icon or other indicator of SSL, as shown in Figure 12.3.

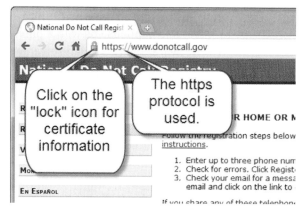

Figure 12.3 The Google Chrome browser indicates that SSL is being used

FAQ **When some websites are displayed in a browser, there is a color bar in the address area. What's up?**

If a website displays a color bar in the address area of the browser in addition to the lock icon in the status bar, you know that it is using *Extended Validation SSL (EV SSL)*. EV SSL signifies that the business has undergone more rigorous background checks to obtain its digital certificate, including verification of the following:

- The applicant owns the domain.
- The applicant works for the organization.
- The applicant has the authority to update the website.
- The organization is a valid, recognized place of business.

Digital Certificate

SSL enables two computers to communicate securely by posting a digital certificate for authentication. A **digital certificate** is a form of an asymmetric key that also contains information about the certificate, the holder of the certificate, and the issuer of the certificate. The contents of a digital certificate include the following:

- The public key
- The effective date of the certificate

- The expiration date of the certificate
- Details about the certificate authority (the issuer of the certificate)
- Details about the certificate holder
- A digest of the certificate content

VeriSign (http://www.verisign.com) and Entrust (http://www.entrust.net) are well-known certificate authorities.

To obtain a certificate, you request a certificate from a certificate authority and pay the application fee. The certificate authority verifies your identity, issues your certificate, and supplies you with a public/private key pair. You store the certificate in your software, such as a web server, web browser, or e-mail application. The certificate authority makes your certificate publicly known.

FAQ   Do I have to apply for a certificate?

If you are accepting any personal information on your website such as credit card numbers, you should be using SSL. One option is to visit a certificate authority (such as VeriSign or Thawte at http://www.thawte.com) and apply for your own certificate. There may be a waiting period and you will need to pay an annual fee.

As an alternative, your web host provider may let you piggyback on its certificate. Normally, there is a setup and/or monthly fee for this service. Usually, the web host assigns you a folder on its secure server. You place the web pages (and associated files such as images) that need to be securely processed in the folder. When linking to the web pages, you use "https" instead of "http" on your absolute links. Contact your web host provider for details.

SSL and Digital Certificates

A number of steps are involved in the SSL authentication process. The web browser and web server go through initial handshaking steps, exchanging information about the server certificate and keys. Once trust is established, the web browser encrypts the single secret key (symmetric key) that will be used for the rest of the communication. From this point on, all data is encrypted through the secret key. Table 12.2 shows this process.

Table 12.2 SSL encryption process overview

Browser	→	"hello"	→	Server
Browser	←	"hello" + server certificate	←	Server
Browser	←	The server's private key is used to encrypt a message. Only the public key can decrypt this message.	←	Server
The browser now verifies the identity of the web server. It obtains the certificate of certificate authority (CA) that signed the server's certificate. Then the browser decrypts the certificate digest using the CA's public key (held in a root CA certificate). Next, the browser authenticates the server's certificate and checks the expiration date of the certificate. If all is valid, the next step occurs.				
Browser	→	The browser generates a session key and encrypts it with the server public key.	→	Server
Browser	←	The server sends a message that is encrypted with the session key.	←	Server
All future transmissions between the browser and the server are encrypted with the session key.				

At this point, you have a general idea of how SSL works to protect the integrity of information on the Internet, including the information exchanged in e-commerce transactions. The next section takes a closer look at order and payment processing in e-commerce.

 Checkpoint 12.1

1. What are three advantages of e-commerce for an entrepreneur who is just starting a business?

2. What are three risks that businesses face when engaging in e-commerce?

3. Define SSL. How can an online shopper tell that an e-commerce site is using SSL.

12.7 Order and Payment Processing

In B2C e-commerce, the products for sale are displayed in an online catalog. On large sites, these catalog pages are dynamically created using server-side scripts to access databases. Each item usually has a button or image that invites visitors to "Buy Me" or "Add to Cart". Items selected are placed in a virtual shopping cart. When visitors are finished shopping, they click a button or image link which indicates that they want to "Check Out" or "Place Order". At this point, the items in their shopping cart are usually displayed on a Web page with an order form.

Secure ordering is facilitated through the use of SSL. Once an order is placed, there are a number of methods by which to pay for the merchandise or service. The payment methods, called payment models, are cash, check, credit, smart card, and mobile payments.

Cash Model

The **cash model** is the most difficult to implement: How do you send cash through a computer? You don't. You use e-cash. You purchase digital money from a bank and deposit it in a digital wallet. The transfer of funds is immediate. Vendors who provide this service include InternetCash (http://www.internetcash.com) and ECash Direct (http://www.ecashdirect.net).

Check Model

In the **check model**, the consumer writes a digital check to make the purchase. As with real-world checks, the availability of funds must be verified and the funds are not transferred immediately. One vendor that provides this service is Fiserv (formerly CheckFree) at http://www.checkfreecorp.fiserv.com.

Credit Model

Credit card payment processing is a very important component of an e-commerce website. Funds from the customer need to be transferred to the merchant's bank. In order to accept credit cards, the site owner must apply for a merchant account and be approved.

A **merchant account** is a type of business bank account that allows a business to accept credit card payments. You may also need real-time credit card verification using a merchant gateway or third party such as Authorize.Net (http://www.authorizenet.com). While merchant accounts can be expensive, there are low-cost solutions such as PayPal (http://www.paypal.com) and Google Checkout (http://checkout.google.com/seller). Originally intended for consumer-to-consumer credit card sales, PayPal now offers credit card and shopping cart services for business website owners. You can add an online shopping experience to your website in minutes with Google's Checkout Store Gadget (http://storegadgetwizard.appspot.com/storegadgetwizard/).

Smart Card Model

The **smart card** model is widely used in Europe, Australia, and Japan. A smart card is similar to a credit card, but it has an integrated circuit instead of a magnetic strip embedded in it. The smart card is inserted into a smart card reader. For more information about smart cards, visit Smart Card Alliance (http://www.smartcardalliance.org/pages/smart-cards-intro-primer).

Mobile Payment Model

Juniper Research predicts large growth in the area of mobile payments and predicts that by 2015, 2.5 billion people will use a mobile device to make a payment of some type (http://www.ecommercetimes.com/story/72807.html). A **mobile payment**, also called an **m-payment**, is an electronic payment for goods or services using a mobile device such as a smartphone. The emerging trend is to use **near field communication** (**NFC**), described by TechSpot (http://www.techspot.com/guides/385-everything-about-nfc/) as short-range wireless communication that uses a radio frequency to share information between NFC devices in close proximity, such as NFC-equipped smartphones, NFC-ready credit card readers, or NFC-ready ticket gates.

According to *The Wall Street Journal* (http://on.wsj.com/hzmzZt), Google has partnered with several credit card companies to include NFC technology in Android mobile devices that would enable customers to wave the mobile device at a checkout counter reader when making a purchase. The Google Wallet app running on an NFC-equipped Android device can effectively "Make your phone your wallet" (http://www.google.com/wallet/). Google's competition in the field of mobile payments includes the ISIS mobile wallet (http://www.paywithisis.com), PayPal (http://tinyurl.com/paypal2011a), and Visa digital wallet (http://tinyurl.com/visa2011a). Expect more developments in this emerging technology.

12.8 E-Commerce Storefront Solutions

You have probably shopped at online stores and found some easy to work with and others difficult. A large problem for e-commerce sites is abandoned shopping carts—visitors who begin to shop but never place an order. This section explores types of storefront solutions and shopping carts. A number of different e-commerce storefront options are available to business owners and web developers. They range from a simple, instant online storefront supplied by another website to building your own shopping cart system. This section examines some of the options.

Instant Online Storefront

You supply the products, the **instant online storefront** does the rest. There is no need to install software. All you do is use your web browser to point and click your way to a virtual store. You use a template provided by the online storefront and choose features, configure settings, and add your products, uploading images, descriptions, prices, and captions.

There are some disadvantages to this approach. You are limited to the templates offered by the online storefront provider. The number of products that you can sell may also be limited. Your store may have a look and feel that is similar to the other instant stores hosted by the provider. However, this method provides a low-overhead, low-risk approach for a small business owner who has limited technical expertise. The storefront provider will often offer merchant accounts and payment automation.

Some instant storefront solutions are free, with limited service or a limited number of products. Others are fee-based and may charge hosting fees, processing fees, and monthly fees. A few popular instant storefront solutions are Yahoo! (http://smallbusiness.yahoo.com/ecommerce/), Earthstores (http://earthstores.com), and Shopify (http://www.shopify.com). Artists and crafters have found a home on Etsy (http://www.etsy.com) to create instant e-storefronts to display and sell their wares.

Off-the-Shelf Shopping Cart Software

With this approach, software that provides a standardized set of e-commerce features is purchased, installed on your web server, and customized. Many web host providers offer this storefront software, which usually includes a shopping cart, order processing, and optional credit card payment processing. **Shopping cart software** provides an online catalog where your visitors can browse, add items to their virtual shopping cart, and check out through an order form when they are ready to make a purchase. Popular shopping carts offered by web host providers are AgoraCart (http://agoracart.com), osCommerce (http://oscommerce.com), ZenCart (http://www.zen-cart.com), and Mercantec SoftCart (http://www.mercantec.com).

Custom-Built Solutions

Custom building a large-scale e-commerce website entirely from scratch usually requires expertise, time, and a sizable budget! The advantage is that you get exactly what you need. Software development tools for a custom-built site include Adobe Dreamweaver, Microsoft Visual Studio.NET, Adobe ColdFusion, IBM's WebSphere Commerce Studio, a database management system (DBMS), and server-side scripting. Custom-built solutions may also require a **commerce server**, which is a web server that is enhanced with support for certain commerce activities. IBM's WebSphere Commerce Suite and Microsoft's Commerce Server are two choices.

Semi-Custom-Built Solutions on a Budget

If the scope of your e-commerce endeavor is small and you want to avoid the cookie-cutter look of an instant storefront, some other options may be worth considering. These include getting pre-written shopping cart and order processing scripts, hiring a company such as PayPal, and buying e-commerce add-ons to popular web-authoring tools.

There are a number of free shopping cart scripts available on the Web. Check out ASPCode.net (http://aspcode.net), the PHP Resource Index (http://php.resourceindex.com), or Mal's e-commerce (http://www.mals-e.com) for some alternate solutions. The level of difficulty and the exact processing of these solutions vary. Each website has instructions and documentation for its product. Some may require you to register before they provide you with specific HTML. Others may require you to download and install the scripts on your own web server.

PayPal (http://www.paypal.com) offers a shopping cart and payment verification for businesses at a very low cost. PayPal writes the code that you need to place on your web pages in order to interface with them. You only need to copy and paste it in. Google Checkout (https://checkout.google.com/seller) offers a variety of options for adding an e-commerce component to a website, including Buy Now buttons, Check Out buttons, a shopping cart wizard, and checkout store gadget.

A number of Adobe Dreamweaver add-ins, or extensions, provide shopping cart functionality. One easy solution is JustAddCommerce (http://www.richmediatech.com), which allows you to configure and add a shopping cart and order buttons to your pages just as easily as you can add images and tables. Budget-wise solutions such as PayPal, Google Checkout, or JustAddCommerce work best for businesses that fit the standard business model and do not require special processing needs.

Checkpoint 12.2

1. Name three payment models that are commonly used on the Web. Which one is the most popular? Why? Which payment model is expected to see increased use in the future?

2. Have you made purchases online? If so, think about the last item that you purchased. Why did you purchase it online instead of at a store? Did you check to see if the transaction was secure? Why or why not? How will your shopping habits be different in the future?

3. Describe three types of available e-commerce solutions. Which one provides the easiest entry to e-commerce? Why?

Chapter Summary

This chapter introduced basic e-commerce concepts and implementation. Consider taking an e-commerce course to continue your study of this dynamic and growing area of web development. Visit the textbook website at http://www.webdevfoundations.net for examples, the links listed in this chapter, and updated information.

Key Terms

algorithm
asymmetric-key encryption
business-to-business (B2B)
business-to-consumer (B2C)
business-to-government (B2G)
cash model
check model
ciphertext
clear text
commerce server
consumer-to-consumer (C2C)
credit model
cybersquatting

decryption
digest
digital certificate
e-commerce
Electronic Data Interchange (EDI)
encryption
Extended Validation SSL (EV SSL)
fraud
hash functions
instant online storefront
integrity
intellectual property
international commerce

key
merchant account
mobile payment
m-payment
near field communication (NFC)
Secure Sockets Layer (SSL)
security
shopping cart software
smart card
symmetric-key encryption
taxation

Review Questions

Multiple Choice

1. Which of the following is a major function of e-commerce?
   a. using SSL to encrypt orders
   b. adding items to a shopping cart
   c. buying and selling goods
   d. none of the above

2. For businesses, which is an advantage of using e-commerce?
   a. reduced costs
   b. the potential for fraudulent transactions
   c. using shopping carts
   d. none of the above

3. For businesses, which is a potential risk of using e-commerce?
   a. increased customer satisfaction
   b. the possibility of fraudulent transactions
   c. lower overhead costs
   d. none of the above

4. What is a short-range wireless communication that uses a radio frequency to share information between electronic devices?
   a. SSL
   b. NFC
   c. EDI
   d. FTP

5. Which of the following options best describes how a website owner can obtain a digital certificate?
   a. Digital certificates are automatically created when you register for a domain name.
   b. Visit a certificate authority and apply for a digital certificate.
   c. Digital certificates are automatically created when you are listed in a search engine.
   d. none of the above

6. Which of the following issues are uniquely related to international e-commerce?

   a. language and currency conversion

   b. browser version and screen resolution

   c. bandwidth and Internet service provider

   d. none of the above

7. Which of the following acronyms refer to the business-to-consumer e-commerce business model?

   a. B2B

   b. BTC

   c. B2C

   d. C2B

8. Which of the following is a disadvantage of an instant online storefront?

   a. The store is based on a template and may look very similar to other online stores.

   b. The store can be ready in minutes.

   c. The store cannot accept credit cards.

   d. none of the above

9. Which of the following include(s) an online catalog, a shopping cart, and a secure order form?

   a. web host providers

   b. shopping cart software

   c. web server software

   d. e-commerce hosting packages

10. Which of the following is true?

   a. A merchant account allows you to use SSL on your website.

   b. Shopping cart add-ins, or extensions, are available for popular web-authoring tools such as Adobe Dreamweaver.

   c. Instant storefronts are what most large-scale e-commerce sites use.

   d. none of the above

Fill in the Blank

11. An encryption method that uses a single, shared private key is _____.

12. _____ can be described as the transfer of structured data between different companies using networks.

13. A digital certificate is a form of a(n) _____ that also contains additional information about the entity holding the certificate.

14. _____ is a protocol that allows data to be privately exchanged over public networks.

Short Answer

15. List one option for a website that needs to reach audiences that speak different languages.

Hands-On Exercises

1. In this Hands-On Exercise, you will create an instant storefront. Choose one of the following websites that offer free trial online stores: Earthstores (http://earthstores.com), AAcart (http://www.aacart.com), InstanteStore (http://www.instantestore.com), Shopify (http://www.shopify.com), BigCommerce (http://www.bigcommerce.com), or EasyStoreCreator (http://www.easystorecreator.com). Websites are constantly changing their policies, so these sites may no longer offer free trials when you do this assignment. If this is the case, check the textbook's website for updated information, ask your instructor for assistance, or search the Web for free online storefronts or trial stores. If you are certain that you have found a website that offers a free trial store, continue with this exercise and create a store that meets the following criteria:

   - Name: Door County Images

   - Purpose: To sell fine quality prints of Door County scenery

   - Target Audience: Adults age 40+ who have visited Door County; are middle to upper class; and who enjoy nature, boating, hiking, cycling, and fishing

   - Item 1: Print of Ellison Bay at Sunset, Size: 11 inches by 14 inches, Price: $19.95

   - Item 2: Print of Ellison Bay in Summer, Size: 11 inches by 14 inches, Price: $19.95

Create a folder called doorcounty. Copy the following images from the chapter12 folder in the student files to your doorcounty folder: summer.jpg, summer_small.jpg, sunnydays.jpg, sunset.jpg, and sunset_small.jpg. Once you are organized, visit the website you have chosen to host your free store. You will have to log in, choose options, and upload your images. Follow the instructions provided. Most free online store sites have an FAQ section or technical support to help you. Figure 12.4 shows a page from a sample store using a BigCommerce instant storefront. After you have completed your store, print out the browser view of the home page and catalog page.

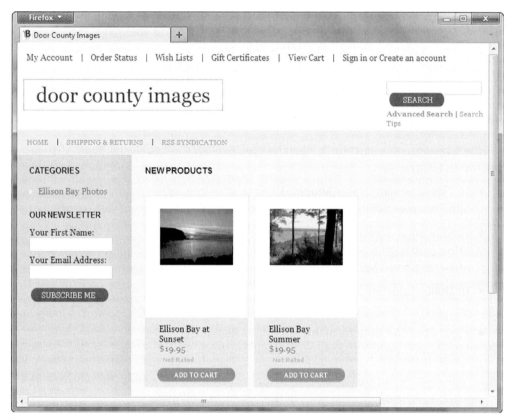

Figure 12.4 An instant store created at BigCommerce (http://www.bigcommerce.com)

Web Research

1. Just how popular is e-commerce? How many of your friends, family members, coworkers, and classmates purchase on the Web? Survey at least 20 people. Determine the following:

   a. How many have purchased an item online?

   b. How many have shopped but not purchased online?

   c. How many purchase online once a year? Once a month? Once a week?

   d. What is their age range (18–25, 26–39, 40–50, or over 50)?

   e. What is their gender?

   f. What is their level of education (high school, some college, college graduate, or graduate school)?

   g. What is their favorite online shopping site?

Create a web page that illustrates your findings. Also comment on the results and draw some conclusions. Search the Web for statistics that support your conclusions. Use the Pew Internet and American Life Project (http://pewinternet.org), eMarketer (http://www.emarketer.com/Products/Reports.aspx), ClickZ (http://www.clickz.com), and E-Commerce Times (http://www.ecommercetimes.com) as starting points for your research. Place your name in an e-mail link on the web page.

2. This chapter provided a number of resources for e-commerce shopping cart and ordering systems. Use them as a starting point. Search the Web for additional resources. Find at least three shopping cart systems that you feel would be easy to use. Create a web page that reports your findings. Organize your page and list the information along with the URLs of the websites you used as resources. Include information such as the product name, a brief description, the cost, and the web server requirements (if any). Place your name in an e-mail link on the web page.

Focus on Web Design

Visit the following sites as a starting point as you explore the web design topic of shopping cart usability:

- 10 Tips to Design Usable Shopping Carts:
  http://www.webdesignerdepot.com/2009/04/10-tips-to-design-usable-shopping-carts

- Fundamental Guidelines of E-Commerce Checkout Design:
  http://uxdesign.smashingmagazine.com/2011/04/06/fundamental-guidelines-of-e-commerce-checkout-design

- Usability Guidelines for Shopping Chart Checkouts:
  http://2helixtech.com/usability-guidelines-for-shopping-cart-checkouts-5491

- 107 Add to Cart Buttons of the Top Online Retailers:
  http://www.getelastic.com/add-to-cart-buttons

Write a one-page report that describes shopping cart usability issues that web designers should be aware of. Cite the URLs of the resources you used.

 WEBSITE CASE STUDY

Adding a Catalog Page for an Online Store

Each of the following case studies has continued throughout most of the text. This chapter adds a catalog page for an online store to the websites. This catalog page will connect to sample shopping cart and order pages on the textbook website at http://www.webdevfoundations.net.

JavaJam Coffee House

See Chapter 2 for an introduction to the JavaJam Coffee House case study. Use the Chapter 9 JavaJam website as a starting point for this case study. As frequently happens with websites, the client, Julio Perez, is pleased with the response to the site and has an idea about a new use for it—selling JavaJam gear, such as T-shirts and coffee mugs. This new page, gear.html, will be part of the main navigation of the site. All pages should link to it. A revised site map is shown in Figure 12.5.

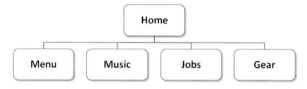

Figure 12.5 Revised JavaJam site map

The Gear page should contain a description, image, and price for each product. It should link to a shopping cart system when the visitor wants to purchase an item. You may access a demonstration shopping cart/ordering system provided by the textbook's website. If you have access to a different shopping cart system, check with your instructor and ask if you can use it instead.

You have four tasks in this case study:

1. Create a new folder for this JavaJam case study.

2. Modify the main navigation on each page to include a link to the new Gear page.

3. Modify the javajam.css external CSS file.

4. Create the new Gear page (gear.html) shown in Figure 12.6.

Hands-On Practice Case Study

Task 1: Create a Folder. Create a folder called javajam12. Copy all of the files from your Chapter 9 javajam9 folder into the javajam12 folder. Copy the javamug.gif and javatshirt.gif images from the chapter12 folder in the student files and save them to your javajam12 folder.

Task 2: Update the Navigation on Each Page. Launch a text editor and open the home page (index.html). Add a new list item and hyperlink in the main navigation area that displays the text "Gear" and links to the file gear.html. See Figure 12.6 for an example of the navigation area. Save the file. Edit the Menu (menu.html), Music (music.html), and Jobs (jobs.html) pages in a similar manner and save each file.

Task 3: Configure the CSS. Launch a text editor and open javajam.css. Before you create the Gear page (gear.html), you will add a new style rule to your javajam.css external style sheet that configures a class named clearright. The clearright class will be used to clear a right float. The style rule is

```
.clearright { clear: right; }
```

Task 4: Create the New Gear Page. One way to be productive is to create pages based on your earlier work. Launch a text editor and open the Music page (music.html). Save

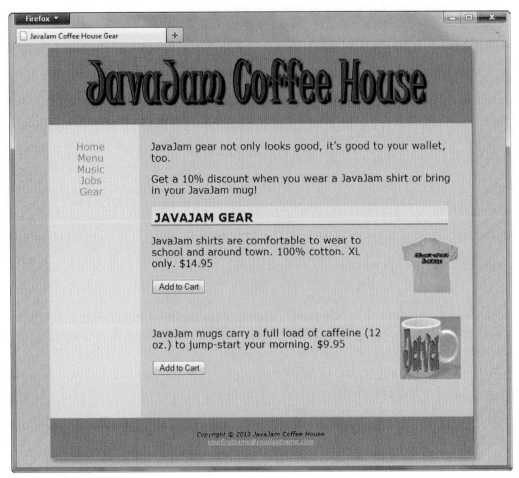

Figure 12.6 New JavaJam Gear page

the file as gear.html. This will give you a head start and ensure that the pages on the website are similar. Perform the following modifications:

a. Change the page title to an appropriate phrase.

b. Delete the contents of the div assigned to the content id.

c. Place each sentence below in a separate paragraph:

JavaJam gear not only looks good, it's good to your wallet, too.

Get a 10% discount when you wear a JavaJam shirt or bring in your JavaJam mug!

d. Code the text "JavaJam Gear" with an h2 element.

e. Configure an image element to display the javashirt.gif graphic. Assign the image to the floatright class.

f. Configure the following text in a paragraph: "JavaJam shirts are comfortable to wear to school and around town. 100% cotton. XL only. $14.95"

g. Code a line break tag below the paragraph. Assign the line break tag to the clearright class.

h. Configure an image element to display the javamug.gif graphic. Assign the image to the floatright class.

i. Configure the following text in a paragraph: "JavaJam mugs carry a full load of caffeine (12 oz.) to jump-start your morning. $9.95".

j. Next you will add a shopping cart button to each item for sale. This is placed in a form. The action on the form is the script called http://www.webdevfoundations.net/scripts/cart.asp. Remember that whenever you use server-side scripts, there will be some documentation or specifications for you to follow. This script processes a limited shopping cart that works with two items only. The gear.html web page will pass information to the script by using hidden fields in the form that contains the button to invoke the script. Please pay careful attention to detail when working on this.

To place the shopping cart button for the T-shirt, add the following code below the paragraph that describes the T-shirt and above the line break tag.

```
<form method="post"
    action="http://www.webdevfoundations.net/scripts/cart.asp">
    <input type="hidden" name="desc1" id="desc1" value="JavaJam Shirt">
    <input type="hidden" name="cost1" id="cost1" value="14.95">
    <input type="submit" value="Add to Cart">
</form>
```

This HTML invokes a server-side script that processes a demonstration shopping cart. The hidden fields named desc1 and cost1 are sent to the script when the Submit button is clicked. These indicate the name and cost of the item.

The process for adding the shopping cart button for the mug is similar, using hidden form fields named desc2 and cost2. Add the following code below the paragraph that contains the description of the mug.

```
<form method="post"
    action="http://www.webdevfoundations.net/scripts/cart.asp">
    <input type="hidden" name="desc2" id="desc2" value="JavaJam Mug">
    <input type="hidden" name="cost2" id="cost2" value="9.95">
    <input type="submit" value="Add to Cart">
</form>
```

Save your page and test it in a browser. It should look similar to the one shown in Figure 12.6. Click the Add to Cart button for the JavaJam shirt. The demonstration shopping cart will display and your screen should look similar to the one shown in Figure 12.7.

Figure 12.7 A Shopping Cart page created by the server-side script that processes the shopping cart and order

Experiment with the cart and try to purchase both items. Simulate placing an order, as shown in Figure 12.8. The shopping cart and order pages are for demonstration purposes only.

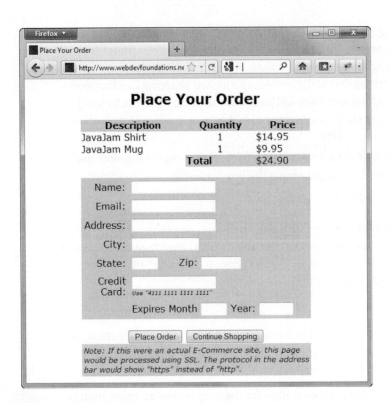

Figure 12.8 An Order page created by the server-side script that processes the shopping cart order

FAQ   How does the cart.asp server-side script work?

The cart.asp file is an ASP script. It is coded to accept a number of form fields and to process them. It creates a web page based on the values and fields that were passed to it. Table 12.3 shows the form fields and values used by the cart.asp file.

Table 12.3 Specifications for cart.asp

Script URL	http://www.webdevfoundations.net/scripts/cart.asp	
Processing	This script accepts product and price information, displays a shopping cart, and finally displays an order page.	
Limitation	This script can only handle two products.	
Input Elements	desc1	Contains the description of the first product. It is displayed on the Shopping Cart page.
	cost1	Contains the per item cost of the first product. It is displayed on the Shopping Cart page.
	desc2	Contains the description of the second product. It is displayed on the Shopping Cart page.
	cost2	Contains the per item cost of the second product. It is displayed on the Shopping Cart page.
	view	If the value is "yes", the shopping cart is displayed.
Output	Shopping Cart web page	Displays the shopping cart. The web page visitor is given the option to continue shopping or to display the Order page to place an order.
	Order web page	Displays an order form. The web page visitor is given the option to place the order or to continue shopping.
	Order Confirmation page	Displays a message to confirm that an order was placed. If this were an actual website, the order would also be saved in a server-side file or database.

Fish Creek Animal Hospital

See Chapter 2 for an introduction to the Fish Creek Animal Hospital case study. You will use the Chapter 9 fishcreek9 folder as the starting point for this case study.

After a site is initially created, it's typical for a client to think of new ideas for the website. The owner of Fish Creek, Magda Patel, is pleased with the response to the site and has a new use for it—selling sweatshirts and tote bags with the Fish Creek logo. She already has these materials for sale at her front desk in the animal hospital and her customers seem to like them. This new Shop page (shop.html) will be part of the main navigation of the site. All pages should link to it. A revised site map is shown in Figure 12.9.

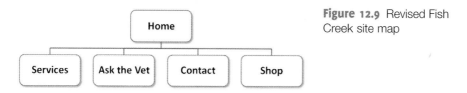

Figure 12.9 Revised Fish Creek site map

The Shop page should contain the description, image, and price of each product. It should link to a shopping cart system when the visitor wants to purchase an item. You may access a demonstration shopping cart/ordering system provided by the textbook's website. If you have access to a different shopping cart system, check with your instructor and ask if you can use it instead.

You have four tasks in this case study:

1. Create a new folder for this Fish Creek case study.

2. Modify the main navigation on each page to include a link to the new Shop page.

3. Modify the fishcreek.css external CSS file.

4. Create the new Shop page (shop.html) shown in Figure 12.10.

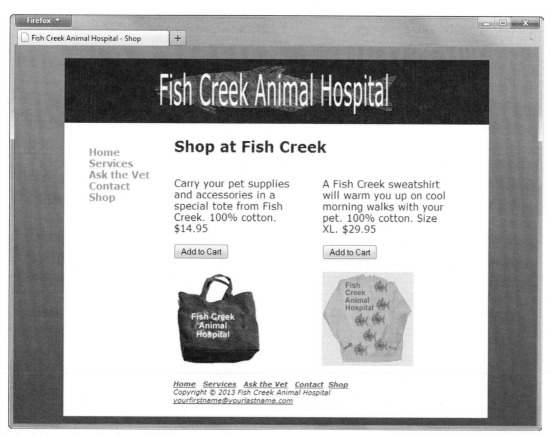

Figure 12.10 New Fish Creek Shop page

Hands-On Practice Case

Task 1: Create a Folder. Create a folder called fishcreek12. Copy all of the files from your Chapter 9 fishcreek9 folder into the fishcreek12 folder. Copy the fishtote.gif and fishsweat.gif images from the chapter12 folder in the student files and save them to your fishcreek12 folder.

Task 2: Update the Navigation on Each Page. Launch a text editor and open the home page (index.html). Add a new list item and hyperlink in the main navigation area that displays the text "Shop" and links to the file shop.html. Add a new hyperlink in the footer navigation area that displays the text "Shop" and links to the file shop.html. See Figure 12.10 for an example of the navigation areas. Save the file. Edit the Services (services.html), Ask the Vet (askvet.html), and Contact (contact.html) pages in a similar manner. Save each file.

Task 3: Configure the CSS. Launch a text editor and open the fishcreek.css file.

a. Configure a class named shop. The shop class will contain the description and Add to Cart form. Configure the shop class with 40% width, left float, 40 pixels of right margin, and 20 pixels of bottom margin. The style rule follows:

```
.shop { width: 40%;
  float: left;
  padding-right: 40px;
  padding-bottom: 20px; }
```

b. Add a style declaration to #footer that clears all floats.

c. Modify the style rules for #wrapper and set the max-width to 960 pixels.

Task 4: Create the New Shop Page. One way to be productive is to create pages based on your earlier work. Launch a text editor and open the home page (index.html). Save the file as shop.html. This will give you a head start and ensure that the pages on the website are similar. Perform the following modifications:

a. Change the page title to an appropriate phrase.

b. Delete the description list and the address/phone information from the page.

c. Configure the following text in an h2 element: "Shop at Fish Creek".

d. Create a div that is assigned to the shop class. The div will contain a description and a form that will process the Add to Cart button. You will configure the description in this step. Type the following descriptive text in a paragraph: "Carry your pet supplies and accessories in a special tote from Fish Creek. 100% cotton. $14.95".

e. Configure the fishtote.gif image below the div element.

f. Create another div that is assigned to the shop class. The div will contain a description and a form that will process the Add to Cart button. You will configure the description in this step. Type the following descriptive text in a paragraph: "A Fish Creek sweatshirt will warm you up on cool morning walks with your pet. 100% cotton. Size XL. $29.95".

g. Configure the fishsweat.gif image below the div element.

h. Next, we will add a shopping cart button to each item for sale. This shopping cart button is placed in a form after the paragraph in each shop div. The action on the form is the ASP script called http://www.webdevfoundations.net/scripts/cart.asp. Remember that whenever you use server-side scripts, there will be some documentation or specifications for you to follow. This script processes a limited shopping cart that works with two items only. The shop.html web page will pass information to the script by using hidden fields in the form that contains the button to invoke the script. Please pay careful attention to detail when working on this.

To place the shopping cart button for the tote, add the following code below the paragraph with the tote's description and within the shop div:

```
<form method="post"
action="http://www.webdevfoundations.net/scripts/cart.asp">
   <input type="hidden" name="desc1" id="desc1" value="Fish
   Creek Tote">
   <input type="hidden" name="cost1" id="cost1" value="14.95">
   <input type="submit" value="Add to Cart">
</form>
```

This HTML invokes a server-side script that processes a demonstration shopping cart. The hidden fields named `desc1` and `cost1` are sent to the script when the Submit button is clicked. These indicate the name and cost of the item.

The process for adding the shopping cart button for the sweatshirt is similar, using hidden form fields named `desc2` and `cost2`. The HTML is

```
<form method="post"
action="http://www.webdevfoundations.net/scripts/cart.asp">
   <input type="hidden" name="desc2" id="desc2" value="Fish
   Creek Shirt">
   <input type="hidden" name="cost2" id="cost2" value="29.95">
   <input type="submit" value="Add to Cart">
</form>
```

i. Configure a line break element assigned to the `clearfloat` class below the second shop div element area.

Save your page and test it in a browser. It should look similar to the one shown in Figure 12.10. Click the Add to Cart button for the tote. The demonstration shopping cart will display and your screen should look similar to the one shown in Figure 12.7. Experiment with the cart and try to purchase both items. You can simulate placing an order, as shown in Figure 12.8. The shopping cart and order pages are for demonstration purposes only.

Pacific Trails Resort

See Chapter 2 for an introduction to the Pacific Trails case study. You will use the Chapter 9 pacific9 folder as the starting point for this case study.

As often happens with websites, the client, Melanie Bowie, is pleased with the response to the site and has an idea about a new use for it—selling books that she's written about yoga and hiking at Pacific Trails Resort. She already has these for sale at the resort front desk and her customers seem to like them. This new Shop page (shop.html) will be part of the main navigation of the site. All pages should link to it. A revised site map is shown in Figure 12.11.

The Shop page should contain the description, image, and price of each book. It should link to a shopping cart system when the visitor wants to purchase an item. You may

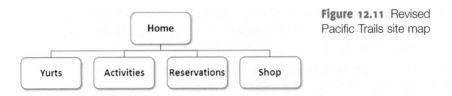

Figure 12.11 Revised Pacific Trails site map

access a demonstration shopping cart/ordering system available on the textbook's website. If you have access to a different shopping cart system, check with your instructor and ask if you can use it instead.

You have four tasks in this case study:

1. Create a new folder for this Pacific Trails case study.

2. Modify the main navigation on each page to include a link to the new Shop page.

3. Modify the pacific.css external CSS file.

4. Create the new Shop page (shop.html) shown in Figure 12.12.

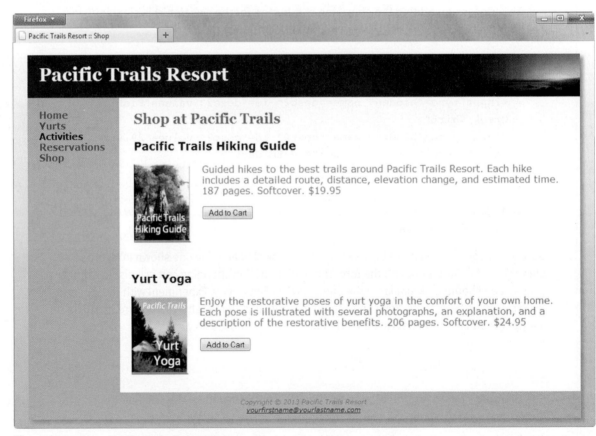

Figure 12.12 New Pacific Trails Resort Shop page

Hands-On Practice Case Study

Task 1: Create a Folder. Create a folder called pacific12. Copy all of the files from your Chapter 9 pacific9 folder into the pacific12 folder. Copy the trailguide.jpg and yurtyoga.jpg images from the chapter12 folder in the student files and save them to your pacific12 folder.

Task 2: Update the Navigation on Each Page. Launch a text editor and open the home page (index.html). Add a new list item and hyperlink in the main navigation area that displays the text "Shop" and links to the file shop.html. See Figure 12.12 for an example of the navigation area. Save the file. Edit the Yurts (yurts.html), Activities (activities.html), and Reservations (reservations.html) pages in a similar manner. Save each file.

Task 3: Configure the CSS. Launch a text editor and open the pacific.css file. Configure a new style rule to add 30 pixels of padding below each form:

```
form { padding-bottom: 30px; }
```

Task 4: Create the new Shop page. One way to be productive is to create pages based on your earlier work. Launch a text editor and open the home page (index.html). Save the file as shop.html. This will give you a head start and ensure that the pages on the website are similar. Perform the following modifications:

a. Change the page title to an appropriate phrase.

b. Change the text within the h2 element to "Shop at Pacific Trails".

c. Delete the coast.jpg image and other home page content, including the paragraph, unordered list, and contact information.

d. Write the HTML to display the trailguide.jpg image.

e. Configure an h3 element to display "Pacific Trails Hiking Guide".

f. Code a paragraph that will display the text description: "Guided hikes to the best trails around Pacific Trails Resort. Each hike includes a detailed route, distance, elevation change, and estimated time. 187 pages. Softcover. $19.95"

g. Configure the Add to Cart button. The visitor will click a button to indicate that they wish to purchase an item. This shopping cart button is placed in a form. For this exercise, the action on the form is the ASP script called http://www.webdevfoundations.net/scripts/cart.asp. Remember that whenever you use server-side scripts, there will be some documentation or specifications for you to follow. This script processes a limited shopping cart that only works with two items. The shop.html web page will pass information to the script by using hidden fields in the form that contains the button to invoke the script. Please pay careful attention to detail when working on this. To add the shopping cart button for the Hiking Guide book below the description paragraph, write the following code:

```
<form method="post"
   action="http://www.webdevfoundations.net/scripts/cart.asp">
   <input type="hidden" name="desc1" id="desc1" value="Hiking Guide">
   <input type="hidden" name="cost1" id="cost1" value="19.95">
   <input type="submit" value="Add to Cart">
</form>
```

This HTML invokes a server-side script that processes a demonstration shopping cart. The hidden fields named desc1 and cost1 are sent to the script when the Submit button is clicked. These indicate the name and cost of the item.

h. Code a line break element assigned to the clearfloat class.

i. Write the HTML to display the yurtyoga.jpg image.

j. Configure an h3 element to display "Yurt Yoga".

k. Code a paragraph that will display the text description: "Enjoy the restorative poses of yurt yoga in the comfort of your own home. Each pose is illustrated with several photographs, an explanation, and a description of the restorative benefits. 206 pages. Softcover. $24.95"

l. Configure the Add to Cart button by writing the following HTML for the form with the shopping cart button:

```
<form method="post"
  action="http://www.webdevfoundations.net/scripts/cart.asp">
  <input type="hidden" name="desc2" id="desc2" value="Yurt Yoga">
  <input type="hidden" name="cost2" id="cost2" value="24.95">
  <input type="submit" value="Add to Cart">
</form>
```

This HTML invokes a server-side script that processes a demonstration shopping cart. The hidden fields named `desc2` and `cost2` are sent to the script when the Submit button is clicked. These indicate the name and cost of the item.

m. Code a line break element assigned to the `clearfloat` class.

Save your page and test it in a browser. It should look similar to the one shown in Figure 12.12. Click the Add to Cart button for one of the books. The demonstration shopping cart will display and your screen should look similar to the one shown in Figure 12.7. Experiment with the cart and try to purchase both items. You can simulate placing an order, as shown in Figure 12.8. The shopping cart and order pages are for demonstration purposes only.

Prime Properties

See Chapter 2 for an introduction to the Prime Properties case study. You will use the Chapter 9 prime9 folder as the starting point for this case study.

The owner, Maria Valdez, would like to showcase the company's services and provide an easy way for clients to choose their thank-you gift. She would like a Services page that will briefly describe the services and offer a form for clients to select their gift. The new Services page (services.html) will be part of the main navigation of the site. All pages should link to it. A revised site map is shown in Figure 12.13.

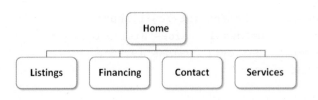

Figure 12.13 Revised Prime Properties site map

The Services page, shown in Figure 12.14, will contain the subheading Services, two short paragraphs of text about the services, and the description and photograph of each gift option. You may access a demonstration shopping cart/ordering system provided by the textbook's website. If you have access to a different shopping cart system, check with your instructor and ask if you can use it instead.

You have three tasks in this case study:

1. Create a new folder for this Prime Properties case study.

2. Modify the main navigation on each page to include a link to the new Services page.

3. Create the new Services page (services.html) shown in Figure 12.14.

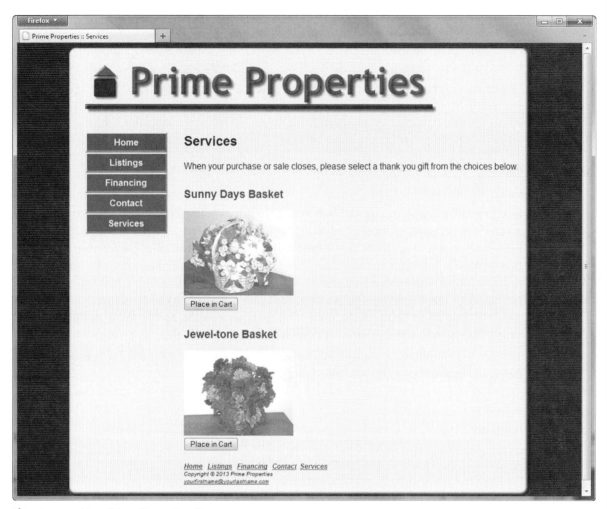

Figure 12.14 New Prime Properties Services page

Hands-On Practice Case Study

Task 1: Create a Folder. Create a folder called prime12. Copy all of the files from your Chapter 9 prime9 folder into the prime12 folder. Copy the jeweltone.jpg and sunnydays.jpg images from the chapter12 folder in the student files and save them to your prime12 folder.

Task 2: Update the Navigation on Each Page. Launch a text editor and open the home page (index.html). Add a new list item and hyperlink in the main navigation area that displays the text "Services" and links to the file services.html. Add a new hyperlink in the footer navigation area that displays the text "Services" and links to the file services.html. See Figure 12.14 for an example of the navigation areas. Save the file. Edit the Listings (listings.html), Financing (financing.html), and Contact (contact.html) pages in a similar manner. Save each file.

Task 3: Create the New Services Page. One way to be productive is to create pages based on your earlier work. Launch a text editor and open the Financing page (financing.html). Save the file as services.html. This will give you a head start and ensure that the pages on the website are similar. Perform the following modifications:

a. Change the page title to an appropriate phrase.

b. Change the Financing heading to Services.

c. Delete the other text and HTML on the page related to the financing content.

d. Place your cursor on the line after the Services heading. Create a paragraph with the following text:

"When your purchase or sale closes, please select a thank you gift from the choices below."

e. Configure an h3 element to display the text "Sunny Days Basket".

f. Configure the sunnydays.jpg image.

g. Configure an h3 element to display the text "Jewel-tone Basket".

h. Configure the jeweltone.jpg.

i. Next, we will add a shopping cart button to each gift item for selection. The action on the form is the ASP script called http://webdevfoundations.net/scripts/cart1.asp. Remember that whenever you use server-side scripts, there will be some documentation or specifications for you to follow. This script processes a limited shopping cart that only works with two items. Because it is designed to function as a gift selector, no prices are displayed. The services.html web page will pass information to the script by using a hidden field in the form that contains the button to invoke the script. Please pay careful attention to detail when working on this.

To place the shopping cart button for the Sunny Days Basket, add the following code below the image tag for the sunnydays.jpg graphic:

```
<form method="post"
action="http://www.webdevfoundations.net/scripts/cart1.asp">
  <input type="hidden" name="desc1" id="desc1"
  value="Sunny Days Basket">
  <input type="submit" value="Place in Cart">
</form>
```

This HTML invokes a server-side script that processes a demonstration shopping cart. The hidden field named desc1 and its value are sent to the script when the Submit button is clicked. This passes the name of the item chosen to the server-side script.

j. The process for adding the shopping cart button for the Jewel-tone Basket is similar, using the hidden form field desc2. The HTML is

```
<form method="post"
action="http://www.webdevfoundations.net/scripts/cart1.asp">
  <input type="hidden" name="desc2" id="desc2"
  value="Jewel-tone Basket">
  <input type="submit" value="Place in Cart">
</form>
```

Save your page and test it in a browser. It should look similar to the one shown in Figure 12.14. Click the Place in Cart button for the Sunny Days Basket. The demonstration shopping cart will display and your screen should be similar to the one pictured in Figure 12.7 (except that no price information will display). Experiment with the cart and try to select both items. You can simulate selecting gifts. The shopping cart and order pages are for demonstration purposes only.

Web Project

See Chapter 5 for an introduction to the Web Project. Review the goals of your website and determine whether they include an e-commerce component. If so, you will add this component to your web project.

Hands-On Practice Case Study

Revise the site map as needed to include the e-commerce component. Perhaps you will add a Products page to your website. Perhaps the Products page already exists and you are just adding functionality to the page. In either case, make sure that the site map and content sheets reflect the new processing.

There are a number of free or low-cost shopping cart providers on the Web. Some are provided in the following list. Your instructor may have additional resources or suggestions. Choose one of the providers from the list in order to add a shopping cart to your website. When you subscribe or sign up for these services, be sure to note any potential costs.

- Mal's e-commerce (free and low-cost service): http://www.mals-e.com

- PayPal (there is a cost per transaction for this service): http://www.paypal.com

- Google Checkout (there is a cost per transaction for this service): http://checkout.google.com/seller/

- JustAddCommerce (free trial): http://www.richmediatech.com

Save and test your page. Experiment with the shopping cart. Welcome to the world of e-commerce!

Web Promotion

You've built it—now what can you do to attract visitors to your website? Once you have visitors, how do you encourage them to return? Getting listed on search engines, site affiliations, and banner ads are some of the topics that are discussed in this chapter.

13.1 **Search Engine Overview**

What do you do when you need to find a website? Most people launch their favorite search engine. A Nielsen/NetRatings survey found that 9 out of 10 web users visit a search engine, portal, or community site every month. These web users also revisit the sites frequently, almost five times per month.

Using a **search engine** is a popular way to navigate the Web and find websites. The PEW Internet and American Life Project (http://www.pewinternet.org/Reports/ 2010/Generations-2010/Activities/All-age-groups.aspx) reports that 87% of American adults use a search engine daily. A Direct Marketing News report (http://www.dmnews.com/cms/dm-news/search-marketing/37367.html) on a Harris Interactive study states that 80% of Internet traffic begins at a search engine.

A search engine listing helps customers find your site and increases the chances that they will make a purchase. Search engine listings can be an excellent marketing tool for your business. To harness the power of search engines and search indexes (sometimes called search directories), it helps to know how they work.

13.2 **Popular Search Engines**

According to NetMarketShare (http://marketshare.hitslink.com/search-engine-market-share.aspx), Google (http://www.google.com) and Yahoo! (http://www.yahoo.com) were the two most popular sites used to search the Web during a recent month. Google was reported to have an overwhelming market share of almost 84%, while the closest competitors were Yahoo (6.21%), Baidu (4.64%), and Microsoft's Bing at http://www.bing.com (3.57%). Check http://marketshare.hitslink.com for the most recent survey results.

Google's popularity has continued to grow since it was founded in the late 1990s. The simple and whimsical interface, combined with quick-loading and useful results, has made it a favorite of web users. The second most popular search engine is Yahoo! Although Yahoo! is now a search engine, it originally was a **search index** (also called a **search directory**). Each site that is submitted for inclusion in a search directory is re-viewed by a person. An example of a current search index is the Open Directory Project (http://www.dmoz.org). It contains a hierarchy of topics and sites related to each topic. In this project, anyone can volunteer to be an editor and site reviewer. There is no cost to submit your site to the Open Directory Project. An added benefit to being listed in the Open Directory Project is that the database containing the approved sites is used by a number of search engines, including Google and Ask.com.

13.3 **Components of a Search Engine**

Search engines have the following components:

- Robot
- Database (also used by search directories)
- Search form (also used by search directories)

Robot

A **robot** (sometimes called a spider or bot) is a program that automatically traverses the hypertext structure of the Web by retrieving a web page document and following the hyperlinks on the page. It moves like a robot spider on the Web, accessing and documenting web pages. The robot categorizes the pages and stores information about the website and the web pages in a database. Various robots may work differently, but, in general, they access and may store the following sections of web pages: title, meta tag descriptions, and some of the text on the page (usually either the first few sentences or the text contained in heading tags). Visit Web Robots Pages (http://www.robotstxt.org) if you'd like more details about web robots.

Database

A **database** is a collection of information which is organized so that its contents can easily be accessed, managed, and updated. A database management system (DBMS), such as Oracle, Microsoft SQL Server, or IBM DB2, is used to configure and manage the database. The web page that displays the results of your search has information from the database accessed by the search engine site. According to Bruce Clay (http://www.bruceclay.com/searchenginerelationshipchart.htm), some search engines receive portions of their content from other search engines. For example, AOL Search receives its primary content from Google.

Search Form

The **search form** is the component of a search engine that you are most familiar with. You have probably used a search engine many times but haven't thought about what goes on "under the hood." The search form is the graphical user interface that allows a user to type in a word or phrase to search for. It is usually simply a text box and a submit button. The visitor to the search engine types in words (called keywords) related to his or her search into the text box. When the form is submitted, the data typed into the text box is sent to a server-side script that searches the database using the keywords entered. The **search results** (also called a result set) are a list of information, such as the URLs for web pages, that meets your criteria. This result set is formatted with a link to each page, along with additional information which might include the page title, a brief description, the first few lines of text, or the size of the page. The type of additional information varies by search engine. Next, the web server at the search engine site sends the **search engine results page (SERP)** to your browser for display.

The order in which the pages are displayed may depend on paid advertisements, alphabetical order, and link popularity (more on this later). Each search engine has its own policy for ordering the search results. Be aware that these policies can change over time.

The components of a search engine (robot, database, and search form) work together to obtain information about web pages, store information about web pages, and provide a graphical user interface to facilitate searching for and displaying a list of web pages that are relevant to the given keywords. Now that you are aware of the components of search engines, let's get to the most important part: how to design your pages to promote your website.

13.4 Search Engine Optimization

If you have followed recommended web design practices, you've already designed your website so that the pages are appealing and compelling to your target audience. How can you also make your site work with search engines? This section provides some suggestions and hints on designing your pages for search engines—a process called **search engine optimization (SEO)**.

Keywords

Spend some time brainstorming about terms and phrases that people may use when searching for your site. Make a list of them. These terms or phrases that describe your website or business are your **keywords**.

Page Titles

A descriptive page title (the text between the `<title>` tags), which includes your company and/or website name, will help your site market itself. It's common for search engines to display the text in the page title in the SERP. The page title is also saved by default when a visitor bookmarks your site and is often included when a visitor prints a page of your site. Avoid using the exact same title for every page; include keywords in the page title that are appropriate for the page. For example, instead of just "Trillium Media Design," configure the page title to include both the company name and the purpose of the page: "Trillium Media Design: Custom E-Commerce Solutions."

Heading Tags

Use structural tags, such as `<h1>`, `<h2>`, and so on, to organize your page content. If it is appropriate for the web page content, also include some keywords in the text contained within the heading tags. Some search engines will give a higher list position if keywords are included in a page title or heading. Also include keywords, as appropriate, within the page text content. However, avoid spamming keywords—that is, do not list them over and over again. The programs behind search engines are becoming more sophisticated all the time and you can actually be prevented from being listed if it is perceived that you are not being honest or are trying to cheat the system.

Description

What is special about your website that would make someone want to visit? With this in mind, write a few sentences about your website or business. This description should be inviting and interesting so that a person searching the Web will choose your site from the list provided by a search engine or search directory. Some search engines will display your description in their search engine results. You might be wondering how these are applied to the actual web pages. The description is placed on a web page by adding an HTML meta tag to the head section.

Description Meta Tag

A **meta tag** is a self-contained tag that is placed in the head section of a web page. You've been using a meta tag to indicate character encoding. There are a number of other uses for meta tags. We'll focus here on providing a description of a website for use by search engines. The **description meta tag** content is displayed on the SERP by some search engines, such as Google. The name attribute indicates the use of the meta tag. The content attribute indicates the values needed for that specific use. The `description` value for the `name` attribute indicates that the use of the meta tag is to provide a description. For example, a description meta tag for a website about a web development consulting firm called Acme Design could be configured as follows:

```
<meta name="description" content="Acme Design, a premier web
consulting group that specializes in e-commerce, web design, web
development, and website redesign.">
```

FAQ   What if I do not want a search engine to index a page?

Sometimes there will be pages that you do not want indexed, perhaps test pages or pages only meant for a small group of individuals (such as family or coworkers). Meta tags can be used for this purpose also. To indicate to a search engine robot that a page should not be indexed and the links should not be followed, do not code a description meta tag in the page. Instead, add a **robots meta tag** to the page as follows:

```
<meta name="robots" content="noindex, nofollow">
```

Linking

Verify that all hyperlinks are working. Each page on your website should be reachable by a text hyperlink. The text should be descriptive (avoid phrases like "More info" and "Click here") and should include keywords as appropriate. Inbound links (sometimes called incoming links) are also a factor in SEO; see the link popularity section later in this chapter.

Images and Multimedia

Be mindful that search engine robots do not "see" the text embedded within your images and multimedia. Configure meaningful alternate text for images. Include relevant keywords in the alternate text. Although some search engine robots, such as Google's Googlebot, have recently added the functionality to index text and hyperlinks contained within Flash media, be aware that a website that depends on the use of technologies such as Flash and Silverlight will be less visible to search engines and may rank lower as a result.

Valid Code

Search engines do not require that your HTML and CSS code pass validation tests. However, code that is valid and well structured is likely to be more easily processed by search engine robots. This may help with your placement in the search engine results.

Content of Value

Probably the most basic, but often overlooked, component of SEO is providing content of value contained within a website that follows web design best practices (see

Chapter 5). Your website should contain high-quality, well-organized content that is of value to your visitors.

13.5 Listing in a Search Engine

Although search engines bring visitors to your website, it is not always easy to get listed in a search engine or search directory. Before you even *think* about submitting your website to a search engine, be sure that it is complete and that you have followed basic SEO techniques (as described in the previous section). Once you're confident that your website is ready, follow the steps listed below to submit your site for consideration by a search engine:

Step 1. Visit the search engine website (such as http://www.google.com or http://www.yahoo.com) and look for the "Add site" or "List URL" link.
This is typically on the home page or the About Us page. Be patient because these links are sometimes not obvious. To submit your website to Google, visit http://www.google.com/submityourcontent/website-owner/ and select the "Add your URL" link.

Step 2. Sign in with your Google account, follow the directions listed on the page, and submit the form to request that your site be added to the search engine. At other search engines, there may be a fee for an automatic listing, called paid inclusion. Currently, there is no fee to submit a site to Google.

Step 3. The spider from the search engine will index your site. This may take several weeks.

Step 4. Several weeks after you submit your website, check the search engine or search directory to see if your site is listed. If it is not listed, review your pages and check whether they are optimized for search engines (see the next section) and display in common browsers.

If the website is for a business, you may want to consider paying for listing consideration in a search engine or directory (often referred to as an express submit or express inclusion), paying for preferential placement in search engine displays (called sponsoring or advertising), and paying each time a visitor clicks the search engine's link to your site. Many businesses regard payment for these types of services as another marketing expense, such as paying for a newspaper ad or a listing in the Yellow Pages.

FAQ   **Is advertising on a search engine worth the cost?**

It depends. How much is it worth to your client to appear on the first page of the search engine results? You select the keywords that will trigger the display of your ad. You also set your monthly budget and the maximum amount to pay for each click. While costs and charges vary by search engine, at this time, Google charges are based on cost per click—you'll be charged each time a visitor to Google clicks on your advertisement. Visit http://google.com/adwords for more information about their program.

If you explore the paid advertising programs that search engines offer, you'll encounter a number of acronyms related to marketing. The most common are listed below:

- **CPC: Cost per click**

    CPC (also referred to as PPC, pay per click) is the price you are charged if you have signed up for a paid sponsor or ad program and a visitor clicks on a link to your website.

- **CPM: Cost per thousand impressions**

  CPM is your cost for every 1,000 times that your ad is displayed on a web page (whether or not the visitor clicks on your ad).

- **CTR: Click-through rate**

  CTR is the ratio of the number of times an ad is clicked on to the number of times an ad is viewed. For example, if your ad was shown 100 times and 20 people clicked on it, your CTR would be 20/100, or 20%.

Map Your Site

Google's Webmaster Guidelines describe two types of site maps that are useful for SEO:

- An HTML site map is a web page with a map of the site that contains a hierarchical list of hyperlinks to the major pages in your website (see Figure 5.14). The information on the site map page is not only helpful for your website visitors, but also may assist search engine robots as they follow hyperlinks on your site.

- An XML **Sitemap** is an XML file that is used by search engines, but it is not accessed by your web page visitors. A Sitemap provides information to a search engine, such as Google, about your website and is essentially a list of pages, along with the following information: date that each page was last modified, an indicator of how frequently each page changes, and a priority level for each page. An excerpt from a Sitemap file (sitemap.xml) is shown below:

```
<url>
  <loc>http://webdevfoundations.net/</loc>
  <lastmod>2011-07-03T08:10:09+00:00</lastmod>
  <changefreq>monthly</changefreq>
  <priority>1.00</priority>
</url>
<url>
  <loc>http://webdevfoundations.net/index.html</loc>
  <lastmod>2011-07-03T08:10:09+00:00</lastmod>
  <changefreq>monthly</changefreq>
  <priority>1.00</priority>
</url>
<url>
  <loc>http://webdevfoundations.net/6e/chapter1.html</loc>
  <lastmod>2011-08-22T15:09:07+00:00</lastmod>
  <changefreq>monthly</changefreq>
  <priority>0.800</priority>
</url>
```

Online Sitemap generators, such as http://www.xml-sitemaps.com will automatically create a Sitemap file, named sitemap.xml, for you. You will need to upload the Sitemap to your website and notify Google of its URL. See http://www.google.com/support/webmasters for more information about Sitemaps.

Alliances

There are a number of alliances between certain search engines and search directories. The Open Directory Project (http://www.dmoz.org) provides directory services for a number of search engines, including Google. Note that these alliances can change over time. Awareness of search engine alliances will help you to maximize the chances of your website turning up when a search is performed.

 ## Checkpoint 13.1

1. Describe the three components of a search engine.

2. What is the purpose of the description meta tag?

3. Is it beneficial for a business to pay for preferential listing? Why or why not?

13.6 Monitoring Search Listings

Although you may want your website to appear instantaneously in search engines and search directories, some time may be required before your site appears in the SERPs. According to Enquiro Search Engine Position (http://searchengineposition.com), it can take from 2 days to 2 weeks for a website to be listed on Google. Also, be mindful that there is no guarantee when you submit your site that it will be listed; however, it is rare that a quality website with content of value is not indexed and included in search engine and search directory listings.

As your sites get listed, it becomes important to determine which keywords are working. Usually, you need to fine-tune and modify your keywords over time. Here are a few methods for determining which keywords are working:

- **Manual Checking.** Visit search engines and type in the keywords. Assess the results. You might consider keeping a record of the search engine, keyword(s), and page ranking.

- **Web Analytics.** The Web Analytics Association (http://www.webanalyticsassociation.org) defines **web analytics** as "the measurement, collection, analysis and reporting of Internet data for the purposes of understanding and optimizing web usage." Every visitor to your website, including those who were referred by search engines, is recorded in your website log files. A **website log** consists of one or more text files that record each visit to your site, capturing information about your visitors and about referring websites. You can discover whether your keywords are successful and which search engines are being used by analyzing your log. You can also determine the days and times that your site is visited, the operating systems and browsers being used, the paths that visitors take through the site, and much more. The log is a rather cryptic text file. See Figure 13.1 for a partial log.

Web analytics software can analyze your log file and create easy-to-use charts and reports. If you have your own website and domain name, many web host providers allow free

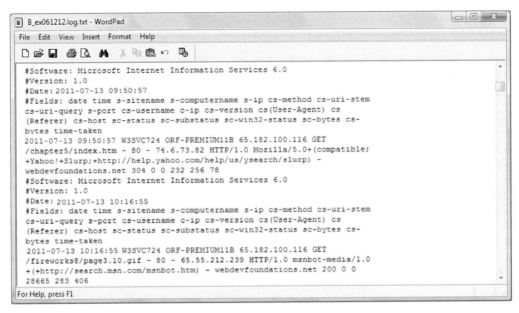

Figure 13.1 A website log file contains useful information, but can be difficult to read

access to the log and may even run web analysis reports as part of the monthly hosting fee. By checking information in the log, you can determine not only what keywords are working, but also which search engines your visitors are using. Webtrends (http://webtrends.com) is a commonly used tool for website log analysis. See Figure 13.2 for information from a log analysis report listing the top 10 keywords used by actual web visitors when searching Google to find a particular website.

Keyword	Visits	Pages Per Visit	Average Time on Site
flash slideshow tutorial	27,097	1.75	00:01:17
adobe flash cs3 tutorial	21,773	6.08	00:07:32
flash cs3 tutorials	15,751	5.71	00:04:56
flash cs3 tutorial	14,346	5.96	00:05:43
flash banner tutorial	6,859	5.32	00:04:05
adobe flash cs3 tutorials	4,943	5.98	00:06:24
fireworks 8 tutorial	4,023	8.20	00:05:23
web development and design foundations with xhtml	3,198	4.17	00:05:02
tutorial flash cs3	3,141	5.06	00:04:46
flash cs5 tutorial	3,120	4.94	00:04:27

Figure 13.2 Partial log file analysis report

Website log analysis is a powerful marketing tool because you can determine exactly how visitors are finding your site. This lets you know which keywords are working and which are not. Perhaps with additional thought, you can add new variations of the productive keywords to your list. If you examine Figure 13.2, you will notice that tutorials are quite popular for this particular website. The developers of this website could add additional tutorials and potentially increase the number of visitors to the site.

Google offers a free web analytics service at http://www.google.com/analytics. The categories of reports provided are as follows:

- Visitors (including a geographical map and browser information)

- Traffic Sources (such as referring sites, keywords, and AdWords)

- Content (including landing pages, paths through the site, and exit pages)

- Goals (tracks business objectives)

Another option is to purchase a program that can help you monitor your search engine positioning. Applications, such as WebPosition (http://webposition.com), can create reports of your search engine rankings, analyze and track keywords, and even submit your sites to search engines.

13.7 Link Popularity

Link popularity is a rating determined by a search engine based on the number of sites that link to a particular website and the quality of those sites. For example, a link from a well-known site such as Oprah Winfrey's website (http://www.oprah.com) would be considered a higher quality link than one from your friend's home page on a free web server. The link popularity of your website can determine its order in the search engine results page. One way to check which sites link to yours is to analyze your log file. Another method is to visit a website that offers a link popularity checking service such as LinkPopularity.com at http://linkpopularity.com to run a report that checks link popularity on a number of search engines. A third method is to visit particular search engines and check for yourself. At Google, type "link:yourdomainname.com" into the search box and the sites that link to yourdomainname.com will be listed. Search engines and search directories are not the only tools you can use to bring visitors to your website. The next section looks at some other options.

13.8 Social Media Optimization

Reach out to your current and potential website visitors with **social media optimization** (SMO), which is described by Rohit Bhargava as optimizing a website so that it is "more easily linked to, more highly visible in social media searches on custom search engines (such as Technorati), and more frequently included in relevant posts on blogs, podcasts and vlogs." The benefits of SMO include increased awareness of your brand and/or site, along with an increase in the number of inbound links (which can help with SEO). Visit the following resources as a starting point as you search for three SMO tips or hints:

- 5 Steps to Expand the Business Value of Social Customer Engagement: http://social-media-optimization.com

- 5 Rules of Social Media Optimization (SMO): http://rohitbhargava.typepad.com/weblog/2006/08/5_rules_of_soci.html

- http://www.toprankblog.com/2009/03/sxswi-interview-rohit-bhargava/

A key principle of SMO is making tagging and bookmarking easy. **Social bookmarking** sites such as Digg (http://digg.com) and Delicious (http://delicious.com) provide a way for people to store, share, and categorize websites. Make it easy for your visitors to add your site to social bookmarking services and social networking services like Twitter and Facebook. You can code hyperlinks to these services yourself or use a content-sharing service such as AddThis (http://www.addthis.com).

Blogs and RSS Feeds

Chapter 1 introduced **blogs**, which are easily updatable and readily available journals on the Web. The power of the blog to share information and elicit comments is being used by businesses of various types (ranging from Nike to Adobe) to build and expand customer relationships. Most blog hosting sites, such as Google's Blogger (http://blogger.com) and WordPress (http://wordpress.com), offer free RSS (Really Simple Syndication or Rich Site Summary) feeds of blog content. The **RSS feed** for a blog is an XML file (with an .rss file extension) that contains a summary of postings with links to a blog or another website. Your customers or business partners can subscribe to the RSS feed and automatically be updated when you've posted new content. RSS feeds are usually identified by an orange button with "XML" or "RSS" in the text. The Firefox browser has a feature called Live Bookmarks, which displays RSS news and blog headlines. There are numerous free and low-cost RSS readers available, including Headline Viewer (http://www.headlineviewer.com) and NetNewsWire (http://netnewswireapp.com). To see a blog in action, visit this textbook's blog at http://webdevfoundations.blogspot.com.

Social Networking

Join groups on social networking sites such as Facebook (http://www.facebook.com), Google+ (http://plus.google.com), or LinkedIn (http://www.linkedin.com) to find and connect with current and potential visitors. Create portable content that promotes your website and publish it on YouTube (http://www.youtube.com), SlideShare (http://www.slideshare.net), and other similar sites. Be active on microblogging sites such as Twitter (http://twitter.com). Bloomberg (http://www.bloomberg.com/apps/news?pid=newsarchive&sid=akXzD_6YNHCk) reported that Dell's use of Twitter resulted in $6.5 million in orders within a two-year period. Blog and tweet about your content. Let viral marketing go to work for you as current and potential visitors find and share your content, which should increase awareness and bring new and returning visitors to your site.

13.9 Other Site Promotion Activities

There are a number of other ways you can promote your website, including Quick Response (QR) codes, affiliate programs, banner ads, banner exchanges, reciprocal link agreements, newsletters, personal recommendations, traditional media advertising, and placement of the URL on all promotional materials.

Quick Response (QR) Codes

A **QR code** is a two-dimensional barcode in a square pattern that is readable by a smartphone camera scan application or a QR barcode reader. The data encoded can be text, a telephone number, or even the URL of a website. ClickZ reports that the popularity of QR codes is increasing because of increased smartphone use

Figure 13.3 QR code for http://webdevfoundations.net

(http://www.clickz.com/clickz/column/2039242/qr-codes-matter). There are many free online QR code generators, including http://qrcode.kaywa.com, http://www.labeljoy.com/en/generate-qr-code.html, and http://www.qrstuff.com. Free apps, such as ScanLife and QR Code Scanner, are available for Apple, Android, and BlackBerry smartphones that use the camera feature to scan the QR code, typically a URL for a website, which is then displayed by the smartphone's web browser. QR codes are useful for promoting a website; include it on your business card or even a T-shirt! The QR code in Figure 13.3 displays the home page of the textbook's website (http://webdevfoundations.net).

Affiliate Programs

The essence of **affiliate programs** is that one website (the affiliate) promotes another website's products or services (the merchant) in exchange for a commission. Both websites benefit from this association. Amazon.com reportedly began the first affiliate marketing program and its Amazon.com Associates program is still going strong. By joining this program, your website can feature books and other products with a link to the Amazon website. If one of your visitors makes a purchase, you get a commission. Amazon benefits because you have delivered an interested visitor who may buy items now or in the future. Your site benefits from the prestige of being affiliated with a known site such as Amazon and the potential for income from the program.

View the Commission Junction website (http://www.cj.com) to see a program that matches websites with potential affiliate programs. Their service allows publishers (website owners and developers) to choose from a wide range of advertisers and affiliate programs. The benefits to web developers include the opportunity to partner with leading advertisers, earn additional revenue from website visitors or ad space, and view real-time tracking and reporting. Visit AssociatePrograms.com (http://www.associateprograms.com) for a directory of affiliate, associate, and referral programs.

Banner Ads

A **banner ad** is typically a graphic image that is used to announce and advertise the name or identity of a site. Banner ads are image hyperlinks that display the advertised site when clicked. You probably see them many times as you surf the Web. They've been around for quite some time; *HotWired*, the first commercial web magazine, introduced the first banner ad in 1994 to promote AT&T.

There is no official size for a banner ad. However, the Interactive Advertising Bureau (http://www.iab.net) provides guidelines for typical ads, including a leaderboard banner (728×90 pixels) and a medium rectangle (300×250 pixels). Visit its website for a full listing of types of ads and common sizes (http://www.iab.net/iab_products_and_industry_services/508676/508767/Ad_Unit). The cost to display your banner ad can vary. Some websites charge by the impression (usually in terms of cost per thousand impressions, or CPM). Others charge for click-throughs only (when the banner ad is clicked). Some search engines sell banner ads and will display your ad on a results page for a keyword that relates to your site (for a fee, of course!).

The effectiveness of banner ads has been a topic of study. If you are like most website visitors, you do not click on banner ads. This means that banner ads do not necessarily generate more immediate visitors to a site. The Interactive Advertising Bureau researched the relationship between banner ads and brand awareness. A ClickZ (http://www.clickz.com/stats/sectors/advertising/article.php/804761) report about this classic study indicates that while standard banner ads helped boost brand awareness, other formats such as skyscrapers (long, skinny ads that run down one side of a page) and larger rectangular ads were three to six times more effective in increasing brand awareness and message association. Media technologies such as audio, video, and Flash also have a greater impact and increase branding effectiveness. Of course, the thinking is that increased brand awareness will increase the likelihood of an actual website visit in the future. If the cost associated with banner ads seems to outweigh their benefits, consider a free option, a banner exchange.

Banner Exchange

While the details of **banner exchange** programs vary, the idea is that you agree to show banners from other sites and they will show your banner. Information on banner exchanges may be found at ExchangeAd (http://www.exchangead.com) and Impressionz (http://www.impressionz.com). Banner exchanges can be beneficial to all parties because of the free advertising.

Reciprocal Link Agreements

A **reciprocal link agreement** is usually between two sites with related or complementary content. You agree to link to each other. The result should be more visitors for each site. If you find a site that you'd like to set up a reciprocal link agreement with, contact its webmaster (usually by e-mail) and ask! Because some search engines partially determine rankings based on the number of quality links to a website, a well-placed reciprocal link can help both sites.

Newsletters

A **newsletter** can bring return visitors to your site. The first step is to collect e-mail addresses. Allow website visitors to opt-in to receive your newsletter by filling out a form. See Figure 13.4 for a sample newsletter subscription form.

Figure 13.4
Sample newsletter subscription form

Offer your visitors some perceived value—timely information on a topic, discounts, and so on. Send out the newsletter with fresh, compelling content regularly. This helps to remind your previous visitors about your site. They may even forward the newsletter to a colleague and bring a new visitor to your site.

Sticky Site Features

Updating your website often and keeping your content fresh will encourage visitors to return to your site. How can you keep them there? Make your website sticky. **Stickiness** is the ability to keep visitors at your site. Display your interesting and compelling content along with features that encourage stickiness, such as news updates, polls and surveys, and chats or message boards.

Personal Recommendations

While forwarding a newsletter is a form of **personal recommendation**, some sites make it even easier to tell a friend about them. They offer a link that is used with a phrase such as "E-mail this article", "Send this page to a friend", or "Tell a colleague about this site". This personal recommendation brings a new visitor who is likely to be interested in the content of your site. See Figure 13.5 for screenshot of the USA.gov website (http://www.usa.gov), showing personal recommendation options.

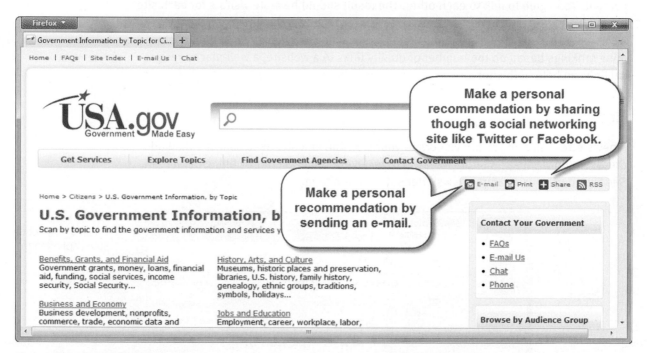

Figure 13.5 The USA.gov site makes it easy to tell friends about interesting articles

Newsgroup and Listserv Postings

Subscribe to relevant Usenet **newsgroups**, **listservs**, or forums related to your website content. Do not reply to postings with an advertisement of your site. Instead, reply to postings when your response can offer assistance or advice. Include a signature line with your website URL. Be subtle! You can get banned from some listservs if the moderator perceives that you are merely advertising. However, by offering friendly, helpful advice in a newsgroup or listserv you can market your website in a subtle, positive manner at no cost other than your Internet connection. Your Internet service provider may provide access to Usenet newsgroups. Google also provides access at http://groups.google.com. Listservs can be run by individuals or by organizations.

Traditional Media Ads and Existing Marketing Materials

Don't forget to mention your website in any print, TV, or radio ads that your organization runs. Include the URL of your website on all brochures, stationery, and business cards. This will help make your website easy to find by your current and potential customers. Depending upon your target audience, also consider including a QR code for your website on printed materials.

 Checkpoint 13.2

1. Are the results returned by various search engines really different? Choose a place, music group, or movie to search for. Enter the same search terms, such as "Door County" into the following three search engines: Google, Yahoo!, and Bing (http://www.bing.com). List the URLs of the top three sites returned by each. Comment on your findings.

2. How can you determine whether your website has been indexed by a search engine? How can you determine which search engines are being used to find your site?

3. List four website promotion methods that do not use search engines. Which would be your first choice? Why?

13.10 Serving Dynamic Content with Inline Frames

How does Edmunds.com (http://www.edmunds.com), the vehicle pricing and review site, display a banner ad on its home page that is hosted and controlled by another organization? How do the Chicago Bears (http://www.chicagobears.com) and ABC (http://abc.com) home pages easily display a variety of multimedia clips? How are the potential customer referrals provided by the Amazon.com Associates program initiated and tracked? How does Google facilitate Ad Sense advertisement displays and click-throughs on third-party websites? At the time this was written, the answer to all of these questions is inline frames. Inline frames are widely used on the Web for a variety of marketing and promotional purposes, including displaying banner ads, playing multimedia that may be hosted on a separate web server, and serving content for associate and partner sites to display. The advantage is separation of control. The dynamic content—such as the banner ad or multimedia clip—can be changed by a project team without allowing them access to change the rest of the website. For example, in the case of the banner ad served by the Edmunds.com website, a third-party organization (such as DoubleClick) has control over the ad content, but is prevented from updating the other items on the Edmunds home page. This is accomplished by configuring the dynamic content (in the form of banner ads) within an inline frame. Let's explore how inline frames are configured.

The iframe Element

An **inline frame**, also called a floating frame, can be placed on the body of any web page, similar to the way you would place an image on a web page. The **iframe element** configures an **inline frame** that displays the contents of another web page within your web page document, which is referred to as *nested browsing*. The iframe element begins with the `<iframe>` tag and ends with the `</iframe>` tag. Fallback content that should be displayed if the browser does not support inline frames (such as a text description or hyperlink to the actual web page) should be placed between the tags. Figure 13.6 shows the use of an inline frame (chapter13/dcwildflowers/index.html in the student files). The white background area is the inline frame; it displays another web page that contains the image of the flower and a text description.

Figure 13.6 The white scrolling area on the page is an inline frame that displays a separate web page

The screenshots shown in Figure 13.7 are of the same web page with different pages displayed in the inline frame area.

Figure 13.7 The same page with different content in the inline frame area

The code for the inline frame that creates this effect is

```
<iframe src="trillium.html" title="Trillium Wild Flower"
  height="160" width="350" name="flower">
  Description of the lovely Spring wild flower, the
  <a href="trillium.html" target="_blank">Trillium</a>
</iframe>
```

Table 13.1 lists iframe element attributes. Commonly used attributes are shown in bold.

Table 13.1 The iframe element attributes

Attribute	Description
src	URL of the web page to be displayed in the inline frame
height	Inline frame height in pixels
width	Inline frame width in pixels
id	Optional; text name, alphanumeric, beginning with a letter, no spaces; the value must be unique and not used for other id values on the same web page document
name	Optional; text name, alphanumeric, beginning with a letter, no spaces; this attribute names the inline frame
sandbox	Optional; disallow/disable features such as plug-ins, scripts, forms (new in HTML5)
seamless	Optional; set seamless="seamless" to configure the browser to more seamlessly display the inline frame content (new in HTML5)
title	Optional; specifies a brief text description that may be displayed by browsers or assistive technologies

YouTube Video in an Inline Frame

YouTube (http://www.youtube.com) is a popular website for sharing videos for both personal and business use. When a video is uploaded to YouTube, the creator can choose to share their video with others. It's easy to display a YouTube video on your web page; just select Share › Embed and then copy and paste the HTML into your web page source code. The code uses an iframe element to display a web page file within your web page. YouTube detects the browser and operating system of your web page visitor and serves the content in an appropriate format—with either Flash or HTML5 video.

 ## Hands-On Practice 13.1

VideoNote
**Configure an
Inline frame**

In this Hands-On Practice, you will launch a text editor and create the web page in Figure 13.8 that displays a YouTube video within an iframe element.

This example embeds the video found at `http://www.youtube.com/watch?v=1QkisJHztHI`. You can choose to display this video or select a different video. The process is to visit the

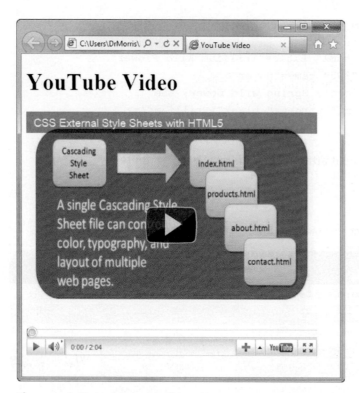

Figure 13.8 Embedding a YouTube video

YouTube page for the video and copy the video identifier, which is the text after the equal sign (=) in the URL. In this example, the video identifier is `1QkisJHztHI`.

Use the chapter2/template.html file as a starting point and configure a web page with the heading "YouTube Video" and an iframe element that displays the video. Code the `src` attribute to display http://www.youtube.com/embed/ followed by the video identifier. In this example, set the `src` attribute to the value `http://www.youtube.com/embed/1QkisJHztHI`. Configure a hyperlink to the YouTube video page as fallback content. The code to display the video shown in Figure 13.8 is

```
<iframe src="http://www.youtube.com/embed/1QkisJHztHI" width="640"
height="385">
  View the <a href="http://www.youtube.com/watch?v=1QkisJHztHI">YouTube
  Video</a>
</iframe>
```

Save your page as youtubevideo.html and display it in a browser. Test your page in different browsers, using different browser versions. Compare your work to Figure 13.8 and chapter13/iframe.html in the student files.

Chapter Summary

This chapter introduced concepts related to promoting your website. The activities involved in submitting websites to search engines and search directories were discussed, along with techniques for optimizing your website for search engines. Other website promotion activities, such as social media optimization, QR codes, banner ads, and newsletters, were also examined. At this point, you should have an idea of what is involved in the other side of website development—marketing and promotion. You can help the marketing staff by creating websites that work with search engines and directories by following the suggestions in this chapter. Visit the textbook website at http://www.webdevfoundations.net for examples, the links listed in this chapter, and updated information.

Key Terms

`<iframe>`
affiliate programs
automated tools
banner ad
banner exchange
blogs
click through rate (CTR)
cost per click (CPC)
cost per thousand impressions (CPM)
database
description meta tag
indexed
inline frame

keywords
link popularity
listservs
manual checking
meta tags
newsgroups
newsletter
pay per click (PPC)
personal recommendation
Quick Response (QR) Code
reciprocal link agreement
robot
robots meta tag
RSS feed

search directory
search engine
search engine optimization (SEO)
search engine results page (SERP)
search form
search index
search results
Sitemap
social bookmarking
social media optimization (SMO)
stickiness
web analytics
website log

Review Questions

Multiple Choice

1. The robot, database, and search form are components of which of the following?

   a. search directory

   b. search engine

   c. both search directories and search engines

   d. search engine optimization

2. In which section of a web page should meta tags be placed?

   a. head

   b. body

   c. comment

   d. CSS

3. What is a first step for search engine optimization?

   a. Join an affiliate program.

   b. Start a blog.

   c. Add a description meta tag to each page.

   d. Create a QR code.

4. Typically, how long can it take between the time you submit your website and the time it is listed in a search engine?

   a. several hours

   b. several weeks

   c. several months

   d. a year

5. Which of the following contains information about which keywords are bringing visitors to your website?
   a. web position log
   b. website log
   c. search engine file
   d. none of the above

6. Which of the following is a rating determined by a search engine based on the number of links to a particular site and the qualities of those links?
   a. line checking
   b. reciprocal linking
   c. link popularity
   d. none of the above

7. Which of the following is the most popular method used by visitors to find websites?
   a. banner ads
   b. hearing about websites on television
   c. search engines
   d. personal recommendations

8. Which of the following is a promotion method whose main purpose is to bring return visitors to your website?
   a. newsletter
   b. banner exchange
   c. TV ad
   d. none of the above

9. Which of the following is the main benefit of a banner ad?
   a. bringing many new visitors to your site
   b. increasing awareness of the website
   c. both bringing many new visitors and increasing awareness of the site
   d. none of the above

10. In which of the following does one website promote another site's products or services in exchange for a commission?
    a. newsletter
    b. affiliate program
    c. search engine optimization
    d. stickiness

Fill in the Blank

11. The ability to keep web page visitors at your site is called _____.

12. Use _____ to indicate that you do not want a web page to be indexed.

13. Frequently used information research resources are _____.

14. In addition to a search engine listing, a website can be promoted by _____.

15. Two-dimensional barcodes that can be scanned by smartphones to access a website are called _____ codes.

Hands-On Exercises

1. Practice writing description meta tags. For each scenario described here, write the HTML to create an appropriate meta tag that includes keywords which may be used by visitors to search for the business.
   a. Lanwell Publishing is a small independent publisher of English as a second language (ESL) books used for secondary school and adult continuing education learners. The website offers textbooks and teacher's manuals.
   b. RevGear is a small specialty truck and auto repair shop in Schaumburg, Illinois. The company sponsors a local drag racing team.
   c. Morris Accounting is a small accounting firm that specializes in tax return preparation and accounting for small businesses. The owner, Greg Morris, is a CPA and Certified Financial Planner.

2. Choose one of the company scenarios listed in Hands-On Exercise 1 (Lanwell Publishing, RevGear, or Morris Accounting). Create a home page for the site that includes a description meta tag, appropriate page titles, and keywords used appropriately in headings. Place an e-mail link to yourself on the web page. Save the page as scenario.html.

3. Choose one of the company scenarios listed in Hands-On Exercise 1. Create a web page that lists at least three possible activities that could be used to promote the site in addition to search engine submission. For each activity, explain why it could be helpful for the website. Place an e-mail link to yourself on the web page. Save the page as promotion.html.

4. Write the HTML and CSS to create a page named inline.html that is configured to display the heading "Web Promotion Techniques", an inline frame that is 400 pixels wide and 200 pixels high, and an e-mail link with your name. Code a web page named marketing.html that lists your three favorite web promotion techniques. Configure the inline frame to display the marketing.html file.

Web Research

1. This chapter discussed a number of website promotion techniques. Choose one technique described in the chapter to research. Obtain information from at least three different websites about the promotion technique you chose. Create a web page that lists at least five hints or facts about the promotion method, along with helpful links that provide additional information on the hint or fact. Provide the URLs of the websites that you used as resources. Place your name in an e-mail link on the web page.

2. Search engine and search directory submission rules are constantly changing. Research a search engine or search directory and determine the following:

   - Are free submissions accepted? If so, are they restricted to noncommercial sites?

   - What types of paid submissions are accepted? How do they work (what is the fee structure, listing guarantee, and so on)?

   - What types of paid advertisements are available? How do they work (what is the fee structure, for example)?

   - Is there any information about the usual time frame for the submission to be listed?

   - Create a web page that describes your findings. Provide URLs of the websites you used as resources. Place your name in an e-mail link on the web page.

Focus on Web Design

Explore how to design your website so that it is optimized for search engines (search engine optimization, or SEO). Visit the following sites as a starting point as you search for three SEO tips or hints:

   - Old Skool Search Engine Success, Step-by-Step:
     http://www.sitepoint.com/article/skool-search-engine-success

   - Designing for Search Engines and Stars:
     http://www.digital-web.com/articles/designing_for_search_engines_and_stars

   - The 52 Top SEO Tips—Here are 10 of Them:
     http://www.seo-writer.com/reprint/top-seo-tips.html

   - Search Engine Watch: http://searchenginewatch.com

   - Search Engine Optimization—Tips for Beginners:
     http://www.youtube.com/watch?v=65PQpHcAonw

Write a one-page report that describes three tips which you found interesting or potentially useful. Cite the URLs of the resources that you used.

WEBSITE CASE STUDY
Meta Tags to Promote Websites

Each of the following case studies continues throughout most of the text. This chapter case study focuses on description meta tags.

JavaJam Coffee House

See Chapter 2 for an introduction to the JavaJam Coffee House case study. Figure 2.25 shows a site map for the JavaJam website. The pages were created in earlier chapters. Use the Chapter 9 JavaJam website as a starting point for this case study. You have three tasks in this case study:

1. Create a new folder for this JavaJam case study.

2. Write a description of the JavaJam Coffee House business.

3. Code a description meta tag on each page in the website.

Hands-On Practice Case Study

Task 1: Create a Folder. Create a folder called javajam13. Copy all of the files from your Chapter 9 javajam9 folder into the javajam13 folder.

Task 2: Write a Description. Review the JavaJam pages that you created in earlier chapters. Write a brief paragraph that describes the JavaJam site. Edit the paragraph down to a description that is only a few sentences and less than 25 words in length.

Task 3: Update Each Page. Open each page in a text editor and add a description meta tag to the head section. Save the files and test them in a browser. They will not look different, but they are much friendlier to search engines!

Fish Creek Animal Hospital

See Chapter 2 for an introduction to the Fish Creek Animal Hospital case study. Figure 2.29 shows a site map for the Fish Creek website. The pages were created in earlier chapters. Use the Chapter 9 Fish Creek website as a starting point for this case study. You have three tasks in this case study:

1. Create a new folder for this Fish Creek case study.

2. Write a description of the Fish Creek Animal Hospital business.

3. Code a description meta tag on each page in the website.

Hands-On Practice Case Study

Task 1: Create a Folder. Create a folder called fishcreek13. Copy all of the files from your Chapter 9 fishcreek9 folder into the fishcreek13 folder.

Task 2: Write a Description. Review the Fish Creek pages that you created in earlier chapters. Write a brief paragraph that describes the Fish Creek site. Edit the paragraph down to a description that is only a few sentences and less than 25 words in length.

Task 3: Update Each Page. Open each page in a text editor and add a description meta tag to the head section. Save the files and test them in a browser. They will not look different, but they are much friendlier to search engines!

Pacific Trails Resort

See Chapter 2 for an introduction to the Pacific Trails Resort case study. Figure 2.33 shows a site map for the Pacific Trails website. The pages were created in earlier chapters. Use the Chapter 9 Pacific Trails website as a starting point for this case study. You have three tasks in this case study:

1. Create a new folder for this Pacific Trails case study.

2. Write a description of the Pacific Trails Resort business.

3. Code a description meta tag on each page in the website.

Hands-On Practice Case Study

Task 1: Create a Folder. Create a folder called pacific13. Copy all of the files from your Chapter 9 pacific9 folder into the pacific13 folder.

Task 2: Write a Description. Review the Pacific Trails pages that you created in earlier chapters. Write a brief paragraph that describes the Pacific Trails site. Edit the paragraph down to a description that is only a few sentences and less than 25 words in length.

Task 3: Update Each Page. Open each page in a text editor and add a description meta tag to the head section. Save the files and test them in a browser. They will not look different, but they are much friendlier to search engines!

Prime Properties

See Chapter 2 for an introduction to the Prime Properties case study. Figure 2.37 shows a site map for the Prime Properties website. The pages were created in earlier chapters. Use the Chapter 9 Prime Properties website as a starting point for this case study. You have three tasks in this case study:

1. Create a new folder for this Prime Properties case study.

2. Write a description of the Prime Properties business.

3. Code a description meta tag on each page in the website.

Hands-On Practice Case Study

Task 1: Create a Folder. Create a folder called prime13. Copy all of the files from your Chapter 9 prime9 folder into the prime13 folder.

Task 2: Write a Description. Review the Prime Properties pages that you created in earlier chapters. Write a brief paragraph that describes the Prime Properties site. Edit the paragraph down to a description that is only a few sentences and less than 25 words in length.

Task 3: Update Each Page. Open each page in a text editor and add a description meta tag to the head section. Save the files and test them in a browser. They will not look different, but they are much friendlier to search engines!

Web Project

See Chapter 5 for an introduction to the Web Project case study. Your task is to add an appropriate description meta tag to each page in the website.

Hands-On Practice Case Study

1. Review the Project Topic Approval document that you created in the Chapter 9 case study. Take a moment to view the pages that you created in earlier chapters. Write a brief paragraph that describes the Web Project website.

2. Launch a text editor and edit the web pages in the project folder. Add a description meta tag to each page. Save your pages and test them in a browser. They will not look different, but they are now friendlier to search engines!

14

A Brief Look at JavaScript

Chapter Objectives   In this chapter, you will learn how to . . .

- Describe common uses of JavaScript in web pages
- Describe the purpose of the Document Object Model (DOM) and list some common events
- Create simple JavaScript using the script element and the `alert()` method
- Use variables, operators, and the if control structure
- Create a basic form data validation script

If a popup window mysteriously appears while you are surfing the Web, you're experiencing the effects of JavaScript. JavaScript is a scripting language and JavaScript commands can be included in an HTML file. Using JavaScript, you can incorporate techniques and effects that will make your web pages come alive! You can display an alert box containing an important message for the user. You can display an image when a user moves the mouse pointer over a link and much more. This chapter introduces JavaScript and some of its capabilities, and provides some samples that you can build on to create your own web pages.

14.1 Overview of JavaScript

There are a variety of methods for adding interactivity to a web page. As you learned in Chapter 7, CSS can be used to achieve a hover effect as you position your mouse pointer over a hypertext link. CSS can also be used for interactive effects, including an image gallery and the new CSS3 transitions and transforms. In Chapter 11, you saw examples of how JavaScript can be used to add interactivity and functionality to web pages.

So, what is JavaScript? It's an object-based, client-side scripting language interpreted by a web browser. JavaScript is considered to be **object-based** because it's used to work with the objects associated with a web page **document**: the browser window, the document itself, and elements such as forms, images, and links. Because JavaScript is interpreted by a browser, it is considered to be a client-side scripting language. A **scripting language** is a type of programming language, but no need to worry! You don't have to be a computer programmer to understand this.

Let's review clients and servers. In Chapter 10, we discussed hosting a website on a web server. As you learned, a web host provider allows you to transfer your files to the web server and stores your website. Visitors to your site (also called users) are able to point their web browsers to your website using the URL provided by your web host provider. As you may recall, the user's web browser is called a client.

JavaScript is interpreted by the client. This means that the JavaScript code, embedded in the HTML document, will be rendered by the browser. The server's job is to provide the HTML document. The web browser's job is to interpret the code in the HTML file and display the web page accordingly. Because all the processing is performed by the client (in this case, the web browser), this is referred to as **client-side processing**. There are programming languages that are executed on the server, which are referred to as server-side programming languages. **Server-side processing** may involve sending e-mail, storing items in a database, or tracking items in a shopping cart. In Chapter 9, you learned how to set the action of a form to point to a server-side script.

In summary, JavaScript is an object-based, client-side scripting language interpreted by a web browser. The JavaScript code is embedded in the HTML file and the web browser interprets it and displays the results as needed.

14.2 The Development of JavaScript

There is a popular misconception that Java and JavaScript are the same. Java and JavaScript are completely separate languages with very little in common. As noted in Chapter 11, Java is an object-oriented programming language. Java is robust, is very technical, and can be used to build large applications for businesses, such as inventory control systems and payroll systems. Sun Microsystems developed Java in the 1990s and designed the language to run on an operating system such as Windows or Unix. The developers of Java also wanted the flexibility that would be available if their language could run in a web browser. Independently, a team at Netscape was developing a scripting language called LiveScript and eventually partnered with Sun Microsystems. This partnership was mutually advantageous as it produced the Java plug-in that enabled web browsers to run Java applets in the browser. The development of

LiveScript continued and was renamed JavaScript. However, JavaScript is not the same as the Java programming language. JavaScript is much simpler than Java. The two languages have more differences than similarities.

14.3 Popular Uses for JavaScript

The uses of JavaScript range from providing some "bells and whistles," such as simple animation and fancy menus, to functionality, such as popping up a new window that contains product information and detecting errors in a form. Let's look at some examples of some of these uses.

Alert Message

An alert message is a popular technique used to draw the user's attention to something that is happening. For instance, a retail website may use an alert message to list errors in an order form or remind the user about an upcoming sale. Figure 14.1 illustrates an alert message that thanks the user for visiting the page. This alert message is displayed when the user is leaving the website and going to a new site.

Figure 14.1 Alert message is displayed when the user leaves the website

Notice that the user must click the OK button before the next page will load. This effectively grabs the user's attention, but it quickly becomes annoying if it is overused.

Popup Windows

And speaking of annoying, a **popup window** is a web browser window that may appear when you interact with a web page by clicking on an image or hovering over a page area, or it may seem to appear somewhat mysteriously. This technique has some legitimate uses, such as popping up an information window that contains a larger picture and description of a product when the user clicks on the product in the main window. Unfortunately, the use of popup windows has been so abused that most browsers allow users to disable popup windows. This also means that the useful popup windows are not displayed. Figure 14.2 shows a popup window that appears when the user clicks the link on the main page.

Figure 14.2 The smaller popup window appears when the user clicks on the link in the larger window

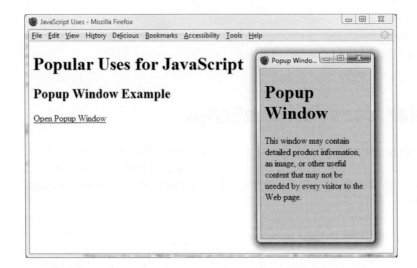

Jump Menus

JavaScript can also be used to create **jump menus** based on a select list as introduced in Chapter 9. The user can select a web page from a select list and click a button to load the selected Web page. Figure 14.3 shows this technique.

Figure 14.3 Jump menu that shows the selection of the Contact Information menu option

In this example, the user selected the Contact Information option from the select list and clicked the Go button. The Contact Information page will load in the browser window.

Mouse Movement Techniques

JavaScript can be used to perform a task based on mouse movement in the browser window. One popular technique is to display a submenu when the user hovers the mouse pointer over a menu item. Figure 14.4 shows this technique.

Figure 14.4 The submenu is displayed when the user hovers over the Products menu item

The window on the left shows the main menu and the window on the right shows the submenu displayed when the user hovers the mouse pointer over the Products menu item. When the user moves the mouse away from the Products menu item, the submenu disappears. Mouse movements also trigger **image swapping**, often referred to as rollover images. An image is displayed on the web page when the page initially loads. When the user positions the mouse pointer on top of the image, the original image is swapped for a new image. When the user moves the mouse away from the image, the original image reappears. Figure 14.5 shows the image-swapping technique. For many years, this technique was commonly used for navigation button bars. However, modern web developers typically use CSS to configure similar effects with the :hover pseudo-class, such as changing the background color or background image of an element.

Figure 14.5 The original image is on the left and the swapped image is on the right with the mouse pointer hovering on the image

In this chapter, we will touch on some of the highlights and concepts involved in using JavaScript. We will create some scripts to demonstrate the use of the alert message, mouseovers, and some of the techniques involved in checking a form for input errors. This chapter offers just a taste of JavaScript, but it will give you on overview of how some of the techniques are developed.

14.4 Adding JavaScript to a Web Page

JavaScript code is embedded in an HTML web page and is interpreted by the web browser. This means that the web browser is capable of understanding the code and running it. The examples in this chapter use the Mozilla Firefox web browser. The code we will create functions in most web browsers. However, we will use Firefox because it will provide us with helpful error messages that will be invaluable when we create and test our pages. If you have not already installed Mozilla Firefox on your computer, visit http://www.mozilla.com/firefox for a free download.

Script Element

When JavaScript code is embedded in an HTML document, it needs to be contained, or encapsulated, in a **script element**. The JavaScript is typed between the opening `<script>` tag and the closing `</script>` tag. Web pages are rendered by the browser from top to bottom. The impact on our scripts is that they will execute wherever they are located in the document. The script element requires a `type` attribute with the value `text/javascript`.

JavaScript Statement Block Template

Within the script tags, we'll use HTML comments before and after a JavaScript statement block. HTML comments are contained between `<!--` and `-->` markup symbols. The `<!--`

denotes the beginning of the HTML comment. The `-->` denotes the end of the HTML comment. JavaScript comment lines begin with `//`. The text on that line is ignored by the browser. We'll use the HTML comment tag at the beginning of the JavaScript statement block to hide JavaScript from older browsers. Some very old browsers will display the JavaScript code rather than execute it. Encapsulating the JavaScript block in HTML comment tags hides the block from older browsers and the code is ignored by browsers that do not support it. Use the JavaScript comment `//` to begin the line with the closing HTML comment. Each JavaScript block will have following structure:

```
<script type="text/javascript">
<!--
... JavaScript code goes here ...
//-->
</script>
```

The JavaScript code is placed inside the statement block. This block can appear anywhere in the HTML document and the code will be executed. Let's see how this works with a Hands-On Practice that will display an alert message.

Alert Message Box

The alert message box is displayed using the **alert()** method. The structure is

```
alert("message to be displayed");
```

VideoNote
JavaScript
Message Box

Each JavaScript command line generally ends with a semicolon (;). Also, JavaScript is **case-sensitive**, which means that there's a difference between uppercase and lowercase characters and it will be important to be precise when typing JavaScript code.

 Hands-On Practice 14.1

In this Hands-On Practice, you will create a simple script with an alert message box. Launch a text editor and type the following HTML and JavaScript code. Note that **alert()** does not contain a space between alert and the opening parenthesis.

```
<!DOCTYPE html>
<html lang="en">
<head>
  <title>JavaScript Practice</title>
  <meta charset="utf-8">
</head>
<body>
<h1>Using JavaScript</h1>
<script type="text/javascript">
<!--
alert("Welcome to my web page!");
// -->
</script>
<h2>When does this display?</h2>
</body>
</html>
```

Save this file as alert.html. Launch Firefox and open your page in the browser. Notice that the first heading appears and then the alert message pops up (see Figure 14.6). After you click the OK button, the second heading appears. This illustrates the top-down processing of the web page and the embedded JavaScript. The JavaScript block is between the headings and that's where the alert message appears as well.

Figure 14.6 JavaScript displays the alert message box (alert.html)

Practice with Debugging

Sometimes your JavaScript code does not work the first time you test it. When this happens, you'll need to **debug** the code—find the errors and correct them.

Let's look at a debugging technique. Edit the JavaScript alert to introduce a typing error:

```
aalert("Welcome to my web page!");
```

Save the file and view it in the browser. Notice that the alert box does not display this time. Firefox will point out some errors in JavaScript code, but we need to open the Error Console in order to see them.

In Firefox, select the menu item Tools > Web Developer > Error Console. The Error Console window will open and the error message will display (see Figure 14.7).

Figure 14.7 The Firefox Error Console displays an error

Notice that the error is displayed, along with the line number where the error was detected. It's useful to create your documents in a text editor that displays the line numbers, but it's not necessary. If you are using Notepad, make use of the Go To feature in the Edit menu. This will allow you to specify a line number and the insertion point will be positioned at the beginning of that line.

Edit the alert.html file to correct the error and test it in the browser. This time the alert box should display after the first heading.

FAQ **Will the Error Console display all of the errors in my JavaScript code?**

The Error Console will display the syntax errors, which include things like missing quotes and items that it does not recognize. Sometimes the error is above the line indicated, particularly if there is a missing parenthesis or quote. The errors displayed indicate that there is something wrong and they serve as a guide as to where the error might be located. Start by looking at the line indicated; if that line looks correct, look at the lines above it.

 Checkpoint 14.1

1. Describe at least three popular uses for JavaScript.
2. How many JavaScript code blocks can be embedded in an HTML document?
3. Describe a method that can be used to find an error in a JavaScript code block.

14.5 Document Object Model Overview

JavaScript can manipulate the elements of an HTML document, such as container tags like paragraphs, spans, and div elements. Elements also include images, forms, and individual form elements such as text boxes and select lists. In order to access these elements, we need to understand a little bit about the Document Object Model (DOM).

In general, an **object** is an entity or a "thing". When using the DOM, the browser window, web page document, and any HTML element are considered to be objects. The browser window is an object. When a web page loads in the browser, the web page is considered to be a document. The document itself is an object. The document can contain objects such as images, headings, paragraphs, and individual form elements such as text boxes. The objects may have properties that can be detected or manipulated. For example, a property of the document is its title. Another property of the document is its background color.

There are actions that can be performed on some objects. For example, the **window object** can display the alert message box or a prompt box. These actions are called **methods**. The command to display an alert message is referred to as a method of the window object. The DOM is the collection of objects, properties, and methods. JavaScript uses the DOM to detect and manipulate the elements in the HTML document.

Let's look at this system of objects, properties, and methods differently. Let's say that your car is an object. It has properties such as color, manufacturer, and year. Your car has elements such as the hood and trunk. The hood and trunk can be opened and closed. If we were to use a programming language to open and close the hood and trunk, the commands might look something like the following:

```
car.hood.open()
car.hood.close()
car.trunk.open()
car.trunk.close()
```

If we wanted to know the color, year, and manufacturer of the car, the commands might look something like the following:

```
car.color
car.year
car.model
car.manufacturer
```

When we use the values, `car.color` might be equal to "silver", `car.manufacturer` might be equal to "Nissan", and `car.model` might be equal to "370Z". We might be able to change the values or only read them without changing them. In this example, car is an object and its properties are hood, trunk, color, year, model, and manufacturer. Hood and trunk could be considered properties as well. Open and close are methods of hood and are also methods of trunk.

With respect to the DOM, we can write to the document using the `write()` method of the document object. The structure is

```
document.write("text to be written to the document");
```

We can use this in JavaScript to write text and HTML tags to a document and the browser will render it. The `alert()` method used in the previous Hands-On Practice is a method of the window object. It can be written as

```
window.alert("message");
```

The window object is assumed to exist and can be omitted. If the window doesn't exist, the script doesn't exist either.

One property of the document is `lastModified`. This property contains the date on which the file was most recently saved or modified and we can access it using `document.lastModified`. This is a read-only property that we can display in the browser window or use for some other purpose.

 ## Hands-On Practice 14.2

In this Hands-On Practice, you will practice using the `write()` method of the document and the `lastModified` property of the document. You will use `document.write()` to add text and some HTML tags to an HTML document. You will also use `document.write()` to write the date the file was last saved to the document.

Open the alert.html file and edit the script block as follows:

```
<!DOCTYPE html>
<html lang="en">
<head>
  <title>JavaScript Practice</title>
  <meta charset="utf-8">
</head>
```

```
<body>
<h1>Using JavaScript</h1>
<script type="text/javascript">
<!--
document.write("<p>Using document.write to add text</p>");
document.write("<h2>Notice that we can add HTML tags too!</h2>");
// -->
</script>
<h3>This document was last modified on:
<script type="text/javascript">
<!--
document.write(document.lastModified);
// -->
</script>
</h3>
</body>
</html>
```

Save this file as documentwrite.html and view it in the browser. The text should display (see Figure 14.8). If the text does not display, open the Error Console and correct any errors that appear.

Figure 14.8 The Firefox browser displays documentwrite.html

JavaScript can be seen in the source code. To confirm this, use the Tools > Web Developer > Page Source menu command to see the source code. Close the source code window when you have finished viewing the code.

FAQ   **Why would I use `document.write` when I can just type the HTML code by itself?**

In practice, you typically wouldn't use `document.write` to generate your web page if you could just type the HTML code by itself. You would use `document.write` in conjunction with other techniques. For instance, you might use JavaScript to detect the time of day and, if it is before noon, use `document.write` to write "Good morning" to the document. If it is afternoon, write "Good afternoon" to the document, and if it is after 6:00 p.m., write "Good evening" to the document.

14.6 Events and Event Handlers

As the user is viewing a web page, the browser detects mouse movement and events. **Events** are actions taken by the web page visitor, such as clicking the mouse, loading pages, or submitting forms. For instance, when you move your mouse pointer over a hypertext link, the browser detects a mouseover event. Table 14.1 lists a few of the events and their descriptions.

Table 14.1 Events and their descriptions

Event	Description
click	The user clicks on an item. This could be an image, hypertext link, or button.
load	The browser displays a web page.
mouseover	The mouse pointer hovers over an item. The mouse pointer does not have to rest on the object. This could be a hypertext link, image, paragraph, or another object.
mouseout	The mouse pointer is moved away from an item that it had previously hovered over.
submit	The user clicks the submit button on a form.
unload	The web page unloads in the browser. This event occurs just before a new web page loads.

When an event occurs, this can trigger some JavaScript code to execute. One widely used technique is to detect the mouseover and mouseout events and swap images or display a menu.

We need to indicate which events will be acted upon and what will be done when an event occurs. We can use an **event handler** to indicate which event to target. An event handler is embedded in an HTML tag as an attribute and indicates some JavaScript code to execute when the event occurs. Event handlers use the event name with the prefix "on". Table 14.2 shows the event handlers that correspond to the events described in Table 14.1. For example, the **onload** event is triggered when browser renders (loads) a web page. When you move your mouse pointer over a text hyperlink, a **mouseover** event occurs and is detected by the browser. If that hyperlink contains an onmouseover event handler, the JavaScript code indicated by the event handler will execute. This code might pop up an alert message, display an image, or display a menu. Other event handlers such as **onclick** and **onmouseout** can cause JavaScript code to execute when their corresponding event occurs.

Table 14.2 Events and event handlers

Event	Event Handler
click	onclick
load	onload
mouseover	onmouseover
mouseout	onmouseout
submit	onsubmit
unload	onunload

 Hands-On Practice 14.3

Let's practice using the onmouseover and onmouseout event handlers and alert messages to indicate when the event handler has been triggered. We will use simple hypertext links and embed the event handlers in the anchor tags. We will not need the <script> block because event handlers are placed as attributes within the HTML tags. We'll place the hypertext links in an unordered list so that there's a lot of room in the browser window to move the mouse pointer and test our script.

Open a text editor and enter the code shown below. Note the use of the double and single quotes in the `onmouseover` and `onmouseout` event handlers. We need quotes around the message in the `alert()` method and we need quotes that encapsulate the JavaScript for the event handler. HTML and JavaScript will allow us to use either double quotes or single quotes. The rule is that they must match in pairs. So when you have a situation where you need two sets of quotes, you can use both double and single quotes. Use double quotes for the outer set and single quotes for the inner set. In the anchor tag, the # symbol is used for the href value because we don't need the functionality of loading another web page. We need the hypertext link to sense mouseover and mouseout events.

```
<!DOCTYPE html>
<html lang="en">
<head>
  <title>JavaScript Practice</title>
  <meta charset="utf-8">
</head>
<body>
<h1>Using JavaScript</h1>
<ul>
  <li><a href="#" onmouseover="alert('You moused over');">Mouseover
  test</a></li>
  <li><a href="#" onmouseout="alert('You moused out');">Mouseout
  test</a></li>
</ul>
</body>
</html>
```

Save this file as mouseovertest.html and load it in the browser. Move your mouse on top of the Mouseover test link. As soon as your mouse touches the link, the mouseover event occurs and the `onmouseover` event handler is triggered. This displays the alert box (see Figure 14.9).

Figure 14.9 Demonstration of onmouseover

Click the OK button and position your mouse pointer over the Mouseout test link. Notice that nothing happens. This is because the mouseout event has not occurred yet.

Move the mouse pointer away from the link. As soon as the mouse pointer is no longer on the link, the mouseout event occurs and the `onmouseout` event handler is triggered. This displays the alert box (see Figure 14.10). A suggested solution can be found in the student files (chapter14/mouseovertest.html).

Figure 14.10 Demonstration of onmouseout

You can combine event handlers in one hypertext link. This is the essence of the image-swapping technique. The `onmouseover` event handler changes the image to a new image and the `onmouseout` event handler changes the image back to the original image. This technique is beyond the scope of this chapter, but perhaps this demonstration sheds some light on how image swapping is accomplished.

Checkpoint 14.2

1. With respect to objects, describe the difference between a property and a method. Feel free to use words like thing, action, description, attribute, and so on.

2. What is the difference between an event and an event handler?

3. Where are event handlers placed in the HTML document?

14.7 Variables

Sometimes we need to be able to collect information from the user. A simple example is prompting the user for a name and writing the name to the document. We would store the name in a **variable**. You probably took a math course at some point and used x and y as variables in equations as placeholders for values. The same principle applies when using variables in JavaScript. (We won't do any tricky math here, so relax!) JavaScript variables are also placeholders for data and the value of the variable can change. Robust programming languages like C++ and Java have all kinds of rules for variables and their data types. JavaScript is very loose that way. We won't have to worry about what type of data is contained in a variable.

FAQ   **Are there any tips for creating variable names?**

Creating the name of a variable is really something of an art form. First of all, you want to create a variable name that describes the data it contains. The underscore, or an uppercase character, can be used for readability to indicate more than one word. Do not use other special characters, though. Stick to letters and numbers. Be careful not to use JavaScript **reserved words** or

keywords, such as `var`, `return`, `function`, and so on. A list of JavaScript keywords can be found at http://www.webreference.com/javascript/reference/core_ref. The following are some variable names that could be used for a product code:

- `productCode`
- `prodCode`
- `product_code`

Writing a Variable to a Web Page

Before we use a variable, we can declare it with the JavaScript `var` keyword. This step isn't necessary, but it is good programming practice. We can assign data to a variable using the assignment operator, the equal sign (=). A variable can contain a number or a string. A **string** is encapsulated in quotes and can contain alphabetic characters, spaces, numbers, and special characters. For instance, a string can be a last name, e-mail address, street address, product code, or paragraph of information. Let's do a practice exercise that assigns data to a variable and writes it to the document.

 Hands-On Practice 14.4

In this Hands-On Practice, you will declare a variable, assign string data to it, and write it to the document.

Open a text editor and type the following:

```
<!DOCTYPE html>
<html lang="en">
<head>
  <title>JavaScript Practice</title>
  <meta charset="utf-8">
</head>
<body>
<h1>Using JavaScript</h1>
<h2>Hello
<script type="text/javascript">
<!--
var userName;
userName = "Karen";
document.write(userName);
// -->
</script>
</h2>
</body>
</html>
```

Notice that the `<h2>` tag is placed before the script block and the `</h2>` tag is placed after the script block. This renders the value of `userName` in the `<h2>` heading format. There is also a single space after the "o" in "Hello". If you miss this space, you'll see the `userName` value displayed right after the "o".

Notice that the variable is mixed case. This is a convention used in many programming languages to make the variable readable. Some developers might use an underscore, like user_name. Selecting a variable name is somewhat of an art form, but try to select names that indicate the contents of the variable.

Also notice that the `document.write()` method does not contain quotes. The contents of the variable will be written to the document. If we had used quotes around the variable name, the variable name itself would be written to the document and not the contents of the variable.

Save this document as variablewrite.html and load it in the browser. Figure 14.11 shows the variablewrite.html file in the browser.

Figure 14.11 Browser with variablewrite.html displayed

Chopping up the `<h2>` heading so that it is placed before and after the script is a bit cumbersome. We can combine strings using the plus (+) symbol. You'll see later in this chapter that the plus symbol can also be used to add numbers. The practice of combining strings using the plus symbol is called **concatenation**. Let's concatenate the `<h2>` information as a string with the `userName` value and the `</h2>` tag.

Edit the variablewrite.html document as follows:

```
<!DOCTYPE html>
<html lang="en">
<head>
  <title>JavaScript Practice</title>
  <meta charset="utf-8">
</head>
<body>
<h1>Using JavaScript</h1>
<script type="text/javascript">
<!--
var userName;
userName = "Karen";
document.write("<h2>Hello " + userName + "</h2>");
// -->
</script>
</body>
</html>
```

Be sure to remove the `<h2>` and `</h2>` information above and below the script block. Save the file as variablewrite2.html and display it in the browser window. You should not see any difference in the document in the browser.

Collecting Variable Values Using a Prompt

To demonstrate the interactive aspect of JavaScript and variables, we can use the `prompt()` method to request data from the user and write this data to the web page. For example, we will build on Hands-On Practice 14.4 and prompt the user for a name rather than hard code this data in the userName variable.

The `prompt()` method is a method of the window object. We could use `window.prompt()`, but the window object is assumed, so we can write this simply as `prompt()`. The `prompt()` method can provide a message to the user. This method is generally used in conjunction with a variable so that the incoming data is stored in a variable. The structure is

```
someVariable = prompt("prompt message");
```

When this command executes, a prompt box pops up that displays the message and an input box for data entry. The user types in the prompt box, clicks the OK button, and the data is assigned to the variable. Let's add this feature to the variablewrite2.html file.

Hands-On Practice 14.5

In this Hands-On Practice, you will use the `prompt()` method to gather data from the user and write it to the document.

Edit the variablewrite2.html file as follows:

```
<script type="text/javascript">
<!--
var userName;
userName = prompt("Please enter your name");
document.write("<h2>Hello " + userName + "</h2>");
// -->
</script>
```

Only the `userName` variable assignment command has changed. The data typed by the user will be assigned to the variable `userName`.

Save the file as variablewrite3.html and display it in the browser. The prompt box will appear and you can type a name in the input box and click the OK button (see Figure 14.12). The name should appear in the browser window.

Figure 14.12 The prompt box is displayed in the browser when the web page is loaded

Let's do a variation on this and allow the user to type a color name. The user's preference will be used as the background color of the document. We will use the `bgColor` property of the document object and set it to the user's color preference. Be sure that an uppercase C is used when typing `bgColor`.

Edit the variablewrite3.html document as follows and save it as changebackground.html:

```
<script type="text/javascript">
<!--
var userColor;
userColor = prompt("Please type the color name blue or red");
document.bgColor = userColor;
// -->
</script>
```

We are prompting the user to type the color name "blue" or "red". You know from your HTML experience that there are more options for color names. Feel free to experiment!

Save the document and display it in the browser. The prompt box will appear and you can type a color name and click the OK button. You should notice the background color change immediately.

14.8 Introduction to Programming Concepts

Until now, we have used the DOM to access properties and methods for the window and document. We have also used some simple event handlers. There is another aspect of JavaScript that is more like programming. In this section, we'll touch on just a small part of this to get a feel for the power of using programming concepts and build on this later to test input on a form.

Arithmetic Operators

When working with variables, it is often useful to be able to do some arithmetic. For instance, you may be creating a web page that calculates the tax on a product. Once the user has selected a product, you can use JavaScript to calculate the tax and write the result to the document. Table 14.3 shows a list of **arithmetic operators**, descriptions, and some examples.

Table 14.3 Commonly used arithmetic operators

Operator	Description	Example	Value of Quantity
=	Assign	quantity = 10	10
+	Addition	quantity = 10 + 6	16
−	subtraction	quantity = 10 − 6	4
x	multiplication	quantity = 10 × 2	20
/	division	quantity = 10 / 2	5

Programming languages differ greatly in capabilities, but they all have a few things in common. They all allow the use of variables and have commands for decision making, command repetition, and reusable code blocks. Decision making would be used when different outcomes are required, depending on the input or action of the user. In the next Hands-On Practice, we will prompt the user to enter a number and write different text on the web page document based on the value entered. Repetition of commands comes in handy when performing a similar task many times. For instance, it is tedious to create a select list containing the numbers 1 through 31 for the days of the months. We can use JavaScript to do this with a few lines of code. Reusable code blocks are handy when you want to refer to a block of code in an event handler rather than typing many commands in the HTML tag's event handler. Because this chapter is meant to be a very brief introduction, it is beyond our scope to elaborate further. We will touch on decision making and reusable code in the Hands-On Practice.

Decision Making

As we've seen, we can use variables in JavaScript. We may wish to test the value of a variable and perform different tasks based on the value of the variable. For instance, perhaps an order form requires that the user enter a quantity greater than 0. We could test the quantity input box to verify that the number entered is greater than 0. If the quantity is not greater than 0, we could pop up an alert message that instructs the user to enter a quantity greater than 0. The `if` control structure will be

```
if (condition) {
... commands to execute if condition is true
} else {
... commands to execute if condition is false
}
```

Notice that there are two types of grouping symbols used: parentheses and brackets. The parentheses are placed around the condition and the brackets are used to encapsulate a block of commands. The `if` statement includes a block of commands to execute if the condition is true and a block of commands to execute if the condition is false. The brackets are aligned so that you can easily see the opening brackets and closing brackets. It's very easy to miss a bracket when you're typing and then you would have to hunt for the missing bracket. Aligning them makes it much easier to track them visually. As you are typing JavaScript code, remember that parentheses, brackets, and quotes always are used in pairs. If a script isn't working as intended, verify that each of these items has a "partner."

If the condition evaluates as true, the first command block will be executed and the else block will be skipped. If the condition is false, the first command block will be skipped and the else block will execute.

This overview should give you a sense of how conditions and the `if` control structure can be useful. The condition must be something that can be evaluated as either true or false. We can think of this as a mathematical condition. The condition will generally make use of an operator. Table 14.4 lists commonly used **comparison operators**. The examples in Table 14.4 could be used as conditions in an `if` control structure.

Table 14.4 Commonly used comparison operators

Operator	Description	Example	Sample Values of a Quantity that Would Result in True
= =	Double equal signs (equivalent); "is exactly equal to"	`quantity = = 10`	10
>	Greater than	`quantity > 10`	11, 12 (but not 10)
> =	Greater than or equal to	`quantity > = 10`	10, 11, 12
<	Less than	`quantity < 10`	9, 8 (but not 10)
< =	Less than or equal to	`quantity < = 10`	10, 9, 8

FAQ   What can I do when my JavaScript code doesn't seem to be working?

You can try the following debugging techniques:

- Open the Error Console in Firefox (Tools > Web Developer > Error Console) to see if there are any errors. Common errors include missing a semicolon at the end of a line and typing errors in commands.

- Use `alert()` to print variables to verify the contents. For instance, if you have a variable named quantity, try `alert(quantity);` to see what is contained in the variable.

- Ask a classmate to look at your code. It's difficult to edit your own code because you tend to see what you think you wrote rather than what you actually wrote. It's easier to edit someone else's code.

- Try to explain your code to a classmate. Often, talking through the code will help you uncover errors.

- Verify that you are not using any JavaScript reserved words as variable names or function names. See the Core JavaScript 1.5 Reference Manual (http://www.webreference.com/javascript/reference/core_ref) for a list of reserved words.

Hands-On Practice 14.6

In this Hands-On Practice, you will code the quantity example described earlier. The user will be prompted for a quantity and must enter a quantity greater than 0. We will assume that the user will enter a number. If the user enters a value of 0 or a negative number, there will be an error message displayed. If the user enters a value greater than 0, a message will be displayed thanking the user for the order. We will use a prompt and will write messages to the document.

Open a text editor and enter the following:

```
<!DOCTYPE html>
<html lang="en">
<head>
  <title>JavaScript Practice</title>
  <meta charset="utf-8">
</head>
```

```
<body>
<h1>Using JavaScript</h1>
<script type="text/javascript">
<!--
var quantity;
quantity = prompt("Type a quantity greater than 0");
if (quantity <= 0) {
   document.write("<p>Quantity is not greater than 0.</p>");
   document.write("<p>Please refresh the web page.</p>");
} else {
   document.write("<p>Thank you for your order!</p>");
}
// -->
</script>
</body>
</html>
```

Save this document as quantityif.html and display it in a browser. If the prompt box does not appear, remember to check the Error Console for errors. When the prompt box appears, type the number 0 and click the OK button. You should see the error message you have created in the browser window (see Figure 14.13).

Figure 14.13 The browser on the left shows the prompt box with input of 0 and the browser on the right shows the result

Now, refresh the page and enter a value greater than 0 (see Figure 14.14).

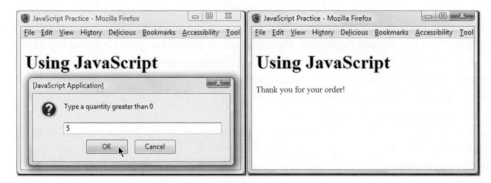

Figure 14.14 The browser on the left shows the prompt box with an input value that is greater than 0 and the browser on the right shows the result

Functions

In Hands-On Practice 14.6, you coded a prompt box that pops up as soon as the page loads. What if we prefer to allow the user to decide when a particular script should be interpreted or run by the browser? Perhaps we could use an onmouseover event handler and run the script when the user moves the mouse pointer over a link or image. Another method, perhaps more intuitive for the user, is to make use of a button and direct the user to click the button to run the script. The web page visitor doesn't need to be aware that a script will run, but can click a button to initiate some sort of functionality.

Three types of buttons were introduced in Chapter 9:

- A submit button, `<input type="submit">`, is used to submit a form.

- A reset button, `<input type="reset">`, is used to clear values entered on a form.

- The third type of button, `<input type="button">`, does not have any default action related to forms.

In this section, we will make use of the button, `<input type="button">`, and the `onclick` event handler to run a script. The onclick event handler can run a single command or multiple commands. The sample HTML is

```
<input type="button" value="Click to see a message"
  onclick="alert('Welcome!');">
```

In this sample, the button will display the text "Click to see a message". When the user clicks the button, the click event occurs and the `onclick` event handler executes the `alert('Welcome!');` statement. The message box appears. This method is very effective when there is only one JavaScript statement to execute. It quickly becomes unmanageable when there are more statements to execute. When that happens, it makes sense to place all JavaScript statements in a block and somehow point to the block to execute. If the statement block has a name, we can execute the block by pointing to the name. In addition to providing a shortcut name, this code is also easily reused. We can provide a name for a statement block by creating a function.

A **function** is a block of JavaScript statements with a specific purpose that can be run when needed. A function can contain a single statement or a group of statements and is defined as

```
function function_name() {
... JavaScript statements
}
```

The function definition starts with the keyword `function` followed by the name of the function. The parentheses are required and more advanced functions make use of them. You can choose a name for the function just like you choose a name for a variable. The function name should indicate the purpose of the function. The statements are contained within the brackets. The block of statements will execute when you **invoke**, or call, the function.

Here's an example of a function definition:

```
function showAlerts() {
  alert("Please click OK to continue.");
  alert("Please click OK again.");
  alert("Click OK for the last time to continue.");
}
```

The function can be invoked using

```
showAlerts();
```

Now, we could include the `showAlerts()` function call in a button as

```
<input type="button" value="Click to see alerts."
onclick="showAlerts();">
```

When the user clicks the button, the `showAlerts()` function will be called and the three alert messages will appear one after the other. Typically, function definitions are placed in the head section of the HTML document. This loads the function definition code, but it does not execute or run until it is invoked. This ensures that the function definition is loaded and ready to use before the function is called.

 Hands-On Practice 14.7

In this Hands-On Practice, you will edit the quantityif.html document to move the prompting script into a function and call it with an `onclick` event handler. There are a few things to note. The script has been moved into the head section and is included in a function definition. The `document.write()` methods have been changed to `alert()` methods and the messages have been altered slightly. The `document.write()` methods will not work well after the page has already been written, as is the case in this exercise. Also, there have been some comments added to the end brackets for the `if` statement and the function definition. These comments can help you keep track of the code blocks within the script. The indentation of the code blocks also helps to identify which brackets begin and end various statements. Launch a text editor and edit the quantityif.html file as follows:

```
<!DOCTYPE html>
<html lang="en">
<head>
  <title>JavaScript Practice</title>
  <meta charset="utf-8">
<script type="text/javascript">
<!--
function promptQuantity() {
    var quantity;
    quantity = prompt("Please type a quantity greater than 0");
    if (quantity <= 0) {
        alert("Quantity is not greater than 0.");
    } else {
        alert("Thank you for entering a quantity greater than 0.");
    } // end if
```

```
} // end function promptQuantity
// -->
</script>
</head>
<body>
<h1>Using JavaScript</h1>
<input type="button" value="Click to enter quantity"
onclick="promptQuantity();">
</body>
</html>
```

Save the document as quantityif2.html and display it in a browser. Open the Error Console to check whether there are typing errors when you run the script.

Click the button to test the script. If the prompt box does not appear, check the Error Console and correct any errors. Figure 14.15 shows the browser and the prompt box after the button has been clicked, as well as the resulting alert box. Be sure to test for a value larger than 0 and a value of 0 or less.

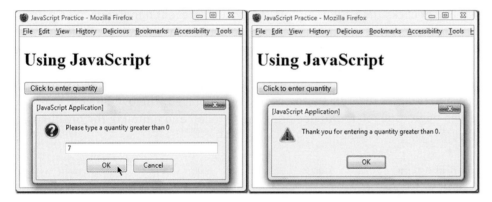

Figure 14.15 The browser on the left shows the prompt box and input; the browser on the right shows the alert box displayed after the input

Checkpoint 14.3

1. Describe a method that can be used to gather a piece of data such as the user's age.

2. Write the JavaScript code to display an alert message for users who are under 18 years old and a different alert message for users who are 18 years or older.

3. What is a function definition?

14.9 Form Handling

As you discovered in Chapter 9, the data from a web form can be submitted to a CGI or a server-side script. This data can be added to a database or used for some other purpose; therefore, it is important that the data submitted by a user is as accurate as possible. When the user enters information in a form, there is always a chance that the information will be incorrect or inaccurate. This is particularly true when text input boxes are used because the user can easily mistype data. Often, the form data is checked for invalid data before it is submitted. Form data validation can be done by the server-side script, but it can also be done client-side, using JavaScript. Again, this topic is simplified here, but we can get a sense of how this might be done.

When the user clicks the form's submit button, the submit event occurs. We can make use of the **onsubmit** event handler to call a function that tests form data for validation. This technique is referred to as **form handling**. The web developer can validate all form input, some input, or just one form input. The following list is a selection of some types of things that might be validated:

- Required fields such as name and e-mail address
- A required check box to acknowledge a license agreement
- A radio button that indicates a method of payment or a delivery option
- A value entered that is numeric and must be within a particular range

When the user clicks the submit button, the onsubmit event handler invokes a function that tests all of the appropriate form elements for valid data. Then the validation function confirms that the data is valid (true) or not valid (false). The form is submitted to the URL indicated in the form action attribute if the data is valid (true). The form would not be submitted if the data is not valid (false) and some indication to the user regarding errors would be displayed. The overall structure of the web page code related to declaring the function and handling the onsubmit event is

```
... HTML begins the web page
function validateForm() {
   ... JavaScript commands to test form data go here
  if form data is valid
      return true
  else
      return false
}
... HTML continues
<form method="post" action="URL" onsubmit="return validateForm();">
... form elements go here
<input type="submit" value="submit form">
</form>
... HTML continues
```

A new concept with regard to functions is indicated here. A function can encapsulate a group of statements, but it can also send a value back to where it was invoked, or called. This is referred to as "returning a value" and the JavaScript keyword `return` is used in the JavaScript code to indicate the value that will be sent back. Our example will return a value of true if the data is valid and a value of false if the data does not pass our validation tests. Notice that the onsubmit event handler also contains the keyword `return`. It works like this: If the validateForm() function returns a value of true, the onsubmit event handler becomes return true and the form is submitted. If the validateForm() function returns a value of false, the onsubmit event handler becomes return false and the form is not submitted. Once a function returns a value, it is finished executing, even if there are more statements in the function.

Hands-On Practice 14.8

In this Hands-On Practice, you will create a form with inputs for name and age, and use JavaScript to validate the data verifydata in the name field and a value for age of 18 or greater. If there is nothing in the name field, an alert message will be displayed that indicates an error. If the age value entered is less than 18, an alert message will be displayed that indicates an error. If all data is valid, an alert message will be displayed indicating that the data is valid and the form will be submitted.

Let's start by creating the form. Open a text editor and type the HTML below. Notice that the `onsubmit` form handler is embedded in the `<form>` tag and we will add the JavaScript code later. CSS is used to align and add space around the form elements.

```
<!DOCTYPE html>
<html lang="en">
<head>
  <title>JavaScript Practice</title>
  <meta charset="utf-8">
<style>
input { display: block;
        padding-bottom: 10px;
        width: 250px;
        text-align: right; }
label { float: left; }
</style>
</head>
<body>
<h1>JavaScript Form Handling</h1>
<form method="post"
      action="http://webdevfoundations.net/scripts/formdemo.asp"
      onsubmit="return validateForm();">
<label for="userName">Name: </label>
<input type="text" name="userName" id="userName">
<label for="userAge">Age: </label>
<input type="text" name="userAge" id="userAge">
<input type="submit" value="Send information" id="submit">
</form>
</body>
</html>
```

Save the file as formvalidation.html and view it in the browser. Figure 14.16 shows the form in the browser.

Figure 14.16 The formvalidation. html file displayed in the browser

Feel free to click the submit button. You will notice that the inputs will be submitted. For the moment, we have not coded the `validateForm()` function, so the form simply submits.

Accessing form inputs is a little tricky. The form is a property of the document object. Each form element is a property of the form object. A property of a form element can be a value. So, the HTML for accessing the contents of an input box could look something like this:

```
document.forms[0].inputbox_name.value
```

The form is identified by `forms[0]` to indicate which form will be used. An HTML document can contain multiple forms. Note that there is an `s` in `forms[0]`. The first form is `forms[0]`. To access the value in the `userAge` input box, we will need to use `document.forms[0].userAge.value`. This is a mouthful, for sure.

Also, notice that the values `true` and `false` are not enclosed in quotes. This is important because `true` and `false` are not strings, they are JavaScript reserved words, or keywords, and represent special values. If you add quotes to them, they become strings and this function will not work properly.

Let's start by adding the code to validate the age. Edit the formvalidation.html file to add the following script block in the head section above the `</head>` tag:

```
<script type="text/javascript">
<!--
function validateForm() {
if (document.forms[0].userAge.value < 18) {
    alert ("Age is less than 18. You are not an adult.");
    return false;
} // end if
alert ("Age is valid.");
return true;
} // end function validateForm
// -->
</script>
```

The validateForm() function will check the age in the `userAge` input box. If it is less than 18, the alert message will be displayed and a value of false will be returned and the function will finish executing. The onsubmit event handler will become return false and the form will not be submitted. If the value for age is 18 or greater, the statements in the `if` structure will be skipped and the `alert("Age is valid.");` will execute. After the user clicks the OK button in the alert message, the statement `return true;` will execute and the onsubmit event handler will become return true; thus, the form will be submitted. Let's test this out!

Type a value less than 18 in the `userAge` input box and click the submit button. If the form submits right away, there is likely an error in the JavaScript code. If this happens, open the Error Console and correct the errors indicated. Figure 14.17 shows the input in the Age box and the alert message displayed after clicking the submit button.

Figure 14.17 The validateform.html file displayed in a browser with input for age that is less than 18 (notice the alert message)

Click the OK button and type a value for age that is 18 or greater in the `userAge` input box. Click the submit button. Figure 14.18 shows the input in the `userAge` input box, the alert message displayed after the submit button has been clicked, and the resulting web page after the form has been submitted.

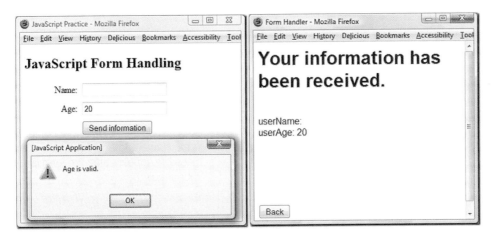

Figure 14.18 The validateform.html file displayed in a browser with input for age greater than or equal to 18 (notice the alert message); the browser on the right shows the resulting web page after the form is submitted

Now, let's add another if statement to validate the name. To ensure that something has been entered in the `userName` input box, we will test to see if the value of the input box is empty. The **null** string (no characters) is represented by two double quotes ("") or two single quotes ('') without a space or any other character in between. We can compare the value of the `userName` text box to the null string. If the value of the `userName` box is equal to the null string, then we know that the user did not enter any information in this box. In our example, we will be sending only one error message at a time. If the user does not have a name in the `userName` box and also does not have an appropriate age in the `userAge` box, the user will only see the `userName` error message displayed. After the user corrects the name and resubmits the information, the user will see the `userAge` error message displayed. This is very basic form processing, but it gives you an idea of how form handling might be accomplished. More sophisticated form processing would verify each form field and indicate all errors each time the form is submitted.

Let's add the code to validate the `userName` data. Edit the formvalidation.html file and modify the following script block. Note that two equal signs represent equivalency in the `if` statement. Some students find it helpful to read the two equal signs (==) as "is exactly equal to".

```
<script type="text/javascript">
<!--
function validateForm() {
if (document.forms[0].userName.value == "") {
    alert("Name field cannot be empty.");
    return false;
} // end if
if (document.forms[0].userAge.value < 18) {
    alert("Age is less than 18. You are not an adult.");
    return false;
} // end if
alert("Name and age are valid.");
return true;
} // end function validateForm
// -->
</script>
```

Save the document and refresh it in the browser window. Click the submit button without entering data in the Name or Age input boxes. Figure 14.19 shows the alert message displayed when no data has been input and the submit button has been clicked.

Figure 14.19 The validateform.html file displayed in the browser without input in the Name and Age boxes; the alert message appears after the form is submitted

Click the OK button, enter some text in the Name input box, and submit the form again. Figure 14.20 shows data in the Name input box and the alert message that appears as a result of validating the age. The age input box does not contain an age and this is interpreted as a value of 0.

Figure 14.20 The validateform.html file displayed in the browser with input in the Name box and without input in the Age box; the alert message appears after the submit button is clicked

Click the OK button and enter a value for age that is 18 or greater. Click the submit button. Figure 14.21 shows data in the Name and Age input boxes and the alert message that displays after the submit button has been clicked. It also shows the resulting web page after successful submission when all data is valid.

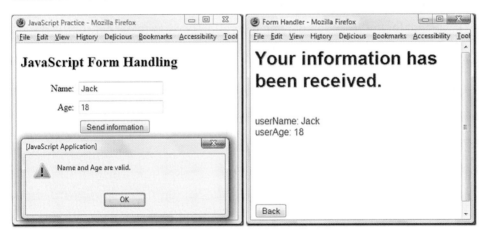

Figure 14.21 The validateform.html file displayed in the browser with valid input in the Name and Age boxes and alert message; the browser on the right shows the web page displayed after valid input has been submitted

Checkpoint 14.4

1. What is meant by the term "form data validation"?

2. Give three examples of form data that may require validation.

3. An HTML document contains the `<form>` tag as follows:

```
<form method="post"
action="http://webdevfoundations.net/scripts/formdemo.asp"
onsubmit="return validateForm();">
```

What happens when the user clicks the submit button?

14.10 **Accessibility and JavaScript**

**Focus on
Accessibility**

The interactivity and functionality that JavaScript can add to a web page is exciting. However, be aware that some visitors may have JavaScript disabled, may not be able to see your visual effect, or may be unable to manipulate the mouse. WCAG 2.0 and Section 508 require that your site is functional at a basic level, even if your visitor's browser does not support JavaScript. If you use JavaScript to handle mouse events in your site navigation, you should also provide plain-text navigation that does not require a mouse and can be easily accessed by a screen reader. If you use JavaScript for form validation, provide an e-mail address to allow physically challenged visitors to contact your organization and obtain assistance.

14.11 **JavaScript Resources**

This chapter has barely scratched the surface regarding the uses of JavaScript in web development. You may wish to do further research using some of the following online resources:

- JavaScript Tutorial: http://www.w3schools.com/JS

- JavaScript for the Total Non-Programmer: http://www.webteacher.com/javascript

- JavaScript Tutorial: http://echoecho.com/javascript.htm

- Core JavaScript 1.5 Reference Manual:
  http://www.webreference.com/javascript/reference/core_ref

- Creating Accessible JavaScript: http://webaim.org/techniques/javascript

Chapter Summary

This chapter introduced the use of JavaScript as a client-side scripting language in web pages. You learned how to embed script blocks in web pages, display an alert message, use an event handler, and validate a form. Visit the textbook website at http://www.webdevfoundations.net for examples, the links listed in this chapter, and updated information.

Key Terms

alert()	events	onclick
prompt()	form handling	onload
<script>	function	onmouseout
write()	if	onmouseover
arithmetic operators	image swapping	onsubmit
case-sensitive	invoke	popup window
client-side processing	jump menus	reserved words
comments	keywords	scripting language
comparison operators	methods	server-side processing
concatenation	mouseover	var
debug	null	variable
document	object	window object
event handler	object-based	

Review Questions

Multiple Choice

1. Which of the following JavaScript statements will write the words "Hello World" on an HTML page?

   a. `document.write("Hello World");`

   b. `browser.write("Hello World");`

   c. `context.write("Hello World");`

   d. `window.write("Hello World");`

2. Which of the following interprets JavaScript?

   a. server

   b. operating system in client machine

   c. browser

   d. compiler

3. Which of the following cannot be achieved by JavaScript?

   a. client-side validation

   b. server-side validation

   c. creating popup windows

   d. mouse movement techniques

4. Which of the following JavaScript methods displays a message?

   a. write()

   b. alert()

   c. message()

   d. None of the above.

5. Which of the following JavaScript methods allows users to input a value?

   a. `prompt()`

   b. `alert()`

   c. `message()`

   d. `write()`

6. Which of the following is not true about JavaScript scripts?

   a. The scripts should be enclosed within the `<script>` and `</script>` tags.

   b. The scripts can be put in both the body and the head section at the same time.

   c. The scripts cannot be placed in external files.

   d. The scripts can be placed in external files with the .js file extension.

7. Which of the following is not true about JavaScript?

   a. JavaScript statements are optionally ended by a semicolon (;).
   b. JavaScript statements are executed by the browser in the sequence they are written.
   c. JavaScript statements can be grouped together in blocks enclosed in curly braces.
   d. JavaScript is not case-sensitive.

8. Which of the following is not a permissible variable name in JavaScript?

   a. `username`
   b. `$username`
   c. `_username`
   d. `user+name`

9. Which of the following is not a conditional statement?

   a. `x = 5;`
   b. `x == 5;`
   c. `x >= 5;`
   d. `x <= 5;`

10. What would be the value of x after the statement var `x = "7" + 6` is executed?

    a. 7, a string
    b. 13, a number
    c. 76, a string
    d. 6, a number

Fill in the Blank

11. The comparison operator that checks for the exactly equal to condition is _____.

12. A _____ is a select list that allows the user to select an option to load another web page.

13. The _____ object can display the alert message box or a prompt box using respective methods.

14. We do not need to declare a _____, but we could choose to do so with the `var` statement.

15. The `<button>` can be used with a(n) _____ event handler to run a script when the user clicks a button.

Short Answer

16. Describe at least three popular uses for JavaScript.

17. Describe how you could debug JavaScript code when it is not working properly.

Apply Your Knowledge

1. **Predict the Result.** Given the following code, give a brief description of the page.

```
<!DOCTYPE html>
<html lang="en">
<head>
<title>JavaScript Practice</title>
<meta charset="utf-8">
</head>
<body>
<script type="text/javascript">
<!--
document.write("<h2>Hello There!</h2>");
var name = prompt("What's your name?", "User");
document.write("Hello " + name);
// -->
</script>
</body>
</html>
```

2. Fill in the Missing Code. This web page should greet the visitor according to the time of the day. If it is earlier than midday, it should say "Good Morning"; otherwise, it should say "Good Day". The missing code is indicated by "_". Fill in the missing code.

```html
<!DOCTYPE html>
<html lang="en">
<head>
<title>JavaScript Practice</title>
<meta charset="utf-8">
<script type="text/javascript">
<!--
function greetings() {
var today = new Date();
var hour = today.getHours();
__(hour<12)
    {
    document.write("<p><strong>Good Morning!</strong></p>");
    }

__
    {
    document.write("<p><strong>Good day!</strong>");
    }
}
// -->
</script>
</head>
<body>
<h1>Using JavaScript</h1>
<input type="button" value="click me" onclick="__">
</body>
</html>
```

3. Find the Error. When this page is loaded in the web browser, it is supposed to display an error message if the user has not typed any data in the Name input box. It is not working properly, so the form is submitted regardless of the missing input. Fix the errors so that the form does not submit if there is no information in the Name input box. Correct the errors and describe the process you followed.

```html
<!DOCTYPE html>
<html lang="en">
<head>
<title>JavaScript Practice</title>
<meta charset="utf-8">
<script type="text/javascript">
<!--
function validateForm() {
if (document.forms[0].userName.value == "" ) {
    aert("Name field cannot be empty.");
    return false;
} // end if
aert("Name and age are valid.");
return true;
} // end function validateForm
```

```
    // -->
    </script>
    </head>
    <body>
    <h1>JavaScript Form Handling</h1>
    <form method="post"
    action="http://webdevfoundations.net/scripts/formdemo.asp"
        onsubmit="return validateUser();">
      <label>Name: <input type="text" name="userName"></label>
      <br>
      <input type="submit" value="Send information">
    </form>
    </body>
    </html>
```

Hands-On Exercises

1. Practice writing event handlers.
   a. Write the HTML tag and event handler to pop up an alert message that greets the user and displays the current date and time.
   b. Write the HTML tag and event handler to pop up an alert message that greets the user and changes the background color of the page to green.
   c. Write the HTML tag and event handler to change the colors of the input text fields to light blue when these fields are focused on.

2. Create a web page that will pop up an alert message and change the background color of the page when an image is loaded. Use a script block in the head section for this task.

3. Create a web page that has a hyperlink and an image. When the user moves the mouse pointer over the hypertext link, the image is changed to a different one. When the user moves the mouse pointer away from the image, the original image returns.

4. Create a web page that will prompt the user to enter his/her name, school, and state, and then write the information on the web page in such a way that all this information comes under different level headings.

5. Continue with Hands-On Practice 14.8. Add a text box for the user's city. Ensure that this text box is not empty when the form is submitted. If the city text box is empty, pop up an appropriate alert message and do not submit the form. If the city text box is not empty and the other data is valid, submit the form.

Web Research

1. Use the resources listed in this chapter as a starting point, but also search the Web for additional resources on JavaScript. Create a web page that lists at least five useful resources, along with a brief description of each. Organize your web page with a list that provides the name of the site, the URL, a brief description of what is offered, and a recommended page (such as a tutorial, free script, and so on) for each resource. Place your name in an e-mail link on the web page.

2. Use the resources listed in the chapter as a starting point, but also search the Web for additional resources on JavaScript. Find either a tutorial or a free download that uses JavaScript. Create a web page that uses the code or download that you found. Describe the effect and list the URL of the resource on the web page. Place your name in an e-mail link on the web page.

WEB SITE CASE STUDY
Adding JavaScript

Each of the following case studies has continued throughout most of the text. This chapter adds JavaScript to selected web pages from each of the case studies.

JavaJam Coffee House

See Chapter 2 for an introduction to the JavaJam Coffee House case study. Figure 2.25 shows a site map for the JavaJam website. The pages were created in earlier chapters. Use the web pages indicated in this exercise from the Chapter 9 javajam9 folder. You have three tasks in this case study:

1. Create a new folder for this JavaJam case study.

2. Add the date that the document was last modified to the bottom of the Music page (music.html).

3. Add an alert message to the Music page.

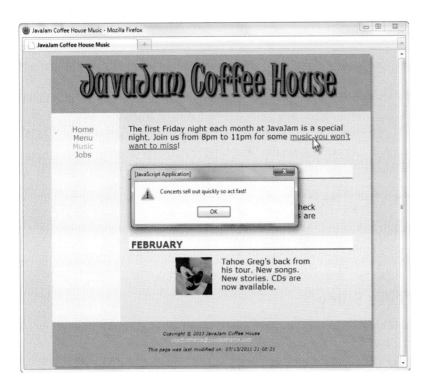

Figure 14.22 JavaJam Music page with the mouseover alert for performers' descriptions and the date last modified

Hands-On Practice Case Study

Task 1: Create a Folder. Create a folder called javajam14. Copy all the files from your Chapter 9 javajam9 folder into the javajam14 folder.

Task 2: Add a Date to the Music Page. Launch a text editor and open the music.html file. You will add the date that the document was last modified to the bottom of the music.html page. Modify the page as follows:

- In the page footer section after the e-mail link, add a script block that will write the following message to the document:

  "This page was last modified on: date"

- Use the `document.lastModified` property to print the date.

Task 3: Display an Alert Message on the Music Page. Launch a text editor and open the music.html file. You will add JavaScript to the music.html page so that an alert message will pop up when the user places the mouse over the phrase "music you won't want to miss!" The alert message will indicate "Concerts sell out quickly so act fast!" Modify the page as follows:

- Add a hypertext link to the first paragraph with an onmouseover event handler as follows:

  ```
  <a href="#" onmouseover=
  "alert('Concerts sell out quickly so act fast!');">music you
  won&rsquo;t want to miss!</a>
  ```

Save the music.html page and test it in the browser. Figure 14.22 shows the alert message when a user places their mouse pointer over the hyperlinked phrase. It also shows the date that the page was last modified.

Fish Creek Animal Hospital

See Chapter 2 for an introduction to the Fish Creek Animal Hospital case study. Figure 2.29 shows a site map for the Fish Creek website. The pages were created in earlier chapters. Use the web pages indicated in this exercise from the Chapter 9 fishcreek9 folder. You have three tasks in this case study:

1. Create a new folder for this Fish Creek case study.

2. Add the date last modified to the home page (index.html).

3. Add form validation to the Contact page (contact.html).

Hands-On Practice Case Study

Task 1: Create a Folder. Create a folder called fishcreek14. Copy all the files from your Chapter 9 fishcreek9 folder into the fishcreek14 folder.

Task 2: Add a Date to the Home Page. Launch a text editor and open the index.html file. You will add the date that the document was last modified to the bottom of the music. html page. Modify the page as follows:

- In the page footer section after the e-mail link, add a script block that will write the following message to the document:

  "This page was last modified on: date"

- Use the `document.lastModified` property to print the date

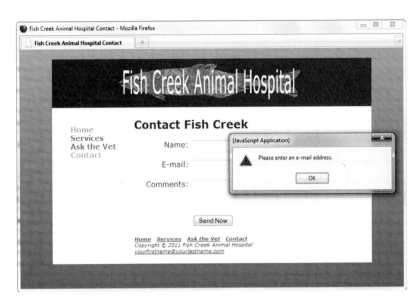

Figure 14.23 Fish Creek Animal
Hospital Contact page

Task 3: Add Form Data Validation to the Contact Page. Launch a text editor and open
the contact.html file. You will add form data validation to the Contact page (contact.html)
that requires an e-mail address to be entered.

- Add a script block to the head section as follows:

```
<script type="text/javascript">
<!--
function validateForm() {
if (document.forms[0].myEmail.value == "" ) {
    alert("Please enter an e-mail address.");
    return false;
} // end if
return true;
} // end function validateForm
// -->
</script>
```

- Edit the <form> tag as follows:

```
<form method="post" action=
"http://webdevbasics.net/scripts/fishcreek.php"
onsubmit="return validateForm();">
```

- Verify that the input textbox that accepts the visitor's e-mail address has a name
  attribute with the value of myEmail. Sample code is

```
<input type="text" name="myEmail" id="myEmail">
```

- Save the file and load it in a browser. Test it by clicking the submit button without
  typing in the e-mail input box. The alert box should pop up and the form should
  not be submitted (see Figure 14.23). Test it again by entering information in the
  e-mail input box and submit again. The form should be submitted successfully
  and a confirmation page should appear.

Pacific Trails Resort

See Chapter 2 for an introduction to the Pacific Trails case study. Figure 2.33 shows a site map for the Pacific Trails Resort website. The pages were created in earlier chapters. Use the web pages indicated in this exercise from the Chapter 9 pacific9 folder. You have three tasks:

1. Create a new folder for this Pacific Trails case study.

2. Add an alert message that displays a message when the browser renders the Yurts page (yurts.html).

3. Add form data validation to the Reservations page (reservations.html) that requires an e-mail address to be entered.

Hands-On Practice Case Study

Task 1: Create a Folder. Create a folder called pacific14. Copy all of the files from your Chapter 9 pacific9 folder into the pacific14 folder.

Task 2: Display an Alert Message on the Yurts Page. Launch a text editor and open the yurts.html file. You will add JavaScript to the yurts.html page so that an alert message will pop up when the page is displayed in the browser.

- Edit the body tag as follows:

```
<body onload=
"alert('Today only - 10% off on a weekend - coupon code ZenTen');">
```

- The load event occurs when the web page begins to load in the browser. The onload event handler in this case pops up an alert message.

Save the file and test it in the browser. Your display should be similar to Figure 14.24.

Figure 14.24 A message displays when the Yurts page is loaded by the browser

Task 3: Add Form Data Validation to the Reservations Page. Launch a text editor and open the reservations.html file. You will add form data validation to the Reservations page (reservations.html) that requires an e-mail address to be entered.

- Add a script block to the head section as follows:

```
<script type="text/javascript">
<!--
function validateForm() {
if (document.forms[0].myEmail.value == "" ) {
    alert("Please enter an e-mail address.");
    return false;
} // end if
return true;
} // end function validateForm
// -->
</script>
```

- Edit the `<form>` tag as follows:

```
<form method="post" onsubmit="return validateForm();"
action="http://webdevbasics.net/scripts/pacific.php">
```

- Verify that the input textbox that accepts the visitor's e-mail address has a name attribute with the value of myEmail. Sample code is

```
<input type="text" name="myEmail" id="myEmail">
```

- Save the file and load it in a browser. Test it by clicking the submit button without typing in the e-mail input box. The alert box should pop up and the form should not be submitted (see Figure 14.25). Test it again by entering information in the e-mail input box and submit again. The form should be submitted successfully and a confirmation page should appear.

Figure 14.25 The Reservations page indicates that an e-mail address was not entered

Prime Properties

See Chapter 2 for an introduction to the Prime Properties case study. Figure 2.37 shows a site map for the Prime Properties website. The pages were created in earlier chapters. Use the web pages indicated in this exercise from the Chapter 9 prime9 folder. You have three tasks in this case study.

1. Create a new folder for this Prime Properties case study.

2. Add the date last modified to the footer section of the Listings page (listings.html).

3. Add onmouseover event handlers to the listing numbers on the listings.html page so that when the user hovers the mouse pointer over the listing number, an alert message pops up reminding the user to click the contact link to contact an agent for more information.

Hands-On Practice Case Study

Task 1: Create a Folder. Create a folder called prime14. Copy all the files from your Chapter 9 prime9 folder into the prime14 folder.

Task 2: Add a Date to the Listings Page. Launch a text editor and open the listings.html file. You will add the date that the document was last modified to the bottom of the listings.html page. Modify the page as follows:

- In the page footer section after the e-mail link, add a script block that will write the following message to the document:

  "This page was last modified on: date"

- Use the `document.lastModified` property to print the date.

Save the file and test it in a browser.

Task 3: Display an Alert Message on the Listings Page. Launch a text editor and open the listings.html file. You will add onmouseover event handlers to the listing numbers on the page so that when the user hovers the mouse pointer over the listing number, an alert message pops up reminding the user to click the contact link to contact an agent for more information.

- Add the following code for the first listing number:

```
<a href="#" onmouseover=
"alert('Please contact us for more information.');"> Listing
#3432535</a>
```

- Similarly, add this code to the paragraph for the second listing.

Save the file and test it in a browser. The alert box should pop up when you move the mouse pointer over the listing link. Your web page should look similar to Figure 14.26.

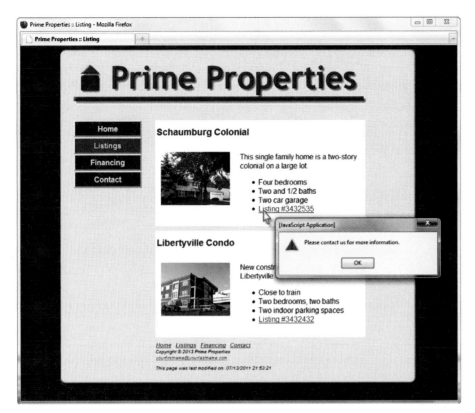

Figure 14.26 The new Prime Properties Listings page

Web Project

See Chapter 5 for an introduction to the Web Project case study. Review the goals of your website and determine whether the use of JavaScript in order to add interactivity would add value to your site. If so, add it appropriately. Check with your instructor regarding the required use of interactivity in your Web project.

Select one or more from the following:

- Choose one of the examples from the chapter to add an alert message to grab the user's attention with regard to important information.

- Choose one of the examples from the chapter to add data validation to a form on your website. Consider using one or more of the following validation rules:

  - Required information such as name, address, e-mail, phone number

  - Numeric information within bounds such as a quantity greater than 0 or age greater than 18

Decide where to apply the interactive technology to your site. Modify the page(s), save the page(s), and test it in a browser.

Web Developer's Handbook

In the following Appendices you will find a variety of resources that can help you be a more productive web developer.

APPENDIXES

Appendix A. HTML5 Quick Reference contains a list of commonly used HTML5 elements and attributes

Appendix B. XHTML Quick Reference contains a list of commonly used XHTML elements and attributes

Appendix C. Special Entity Characters contains a list of codes needed to display symbols and other special characters on web pages

Appendix D. CSS Property Reference contains a list of commonly used properties and values

Appendix E. WCAG 2.0 Quick Reference lists the WCAG 2.0 accessibility principles and the textbook chapters that discuss related coding or design techniques

Appendix F. The Web-Safe Color Palette provides examples of each color along with hexadecimal and decimal RGB values

Appendix G. FTP Tutorial provides a brief introduction to using File Transfer Protocol

HTML5 Quick Reference

Commonly Used HTML5 Elements

Element	Purpose	Commonly Used Attributes
`<!-- -->`	Comment	*Not applicable*
`<a>`	Anchor tag: configures hyperlinks	accesskey, class, href, id, name, rel, style, tabindex, target, title
`<abbr>`	Configures an abbreviation	class, id, style
`<address>`	Configures contact information	class, id, style
`<area>`	Configures an area in an image map	accesskey, alt, class, href, hreflang, id, media, shape, style, tabindex, target
`<article>`	Configures an independent section of a document as an article	class, id, style
`<aside>`	Configures tangential content	class, id, style
`<audio>`	Configures an audio control native to the browser	autoplay, class, controls, id, loop, preload, src, style, title
`<b>`	Configures bold text with no implied importance	class, id, style
`<blockquote>`	Configures a long quotation	class, id, style
`<body>`	Configures the body section	class, id, style
` `	Configures a line break	class, id, style
`<button>`	Configures a button	accesskey, autofocus, class, disabled, form, formaction, formenctype, formmethod, formtarget, formnovalidate, id, name, type, style, value
`<canvas>`	Configures dynamic graphics	class, height, id, style, title, width
`<caption>`	Configures a caption for a table	align (obsolete), class, id, style
`<cite>`	Configures the title of a cited work	class, height, id, style, title, width
`<code>`	Configures a fragment of computer code	class, id, style
`<col>`	Configures a table column	class, id, span, style

(Continued)

Element	Purpose	Commonly Used Attributes
`<colgroup>`	Configures a group of one or more columns in a table	`class, id, span, style`
`<command>`	Configures an area to represent commands	`class, id, style, type`
`<data>`	Provides a machine-readable format for text content	`class, id, style, value`
`<datalist>`	Configures a control that contains one or more option elements	`class, id, style`
`<dd>`	Configures a description area in a description list	`class, id, style`
`<del>`	Configures deleted text (with strikethrough)	`cite, class, datetime, id, style`
`<details>`	Configures a control to provide additional information to the user on demand	`class, id, open, style`
`<dfn>`	Configures the definition of a term	`class, id, style`
`<div>`	Configures a generic section or division in a document	`align (obsolete), class, id, style`
`<dl>`	Configures a description list (formerly called a definition list)	`class, id, style`
`<dt>`	Configures a term in a description list	`class, id, style`
`<em>`	Configures emphasized text (usually displays in italics)	`class, id, style`
`<fieldset>`	Configures a grouping of form elements with a border	`class, id, style`
`<figcaption>`	Configures a caption for a figure	`class, id, style`
`<figure>`	Configures a figure	`class, id, style`
`<footer>`	Configures a footer area	`class, id, style`
`<form>`	Configures a form	`accept-charset, action, autocomplete, class, enctype, id, method, name, novalidate, style, target`
`<h1> … <h6>`	Configures headings	`align (obsolete), class, id, style`
`<head>`	Configures the head section	*Not applicable*
`<header>`	Configures a header area	`class, id, style`
`<hgroup>`	Configures a heading group	`class, id, style`
`<hr>`	Configures a horizontal line; indicates a thematic break in HTML5	`class, id, style`
`<html>`	Configures the root element of a web page document	`lang, manifest`
`<i>`	Configures italic text with no particular emphasis or importance	`class, id, style`
`<iframe>`	Configures an inline frame	`class, height, id, name, sandbox, seamless, src, style, width`
`<img>`	Configures an image	`alt, class, height, id, ismap, name, src, style, usemap, width`
`<input>`	Configures an input control: text box, email text box, URL text box, search text box, telephone number text box, scrolling text box, submit button, reset button, password box, calendar control, slider control, spinner control, color-well control, or hidden field form control	`accesskey, autocomplete, class, checked, disabled, form, id, list, max, maxlength, min, name, pattern, placeholder, readonly, required, size, step, style, tabindex, type, value`
`<ins>`	Configures text that has been inserted into a document	`cite, class, datetime, id, style`
`<kbd>`	Configures a representation of user input	`class, id, style`
`<keygen>`	Configures a control that generates a public-private key pair or submits the public key	`autofocus, challenge, class, disabled, form, id, keytype, style`
`<label>`	Configures a label for a form control	`class, for, form, id, style`
`<legend>`	Configures a caption for a fieldset element	`class, id, style`

Element	Purpose	Commonly Used Attributes
`<li>`	Configures a list item in an unordered or ordered list	`class, id, style, value`
`<link>`	Associates a web page document with an external resource	`class, href, hreflang, id, rel, media, sizes, style, type`
`<map>`	Configures an image map	`class, id, name, style`
`<mark>`	Configures text as marked (or highlighted) for easy reference	`class, id, style`
`<menu>`	Configures a list of commands	`class, id, label, style, type`
`<meta>`	Configures metadata	`charset, content, http-equiv, name`
`<meter>`	Configures a visual gauge of a value	`class, id, high, low, max, min, optimum, style, value`
`<nav>`	Configures an area with navigation hyperlinks	`class, id, style`
`<noscript>`	Configures content for browsers that do not support client-side scripting	
`<object>`	Configures an embedded object	`classid, codebase, data, form, height, name, id, style, title, tabindex, type, width`
`<ol>`	Configures an ordered list	`class, id, reversed, start, style, type`
`<optgroup>`	Configures a group of related options in a select list	`class, disabled, id, label, style`
`<option>`	Configures an option in a select list	`class, disabled, id, selected, style, value`
`<output>`	Configures the results of a calculation	`class, for, form, id, name, style`
`<p>`	Configures a paragraph	`class, id, style`
`<param>`	Configures a parameter for plug-ins	`name, value`
`<pre>`	Configures preformatted text	`class, id, style`
`<progress>`	Configures a visual progress indicator	`class, id, max, style, value`
`<q>`	Configures quoted text	`class, id, style`
`<rp>`	Configures a ruby parenthesis	`class, id, style`
`<rt>`	Configures ruby text component of a ruby annotation	`class, id, style`
`<ruby>`	Configures a ruby annotation	`class, id, style`
`<s>`	Configures text that is no longer accurate or relevant	`class, id, style`
`<samp>`	Configures sample output from a computer program or system	`class, id, style`
`<script>`	Configures a client-side script (typically, JavaScript)	`async, charset, defer, src, type`
`<section>`	Configures a section of a document	`class, id, style`
`<select>`	Configures a select list form control	`class, disabled, form, id, multiple, name, size, style, tabindex`
`<small>`	Configures a disclaimer in small text size	`class, id, style`
`<source>`	Configures a media file and MIME type	`class, id, media, src, style, type`
`<span>`	Configures a generic section of a document with inline display	`class, id, style`
`<strong>`	Configures text with strong importance (typically displayed as bold)	`class, id, style`
`<style>`	Configures embedded styles in a document	`media, scoped, type`
`<sub>`	Configures subscript text	`class, id, style`
`<summary>`	Configures text as a summary, caption, or legend for a details control	`class, id, style`
`<sup>`	Configures superscript text	`class, id, style`
`<table>`	Configures a table	`class, id, style, summary`

(Continued)

Element	Purpose	Commonly Used Attributes
`<tbody>`	Configures the body section of a table	`class, id, style`
`<td>`	Configures a table data cell in a table	`class, colspan, id, headers, rowspan`
`<textarea>`	Configures a scrolling text box form control	`accesskey, autofocus, class, cols, disabled, id, maxlength, name, placeholder, readonly, required, rows, style, tabindex, wrap`
`<tfoot>`	Configures the footer section of a table	`class, id, style`
`<th>`	Configures a table header cell in a table	`class, colspan, id, headers, rowspan, scope, style`
`<thead>`	Configures the head section of a table	`class, id, style`
`<time>`	Configures a date and/or time	`class, datetime, id, style`
`<title>`	Configures the title of a web page document	
`<tr>`	Configures a row in a table	`class, id, style`
`<track>`	Configures a subtitle or caption track for media	`class, default, id, kind, label, src, srclang, style`
`<u>`	Configures text conventionally styled with an underline	`class, id, style`
`<ul>`	Configures an unordered list	`class, id, style`
`<var>`	Configures text as a variable or placeholder	`class, id, style`
`<video>`	Configures a video control native to the browser	`autoplay, class, controls, height, id, loop, poster, preload, src, style, width`
`<wbr>`	Configures a line-break opportunity	`class, id, style`

XHTML Quick Reference

Commonly Used XHTML Elements

Element	Purpose	Commonly Used Attributes
`<!-- -->`	Comment	*Not applicable*
`<a>`	Anchor tag: configures hyperlinks	accesskey, class, href, id, name, style, tabindex, target, title
`<abbr>`	Configures an abbreviation	class, id, style
`<acronym>`	Configures an acronym	class, id, style
`<address>`	Configures contact information	class, id, style
`<area />`	Configures an area in an image map	accesskey, alt, class, coords, href, id, nohref, shape, style, tabindex, target
`<b>`	Configures bold text	class, id, style
`<big>`	Configures large text size	class, id, style
`<blockquote>`	Configures a long quotation	class, id, style
`<body>`	Configures the body section	alink (deprecated), background (deprecated), bgcolor (deprecated), class, id, link (deprecated), style, text (deprecated), vlink (deprecated)
` `	Configures a line break	class, id, style
`<button>`	Configures a button	accesskey, class, disabled, id, name, type, style, value
`<caption>`	Configures a caption for a table	align (deprecated), class, id, style
`<dd>`	Configures a definition area in a definition list	class, id, style
`<del>`	Configures deleted text (with strikethrough)	cite, class, datetime, id, style
`<div>`	Configures a section or division in a document	align (deprecated), class, id, style
`<dl>`	Configures a definition list	class, id, style
`<dt>`	Configures a term in a definition list	class, id, style
`<em>`	Configures emphasized text (usually displays in italics)	class, id, style
`<fieldset>`	Configures a grouping of form elements with a border	class, id, style

(Continued)

Element	Purpose	Commonly Used Attributes
`<form>`	Configures a form	`accept, action, class, enctype, id, method, name, style, target` (deprecated)
`<h1>...<h6>`	Configures headings	`align` (deprecated)`, class, id, style`
`<head>`	Configures the head section	
`<hr />`	Configures a horizontal line	`align` (deprecated)`, class, id, size` (deprecated)`, style, width` (deprecated)
`<html>`	Configures a web page document	`lang, xmlns, xml:lang`
`<i>`	Configures italic text	`class, id, style`
`<iframe>`	Configures an inline frame	`align` (deprecated)`, class, frameborder, height, id, marginheight, marginwidth, name, scrolling, src, style, width`
`<img />`	Configures an image	`align` (deprecated)`, alt, border` (deprecated)`, class, height, hspace` (deprecated)`, id, name, src, style, width, vspace` (deprecated)
`<input />`	Configures a text box, scrolling text box, submit button, reset button, password box, or hidden field form control	`accesskey, class, checked, disabled, id, maxlength, name, readonly, size, style, tabindex, type, value`
`<label>`	Configures a label for a form control	`class, for, id, style`
`<legend>`	Configures a caption for a fieldset element	`align` (deprecated)`, class, id, style`
`<li>`	Configures a list item in an unordered or ordered list	`class, id, style`
`<link />`	Associates a web page document with an external resource	`class, href, id, rel, media, style, type`
`<map>`	Configures an image map	`class, id, name, style`
`<meta />`	Configures metadata	`content, http-equiv, name`
`<noscript>`	Configures content for browsers that do not support client-side scripting	*Not applicable*
`<object>`	Configures an embedded object	`align, classid, codebase, data, height, name, id, style, title, tabindex, type, width`
`<ol>`	Configures an ordered list	`class, id, start` (deprecated)`, style, type` (deprecated)
`<optgroup>`	Configures a group of related options in a select list	`class, disabled, id, label, style`
`<option>`	Configures an option in a select list	`class, disabled, id, selected, style, value`
`<p>`	Configures a paragraph	`align` (deprecated)`, class, id, style`
`<param />`	Configures a parameter for an object element	`name, value`
`<pre>`	Configures preformatted text	`class, id, style`
`<script>`	Configures a client-side script (typically, JavaScript)	`src, type`
`<select>`	Configures a select list form control	`class, disabled, id, multiple, name, size, style, tabindex`
`<small>`	Configures small text size	`class, id, style`
`<span>`	Configures an inline-level section of a document	`class, id, style`
`<strong>`	Configures strong text (typically displayed as bold)	`class, id, style`
`<style>`	Configures embedded styles in a web page document	`type, media`
`<sub>`	Configures subscript text	`class, id, style`
`<sup>`	Configures superscript text	`class, id, style`
`<table>`	Configures a table	`align` (deprecated)`, bgcolor` (deprecated)`, border, cellpadding, cellspacing, class, id, style, summary, title, width`

Element	Purpose	Commonly Used Attributes
`<tbody>`	Configures the body section of a table	`align`, `class`, `id`, `style`, `valign`
`<td>`	Configures a table data cell in a table	`align`, `bgcolor` (deprecated), `class`, `colspan`, `id`, `headers`, `height` (deprecated), `rowspan`, `style`, `valign`, `width` (deprecated)
`<textarea>`	Configures a scrolling text box form control	`accesskey`, `class`, `cols`, `disabled`, `id`, `name`, `readonly`, `rows`, `style`, `tabindex`
`<tfoot>`	Configures the footer section of a table	`align`, `class`, `id`, `style`, `valign`
`<th>`	Configures a table header cell in a table	`align`, `bgcolor` (deprecated), `class`, `colspan`, `id`, `height` (deprecated), `rowspan`, `scope`, `style`, `valign`, `width` (deprecated)
`<thead>`	Configures the head section of a table	`align`, `class`, `id`, `style`, `valign`
`<title>`	Configures the title of a web page document	
`<tr>`	Configures a row in a table	`align`, `bgcolor` (deprecated), `class`, `id`, `style`, `valign`
`<ul>`	Configures an unordered list	`class`, `id`, `style`, `type` (deprecated)

Special Entity Characters

The table that follows lists a selection of special entity characters in order of numeric code. The most commonly used special characters are shown in bold. The W3C's list of special characters is found at http://www.w3.org/MarkUp/html-spec/html-spec_13.html.

Entity Name	Numeric Code	Descriptive Code	Character
Quotation mark	`&#34;`	`&quot;`	"
Ampersand	`&#38;`	`&amp;`	&
Apostrophe	`&#39;`		'
Less than sign	`&#60;`	`&lt;`	<
Greater than sign	`&#62;`	`&gt;`	>
Vertical bar	`&#124;`		|
Left single quotation mark	`&#145;`	`&lsquo;`	'
Right single quotation mark	`&#146;`	`&rsquo;`	'
Nonbreaking space	` `	` `	**a blank space**
Inverted exclamation	`&#161;`	`&iexcl;`	¡
Cent sign	`&#162;`	`&cent;`	¢
Pound sterling sign	`&#163;`	`&pound;`	£
General currency sign	`&#164;`	`&curren;`	†
Yen sign	`&#165;`	`&yen;`	¥
Broken vertical bar	`&#166;`	`&brvbar;`	¦
Section sign	`&#167;`	`&sect;`	§
Umlaut	`&#168;`	`&uml;`	¨
Copyright symbol	`&#169;`	`&copy;`	©
Feminine ordinal	`&#170;`	`&ordf;`	a
Left angle quote	`&#171;`	`&laquo;`	<<
Not sign	`&#172;`	`&not;`	¬
Soft hyphen	`&#173;`	`&shy;`	-

(Continued)

Entity Name	Numeric Code	Descriptive Code	Character
Registered trademark symbol	`&#174;`	`&reg;`	®
Macron	`&#175;`	`&macr;`	¯
Degree sign	`&#176;`	`&deg;`	°
Plus or minus	`&#177;`	`&plusmn;`	±
Superscript two	`&#178;`	`&sup2;`	²
Superscript three	`&#179;`	`&sup3;`	³
Acute accent	`&#180;`	`&acute;`	´
Micro (Mu)	`&#181;`	`&micro;`	µ
Paragraph sign	`&#182;`	`&para;`	¶
Middle dot	`&#183;`	`&middot;`	·
Cedilla	`&#184;`	`&cedil;`	¸
Superscript one	`&#185;`	`&sup1;`	¹
Masculine ordinal	`&#186;`	`&ordm;`	º
Right angle quote	`&#187;`	`&raquo;`	>>
Fraction one-fourth	`&#188;`	`&frac14;`	¼
Fraction one-half	`&#189;`	`&frac12;`	½
Fraction three-fourths	`&#190;`	`&frac34;`	¾
Inverted question mark	`&#191;`	`&iquest;`	¿
Small e, grave accent	`&#232;`	`&egrave;`	è
Small e, acute accent	`&#233;`	`&eacute;`	é
En dash	`&#8211;`	`&ndash;`	–
Em dash	`&#8212;`	`&mdash;`	—

CSS Property Reference

Commonly Used CSS Properties

Property	Description
background	Shorthand to configure all the background properties of an element Value: `background-color background-image background-repeat background-position`
background-attachment	Configures a background image as fixed in place or scrolling Value: `scroll` (default) or `fixed`
background-clip	CSS3; configures the area to display the background Value: `border-box`, `padding-box`, or `content-box`
background-color	Configures the background color of an element Value: Valid color value
background-image	Configures a background image for an element Value: `url` (*file name or path to the image*), `none` (default) Optional new CSS3 functions: `linear-gradient()` and `radial-gradient()`
background-origin	CSS3; configures the background positioning area Value: `padding-box`, `border-box`, or `content-box`
background-position	Configures the position of a background image Value: Two percentages, pixel values, or position values (`left`, `top`, `center`, `bottom`, `right`)
background-repeat	Configures how the background image will be repeated Value: `repeat` (default), `repeat-y`, `repeat-x`, or `no-repeat`
background-size	CSS3; configures the size of the background images Value: Numeric value (px or em), percentage, `contain`, `cover`
border	Shorthand to configure the border of an element Value: `border-width border-style border-color`
border-bottom	Configures the bottom border of an element Value: `border-width border-style border-color`
border-collapse	Configures the display of borders in a table Value: `separate` (default) or `collapse`

(Continued)

Property	Description
border-color	Configures the border color of an element Value: Valid color value
border-image	CSS3; configures an image in the border of an element See http://www.w3.org/TR/css3-background#the-border-image
border-left	Configures the left border of an element Value: `border-width border-style border-color`
border-radius	CSS3; configures rounded corners Value: One to four numeric values (px or em) or percentages that configure the radius of the corners. If a single value is provided, it configures all four corners. The corners are configured in order of top left, top right, bottom right, and bottom left. Related properties: `border-top-left-radius`, `border-top-right-radius`, `border-bottom-left-radius`, and `border-bottom-right-radius`
border-right	Configures the right border of an element Value: `border-width border-style border-color`
border-spacing	Configures the space between table cells in a table Value: Numeric value (px or em)
border-style	Configures the style of the borders around an element Value: `none` (default), `inset`, `outset`, `double`, `groove`, `ridge`, `solid`, `dashed`, or `dotted`
border-top	Configures the top border of an element Value: `border-width border-style border-color`
border-width	Configures the width of an element's border Value: numeric pixel value (such as 1px), `thin`, `medium`, or `thick`
bottom	Configures the offset position from the bottom of a containing element Value: Numeric value (px or em), percentage, or `auto` (default)
box-shadow	CSS3; configures a drop shadow on an element Values: Three or four numerical values (px or em) to indicate horizontal offset, vertical offset, blur radius, spread distance (optional), and a valid color value. Use the `inset` keyword to configure an inner shadow.
caption-side	Configures the placement of a table caption Value: `top` (default) or `bottom`
clear	Configures the display of an element in relation to floating elements Value: `none` (default), `left`, `right`, or `both`
color	Configures the color of text within an element Value: Valid color value
display	Configures how and whether an element will display Value: `inline`, `none`, `block`, `list-item`, `table`, `table-row`, or `table-cell`
float	Configures the horizontal placement (left or right) of an element Value: `none` (default), `left`, or `right`
font-family	Configures the font typeface of text Value: List of valid font names or generic font family names
font-size	Configures the font size of text Value: Numeric value (px, pt, em) percentage value, `xx-small`, `x-small`, `small`, `medium` (default), `large`, `x-large`, `xx-large`, `smaller`, or `larger`
font-stretch	CSS3; configures a normal, condensed, or expanded face from a font family Value: `normal` (default), `wider`, `narrower`, `condensed`, `semi-condensed`, `expanded`, or `ultra-expanded`
font-style	Configures the font style of text Value: `normal` (default), `italic`, or `oblique`

Property	Description
`font-variant`	Configures whether text is displayed in small-caps font Value: `normal` (default) or `small-caps`
`font-weight`	Configures the weight (boldness) of text Value: `normal` (default), `bold`, `bolder`, `lighter`, `100`, `200`, `300`, `400`, `500`, `600`, `700`, `800`, or `900`
`height`	Configures the height of an element Value: Numeric value (px or em), percentage, or `auto` (default)
`left`	Configures the offset position from the left of a containing element Value: Numeric value (px or em), percentage, or `auto` (default)
`letter-spacing`	Configures the space between text characters Value: Numeric value (px or em) or `normal` (default)
`line-height`	Configures the line height of the text Value: Numeric value (px or em), percentage, multiplier numeric value, or `normal` (default)
`list-style`	Shorthand to configure the properties of a list Value: `list-style-type` `list-style-position` `list-style-image`
`list-style-image`	Configures an image as a list marker Value: `url` (*file name or path to the image*) or `none` (default)
`list-style-position`	Configures the position of the list markers Value: `inside` or `outside` (default)
`list-style-type`	Configures the type of list marker displayed Value: `none`, `circle`, `disc` (default), `square`, `decimal`, `decimal-leading-zero`, `Georgian`, `lower-alpha`, `lower-roman`, `upper-alpha`, or `upper-roman`
`margin`	Shorthand to configure the margin of an element Value: One to four numeric values (px or em) or percentages, `auto`, or 0
`margin-bottom`	Configures the bottom margin of an element Value: Numeric value (px or em), percentage, `auto`, or 0
`margin-left`	Configures the left margin of an element Value: Numeric value (px or em), percentage, `auto`, or 0
`margin-right`	Configures the right margin of an element Value: Numeric value (px or em), percentage, `auto`, or 0
`margin-top`	Configures the top margin of an element Value: Numeric value (px or em), percentage, `auto`, or 0
`max-height`	Configures the maximum height of an element Value: Numeric value (px or em), percentage, or `none` (default)
`max-width`	Configures the maximum width of an element Value: Numeric value (px or em), percentage, or `none` (default)
`min-height`	Configures the minimum height of an element Value: Numeric value (px or em), percentage, or `none` (default)
`min-width`	Configures the minimum width of an element Value: Numeric value (px or em), percentage, or `none` (default)
`opacity`	CSS3; configures the transparency of an element and its child elements Value: Numeric value between 1 (fully opaque) and 0 (completely transparent)
`overflow`	Configures how content should display if it is too large for the area allocated Value: `visible` (default), `hidden`, `auto`, or `scroll`
`padding`	Shorthand to configure the padding of an element Value: One to four numeric values (px or em) or percentages, or 0

(*Continued*)

Property	Description
padding-bottom	Configures the bottom padding of an element Value: Numeric value (px or em), percentage, or 0
padding-left	Configures the left padding of an element Value: Numeric value (px or em), percentage, or 0
padding-right	Configures the right padding of an element Value: Numeric value (px or em), percentage, or 0
padding-top	Configures the top padding of an element Value: Numeric value (px or em), percentage, or 0
page-break-after	Configures the page break after an element Value: auto (default), always, avoid, left, or right
page-break-before	Configures the page break before an element Value: auto (default), always, avoid, left, or right
page-break-inside	Configures the page break inside an element Value: auto (default) or avoid
position	Configures the type of positioning used to display an element Value: static (default), absolute, fixed, or relative
right	Configures the offset position from the right of a containing element Value: Numeric value (px or em), percentage, or auto (default)
text-align	Configures the horizontal alignment of text within an element Value: left (default), right, center, or justify
text-decoration	Configures the decoration added to text Value: none (default), underline, overline, line-through, or blink
text-indent	Configures the indentation of the first line of text Value: Numeric value (px or em) or percentage
text-outline	CSS3; configures an outline around text displayed within an element Value: One or two numerical values (px or em) to indicate thickness and (optionally) blur radius, and a valid color value
text-shadow	CSS3; configures a drop shadow on the text displayed within an element Values: Three or four numerical values (px or em) to indicate horizontal offset, vertical offset, blur radius, or spread distance (optional), and a valid color value
text-transform	Configures the capitalization of text Value: none (default), capitalize, uppercase, or lowercase
top	Configures the offset position from the top of a containing element Value: Numeric value (px or em), percentage, or auto (default)
transform	CSS3; configures change or transformation in the display of an element Value: A transform function such as scale(), translate(), matrix(), rotate(), skew(), or perspective()
transition	CSS3; shorthand property to configure the presentational transition of a CSS property Value: List the value for the transition-property, transition-duration, transition-timing-function, and transition-delay, separated by spaces; default values can be omitted, but the first time unit applies to transition-duration
transition-delay	CSS3; Indicates the beginning of the transition Value: 0 (default) configures no delay; otherwise use a numeric value to specify time (usually in seconds)
transition-duration	CSS3; Indicates the length of time to apply the transition Value: 0 (default) configures an immediate transition; otherwise use a numeric value to specify time (usually in seconds)

Property	Description
`transition-property`	CSS3; Indicates the CSS property that the transition applies to Value: A list of applicable properties is available at http://www.w3.org/TR/css3-transitions
`transition-timing-function`	CSS3; Configures changes in the speed of the transition by describing how intermediate property values are calculated Value: `ease` (default), `linear`, `ease-in`, `ease-out`, or `ease-in-out`
`vertical-align`	Configures the vertical alignment of an element Value: Numeric value (px or em), percentage, baseline (default), `sub`, `super`, `top`, `text-top`, `middle`, `bottom`, or `text-bottom`
`visibility`	Configures the visibility of an element Value: `visible` (default), `hidden`, or `collapse`
`white-space`	Configures white space inside an element Value: `normal` (default), `nowrap`, `pre`, `pre-line`, or `pre-wrap`
`width`	Configures the width of an element Value: Numeric value (px or em), percentage, or `auto` (default)
`word-spacing`	Configures the space between words within text Value: Numeric value (px or em) or `auto` (default)
`z-index`	Configures the stacking order of an element Value: Numeric value or `auto` (default)

WCAG 2.0 Quick Reference

Perceivable

- **1.1 Text Alternatives:** Provide text alternatives for any nontext content so that it can be changed into other forms people need, such as large print, Braille, speech, symbols, or simpler language. *You configure images (Chapter 4) and multimedia (Chapter 11) on web pages and provide for alternative text content.*

- **1.2 Time-Based Media:** Provide alternatives for time-based media. *You don't create time-based media in this textbook, but keep this option in mind for the future if you create animation or use client-side scripting for features such as interactive slide shows.*

- **1.3 Adaptable:** Create content that can be presented in different ways (for example, simpler layout) without losing information or structure. *In Chapter 2, you use block elements (such as headings, paragraphs, and lists) to create single-column web pages. You create multicolumn web pages in Chapter 6 and Chapter 7. You use HTML tables in Chapter 8 to configure information.*

- **1.4 Distinguishable:** Make it easier for users to see and hear content, including separating foreground from background. *You are aware of the importance of good contrast between text and background.*

Operable

- **2.1 Keyboard Accessible:** Make all functionality available from a keyboard. *In Chapter 2, you configure hyperlinks to named fragment identifiers on a web page. The label element is introduced in Chapter 9.*

- **2.2 Enough Time:** Provide users enough time to read and use content. *You don't create time-based media in this textbook, but keep this option in mind for the future if you create animation or use client-side scripting for features such as interactive slide shows.*

- **2.3 Seizures:** Do not design content in a way that is known to cause seizures. *Be careful when you use animation created by others; web pages should not contain elements that flash more than three times in a one-second period.*

- **2.4 Navigable:** Provide ways to help users navigate, find content, and determine where they are. *In Chapter 2, you use block elements (such as headings and lists) to organize web page content. In Chapter 6, you learn to structure navigation links within an unordered list. In Chapter 7, you configure hyperlinks to named fragment identifiers on a web page.*

Understandable

- **3.1 Readable:** Make text content readable and understandable. *You explore techniques used in writing for the Web in Chapter 5.*

- **3.2 Predictable:** Make web pages appear and operate in predictable ways. *The web pages you create are predictable, with clearly labeled and functioning hyperlinks.*

- **3.3 Input Assistance:** Help users avoid and correct mistakes. *You learn to use HTML form controls in Chapter 9 that cause a supporting browser to validate basic form information and display error messages. Note that client-side scripting can be used to edit web page forms and provide additional feedback to users.*

Robust

- **4.1 Compatible:** Maximize compatibility with current and future user agents, including assistive technologies. *You provide for future compatibility by writing code that follows W3C Recommendations (standards).*

The WCAG 2.0 Quick Reference List entries are copyright © 2008 World Wide Web Consortium (Massachusetts Institute of Technology, European Research Consortium for Informatics and Mathematics, Keio University). All Rights Reserved. http://www.w3.org/Consortium/Legal/2002/copyright-documents-20021231.

Resources

You'll find the most up-to-date information about WCAG 2.0 at the following resources:

- Overview of WCAG 2.0   http://www.w3.org/TR/WCAG20/Overview
- Understanding WCAG 2.0   http://www.w3.org/TR/UNDERSTANDING-WCAG20
- How to Meet WCAG 2.0   http://www.w3.org/WAI/WCAG20/quickref
- Techniques for WCAG 2.0   http://www.w3.org/TR/WCAG-TECHS

Web-Safe Color Palette

Web-safe colors look the most similar on various computer platforms and computer monitors. Back in the day of eight-bit color it was crucial to use web-safe colors. Since most modern video drivers support millions of colors the use of web-safe colors is now optional. The hexadecimal and decimal RGB values are shown for each web-safe color in the palette above.

G

FTP Tutorial

Publish with File Transfer Protocol (FTP)

Once you obtain your web hosting space, you'll need to upload your files. Although your web host may offer a web-based file manager application for client use, a common method of transferring files is to use File Transfer Protocol (FTP). A protocol is a convention or standard that enables computers to speak to one another. FTP is used to copy and manage files and folders over the Internet. FTP uses two ports to communicate over a network—one for the data (typically port 20) and one for control commands (typically port 21). See http://www.iana.org/assignments/port-numbers for a list port numbers used on the Internet.

FTP Applications

There are many FTP applications available for download or purchase on the Web, including the following:

- **Filezilla**
  - Windows, Mac, Linux Platform
  - http://filezilla-project.org
  - Free download
- **SmartFTP**
  - Windows
  - http://www.smartftp.com
  - Free download
- **CuteFTP**
  - Windows, Mac
  - http://www.cuteftp.com
  - Free trial download, academic pricing available

- **WS_FTP**
  - Windows
  - http://www.ipswitch.com
  - Free trial download

Connecting with FTP

Your web host will provide you with the following information along with any other specifications, such as whether the FTP server requires the use of active mode or passive mode:

FTP Host: Your FTP Host

Username: Your Account Username

Password: Your Account Password

Overview of Using an FTP Application

This section focuses on FileZilla, a free FTP application with versions for the Windows, Mac, and Linux platforms. A free download of FileZilla is available at http://filezilla-project.org/download.php?type=client. After you download an FTP application of your choice, install the program on your computer, using the instructions provided.

Launch and Login

Launch Filezilla or another FTP application. Enter the information required by your web host (such as FTP host, username, and password) and initiate the connection. An example screenshot of FileZilla after a connection is shown in Figure F.1.

As you examine Figure F.1, notice the text boxes near the top of the application for the Host, Username, and Password information. Under this area is a display of messages from the FTP server. Review the area to confirm a successful connection and the results of file transfers. Next, notice that the application is divided into a left panel and a right panel. The left panel is the local site—it displays information about your local computer and allows you to navigate to your drives, folders, and files. The right panel is the remote site—it displays information about your website and provides a way to navigate to its folders and files.

Uploading a File

It's really easy to transfer a file from your local computer to your remote website: Just select the file with your mouse in the left panel (local site list) and drag it to the right panel (remote site list).

Downloading a File

If you need to download a file from your website to your local computer, just drag the file with your mouse from the right panel (remote site list) to the left panel (local site list).

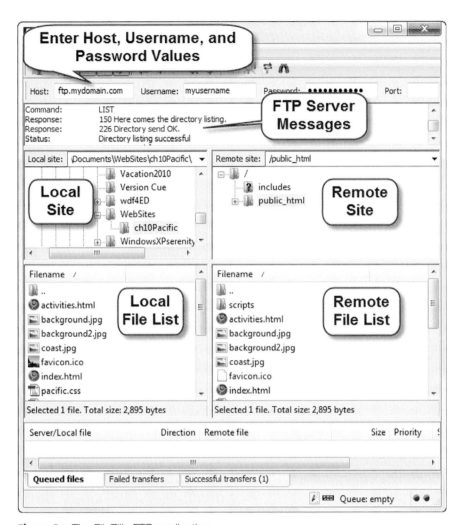

Figure F.1 The FileZilla FTP application

Deleting a File

To delete a file on your website, right-click on the file name (in the right panel) and select Delete from the context-sensitive menu.

And There's More!

Feel free to explore the other functions offered by FileZilla (and most FTP applications). Right-click on a file in the remote site list to display a context-sensitive menu with several options, including renaming a file, creating a new directory (also known as a folder), and viewing a file.

Answers

Chapter 1

Checkpoint 1.1

1. The Internet is a public, globally connected network of computer networks. The Web is a graphical user interface to information stored on computers running web servers connected to the Internet. The Web is a subset of the Internet.

2. The commercialization and exponential growth of the Internet that began in the early 1990s was due largely to a convergence of technologies, including the development of personal computers with graphical operating systems, widespread availability of Internet connection services, the removal of the restriction of commercial use on NSFnet, the development of the World Wide Web by Tim Berners-Lee at CERN, and the development of a graphical browser (called Mosaic) at the NCSA. These events combined to provide the commercial incentive and an easy way to share and access information in a manner that had never been experienced.

3. Universal design is a very important concept for web developers because the websites that they create should be usable by all people. Not only is this the right thing to do, but in developing websites for the government or for educational institutions, access to technology (including websites) is mandated by law.

Checkpoint 1.2

1. An example of a web client is a computer running a browser software application such as Internet Explorer. Typically, the computer is connected to the Internet only when needed. The web browser software uses HTTP to request web pages and related resources from a web server. A web server is a computer that is continually connected to the Internet and that runs some type of web server software application. It uses the HTTP protocol to receive requests for web pages and related resources. It responds to these requests and sends the resources.

2. In this chapter, several protocols are discussed that use the Internet but not the Web. E-mail messages are transmitted via the Internet. SMTP (Simple Mail Transfer Protocol) is used to send e-mail messages. POP (Post Office Protocol) and IMAP (Internet Message Access Protocol) can be used to receive e-mail messages. FTP (File Transfer Protocol) can be used to exchange (send and receive) files with a computer connected to the Internet.

3. A URL (Uniform Resource Locator) represents the address of a resource that is available on the Internet. A URL consists of a protocol, a domain name, and the hierarchical location of the file or resource. An example of a URL is http://www.webdevfoundations.net/chapter1/index.htm. A domain name locates an organization or other entity on the Internet and is associated with a unique numeric IP address. A domain name is part of a URL.

Review Questions

1. a
2. a
3. c
4. b
5. a
6. True
7. True
8. False
9. False
10. SGML
11. XHTML
12. HTML
13. HTML5
14. microblogging
15. TCP

Chapter 2

Checkpoint 2.1

1. HTML (Hypertext Markup Language) was developed by Tim Berners-Lee at CERN, using SGML. HTML is the set of markup symbols or codes placed in a file intended for display on a web browser. HTML configures a platform-independent display of information. Each markup code is referred to as an element (or tag).

2. No expensive software is required to create and code web pages. You can use a Windows or Mac text editor application that is part of the operating system. Free text editors and web browsers are also available for download.

3. The body element.

Checkpoint 2.2

1. Search engines use headings to index the structure and content of a web page. When a page is indexed by search engines, it is easily accessible to the users who use the search engines for any information that is provided in the page.

2. There are three types of lists: description lists, ordered lists, and unordered lists. Yes, nested lists can be created in HTML.

3. The purpose of the blockquote element is to format a long quotation by indenting a section of text on a web page. Empty space is placed above and below the text contained in the blockquote element. The text is indented from both the left and right margins.

Checkpoint 2.3

1. The div element configures a structural block area, or division, on a web page, with empty space above and below. It is used mostly for formatting an area of a web page, such as a logo, navigation, or footer area. It is also useful for configuring a section that contains other block display elements, such as <p>, <ul>, <blockquote>, and other <div> elements.

2. The anchor element ‹a› is used for creating a hyperlink of a word, a group of words, or an image that allows the user to jump to a new page or another section within the current page.

3. To create an e-mail link, the href value should begin with "mailto:" followed by the e-mail address.

4. Example: <a href = "contact.html">Contact Us</a>

Review Questions

1. c

2. a

3. b

4. d

5. d

6. a

7. a

8. c

9. b

10. b

11. <meta>

12.

13. <li>

14. Left alignment

15. disc; square; circle; disc

16. It is good practice to place the e-mail address both on the web page and within the anchor tag. Not everyone has an e-mail program configured with his or her browser. By placing the e-mail address in both places, you increase usability for all your visitors.

Chapter 3

Checkpoint 3.1

1. Reasons to use CSS on a web page include the following: greater control of typography and page layout, separation of style from structure, potentially smaller web page documents, and easier site maintenance.

2. Because visitors may set their browsers to certain colors, it is a good idea when changing a text or background color to configure both the text color and the background color properties to provide good contrast between text and background.

3. Embedded styles are coded once in the header section of the web page and apply to the entire page. This practice is more efficient than using inline styles to code individual styles on HTML elements.

Checkpoint 3.2

1. Embedded styles can be used to configure the text and color formatting for an entire web page. Embedded styles are placed in the head section of a web page. The `<style>` tag is used to contain the CSS selectors and properties that configure the embedded styles.

2. External styles can be used to configure the text and color formatting for some or all of the pages on a website in one file. This single file can be changed, and all the web pages associated with it will display the new styles the next time they are rendered in a browser. External styles are placed in a separate text file that uses a .css file extension. Web pages use the `<link>` tag to indicate that they are using an external style sheet.

3. `<link rel="stylesheet" href="mystyles.css">`

Review Questions

1. a
2. b
3. a
4. c
5. d
6. c
7. b
8. a
9. a
10. b
11. c
12. selector; declarations
13. property; value
14. text-decoration
15. div; span

Chapter 4

Checkpoint 4.1

1. Yes. It styles a level one heading element with text color green. The border around the element is solid and 5 pixels thick. On the top, the right, and the left sides, the border color is red. However, the bottom border color is green.

2. Yes. The border-style property can have from one to four values for four borders. It is the same with the other border properties, i.e., border-width and border-color.

3. True. You need to set the borders first using the border-style property.

Checkpoint 4.2

1. The alt attribute specifies the alternative text.

   The code should be

   ```
   <imgsrc="logo.gif" height="200" width="300" alt="Company Name">
   ```

2. body {background:#FFCC99 url(myfile.gif) no-repeat right top;}

3. The browser will display the background color immediately. Then, the browser will render the background image and repeat the image as specified in the CSS. The background color will appear in areas not covered by the background image.

Checkpoint 4.3

1. Answers will vary with the site that you choose to review. Suggested solution: The page reviewed is the home page of a travel soccer league. The URL is http://www.alithsa.org. Image links are used for the main navigation of the site. Each image link contains a rectangle with text and a soccer ball. There is good contrast between the black text and the background color of either yellow or green. Yellow background is used to indicate the current page. Because of the alt attribute values used, this page would not be accessible to a visitor who cannot see the images. Currently, every graphic has the same value for the alt attribute "Picture". To improve accessibility, the alt attribute values on each image tag should be modified to contain brief descriptive phrases. On the plus side, the page does display plain text links in the footer section. The images used as navigation links on this page contribute to the fun, sporty attitude of the site. The accessibility of the page needs to be improved.

2. The image, map, and area elements work together to create a functioning image map. The <img> tag configures the image that will be used for the map and

contains a usemap attribute whose value corresponds to the id value on the `<map>` tag associated with the image. The `<map>` tag is a container tag and surrounds one or more `<area>` tags. There is one self-contained `<area>` tag for each clickable hotspot on the image map. See the working example on the textbook website at http://webdevfoundations.net/6e/chapter4.html.

3. False. There is a trade-off between the quality of the image and the file size. The goal should be to save images that use the smallest file size which provides acceptable display quality.

Review Questions

1. b
2. c
3. b
4. b
5. a
6. c
7. b
8. a
9. d
10. d
11. zero
12. figcaption
13. progress; meter
14. image; selectable, hotspots
15. background-size property

Chapter 5

Checkpoint 5.1

1. The four basic principles of design are repetition, contrast, proximity, and alignment. Descriptions of school home pages and how these principles are applied will vary.

2. Best practices for writing for the Web include the following: short paragraphs, bullet points, common fonts, white space, multiple columns if possible, bold or emphasized important text, and correct spelling and grammar.

   Answers will vary. The following suggested solution adds interest with bullet points, places emphasis on important phrases, and includes editing of the original text:

   Acme, Inc., is a new laboratory instrument repair and service company. At this time, our staff has a combined total of 30-plus years of specimen preparation instrumentation service and repair.

   - **EPA Refrigeration Certified**
     Acme, Inc., technicians are factory trained and equipped with the best diagnostic and repair equipment available.

   - **Fully Insured**
     Our workers are fully covered by workman's compensation insurance. A proof-of-insurance certificate can be provided upon request.

   - **Convenient Location**
     Repair shop facilities and offices are located in Chicago, Illinois.

   - **Service History**
     Your equipment is important to us. A detailed repair history is kept and is available to our service technicians.

- **Rates**
  - Labor and travel, $100.00 per hour
  - 2-hour minimum
  - $0.40 per mile and all related expenses
  - Parts are not included

3. http://www.walmart.com is an e-commerce site. It is designed to appeal to the general public—note the white background and high contrast and the use of tabbed navigation, product hierarchy, and site search. This design meets the needs of its target audience: teen and adult shoppers. http://www.sesameworkshop.org/sesamestreet is geared toward young children and their parents. It is bright and colorful with much interactivity and animation, all of which is appealing to the target audience. http://www.mugglenet.com is a fan site designed to appeal to teens and young adults. It is a dark, mysterious site with much interaction—the forums are very busy. This site appeals to its niche audience.

Checkpoint 5.2

1. Answers will vary.

2. Answers will vary.

3. Best practices for using graphics on web pages include the following: careful choice of colors (Appendix F is recommended for the most similar cross-platform display), use of necessary images only, use of images as small as possible, a usable site even if images are not displayed, and use of the alt attribute to configure text descriptions for images. Recommendations for school home pages will vary.

Review Questions

1. c
2. b
3. b
4. b
5. d
6. d
7. c
8. a
9. c
10. b
11. hierarchical
12. do not
13. Web Accessibility Initiative (WAI)
14. Student answers will vary. Issues to be aware of in designing for the mobile web include small screen size, low bandwidth, awkward controls, limited processor and memory, and reduced support of font typefaces and color.

15. Student answers will vary. The four principles that are essential to complying with WCAG 2.0 are as follows: **P**erceivable, **O**perable, **U**nderstandable, and **R**obust.

   1. Content must be **P**erceivable
   2. Interface components in the content must be **O**perable
   3. Content and controls must be **U**nderstandable
   4. Content should be **R**obust enough to work with current and future user agents, including assistive technologies

Chapter 6

Checkpoint 6.1

1. The components of the box model, from innermost to outermost, are the content, padding, border, and margin.

2. The position property is used to position the elements in your document. There are four possible values of this property: static, relative, absolute, and fixed.

3. The purpose of the float property is to shift the display of an element to the right or left side of the container element.

Checkpoint 6.2

1. The page layout is jello. The content has a percentage width with a centered layout that takes up 80% of the browser viewport. A minimum width is configured to avoid awkward wrapping of text when the browser is resized.

2. Contextual selectors allow you to apply style properties to select elements, based on their context or relation to another element.

3. Configure an HTML element selector if the style is expected to be applied every time that tag is used. Configure an id if the style is for a specific element that is expected to occur only once on a page. Configure a class if the style is expected to be applied to a variety of different HTML elements.

Checkpoint 6.3

1. The div element is a multipurpose generic element that configures a section or division of a web page. HTML5 introduces new elements for configuring web page areas intended to be more specific in their semantic purpose. Depending on the target audience for a website, it may be appropriate to use new HTML5 elements instead of div elements to configure page areas for navigation (the nav element), logo header (header and hgroup elements), footer (footer element), sidebar (aside element), articles (article element), images/charts (figure and figcaption elements), and page sections (section element). As time goes on and browser support increases, use of these new HTML5 elements is expected to be the norm.

2. The article element is intended to contain an independent entry, such as a blog posting, comment, or e-zine article that could stand on its own and be syndicated or distributed.

3. The hgroup element is intended to group multiple heading elements.

Review Questions

1. a
2. a
3. a
4. c
5. b
6. c
7. c
8. d

9. d

10. b

11. static

12. left

13. aside

14. float

15. margin

Chapter 7

Checkpoint 7.1

1. Organizing a website into folders can help increase productivity by arranging the files into file type (such as images or media), file function (web page or script), and/or website section (products, services, and so on). Using folders and subfolders can be helpful when a project team (see Chapter 10) is developing a large website.

2. The target attribute configures a hyperlink to open the file in a new browser window or tab.

3. Advantages of using CSS sprites on a website include reduced bandwidth (a condensed sprite image typically will have lower file size than multiple individual images will have), reduced number of http requests by the browser (only one request must be made for the sprite image, instead of multiple requests for individual image files), and quick display of individual images in the sprite, which are configured to display in response to mouse movement.

Checkpoint 7.2

1. Web page areas can be configured specifically for hard copy. For example, navigation areas can be hidden, page breaks can be configured, and font typeface can configured in serif fonts. In addition, content useful for a person with a hard copy—such as a contact phone number or even a map—can be configured to display and print on the hard copy.

2. A single-column page layout with a small header, key navigation links, content, and page footer works well for mobile device display. Heading elements and lists are well suited for mobile web pages. Eliminate content that is not essential for mobile use. Avoid the use of tables and absolute positioning when configuring pages for mobile display.

3. False. Although well intended, `media="handheld"` is not a reliable way to target mobile devices. CSS media queries are used instead.

Review Questions

1. a

2. a

3. c

4. b

5. c

6. a

7. b

8. c

9. c	**13.** One Web
10. b	**14.** minimal
11. media = "print"	**15.** only
12. media queries	

Chapter 8

Checkpoint 8.1

1. Tables are often used to organize tabular information on a web page.

2. The colspan and rowspan attributes are applied to the table header and table data elements. The colspan and rowspan attributes are used for defining cells that span more than one column and more than one row, respectively.

3. The headers attribute in a ‹td› tag is used for associating the tabledata cell values with their corresponding headers.

Checkpoint 8.2

1. The respective CSS properties are padding and border-spacing.

2. The border-collapse property is used to define whether the table borders are collapsed into a single border or separated.

Review Questions

1. a	**9.** c
2. c	**10.** d
3. d	**11.** background-color
4. b	**12.** :first-of-type
5. b	**13.** :last-of-type
6. c	**14.** align
7. a	**15.** scope
8. b	

Chapter 9

Checkpoint 9.1

1. Although either solution would be appropriate, the solution that uses three input boxes (first name, last name, and e-mail address) is the more flexible solution. These separate values could be stored in a database by server-side processing, where they could easily be selected and placed into personalized e-mail messages. This approach provides the most useful functionality of the collected information in future manipulations.

2. There are a number of possible solutions for this design question. If the responses are short and of about equal length, perhaps a group of radio buttons would be appropriate. If the responses are lengthy or of widely varying lengths, a select list would be a good choice. Radio button groups can accept only one response per group. By default, select lists accept only one response. Check boxes would not be appropriate because they allow more than one response to be selected.

3. False. In a radio button group, the name attribute is used by the browser to process separate elements as a group.

Checkpoint 9.2

1. The fieldset element creates a visual border around the elements contained within the fieldset. The border can help to organize form elements and increase the usability of the form. The legend element is used to provide a text description of the area bounded by the fieldset element, further increasing the usability of the form for visitors using browsers that support these tags.

2. The accesskey attribute allows a visitor to select an element immediately by using the keyboard instead of a mouse. This approach improves the accessibility of the page and can be very helpful to mobility-impaired visitors. The W3C recommends providing a visual cue of an underlined letter, bold letter, or message that indicates the hot keys to press to activate an element.

3. The web designer and client decide which is used: standard submit button, image button, or button tag. However, it makes sense to use the simplest possible technology that provides the needed functionality. In most cases, this is the standard submit button. Visually challenged visitors using a screen reader will hear that a submit button has been encountered. Submit buttons automatically invoke the server-side processing configured in the form tag.

   An image button will also automatically invoke the server-side processing configured for the form and can be more accessible if configured with the alt and accesskey attributes. Unless there is a very good reason or a very insistent client, avoid the button element for standard web forms—avoid choosing a complex solution when a basic submit button can be used.

Checkpoint 9.3

1. A web browser requests web pages and their related files from a web server. The web server locates the files and sends them to your web browser. Then the web browser renders the returned files and displays the requested web pages. Server-side processing is required to save and handle information entered by web page visitors. The action attribute on a form element specifies the script or program that the web server should invoke and pass the form data to. The script or program returns a result (often a web page) that is sent from the web server to the browser for display.

2. The server-side script developer and the web page designer must work together to get both parts of the form processing—the front-end web page and the back-end server-side script—working together. They need to communicate regarding the method (get or post) to be used by the form and the location of the server-side script. Because the names of the form elements are often used by the server-side script as variable names, the form element names are usually specified at this time.

Review Questions

1. a

2. d

3. a

4. b

5. b

6. c

7. b

8. a

9. d

10. d

11. d

12. legend

13. accesskey

14. input; datalist; option

15. The following form controls could provide a way for a web page visitor to select a color: an input text box for free-form entry of a color value, an HTML5 datalist with one option element for each color choice, a radio button group with one radio button for each color choice, a select list with one option element for each color choice, and an HTML5 color-well form control (although this is not yet well supported by browsers and will usually result in the display of an input text box).

Chapter 10

Checkpoint 10.1

1. The project manager directs the website development process—creating the project plan and schedule. He or she must keep the big picture in mind while communicating with the staff and coordinating team activities. The project manager is accountable for meeting project milestones and producing results.

2. A large-scale web project is much more than brochure-ware—it is often a complex information application that the company depends on. Such an application needs the special talents of a wide variety of individuals—including experts in graphics, organization, writing, marketing, coding, database administration, and so on—one or two people simply cannot fulfill all these roles and create a quality website.

3. Answers will vary. Different testing techniques include the unit testing done by individual web developers, automated testing performed by link checker programs, code testing and validation performed by code validation programs, and usability testing achieved by watching typical web visitors use a website to perform tasks.

Checkpoint 10.2

1. A virtual web host that offers reliability and scalability would meet the needs of a small company for its initial web presence. The web host chosen should offer higher-end packages with scripting, database, and e-commerce capabilities to allow for future growth.

2. A dedicated web server is owned and supported by the web host company. The client company may choose to administer it or may pay the web host company to perform this task. A co-located server is owned by the client company and housed at the web host provider. This configuration offers both the advantage of a reliable Internet connection at the web host and full control of the administration and support of the web server.

3. If your website is down and your web host is not responding to technical support requests, it doesn't matter that you are saving $5.00 per month. When comparing web host plans, check prices to know the currently prevailing fees. If the charges of a particular Web host seem abnormally low, the company is probably cutting corners. Do not base your choice on price alone.

Review Questions

1. d
2. a
3. c
4. b
5. d
6. a
7. d
8. a
9. a
10. c
11. usability testing
12. graphic designer
13. UNIX and Linux
14. A careful review of your competitor's web presence helps you design a site that will stand out from the rest and be more appealing to your shared customer base. Note both the good and bad components of your competitors' sites.

15. Contacting technical support can give you a general idea of the responsiveness of the web host provider to issues and problems. If the technical support staff is slow getting back to you at this point, don't be surprised if you get the same type of service when you have a problem and need immediate help. While not fail-safe, a quick response to a simple question at least gives the appearance of a well-organized, professional, and responsive technical support staff.

Chapter 11

Checkpoint 11.1

1. Answers will vary and will include RealPlayer, Windows Media Player, Apple QuickTime, Adobe Reader, Adobe Flash Player, and Adobe Shockwave Player. Review Section 11.1 for more information.

2. Issues include bandwidth, unreliability of the delivery of the media because of platform, browser, and plug-in issues, and accessibility. It is a good idea to have alternate content available that does not rely on media alone.

3. Although Flash has good support on desktop browsers, not all your web page visitors are able to use Flash: The technology is currently not supported by iPad and iPhone mobile devices. While the accessibility of Flash content has improved, "plain" HTML web pages are still more easily accessible. The Flash .swf files take up bandwidth and slow the delivery of pages. If most of your target audience uses a dial-up connection or mobile devices, slower delivery may be a concern.

Checkpoint 11.2

1. HTML5 video and audio elements provide for native display of media by browsers—no need for plug-ins. These elements can be configured with fallback content, such as hyperlinks to the media, for browsers that do not support the new HTML5 elements.

2. The transform property allows you to rotate, scale, skew, or move an element with CSS.

3. After download, a Java applet must be interpreted by the Java Virtual Machine in the web browser before the applet runs. The time taken for interpretation can cause a delay before the applet is displayed on the page. Also, visitors with mobile devices may not be using a browser that supports Java.

Checkpoint 11.3

1. JavaScript can be used to add a wide range of interactive effects to a web page, including form validation, popup windows, jump menus, message boxes, image rollovers, status message changes, calculations, and so on.

2. The foundation for Ajax is Standards-based HTML and CSS. Other technologies used in Ajax include the DOM, JavaScript, and XML.

3. The HTML5 canvas element provides an API to web developers that allows them to configure dynamic graphics with JavaScript.

Review Questions

1. b

2. d

3. d

4. c

5. a

6. a

7. d

8. b

9. d

10. b

11. transform

12. transition

13. canvas

14. Java Virtual Machine (JVM)

15. asynchronous

16. Answers will vary but may include the following: large file size to download, uneven support of browser plug-ins, and the time, talent, and software required to create audio or video content.

17. Creative Commons at http://creativecommons.org provides a free service that allows authors and artists to register a type of a copyright license. The Creative Commons license informs others exactly what they can and cannot do with the creative work.

Chapter 12

Checkpoint 12.1

1. There are many advantages to engaging in e-commerce, especially for a small business owner who must watch costs carefully. Advantages include very low overhead, 24/7 business hours, and global sales potential.

2. There are risks in any business venture, including e-commerce. Risks associated with e-commerce include increased competition, fraudulent transactions, and security issues.

3. SSL (Secure Sockets Layer) is a protocol that allows data to be privately exchanged over public networks such as the Internet. An online shopper can check the following to determine whether SSL is being used:

   - The https protocol, rather than http, will display in the browser address bar.

   - The browser may display a lock icon. If this icon is clicked, information about the digital certificate and encryption level being used will display.

Checkpoint 12.2

1. Three payment models commonly employed on the Web are cash, check, and credit. Credit is the most popular. Consumers are used to using credit cards. Processes for accepting credit cards at stores are easily adapted to online use. Mobile payments are expected to increase in the future.

2. Answers will vary. People make online purchases for many reasons, including the following: convenience, lower cost, and ease of shipping. If you did not check for SSL the last time you purchased an item on the Web, most likely you'll look for it in the future.

3. E-commerce solutions include instant storefronts, off-the-shelf shopping cart software that you or your web host installs, and custom solutions. The easiest entry to e-commerce is an instant storefront. Although this solution does not provide the most flexibility, you can get a store up and running in an afternoon. An easy semi-custom solution would be to create your own website but use PayPal or Google Checkout to process the shopping cart and credit card transactions.

Review Questions

1. c	**10.** b
2. a	**11.** symmetric encryption
3. b	**12.** EDI
4. b	**13.** asymmetric key
5. b	**14.** SSL
6. a	**15.** The website developers may use an automatic translation program or other customized web translation service.
7. c	
8. a	
9. d	

Chapter 13

Checkpoint 13.1

1. Three components of a search engine are the robot, database, and search form. The robot is a special program that "walks" the Web and follows links to sites. The robot updates the search engine's database with the information it finds. The search form is the graphical user interface that is used to request a search by a visitor to the search engine site.

2. Use the description meta tag to provide a brief description of the website. The information in the description meta tag may be used by search engines when they index your website. Some search engines, such as Google, display the description meta tag information on the search engine results page (SERP).

3. Yes, it may be beneficial for a business to pay for preferential listing. If your business is listed in the first page of search results, visitors are more likely to find your site than if you are in the hundredth page of search results. Paid programs for preferential listing such as Google's AdWords should be carefully considered and may be a good match for the marketing goals of an organization.

Checkpoint 13.2

1. Answers will vary. In most cases, the top three sites returned for a particular search phrase will not be the same. Consider optimizing your site so that currently the most popular search engine displays the site as high as possible in its results list.

2. A brute force method is to experiment by visiting a search engine, typing in keywords, and checking for your site in the search results. If your web site host provides you with web log reports, you can easily tell by examining the reports. You'll see the names of the robot/spider programs—Googlebot is the name of Google's spider (see http://www.robotstxt.org for more information on search engine robots). The web log reports will also itemize both the search engines used by visitors and the keywords used to locate your site.

3. Answers will vary. Website promotion methods that do not use search engines include the following: affiliate programs, banner ads, banner exchanges, reciprocal link agreements, newsletters, sticky site features such as polls, forums, surveys, QR codes, personal recommendations, newsgroup/listserv postings, social media marketing techniques, blog postings, RSS feeds, traditional media ads, and existing paper marketing materials. Any of these are valid as a first choice—depending on the needs of the organization. The newsletter technique is an interesting promotion method. Place a form on a web page to allow visitors to opt into your newsletter. Send them a periodic e-mail with information of value related to your site (possibly even special offers). This approach encourages visitors to return to your site. They may even forward your e-mail to a friend.

Note: Be sure to provide a way for visitors to opt out of the newsletter. For example, newsletters sent by TechLearning News include the following message:

"UNSUBSCRIBE
To unsubscribe from this type of e-mail, please reply to this message.
unsubtechlearning@news.techlearning.com"

Review Questions

1. b

2. a

3. c

4. b

5. b

6. c

7. c

8. a

9. b

10. b

11. stickiness

12. `<meta name="robots" description="noindex, nofollow">`

13. search engines

14. a variety of methods, including affiliate programs, banner ads, banner exchanges, reciprocal link agreements, blog posting, RSS feeds, newsletters, personal recommendations, social bookmarking, and traditional media advertising, or including a URL or QR code on all promotional materials

15. QR codes

Chapter 14

Checkpoint 14.1

1. JavaScript can be used for rollover images, form data validation, popup windows, interactivity such as alert messages and prompts, and mathematical calculations for tasks such as determining tax.

2. There is no limit to the number of script blocks that can be embedded in an HTML document.

3. You can use the JavaScript Console in Firefox to find an error. You could also look through your code, paying particular attention to names of objects, properties, methods and statements, and missing semicolons.

Checkpoint 14.2

1. An object is a thing, a property is an attribute, and a method is an action.

2. An event is an occurrence such as clicking a mouse, loading a page, or placing the mouse over an area on the page. An event handler is an attribute embedded in an HTML tag such as onclick, onload, and onmouseover, that points to JavaScript code to execute when the corresponding event occurs.

3. Event handlers are embedded in HTML tags and are not placed in separate script blocks.

Checkpoint 14.3

1. The prompt() method could be used to gather a piece of data such as the user's age. The prompt() method should be used in conjunction with a variable so that the data will be stored in the variable.

2. The code might look something like the following:

```
if (userAge < 18) {
  alert("You are under 18");
} else {
  alert("You are 18 or older");
}
```

3. A function definition begins with the keyword function, followed by the name of the function and some JavaScript statements. It defines a function, and calling that function results in the execution of the statements within it.

Checkpoint 14.4

1. Form data validation refers to checking form input against validation rules and not allowing the form to be submitted if the data does not conform to the rules.

2. Answers may vary, but may include required fields such as name, e-mail address, and phone number. Numeric fields may require validation to ensure that they are within particular bounds—for example, order quantity greater than 0 and age between 1 and 120.

3. When the user clicks the submit button, the submit event occurs and the onsubmit event handler executes the return validateForm() command. The validateForm function runs and tests the form data for validation. If the data is valid, validateForm() returns the value of true, and the form is submitted. If the data is not valid, validateForm() returns the value of false and the form is not submitted.

Review Questions

1. a

2. c

3. b

4. b

5. a

6. c

7. d

8. d

9. a

10. c

11. = =

12. jump menu

13. window

14. variable

15. onclick

16. Common uses for JavaScript include rollover images, form data validation, popup windows, interactivity such as alert messages and prompts, and mathematical calculations.

17. The following techniques can be used in debugging JavaScript: Check the JavaScript code carefully for syntax errors. Verify that quotation marks, braces, and parentheses are used in pairs. Check for missing semicolons. Verify that your code uses the correct case (uppercase and lowercase characters) in variable, object, property, and method names. Use the JavaScript Console to help with debugging—it will provide some information about the error. Use an `alert()` to display the values of variables or to display messages as your script is running.

Index

Credits

Figures 4.14, 9.25, 9.33, 9.34, 9.35, 9.37, 9.44, 9.47, 11.13 © Opera Software A/S

Figure 5.9 © Dmitriy Shironosov/Shutterstock Images LLC

The Web Design Best Practices Checklist (Table 5.1) © Terry Ann Morris (http://www.terrymorris.net)

Figure 10.5 (flat-screen monitor, keyboard, mouse) © jossnat/Shutterstock Images LLC

Figure 10.5 (laptop) © portfolio/Shutterstock Images LLC

Figure 10.5 (mobile device) © valkos/Shutterstock Images LLC

Page 199, Web Content Accessibility Guidelines 2.0 (WCAG 2.0) recommended by the W3C's Web Accessibility Initiative (WAI) © W3C (World Wide Web Consortium)

Table 12.1 © Pew Internet & American Life Project

Appendix E, "WCAG 2.0 Quick Reference" © W3C (World Wide Web Consortium)

The documents and related graphics contained herein could include technical inaccuracies or typographical errors. Changes are periodically added to the information herein. Microsoft and/or its respective suppliers may make improvements and/or changes in the product(s) and/or the program(s) described herein at any time. Partial screen shots may be viewed in full within the software version specified.